# books are worth more than t."
didate

## HOW THE EXPERTS HELP YOU PASS:

- **PROVEN TEACHING METHODOLOGY** Text based on thousands of hours of classroom experience — Global gets people certified. (150,000 professionals can't be wrong!)

- **MORE PRACTICE TESTS** More practice exam questions than any other study guide/CD-ROM—hundreds! Includes hyperlinks from questions to answers in electronic book.

- **AUTHORITATIVE INFORMATION** Developed and reviewed by master MCSE and MCT professionals.

- **EXAM WATCH** Warnings based on post-exam research identifying troublesome exam questions.

| MCSE Windows NT 4.0 Certification Track — Candidates must pass 4 core and 2 elective exams | MCSE + Internet Windows NT 4.0 Certification Track — Candidates must pass 7 core and 2 elective exams | |
|---|---|---|
| CHOOSE 4 CORE & 2 ELECTIVE | CHOOSE 7 CORE & 2 ELECTIVE | CERTIFICATION PRESS STUDY GUIDES |
| CORE | CORE | MCSE Windows NT Server 4.0 Study Guide (Exam 70-67) 0-07-882491-5 |
| CORE | CORE | MCSE Windows NT Server 4.0 in the Enterprise Study Guide (Exam 70-68) 0-07-882490-7 |
| CORE | CORE | |
| CORE | CORE | MCSE Windows NT Workstation 4.0 Study Guide (Exam 70-73) 0-07-882492-3 |
| CORE | CORE | MCSE Windows 98 Study Guide (Exam 70-98) 0-07-882532-6 |
| CORE | CORE | MCSE Networking Essentials Study Guide (Exam 70-58) 0-07-882493-1 |
| ELECTIVE | CORE | MCSE Microsoft TCP/IP on Windows NT 4.0 Study Guide (Exam 70-59) 0-07-882489-3 |
| ELECTIVE | CORE | MCSE Internet Information Server 4.0 with Proxy Server 2.0 and Internet Explorer Administration Kit 1.1 Study Guide (Exams 70-87, 70-79, 70-88) 0-07-882560-1 |
| ELECTIVE | CORE | MCSE Internet Information Server 4.0 with Proxy Server 2.0 and Internet Explorer Administration Kit 1.1 Study Guide (Exams 70-87, 70-79, 70-88) 0-07-882560-1 |
| ELECTIVE | ELECTIVE | |
| ELECTIVE | | |
| ELECTIVE | ELECTIVE | |
| ELECTIVE | ELECTIVE | |
| ELECTIVE | ELECTIVE | |
| ELECTIVE | ELECTIVE | MCSE System Administration for SQL Server™ Study Guide (Exam 70-28) |
| ELECTIVE | ELECTIVE | MCSE Exchange Server 5.5 Study Guide (Exam 70-81) 0-07-882488-5 |
| ELECTIVE | ELECTIVE | MCSE Internet Information Server 4.0 with Proxy Server 2.0 and Internet Explorer Administration Kit 1.1 Study Guide (Exams 70-87, 70-79, 70-88) 0-07-882560-1 |

**MICROSOFT CERTIFIED SYSTEMS ENGINEER**

# MCSE Internet Information

# Server 4.0 Study Guide

## (Exams 70-87, 70-88, 70-79)

Syngress Media, Inc.

Osborne McGraw-Hill

Berkeley  New York  St. Louis  San Francisco  Auckland  Bogotá  Hamburg  London  Madrid  Mexico City
Milan  Montreal  New Delhi  Panama City  Paris  São Paulo  Singapore  Sydney  Tokyo  Toronto

Osborne McGraw-Hill
2600 Tenth Street
Berkeley, California 94710
U.S.A.

For information on translations or book distributors outside the U.S.A.,
or to arrange bulk purchase discounts for sales promotions, premiums, or
fund-raisers, please contact Osborne/**McGraw-Hill** at the above address.

MCSE Internet Information Server 4.0 Study Guide (Exams 70-87, 70-88, 70-79)

1234567890 DOC DOC 901987654321098

ISBN 0-07-882560-1

| **Publisher** | **Copy Editor** | **Illustrators** |
|---|---|---|
| Brandon A. Nordin | Sarah Lemaire | Lance Ravella |
| | | Brian Wells |
| **Editor-in-Chief** | **Indexer** | |
| Scott Rogers | Valerie Robbins | **Series Design** |
| | | Roberta Steele |
| **Acquisitions Editor** | **Proofreader** | Arlette Crosland |
| Gareth Hancock | Stefany Otis | |
| | | **Cover Design** |
| **Project Editor** | **Computer Designers** | Regan Honda |
| Cynthia Douglas | Ann Sellers | |
| | Mickey Galicia | **Editorial Management** |
| **Technical Editor** | Roberta Steele | Syngress Media, Inc. |
| Sean Wallbridge | Jean Butterfield | |
| David W. Egan | | |

## From Global Knowledge Network

At Global Knowledge Network we strive to support the multiplicity of learning styles required by our students to achieve success as technical professionals. In this series of books, it is our intention to offer the reader a valuable tool for successful completion of the MCSE Certification Exam.

As the world's largest IT training company, Global Knowledge Network is uniquely positioned to offer these books. The expertise gained each year from providing instructor-led training to hundreds of thousands of students worldwide has been captured in book form to enhance your learning experience. We hope that the quality of these books demonstrates our commitment to your lifelong learning success. Whether you choose to learn through the written word, computer-based training, Web delivery, or instructor-led training, Global Knowledge Network is committed to providing you the very best in each of those categories. For those of you who know Global Knowledge Network, or those of you who have just found us for the first time, our goal is to be your lifelong competency partner.

Thank you for the opportunity to serve you. We look forward to serving your needs again in the future.

Warmest regards,

Duncan Anderson
Chief Operating Officer, Global Knowledge Network

January 12, 1998

Dear Osborne/McGraw-Hill Customer:

Microsoft is pleased to inform you that Osborne/McGraw-Hill is a participant in the Microsoft® Independent Courseware Vendor (ICV) program. Microsoft ICVs design, develop, and market self-paced courseware, books, and other products that support Microsoft software and the Microsoft Certified Professional (MCP) program.

To be accepted into the Microsoft ICV program, an ICV must meet set criteria. In addition, Microsoft reviews and approves each ICV training product before permission is granted to use the Microsoft Certified Professional Approved Study Guide logo on that product. This logo assures the consumer that the product has passed the following Microsoft standards:

- The course contains accurate product information.
- The course includes labs and activities during which the student can apply knowledge and skills learned from the course.
- The course teaches skills that help prepare the student to take corresponding MCP exams.

Microsoft ICVs continually develop and release new MCP Approved Study Guides. To prepare for a particular Microsoft certification exam, a student may choose one or more single, self-paced training courses or a series of training courses.

You will be pleased with the quality and effectiveness of the MCP Approved Study Guides available from Osborne/McGraw-Hill.

Sincerely,

*Becky Kirsininkas*

Becky Kirsininkas
ICV Program Manager
Microsoft Training & Certification

## ABOUT SYNGRESS MEDIA

**Syngress Media** creates books and software for Information Technology professionals seeking skill enhancement and career advancement. Its products are designed to comply with vendor and industry standard course curricula, and are optimized for certification exam preparation. Visit the Syngress web site at www.syngress.com.

## ABOUT THE CONTRIBUTORS

**Shane Clawson** is a principal in Virtual Engineering, a consulting and engineering firm specializing in network consulting and technology process re-engineering. Shane has more than 20 years' experience as an instructor in the networking field. He is a Microsoft Certified System Engineer (MCSE) and a Microsoft Certified Trainer (MCT) who has been working with NT since its inception. He specializes in Microsoft networking and BackOffice products. Shane can be reached at ShaneCSE@msn.com.

**Richard H. Luckett** (MCSE) is currently a consultant for Comms People specializing in enterprise messaging systems and security. He has worked in the networking industry for more than eight years. For the past three years, Richard has worked to design, implement, deploy and integrate Microsoft's BackOffice solutions for the U.S. Government and many publicly and privately held corporations.

## Technical Review by:

**Sean Wallbridge** is a network systems engineer and consultant specializing in BackOffice and Intranet solutions. When not writing, geeking, or just plain getting into trouble, he enjoys spending time with his wife Wendy, Murphy the Basset Hound from Hell, and their two cats, Gidget and Elvis. Sean is a Microsoft Certified Systems Engineer (MCSE 3x/4x) specializing in Internet technologies (MCSE+Internet). Sean also maintains the Compaq Accredited Systems Engineer (ASE), Microsoft Certified Trainer (MCT), Microsoft Sales Specialist (MSS) and trainer, Novell CNA and Intolerable Nuisance Husband (INH) designations.

**David W. Egan** is an engineer and a Microsoft Certified Trainer. David has 20 years of programming and operating system experience. After receiving a BASc in Engineering in 1978 from the University of Toronto, David started his career working in the oilfield industry performing computerized, geological, downhole, formation testing in both North and South America.

After this David programmed in assembler and C for several years. Following this was a two-year lecturing position at a college in Southeast Asia teaching programming and hardware design. This led to four years as a VMS and UNIX instructor at Digital Equipment Corporation. For the past six years, David has been writing course material and technical books, as well as consulting and teaching VMS, UNIX, and NT.

David lives with his wife and two children in the Vancouver, British Columbia area.

# ACKNOWLEDGMENTS

We would like to thank the following people:

- Richard Kristof of Global Knowledge Network for championing the series and providing us access to some great people and information. And to Patrick Von Schlag, Robin Yunker, David Mantica, Stacey Cannon, and Kevin Murray for all their cooperation.

- To all the incredibly hard-working folks at Osborne/McGraw-Hill: Brandon Nordin, Scott Rogers, and Gareth Hancock for their help in launching a great series and being solid team players. In addition, Cynthia Douglas, Steve Emry, Anne Ellingsen, Bernadette Jurich, and Jody McKenzie for their help in fine-tuning the book.

- Thanks to John Phillips of Self Test Software, John Rose of Transcender Corporation, Parmol Soni of Microhard Technologies, and Michael Herrick of VFX Technologies.

- To Holly Heath at Microsoft, Corp. for being patient and diligent in answering all our questions.

# CONTENTS

# PREFACE

This book's primary objective is to help you prepare for and pass the required MCSE exam so you can begin to reap the career benefits of certification. We believe that the only way to do this is to help you increase your knowledge and build your skills. After completing this book, you should feel confident that you have thoroughly reviewed all of the objectives that Microsoft has established for the exam.

## In This Book

This book is organized around the actual structure of the Microsoft exam administered at Sylvan Testing Centers. Most of the MCSE exams have six parts to them: Planning, Installation and Configuration, Managing Resources, Connectivity, Monitoring and Optimization, and Troubleshooting. Microsoft has let us know all the topics we need to cover for the exam. We've followed their list carefully, so you can be assured you're not missing anything.

## In Every Chapter

We've created a set of chapter components that call your attention to important items, reinforce important points, and provide helpful exam-taking hints. Take a look at what you'll find in every chapter:

- Every chapter begins with the **Certification Objectives**—what you need to know in order to pass the section on the exam dealing with the chapter topic. The Certification Objective headings identify the objectives within the chapter, so you'll always know an objective when you see it!

- **Exam Watch** notes call attention to information about, and potential pitfalls in, the exam. These helpful hints are written by MCSEs who have taken the exams and received their certification—who better to tell you what to worry about? They know what you're about to go through!

- **Certification Exercises** are interspersed throughout the chapters. These are step-by-step exercises that mirror vendor-recommended labs. They help you master skills that are likely to be an area of focus on the exam. Don't just read through the exercises; they are hands-on practice that you should be comfortable completing. Learning by doing is an effective way to increase your competency with a product.

- **From the Classroom** sidebars describe the issues that come up most often in the training classroom setting. These sidebars give you a valuable perspective into certification- and product-related topics. They point out common mistakes and address questions that have arisen from classroom discussions.

- **Q & A** sections lay out problems and solutions in a quick-read format:

## QUESTIONS AND ANSWERS

| | |
|---|---|
| I am the administrator for our Windows NT Server and the IIS server. Will I be using MTS? | MTS is for programmers who wish to write programs to take advantage of the features that programming for MTS can provide. |

- The **Certification Summary** is a succinct review of the chapter and a re-statement of salient points regarding the exam.

- The **Two-Minute Drill** at the end of every chapter is a checklist of the main points of the chapter. It can be used for last-minute review.

- The **Self Test** offers questions similar to those found on the certification exams, including multiple choice, true/false questions, and fill-in-the-blank. The answers to these questions, as well as explanations of the answers, can be found in Appendix A. By taking the Self Test after completing each chapter, you'll reinforce what you've learned from that chapter, while becoming familiar with the structure of the exam questions.

## Some Pointers

Once you've finished reading this book, set aside some time to do a thorough review. You might want to return to the book several times and make use of all the methods it offers for reviewing the material:

1. *Re-read all the Two-Minute Drills,* or have someone quiz you. You also can use the drills as a way to do a quick cram before the exam.

2. *Re-read all the Exam Watch notes.* Remember that these are written by MCSEs who have taken the exam and passed. They know what you should expect—and what you should be careful about.

3. *Review all the Q & A scenarios* for quick problem solving.

4. *Re-take the Self Tests.* Taking the tests right after you've read the chapter is a good idea, because it helps reinforce what you've just learned. However, it's an even better idea to go back later and do all the questions in the book in one sitting. Pretend you're taking the exam. (For this reason, you should mark your answers on a separate piece of paper when you go through the questions the first time.)

5. *Take the on-line tests.* Boot up the CD-ROM and take a look. We have more third-party tests on our CD than any other book out there, so you'll get quite a bit of practice.

6. *Complete the exercises.* Did you do the exercises when you read through each chapter? If not, do them! These exercises are designed to cover exam topics, and there's no better way to get to know this material than by practicing.

7. *Check out the web site.* Global Knowledge Network invites you to become an active member of the Access Global web site. This site is an online mall and an information repository that you'll find invaluable. You can access many types of products to assist you in your preparation for the exams, and you'll be able to participate in forums, on-line discussions, and threaded discussions. No other book brings you unlimited access to such a resource. You'll find more information about this site in Appendix C.

# MCSE Certification

Microsoft offers several levels of certification. You can find information on the certification and tests at www.microsoft.com/train_cert. The information contained in this book will help you in attaining your Microsoft Certified System Engineer (MCSE) and MCSE + Internet Certification.

To attain the MCSE, you must pass six exams: four core exams and two electives. You need a network exam, a desktop operating system exam, and both Windows NT Server and Windows NT Server in the Enterprise exams for the core requirements. You also need two elective exams covering other products. The IIS 4.0 exam and the Proxy Server exam are electives.

For the MCSE + Internet, the following table details which exams you need to pass:

| MCSE + Internet Core Exams (Seven Required): | |
|---|---|
| Exam 70-058: | Networking Essentials |
| Exam 70-059: | Internetworking with TCP/IP on Windows NT 4.0 |
| Exam 70-063: | Implementing and Supporting Windows 95 |
| Exam 70-073: | **OR** <br><br> Implementing and Supporting Windows NT Workstation 4.0 |
| Exam 70-067: | Implementing and Supporting Windows NT Server 4.0 |
| Exam 70-068: | Implementing and Supporting Windows NT Server 4.0 in the Enterprise |
| Exam 70-077: | Implementing and Supporting Internet Information Server 3.0 and Microsoft Index Server 1.1 |
| Exam 70-087: | **OR** <br><br> Implementing and Supporting Internet Information Server 4.0 |
| Exam 70-079: | Implementing and Supporting Internet Explorer 4.0 by Using the Internet Explorer Administration Kit |

This book will help you with Exams 70-087 and 70-079. It will also prepare you for Exam 70-088 on Proxy Server, which is not listed in the above table, but qualifies as an elective exam.

# The CD-ROM Resource

This book comes with a CD-ROM full of supplementary material you can use while preparing for the MCSE exams. We think you'll find our book/CD package one of the most useful on the market. It provides all the sample tests available from testing companies such as Transcender, MicroHard, Self Test Software, and VFX Technologies. In addition to all these third-party products, you'll find an electronic version of the book, where you can look up items easily, search on specific terms, and link to a test bank of questions created especially for this book. There's more about this resource in Appendix C, "About the CD."

# How to Take a Microsoft Certification Examination

**by John C. Phillips, Vice President of Test Development,
Self Test Software
(Self Test's PEP is the official Microsoft practice test.)**

## Good News and Bad News

If you are new to Microsoft certification, we have some good news and some bad news. The good news, of course, is that Microsoft certification is one of the most valuable credentials you can earn. It sets you apart from the crowd, and marks you as a valuable asset to your employer. You will gain the respect of your peers, and Microsoft certification can have a wonderful effect on your income.

The bad news is that Microsoft certification tests are not easy. You may think you will read through some study material, memorize a few facts, and pass the Microsoft examinations. After all, these certification exams are just computer-based, multiple-choice tests, so they must be easy. If you believe this, you are wrong. Unlike many "multiple guess" tests you have been exposed to in school, the questions on Microsoft certification examinations go beyond simple factual knowledge.

The purpose of this introduction is to teach you how to take a Microsoft certification examination. To be successful, you need to know something about the purpose and structure of these tests. We will also look at the latest innovations in Microsoft testing. Using *simulations* and *adaptive testing*, Microsoft is enhancing both the validity and security of the certification process. These factors have some important effects on how you should prepare for an exam, as well as your approach to each question during the test.

We will begin by looking at the purpose, focus, and structure of Microsoft certification tests, and examine the effect these factors have on the kinds of questions you will face on your certification exams. We will define the structure of examination questions and investigate some common formats. Next, we will present a strategy for answering these questions. Finally, we will give some specific guidelines on what you should do on the day of your test.

## Why Vendor Certification?

The Microsoft Certified Professional program, like the certification programs from Lotus, Novell, Oracle, and other software vendors, is maintained for the ultimate purpose of increasing the corporation's profits. A successful vendor certification program accomplishes this goal by helping to create a pool of experts in a company's software, and by "branding" these experts so that companies using the software can identify them.

We know that vendor certification has become increasingly popular in the last few years because it helps employers find qualified workers, and because it helps software vendors like Microsoft sell their products. But why vendor certification rather than a more traditional approach like a college degree in computer science? A college education is a broadening and enriching experience, but a degree in computer science does not prepare students for most jobs in the IT industry.

A common truism in our business states, "If you are out of the IT industry for three years and want to return, you have to start over." The problem, of course, is *timeliness*; if a first-year student learns about a specific computer program, it probably will no longer be in wide use when he or she graduates. Although some colleges are trying to integrate Microsoft certification into their curriculum, the problem is not really a flaw in higher education, but a characteristic of the IT industry. Computer software is changing so rapidly that a four-year college just can't keep up.

A marked characteristic of the Microsoft certification program is an emphasis on performing specific job tasks rather than merely gathering knowledge. It may come as a shock, but most potential employers do not care how much you know about the theory of operating systems, networking, or database design. As one IT manager put it, "I don't really care what my employees know about the theory of our network. We don't need someone to sit at a desk and think about it. We need people who can actually do something to make it work better."

You should not think that this attitude is some kind of anti-intellectual revolt against "book learning." Knowledge is a necessary prerequisite, but it is not enough. More than one company has hired a computer science graduate as a network administrator, only to learn that the new employee has no idea how to add users, assign permissions, or perform the other day-to-day tasks necessary to maintain a network. This brings us to the second major characteristic of Microsoft certification that affects the questions you must be prepared to answer. In addition to timeliness, Microsoft certification is also job task oriented.

The timeliness of Microsoft's certification program is obvious, and is inherent in the fact that you will be tested on current versions of software in wide use today. The job task orientation of Microsoft certification is almost as obvious, but testing real-world job skills using a computer-based test is not easy.

## Computerized Testing

Considering the popularity of Microsoft certification, and the fact that certification candidates are spread around the world, the only practical way to administer tests for the certification program is through Sylvan Prometric testing centers. Sylvan Prometric provides proctored testing services for Microsoft, Oracle, Novell, Lotus, and the A+ computer technician certification. Although the IT industry accounts for much of Sylvan's revenue, the company provides services for a number of other businesses and organizations, such as FAA pre-flight pilot tests. In fact, most companies that need secure test delivery over a wide geographic area use the services of Sylvan Prometric. In addition to delivery, Sylvan Prometric also scores the tests and provides statistical feedback on the performance of each test question to the companies and organizations that use their services.

Typically, several hundred questions are developed for a new Microsoft certification examination. The questions are first reviewed by a number of subject matter experts for technical accuracy, and then are presented in a beta test. The beta test may last for several hours, due to the large number of questions. After a few weeks, Microsoft Certification uses the statistical feedback from Sylvan to check the performance of the beta questions.

Questions are discarded if most test takers get them right (too easy) or wrong (too difficult), and a number of other statistical measures are taken of each question. Although the scope of our discussion precludes a rigorous treatment of question analysis, you should be aware that Microsoft and other vendors spend a great deal of time and effort making sure their examination questions are valid. In addition to the obvious desire for quality, the fairness of a vendor's certification program must be legally defensible.

The questions that survive statistical analysis form the pool of questions for the final certification examination.

# Test Structure

The kind of test we are most familiar with is known as a *form* test. For Microsoft certification, a form usually consists of 50–70 questions and takes 60–90 minutes to complete. If there are 240 questions in the final pool for an examination, then four forms can be created. Thus, candidates who retake the test probably will not see the same questions.

Other variations are possible. From the same pool of 240 questions, *five* forms can be created, each containing 40 unique questions (200 questions) and 20 questions selected at random from the remaining 40.

The questions in a Microsoft form test are equally weighted. This means they all count the same when the test is scored. An interesting and useful characteristic of a form test is that you can mark a question you have doubts about as you take the test. Assuming you have time left when you finish all the questions, you can return and spend more time on the questions you have marked as doubtful.

Microsoft may soon implement *adaptive* testing. To use this interactive technique, a form test is first created and administered to several thousand certification candidates. The statistics generated are used to assign a weight, or difficulty level, for each question. For example, the questions in a form might be divided into levels one through five, with level one questions being the easiest and level five the hardest.

When an adaptive test begins, the candidate is first given a level three question. If it is answered correctly, a question from the next higher level is presented, and an incorrect response results in a question from the next lower level. When 15–20 questions have been answered in this manner, the scoring algorithm is able to predict, with a high degree of statistical certainty, whether the candidate would pass or fail if all the questions in the form were answered. When the required degree of certainty is attained, the test ends and the candidate receives a pass/fail grade.

Adaptive testing has some definite advantages for everyone involved in the certification process. Adaptive tests allow Sylvan Prometric to deliver more tests with the same resources, as certification candidates often are in and out in 30 minutes or less. For Microsoft, adaptive testing means that fewer test questions are exposed to each candidate, and this can enhance the security, and therefore the validity, of certification tests.

One possible problem you may have with adaptive testing is that you are not allowed to mark and revisit questions. Since the adaptive algorithm is interactive, and all questions but the first are selected on the basis of your response to the previous question, it is not possible to skip a particular question or change an answer.

# Question Types

Computerized test questions can be presented in a number of ways. Some of the possible formats are used on Microsoft certification examinations, and some are not.

### True/False

We are all familiar with True/False questions, but because of the inherent 50 percent chance of guessing the correct answer, you will not see questions of this type on Microsoft certification exams.

### Multiple Choice

The majority of Microsoft certification questions are in the multiple-choice format, with either a single correct answer or multiple correct answers. One interesting variation on multiple-choice questions with multiple correct answers is whether or not the candidate is told how many answers are correct.

EXAMPLE:

Which two files can be altered to configure the MS-DOS environment? (Choose two.)

Or

Which files can be altered to configure the MS-DOS environment? (Choose all that apply.)

You may see both variations on Microsoft certification examinations, but the trend seems to be toward the first type, where candidates are told explicitly how many answers are correct. Questions of the "choose all that apply" variety are more difficult, and can be merely confusing.

## Graphical Questions

One or more graphical elements are sometimes used as exhibits to help present or clarify an exam question. These elements may take the form of a network diagram, pictures of networking components, or screen shots from the software on which you are being tested. It is often easier to present the concepts required for a complex performance-based scenario with a graphic than with words.

Test questions known as *hotspots* actually incorporate graphics as part of the answer. These questions ask the certification candidate to click on a location or graphical element to answer the question. As an example, you might be shown the diagram of a network and asked to click on an appropriate location for a router. The answer is correct if the candidate clicks within the *hotspot* that defines the correct location.

## Free Response Questions

Another kind of question you sometimes see on Microsoft certification examinations requires a *free response* or type-in answer. An example of this type of question might present a TCP/IP network scenario and ask the candidate to calculate and enter the correct subnet mask in dotted decimal notation.

## Knowledge-Based and Performance-Based Questions

Microsoft Certification develops a blueprint for each Microsoft certification examination with input from subject matter experts. This blueprint defines the content areas and objectives for each test, and each test question is created to test a specific objective. The basic information from the examination blueprint can be found on Microsoft's web site in the Exam Prep Guide for each test.

Psychometricians (psychologists who specialize in designing and analyzing tests) categorize test questions as knowledge-based or performance-based. As the names imply, knowledge-based questions are designed to test knowledge, while performance-based questions are designed to test performance.

Some objectives demand a knowledge-based question. For example, objectives that use verbs like *list* and *identify* tend to test only what you know, not what you can do.

EXAMPLE:
Objective: Identify the MS-DOS configuration files.
Which two files can be altered to configure the MS-DOS environment? (Choose two.)

    A. COMMAND.COM

    B. AUTOEXEC.BAT

    C. IO.SYS

    D. CONFIG.SYS
    **Correct answers: B,D**

Other objectives use action verbs like *install, configure,* and *troubleshoot* to define job tasks. These objectives can often be tested with either a knowledge-based question or a performance-based question.

EXAMPLE:
Objective: Configure an MS-DOS installation appropriately using the PATH statement in AUTOEXEX.BAT.

Knowledge-based question:

What is the correct syntax to set a path to the D:\APP directory in AUTOEXEC.BAT?

A. SET PATH EQUAL TO D:\APP

B. PATH D:\APP

C. SETPATH D:\APP

D. D:\APP EQUALS PATH

Correct answer: **B**

Performance-based question:

Your company uses several DOS accounting applications that access a group of common utility programs. What is the best strategy for configuring the computers in the accounting department so that the accounting applications will always be able to access the utility programs?

A. Store all the utilities on a single floppy disk, and make a copy of the disk for each computer in the accounting department.

B. Copy all the utilities to a directory on the C: drive of each computer in the accounting department, and add a PATH statement pointing to this directory in the AUTOEXEC.BAT files.

C. Copy all the utilities to all application directories on each computer in the accounting department.

D. Place all the utilities in the C:\DOS directory on each computer, because the C:\DOS directory is automatically included in the PATH statement when AUTOEXEC.BAT is executed.

Correct answer: **B**

Even in this simple example, the superiority of the performance-based question is obvious. Whereas the knowledge-based question asks for a single fact, the performance-based question presents a real-life situation and requires that you make a decision based on this scenario. Thus, performance-based questions give more bang (validity) for the test author's buck (individual question).

# Testing Job Performance

We have said that Microsoft certification focuses on timeliness and the ability to perform job tasks. We have also introduced the concept of performance-based questions, but even performance-based multiple-choice questions do not really measure performance. Another strategy is needed to test job skills.

Given unlimited resources, it is not difficult to test job skills. In an ideal world, Microsoft would fly MCP candidates to Redmond, place them in a controlled environment with a team of experts, and ask them to plan, install, maintain, and troubleshoot a Windows network. In a few days at most, the experts could reach a valid decision as to whether each candidate should or should not be granted MCSE status. Needless to say, this is not likely to happen.

Closer to reality, another way to test performance is by using the actual software, and creating a testing program to present tasks and automatically grade a candidate's performance when the tasks are completed. This *cooperative* approach would be practical in some testing situations, but the same test that is presented to MCP candidates in Boston must also be available in Bahrain and Botswana. Many Sylvan Prometric testing locations around the world cannot run 32-bit applications, much less provide the complex networked solutions required by cooperative testing applications.

The most workable solution for measuring performance in today's testing environment is a *simulation* program. When the program is launched during a test, the candidate sees a simulation of the actual software that looks, and behaves, just like the real thing. When the testing software presents a task, the simulation program is launched and the candidate performs the required task. The testing software then grades the candidate's performance on the required task and moves to the next question. In this way, a 16-bit simulation program can mimic the look and feel of 32-bit operating systems, a complicated network, or even the entire Internet.

Microsoft has introduced simulation questions on the certification examination for Internet Information Server 4.0. Simulation questions provide many advantages over other testing methodologies, and simulations are expected to become increasingly important in the Microsoft certification program. For example, studies have shown that there is a very high correlation between the ability to perform simulated tasks on a computer-based test and the ability to perform the actual job tasks. Thus, simulations enhance the validity of the certification process.

Another truly wonderful benefit of simulations is in the area of test security. It is just not possible to cheat on a simulation question. In fact, you will be told exactly what tasks you are expected to perform on the test. How can a certification candidate cheat? By learning to perform the tasks? What a concept!

# Study Strategies

There are appropriate ways to study for the different types of questions you will see on a Microsoft certification examination.

## Knowledge-Based Questions

Knowledge-based questions require that you memorize facts. There are hundreds of facts inherent in every content area of every Microsoft certification examination. There are several keys to memorizing facts:

- **Repetition** The more times your brain is exposed to a fact, the more likely you are to remember it.

- **Association** Connecting facts within a logical framework makes them easier to remember.

- **Motor Association** It is often easier to remember something if you write it down or perform some other physical act, like clicking on a practice test answer.

We have said that the emphasis of Microsoft certification is job performance, and that there are very few knowledge-based questions on Microsoft certification exams. Why should you waste a lot of time learning file names, IP address formulas, and other minutiae? Read on.

## Performance-Based Questions

Most of the questions you will face on a Microsoft certification exam are performance-based scenario questions. We have discussed the superiority of these questions over simple knowledge-based questions, but you should remember that the job task orientation of Microsoft certification extends the knowledge you need to pass the exams; it does not replace this knowledge. Therefore, the first step in preparing for scenario questions is to absorb as many facts relating to the exam content areas as you can. In other words, go back to the previous section and follow the steps to prepare for an exam composed of knowledge-based questions.

The second step is to familiarize yourself with the format of the questions you are likely to see on the exam. You can do this by answering the questions in this study guide, by using Microsoft assessment tests, or by using practice tests. The day of your test is not the time to be surprised by the convoluted construction of Microsoft exam questions.

For example, one of Microsoft Certification's favorite formats of late takes the following form:

**Scenario:** You have a network with...

**Primary Objective:** You want to...

**Secondary Objective:** You also want to...

**Proposed Solution:** Do this...

What does the proposed solution accomplish?

    A.  satisfies the primary and the secondary objective

    B.  satisfies the primary but not the secondary objective

    C.  satisfies the secondary but not the primary objective

    D.  satisfies neither the primary nor the secondary objective

This kind of question, with some variation, is seen on many Microsoft Certification examinations.

At best, these performance-based scenario questions really do test certification candidates at a higher cognitive level than knowledge-based questions. At worst, these questions can test your reading comprehension and test-taking ability rather than your ability to use Microsoft products. Be sure to get in the habit of reading the question carefully to determine what is being asked.

The third step in preparing for Microsoft scenario questions is to adopt the following attitude: Multiple-choice questions aren't really performance-based. It is all a cruel lie. These scenario questions are just knowledge-based questions with a little story wrapped around them.

To answer a scenario question, you have to sift through the story to the underlying facts of the situation, and apply your knowledge to determine the correct answer. This may sound silly at first, but the process we go through in solving real-life problems is quite similar. The key concept is that every scenario question (and every real-life problem) has a fact at its center, and if we can identify that fact, we can answer the question.

### Simulations

Simulation questions really do measure your ability to perform job tasks. You must be able to perform the specified tasks. There are two ways to prepare for simulation questions:

1. Get experience with the actual software. If you have the resources, this is a great way to prepare for simulation questions.

2. Use official Microsoft practice tests. Practice tests are available that provide practice with the same simulation engine used on Microsoft certification exams. This approach has the added advantage of grading your efforts.

# Signing Up

Signing up to take a Microsoft certification examination is easy. Sylvan operators in each country can schedule tests at any testing center. There are, however, a few things you should know:

1. If you call Sylvan during a busy time period, get a cup of coffee first, because you may be in for a long wait. Sylvan does an excellent job, but everyone in the world seems to want to sign up for a test on Monday morning.

2. You will need your social security number or some other unique identifier to sign up for a Sylvan test, so have it at hand.

3. Pay for your test by credit card if at all possible. This makes things easier, and you can even schedule tests for the same day you call, if space is available at your local testing center.

4. Know the number and title of the test you want to take before you call. This is not essential, and the Sylvan operators will help you if they can. Having this information in advance, however, speeds up the registration process.

# Taking the Test

Teachers have always told you not to try to cram for examinations, because it does no good. Sometimes they lied. If you are faced with a knowledge-based test requiring only that you regurgitate facts, cramming can mean the difference between passing and failing. This is not the case, however, with Microsoft certification exams. If you don't know it the night before, don't bother to stay up and cram.

Instead, create a schedule and stick to it. Plan your study time carefully, and do not schedule your test until you think you are ready to succeed. Follow these guidelines on the day of your exam:

1. Get a good night's sleep. The scenario questions you will face on a Microsoft certification examination require a clear head.

2. Remember to take two forms of identification—at least one with a picture. A driver's license with your picture, and social security or credit cards are acceptable.

3. Leave home in time to arrive at your testing center a few minutes early. It is not a good idea to feel rushed as you begin your exam.

4. Do not spend too much time on any one question. If you are taking a form test, take your best guess and mark the question so you can come back to it if you have time. You cannot mark and revisit questions on an adaptive test, so you must do your best on each question as you go.

5. If you do not know the answer to a question, try to eliminate the obviously wrong answers and guess from the rest. If you can eliminate two out of four options, you have a 50 percent chance of guessing the correct answer.

6. For scenario questions, follow the steps we outlined earlier. Read the question carefully and try to identify the facts at the center of the story.

Finally, I would advise anyone attempting to earn Microsoft MCSE certification to adopt a philosophical attitude. Even if you are the kind of person who never fails a test, you are likely to fail at least one Microsoft certification test somewhere along the way. Do not get discouraged. If Microsoft certification were easy to obtain, more people would have it, and it would not be so respected and so valuable to your future in the IT industry.

# MCSE
## MICROSOFT CERTIFIED SYSTEMS ENGINEER

# 1

# Overview of Internet Information Server 4.0

## CERTIFICATION OBJECTIVES

I nternet Information Server (IIS) is Microsoft®'s Web server software that services requests from Web browsers running on client computers. IIS runs on Windows NT Server and provides connectivity to your organization's Web site.

This chapter identifies the MCSE + Internet certification objectives and describes how this book can help you meet those objectives. This chapter also describes how IIS has evolved as a product and then briefly introduces you to the functions and components of IIS 4.0, most of which are covered in more detail later in this book.

## Why Read This Book?

This book has two objectives: First, to learn to use Microsoft Internet technologies and second, to pass three Microsoft certification tests.

If either one or both of those objectives match your desires, then read this book. Be prepared to accomplish both objectives as you go through the book. I believe that both objectives go hand in hand. For most people, it will be difficult (if not impossible) to pass the Microsoft certification tests without a fundamental understanding of and hands-on experience with the product.

When you have completed this book, you will have installed and configured and used Internet Information Server, Proxy Server, and Internet Explorer. You will be able to use this baseline knowledge to set up a reasonably secure Web site for your organization.

Let's talk about Microsoft certification. First, professionals attain professional certification as a means of validating their knowledge and experience. We see this in everyday life. In fact, I submit that the overwhelming majority of us demand it from the professional with whom we interact. For example, if you go to see a doctor, you expect the doctor to know what he is doing to have been awarded the professional credential "M.D." There are people who may have a great deal of knowledge and skill in treating the ailments of human beings who are not certified as Medical Doctors. Most of us probably stay away from these practitioners, opting to see those individuals who are. In some respect, being certified doesn't mean you are competent; it means that you were able to pass a number of tests. But don't let that philosophy sidetrack you. You are better off being competent and certified than just being competent. A true professional carries professional credentials and is appropriately compensated for them.

Second, the certification exams are rigorous. You must be prepared if you expect to pass the tests and you must be prepared to persevere to obtain your objective. This book, and others in this series, will give you all the skills you need to pass the exams.

## CERTIFICATION OBJECTIVE 1.01

# Scope of This Book

This book covers Internet Information Server 4.0, Proxy Server 2.0, and Internet Explorer 4.0, in that order. Each chapter includes a list of certification objectives, a discussion about the technology involved, exercises aimed at building your understanding and skills, a certification summary, a two-minute, hard-hitting drill on the material in the chapter, and some practice questions.

To follow along, you need hardware and software so that you can do the exercises. There is no substitute for hands-on experience, both from the point of view of developing your skills and from becoming comfortable with the information needed to pass the certification tests.

We start with Microsoft's disclaimer: "This exam preparation guide was published December 2, 1997, and is subject to change at any time without prior notice and at Microsoft's sole discretion." The following section describes Microsoft's certification objectives for IIS 4.0.

## Microsoft Objectives

This certification exam measures your ability to implement, administer, and troubleshoot information systems that incorporate Internet Information Server 4.0.

## Planning

Choose a security strategy for various situations. Security considerations include:

- Controlling anonymous access
- Controlling access to known users and groups
- Controlling access by host or network
- Configuring SSL to provide encryption and authentication schemes
- Identifying the appropriate balance between security requirements and performance requirements

Choose an implementation strategy for an Internet site or an intranet site for stand-alone servers, single-domain environments, and multiple-domain environments. Tasks include:

- Resolving host header name issues using a HOSTS file, or DNS, or both
- Choosing the appropriate operating system on which to install IIS

Choose the appropriate technology to resolve specified problems. Technology options include:

- WWW service
- FTP service
- Microsoft Transaction Server
- Microsoft SMTP Service
- Microsoft NNTP Service
- Microsoft Index Server
- Microsoft Certificate Server

## Installation and Configuration

Install IIS. Tasks include:

- Configuring a Microsoft Windows NT Server 4.0 computer for the installation of IIS
- Identifying differences made to a Windows NT Server 4.0 computer by the installation of IIS

Configure IIS to support the FTP service. Tasks include:

- Setting bandwidth and user connections
- Setting user logon requirements and authentication requirements
- Modifying port settings
- Setting directory listing style
- Configuring virtual directories and servers

Configure IIS to support the WWW service. Tasks include:

- Setting bandwidth and user connections
- Setting user logon requirements and authentication requirements
- Modifying port settings
- Setting default pages
- Setting HTTP 1.1 host header names to host multiple Web sites
- Enabling HTTP keep-alives

Configure and save consoles using Microsoft Management Console (MMC).
Verify server settings by accessing the metabase.
Choose the appropriate administration method.
Install and configure Certificate Server.

Install and configure Microsoft SMTP Service.
Install and configure Microsoft NNTP Service.
Customize the installation of Site Server Express (SSE) Content Analyzer.
Customize the installation of SSE Usage Import and Report Writer.

### Configuring and Managing Resource Access

Create and share directories with appropriate permissions. Tasks include:

- Setting directory-level permissions
- Setting file-level permissions

Create and share local and remote virtual directories with appropriate permissions. Tasks include:

- Creating a virtual directory and assigning an alias
- Setting directory-level permissions
- Setting file-level permissions

Create and share virtual servers with appropriate permissions. Tasks include:

- Assigning IP addresses

Write scripts to manage the FTP service or the WWW service.
Manage a Web site by using Content Analyzer. Tasks include:

- Creating, customizing, and navigating WebMaps
- Examining a Web site using the various reports provided by Content Analyzer
- Tracking links by using a WebMap

Configure Microsoft SMTP Service to host personal mailboxes.
Configure Microsoft NNTP Service to host a newsgroup.
Configure Certificate Server to issue certificates.
Configure Index Server to index a Web site.
Manage MIME types.

Manage the FTP service.
Manage the WWW service.

### Integration and Interoperability

Configure IIS to connect to a database. Tasks include:

■ Configuring ODBC

Configure IIS to integrate with Index Server. Tasks include:

■ Specifying query parameters by creating the .IDQ file

■ Specifying how the query results are formatted and displayed to the user by creating the .HTX file

### Running Applications

Configure IIS to support server-side scripting.
Configure IIS to run ISAPI applications.

### Monitoring and Optimization

Maintain a log for fine-tuning and auditing purposes. Tasks include:

■ Importing log files into a Usage Import and Report Writer database

■ Configuring the logging features of the WWW service

■ Configuring the logging features of the FTP service

■ Configuring Usage Import and Report Writer to analyze logs created by the WWW service or the FTP service

■ Automating the use of Usage Import and Report Writer

Monitor performance of various functions by using Performance Monitor. Functions include HTTP and FTP sessions.
Analyze performance. Performance issues include:

■ Identifying bottlenecks
■ Identifying network-related performance issues

■ Identifying disk-related performance issues

Identifying CPU-related performance issues
Optimize performance of IIS.
Optimize performance of Index Server.
Optimize performance of Microsoft SMTP Service.
Optimize performance of Microsoft NNTP Service.
Interpret performance data.
Optimize a Web site by using Content Analyzer.

### Troubleshooting

Resolve IIS configuration problems.
Resolve security problems.
Resolve resource access problems.
Resolve Index Server query problems.
Resolve setup issues when installing IIS on a Windows NT Server 4.0 computer.
Use a WebMap to find and repair broken links, hyperlink texts, headings, and titles.
Resolve WWW service problems.
Resolve FTP service problems.

**CERTIFICATION OBJECTIVE 1.02**

# Required Hardware and Software

From a hardware point of view, you need at least two PCs. You will configure one to be a domain controller and the other to be a member server. The domain controller will have two Network Interface Cards (NICs). The computer with two NICs will be used for our Proxy Server later. Each PC should have the following components:

■ Pentium CPU

■ 32MB RAM

■ 1GB unused disk space

- Mouse
- VGA adapter
- CD-ROM

For software, you need Windows NT Server 4.0, Proxy Server 2.0, Internet Explorer 4.01, Windows NT Option Pack 4.0 and Windows NT Server Service Pack 3 (SP3).

This book approaches the exercises as though you are starting with a clean, new network. If you are working with an established network, you must make the appropriate adjustments, but it shouldn't be too hard.

## General Requirements for IIS

To install Internet Information Server 4.0, you need the Windows NT 4.0 Option Pack, which contains the IIS software, as well as the add-on products.

You must have Windows NT Server and Service Pack 3 (SP3) installed. It does not have to be installed as a domain controller or in a Windows NT domain environment. However, in this book you will be using the security features of a domain, so some exercises will require that the Windows NT Server be either a domain, controller or a member server in a Windows NT domain.

| Hardware | Required | Recommended |
|---|---|---|
| CPU | 486/66 | P-90 or greater |
| RAM | 32MB | 64MB |
| Unused Disk Space | 50MB | 300MB plus publishing space |

## The Internet

The Internet is the mythical place where people go to "surf" the World Wide Web (WWW) and connect to FTP sites. We tend to talk about the Internet as though it was one object, like saying, "I have a glass." But the Internet is composed of many (perhaps thousands) different networks all linked together.

The transport protocol of the Internet is TCP/IP. Therefore, your IIS server must have TCP/IP as its transport protocol.

## Connecting to the Internet

To connect to the Internet, you need an Internet Service Provider (ISP). The ISP's job is to provide you connectivity to the Internet. The ISP may offer various types of connections ranging from dial-up line to dedicated leased line. The line speed of the connection can be important. The faster your line speed, the more information that can be transmitted in a given period of time. Keep in mind that even relatively slow links of 56 Kbps may be faster than the throughput of the Internet at any given time due to congestion at the ISP or at some point in between. There are much higher speed connections you can get from various telecom providers if you really need high throughput from and to your site, such as a T1 or T3 connection. Talk to your ISP.

## Your Domain Name

If you are going to have your Web and FTP server connected to the Internet, you'll need an Internet domain name. This is entirely different than a Windows NT Domain; the two have nothing in common. You start with a request to register (or reserve) a domain name for your organization. You may do this on-line at www.internic.com or ask your ISP to do it for you. Each domain name must be unique, so someone else may have registered your favorite name. If you are not going to be on the Internet, but your server will be on an intranet, you'll need to create a domain name for yourself using the DNS service available with most operating systems, including Windows NT 4.0. The creation of this DNS primary and secondary service is mandatory for connection to the Internet but not within the scope of this book.

# History of IIS

Microsoft released Internet Information Server (IIS) Version 4.0 to production late in 1997. Version 4.0 is the latest product in the Internet Information Server series. IIS 4.0 adds significant features and tighter integration of other products and technologies than did the earlier versions. The IIS technology evolution of the past months can be classified as "remarkable" due to the progress this product has shown in a relatively short period of time. The product has evolved in less than 24 months and will evolve even further. Part of the reason for this is the fast pace of change of Internet technology and of technology in general. There was a period in time that you might expect to use software and hardware products for many years before feeling the need to "update" them with newer products. Now, we measure the useful life of such products in months rather than years. And, the rate at which the changes are occurring is decreasing.

IIS 2.0 is included with the Windows NT Server CD-ROM and only runs on Windows NT Server. IIS is not technically part of the Windows NT Server operating system, but is an add-on product. Microsoft does not charge for IIS. IIS 2.0 offered the basic functionality with a Hypertext Transfer Protocol (HTTP) server, an FTP server, and a Gopher server. There were not many add-on products that would enhance its Internet or intranet functionality. IIS 2.0 is fully integrated with Windows NT domain security and you can use the added security offered by Windows NT's NTFS file system.

IIS 3.0 added support for Active Server Pages, a significant feature, and added the ability to use Open Database Connectors (ODBC) to get and put data into SQL Server. Microsoft only included ODBC drivers for SQL Server in IIS 3.0. You had to get other database drivers directly from the other database publishers. Like its predecessor, IIS 3.0 offered WWW server, FTP server, and a Gopher server and is fully integrated with the Windows NT domain security. In independent tests, IIS 3.0 turned in outstanding performance figures, finishing at the top or near the top in these tests. And, there is no charge for IIS 3.0! In fact, if you install Windows NT Service Pack 3 (SP3) and IIS 2.0 is installed at the time, the Service Pack will upgrade IIS 2.0 to IIS 3.0 as part of the process.

## CERTIFICATION OBJECTIVE 1.03

# Overview of IIS 4.0

IIS 4.0 is a significant enhancement to IIS 3.0 in terms of the features and integration of other products that it offers. IIS 4.0 offers a great deal more capability than IIS 3.0. However, IIS 4.0 no longer offers support for Gopher server. This functionality has mostly been replaced by the WWW. IIS 4.0 still supports an FTP server.

IIS 4.0 is part of the Windows NT 4.0 Option Pack that includes features and add-on products such as:

- Index Server
- Transaction Server
- Certificate Server
- Microsoft Management Console (MMC)
- Microsoft Site Server Express
- Network News Transfer Protocol (NNTP)
- Simple Mail Transfer Protocol (SMTP) Service
- Microsoft Message Queue Service
- Data Access Tools
- RAS Connectivity
- Microsoft Script Debugger
- Support for Secure Sockets 3.0

This book will explain and illustrate many of these features. Most of these features are new with the Option Pack.

## CERTIFICATION OBJECTIVE 1.04

# Why Use IIS?

If you are using Windows NT Server, then this product is a natural. It is fully integrated with the operating system, and according to some (like Microsoft) has the following features:

- It is fast.
- It is free.

- It has good flexibility.

- It offers outstanding capabilities.

- It will support small, medium, and large organizations.

- It is easy to configure and easy to use.

Other than that, I can't think of a single thing to recommend it.

**CERTIFICATION OBJECTIVE 1.05**

# IIS Architecture

The design goals for Internet Information Server were:

- **Performance**   Make IIS as fast as practical while using the minimum amount of resources.

- **Integration**   Integrate with Windows NT Server and domain security. A comprehensive set of add-on products is integrated with IIS.

- **Extensibility**   Support Internet Server Application Programming Interface (ISAPI) and Multipurpose Internet Mail Extensions (MIME).

- **Comprehensive Integration**   Integrate additional services, such as Active Server Pages, Java support, Jscript, Visual Basic, Index Server, NetShow, CGI scripts, and Transaction Server.

Standard Internet services (WWW and FTP, for example) run in a process called InetInfo. This process can be viewed using Task Manager. This process contains the shared thread pool, cache logging, and SNMP service.

When you start a process, it spawns one or more *threads*. A thread is a unit of instruction. A *thread pool* is all of the threads within a process. Threads share the same memory address space. Using threads to accomplish tasks is faster than spawning a new process for the task.

Both the HTTP and FTP services run in the same process and share the same cached information such as account information.

**CERTIFICATION OBJECTIVE 1.06**

# Internetworking

Internetworking computers together has been around a long time, probably since the advent of the second computer. Connecting computers together can take many forms. Connecting computer networks together can also take many forms. Some networks are proprietary in form; the protocols by which they communicate are the property of their respective vendors. For example, IBM makes use of a network protocol and architecture called SNA, which is proprietary to IBM. IBM did not publish how it worked so it was difficult for others to make products that coexisted because they had to guess how it worked. Some networks are "open" in form; the protocols by which the network operates are published and freely available to those who are interested. This makes the task of designing equipment and interoperating with the network a much simpler task. Internet protocols are open for all.

## The "*little i*" internet

An *internetwork* is two or more networks connected together. If you have an office in Washington, D.C. and an office in San Diego and the two offices are connected together, this may be described as an internetwork (with a little "i"). This network is called a *private network* if it is not available for use by those outside your organization. As a point of reference, any time you connect offices using public networks you have an internetwork.

## The "*big I*" Internet

The Internet is the subject of countless articles, books, and discussions. The Internet is not a single network, but an amalgam of many smaller networks all interconnected with the purpose of allowing users anywhere to connect to resources anywhere on the greater network. By definition, if your network is connected to the Internet, then it is accessible to anyone anywhere who is using the Internet. You can, of course, restrict access to your network by those outside your network. And, you can restrict where people on your network can go on the Internet.

## Extranet

A new catch phrase, *extranet*, has surfaced in our industry. An extranet is a private internal network combined with another private network toward the purpose of facilitating interorganization communication or business processes.

The most typical example of an extranet is linking your customer's network with yours so your customer can process orders and access information without putting the traffic on the public Internet.

### CERTIFICATION OBJECTIVE 1.07

## Intranets

An *intranet* is an internal network using Internet technology, such as HTTP servers. By definition, an intranet is not connected to other networks or to the Internet. If your internal network is connected to the Internet, it is not an intranet. Using a product like Microsoft Proxy Server allows you to have an intranet for your users to access, while also allowing the users to surf the Internet.

### CERTIFICATION OBJECTIVE 1.08

## New Features of IIS

IIS 4.0 supports a whole host of new features. This section briefly lists the major new features. Some of these features are covered in more detail later in the book.

## NNTP Service

NNTP is a standards-based, commercial duty server for hosting electronic discussion groups called *newsgroups*. Newsgroups can be private or public. NNTP supports secure authentication and can be encrypted.

## SMTP Service

SMTP is a standards-based mail server and is used throughout the Internet. It is highly scalable and allows for the partitioning of mailboxes across multiple servers. User mailboxes can be moved easily between servers. It is used in conjunction with Post Office Protocol Version 3 (POP3).

## Microsoft Script Debugger

Script Debugger is a built-in tool aimed at making it easier to follow script execution in order to find problems in the script execution. Script debugger can be used with client-based scripts or server-based scripts.

## Microsoft Transaction Server

Transaction Server provides a stable run-time environment for high performance applications. It has a graphical administration tool for managing these applications and server process throughout an organization.

## Microsoft Management Console (MMC)

Management Console is a new tool featured when you install IIS 4.0. It is intended to be the standard console in Windows NT 5.0. Applications written for managing services, called *plug-ins*, are written to run in MMC. MMC provides administrators with one common tool with which to manage all services running on Windows NT.

## Microsoft Site Server Express

Site Server Express is a tool that can be used to help analyze how information is organized at your site. The Content Analyzer provides a visual picture of the content of a Web site including link management and reporting functionality.

# Microsoft Certificate Server

Certificate Server is used to provide and manage digital certificates. Digital certificates are used to secure e-mail and to authenticate clients to the servers on the Internet or intranet.

# Microsoft Data Access Components

The Data Access Components services make it easy to use databases with an expanded support for a variety of connections such as ActiveX data objects and OLEDB.

# Microsoft Message Queue (MSMQ)

MSMQ provides applications the ability to communicate with each other by sending and receiving messages. MSMQ uses asynchronous communication and a store-and-forward methodology. MSMQ keeps messages in a queue. The queues protect the messages from being lost while in transit and provide the place for receivers to look for new messages. MSMQ is integrated with Transaction Server.

# Microsoft Internet Connection Services for RAS

Internet Connection Services for Remote Access Service (RAS) is a set of software components designed to help corporations and ISPs build comprehensive Internet access solutions, including dial-up virtual private networks (VPNs). With Internet Connection Services for RAS, you can provide your subscribers or your employees with a seamless connection experience, a global dial-up service, and secure connections over the Internet to a private network.

# Secure Sockets 3.0

Secure Sockets 3.0 is the new standard for secure sockets. Secure sockets provide a mechanism for transmitting and receiving encrypted traffic and for authenticating the client to the server.

**CERTIFICATION OBJECTIVE 1.09**

# Other Microsoft Products

Microsoft offers other products that are designed to run specifically on Windows NT Server. These products are bundled together in the Microsoft Back Office suite. The suite includes System Management Server, SNA Server, SQL Server, and Proxy Server. This section describes two of the major products that use the Internet Information Server.

### SQL Server

SQL Server is part of Microsoft's Back Office suite of client/server applications. SQL Server is an ANSI-compliant SQL (pronounced "seeqwell") Server. IIS provides a connector to SQL Server.

### Exchange Server

Exchange Server is Microsoft's advanced e-mail and Groupware server. IIS integrates with Exchange Server and makes use of facilities such as Exchange Server's SMTP server and POP3 server.

## CERTIFICATION SUMMARY

This introduction gives you the foundation for the rest of the book. This chapter discussed the IIS evolution and the goals of the book. It also covered what certification is, why you want it, and what it will take for you to accomplish it. You have the road map for the skills required to pass the certification test for Internet Information Server. Now, let's go on to Chapter 2 and begin the learning experience.

# 2

# Installing the Server and Client

I nternet Information Server (IIS) uses the client/server paradigm. The server part is IIS, and there are client parts such as Web browsers.

This chapter shows you how to set up Windows NT Server in preparation for installing Internet Information Server. Then this chapter will describe how to install Internet Explorer 4.01 and how to install Internet Information Server 4.0 by upgrading the IIS that is currently installed.

As a prerequisite, I will assume that you have a sound working knowledge of Windows NT Server and Microsoft's domain environments. This book does not cover Windows NT Server except as it directly relates to IIS. The exercises will not include detailed instructions on configuring Windows NT Server, but will include generalized instructions such as "Creating a User account." You will need to be familiar with the "how to." That is, you will need to click Start, then click Programs | Administrative Tools | User Manager | User | New User.

Note that you must have Internet Explorer 4.01 (or later) installed before you can install IIS 4.0. IIS 4.0 is part of the Windows NT 4.0 Option Pack that contains all of the applicable add-ons to help you manage your site and make it more functional. The Installation Wizard makes the installation of IIS very easy.

**CERTIFICATION OBJECTIVE 2.01**

# Setting Up Windows NT Server

Internet Information Server only runs on Windows NT Server. Internet Information Server 4.0 only installs on Windows NT Server 4.0 with Service Pack 3 installed (SP3 was the current service pack at the time of this writing).

## Planning for Your IIS Server

There are two situations in which you may be installing IIS 4.0. One situation is when you have a previous version of IIS installed and the other is when there is no IIS installed. The IIS 4.0 Installation Wizard automatically detects the proper condition and starts up the appropriate wizard. If you have a previous instance of IIS installed, then you are presented with a choice of "Upgrade Only" or "Upgrade Plus." Upgrade Only installs replacement components for the services already installed and Upgrade Plus installs additional components found in IIS 4.0.

Which services you install depend on what you want to accomplish. The basic rule is to only install services that you need, rather than installing all components. If you want to have a presence on the World Wide Web (WWW) where you will publish information and documents for retrieval or collect information from your customers or visitors to your site, then you would install the WWW service. A Web server is also known as an HTTP (Hypertext Transfer Protocol) server. The one limitation of a Web server is that clients cannot upload files to you. You can collect information from users by presenting them with a form to fill out on-line, but they cannot send you a file containing the same information.

If you want to transfer files between your site and your clients, then install the File Transfer Protocol (FTP) service. Once the client establishes a session with your FTP server, the client can send and receive files. The server in this case is passive. Effectively, the client is the one doing the uploading (sending) and the downloading (receiving.) The FTP server does not just send a file to the client; the client gets it. FTP sessions may be done from a command prompt. Those sessions are not GUI-based like the Web browsers using the HTTP server, although you can use the browser to establish the FTP session.

Internet Information Server 4.0 does not support Gopher services as its predecessors did, so you cannot use Gopher from Windows NT. This will be of little concern for most organizations. Many people believe the time for Gopher has come and gone and that its use will diminish to nothing in the near future.

## Windows NT Server Hardware Requirements

There are no unique requirements to support IIS server on Windows NT Server. Table 2-1 summarizes the requirements for Windows NT Server.

Table 2-2 summarizes the requirements to support IIS on Windows NT Server. When you evaluate the requirements for memory and disk space, keep in mind what you intend to do with the IIS. Memory requirements provide enough memory for adequate performance for the basic IIS server operation with a "few" users with sessions. You will need more memory available for times when more users establish sessions with the server. The exact amount of memory depends on the number of users with concurrent sessions, the size of the pages that they open, and how robust you want the server performance to be. We ran some tests and found that having between 150 and 250KB per concurrent users gave us adequate performance. This means that if you have 100 users with concurrent sessions, you might want to have 25MB on hand to service those 100 users. If you take the minimum requirement for Windows NT, which is 16MB, and add 25MB for IIS, it makes a total of 41MB. On most Pentium servers, you need 64MB of RAM to cover that scenario. As a point of reference, 100 concurrent users is a light-duty server in some circumstances. Look what happens if you want to support 1000 concurrent users at your server.

The disk space listed is just the space for IIS server. You should provide your server with enough disk space to cover your publishing objectives, plus some extra for reserve. Installing all the components that come with IIS 4.0 takes slightly more than 170MB of drive space for just the programs. For publishing space, we recommend you calculate what you think you will want

| **TABLE 2-1** | | | |
| :-- | :-- | :-- | :-- |
| Requirements for Windows NT Server | **Component** | **Requirement** | **Recommended** |
| | CPU | 486/33 | Pentium 90 or better |
| | Memory | 16MB | 32MB or more |
| | Disk space | 130MB | 400MB |
| | Monitor | VGA | Super VGA |

| **TABLE 2-2** | | | |
| :-- | :-- | :-- | :-- |
| Requirements for IIS 4.0 | **Component** | **Requirement** | **Recommended** |
| | CPU | 486/50 | Pentium 90 or better |
| | Memory | 16MB | 32–64MB |
| | Disk space | 50MB to install just the bare minimum components. | 1GB. This space requirement could vary depending upon publishing volumes sizes. |

to have, and then use 150 percent of that number as your minimum disk space available before you start to build your site.

## Configuring Windows NT Server

The following exercise assumes that you have Windows NT Server installed and configured according to Table 2-3.

If you do not have Windows NT Server configured as in Table 2-3, it is helpful to reconfigure the server to match the conditions described in that table. It may make following along in the exercises a bit easier. If your server configuration does not match, then you must translate the exercise instructions to meet your configuration.

**TABLE 2-3**

Windows NT Server Parameters for Exercises

| Parameter | Server01 | Server02 |
|---|---|---|
| Operating system version | Windows NT Server 4.0 | Windows NT Server 4.0 |
| Service pack | None | None |
| Server role | Domain controller | Member server |
| Domain name | Domain | Domain |
| Server computer name | Server01 | Server02 |
| Protocols | TCP/IP | TCP/IP |
| IP address | 201.200.199.253 | 201.200.199.252 |
| Subnet mask | 255.255.255.0 | 255.255.255.0 |
| Default gateway | Blank | Blank |
| Internet Information Server | Not installed | Not installed |
| DHCP, DNS, WINS, RAS | Not installed | Not installed |
| User account policies | Left at installation default | Left at installation default |
| System and boot partition | C: Drive at least 500MB free; FAT | C: Drive at least 500MB free; FAT |
| Additional partitions | D: Drive at least 200MB free; NTFS | D: Drive at least 200MB free; NTFS |

# FROM THE CLASSROOM

## IIS Performance: RAM and Disk Subsystems

The two most important factors affecting performance of your Internet server are RAM and the performance of the disk subsystem. These interest students greatly. The architecture of current Intel-based servers allows for a great deal more RAM than the older servers. Windows NT makes use of as much RAM as you can put in the machine and will allocate RAM to its various caches. In IIS, each additional user connection needs some RAM for its process. Other processes that you might run, such as CGI scripts, have memory needs of their own.

Disk subsystem evolution has some interesting facets. Reliability and performance are the two more critical factors. The costs of modern drives typically used in Intel-based servers has come down so much in price that it is a nonissue for all but the most cost-sensitive operations. We can find multimegabyte hard drives from reputable manufacturers for costs that were unattainable a few years ago. 4GB hard drives for wide SCSI systems are easily found for below $500 today. Even the larger 9GB drives are typically less than $100 per megabyte. Of course, there are more expensive drives that offer high performance, higher spindle rotation speeds, and on-board cache. Cost does not have to be an indicator of the reliability of the drive. Modern drive manufacturers boast MTBFs (Mean Times Between Failure) in the 100,000 hours range.

Running 7 hours a day every day of the year, you could expect the drive to last for longer than 11 years!

Performance of the disk subsystem is an important factor in the performance of your Internet Information Server. Generally speaking, the faster the rotation speeds, the better the performance. Ultra IDE drives have much better throughput than standard IDE drives. If your disk subsystems allow for concurrent access, the RAID 5 can offer both a moderate increase in performance as well as a degree of safety through its fault-tolerant design. Windows NT offers the option of configuring a RAID 5 array through its software interface. This is a feature bundled with Windows NT at no cost. Because Windows NT RAID is all done in software, it has memory requirements of its own. And while it offers the standard fault tolerance of RAID 5, it does not support "hot swap" of the failed member of the array. You will need to shut down the server twice to fix a failed member: once to replace the failed drive and once to regenerate the array with the new drive installed. A hardware RAID generally allows you to replace the failed drive while the system is still running and regenerate the array dynamically without having to take the server down. And on the other hand, a hardware-based RAID array is much more expensive. To some degree, you are trading off performance and cost vs. features and cost.

## CERTIFICATION OBJECTIVE 2.02

# Installing IIS 2.0

We are going to install Internet Information Server 2.0 because that is what comes with Windows NT Server when you buy it. The exercises to follow will take you through:

- Installing IIS 2.0
- Installing Internet Explorer 4.01
- Upgrade IIS 2.0 to 3.0 by adding the Service Pack 3
- Installing Internet Information Server 4.0.

You may recall from earlier discussions that IIS 4.0 requires Windows NT Server 4.0 with SP3 installed. Don't forget that IIS requires TCP/IP installed as the transport protocol. It also requires that Internet Explorer 4.01 be installed as well. We will do that as part of the exercises.

A word about the exercises before we get started. You must do the exercises in order. Read each and every step. Do not assume you know where the exercise is headed. Each step in the exercise should be done in order. The exercises in this book use the "build" method; later exercises depend upon one or more of the preceding exercises being completed successfully for the subsequent exercises to work.

To begin an installation of IIS 2.0, you launch the IIS Installation Wizard from the I386\INTSRV folder. The dialog box illustrated in Figure 2-1 appears.

The Setup Wizard takes you through a brief series of dialogs and then your setup will be complete. Refer to Figure 2-2 to see what options are available under IIS 2.0. Notice the Change Directory button. You use this if you want to install the IIS operating files into another folder. We are going to use the defaults for the installation since it is hard to predict what type of configuration that your computer will support. This book will use both FAT and NTFS partitions to create Web content. This is the reason that we have set up both partitions. I have elected to use the FAT partition as the system

IIS 2.0 setup

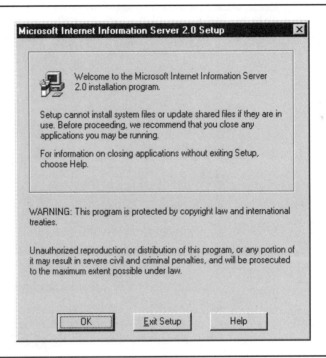

and boot partitions because this might be easier for you to uninstall after we are done. We are putting some of our Web content on the same drive as the operating system files because we are using just two partitions for the exercises. If this were a production server, you would not put Web content on the boot partition for performance reasons. If the Web server operation is real critical to you, then you might consider putting the Web content on a RAID 5 array for performance and for security.

After you select the options, you are asked where you want to have your publishing directories. Refer to Figure 2-3 for this option. You may also change the location of the root folders for your services to accommodate a different structure. You might do this to put them on a drive with more free space available. Although as you will see in Chapter 8, which describes virtual servers and virtual directories, needing more drive space is not as limiting a factor as it might seem at first. It is probably more critical to the FTP service than to the WWW service.

**FIGURE 2-2**

IIS setup options

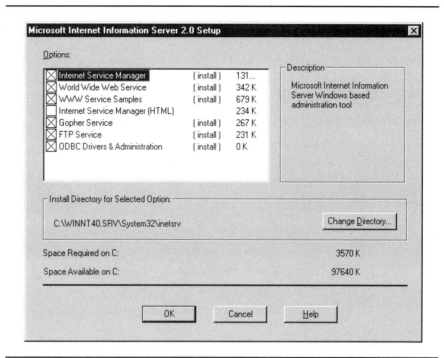

If the default folders do not exist, the Installation Wizard asks you if you want to create them. Obviously you do want to create them, otherwise you would not be installing IIS. Figures 2-4 and 2-5 illustrate the procedures for creating program and publishing directories.

If you have the Guest account enabled, you see a message like the one in Figure 2-6. It is not a good idea to have the Guest account enabled on your IIS server. Chapter 4 will discuss why you don't want the Guest account enabled and other security considerations.

You will be asked about installing ODBC drivers as illustrated in Figure 2-7. These drivers allow you to connect to Microsoft's SQL Server. IIS 4.0 comes with a much broader set of ODBC drivers that allow you to publish data contained in your database. You can also use SQL Server to log activity information about your IIS services. We will discuss security and logging in more detail in Chapter 4.

**FIGURE 2-3**

Default publishing folders

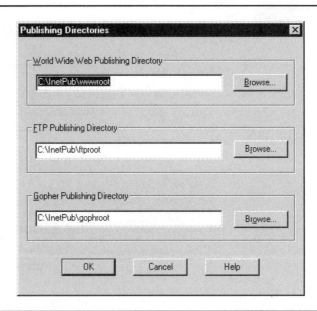

**FIGURE 2-4**

Create program directory

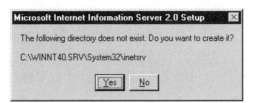

**FIGURE 2-5**

Create publishing
directories

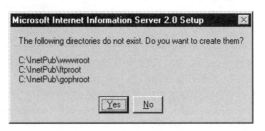

FIGURE 2-6

Warning about Guest
account

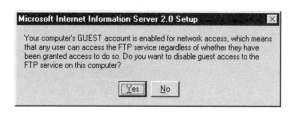

And, the final step: Notification that the installation has been successful!
See Figure 2-8.

## Verifying Server Configuration

Purpose: To verify system configuration prior to installing IIS 2.0. This will help
you see the changes when the IIS installation makes them.

*Do this exercise from both computers.*

1. Log on as Administrator.
2. Open the Services applet.
3. Check the listing to see if FTP, Gopher, or World Wide Web services
   are present.
4. Record the results. If you can see that these services are present, then
   you have IIS installed. You should uninstall IIS by using the Add/Remove
   Programs applet in the Control Panel before proceeding with this exercise.

FIGURE 2-7

Installing ODBC drivers

**FIGURE 2-8**

Successful installation

5. Close the Services applet.

6. Open User Manager for Domains.

7. Look at which user accounts are present. Look in particular for any user accounts that begin with the letter "I."

8. Record the results.

9. Close User Manager for Domains.

*Answers to steps in this exercise:*

4. FTP, Gopher, and WWW should not be present. If they are, IIS is installed and you should remove it.

8. Administrator and Guest.

**EXERCISE 2-2**

## Installing IIS 2.0

Purpose: To install Internet Information Server 2.0. You will install IIS 2.0 on one computer only so that you can see the installation and you can experience upgrading IIS 2.0 to IIS 4.0 in a later exercise. You will install IIS on only one computer at this time, leaving the other computer for the exercise installing IIS 4.0 on a computer that has no previous copies of IIS installed.

*Do this exercise from the domain controller only.*

1. Locate the INETSRV folder on the Windows NT Server distribution CD-ROM. It is under the I386 folder.

2. Double-click the INETSTP.EXE file. That will launch the Setup Wizard.

3. Click OK on the Server 2.0 setup box.

4. Click OK to accept the default options. Note the folder into which the IIS operating files will be installed.

5. Click Yes if asked to create a directory.

6. Click Yes to accept the default publishing folders.

7. Click Yes if asked to create the directories.

8. If the Internet Domain name warning dialog appears, click OK.

9. Click OK on the ODBC dialog box to accept as is.

10. Click OK on the Successful Installation dialog box.

11. You are done with the installation of IIS 2.0

---

**CERTIFICATION OBJECTIVE 2.03**

# Changes Made to Windows NT During Installation

During the installation of Internet Information Server, the installation process makes changes to Windows NT Server automatically and without your input. These changes are in addition to the changes that you were prompted about during the installation of IIS. You cannot stop or modify these changes. These changes are visible using the Services applet, using User Manager for Domains, and using a registry-editing tool.

## Changes to User Manager

During the installation process, IIS will create a user account name "IUSR_*Servername*" *where Servername* is the name of the computer, as illustrated in Figure 2-9. This account is necessary for users to connect to your Internet services such as FTP and WWW. This is the account that users need when they log on anonymously.

The IUSR account is assigned a password during installation, as illustrated in Figure 2-10. Do not change the password here. Notice that the Password Never Expires and the User Cannot Change Password boxes are checked. These are important considerations. Leave these boxes checked.

Note which groups the IUSR account is a member (see Figure 2-11). Chapter 4 describes why this particular account is set up this way.

## Changes to the Registry

The installation process makes necessary changes to the registry so the Internet services will function, as illustrated in Figures 2-12 and 2-13. There are some registry entries that you must make yourself if you want to tune the system performance. These registry entries cannot be made from Internet Service

User Manager with IUSR account

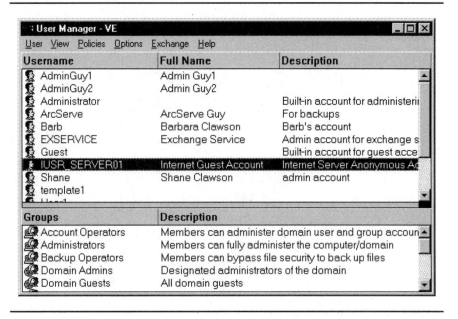

FIGURE 2-10

IUSR account properties

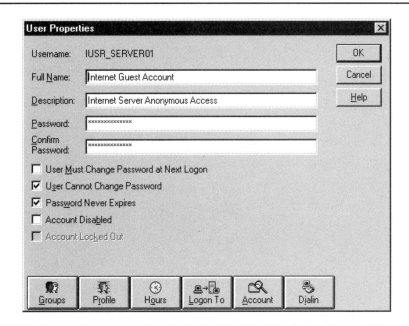

FIGURE 2-11

Group membership for the
IUSR account

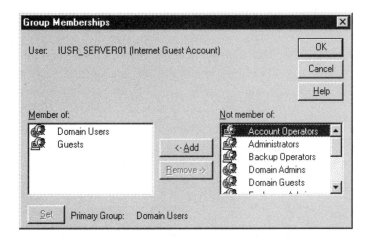

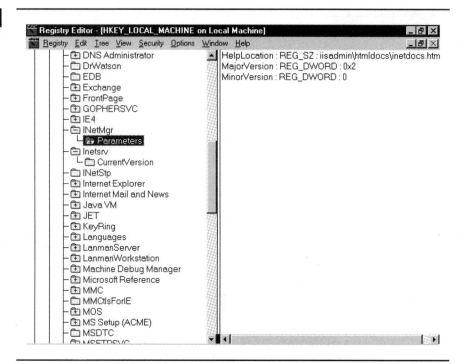

**FIGURE 2-12**

Registry; Local Machine;
Software hive;
Microsoft key

Manager, but must be made directly to the registry. Consider the parameter DisableMemoryCache. This entry will disable the server cache and cannot be set from Internet Service Manager. You should not change this variable without understanding what the ramifications are. It is an example of a setting, that if you wanted to change it, you would have to do so in the registry. The tree structure is:

```
HKEY_LOCAL_MACHINE\SYSTEM
 \CurrentControlSet
 \Services
 \InetInfo
  \Parameters
```

## Changes Visible with the Services Applet

As you can see in Figure 2-14, after installing IIS, three new services are installed in Windows NT Server as a result of having selected the defaults in

**FIGURE 2-13**

Registry; System hive;
Current Control Set;
Services key

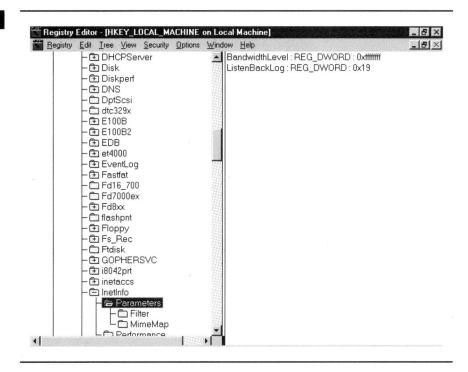

the installation: FTP, Gopher, and WWW services. These are the default services and they are configured to start automatically.

## Changes to Performance Monitor

The IIS installation process also adds the appropriate objects to Performance Monitor, as you can see in Figure 2-15. Performance Monitor is a major tool for optimizing and troubleshooting Windows NT. The objects added are FTP, Gopher, and HTTP objects. With these objects and their associated counters, Performance Monitor can now be used to help tune and troubleshoot Internet Information Server.

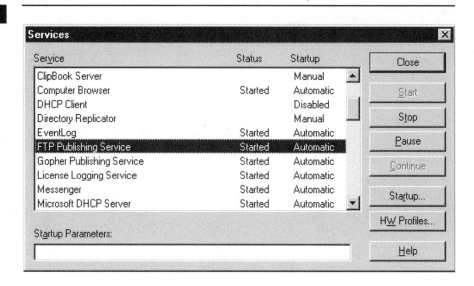

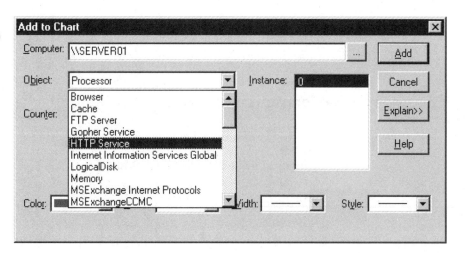

## Verifying Installed Components and Functionality

Purpose: To verify the changes discussed previously were made to your system. Test that the FTP and WWW services are functional and that you can establish a session with each of them.

*Do this exercise from the domain controller only.*

1. Ensure that you are logged on as Administrator. If you are unsure how to tell, press CTRL-ALT-DEL and the resulting dialog will display the username of the user currently logged on. If the user is not Administrator, then click the Logoff option and log back in as Administrator.

2. Open the Services applet.

3. Check the listing to see if FTP, Gopher, or World Wide Web services are present.

4. Record the results.

5. Close the Services applet.

6. Open User Manager for Domains.

7. Look at which user accounts are present. Look in particular for any user accounts that begin with the letter "I."

8. Record the results.

9. Close User Manager for Domains.

10. Open Performance Monitor.

11. Click the menu item Option.

12. Change the number in the Vertical Maximum box to 5.

13. Click OK.

14. Position Performance Monitor in a window at the top of your screen so that it is about one-half the size of your screen.

15. Open a command prompt. Put it in a window and position it at the bottom of the screen so that you can see both the command prompt window and the Performance Monitor window with a minimum overlap.

    You are going to add the FTP object and a counter to the chart in the following steps. Then you will establish an FTP session with your FTP server. The performance monitor will log the connection attempts as you make the attempts. This is why it is important to see both windows at the same time.

You may want to familiarize yourself with the following steps first, before you execute them. The default graph time in Performance Monitor is 100 seconds. You will have to complete the steps within that time, before the sweep bar wraps. There will be enough time if you move along without hesitation.

16. Click the menu item Edit.

17. Click Add to Chart.

18. In the Object dialog box, click the drop-down arrow on the right side.

19. Locate the object FTP Server and select it.

20. What is the default counter for the object?

21. Select the counter Connection Attempts.

22. Click Add. Click Done.

23. Go to the command prompt window.

24. Type **ftp server01** and press ENTER.

25. Type **anonymous** and press ENTER.

26. Press ENTER to accept a blank password. Observe in the Performance Monitor window that the red line has moved up to 1 on the vertical scale.

27. Type **BYE** and press ENTER. Press the up arrow. This should display ftp server01.

28. Press ENTER.

29. What happens to the red line in Performance Monitor?

30. Close Performance Monitor.

31. Close the command prompt.

*Answers to steps in this exercise:*

4. FTP, Gopher, and WWW should now be present.

8. The additional account IUSR_Server01 should be present.

20. Bytes Total/sec.

29. It increments by one unit.

**CERTIFICATION OBJECTIVE 2.04**

# Setting Up Internet Explorer

Chapter 22 covers Internet Explorer 4.01 as we prepare for the certification test for Internet Explorer Administration Kit. This is one of the certification tests that will lead to having the "+ Internet" designation. IE 4.*x* is a substantially different program than its predecessors. With the new versions, Microsoft has introduced something called "Active Desktop." In addition to Windows NT Server 4.0, SP3, TCP/IP, and Internet Explorer 4.01 must be installed.

There are different versions of Internet Explorer (IE) for each operating system. You will need the proper version for your operating system. You launch the Setup Wizard by running IE4SETUP.EXE, as illustrated in Figure 2-16. Like most Setup Wizards, Internet Explorer Setup Wizard does most of the work for you.

**FIGURE 2-16**

IE Setup screen

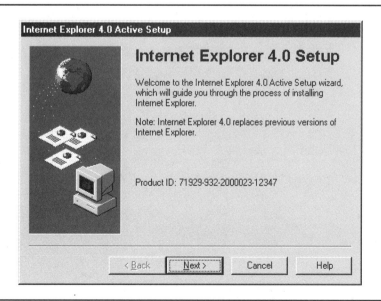

*You need to have Internet Explorer 4.0 installed first, before you can install Internet Information Server for the Windows NT 4.0 Option Pack. The key is to have IE 4.0, not an earlier version. So that you know, if you try to install IIS 4.0 without IE 4.0, the installation will stop and direct you to install IE 4.0 first.*

Figure 2-17 contains the licensing information.

Figure 2-18 contains the installation options for Internet Explorer. There are three options: Browser Only, Standard Installation, and Full Installation. These options are described in more detail in the section about Internet Explorer.

Next, the Installation Wizard asks which desktop environment you would like to have. As an optional component, it will install the Active Desktop or you can select No to use the standard Windows Explorer desktop. Figure 2-19 contains the Windows Desktop Update dialog box. This additional component is described in Chapter 22.

The next screen (see Figure 2-20) asks about the destination folder for the IE files. You may put them anywhere you want, but I recommend the default path unless you have a well thought-out reason otherwise.

---

**FIGURE 2-17**

Licensing information

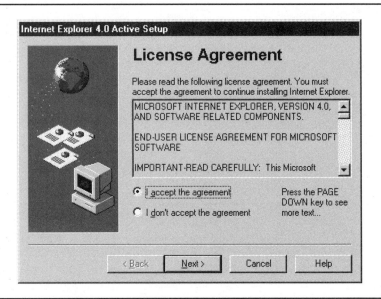

**FIGURE 2-18**

IE installation options

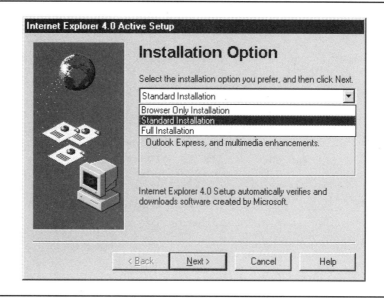

**FIGURE 2-19**

Options for installing
Active Desktop

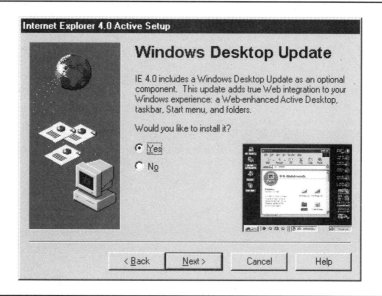

**FIGURE 2-20**

Selecting a folder for
Internet Explorer
program files

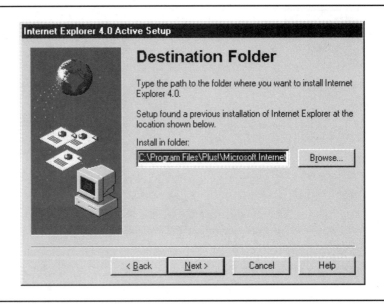

The next screen, illustrated in Figure 2-21, asks to create the folder, if it
does not exist. If you do not see this screen, it means that the folder
already exists.

The Setup Wizard will install the required files and then briefly bring up a
box that says it is configuring the system (see Figure 2-22). After it is done, the
Setup Wizard asks to restart your computer.

**FIGURE 2-21**

Create folder message

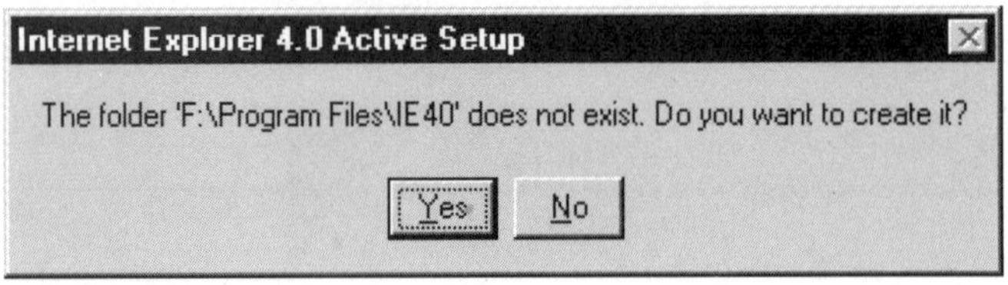

> **Internet Explorer 4.0 Active Setup**  ☒
>
> The folder 'F:\Program Files\IE40' does not exist. Do you want to create it?
>
>      [ Yes ]    [ No ]

**FIGURE** 2-22

Installing, configuring, and
successful completion
screens

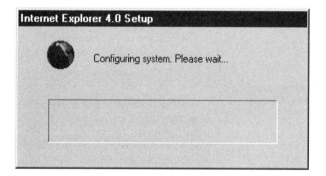

After you restart the server and log on, IE will finish configuring itself and present you with the screen in Figure 2-23. This allows a new user easy access to IE for taking a "tour" of the new product and registering the product with Microsoft. A more experienced user may not need or want to take this tour. Internet Explorer is discussed in more detail in Chapter 22. You may close this dialog box without negative consequences.

### Installing Internet Explorer 4.0

Purpose: To install Internet Explorer 4.0 and test its functionality. You must have IE 4.0 installed prior to installing IIS 4.0.

*Complete this exercise at both computers.*

1. Ensure that you are logged on as Administrator.
2. Locate the file named IE40SETUP.EXE and run it.
3. Click Next on the initial setup screen.
4. Select "I Accept" and click Next on the license agreement.
5. Ensure that Standard Installation is selected and click Next.

FIGURE 2-23

Initial startup screen for IE 4.0

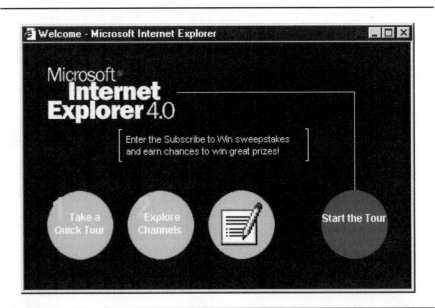

6. Select the No radio button to install the standard desktop and click Next. Pay close attention here and make sure that you selected the No radio button. You can always use the Back button to make sure of a setting.

7. Click Next to accept the default location for the folder.

8. Click Next if asked to create the folder.

9. Click Restart when asked to restart your computer.

10. Log on as Administrator.

11. If the initial screen that allows you take a tour appears, close it by clicking the "x" box in the upper right-hand corner.

12. Double-click the IE icon on the desktop to launch Internet Explorer.

13. In the URL address line box, type **serverxx**, where *xx* is the number associated with the computer name. This should connect to the default.htm Web page found in the INETPUB\WWWROOT folder. (Note: You will only be able to do this at the domain controller because you haven't installed IIS on the member server yet.)

14. Close IE.

15. Take a 20-minute break. When you get back, we will install IIS 4.0!

**CERTIFICATION OBJECTIVE 2.05**

# Upgrading IIS 2.0 to 3.0

Upgrading IIS 2.0 to 3.0 is easy and straightforward. You install Service Pack 3 (SP3). When you install the Service Pack, if IIS 2.0 is installed, it will upgrade it to version 3.0 automatically. No other actions are required on your part. If you install SP3 and IIS is not installed, then nothing will happen about IIS. The Service Pack will not install IIS 3.0, unless it finds a previous version of IIS already installed.

As a general note, Microsoft service packs only install updated files for files that it finds already installed. If it finds no IIS files, then no updated files will be installed. This is why you must reapply the Service Pack after you add any new services or such. So if you install IIS after you install the Service Pack, you must reapply the Service Pack to upgrade IIS 2.0 to version 3.

You can also download IIS 3.0 from the Microsoft Web site and install it directly without using the Service Pack. However, most people will want to update to SP3 for other reasons, which will also upgrade the Internet server files.

*There is no reason to upgrade IIS 2.0 to IIS 3.0 if you want to install IIS version 4.0. You can run the Setup Wizard and upgrade directly from IIS 2.0 to IIS 4.0 without the intermediate step of going to IIS 3.0.*

## CERTIFICATION OBJECTIVE 2.06

# Upgrading IIS 3.0 to 4.0

Upgrading from IIS 3.0 to IIS 4.0 is also a simple process. The Installation Wizard takes care of most of the work for you. You install IIS 4.0 from the Windows NT Option Pack 4.0. The Option Pack contains lots of other programs, in addition to IIS. These programs are described in more detail in other chapters of this book.

During an upgrade installation you have two options. You can upgrade the basic installed components or you can do an upgrade "plus" which installs other components that may be typically used in the Internet Information Server environment.

## Installing IIS 4.0

Begin the IIS 4.0 installation from the Windows NT Option Pack 4.0 folder by running SETUP.EXE. As a prerequisite to running the setup program, you must have SP3 installed. First, let's discuss an installation upgrade from a previous version of IIS. If you are running the Gopher service with the

**FIGURE 2-24**

Advisory message about
Gopher support

previous version, the start of the setup is a bit different. Under this condition, running setup brings up the screen in Figure 2-24. Otherwise, you see the screen as in Figure 2-25.

The next screen in the installation is the Option Pack screen, shown in Figure 2-25.

**FIGURE 2-25**

Option Pack setup screen

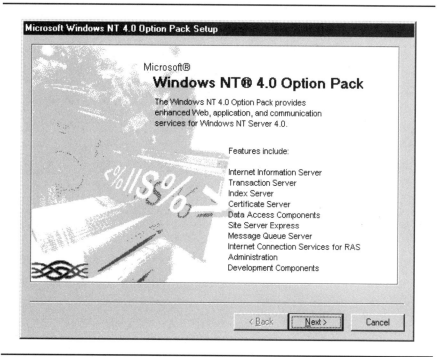

Clicking Next brings up the licensing screen shown in Figure 2-26.

After accepting the licensing agreement, you must choose between a simple upgrade of services and an Upgrade Plus, as illustrated in Figure 2-27.

The screen in Figure 2-28 appears as the installation is completing. After the Installation Wizard completes copying of files, it asks to restart your computer so that it can initialize the new services.

IIS 4.0 license agreement

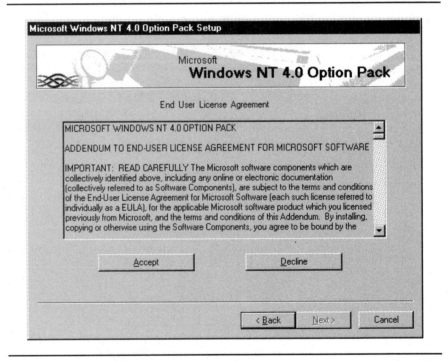

**FIGURE 2-27**

Installation options for
IIS 4.0

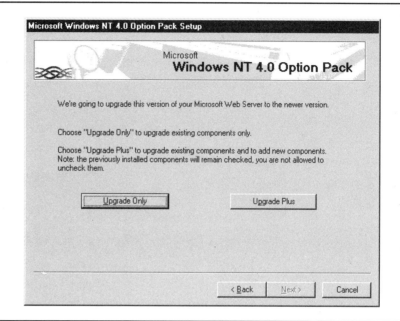

**FIGURE 2-28**

Completing the installation

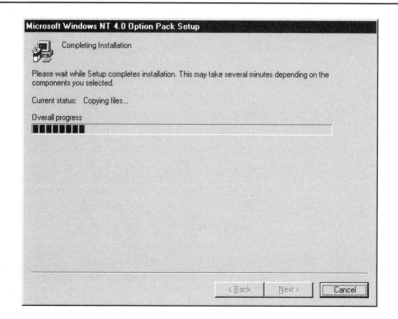

## Installing IIS 4.0

Purpose: To install IIS 4.0 by using the upgrade. Then explore the changes that were made.

*Complete this step from the domain controller only.*

1. Ensure that you are logged on as Administrator.
2. Locate the Windows NT 4.0 Option Pack folder.
3. Double-click the SETUP.EXE file to launch the Installation Wizard.
4. Click OK to acknowledge the No Gopher support message.
5. Click Next on the Windows NT 4.0 Option Pack setup screen.
6. Select "I Accept" and click Next on the licensing agreement form.
7. Select the Upgrade Only option.
8. Click Next.
9. Click Next when the files finish installing.
10. Click Finish.
11. Click Yes when prompted to restart.
12. After your computer restarts, make sure that you are logged on as Administrator.
13. Open up the Services applet.
14. What are the four services installed by IIS?
15. Open User Manager for Domains. What IIS account(s) are there?
16. Close User Manager for Domains.

*Answers to steps in this exercise.*

14. FTP, IIS Admin, MSDTC, and World Wide Web Publishing Service.
15. New accounts IUSR_Server01 and IWAM_Server01 should be present.

There are new services installed as a result of the upgrade of IIS (see Figure 2-29). Figure 2-30 shows the new user account in User Manager for Domains.

**FIGURE 2-29**

Services installed by IIS 4.0

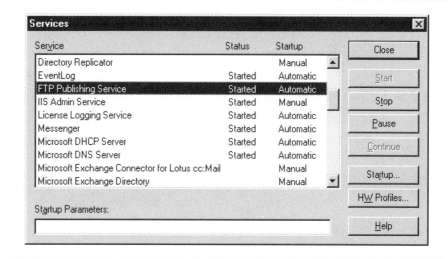

**FIGURE 2-30**

IIS 4.0 accounts in User Manager

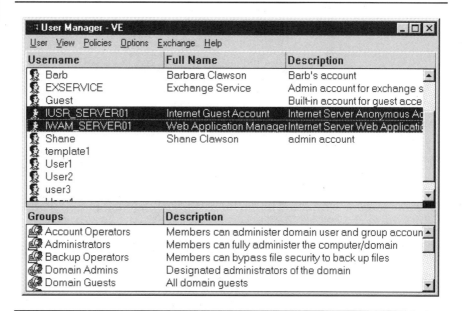

## Installing IIS 4.0 as a New Installation

You begin the installation of IIS the same way as installing over a previous version. The choices and screens will be a bit different when installing IIS on a server that does not have a previous version installed. Starting the installation brings up the Option Pack screen illustrated in Figure 2-31.

The next screen is the same licensing screen you have seen before. Figure 2-32 contains a different dialog box than the ones you saw during an upgrade. Only during an IIS installation on a server without a previous IIS installation will you get a choice of Minimum, Typical, or Custom installation. A Typical installation installs the FTP and WWW services; a Custom installation allows you to specifically select what you want installed.

**FIGURE 2-31**

Option Pack setup screen

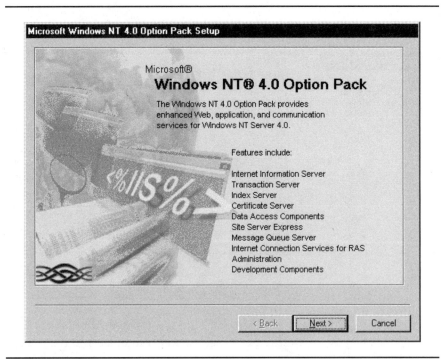

**FIGURE 2-32**

Option Pack with three
installation options

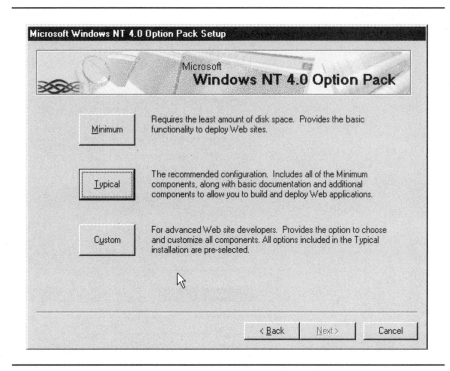

Figure 2-33 contains the screen that comes from selecting the
Custom option.

If you select Internet Information Server and then click Show
Subcomponents, you can choose which components you wish to install, as
illustrated in Figure 2-34.

The next screen (Figure 2-35) asks you where you want the files for the
Microsoft Transaction Server (MTS).

Following that, select theAadministration mode for MTS, as illustrated in
Figure 2-36. This chapter discusses MTS later.

Now the installation will complete. All that remains is to click Finish and
restart your computer when asked.

**FIGURE 2-33**

Custom installation screen

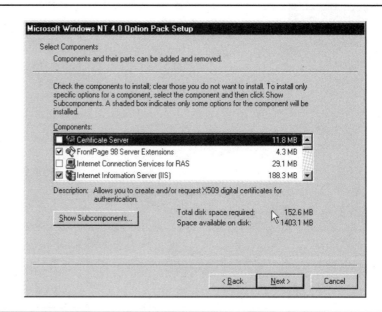

**FIGURE 2-34**

Selecting IIS components

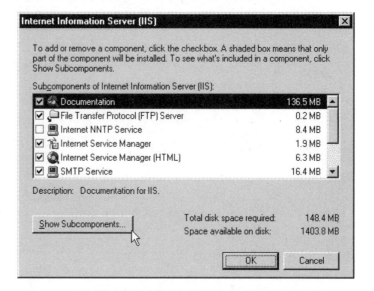

**FIGURE 2-35**

Selecting a folder for
MTS files

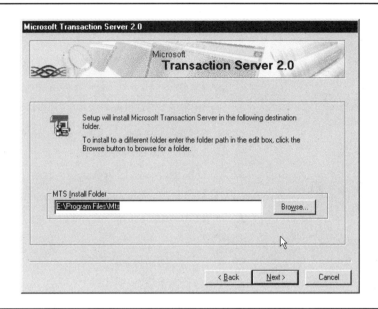

**FIGURE 2-36**

Configuring administration
for MTS

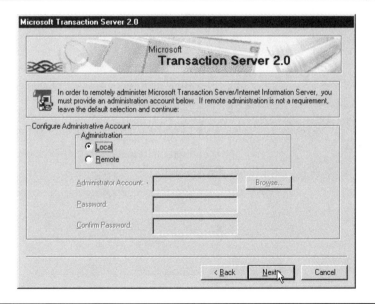

### Installing IIS on a New Machine

Purpose: To install Internet Information Server as a new installation.

*Complete this procedure from the member server only.*

1. Ensure that you are logged on as Administrator.

2. Locate the Windows NT 4.0 Option Pack folder.

3. Double-click the SETUP.EXE file to launch the Installation Wizard.

4. Click Next on the Setup screen.

5. Click Accept on the licensing screen.

6. Click Custom to install the selected components.

7. Select Internet Information Server by clicking on the name *and not the check box.*

8. Click Show Subcomponents.

9. Uncheck the following services:

   ■ Front Page 98 Server Extension

   ■ Microsoft Index Server

   ■ Microsoft Script Debugger

   ■ Windows Scripting Host

10. Ensure that Internet NNTP Server and SMTP Services are *unchecked.*

11. Click the OK button on the IIS dialog box.

12. Click Next.

13. Click Next to accept the default file locations.

14. Click Next to accept the default location for Transaction Server file location.

15. Click Next to accept local administration for Transaction Server.

16. Click Finish.

17. Click Yes when asked to Restart.

**CERTIFICATION OBJECTIVE 2.07**

# Other Web Clients

There are other Web clients besides the Internet Explorer 4.01. Some of them are from companies other than Microsoft or Netscape. Mosaic is probably one of the better known "also-rans." Any browser that supports HTTP 1.1 is what you need to connect to IIS.

## Other Versions of Internet Explorer

Previous versions of Internet Explorer prior to IE 4.0 can connect to IIS 4.0 servers. In the version 3.*x* series, IE 3.02 is the current version. It is a stable and fairly robust browser. It features reasonable security and supports frames and ActiveX. But by comparison, IE 4.0 has much tighter security and sports new features that the older browsers just can't match.

## Netscape Navigator

Netscape's Navigator is a substantial browser with a large installed base. Navigator pioneered the GUI browser technology. The current version of Netscape Navigator is 4.*x*. It started as a shareware product and after the company went public, Netscape charged for its browser while the Microsoft offering was then, and is now, free of charge. As of this writing, Netscape now offers its Navigator product without charge.

Navigator does have one shortcoming when connecting to IIS when you are using domain security authentication and Microsoft challenge and response security. Currently, Navigator does not support the Microsoft challenge and response security. If you set this mode, your clients will not be able to connect to your Web server using Navigator.

# CERTIFICATION SUMMARY

Internet Information Server 4.0 runs only on Windows NT Server 4.0 with SP3 installed. Internet Explorer 4.01 must be installed first before you can install IIS 4.0. IIS 4.0 is part of the Windows NT 4.0 Option Pack, along with other components. You may install IIS 4.0 on a server (or domain controller) with a previous version of IIS installed or on a server with no previous version of IIS installed. The Installation Wizard detects a previous version of the program automatically and presents you with the proper dialog boxes. If you are upgrading, you have two choices, Upgrade and Upgrade Plus. If it is a new installation, you have three choices: Minimum, Typical, or Custom. The installation process makes changes to your system. It installs additional services, creates user accounts, modifies the registry, and adds objects to Performance Monitor.

 # TWO-MINUTE DRILL

- ❑ Internet Information Server installs on Windows NT Server.
- ❑ IIS 4.0 is part of Windows NT 4.0 Option Pack.
- ❑ IIS 4.0 needs Windows NT Server version 4.0.
- ❑ IIS 4.0 needs Service Pack 3 (SP3) installed on Windows NT Server.
- ❑ IIS 4.0 needs IE 4.01 (or later) installed first.
- ❑ You can do a basic upgrade of existing IIS servers during installation.
- ❑ You can upgrade IIS and add additional components during installation.
- ❑ IIS 4.0 installation automatically detects previous versions of IIS.
- ❑ You can do an installation of IIS 4.0 without a previous version of IIS installed first.
- ❑ You need a 486/50 and 32MB of RAM for IIS 4.0.
- ❑ On a new installation of IIS, you have three choices of installation types: Minimum, Typical, and Custom.
- ❑ IIS needs a minimum of 50MB of free disk space to install.
- ❑ The more options you install, the more disk space you need.
- ❑ The Typical installation needs approximately 70MB of drive space.
- ❑ IIS 4.0 no longer offers Gopher support.
- ❑ Typical installation installs FTP and WWW services. The installation configures these services to start automatically.
- ❑ Installation creates two new user accounts.

❏ New to IIS is the Microsoft Management Console (MMC).

❏ You use MMC to access Internet Service Manager.

❏ IIS installation automatically establishes the necessary folders during installation.

❏ You can install IIS on a domain controller or on a member server.

❏ During a new installation, you can select which components to install by selecting Custom installation.

❏ During an upgrade installation, you only have two choices: Upgrade and Upgrade Plus.

# SELF TEST

The following Self Test questions will help you measure your understanding of the material presented in this chapter. Read all the choices carefully, as there may be more than one correct answer. Choose all correct answers for each question.

1. Which operating systems support IIS 4.0?

   A. Windows NT Server 3.51

   B. Windows NT Workstation

   C. Windows NT Server 4.0

   D. UNIX

2. What are the minimum hardware requirements for IIS 4.0?

   A. 32MB RAM

   B. 64MB RAM

   C. Pentium

   D. 486/50

3. Which service would you use if you wanted to send and receive files using IIS?

   A. RAS

   B. FTP

   C. WWW

   D. HTTP

4. Which service that was supported under previous versions of IIS is no longer supported under IIS 4.0?

   A. FTP

   B. TFTP

   C. Internet Service Manager

   D. Gopher

5. Which transport protocol should be installed for IIS?

   A. TCP/IP

   B. NetBEUI

   C. TCP/IP and NetBEUI

   D. NetBIOS

6. Which items need to be installed prior to IIS 4.0?

   A. Windows NT Server 4.0

   B. Service Pack 3

   C. RAS

   D. IE 4.01

7. You have IIS 2.0 installed on your server and want to upgrade to IIS 4.0. What steps are required?

   A. Install IIS 3.0 first.

   B. Create a new anonymous user.

   C. Nothing.

   D. Remove IIS 2.0 and install IIS 4.0.

8. During an installation of IIS 4.0 on a server with a previous version of IIS installed, which installation options are available to you?

   A. Typical

   B. Upgrade

C. Upgrade Plus

D. Custom

9. Which command do you run to upgrade IIS 3.0 to IIS 4.0?

A. Upgrade

B. Update

C. Setup

D. Run Service Pack 3

10. Where do you find the IIS 4.0 distribution files for installation?

A. Windows NT 4.0 Option Pack

B. IIS 4.0 folder

C. With the service pack

D. WINNT/SYSTEM32 folder

11. During a Typical installation, what publishing services are installed by IIS 4.0?

A. FTP

B. TFTP

C. Gopher

D. WWW

12. Which three installation options are available when you install IIS 4.0 on a server that does not have a previous version of IIS installed?

A. Typical

B. Upgrade

C. Custom

D. Minimum

13. Which browsers can connect to an IIS 4.0 server?

A. Only Microsoft browsers

B. IE 4.01

C. Only browsers that support frames

D. Netscape Navigator

# 3

# Managing Internet Information Server

There are several tools that can be used to manage your IIS server. You can use the Internet Service Manager (ISM). There is also an HTML version of the ISM as well. You access the ISM through a new utility Microsoft has named the Microsoft Management Console (MMC). This chapter will describe how you can access ISM using the MMC.

This chapter also provides an introduction to the IIS service property sheets. Property sheets are discussed in greater detail in the chapters devoted to the individual services.

The exercises in this chapter serve as learning reinforcement tools to:

- Configure and save consoles using Microsoft Management Console (MMC).

- Verify server settings by accessing the metabase.

- Choose an appropriate administration method.

- Access service property sheets.

**CERTIFICATION OBJECTIVE 3.01**

# Microsoft Management Console

MMC is a system management tool included in the release of Windows NT Server 5.0. It is also included in the Windows NT 4.0 Option Pack. MMC is installed as part of the installation of IIS 4.0. The MMC does not provide any functional management by itself. Its purpose is to provide the common environment for other system management tools such as Internet Service Manager and Microsoft Transaction Server. When these tools are used with MMC, they are known as *snap-ins*. The snap-in provides the actual functionality while the MMC provides the common environment for the snap-ins. MMC is also a single utility that you can use to access all of your administration and management tools; a common console for them all.

By providing MMC, Microsoft has also provided a tool for other vendors and developers to use. They can write their programs as snap-ins. You can add their snap-in to your MMC, thereby preserving the concept of going to a single place (tool) for all of your management tools. This facility makes MMC a valuable shared management tool for cross-application management by providing the framework for you to access multiple network and system management programs.

Microsoft also plans to accommodate all of their BackOffice management tools as snap-ins for MMC. Other third-party vendors will have snap-ins too, such as Wang's Image Edit Controls. You can also create additional snap-ins yourself.

## Benefits of MMC

MMC simplifies the tasks of managing your environment and administering your servers. Microsoft lists three benefits to having MMC:

- Customization
- Integration and commonality
- Flexibility

You can customize MMC in a variety of different ways. You can set up a console configured to include the exact administrative tools that you want for a particular situation. You can save this console configuration and call it up later. You can create multiple consoles. You send the configuration files to others for them to use. By customizing, you have only the tools that you need to perform your tasks, rather than all of the tools cluttering up the environment, especially when you only actually use a few of those tools.

As noted earlier, MMC provides the framework for the snap-in tools to use. You only have to go to one place to access all the tools that you need to perform your tasks. And because the snap-ins are under the common framework of MMC, they must conform to the MMC specifications and conventions. This results in a common look and feel to all of the snap-ins and makes it easier and faster to learn a new tool.

MMC is flexible enough to accommodate different tools and different configurations. The next section describes the MMC and how to configure and use it.

## Using MMC

MMC is installed when you install IIS 4.0. When you did the new installation, selected Custom from the installation options, and then selected Internet Information Server and Show Subcomponents, you may have seen that MMC was already selected to be installed as part of the default installation.

Start the MMC by launching it from the Windows NT 4.0 Option Pack group, as illustrated in Figure 3-1. Opening MMC uses about 5MB of RAM on a Windows NT system. This is in addition to the RAM being used by any other processes.

Click on Microsoft Internet Information Server to display Internet Service Manager and Internet Service Manager (HTML) as shown in the following

---

**FIGURE 3-1**

Starting the MMC by launching Internet Service Manager

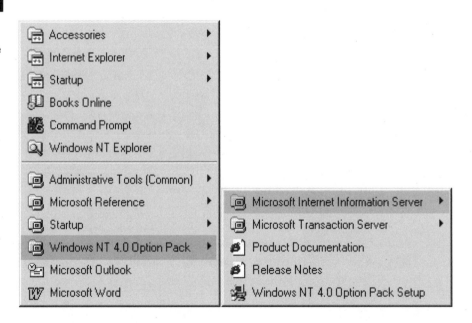

---

illustration. If you did not install the HTML version of the Internet Service Manager, that option will not appear on the menu.

Selecting the Internet Service Manager launches MMC. (You can also start ISM by double-clicking on a .MSC file in Windows NT Explorer, as illustrated in Figure 3-2.) By default, the two snap-ins for Internet Information Server and Transaction Server are installed. The MMC has two *panes*, a left pane and a right pane. The left pane is called the *scope* pane and shows the tree view of the *namespace*. Namespace is the terminology used to describe the hierarchy of the objects. Each item or object is called a *node*. Nodes may be

**FIGURE 3-2**

Microsoft Management
Console

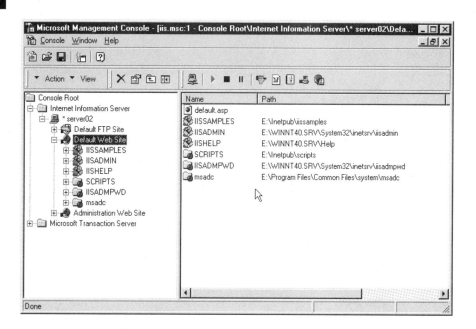

objects or tasks. Some objects are called *container* objects. Container objects can contain other objects or tasks. An object that cannot contain other objects is known as a *leaf* object.

*exam*
*Watch*

**Remember that the Console settings are saved in a FILENAME.MMC file.**

The right pane is called the *results* pane. It is analogous to the right pane in Windows NT Explorer. When you select an object or node in the scope pane, the results pane displays a list of all of the objects and tasks that are available within that node. Referring to Figure 3-2, note that Default Web Site is selected in the scope pane. In the results pane you see DEFAULT.ASP, IISSAMPLES, IISADMIN, IISHELP, etc.

The MMC has three menu bars. The bottom menu bar is called the *rebar* menu and is illustrated next. The rebar menu consists of an Action pull-down menu and a View pull-down menu, plus two other *bands*. Notice the band at the far right-hand side of the bar. The last five icons are Key Manager, Performance Monitor, Event Viewer, Server Manager, and User Manager for Domains. These icons launch the same programs as the icons found in the Administrative Tools group.

A band is an area of the menu bar that contains additional tools. These two areas are to the right of the View pull-down menu. The tools in these bands change to reflect which object is selected in the scope pane. To illustrate the different rebar displays, the previous illustration showed the Default Web Site, while the next illustration shows the Transaction Server rebar layout.

*exam*
*Watch*

**The bands in the rebar are context sensitive, depending on the object selected.**

You can configure the MMC to display multiple windows simultaneously, as illustrated in Figure 3-3. You accomplish this by right-clicking the node in the scope pane and selecting New window from the pop-up window. This creates a new window with the selected node at the top of the namespace in the scope pane. This enables you to create different views in separate windows and switch between the windows or view multiple parts of the console together, each in its own window.

You can save a particular arrangement of a console, allowing you to retrieve this console later with the same snap-ins loaded and the same windows saved. You save and open the console from the Console menu. Console files are saved with a .msc extension and can be sent for use by others.

**FIGURE 3-3**

MMC with two windows tiled horizontally

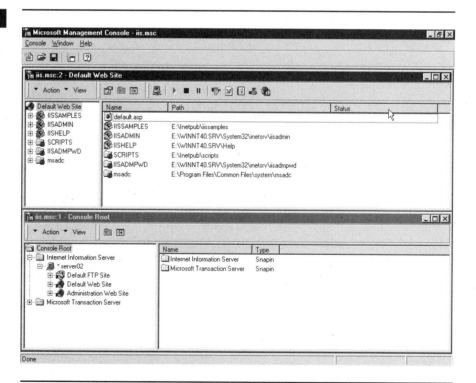

## Configuring Microsoft Management Console

Purpose: To configure the MMC, save the console and open the console using the file that was previously saved.

*Complete this exercise from either computer.*

1. Ensure that you are logged on as Administrator.
2. Click the Start button on the task bar.
3. Select Programs.
4. Select Windows NT 4.0 Option Pack.
5. Select Microsoft Internet Information Server.
6. Select Internet Service Manager.
7. Left-click the plus (+) key next to the folder labeled Internet Information Server to expand the object.
8. Which objects are displayed?
9. Expand the object Default Web Site.
10. Left-click once on the name IISADMIN.
11. What appears in the results pane?
12. Right-click IISADMIN and study the pop-up windows for a minute.
13. Select properties.
14. What tabs are available?
15. Click Cancel.
16. Click the menu item Window and observe which windows are available.
17. Right-click the object Default Web Site.
18. Select New window from here.
19. Observe the changes in the scope pane and the title bar.
20. Click the menu item Window and observe which windows are available.
21. Which windows are now available?

22. Click the menu item Window and select Tile Horizontally.
23. Click the menu item Console.
24. Select Save As.
25. Which folder is the default to save the console file?
26. Enter the filename **console01** and click Save.
27. Note the title bars now read CONSOLE01.MSC.
28. Close the MMC.
29. Right-click My Computer.
30. Select Find and enter **\*.msc** in the named box. To make the search shorter, you might select the C: drive rather than My Computer.
31. Find the file console.msc and double-click it.
32. Did the MMC launch with the split windows as saved?
33. Close the MMC.

*Answers to the steps in this exercise:*

8. Default FTP site, Default Web Site, and Administration Web Site.
11. The object contained is IISADMIN, a list of .ASP files.
14. Virtual Directory, Documents, Directory Security, HTTP Headers, and Custom Errors.
25. <winnt_root>\system32\inetsrv
32. Yes.

## CERTIFICATION OBJECTIVE 3.02

# Microsoft Internet Service Manager

The Internet Service Manager (ISM) is the primary tool used to manage the IIS services. You can manage any IIS server from anywhere in the world using Internet Service Manager, not just your local IIS server computer. The IIS configuration parameters are stored in a database called the *metabase*. Most of the metabase parameters are set using the IIS. Windows NT still stores some

IIS information in the registry but many items that previous IIS versions kept in the registry are now kept in the metabase. The metabase offers the following advantages:

- Speed
- More flexibility
- Easier to expand
- Scriptable
- Easier for remote administration

exam
**W**atch

*You manage the IIS with the ISM. You access the ISM through the MMC.*

Access the ISM through the MMC. Start the process through the Windows NT 4.0 Option Pack by selecting Internet Information Server and then selecting the Internet Service Manager. This shortcut launches the file iis.msc, which in turn launches the MMC, resulting in the screen in Figure 3-4. You can also click on a .MSC file in Windows NT Explorer to launch ISM.

---

**FIGURE 3-4**

Accessing Internet Service
Manager through MMC

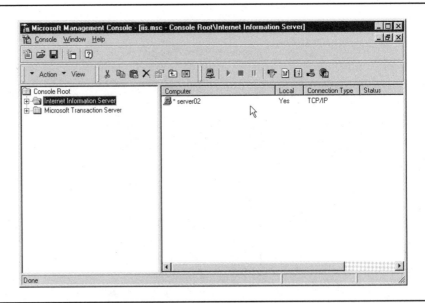

---

## FROM THE CLASSROOM

### Getting Used to MMC

Working with Microsoft Management Console (MMC) can be quite interesting for the students, especially for those students who have previous experience using Internet Service Manager (ISM). They can still access Internet Service Manager through the MMC, but it seems to take a little while to make the adjustment. Most people we have talked with seem to like the MMC concept and find that once they make the transition, they are ready to explore MMC further.

Getting used to the new look of Internet Service Manager can take some time. It has a completely different look and feel to the interface than the old Internet Service Manager. One of our students was completely unnerved because she could not create a virtual server or a virtual directory using the new interface. She had previously done these tasks many times before. After some practice, she was able to

understand how to navigate the new interface and how to manipulate the objects and property sheets. For just a moment, I wasn't sure that she was going to make the transition, or at least make it while she still had hair on her head!

Another new feature that takes the students by surprise is the rebar and the bands. It seemed to confuse some students that the icons on the band change with each selected object. After using the interface for a while, they did become comfortable with it.

There is a whole new set of terminology for the students to become used to. This causes both chuckles and groans from the students. Getting used to the results pane and the scope pane and being told to go to the rebar or to select an icon from inside the band can be quite intimidating until you become comfortable hearing the new terms.

## CERTIFICATION OBJECTIVE 3.03

# Service Manager Views

When you start IIS.MSC, it connects you to the local machine and the Internet Information Server and the Transaction Server. You can view which servers are connected by expanding the Internet Information Server folder. You can view which services are installed on that server by clicking on the plus (+) key to the left of the server to expand the tree or by double-clicking the server icon or name. See Figure 3-5.

You can add other servers to the console display so that you can manage their services from this console as well. You add servers by a right-click on either the Internet Information Server folder or any server icon displayed. Then select Connect from the pop-up dialog box and enter the name of the server. After a brief pause, the new server is displayed under the Internet Information Server folder. You can also use the Connect Server icon on the rebar, as shown next. Figure 3-6 illustrates the MCC with two servers connected.

**FIGURE 3-5**

Viewing the server and installed services

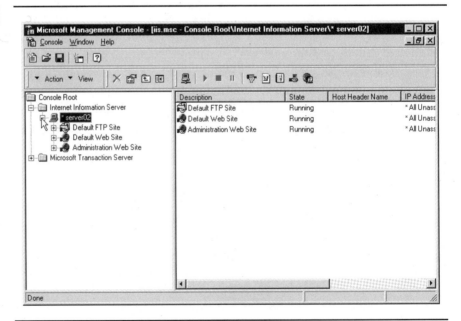

**FIGURE 3-6**

MMC with two servers
connected

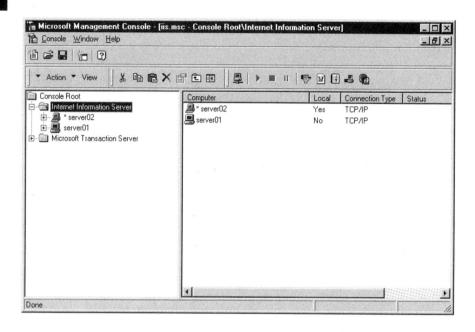

**EXERCISE 3-2**

## Expanding MMC

Purpose: To add another server to the console.

*Complete this procedure from both computers.*

1. Ensure that you are logged on as Administrator.
2. Open the MMC.
3. Expand the Internet Information Server folder.
4. Which servers are listed?
5. Right-click the Internet Information Server folder.
6. Click on Connect in the pop-up menu.
7. Enter the name of the other server in the dialog box.
8. Click OK.

9. Save this console as the file named "console with server*xx*" where *xx* is the number of the server that you added.

*Answers to the steps in this exercise:*

4. Server*xx*, depending upon which computer you are using.

**CERTIFICATION OBJECTIVE 3.04**

# Introduction to the Property Sheets

Each service has an associated *property sheet.* You use this property sheet to set the parameters for the particular service. In the installation you have set up, there are three property sheets of immediate interest:

- Properties for the server
- Properties for the WWW service
- Properties for the FTP service

There are also property sheets for the other objects such as IISADMIN, IISHELP, IISADMPWD, etc.

## WWW

You can display the property sheet of the WWW service by right-clicking the Default Web Site and selecting Property from the pop-up menu. There are nine tabs associated with this property sheet (see Figure 3-7). The tabs are:

- Web Site
- Operators
- Performance
- ISAPI Filters
- Home Directory

- Documents
- Directory Security
- HTTP Headers
- Custom Errors

Chapter 6 will describe many of these tabs in greater detail.

---

**FIGURE 3-7**

Default Web Site properties

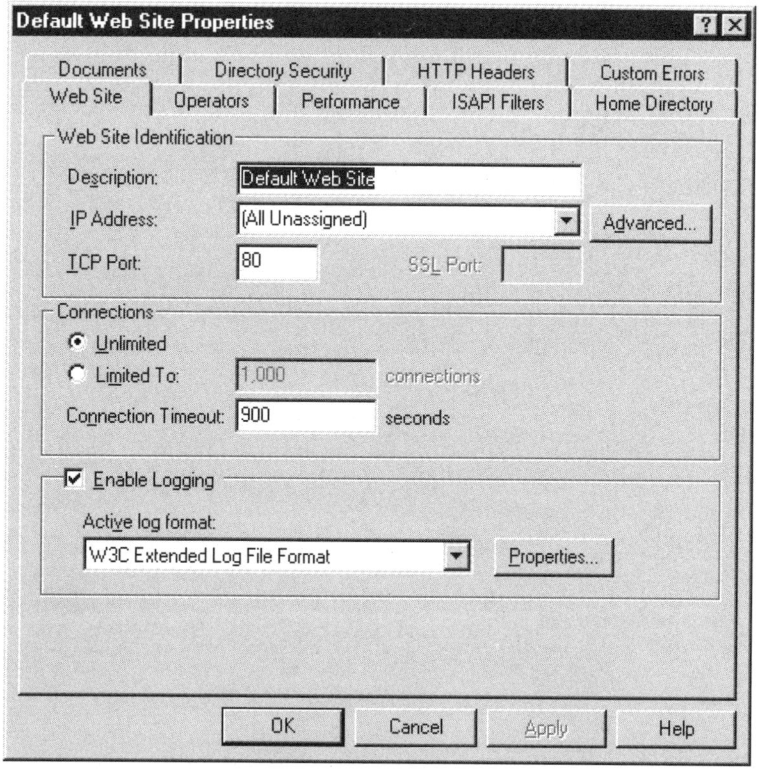

# FTP

You can bring up the property sheet of the FTP service by right-clicking the Default FTP Site and selecting Property from the pop-up menu. There are five tabs associated with this property sheet (see Figure 3-8). The tabs are:

■ FTP Site

■ Security Accounts

■ Messages

■ Home Directory

■ Directory Security

**FIGURE 3-8**

Default FTP Site properties

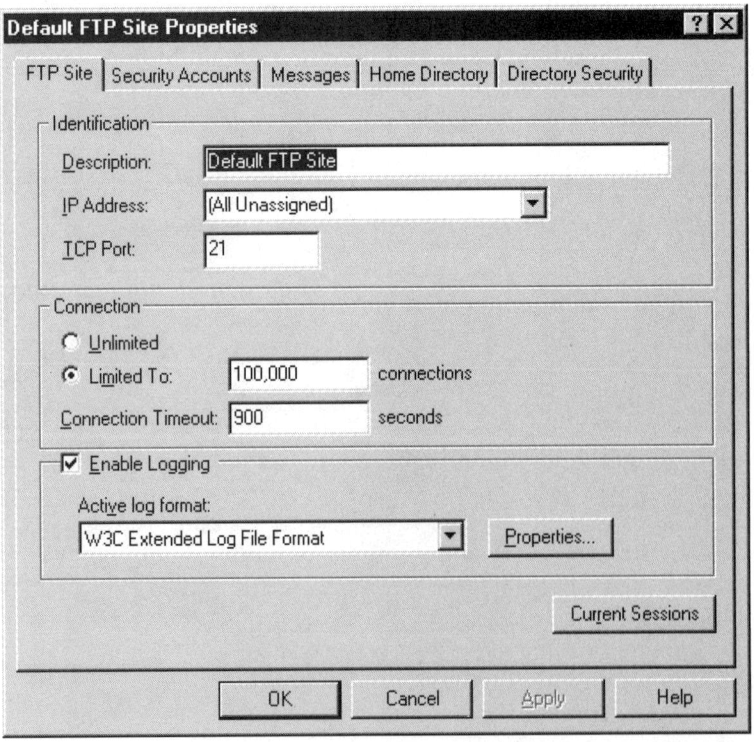

# Using Internet Services Manager HTML Version

Microsoft also includes an HTML version of the Internet Service Manager, illustrated in Figure 3-9. With Internet Explorer (IE) 4.01, you can open the HTML version and connect to the local site. By default, the HTML version is configured to allow access only to the machine. If you want to access Internet Information Servers elsewhere on the network, you have to configure the IIS server to allow for this. Use some caution when configuring your IIS server to allow for remote connections.

Remember that you can administer a remote IIS server using the Internet Service Manager through the MMC. To access this tool, you must first log on and have your account validated. While you can configure the remote IIS to

---

**FIGURE 3-9**

HTML version of Internet Service Manager

use Windows challenge authentication, be careful which configuration parameters you set.

Using the browser to do administration is also known as *HTML Administration (HTMLA)*. HTMLA relies heavily on the architecture of Common Object Model (COM) which is the foundation for OLE (object linking and embedding) and Distributed Common Object Model (DCOM) for its distributed services. DCOM is the Microsoft approach to what other vendors do with COBRA (Common Object Request Broker Architecture).

<table>
<tr><td>EXERCISE 3-3</td></tr>
</table>

## Using HTMLA

Purpose: To explore the property sheets associated with the FTP and WWW service. To use the HTMLA to examine the same properties toverify they are the same items in both versions of ISM.

*Complete these procedures from both computers.*

1. Ensure that you are logged on as Administrator.
2. Ensure that the MMC is open.
3. Expand Internet Information Server.
4. Expand your server.
5. Right-click the Default Web Site icon.
6. Select Properties.
7. The Web Site tab should be in the foreground. What is the default TCP Port?
8. Click the Advanced button next to the IP Address dialog box.
9. What is the default SSL port?
10. Click Cancel twice to close the Default Web Site Properties box.
11. Expand the Default Web Site.
12. Right-click the IISSAMPLES object.
13. Click Browse. This starts Internet Explorer.
14. What message is displayed in the browser?
15. Minimize the browser.
16. Right-click the IISSAMPLES object.

17. Select Properties.
18. In the Virtual Directory tab, Content Control, check Directory browsing allowed.
19. Click OK.
20. Restore the browser.
21. Click the Refresh button. The screen will update.
22. What is displayed in the browser?
23. Close the browser.
24. Right-click the IISSAMPLES object.
25. Select Properties.
26. In the Virtual Directory tab, Content Control, clear Directory browsing allowed.
27. Click OK.
28. Close the MMC.
29. Click No when prompted to save the settings.
30. Click the Start button.
31. Point to Programs.
32. Point to Windows NT 4.0 Option Pack.
33. Point to Microsoft Internet Information Server.
34. Click Internet Service Manager (HTML).
35. Internet Explorer should open and connect to your site.
36. Click the plus key to the left of Default Web Site.
37. Click the Default Web Site.
38. What is the default TCP Port?
39. Click the Advanced button next to the IP Address dialog box. This should open a separate window.
40. What is the default SSL port listed under secure bindings?
41. Close this ISM screen by clicking cancel at the bottom.
42. Close Internet Explorer.

*Answers to the steps in this exercise:*

7. Port 80.

9. Port 443

14. Directory browsing forbidden.

22. The directory structure.

38. Port 80.

40. Port 443

# CERTIFICATION SUMMARY

Microsoft has a new management unification tool called the Microsoft Management Console. This utility provides no functionality itself, but provides the framework for the actual utilities, called snap-ins. The Internet Service Manager is one such snap-in.

The Internet Information Server has objects and tasks associated with it. Objects, such as the FTP service and the WWW service, have properties. The properties are managed from the ISM. The configuration parameters are kept in a database called the metabase. Most of the metabase parameters can be set with the ISM interface. You can also edit the metabase directly, but this is seldom recommended.

You can also administer the Internet Information Server from the Internet Explorer using the Internet Information Server HTML version, also called HTMLA.

 # TWO-MINUTE DRILL

❑ You manage the Internet Information Server with the Internet Service Manager (ISM).

❑ ISM is a snap-in to MMC.

❑ MMC provides a platform framework for management tools.

❑ Snap-ins can be written by third-party vendors.

❑ Snap-ins can be written by system administrators.

❑ MMC snap-ins should have a common look and feel, making them easier to use.

❑ The MMC environment can be customized.

❑ These MMC customized views can be saved and retrieved later.

❑ There are two panes in the MMC: The scope pane contains nodes and the results pane shows the objects and tasks of a node.

❑ The last toolbar in the MMC is called the rebar. The rebar has three bands: The first band contains the Action and View menus. The contents of the other two bands varies depending on the node selected.

❑ Right-clicking on an object brings a pop-up menu into view.

❑ You access object properties from this pop-up menu.

❑ IIS parameters are kept in the metabase.

❑ You can use Internet Explorer to do IIS administration. This is also called HTMLA.

❑ IIS servers can be administered locally.

❑ IIS servers can be administered remotely.

# SELF TEST

The Self Test questions will help you measure your understanding of the material presented in this chapter. Read all the choices carefully, as there may be more than one correct answer. Choose all correct answers for each question.

1. What tools are available to manage IIS?

    A. Regedt32

    B. Server Manager

    C. Internet Service Manager

    D. Internet Service Manager HTML

2. Which tool provides the framework for snap-ins?

    A. Internet Service Manager

    B. Microsoft Management Console

    C. Internet Information Server

    D. Services Manager

3. Which of the following statements are true of MMC?

    A. It provides the framework for you to access multiple management programs.

    B. It modifies the registry.

    C. Only Microsoft programs can be added to MMC.

    D. Third-party programs can be written to run in MMC.

4. Which of the following characteristics are benefits of MMC?

    A. It can be customized.

    B. It provides integration.

    C. It is flexible.

    D. It is transportable.

5. How do you start the MMC?

    A. Go to Administrative Tools and select Management Console.

    B. Select Windows NT 4.0 Option Pack | Microsoft Internet Information Server, then select Internet Information Server.

    C. Double-click on a .MSC file.

    D. Enter **ISM.EXE** at the Run command.

6. What is contained in the scope pane of the MMC?

    A. A tree view of the namespace

    B. Nodes

    C. Registry entries

    D. Files

7. Which of the following statements is true of the MMC menu bars?

    A. MMC has two menu bars.

    B. The last menu bar is called the rebar.

    C. The rebar has three bands

    D. You can add other menu bars to MMC through the Console menu item.

8. Which of the following is true of the MMC?

    A. The item contained in the last two bands of the rebar changes depending on the object selected.

B. You can configure the MMC to display multiple windows.

C. You can save console configurations.

D. You cannot save console configurations.

9. What is the best way to make configuration changes to IIS?

   A. Edit the registry.

   B. Use the Internet Service Manager.

   C. Edit the metabase.

D. Use the Windows NT 4.0 Option Pack Setup program.

10. How do you add another server to your console view?

   A. Open Server Manager and select Add Computer account.

   B. Edit the metabase.

   C. Click the Connect button on the rebar.

   D. You cannot add another IIS machine to the console view.

# 4

# Security and IIS

T here are many aspects to security, many of which are beyond the scope of this book. However, the following security axiom applies to most situations, including Windows NT Server and Internet Information Server:

*No system is secure from a knowledgeable user and idiots.*

To illustrate both points, consider a typical organization's IT shop. Can an organization prevent a system administrator from doing damage to the system? Not really; the best you can do is to put some obstacles in the way and maintain an audit trail to see who did the damage. You cannot stop a knowledgeable user such as a system administrator from doing damage if they are determined to do so. As a consultant, I am called upon frequently by my customers to discuss security, generally *after* a security breach has occurred.

Many times clients ask how they can limit the capabilities of a system administrator and minimize the potential damage a system administrator can do. The analogy I use most often is the one where the data center is in a room secured by a door and a cipher lock. (A cipher lock is one where you enter a code on a keypad and the lock unlatches and you can enter the computer room.) So I rephrase the question asked by clients in this metaphor, "How can I prevent the system administrator, to whom I gave the combination to the lock so they can gain access to do their work, from gaining access for the purpose of doing damage?" The obvious answer is not to give the administrator the code for the lock. The point is you have to trust your administrators. If you don't, then you have to fix *that* problem.

The second security issue is that of "idiots." Many times, I walk the halls of a client's organization. I can tell visually whether their security system for protecting their data is overengineered without talking to any users or doing any formal study or even any hard work. Let me illustrate this point by asking, "What do users do when faced with a password security system that is rigid and demanding (frequent password changes, long passwords, not reusing passwords, etc.)?" The users write their passwords down on little yellow pieces of paper and they put them where? They put them on the monitor, under the phone, in their center or right-hand desk drawer, under the desk pad behind the picture of their family, and so on. How secure is a system when the system security code is out in the open, or poorly hidden? Not at all secure!

Your organization is better off to have simple passwords that change yearly than to have "idiot behavior" that leaves system passwords unprotected. If you smile after reading this because you know this is typical behavior in your organization, you might want to rethink your security non-system. And, if your face turns stone cold after reading this because you know this behavior does not happen in your organization, you might want to lazily wander around the corridors of your organization, with your eyes open!

## CERTIFICATION OBJECTIVE 4.01

# IIS Security Overview

Internet Information Server (IIS) has multiple security features designed to keep the server and its data as safe as possible from intruders and hackers. IIS security is based on the foundation of Windows NT, which is an excellent platform for security protection. Securing an IIS server is a combination of configuring Windows NT Server security and the individual IIS service security options. When you connect the IIS to the Internet, a firewall can be configured to provide additional security services. Microsoft Proxy Server can be used as a firewall for such a purpose.

exam
ⓦatch

*IIS takes advantage of the security features of Windows NT Server. Mandatory logon and NTFS are two big ones.*

The first step in securing the Internet Information Server is to practice good security on Windows NT Server. Windows NT Server has two key features to assist in securing the IIS server and its WWW service and its FTP service:

- Windows NT account and mandatory logon security
- Windows NT Server file system NTFS

Windows NT Server helps secure its resources and your assets by requiring valid user accounts in order to access these resources. Every operation on the server identifies who is performing the operation for the security system. You can control access to all the computer resources by limiting the authority these accounts have.

One of the primary causes of unauthorized access to your system is being complacent about the passwords associated with the user accounts. To avoid unauthorized access, encourage users to choose difficult-to-guess passwords. Such passwords are generally long and use mixed-case characters (uppercase and lowercase alphabetic characters). You can also mix numeric characters with special characters such as the pound sign (#) or the exclamation mark (!). In some cases, a password of at least 10 characters in length of mixed-case characters, using alphanumeric with one or two embedded special characters, is considered virtually unbreakable by a hacker using a data dictionary routine.

Another security technique is to limit the number of people who have administrative accounts. Only authorize those employees who absolutely require access to administrative accounts. In addition, users who have administrative accounts should also have regular, user-level accounts. When performing administrative tasks, those users can log on using the administrative account. When performing non-administrative tasks, users should log on using the regular user account. Users should log on with only enough authority to do the task at hand. Using a word processor does not require administrative-level authority. Therefore, the user should not log on with an administrative account to perform word processing functions.

In addition to these techniques, applying strict account policies is another good policy. Regular and enforced password changes are vital. The password uniqueness function in Windows NT prevents users from reusing the same password.

exam
⚠️atch

*Enforcing other account policies such as password uniqueness and minimum password age can improve security.*

Enforcing periodic password changes is important in the event that an account becomes compromised and an unauthorized user has obtained a user account and password. The password change forces the unauthorized user to search again for an available password.

Another good security practice is to secure the resource access using the NTFS file system. By setting your drives with NTFS security, you have additional security features for the files and folders contained on your IIS server. Using NTFS permissions, you can specify which users have which access type to files and folders. In the event that there are conflicts between your NTFS settings and the IIS security settings, the most restrictive settings are in effect.

## The Cost of Poor Security

Companies that have a minimal security system or a poorly designed security system are suffering enormous losses. The cost of a well-designed security system can be far less than the cost of unauthorized access. In addition to unauthorized access, you can incur substantial costs in the analysis of the intrusion after the fact.

The United States Senate Subcommittee on Permanent Investigations concluded that the cost of unauthorized access to businesses worldwide was more than $800 million in 1995. U.S.-based companies accounted for more than half of the reported losses. This study also concluded that many of these security breaches were never reported out of fear of bad publicity surrounding such a breach.

## Even Secure Systems Are Not Safe from Attack

In 1995, the computer networks of the Department of Defense (DOD) experienced more than 250,000 unauthorized attacks. It is expected that the rate of the attacks will double every year for the foreseeable future. Some analysts believe that these attacks on the DOD networks were successful about two-thirds of the time. While some of the attacks on the DOD system were only a nuisance, some of the attacks were real threats to national security.

In early 1995, the United States Air Force reported that in one of its computer laboratories in New York state, a pair of intruders were successful in gaining unauthorized access to the lab's computer systems more than 150 times. During these unauthorized accesses, the intruders were successful in collecting user IDs and passwords, which allowed the users to break into more than 100 other computer systems attached to the Internet.

Unauthorized attacks and intrusions know no age limit. One of the perpetrators in the attacks on the Air Force laboratory was a 16-year-old boy.

## Security Classifications

The Department of Defense views network security very seriously. To assist in evaluating how secure computer operating systems are, the Department of Defense uses a security standard number 5200.28 entitled "Trusted Computer System Evaluation Criteria." This standard is also called "The Orange Book." The Orange Book provides technical criteria for evaluating hardware and software security, along with evaluation methodologies that support a data security model. The Orange Book categorizes security in four different levels. The levels are:

- Level D
- Level C
- Level B
- Level A

Level D systems offer minimal protection. Operating systems such as MS-DOS fall into this level because they allow open and generally unrestricted access. Level C protection is grouped into two categories: C1 and C2. C1 security is known as *Discretionary Security Protection*, and C2 security is known as *Controlled Access Protection*. There is a difference between being C2-certified by the National Computer Security Center (NCSC) and complying with DOD Orange Book level C2 security. Windows NT is in the C2 security level of the DOD Orange Book.

Level B security specifies mandatory protection. It also specifies that the system must provide mathematical documentation of its security and its ability to maintain its system security even when the system is down. Level B has three categories:

- **B1**  Labeled security protection
- **B2**  Structured protection
- **B3**  Security domains

Level A is the highest security protection accorded to the computer systems in the Orange Book and is known as *Verified Security*.

**CERTIFICATION OBJECTIVE 4.02**

# What Are Security Risks?

A security risk is any entry point into your system or business. There are many potential entry points into the business of your organization, some of which may not receive a great deal of attention. Consider the analogy of a fortress to represent a security system. You construct an impenetrable fortress with steel and brick walls. You enclose the fortress on all four sides and the top, with no windows, no doors, no entry points, no exit points; the fortress is fairly secure. Then you add a doorway to the fortress. You have now created a security risk, and that security risk entry point should be guarded against unauthorized access. Some of the techniques used to secure a doorway into a facility include well-known techniques such as locks and keys, or security personnel at the doorway to check entry access permission of people coming into and going out of the doorway.

The more doorways and windows you put in your system, the easier and more convenient it is for you and your coworkers to gain access to the fortress in order to do your work. Unfortunately, the easier it is for you to gain access means that there are more potential doorways, and the easier it is for others to gain unauthorized access to the system. Remember, every new doorway you create to the system is a new doorway through which unauthorized access may occur. Things that you may do as a network administrator and your users may do every day as part of your network practices may be creating doorways into your system through which unauthorized access can occur. For example, you have a computer system that is a stand-alone computer system in your office. When you are not in your office, your office door is always closed and locked. This office doorway represents a potential entry point for unauthorized access into your office and into your computer system. This is not a problem, you say, because you always keep your office door locked. Except that one day, when you are in a rush to get to a meeting or another emergency, you go blowing out of your office, close the door as you have done a thousand times before but the door does not lock or fully close. The doorway to your system is now open.

A stand-alone computer may be fairly secure, or can be made so, in that context. Put that same computer on a network, and you have opened a potential doorway into the system. Create a share point on that computer that is now the network, and you have opened yet another doorway for potential access to the system. Connect your network to another network within your company, and you have created a potential doorway for more users to gain access to your system. Take the same, small intra-company network and attach it to the Internet, and you have now created a giant doorway for potentially millions of users to gain access to your system. This is a security risk. The fact that connecting to the Internet is common does not make it any less of a security risk.

It is probably a mistake to assume that knowledgeable (or even unknowledgeable) users, hackers, and crackers will not exploit the security risks that you created. Ernst & Young's Fourth Annual Information Security Survey was conducted by interviewing more than 1,300 IT executives in North America. The following is a summary of some of the statistics of that survey:

- More than 50 percent of those surveyed indicated that they had suffered financial loss from security breaches.

- 70 percent of those who said they suffered financial losses were unable to calculate the amount of the loss, although many believed it to be substantial.

- More than 25 percent of those who were able to calculate the financial loss from security breaches estimated those losses at more than $250,000.
  In some cases, the loss was in the one-million-dollar range.

- Almost two-thirds of those surveyed indicated that their losses were due to virus attacks. One-third of those surveyed discovered attacks on the system by insiders (employees and other trusted people). 17 percent of those surveyed said that they had discovered attacks on the system by outsiders.

Stated another way, these statistics reveal the stark reality that one out of every two organizations suffers unauthorized access that causes financial loss.

## Back Doors

As the name implies, a back door is a way into the system, sometimes through the legitimate system security and sometimes around the legitimate system security. Many administrators create an innocent back door in the form of an extra administrator's account that has an easy-to-remember user ID and password. The theory behind such an account is that should the regular administrator account become corrupt or the password be forgotten, there is this immediate back door into the system to gain administrative access to fix potential account problems.

Other sources of back doors are contractors and other support personnel who periodically use your system. One technique that administrators use when doing work for another company is to create an account for themselves with administrative privileges. This is often done innocently enough to facilitate access to the system by the contractor. In many cases, the network administrator for the company itself creates an administrative account for the contractor. When the contractor finishes his or her job and leaves, the account created for the contractor is a potential back door if not immediately deleted from the system.

Another possible back door exists with Windows NT 4.0 with Service Pack 2 installed. Under that configuration, it is possible for someone to add a SYSTEM.DLL (an executable program) that can be used to intercept and record any password changes on the system. This program can store the password information in a place where a cracker would have access.

## Intruder Categories

There are three generic terms used to describe intruders and others who attempt to gain unauthorized access to systems. They are:

- Hackers
- Crackers
- Phreaks

The terms hacker, cracker, and phreak apply to people with similar "hobbies," but there are some important differences.

A *hacker* is an independent-minded, generally law-abiding computer enthusiast. Typically, hackers are very interested in computer systems. A hacker delights in gaining an intimate understanding of the internal workings of computer systems and computer networks in particular. Hackers are usually harmless, although many times people use the term "hacker" to refer to both good and bad (malicious).

*Cracker* is a term that describes a person who gains access or attempts to gain access to your system or computer network with malicious intent. A cracker will illegally gain access to computer systems for fun, profit, or personal gain. A cracker may not always harm a computer system or network when gaining access. However, crackers definitely perpetrate a computer crime, whether they realize it or not.

*Phreaks* are mischievous individuals who delight in manipulating telephone equipment and other communications equipment. Phreaks have been around for several decades, and in their early existence, broke into telephone systems in an effort to make long-distance calls without charges. As computer systems became prevalent and information was stored in bulletin board systems (BBSs), many BBSs were accessible only by long-distance phone calls. To gain access, phreaks used all types of ploys, including tone-producing devices to trick telephone company switches. Today, phone system equipment has become more sophisticated, making phreaking an extremely dangerous game to play because tracking down the phreak is relatively easy.

## Spoofing

*Spoofing* occurs when IP packets from one computer are made to look like packets from a trusted system. Spoofing lets an intruder on a TCP/IP network impersonate a computer as if it is on your local network. In other words, someone from outside your firewall on the Internet can send a packet to your firewall, and that packet will look like it came from a computer on your network.

This technique can be especially dangerous if you allow connections without a password. If computers on your network allow session authentication based on an IP address from the host, then the network believes that the incoming connection request originated from the trusted local host and therefore does not require a password. It is entirely possible for forged packets to penetrate a firewall if that firewall is not configured to block incoming packets that have source addresses of the local network or the local domain. This attack may still be possible even if no session packets can be routed back to the attacker. This attack does not necessarily need to use the source routing option of the IP protocol. Network configurations that are potentially vulnerable to IP spoofing attacks are:

- Networks that have routers
- External networks where the router supports multiple internal interfaces
- Networks that have routers with at least two interfaces that support subnetting on the internal network
- Networks that have proxy firewalls where the proxy system uses the source IP address for authentication

IP spoofing attacks can be very difficult to detect. One of the best defenses against IP spoofing is to filter packets as they enter your router from the Internet, denying access to any packet that claims to have originated inside your local network. This technique is known as an *input filter* and is supported by most major router manufacturers.

## Keystroke Grabbing

A *keystroke grabber* is a piece of software installed on a computer that records the user's keystrokes (keys on the keyboard that the user presses). It writes those keystrokes to a file. One purpose of a keystroke grabber is to record the user login ID and password. The cracker then returns to the system, retrieves the grabber file that was created, and can view the username and password from the file. Since this file records all keystrokes that are pressed, if the user is typing a confidential memo, the unauthorized person can reconstruct that memo simply by examining the file created by the keystroke grabber.

The system cracker has to install the keystroke grabber file either by physically accessing the computer to install the file or by installing it across the network. Installing grabber files across the network can be quite insidious. These programs can be installed by unaware users doing tasks that they normally do such as searching the Internet, or connecting to a Web site. Grabber files can also be installed by executing a program unintentionally on the Web site that delivers the keystroke grabber program, installs it on the user's hard drive, and then activates it, leaving the user entirely unaware that the keystroke grabber program has ever been installed.

Microsoft Windows NT, by way of the mandatory logon initiated by the CTRL-ALT-DEL sequence, makes installing keystroke grabber programs from the local system extremely difficult to do. Microsoft intentionally chose the CTRL-ALT-DEL keystroke sequence because that keystroke sequence generates a hardware interrupt. It is not possible for software programs to emulate a hardware interrupt. This means that even if a user has access to a Windows NT computer while someone is logged on and manages to install a keystroke grabber program, that program cannot become active and emulate the environment created when the user presses CTRL-ALT-DEL. Since the program cannot emulate the hardware interrupt, there is no way to keep Windows NT from seeing the CTRL-ALT-DEL command. Once that happens, the security system is invoked, the program does not see the keystrokes, and they are not recorded. This same security feature is not available in other operating systems such as Windows 95.

## Denial of Service

With a denial of service (DoS) attack, there may not be an actual intrusion on your network or attempted unauthorized access. The person originating the denial of service attack is attempting to make legitimate requests of your system in such a fashion that it "busies out" your server so that no other authorized access can get to the server. This happens because the server is busy with the work sent under the denial of service attack.

Stated in other words, the purpose of this attack is to bombard a system with unnecessary traffic on a certain port or group of ports, rendering those services unavailable to respond to genuine requests. A denial of service attack can originate from any TCP/IP-based service or computer on the Internet. Protecting and configuring your network against denial of service attacks can be tricky.

Detecting a denial of service attack may be self-evident. If your e-mail server does not seem to be sending or receiving e-mail, or your Web server has stopped responding or has become incredibly slow, it could be due to a denial of service attack. These significant drops in performance that are abnormal in the normal usage pattern of your server can mean that the computer has been busied out by a denial of service attack.

While actually realizing that you have been a victim of a denial of service attack may be easy, preventing one can be quite difficult. Fixing one may require you to shut down your server, making it unavailable for access, which means that your user community has been denied the services a little while longer.

To detect a denial of service attack in the early stages and find out who initiated this attack requires certain tools. A *network analyzer* allows you to examine the packets on your network and capture those packets so you can examine the source address of the request that is attempting to busy out your server.

This attack is a current topic. As I am writing this book, Microsoft has announced a new attack called the Tear II and has posted fixes to it on their Web site.

## Update on Network Denial of Service Attacks (Teardrop/NewTear/Bonk/Boink)

*Microsoft is responsive to publishing information and fixes about denial of service attacks. The following is quoted from the Microsoft Web site, Security section:*

*Posted March 3, 1998; Last Updated March 6, 1998*

Since March 2, 1998, there have been numerous reports of malicious network-based, denial-of-service attacks launched against Internet-connected systems. We were notified of these attacks, which affected some Internet-connected Microsoft Windows NT and Windows 95 systems, by customers and security alert organizations, including CIAC and CERT. This issue was also reported on the NTBUGTRAQ mailing list. Special thanks to Russ Cooper, the list moderator, for his assistance in this issue.

Based on analysis of data received from customers and alert groups, this is not a new issue. Systems that contain up-to-date patches were not vulnerable to this wave of attacks. This vulnerability exploited by this attack was addressed by a patch issued in early January. The attack is called by various names, including Teardrop2, NewTear, Bonk, Boink. These are all varied attacks that exploit the same vulnerability, which was addressed in the patch released in January.

For more information specifically on the NewTear/Bonk/Boink attack and the available updates for that vulnerability, please read our bulletin on that issue.

## What Microsoft Is Doing

Since the attacks began, we have worked with customers and security response organizations to obtain network traces of the attacks in action, as well as Windows NT memory dumps from affected machines. The network traces indicate an exploit that uses a fragmented UDP network packet to cause a failure similar to the NewTear/Bonk/Boink issue from early in January. None of the attacked machines from which we obtained memory dumps had the latest patches installed, and the memory dumps indicated a failure consistent with the NewTear/Bonk/Boink attack.

Additionally, replaying the network traces we obtained from attacked customers against patched systems had no effect, while these same traces replayed against an unpatched system caused it to crash. This was further evidence that the widespread attack since Monday was a NewTear/Bonk/Boink-type attack.

We will continue to work with customers who are affected by this issue, and with the security response organizations to ensure that there is no new issue here, and to ensure that all customers are aware of the security updates necessary to protect against these network denial of service attacks. The following are some alerts that have been posted by other alert organizations on this issue:

> CERT Coordination Center (Carnegie Mellon University)
>
> CIAC (Lawrence Livermore National Laboratory)
>
> NASIRC (NASA)
>
> internetMCI Security Engineering

Additional information and discussion is available on a number of newsgroups, including the NTBUGTRAQ.

## What Customers Should Do

Customers in large corporations, or campus-style networks should contact their network administrators if they are being attacked. Additionally, reporting these incidents to a response organization like CERT could assist in determining the scope of this attack. In some cases it is useful to work with your Internet Service Provider, or upstream Internet Service Provider to attempt to determine the source of an ongoing attack. It might also be appropriate to notify law enforcement officials (see the end of this document for details).

Customers should evaluate their current environment to determine their exposure, and install all relevant security updates. Information about available updates is included in the following sections.

## Windows NT 4.0

Customers should install Windows NT 4 Service Pack 3. The following post-SP3 hot fixes relating to possible denial of service attacks are also available. These patches can be installed in any order relevant to each other.

- LSA Denial of Service Fix
- Simple TCP/IP Services Denial of Service Fix
- NewTear/Bonk/Boink TCP/IP Denial of Service Fix
- IIS Denial of Service Fix (only if you have IIS 2.0 or 3.0 installed)
- SMB/CIFS Denial of Service Fix

**Note:** There were earlier TCP/IP denial of service fixes for Windows NT (icmp-fix, oob-fix, land-fix) that are superceded by the ones listed above.

**CERTIFICATION OBJECTIVE 4.03**

# Why Are Systems Hacked?

One reason systems are attacked is because they are there. There is a personality type who climbs a mountain simply because the mountain is there. In computer terms, this personality type wants to gain access simply because the system is there or because they are told they cannot have access. Typically, this type of attack is not designed to be malicious or to cause any damage. Once access is gained, the interest of the hacker often goes away and he moves on to the next system to which he does not have access.

Systems are also attacked with malicious intent. Amazingly enough, there are some individuals who will attack a system intending to disrupt it, such as with denial of service attacks, but who do not think that such an attack is wrong or unethical. Typical of this person's philosophy is the concept that if the company did not want the system to be attacked, then it should not have created the system.

Systems are attacked to gain information. The information in your organization is an asset. This information frequently has immediate and potential financial value. Your competitors (and even friends) may be very interested in what you are doing or not doing. Do not underestimate the risk from friends.

You might want to have a disclaimer on your Web site that states this site "is for authorized users only." If you say "Welcome to the site..." and someone hacks into your site, you may not be able to take legal action because you said "Welcome."

# Security Countermeasures

There are a variety of security measures you should employ on your network to reduce the possibility of unwanted and unauthorized access. This is especially important if your network is connected to the Internet.

## Authenticating Users

Authenticating users is a way to distinguish legitimate users from those trying to gain unauthorized access. Authenticating users and using this authentication to provide them with information, content, and other services is a fundamental part of security.

## Resource Access Control

Using the NTFS file system as the basis of your resource access control allows you to implement "granular" access control over authorized users' access to resources. NTFS allows you to differentiate which resources particular users may have access to and what type of access they may have.

## Encryption

Encrypting data, especially sensitive data, on the Internet is fast becoming a security must. Encrypting your logon IDs and passwords should be considered a top security priority.

## Auditing and Logging

Enabling auditing on Windows NT and logging user activity helps you keep track of access by authorized users and potential access by unauthorized users. In some cases, just the knowledge that the system is being monitored is sufficient to deter some from attempting unauthorized access.

Monitoring your systems for availability and early warning signs of possible unauthorized access is always a good idea. You can monitor TCP/IP services with a number of programs that have been engineered specifically for that purpose. Some programs are for monitoring services at the port level, and some programs monitor services at the service level. These programs can generate alerts and alarms and can even page you or send you an e-mail message if unauthorized access is attempted.

Windows NT Server comes with robust auditing capabilities. Windows NT writes its audited events in the security log. Of course, if the audited events are to be of any value to you, you must review the security log regularly.

On a fairly busy server, audited events can generate a tremendous amount of information. Therefore, you should audit only key events and critical pieces of information; do not audit all events. This technique keeps you from being overwhelmed by a great deal of information; truly important information can be lost in a deluge of audited events.

## Block Unwanted TCP/IP Ports

TCP relies on ports to perform its tasks. You may want to routinely scan the TCP/IP ports on the servers on your network with an eye for finding ports that should not be listening. You are looking for unwanted services that may be running. These services are sometimes known as *rogue services*. Intruders are known for installing rogue services on inconspicuous TCP/IP ports. You should plan to monitor TCP ports 137, 138, and 139, which allow direct network connections to shared Windows NT Server resources. You may want to block all access to these ports. A convenient place to block access to these ports is your router. This prevents a potential intruder from gaining direct network access to your RAS server.

Windows NT Server 4.0 includes rudimentary TCP/IP filtering mechanisms. While this feature may be quite primitive and does not support access control logging or other advanced features that are found in most firewalls, it does behave as a filter that adds a layer of network security to your system. You can access these port filters through the Network applet by selecting the TCP/IP protocol and clicking on the Advanced button. Then click Enable Security in the Configure button, and it brings up a dialog box in which you configure the filters. Your choices are to commit all or only certain TCP ports and UDP ports to be active.

## Other Security Techniques

TCP/IP networks can be made more secure in the following ways:

- Firewalls
- Packet filters
- Proxy servers and application gateways
- Second-level gateways
- Physical isolation
- Protocol isolation
- Monitoring and auditing

### Firewalls

Among network engineers with networks connected to the Internet today, you often hear the term *firewall* used. A firewall is a generic term for a mechanism (hardware or software) for protecting your network from an outside attack.

According to a study done by the International Data Corporation, the affect of outside attacks by unauthorized users has sent worldwide firewall sales from about 10,000 units shipped in 1995 to a projected 1.5 million units in the year 2000. The cost of a typical firewall today is between $16,000 and $20,000. Some industry analysts predict that by the year 2000, the cost of an average firewall could be under $1,000.

Many network administrators believe that because they have a firewall installed between their network and the Internet, they are secure from unauthorized entry. This is not the case. Even with a firewall in place on your network, you can still be exposed to intruder attacks and unauthorized access.

There are a number of security professionals whose sole job it is to evaluate organizations' computer network security. These individuals deliberately try to penetrate the security systems of a network, even those networks protected by firewalls. Many corporations and government agencies are unpleasantly surprised by these results. These security professionals are able to gain unauthorized access to many networks, often for a number of weeks before they are detected.

One of the reasons that these attempts are successful is that firewall system logs are not properly scrutinized by network administrators. While the firewall log records attempts of unauthorized access, it is estimated that 50 to 60 percent of all unauthorized access attempts actually get through. In some cases, there is sufficient inattention from network administrators who assume that because they have a firewall installed, their networks are secure.

## Packet Filters

The purpose of a packet filter is to limit packet traffic to and from hosts on your network and the Internet. Packet filters operate on a set of rules that you define. Packet filters come in two general varieties: those that are hardware-based and those that are software-based. A hardware packet filter is typically a stand-alone router that filters packets as they enter and leave the router. A software packet filter runs on a network server. Windows NT Server 4.0 has a built-in rudimentary packet filter for its TCP/IP protocol stack.

A TCP/IP packet traveling through the Internet contains a source IP address, a destination IP address, and a destination port number. A packet filter looks at this information and then decides how to handle the packet based on rules that you establish for each packet type and port number. As the packets go through the router, the router compares each packet in turn with the defined set of rules and decides whether the packet can pass or should be blocked.

Packet filters can be set to deny all access to the network, in which case you must expressly configure which packets should be able to pass.

The disadvantage of packet filters is that they simply look at the packet and decide how to handle the packet based on the port number or IP addresses. These devices can sometimes be fooled, with a technique called *spoofing*, into thinking that a particular packet string is actually authorized traffic when in fact, it may not be.

## Proxy Servers and Application Gateways

A *proxy server* is a server that is entitled to act on behalf of other computers on the network. A proxy server may also be referred to as an *application gateway*. Proxy servers act as mediators between two systems attempting to communicate with each other across the Internet. Microsoft Proxy Server, discussed later in this book, is an example of a proxy server.

Proxy servers protect the identity of the host. The source IP address of the host is never revealed to any system other than the proxy server. This can improve network security because intruders do not know the true IP address of the host and without this, it is extremely difficult to gain unauthorized access to or to attack the host. Proxy servers can be an economical and reliable way to protect your computer system from unauthorized access. Proxy servers used in conjunction with packet filters can greatly strengthen network security. One of the weaknesses of proxy servers is that they can be very complex to configure, and even a minor configuration mistake can leave your network open to attack when you consider yourself to be protected.

## Second-Level Gateways

*Second-level gateways* are similar to application gateways except that second-level gateways verify the TCP or UDP session. The second-level gateway approach is to avoid any direct physical contact between the Internet and any host on the internal network. In this scenario, a proxy address is used as a contact to the outside source. Once information is transferred to that address, the proxy transfers information to the appropriate internal destination. By using this technique, hackers are limited to the amount of information they can get about individual machines. Second-level gateways generally do not examine individual packets of information once they verify the address. Second-level gateways are rarely used stand-alone; they are commonly part of a larger security scheme.

## Physical Isolation

Physical isolation means isolating systems on your network by placing them where they cannot be reached by TCP/IP traffic and anyone outside your immediate network. With a physically isolated system, your only choice for gaining access to the system or network is through the physical facility where the system resides. Controlling access to the physical facility is much easier than controlling network access.

## Protocol Isolation

Protocol isolation is a technique that uses protocols not commonly supported by the Internet as a primary means of network communication. For example, using NetBEUI on your internal LAN is a form of protocol isolation. Systems from the outside world on the Internet are generally running the TCP/IP protocol. In order to gain access to your internal network that is running NetBEUI, they also have to be running the NetBEUI protocol. When you need access to the Internet, which usually requires TCP/IP, you go through a proxy server or application gateway.

## Packet Sniffers

A *packet sniffer* for a data monitor camps on the network and captures each packet on the network. With a packet sniffer or monitor, a potential cracker does not need a tool like a keystroke grabber to discern usernames and passwords. If you allow remote logon across the network and a potential cracker is monitoring the traffic, your logon request (user ID and password) goes across the network in the data packets. The potential cracker is able to capture those packets and to see the username and password. Any information that is unencrypted while sent across the network is potentially useful to the cracker. For example, FTP logons (the account used to log on and its password) are sent across the network in clear text.

Do not be lulled into a false sense of security because you have encrypted data or logon requests on your network. While data encryption may present an insurmountable object to some, to a knowledgeable and determined cracker, encryption schemes run anywhere from a mild nuisance to a new professional challenge. Data encryption can be and is broken regularly.

Hardware-based analyzers generally must be connected to the physical cable on your network in order to capture data packets. However, software-based programs may be run from any workstation including a dial-up link. A packet sniffer can be as valuable a tool to you as it is to the professional cracker.

# FROM THE CLASSROOM

## Top List of Security Items to Watch

The following is a quick checklist of things to do or not to do relative to security for your site.

1. Physically secure your environment. This means secure your building, your computers, and your network.

2. Enforce the security policies. It won't help to have elaborate security schemes if people don't pay attention or try to circumvent them.

3. Limit the number of people who have administrative authority to the absolute number necessary and not the number that is convenient. Too many administrators create security risks. There are two important issues to remember here: One, it is very hard to keep a determined administrator from doing damage and two, a substantial amount of damage to systems is done by employees, not outsiders.

4. Only log on with enough authority to do the task at hand. In other words, you do not need to log on as an administrator to use the word processor.

5. Log off. I am amazed at the number of clients that I visit who do not log off when they leave the computer. They leave their computer while they are logged on as administrator! I have even seen this happen when the administrator is logged on at a user's station while troubleshooting a problem.

6. Password-protected screen savers may leave a security hole. I know some administrators who leave their computer on and attempt to prevent access to their computer using a screen saver that is password protected. This approach is better than not logging off at all but less secure than logging off. Your system will be unsecured for whatever time it takes for the screen saver to be invoked.

7. Security is more about catching violations than it is in preventing violations. You must monitor, check, and double-check the security system that is in place to watch for unauthorized access. The relevant question is not "Will you be hacked?" but "Will you know that you have been hacked?"

# Windows NT Domain and Security

Internet Information Server is the security foundation established by Windows NT Server. The Windows NT security system requires a logon validation in order to gain access. This is true of logging on locally and accessing the computer through the network. The security system continues in force even after you have logged on. Everything you do in Windows NT has to be done with a security context and with access authority. Unless you have the proper security context and access authority, you cannot perform operations you may need to. This is also true if you are trying to log on at the local console. If you do not have the right to log on locally, you will not be allowed to log on even though you have a valid account.

The same is true of attempting to access the computer from the network. You may have a valid account and have access permission to the files on an NTFS partition, but without the security context of accessing the computer from the network, you will not be able to access your files.

## The IUSR Account

When you install IIS, it creates two accounts. One of those is the IUSR_*computername* account. This account is granted the Log On Locally user right. These are the account credentials that users present when they access the Web service or the FTP service.

IIS setup also installs an IWAM_*computername* account for Web administration. Figure 4-1 shows the description of both these accounts.

Windows NT's security system requires users to present valid credentials in order to access the system. These credentials take the form of a username and password. Every process within Windows NT must have a security context. Users that access the IIS will have Log On Locally access but will not have the right to access this computer from the network. The significance of this is that without the right to access the computer from the network, a user cannot access

**FIGURE 4-1**          User Manager with IUSR and IWAM account

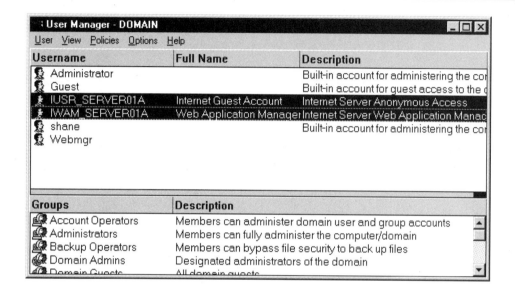

the file services of the server. This limits the amount of potential damage a user can inflict.

e x a m
ⓦ a t c h

*The account IUSR_computername must have the Log On Locally right so that anonymous users can gain access.*

Windows NT Server assigns the built-in group Everyone the right to access the computer from the network as the default. As the administrator, it is up to you to remove this group from that user's rights if necessary.

Along the same line, you should have good physical security for your IIS server. Because users who access the Web or FTP server never have access to the physical server to log on at the console, the Log On Locally right provides only minimum exposure.

## Anonymous

When you access the IIS services, both the HTTP server and the FTP server, you access it using an Anonymous account for logon. You can set the FTP server so that clients may only log on using the Anonymous account, as illustrated in Figure 4-2.

When a user logs on to an FTP server, the logon credentials are sent across the network in clear text. Sending your logon credentials for the Anonymous account in clear text is not a big concern. If you do not restrict the logon to only Anonymous, then users may log on to the FTP server using their Windows NT account. This means that the user's Windows NT username and password are going to be transmitted over the network in clear text. This may not be an acceptable security risk.

**FIGURE 4-2**

Configuring anonymous logon

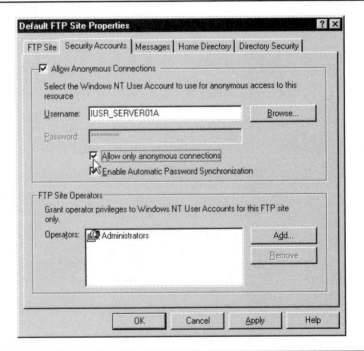

From the HTTP server point-of-view, you cannot restrict a client request to only Anonymous in the same way as you can with FTP. Figure 4-3 shows how you configure HTTP authentication methods.

The default is to allow anonymous access and require Windows NT Challenge/Response methods when the user tries to access an object restricted by the NTFS file system Access Control List (ACL). The Windows NT Challenge/Response method encrypts the username and password. To support this method, your browser must support Windows NT Challenge/Response. Currently, only Internet Explorer 3.x (and later) browsers support this authentication method.

## Using Windows NT Domain Accounts

You can restrict access to valid Windows NT domain accounts. By doing this, users attempting to access either the FTP or HTTP servers must present valid

---

**FIGURE 4-3**

Configuring HTTP
authentication methods

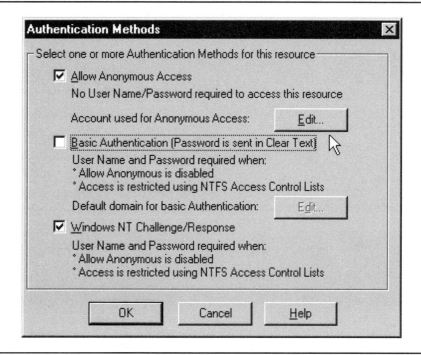

Windows NT account credentials to gain access to the system. As noted before, authentication to the FTP server is done in clear text. This can be a serious limitation if security is a concern. Anyone using a packet analyzer will be able to see the username and password. With the valid username and password, potential hackers have access to other resources on the server or your network.

With HTTP access, using a Windows NT account is more secure than FTP. First, the browser you use needs to support Windows NT's Challenge/Response authentication protocol. The username and password are sent encrypted across the network. This means that using a packet analyzer to determine the username and password would not be sufficient. The person attempting to discern the logon credentials would also need to break the encryption.

## Using NTFS Volumes

You can secure data on your IIS server using NTFS file system security. With NTFS, you are able to set access control on an object-by-object basis for any file on that partition. This security is in effect for access by users through either the FTP or HTTP servers.

exam
ⓦatch

*You can use NTFS security to further protect your data published through the FTP or HTTP servers.*

While it is beyond the scope of this book to define exactly how you set NTFS permissions, the point is that you can use NTFS to protect your content. You can also elect to put your data on a FAT partition, but in so doing, you lose the benefits of an NTFS partition.

## QUESTIONS AND ANSWERS

| | |
|---|---|
| I hear a lot about Windows NT being hacked when I surf the Internet. I am concerned that Windows NT is not secure enough for the Internet. Should I be concerned? | The Windows NT operating system can be made very secure, secure enough for the Internet. But it is up to you to make it secure by configuration and practices. |

# QUESTIONS AND ANSWERS

| | |
|---|---|
| What are "password-breakers?" Will users be able to find my administrator password? | All of the password-breaker programs that I have reviewed require that the program be installed on the local machine while you are logged in as an administrator. If you have unauthorized access of the computer by the administrator account, you have another type of problem. |
| Yes, but I read that hackers can "break out" of the Web server and install a password breaker program remotely and then come back in later and get the password. | It is not possible to break out of the HTTP or the FTP session and access other areas of the drive if you configure Windows NT and IIS security properly. One of the techniques we use is to shut down the Server service on IIS machines. |
| Well, if you can't hack into a Windows NT Server, then why does Microsoft post all of the security patches to the Web? | Hacking and denial of service are two different issues. Most of the attacks against Windows NT systems are denial of service attacks rather than actual hacks where users are able to gain access. |
| Aren't DoS attacks a significant issue? | Yes, they are. As Microsoft "sees" how another attack is successful, they are very responsive to posting a fix to the attack. |

## CERTIFICATION OBJECTIVE 4.06

# TCP/IP Port Security Features

You can set the TCP port numbers used by both the FTP and HTTP servers to monitor an incoming connection request. The TCP port numbers are discussed in greater detail in Chapters 5 and 6. By changing the default port assignments, users attempting to connect to your FTP or HTTP servers need to specify the port number during the connection attempt or they will not be able to connect.

This offers some degree of security. While this technique may be a deterrent for some, it is not much of an obstacle for the knowledgeable or determined hacker. Changing the default port assignments is not a good technique for servers that are accessed by the general public because there is no effective way for you to let them know what port number to use. It might also be a problem for unsophisticated users of the Internet because they would have to specify the port number in the URL. Many users are challenged enough just specifying the basic URL of the server and domain name.

## IIS Security

You can set security for your FTP and HTTP servers based on IP addresses, as illustrated in Figure 4-4.

You can either grant access to all computers or deny access to all computers. You then manage security by exception. For example, the default is to grant all IP addresses access to the Web site. You deny access to the Web site by IP address, a range of IP addresses, or by a domain name. You can also do the reverse; you can deny all IP address access, then grant access by IP address, a range of IP addresses, or by domain name.

**FIGURE 4-4**

Setting IP security

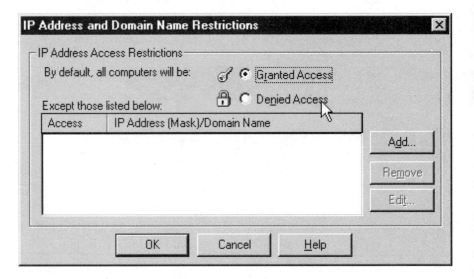

## CERTIFICATION OBJECTIVE 4.07

# Secure Sockets Layer

The IIS server has a feature called Secure Sockets Layer (SSL). The SSL feature utilizes a technique known as *public key encryption* to shield the session key from interception during transmission. This public key algorithm is comprised of two separate keys: a public key and a private key. The *private key* is held by the owner of the key pair. The *public key* can be distributed to those who request it. The public key algorithm specifies that one of the keys is used to encrypt the message and the other key is required to decrypt the message.

exam
ⓦatch

### IIS supports SSL Version 3.0.

Digital signatures and digital envelopes are used to produce two different but related processes. Creating a digital signature involves using the sender's private key. Creating the digital envelope uses the intended recipient's public key.

*Digital signatures* are used to confirm authorship and not to encrypt messages. The sender of the message uses his private key to generate the digital signature string in the message. The recipient of the message uses that sender's public key to validate the digital signature. Digital signatures are used to verify that the person who claims to be the author in fact sends the message.

A *digital envelope* is created to send a private message that can be read only by the specific recipient intended. When creating the digital envelope, the sender encrypts the message using the recipient's public key. This message can only be decrypted by the recipient's private key. No other private key will work.

The Secure Sockets Layer (SSL) 3.0 protocol has been implemented in the IIS Web server as a security feature. This layer provides a secure way of establishing an encrypted communication link with users. SSL guarantees the authenticity of the Web content while reliably identifying the identity of users accessing a Web site. IIS server also supports the Private Communication Technology (PCT) 1.0 protocol.

To encrypt all data between the Web client and the Web server, an SSL session is established in the following manner:

- The Web browser establishes a secure link with the Web server.
- The Web server sends the browser a copy of its digital certificate, along with its public key.
- The Web browser and the server negotiate which degree of encryption to use for secure communications. This encryption uses either the 40-bit or 128-bit algorithm. The stronger, 128-bit encryption is currently allowed only in the United States and Canada. The U.S. government imposes this restriction.
- The Web browser generates a session key and encrypts it with the server's public key. The Web browser then sends the encrypted session key to the Web server.
- The server decrypts the session key using its private key and sets up the secure channel.
- The client and the server then use the session keys to encrypt and decrypt the transmitted data.

# CERTIFICATION SUMMARY

This chapter covered the basic concepts of security and described the most effective methods for securing your environment and data. You achieve security as part of an integrated and coordinated practice. IIS is integrated into Windows NT Server. Windows NT Server uses mandatory logons and NTFS file permissions to secure the system and the Internet Information Server can make use of these security features as well. Some of these security systems allow Windows NT to be designated as a C2-compliant system.

Different security risks were discussed. Every time you do something to make your computer more accessible, you increase the security risk of unauthorized access. Hackers and crackers may attempt to gain unauthorized access to your systems. With good security practices and regular audits, you can limit the exposure you have. But no system is 100 percent invulnerable.

One of the most common types of attacks on secure systems is a denial of service attack. This is not an attack where the attacker actually gains access. Just the opposite may be true; the attacker cannot gain access. DoS prevents anyone from accessing the system by causing the system to become so busy that no productive work can be done. Or a DoS attack may be so disruptive to the server that the server actually fails. In either case, others are being denied access to the server. You can get more information from Microsoft at www.microsoft.com/security.

This chapter also discussed some security countermeasures and other common techniques that may be used to improve security and combat unauthorized access.

# ✓ TWO-MINUTE DRILL

- ❑ No system is totally secure.
- ❑ Administrators always have access.
- ❑ Limit the number of administrators of your system to only those persons with a critical need to access the system.
- ❑ Security policies should be designed for users to use, not for users to circumvent.
- ❑ IIS security is fully integrated with Windows NT's security system.
- ❑ Passwords should be changed regularly.
- ❑ Use other strict account policies.
- ❑ Set minimum password age and password uniqueness to improve security.
- ❑ Use NTFS for the published data.
- ❑ Remove the group Everyone from NTFS permissions.
- ❑ Remove the group Everyone from key user rights.
- ❑ Windows NT is designated as C2 compliant.
- ❑ You must make Windows NT C2 compliant. It is not so by default.
- ❑ Spoofing occurs when IP packets from one computer are made to look like packets from a trusted system.

❑ A denial of service attack is an attack aimed at making your server unavailable to the community.

❑ IIS installs an IUSR_*computername* account through installation.

❑ You can configure the FTP server to accept only anonymous logons.

❑ FTP passwords are sent in clear text.

❑ You can configure the HTTP server to use Windows NT Challenge/Response security.

❑ Windows NT Challenge/Response security encrypts the username and password.

❑ You can use a Windows NT account, instead of the Anonymous account to gain access to the FTP or HTTP server.

❑ You can use NTFS file and folder security to further protect your data.

❑ You can change the default TCP ports monitored by the FTP and HTTP servers.

❑ You can deny access to certain IP addresses.

❑ You can deny access to all IP addresses, then grant access to select IP addresses.

❑ IIS supports Secure Sockets Layer.

❑ SSL uses a public key/private key security system.

# SELF TEST

The following Self Test questions will help you measure your understanding of the material presented in this chapter. Read all the choices carefully, as there may be more than one correct answer. Choose all correct answers for each question.

1. Which of the following statements describes good password policies?

    A. Have the same password for all users.

    B. Use password uniqueness to ensure that the same passwords are not reused too often.

    C. Make the username and password be the same string.

    D. Use long passwords, mixing the case and including numerals.

2. Which of the following are good practices for Windows NT accounts?

    A. Restrict membership in the Administrator group.

    B. Delete the IUSR account so that it will not be compromised.

    C. Use the built-in group Everyone.

    D. Administrator should always log on using their admin account.

3. Under which DOD security classification can Windows NT be made to be compliant?

    A. D

    B. B3

    C. A1

    D. C2

4. Which of the following statements best decribes IP spoofing?

    A. A firewall set up to restrict access

    B. An intruder impersonating a computer on your local network

    C. An intruder impersonating a computer from outside your network

    D. Using a packet analyzer in an attempt to discover your password

5. Which of the following is true of a denial of service attack?

    A. A denial of service attack is the same thing as IP spoofing.

    B. A denial of service attack is used to discover user's passwords.

    C. You cannot detect a denial of service attack.

    D. A denial of service attack may originate from any computer on the Internet.

6. Which accounts does IIS create during installation?

    A. IUSR_*computername*

    B. Administrator

    C. IWAM_*computername*

    D. Anonymous

7. Which of the following is true about the IUSR account?

   A. It has the Log On Locally rights.

   B. It has the right to access the computer from the network.

   C. It is part of the group Everyone.

   D. It is the administrative account used to access the HTTP server.

8. Which of the following are valid FTP authentication methods?

   A. Allow anonymous

   B. Allow only anonymous

   C. Windows NT Challenge/Response

   D. Log on with your Windows NT domain account

9. Which of the following are valid HTTP authentication methods?

   A. Allow anonymous

   B. Allow only anonymous

   C. Windows NT Challenge/Response

   D. HTTP doesn't use authentication, only FTP.

10. Which of the following security tools does IIS use?

   A. Logon authentication

   B. NTFS file permissions

   C. FTP data encryption

   D. Secure Sockets Layer 3.0

# 5

# FTP Service

T he FTP service is installed when you select the Typical installation from the Windows NT 4.0 Option Pack. File Transfer Protocol (FTP) uses the Transmission Control Protocol (TCP) to transfer files between the FTP client and the FTP server. FTP was one of the earliest protocols used on the Internet. The HTTP servers have supplanted much of the work that was done in the past by FTP. HTTP servers are convenient for clients to download files but they do not support uploading of files. To do that, you must still use the FTP protocol.

To transfer files over the Internet, one computer must be functioning as an FTP server and one computer must be an FTP client. Using Windows NT, your computer can be both an FTP server and an FTP client. The client issues commands to the server and the server responds. File transfers are always initiated by the client and never by the server. It is not possible for the server to send files automatically to the client.

exam
ⓦatch

*The client must always initiate the connection to the server. In this respect, the server is always passive.*

## CERTIFICATION OBJECTIVE 5.01

# TCP

FTP uses the TCP protocol to do all of its work. TCP is a *connection-oriented protocol*. A connection-oriented protocol establishes a session between the client and the server before any information is exchanged. This session remains established until it is torn down, typically by the process that initiated the session. This is a bidirectional connection; traffic can travel in both directions during the session. One feature of a connection-oriented protocol is that the protocol itself provides for error recovery and is more reliable. Because the TCP protocol performs error correction, the application using TCP does not have to provide for error correction. The programmer is free to concentrate on the application's semantics without having to also incorporate mechanisms to ensure that the other party reliably receives data. This reliable receipt of information is also called *guaranteed end delivery*.

# TCP Features

The most important features of the TCP protocol include:

- **Acknowledgment**   When sending a packet, the sending computer expects to "hear back" from the receiving computer that it received the data packet. This is called an *acknowledgment (ACK)*. If the sending computer does not get an ACK from the receiving computer, the sending computer assumes that the receiving computer never received the data packet and retransmits the packet. The sender continues to resend the packet until it receives an ACK, or the process times out.

- **Checksum**   The *checksum* is a calculation done by the sending computer and is attached to the data packet. When the receiving computer gets the packet it calculates the checksum on the data and compares that value to the checksum value contained in the packet (the one calculated by the sending computer). If the two values are the same, the receiver assumes that the data was transmitted without error. If the two values are different, the receiving station sends a *negative acknowledgment (NACK)* back to the sender. The sender recalculates the checksum and retransmits the packet. This process is repeated until the packet is received error free (the checksum values match) or the process times out.

- **Flow Control**   When two computers are transmitting packets back and forth, there must be some agreement about when to stop if one side gets too many packets. This process is called *flow control*. If packets are received faster than the computer can process them, data will be lost. By invoking flow control, the receiving computer can ask the sending computer to stop transmitting until it has time to catch up. When the receiving computer is ready for more packets, it "turns off" flow control and the sending computer starts sending packets again until it is done sending them, or until it gets a stop sending (flow control) message from the receiving computer.

- **Retransmission**   Retransmission is the term used when the sender resends data packets that it sent previously. If the receiving station sends a NACK, then the sending station retransmits the packets. If the sending station does not get an ACK, it assumes the packets were lost or corrupted and resends the packets. It continues to send the packets until it no longer receives a NACK or until it receives an ACK. This is automatically done by the protocol without user intervention and generally without the user even being aware that it is happening.

■ **Sequencing**   When data is being sent, it is divided up into segments and put in an "envelope" called a packet. The actual data is most likely put into multiple packets and sent on to its destination. The path to the destination can be different for each data packet. Packets can arrive in an order different than the order in which they were sent. If the receiving computer reassembles the data from the out-of-order packets, then the data is useless. To prevent this, the protocol assigns a sequence number to each packet as it is sent. When the packets arrive, the receiving computer reassembles them in the order indicated by the sequence numbers.

## Trivial File Transfer Protocol (TFTP)

Trivial File Transfer Protocol (TFTP) is distinct from FTP. TFTP uses the UDP (User Datagram Protocol) as its transport protocol. UDP is a *connectionless protocol*. TFTP differs from a connection-oriented protocol like TCP in the following ways:

■ There is no guarantee of end delivery. TFTP does not provide for error-checking in the protocol so there is no guarantee that what you send will be received without errors.

■ TFTP does not set up a bidirectional session with the other end. Think of this as a "send and forget" type of protocol. It does not wait for an ACK from the receiving station and therefore has no idea if the packet was ever received.

■ TFTP is faster than TCP since it doesn't have the overhead of setting up a session and going through acknowledgments and error control.

■ Because it can be less reliable than TCP, TFTP should be used only for traffic that is not critical and where speed is more important than data reliability.

■ You can still use UDP if you include error-handling procedures in your application.

**Internet Information Server is not a TFTP server. You can use Windows NT as a TFTP client.**

# Managing the FTP Service

Managing the FTP service is done through the Microsoft Management Console (MMC) and the Internet Service Manager (ISM). You can stop and start the FTP service from the ISM. Figure 5-1 contains the MMC window which shows the FTP service stopped. You can also start and stop the FTP service using the Services applet in the Control Panel.

**FIGURE 5-1**     Stopping and starting the FTP service

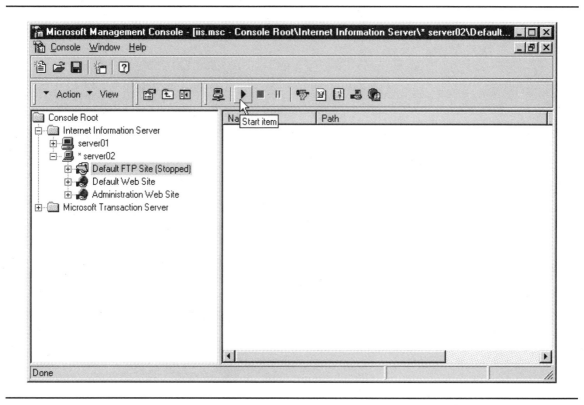

If you start or stop the FTP service using the ISM interface, it may take a while for the Control Panel applet to update the status to reflect the change. In several test cases that I ran, I had to close and restart the Services applet in order for the changes to show up. This was true even if the Services applet was initially opened after the changes were made in the ISM applet.

**CERTIFICATION OBJECTIVE 5.03**

# FTP Ports

A *socket* represents the endpoint of a network connection. Two numbers identify TCP sockets:

- **IP address**   The IP address identifies the computer on the network.
- **TCP port number**   The TCP port number identifies a process or application at the computer.

An example of such a number is 201.200.199.250(20).

A *TCP port* is the address of a server on an Internet Protocol (IP) network. When an application uses TCP, it calls an assigned port for access. For example, the FTP service always monitors TCP port 21 for activity.

TCP ports are divided into two general categories: *well-known ports* and *dynamic ports.* A TCP port can be referred to by several different names, including:

- TCP port number
- Port address
- TCP port
- Port number
- Port
- Data port

These terms all refer to a TCP port.

TCP ports can be numbered from 0 to 65,535. Port numbers 0 through 1023 are reserved for server-side use and never change. Port numbers 0 through 1023 are called well-known ports because they never change. These well-known ports are preassigned by the Internet Assigned Numbers Authority (IANA). You can always expect FTP to monitor port 21 in a standard configuration.

Ports 1024 through 65,535 are reserved for client-side applications. These port numbers are assigned dynamically by the operating system when an application makes a request for service. An application may be assigned a given port number on one occasion and another port number on a different occasion, even though the application may be performing the same function on both occasions.

A server-side application that uses TCP always has at least one preassigned, or well-known, port number. By way of example, FTP uses two port numbers for its service:

- Port 20 for data
- Port 21 for control

These well-known port numbers can be found in RFC (Request for Comments) 1700 which can be accessed at www.internic.net. RFC is the way the Internet defines standards. Listed next are some well-known port numbers. You can see these port numbers listed in the <winnt_root>\ system32\drivers\ etc\Services file (see Table 5-1).

| TABLE 5-1 | Service Name | Port Number | Description |
| --- | --- | --- | --- |
| Well-Known Ports for TCP and UDP | echo | 7/tcp | |
| | echo | 7/udp | |
| | discard | 9/tcp | sink null |
| | discard | 9/udp | sink null |
| | systat | 11/tcp | |
| | systat | 11/tcp | users |
| | daytime | 13/tcp | |
| | daytime | 13/udp | |

**TABLE 5-1**

Well-Known Ports for TCP and UDP (*continued*)

| Service Name | Port Number | Description |
| --- | --- | --- |
| netstat | 15/tcp | |
| qotd | 17/tcp | quote |
| qotd | 17/udp | quote |
| chargen | 19/tcp | ttytst source |
| chargen | 19/udp | ttytst source |
| ftp-data | 20/tcp | |
| ftp | 21/tcp | |
| telnet | 23/tcp | |
| smtp | 25/tcp | mail |
| time | 37/tcp | time server |
| time | 37/udp | time server |
| rlp | 39/udp | resource   # resource location |
| name | 42/tcp | name server |
| name | 42/udp | name server |
| whois | 43/tcp | nickname   # usually to sri-nic |
| domain | 53/tcp | name server   # name-domain server |
| domain | 53/udp | name server |
| name server | 53/tcp | domain   # name-domain server |
| name server | 53/udp | domain |
| mtp | 57/tcp | # deprecated |
| bootp | 67/udp | # boot program server |
| tftp | 69/udp | |
| rje | 77/tcp | netrjs |
| finger | 79/tcp | |
| link | 87/tcp | ttylink |
| supdup | 95/tcp | |

TABLE 5-1

Well-Known Ports for TCP and UDP (*continued*)

| Service Name | Port Number | Description |
| --- | --- | --- |
| hostnames | 101/tcp | hostname   # usually from sri-nic |
| iso-tsap | 102/tcp | |
| dictionary | 103/tcp | webster |
| x400 | 103/tcp | # ISO Mail |
| x400-snd | 104/tcp | |
| csnet-ns | 105/tcp | |
| pop | 109/tcp | Post Office |
| pop2 | 109/tcp | # Post Office |
| pop3 | 110/tcp | Post Office |
| portmap | 111/tcp | |
| portmap | 111/udp | |
| sunrpc | 111/tcp | |
| sunrpc | 111/udp | |
| auth | 113/tcp | authentication |
| sftp | 115/tcp | |
| path | 117/tcp | |
| uucp-path | 117/tcp | |
| nntp | 119/tcp | usenet   # Network News Transfer |
| ntp | 123/udp | ntpd ntp   # network time protocol (exp) |
| nbname | 137/udp | |
| nbdatagram | 138/udp | |
| nbsession | 139/tcp | |
| NeWS | 144/tcp | news |
| sgmp | 153/udp | sgmp |
| tcprepo | 158/tcp | repository   # PCMAIL |
| snmp | 161/udp | snmp |
| snmp-trap | 162/udp | snmp |

| TABLE 5-1 |
|---|

Well-Known Ports for TCP and UDP (*continued*)

| Service Name | Port Number | Description |
|---|---|---|
| print-srv | 170/tcp | # network PostScript |
| vmnet | 175/tcp | |
| load | 315/udp | |
| vmnet0 | 400/tcp | |
| sytek | 500/udp | |
| biff | 512/udp | comsat |
| exec | 512/tcp | |
| login | 513/tcp | |
| who | 513/udp | whod |
| shell | 514/tcp | cmd   # no passwords used |
| syslog | 514/udp | |
| printer | 515/tcp | spooler   # line printer spooler |
| talk | 517/udp | |
| ntalk | 518/udp | |
| efs | 520/tcp | # for LucasFilm |
| route | 520/udp | router routed |
| timed | 525/udp | timeserver |
| tempo | 526/tcp | newdate |
| courier | 530/tcp | rpc |
| conference | 531/tcp | chat |
| rvd-contro | 531/udp | MIT disk |
| netnews | 532/tcp | readnews |
| netwall | 533/udp | # -for emergency broadcasts |
| uucp | 540/tcp | uucpd   # uucp daemon |
| klogin | 543/tcp | # Kerberos authenticated rlogin |
| kshell | 544/tcp | cmd   # and remote shell |

| TABLE 5-1 |
|---|
| Well-Known Ports for TCP and UDP (*continued*) |

| Service Name | Port Number | Description |
|---|---|---|
| new-rwho | 550/udp | new-who<br># experimental |
| remotefs | 556/tcp | rfs_server rfs# Brunhoff remote filesystem |
| rmonitor | 560/udp | rmonitord<br># experimental |
| monitor | 561/udp | # experimental |
| garcon | 600/tcp | |
| maitrd | 601/tcp | |
| busboy | 602/tcp | |
| acctmaster | 700/udp | |
| acctslave | 701/udp | |
| acct | 702/udp | |
| acctlogin | 703/udp | |
| acctprinte | 704/udp | |
| elcsd | 704/udp | # errlog |
| acctinfo | 705/udp | |
| acctslave2 | 706/udp | |
| acctdisk | 707/udp | |
| kerberos | 750/tcp | kdc   # Kerberos authentication—tcp |
| kerberos | 750/udp | kdc   # Kerberos authentication—udp |
| kerberos_m | 751/tcp | # Kerberos authentication |
| kerberos_m | 751/udp | # Kerberos authentication |
| passwd_ser | 752/udp | # Kerberos passwd server |
| userreg_se | 753/udp | # Kerberos userreg server |
| krb_prop | 754/tcp | # Kerberos slave propagation |

**TABLE 5-1**

Well-Known Ports for
TCP and UDP (*continued*)

| Service Name | Port Number | Description |
|---|---|---|
| erlogin | 888/tcp | # Login and environment passing |
| kpop | 1109/tcp | # Pop with Kerberos |
| phone | 1167/udp | |
| ingreslock | 1524/tcp | |
| maze | 1666/udp | |
| nfs | 2049/udp | # sun nfs |
| knetd | 2053/tcp | # Kerberos de-multiplexor |
| eklogin | 2105/tcp | # Kerberos encrypted rlogin |
| rmt | 5555/tcp | rmtd |
| mtb | 5556/tcp | mtbd    # mtb backup |
| man | 9535/tcp | # remote man server |
| w | 9536/tcp | |
| mantst | 9537/tcp | # remote man server, testing |
| bnews | 10000/tcp | |
| rscs0 | 10000/udp | |
| queue | 10001/tcp | |
| rscs1 | 10001/udp | |
| poker | 10002/tcp | |
| rscs2 | 10002/udp | |
| gateway | 10003/tcp | |
| rscs3 | 10003/udp | |
| remp | 10004/tcp | |
| rscs4 | 10004/udp | |
| rscs5 | 10005/udp | |
| rscs6 | 10006/udp | |
| rscs7 | 10007/udp | |

| | Service Name | Port Number | Description |
|---|---|---|---|
| **TABLE 5-1** | rscs8 | 10008/udp | |
| | rscs9 | 10009/udp | |
| Well-Known Ports for TCP and UDP (*continued*) | rscsa | 10010/udp | |
| | rscsb | 10011/udp | |
| | qmaster | 10012/tcp | |
| | qmaster | 10012/udp | |

## CERTIFICATION OBJECTIVE 5.04

# FTP Connections

FTP is a client/server process and uses two connections: the *control connection* and the *data connection*. These connections may have one of two states:

- **Passive open**   A state waiting for transmission
- **Active open**   A state initiating the transmission

The control connection starts the process between the client and the FTP server. The control connection uses port 21 on the server side and an open port on the client side that is greater than 1023. This connection is maintained for the duration of the session.

The control connection is managed by a set of programs known as the *Protocol Interpreter*.

The data connection is managed by a set of programs known as the Data Transfer Process.

The server maintains a passive open state at port 21 listening for an FTP connection request from the client. When a request arrives, the server sets up the control session and receives FTP commands from the client. This session remains until the user types **Bye** or **Quit**.

The data transfer connection gets set up only when there is data to transfer between the server and the client. After the data transfer is complete, the connection is closed. The next time data is to be transferred, a new data connection is established. The control connection remains open through multiple data transfers. The server data port is always 20.

**CERTIFICATION OBJECTIVE 5.05**

# FTP Commands

FTP commands are issued from the FTP command line. For example, to transfer a file from the server to you, you enter the command **get** *filename.* Table 5-2 lists some of the common FTP commands.

exam
ⓦatch

*You do not need to know all of the FTP commands for the exam, but you should know what open, dir, get, put, bye, and quit do. You should also know how to get to the DOS prompt and back.*

| TABLE 5-2 | Command | Description |
| --- | --- | --- |
| FTP Commands | ! | Returns to the DOS or UNIX shell. FTP is still in session. Type **exit** to return to FTP. |
| | ? | Displays descriptions for FTP commands. |
| | !command | Executes a DOS or UNIX command without leaving the FTP session. |
| | bye | Ends the FTP session with the server and exits FTP. |
| | dir | Lists the server's files and directories. |
| | get, mget | Copies one or more files (using wildcards if necessary) from the server to your computer. |
| | help | Displays descriptions for FTP commands |
| | mkdir | Creates a directory on the server. You need to have the appropriate permission to create a directory. |
| | put, mput | Copies one or more files (using wildcards if necessary) from your computer to the server. |
| | quit | Ends the FTP session with the server and exits FTP. |

# FTP Return Codes

When you enter a command, the FTP server returns a return code or a series of return codes. These codes identify the status of your command. Table 5-3 contains a partial list of return codes and their associated messages. A complete list may be found in RFC 640.

**TABLE 5-3**

Standard FTP
Return Codes

| Code | Description |
| --- | --- |
| 119 | Terminal not available. |
| 120 | Service ready in *nnn* minutes. |
| 125 | Data connection already open; transfer starting. |
| 150 | File status OK; about to open data connection. |
| 151 | User not local. |
| 152 | User unknown. |
| 200 | Command OK. |
| 211 | System status or system help reply. |
| 212 | Directory status. |
| 213 | File Status. |
| 214 | Help message. |
| 220 | Service is ready for new user. |
| 221 | Service closing Telnet connection. |
| 225 | Data connection open; no transfer in progress. |
| 226 | Closing data connection; requested action successful. |
| 227 | Entering passive mode. |
| 230 | User logged in. |
| 250 | Request file action OK. |
| 331 | Username OK, password needed. |
| 350 | Requested file action pending further information. |
| 421 | Service not available. |
| 425 | Can't open data connection. |

**TABLE 5-3**

Standard FTP Return Codes (*continued*)

| Code | Description |
|---|---|
| 426 | Connection closed; transfer aborted. |
| 450 | Requested file action not taken. |
| 530 | Not logged in. |
| 532 | Need account for storing files. |
| 550 | Requested action not taken. |

When you enter an FTP command, a return code and its associated message appears after the command. Figure 5-2 contains an example of command usage and the resulting return codes.

**EXERCISE 5-1**

## Entering FTP Commands

Purpose: To gain experience using FTP commands. To observe various return codes.

*Do this step only from Server01.*

1. Ensure that you are logged in as Administrator.
2. Using Windows NT Explorer, select the \interpub\ftp root folder.

**FIGURE 5-2**

FTP command and return codes

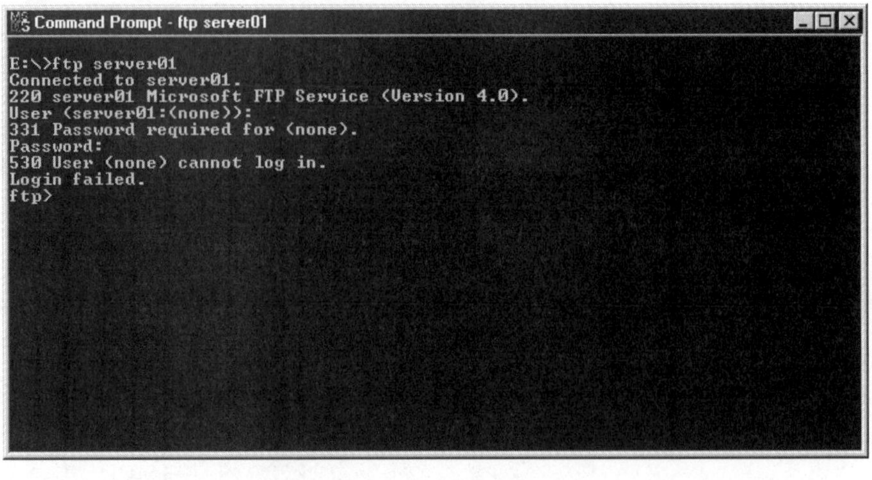
Command Prompt - ftp server01
E:\>ftp server01
Connected to server01.
220 server01 Microsoft FTP Service (Version 4.0).
User (server01:(none)):
331 Password required for (none).
Password:
530 User (none) cannot log in.
Login failed.
ftp>

3. Right-click the right side pane.

4. Click New.

5. Click Text Document.

6. Type **From_Server01** in the dialog box. Press ENTER to create the file.

7. You are done.

*Do these steps only from Server02.*

1. Ensure that you are logged on as Administrator.

2. Open a command prompt.

3. Type **ftp server01** and press ENTER.

4. Which return code was returned?

5. Enter **anonymous** for a username.

6. Press ENTER to supply a null password.

7. Which return codes were returned?

8. Open Internet Service Manager. (Refer to earlier chapters if you do not remember how to do this.)

9. Expand the Server01 site.

10. Right-click the Default FTP Site.

11. Select Properties.

12. Click Current Sessions.

13. Which user is logged on?

14. Return to the command prompt.

15. Type **Bye**.

16. Press the up arrow key. The previous command, **ftp server01**, should be displayed. If it is not displayed, then type **ftp server01**.

17. Press ENTER.

18. Enter **anonymous** for a username.

19. Type **Fred@fun.com** and press ENTER.

20. Return to the MMC, Default FTP Site Properties.

21. Click Current Sessions.

22. Which user is logged on?

23. Return to the command prompt.

24. Change directories to the \inetpub\ftproot folder

25. Type **dir** and press ENTER.

26. What do you see listed?

27. Type **get From_Server01.txt** and press ENTER.

28. Type **bye** to quit the FTP session. Close the command prompt.

29. Click the Cancel button in the Default FTP Site Properties.

*Answers to steps in this exercise:*

4. 220 server01.

7. 331 Anonymous access allowed and 230 Anonymous user logged in.

13. Anonymous.

22. Fred@fun.com.

26. From_Server01.txt file name.

**CERTIFICATION OBJECTIVE 5.06**

# Configuring the FTP Service

Configuring the FTP service is done from the various property sheets. The property sheets are Master, Default, and File. Which property sheet you use depends on what you need to accomplish. The property sheets are similar to those found in the WWW service.

## Master Property Sheet

When Internet Information Server is installed, properties are applied to the Master property sheet, illustrated in Figure 5-3. You get to this sheet by right-clicking on the server icon and selecting Properties.

You configure the FTP and the WWW property sheets from this dialog box. Every virtual FTP site that you create inherits the properties set in the

**FIGURE 5-3**

Master property sheet

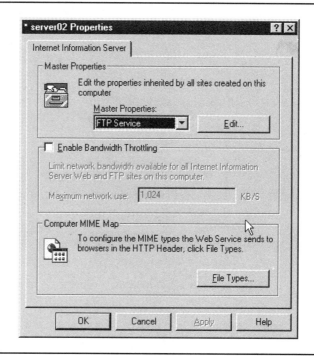

Master property sheet. Clicking the Edit button brings up the service Master property sheet as illustrated in Figure 5-4.

There are six tabs:

- **FTP Site**    Use this tab to set connection limits and logging options.
- **Security Accounts**    Use this tab to set the account used for anonymous logins. You can allow Anonymous Connections or Allow Only Anonymous Connections. You can also set Enable Password Synchronization so that if you change the password here, it also changes in the SAM database.

You can enter messages to be sent to users on the server when:

- They connect.
- They exit.
- The site has the maximum number of connections already.

**FIGURE 5-4**

Master Properties tabs

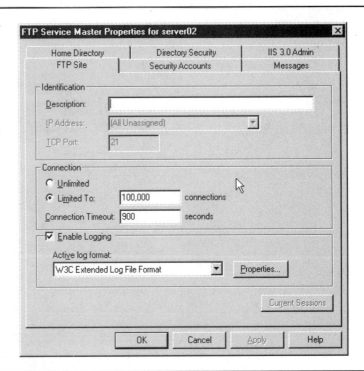

- ■ **Home Directory**  You can set the designated Home Directory for read and write access and you can set the Directory Listing Style.

- ■ **Directory Security**  The default is to grant access to everyone and restrict by IP addresses or domains. You can deny access to everyone and then allow access by exception.

- ■ **IIS 3.0 Admin**  You can use this tab to select one, but only one, IIS 4.0 FTP site to be managed by the ISM that is used with IIS 3.0.

## Default FTP Site

Each IIS installation creates a Default FTP Site. This site initially has the same properties as specified on the Master property sheet. You select the Default FTP Site property sheet by right-clicking the Default FTP Site node and selecting Properties. Figure 5-5 illustrates this property sheet.

**FIGURE 5-5**

Default FTP Site
Properties tabs

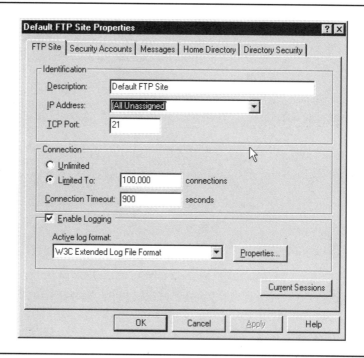

There are five tabs on this property sheet. They are:

- FTP Site
- Security Accounts
- Messages
- Home Directory
- Directory Security

From the FTP Site tab, you can change the listening port of the FTP server. By changing the port, the FTP client has to specify the connection port at the time of connection. Otherwise, the client cannot connect since the default port for the FTP client is port 21. This can give your site a small measure of extra security.

# Files

Files created in the Default FTP Site inherit the properties of that site's property sheet. Files created in a virtual FTP directory inherit the properties of the directory's property sheet.

# Virtual Directories

A *virtual directory* is a directory that appears to be in the ftproot, or home, folder. A virtual directory can be on any server in the same Windows NT domain. Virtual directories created on other servers should be referenced by their Universal Naming Convention (UNC) names.

# Virtual Servers

A *virtual server* can be used to host multiple domain names on the same physical Internet Information Server. You need a unique IP address for each virtual server that you host.

**EXERCISE 5-2**

## Configure the FTP Service

Purpose: To configure the Default FTP Site using the property sheets.

*Complete this exercise from both computers.*

1. Ensure that you logged in as Administrator.
2. Open Internet Service Manager.
3. Right-click the Default FTP Site node.
4. Click Properties.
5. In the Description box, Type **your name FTP Site** (where **your name** is the site name).
6. Click the Messages tab.
7. Enter a message of your choice for a Welcome message.
8. Click Apply.
9. Open a command prompt.
10. Establish an FTP session with your server.

11. Log on as anonymous.

12. Did you get your welcome message?

13. Type **put c:\boot.ini** and press ENTER.

14. What message did you get?

15. Switch back to the Default FTP Site property sheet.

16. Click the Home Directory tab.

17. Check the Write box.

18. Click Apply.

19. Switch to the command prompt.

20. Type **put c:\boot.ini** and press ENTER.

21. What message did you get?

22. Type **dir** and press ENTER.

23. Which files do you see?

*Answers to Steps in this exercise*

12. Hopefully you saw the message that you entered.

14. Access denied.

21. Opening ASCII mode and Transfer complete

23. You should see the boot.ini file and one other if you were successful in a previous exercise.

## CERTIFICATION OBJECTIVE 5.07

# FTP Security

Users can log on using the user name "anonymous." You can restrict your site to only anonymous logons but this precludes users from attempting to log on to the FTP site using their Windows NT account.

# FROM THE CLASSROOM

## Managing FTP Sites

Many students have experience with FTP. The subject is not entirely new to them when they get to class. What is new to many of the students is the Microsoft Management Console (MMC) and how Internet Service Manager (ISM) allows them to create and manage FTP sites. The property sheets are full featured, allowing configuration in great detail.

One of the items of interest to students is the use of the Windows NT security system to help them make their FTP site more secure. By using the NTFS file system, you can set permissions on each object (files and folders). Even though a client can connect to a site, they can only access objects for which they have permission. When you specify Read permission on the folder, clients cannot upload files, but can still download files. When you specify No Access permission, you can keep files on the FTP site and control who can download which files. This built-in security from Windows NT adds more flexibility in managing the FTP site content.

Another item of interest to students is how FTP connections are established. Many students are aware that FTP communications use the TCP protocol. Some are aware that a connection is required and this connection uses a TCP port. Most students are unaware that there are actually two ports used during the FTP session. Port 21 is the port number that most are familiar with for the FTP connection. The server monitors Port 21 while waiting for a connection. Another port used by the FTP process is opened at the client. This port is greater than port 1023, which means it is not a well-known port and the port number changes with each connection. The fact that there are two connections made is not significant in itself, especially in managing an FTP site. The client-side port assignment is taken care of by the protocol itself. It is interesting to observe the reaction of students who consider themselves to be knowledgeable about FTP when they "learn" a new facet about something old and familiar to them.

Life is about learning, and the pursuit continues.

You can also change the port that the server listens on for connections. By default, the FTP server listens on port 21 and the FTP client attempts to connect to port 21. If you change this port at the FTP server, then the computer attempting to make the connection has to manually supply the port number in order to complete the connection. Determining which port your FTP server is using to make a connection is not difficult to an experienced hacker, but it can be quite vexing to others who are trying to get unauthorized access to your site.

You can also use Windows NT user accounts. Keep in mind that the username and password for FTP logins are transmitted in clear text over the Internet. In many cases, this is undesirable.

## Using FTP Security

Purpose: To implement some of the FTP security features.

*Complete this exercise from either computer.*

1. From the previous exercise, you should still have open a command prompt and the property sheet for your FTP site.

2. Switch to the property sheet.

3. Select the Security Accounts tab.

4. Click Allow Only Anonymous connections.

5. Switch to the command prompt.

6. Type **ftp serverxx** and press ENTER.

7. Enter **Administrator** as the user and press ENTER.

8. Press ENTER to accept a blank password.

9. Which message did you get?

10. Type **Bye** and press ENTER.

11. Type **ftp serverxx** and press ENTER.

12. Type **anonymous** and press ENTER.

13. Press ENTER to accept a blank password.

14. Were you able to log on as anonymous?

15. Type **Bye** and press ENTER.

16. Switch to the FTP site property sheet in MMC.

17. Select the FTP Site tab.

18. In the TCP Port dialog box, enter the number **5683**.

19. Click Apply.

20. Switch to the command prompt.

21. Type **ftp serverxx** and press ENTER.

22. Which message did you receive?

23. Type **open serverxx 5683** and press ENTER.

24. Type **anonymous** and press ENTER.

25. Press ENTER to accept a blank password.

26. Were you able to log on as anonymous?

27. Type **Bye** and press ENTER.

28. Switch to the property sheet of the FTP site server.

29. Change the port number back to 21.

30. Click OK.

31. Close the MMC.

32. Answer No if you are asked to save the console settings.

*Answers to steps in this exercise:*

9. Login failed.

14. Yes.

22. ftp: connect:connection refused.

26. Yes. When you specify the port number where the FTP server is listening, you get a connection and can log in.

# CERTIFICATION SUMMARY

The FTP service installs as part of the Typical installation. The FTP service is used to transfer files between the FTP server and an FTP client. The FTP service uses the TCP protocol as its transport protocol. The TCP protocol is robust and provides for automatic error detection.

You manage the FTP service from the MMC using the Internet Service Manager (ISM). You can manage all of the FTP servers in your organization from the ISM. FTP servers listen on port 21 for connections. You can change that port if you wish, but your clients need to know the nonstandard port number in order to connect.

You configure the FTP services using property sheets. You communicate with the FTP server using commands. The server sends you return codes indicating what the server did in response to your command. You can configure your FTP server to be more flexible by configuring the service for virtual directories and virtual servers.

# TWO-MINUTE DRILL

❑ FTP is a client/server process.

❑ Use FTP to transfer files between the server and the client.

❑ The client must initiate the connection.

❑ FTP uses the TCP protocol.

❑ TCP protocol is connection-oriented.

❑ TCP protocol performs automatic error correction and packet retransmission.

❑ TFTP is a command-line utility that uses the UDP protocol.

❑ IIS is not a TFTP server.

❑ Managing the FTP service is done through the Microsoft Management Console (MMC) and the Internet Service Manager (ISM).

❑ You can manage any FTP server using the ISM interface.

❑ You can start and stop the FTP service from ISM.

❑ You can start and stop the FTP service from the Services applet in the Control Panel.

❑ The FTP server monitors port 21 for a connection.

❑ TCP ports are divided into two broad categories: Well-known ports are numbered 0 through 1023 and have assigned functions. Dynamic ports are numbered from 1024 through 65,535 and are assigned as needed by processes.

❑ Some of the dynamic ports are used by companies to support their products or processes.

- ❑ A data transfer connection is set up on port 20.
- ❑ The data transfer connection is closed after the data transfer.
- ❑ The FTP connection is open until closed by the client.
- ❑ The FTP connection can be closed by the server if the connection timeout limit is exceeded (inactivity timeout).
- ❑ The FTP server sends the client a return code to indicate the status of the command issued by the client.
- ❑ You configure the FTP service using property sheets.
- ❑ The Master property sheet is created at installation.
- ❑ Virtual servers inherit the properties of the Master property sheet.
- ❑ Files inherit the properties of the FTP site.
- ❑ A virtual directory is a folder that appears to the client as though it is in the ftproot folder, but it is not.
- ❑ Virtual directories may be on any local drive and any server in the Windows NT domain.
- ❑ A virtual server can be used to host multiple domain names on the same physical Internet Information Server.
- ❑ You can restrict the FTP server to allow only anonymous login.
- ❑ You can use your Windows NT account to log on to the FTP server.
- ❑ Login credentials are sent in clear text over the Internet.
- ❑ You can change the TCP port number your server monitors for a connection.

# SELF TEST

The following Self Test questions will help you measure your understanding of the material presented in this chapter. Read all the choices carefully, as there may be more than one correct answer. Choose all correct answers for each question.

1. To transfer files using FTP, what must be in place?

   A. A default gateway

   B. An FTP server

   C. A WWW server

   D. An FTP client

2. Which protocol does FTP use?

   A. TFTP

   B. IPX

   C. TCP

   D. NetBIOS

3. Which of the following are features of the TCP protocol?

   A. It provides error correction.

   B. It does not provide error correction.

   C. It provides flow control.

   D. It supports TFTP.

4. Which of the following statements about TFTP is true?

   A. It uses UDP protocol.

   B. IIS is a TFTP server.

   C. TFTP is faster than FTP.

   D. TFTP is the newer version of FTP.

5. How can you stop the FTP service?

   A. Using Internet Service Manager

   B. Using Server Manager

   C. By closing Microsoft Management Console

   D. Using the Services applet

6. Which port does the FTP service monitor for a connection request?

   A. 20

   B. 21

   C. 1024

   D. Any available port

7. Which of the following statements is true about sockets?

   A. A socket is an endpoint.

   B. The IP address is part of the socket number.

   C. Sockets are fixed addresses.

   D. The TCP port number is part of the socket number.

8. Which of the following is not true of ports?

   A. There are well-known ports.

   B. Dynamic ports are fixed.

   C. Well-known ports are fixed.

   D. There are only 1500 ports.

9. Which ports does the FTP service use to transfer files?

   A. 20

   B. 21

C. Any port above 1023 set by the client

D. 2

10. Which of the following is not an FTP command?

    A. Dir

    B. Bye

    C. Get

    D. Copy

11. You are preparing to set up several virtual servers on your IIS computer. You want these virtual servers to have properties in common. Which property sheet should you modify?

    A. Default

B. Master

C. IIS

D. MMC

12. You want to set your FTP server to only allow anonymous connections. How can you accomplish this?

    A. Disable the IUSR_*servername* account.

    B. Create an anonymous account in User Manager.

    C. Select the Connections tab and clear all users from the Allowed to Connect box.

    D. Select the Security Accounts tab and check the Allow Only Anonymous Connections box.

# 6

# WWW Service

One of the most popular intranet applications today is publishing on the *World Wide Web (WWW)*, sometimes referred to as W3 or just the Web. Organizations have discovered that the Web is a wonderful place to publish information internally and externally. The WWW service has an intuitive interface that works as well inside the corporate firewall as it does internationally on the Web. The Web is founded on standards developed by the Internet community. The advantage of using standards-based products is communication with others who might be using other software or hardware.

## The World Wide Web

The Web provides information in a graphical format, complete with images, rich-text formatting, and multimedia. The Web also provides an ingenious way of moving around within documents or jumping to other Web sites using *hyperlinks*. Click on a hyperlink and you're on another Web page. This has become so popular that Microsoft has enabled all of its Office products with Web technology.

You do not actually "go" to the Web page as in a login, telnet, or FTP session. Your Web browser requests a Hypertext Markup Language (HTML) page from the remote site specified by the Uniform Resource Locator (URL). As your browser interprets this HTML document while downloading it from the remote site, it may encounter requests for other objects such as pictures. As each picture request is interpreted, the browser may indicate, by a percentage value changing in the bottom line or a filling bar graph, that further downloading is occurring. You can always click the Stop button to discontinue any further downloading of pictures if you are happy with the text-only output. Hyperlinks are usually embedded URLs that, when clicked on, result in the specified Web page being downloaded and interpreted.

The actual display of the HTML page is a function of your browser. Each browser interprets HTML tags differently. Do not be surprised if different browsers display the same HTML page in a different manner.

The Web can tie together many servers throughout the world or within your organization into what appears to users as unified information content. With this power, the Web is preferable to storing information in the form of files on different servers. The Web technology brings information to life. It puts a premium on the information content and not where the information is stored. If you have heard Bill Gates talk about his 15-year-old concept he calls "information at your fingertips," you will recognize why he is so enthusiastic about Internet technologies when you use the Web.

When the Web was in its early stages, content was authored using text editors such as vi in UNIX, Notepad in Windows, and others. Authors composed documents by hand, entering HTML tags themselves. With the advent of HTML editors such as FrontPage by Microsoft and Navigator Gold by Netscape, users can compose their own documents without having to learn HTML. With these powerful tools, Web growth took off and has been in high gear ever since.

## CERTIFICATION OBJECTIVE 6.02

# WWW Service

Hypertext Transfer Protocol (HTTP) was the protocol that led to the World Wide Web. HTTP grew out of a need for a standards-based protocol to simplify the way in which users access information on the Internet. It is a generic, stateless, object-oriented protocol. HTTP is at the application layer of the protocol model. HTTP categorizes data, allowing systems to be built independently of the data being transferred.

## Virtual Servers

The WWW service supports a concept called *virtual servers.* A virtual server can be used to host multiple domain names on the same physical Internet Information Server (IIS). You need a unique IP address for each virtual server that you host.

*Each virtual server requires a unique IP address that is assigned to the Network Interface Card (NIC).*

## Virtual Directories

The WWW and FTP services also support *virtual directories.* A virtual directory is a directory that appears to be in ftproot, the home folder. A virtual directory can be on any server in the same Windows NT domain. Virtual directories created on other servers should be referenced by their Universal Naming Convention (UNC) names.

*Virtual directories may be located on local drives or on remote servers. You should refer to remote drives by the UNC.*

## CERTIFICATION OBJECTIVE 6.03

# HTTP Communication

HTTP is a client/server model. There must be a server-side application and a client-side application. The client and the server interact to perform a specific task.

When a client clicks on a hyperlink, the HTTP protocol performs the following:

1. The client browser uses HTTP to communicate with the server.

2. A connection is established from the client to the server. The server monitors TCP port 80 by default.

3. Once the connection is made, the requested message is sent to the server. The requests are typically for a resource file.

4. Server sends a response message to the client, along with the data the client requested.

5. The server closes the connection unless the client's browser has configured a keep-alive option.

# HTTP Requests

The client communicates with the server in the form of a simple request method. This request method consists of a URL and a protocol version. Here is an example of an HTTP request:

Get http://www.microsoft.com/cert_train/iis HTTP 1.0

This request contains the following elements:

- **Get** Specifies the request method.
- **URL** //www.microsoft.com/cert_train/iis specifies which object to get.
- **HTTP 1.0** The version of the protocol to be used.

The following elements may be used in an HTTP request:

- **Request** Such as "get."
- **Resource** The URL path to the object.
- **Message** The message makes a simple request into a full request and can include additional information such as a MIME (Multipurpose Internet Mail Extensions), request modifiers, and client information.
- **Response** The HTTP response message.

# HTTP Server Response Messages

The client sends a request to the HTTP (Web) server. The server receives the request and responds with a status message. The message includes the protocol version and a success or error code. A MIME message follows containing server information, entity information, and possibly body content. Table 6-1 contains examples of server status messages.

exam
ⓦatch

*Know what the syntax of the request is. Know what a URL is and how to construct it.*

**TABLE 6-1**

HTTP Server Response Messages

| Message | Type | Description |
| --- | --- | --- |
| 2.*xx* | Success | The request was successfully received. |
| 3.*xx* | Redirection | Further action must be taken to complete the request. |
| 4.*xx* | Client error | The request contains bad syntax or the request cannot be fulfilled. |
| 5*xx* | Server error | The server has failed to fulfill a valid request. |
| l*xx*l | Informational | This series has been reserved for future use. It is not currently used. |

## MIME Type Configuration

If your server has files that use different file formats, your server must have a MIME mapping for each different file type or extension. If you don't have this, your client's browser may not be able to retrieve the file. You set these mappings from the HTTP Headers tab in the property sheet, as illustrated in Figure 6-1.

**FIGURE 6-1**

Accessing MIME mappings

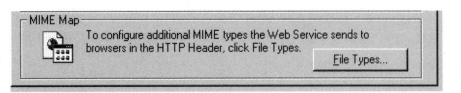

To configure additional MIME mappings, click the New Type button in the File Types dialog box. In the File Types dialog box, enter the extension that is associated with the file in the Associated Extension box. In the Content Type (MIME) box, enter the MIME type followed by the filename extension in the form MIME *type /filename extension,* as illustrated in Figure 6-2. If you are using files with a .my_file extension and do not map this file as a MIME type, then when a client requests the file it will be identified as the default MIME type, which is typically binary.

**FIGURE 6-2**

Creating MIME mappings

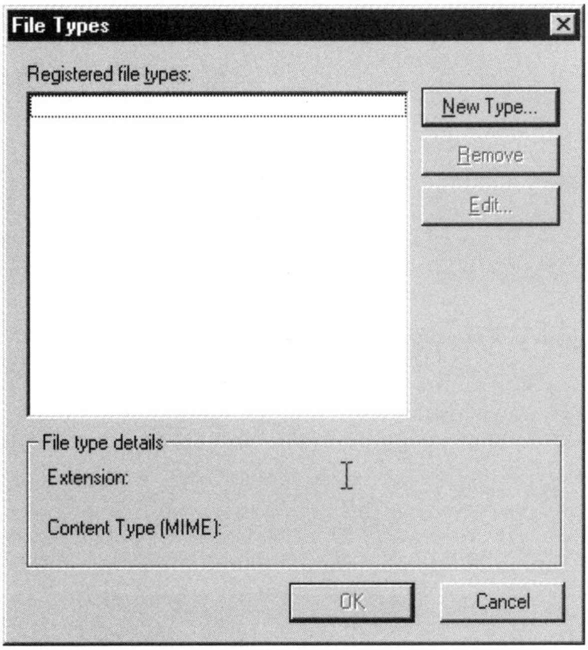

# HTTP Clients and URLs

You need an HTTP client to attach to the Web server. The client is called a *browser*. The two predominant browsers in use today are Microsoft's Internet Explorer (IE) family and Netscape's Navigator family. Interestingly, both programs' current version is Version 4.*x*.

To access a resource on the Web server, you specify three items:

1. **How access is to occur**   The default in IE is HTTP protocol; if you enter a URL like www.microsoft.com, the browser assumes that this is an http://www.microsoft.com request. You can still use the FTP protocol from your browser by simply specifying ftp: where you would normally see http: and using the appropriate FTP site URL. For example, the URL ftp://sunsite.unc.edu/ accesses an FTP site.

2. **The host**   You can use an IP address, a fully qualified domain name (FQDN), or a NetBIOS computer name. You separate the protocol, HTTP or FTP, with a "//," slashes that go the opposite direction from what you use in a DOS path (for example). By default, the browser uses port 80 to connect to the server. If you have configured the server to monitor a different port, use a ":" after the host name, followed immediately by the port number the server is monitoring.

3. **The path to the object**   You must use the entire path to the object. Separate the sections, usually indicating subdirectory names, in the path using a "/" between them.

# HTTP Ports and Connections

The HTTP server monitors port 80 for client connections, as illustrated in Figure 6-3. You change this port by modifying the port number from the Default Web Site property sheet or by changing the values in the Services file

FIGURE 6-3

Modifying the HTTP port

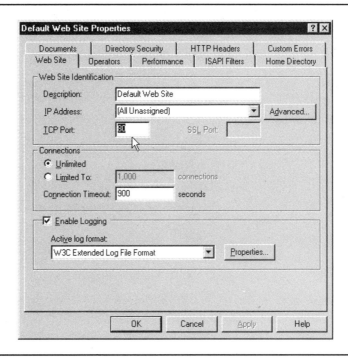

located in the <winnt_root>\system32\drivers\ect folder. Changing the port number on the server requires that the clients specify the same port number when they attempt to connect. This may act as a small security screen because the client needs to know which port is in use but, as in the case with FTP, this is not much of an obstacle to an experienced hacker.

EXERCISE 6-1

## Connecting to Your HTTP Server

Purpose: To demonstrate the ability of your browser to connect to the Web server. You will also modify the TCP port and reconnect to the server specifying the new port number.

*Do this exercise from either computer.*

1. Ensure you are logged on as Administrator.
2. Start Internet Explorer.
3. In the Address box, type **Serverxx.** *xx* as the number of your server.
4. Press ENTER. Your browser should connect to your server.
5. Close IE.

6. Open Internet Service Manager.

7. Expand your server so that you can see the Default Web Site.

8. Right-click the Default Web Site.

9. Click Properties.

10. Ensure that the Web Site is selected.

11. What is the default TCP port?

12. Modify the TCP port number to 3300.

13. Click Apply.

14. Open Internet Explorer.

15. What message did you get?

16. Click OK to clear the error message.

17. In the Address box, type **http://serverxx:3300**.

18. Press ENTER.

19. What happened?

20. Close IE.

21. Switch to the Web property sheet.

22. Set the TCP port to 80.

23. Click Apply.

24. Close the MMC.

*Answers to the steps in this exercise.*

11. Port 80.

15. Internet Explorer cannot open the Internet site.

19. You connected to the server using TCP port 3300.

**CERTIFICATION OBJECTIVE 6.06**

# Configuring WWW Services

You configure the Web services using three property sheets. Which property sheet you use depends upon what object you wish to change. The property sheets are:

- Master
- Default
- File

## Master

When Internet Information Server is installed, properties are applied to the Master property sheet, which is illustrated in Figure 6-4. You select the Master property sheet by right-clicking on the server icon and selecting Properties.

## Default

Each IIS installation creates a Default Web Site. This site initially has the same properties as specified on the Master property sheet. You select the Default Web Site property sheet by right-clicking the Default Web Site node and selecting Properties. Figure 6-5 illustrates the Default property sheet.

---

**FIGURE 6-4**

Master property sheet for WWW Service

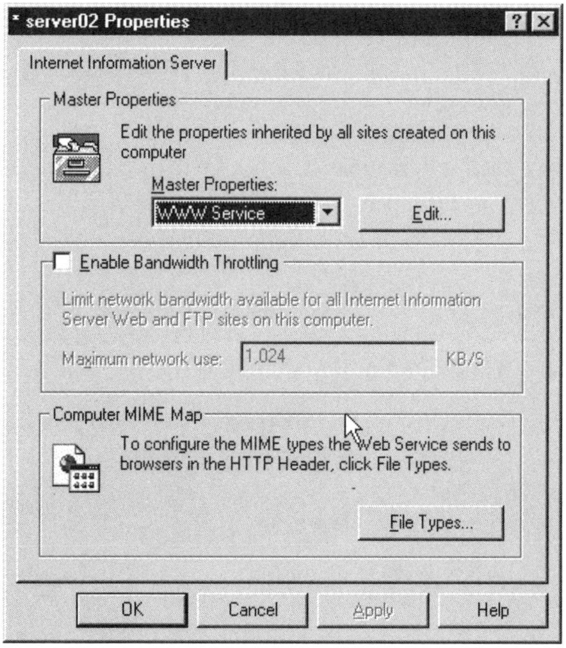

FIGURE 6-5

Default Web Site
property sheet

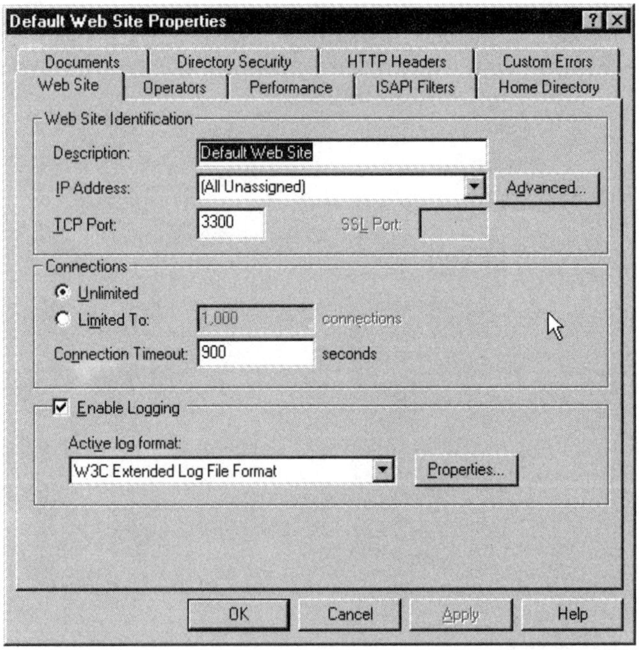

## File

Files created in the Default FTP Site inherit the properties of that site's property sheet. Files created in a virtual FTP directory inherit the properties of the directory's property sheet. Figure 6-6 contains an example of a file's properties.

## Configuring the Default Web Site

You configure the Default Web Site by using the Default Web Site property sheet. The sheet contains nine tabs:

- Web Site
- Operators

FIGURE 6-6

Property sheet for file
IE.GIF

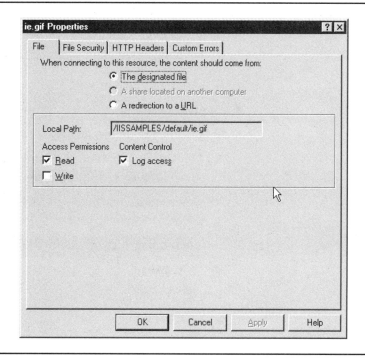

- Performance
- ISAPI Filters
- Home Directory
- Documents
- Directory Security
- HTTP Headers
- Custom Errors

## Web Site

You use the Web Site tab, illustrated in Figure 6-5, to set general parameters about the site including:

- **Web Site Identification**

- **Description**    A name you choose for your site
- **IP Address**    The IP address for this site
- **TCP Port**    The port the server monitors for connections
- **SSL**    Port used by the Secure Socket Layer transmission
- **Connections**
  - **Unlimited**    Allows an unlimited number of connections to the site.
  - **Limited To**    Restricts the number of sessions that can be simultaneously established at the site.
  - **Connection Timeout**    The number of seconds before the server disconnects an inactive user.
- **Enable Logging**    There are three log formats:
  - W3C Extended
  - NCSA common
  - ODBC logging

## Operators

You use the Operators tab to designate users you want to administer specific Web sites. The default is for members of the local administrators group to be able to administer the Web site, as illustrated in Figure 6-7.

## Performance

You use the Performance tab to:

- Adjust performance tuning to the number of expected daily connections. This is different than the maximum number of simultaneous connections you will allow. For example, you can set the maximum number of simultaneous connections to 25,000 and set the anticipated number of daily connections to more than 100,000. However, that means that you expect more than 100,000 daily users to connect to your site, but you will only allow 25,000 to be connected at any one time.

**FIGURE 6-7**

Assigning operators for
a site

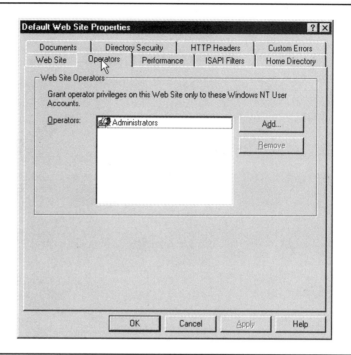

- Check the Enable Bandwidth Throttling box to restrict the Web site.
  The value here overrides the value set at the server computer, even if the
  value set at the site is higher.

- HTTP Keep-Alives is enabled by default. This allows the client to keep
  an open connection with the server, instead of opening a connection for
  each new request. This is enabled by default. Without this enabled,
  each time a client gets a new page from your site, it opens a connection,
  gets the pages, and closes the connection. This is how Web sites work
  without this enhancement. Figure 6-8 illustrates the Performance tab.

## ISAPI Filters

You use the ISAPI tab to set Internet Server Application Programming
Interface (ISAPI) filters. ISAPI can be used to run remote applications. You do
this by requesting a URL that is mapped to a filter, which activates the

**FIGURE 6-8**

Configuring site
performance and
keep-alives

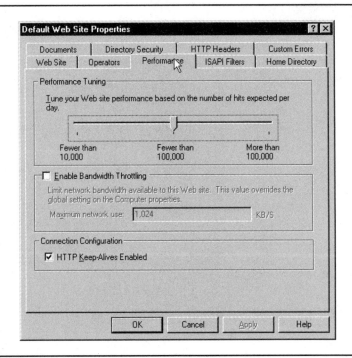

application. ISAPI programs run inside a single process and memory space.
If you use CGI scripts, each time a CGI script runs, it initializes its process,
spawns a thread, and allocates memory. This all takes time and machine
resources. ISAPI calls are faster and consume fewer resources. Figure 6-9
illustrates the ISAPI Filters tab.

## Home Directory

You use the Home Directory tab to change settings and properties for your
home directory. Figure 6-10 contains the Home Directory tab. When you
install IIS, it creates a home directory called wwwroot in the \inetpub folder.
You can have a home directory:

- In a folder on the local server
- In a folder shared on another computer

**FIGURE 6-9**

Configuring ISAPI filters

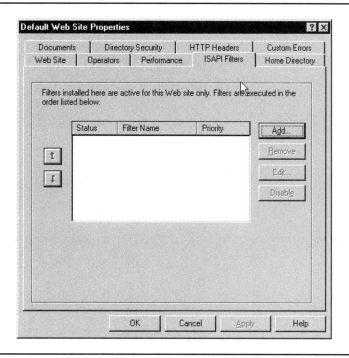

- From a URL redirection

You can set access permissions as follows:

- **Read**  Web clients can read and download files.
- **Write**  Web clients can upload files to the enabled folder. They can change the contents in a write-enabled file. To do this, the client must be using a browser that supports the PUT feature of the HTTP 1.1 standard.

The content control properties are in affect when you are using a local folder or using a folder from a network share. These properties are:

- **Log access**  Record all visits to a folder or a file.
- **Directory browsing allowed**  Show the user a hypertext listing of the folders and files so that the client can navigate through the directory

Setting the properties of
the home directory

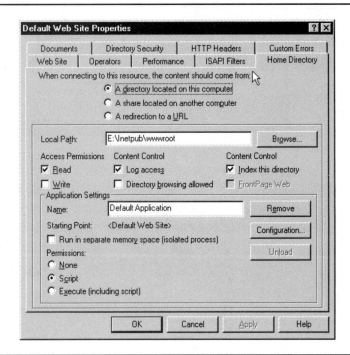

structure. This listing is automatically sent to the client when the
browser request does not contain a specified filename or there is no
default document in the folder.

- **Index this directory**    Instruct Microsoft Index Server to include this
  directory in a full text search of your Web site.

- **FrontPage Web**    Create a Microsoft FrontPage Web site for this
  directory.

With respect to Application Settings in the Home Directory dialog box, an
application is defined as all the folders and files contained within a folder

marked as an application starting point, until another application starting point is reached. To make a folder an application starting point, click the Configuration button. You have the following choices for applications:

- **Run in separate memory**   This option causes the application to run in its own memory space as a separate process on the Web server. Running in its own memory space causes the application to be protected from other processes.

- **Permissions**   This option controls how applications can be run in this folder. You have the following choices:

  - **None**   Any programs or scripts can run in this folder.

  - **Script**   The script engine can run in this folder without setting the Execute permission.

  - **Execute**   Applications can run in this folder, including script and executables (Windows NT binaries).

## Documents

You use the Documents tab to select which default document you will show the user when the browser does not specify a particular HTML file. The default document filename should be "Default.htm." Figure 6-11 illustrates the Documents tab.

You can specify more than one default document by using the Add button. This causes the Web server to go down the list of documents in the order listed until it finds one of the listed documents in the folder.

You can enable Document Footer to have the Web server automatically insert a footer for you. This file can contain HTML formatting instructions for identifying your Web page, but this file should not be an HTML document. This file should only include tags necessary for formatting the appearance of your footer. You must provide a complete path and filename for the footer file.

FIGURE 6-11

Documents tab

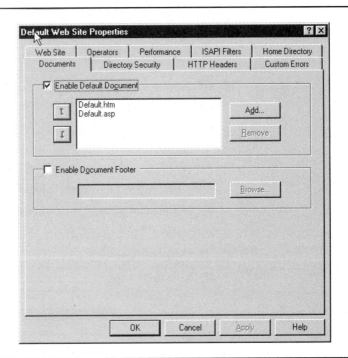

### Directory Security

Use the Directory Security tab to configure your Web server's security features, as illustrated in Figure 6-12. This dialog box includes:

- **Anonymous Access and Authentication Control**   Click the Edit button to select the following options:

  - **Anonymous Access**   Always allow this.

  - **Basic Authentication**   If you select this option, and Allow Anonymous Access is disabled, the user is required to submit a valid set of Windows NT account credentials. The associated password is sent in clear text.

  - **Windows NT Challenge/Response**   A username and password is required if Anonymous Access is disabled, and this access is controlled by NTFS security. The password is encrypted and the client browser must support Windows NT Challenge/Response.

■ **Secure Communications**   Select the Key Manager button to initiate the process of receiving a Secure Socket Layer (SSL) certificate.

■ **IP Address and Domain Name Restrictions**

  ■ **Grant access**   This is the default. Grants access to all computers. You restrict access by denying access to specific IP addresses or domain names.

  ■ **Deny access**   This turns off access. You must grant access by specific IP address or domain name.

---

**FIGURE 6-12**

Setting Web access using the Directory Security tab

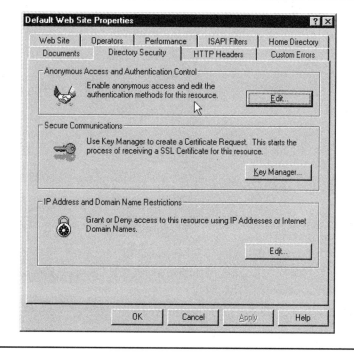

## HTTP Headers

Use the HTTP Headers tab (illustrated in Figure 6-13) to set the values returned to the browser in the header of the HTML page.

Select Enable Content Expiration to include expiration information. This causes the browser to compare the current date to the date in the document. If the date is good, the browser uses the locally cached copy. If the date is old, it does not use the locally cached copy; it attempts to get an updated page.

The Custom HTTP Headers option allows you to send a custom header from your server to the client's browser. Use the Add button to specify the header.

MIME Map is used to set information about files kept on the server. You need to create a map to map specific applications to certain file extensions. For example, you want to match the WINZIP application to files with the .ZIP

**FIGURE 6-13**

HTTP Headers tab

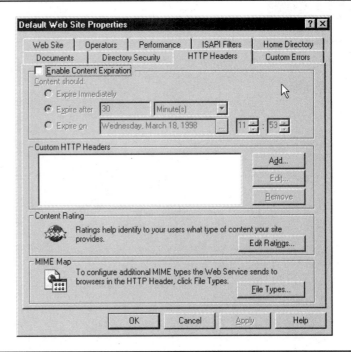

extension. If you do not create this map, the client's browser might not know how to interpret the file type when it is received. The client then has to decode the file manually using a utility program. While this is not difficult, it is nice just to get the file and use it.

## Custom Errors

The Custom Errors property sheet shows the messages that are returned to the browser in the event of an HTTP error. You can use the default HTTP 1.1 error messages supplied, or create your own custom error messages. Figure 6-14 illustrates the Custom Errors tab.

**FIGURE 6-14**

Custom Errors tab

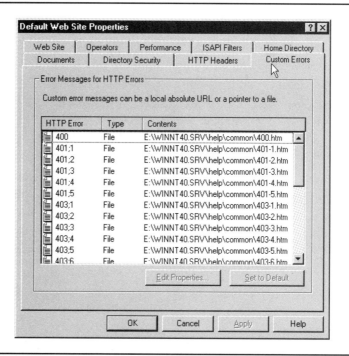

# FROM THE CLASSROOM

## The Reality of Being Virtual at Your IIS Server, but Not Virtual Reality

Students are greatly interested in the capabilities of IIS to extend its root directories (WWW and FTP) by using virtual directories. Several students in a class that I had recently were quite surprised to discover that IIS could use a virtual directory on a remote server. In the marketing hype wars that go on, they were left with the definite perception that IIS does not support this feature. Of course IIS supports a virtual directory on a remote server.

Another new feature of interest to the students is how IIS 4.0 handles virtual servers. IIS 3.0 supported virtual servers by assigning an IP address to the NIC for each virtual server. If you had 10 virtual servers, then you would have 10 IP addresses assigned to the NIC.

IIS Version 4.0 allows you to create multiple virtual servers anchored to the same IP address. This helps preserve available IP addresses. It also helps in the administration of the server. The administrator does not have to fuss with multiple IP addresses when configuring the server.

Multiple IP addresses can have their benefits. If you are configuring a virtual server for a group that is not part of your organization, it might be desirable for that group to use an IP address of its own. This puts forth the image that there is a truly distinct and separate site for that group.

Students familiar with IIS 3.0 can be overwhelmed initially by the changes in administration for the Web service. One of those changes is the Microsoft Management Console (MMC). It takes some students time to adjust to this new concept. However, most students actually like it better, once they get used to it.

Once you get inside the property sheet for the Web server, the shock of how different it is to configure is also evident in the faces of the students. IIS 3.0 had five tabs for configuration. IIS 4.0 has nearly twice that many tabs to set parameters. And some of the configurations are much more robust and easier to set.

**EXERCISE 6-2**

## Configuring the WWW Server

Purpose: To configure the Web server.

*Do this exercise on either computer.*

1. Ensure that you are logged on as Administrator.
2. Open the MMC.
3. Expand your server, if not already expanded.
4. Right-click Default Web Site.
5. Click Properties.
6. In the Description box, change the description to be *your name's* Web Site.
7. In the Connections section, click the radio button for Limited To.
8. In the box to the right, set the connection limit to 5. In a real environment, you would not normally set the limit so low.
9. Click Apply.
10. Open User Manager.
11. Create a new user with the following properties:
    - Username: Webmgr
    - Full Name: Web Manager
    - Description: Account to be used for other Web management
    - Password: Blank (null)
    - Clear the check box User Must Change Password at Next Logon.
    - Check the box Password Never Expires.
12. Click on the Policies menu, then click User Rights. Modify the User Right "Log on locally" to include the group Everyone.
13. Close User Manager.
14. Return to the Default Web Site Properties.

15. Select the Operators tab.

16. Click the Add button.

17. Add the user account Webmgr to the Add Names box.

18. Click OK.

19. The Webmgr account should now be included in the Operators box.

20. Click Apply.

21. Click OK.

22. Close the MMC.

23. Click No to save the console.

# CERTIFICATION SUMMARY

The Web server is a graphical client/server application. It is one of the most popular ways of disseminating information today. On one end is a Web server and on the other end is a client browser. The communication method is the HTTP protocol, a stateless, object-oriented protocol. The client establishes a connection with the server. The client makes this request by specifying the exact resource. The resource request is in the form of a URL. If the client does not specify a filename at the end of the URL, the server sends the default page. If there is no default page in the folder and the server is configured to allow directory browsing, the client receives a directory listing. If there is no home page and directory browsing is not allowed, then the client receives an error message from the server.

You manage the server properties using various property sheets. You must be an administrator or have been given operator permission to change the property sheets.

# TWO-MINUTE DRILL

❑ HTTP was the protocol that led to the development of the World Wide Web.

❑ IIS 4.0 supports HTTP 1.1.

❑ HTTP 1.1 supports both put and get operations.

❑ A virtual directory may be on a local drive.

❑ A virtual directory may be on a remote drive.

❑ Refer to a virtual directory on a remote server by the UNC.

❑ IIS supports virtual servers.

❑ You can have multiple virtual servers on one physical server.

❑ Virtual servers can be assigned to one IP address.

❑ Virtual servers can be assigned a unique IP address to each virtual server.

❑ HTTP is a client/server process.

❑ The WWW server monitors TCP port 80.

❑ Each time the browser makes a request, a new connection is made.

❑ Enabling keep-alives prevents client connections from being closed after a request.

❑ The client communicates with the Web server with a simple request.

❑ The request specifies a Uniform Resource Locator (URL).

❑ The client request can also specify the protocol.

❑ The server responds with a status message.

❑ A 4.*xx* is a client error that contains a bad syntax or a request that cannot be fulfilled.

❑ You need to configure MIME mappings to associate file extensions (file types).

❑ You can connect to the FTP site using the browser.

# SELF TEST

The following Self Test questions will help you measure your understanding of the material presented in this chapter. Read all the choices carefully, as there may be more than one correct answer. Choose all correct answers for each question.

1. What protocol does the WWW use?

   A. FTP

   B. HTTP

   C. IPX

   D. Hyperlink

2. Which of the following statements is true about a virtual server?

   A. IIS can host multiple virtual servers.

   B. A virtual server appears on the network and then disappears.

   C. Each virtual server must have its own IP address.

   D. Each virtual server must have its own network card.

3. Which of the following statements is true of virtual directories?

   A. You create a virtual directory from Windows NT Explorer.

   B. Virtual directories appear as though they are in the wwwroot folder.

   C. Virtual directories can be on a local drive or a network drive.

   D. Virtual directories created on other servers should be referenced by their UNC names.

4. Which port does the WWW service monitor for a client connection?

   A. 20

   B. 21

   C. 70

   D. 80

5. Which characteristics are necessary for you to specify access to a resource on a Web server?

   A. How access is to occur

   B. The MAC address of the server

   C. The host

   D. A path to the object

6. You receive a call from a user stating that he is trying to connect to your Web server and receives the error message, "Internet Explorer cannot open the Internet site…" What may be causing this to happen?

   A. The user does not have TCP/IP loaded.

   B. The default gateway is down.

   C. He is trying to access the Web server using the wrong TCP port number for the server.

   D. The Web server is down.

7. How do you modify which TCP port your Web server monitors?

   A. From ISM, right-click the Web server and select Properties.

   B. Open Server Manager.

   C. Select the TCP port tab.

D. Select the Web Site Identification tab.

8. Jerry has been made responsible for managing the Web site recently. How can you make sure that Jerry will be able to administer the site?

   A. Add Jerry's account to the local administrators group.

   B. Nothing. Jerry should be able to administer the site.

   C. Create a new account for Jerry and make it part of the Domain Users group.

   D. Add Jerry's account to Operators using the Web server's property's sheet.

9. You want to restrict the amount of bandwidth your Web server might use on the network. What is the best way to accomplish this?

   A. Use a slower network card.

   B. Enable bandwidth throttling in the Performance tab.

   C. Limit the number of concurrent users at the server.

   D. Keep the server busy with other processes so that it has less time to service Web requests.

10. Which of the following statements is correct about keep-alives?

   A. Keep-alives keep the server running in the event of a power outage.

   B. A keep-alive restarts a file copy in the event you are accidentally disconnected from the server.

   C. Keep-alives have something to do with life insurance.

   D. Keep-alives maintain the client connection after the request is complete.

# 7

# Domain Name Service (DNS) Server

## CERTIFICATION OBJECTIVES

**D**omain Name Service (DNS) is what allows users to refer to sites on the Internet by name, rather than refer to them by some complicated number that is difficult to remember. This chapter describes the components of DNS and explains how to install, configure, and use DNS on your server.

You may find some sections in this chapter where you feel like you might want more information. An excellent source of additional information is the *MCSE Microsoft TCP/IP on Windows NT 4.0 Study Guide* (Osborne McGraw-Hill). This chapter also contains references to other resources for information such as the RFCs. You should become familiar with TCP/IP, and in particular the Microsoft approach to TCP/IP. Remember, to obtain your MCSE + Internet certification, you also have to pass the TCP/IP exam.

**CERTIFICATION OBJECTIVE 7.01**

# Overview

Before 1980, the Internet consisted of a handful of computers, certainly not more than a few hundred computers. The host name-to-IP address mapping was fairly insignificant. The entire host name-to-IP address resolution effort was contained in a single file called HOSTS.TXT. This file was stored on a host computer at the Stanford Research Institute Network Information Center (SRI-NIC) in Menlo Park, California. Other host computers copied this file as necessary from the host in Menlo Park.

This scheme worked well in the beginning because the host file needed to be updated infrequently. However, as the Internet grew, problems arose due to the ever-increasing size of the host file. The problems included the following:

- The host file became too large.

- The file needed to be updated more than once a day.

- Network traffic on the SRI-NIC host became almost unmanageable.

- The host file used a flat name structure. This required every computer name to be unique across the entire Internet.

These and other problems led the Internet to find a solution for the HOST.TXT file. That solution was the *Domain Name System (DNS)*, a distributed database that uses a hierarchical name structure. DNS is described in RFCs 1034 and 1035.

DNS resolution is a client/server process. It is based on a distributed database management system. DNS uses the application layer, which in turn uses UDP and TCP as its transport protocols.

The purpose of DNS is to resolve *host names* (also known as *computer names* but different from the computer names used by Microsoft networks, which are NetBIOS names) to an IP address. In DNS, the clients are called *resolvers*, and the DNS servers are called *name servers* (*NS*).

DNS is analogous to the white pages of a telephone book. When using a telephone book, a person looks up the name of the person they want to call, then cross-references that name to a telephone number. On the Internet, the user wants to contact a host by its friendly name (for example, www.microsoft.com), and the system contacts the DNS server to resolve the friendly name. The DNS server takes the query for the friendly name and then cross-references it to an IP address.

The resolver passes the name request from the application to the DNS name server. The name request is known as a *query*. A query might ask for the IP address of www.microsoft.com, for example. The resolver sends the query using UDP for increased performance. (The UDP protocol is faster than the TCP protocol because it does not have to set up a session first.) If the resolver does not receive a valid answer, it repeats the query using TCP.

The name server takes the request for the IP address from the resolver and resolves the friendly name to its respective IP address. If the name server is unable to resolve the request, it may forward the request to another name server that can resolve it. The servers are often grouped into different levels that are called *domains*.

Domains assign the different levels that have authority in the hierarchical name structure. At the top of the hierarchy is a domain called the *root domain*. The root domain has no formal name and is signified by a period ("."). The root domain uses a null label. The domains of root domains are called *top-level domains*. The following are the top-level domains:

- **COM**   Commercial organizations
- **EDU**   Educational institutions

- ■ **ORG**  Non-profit organizations
- ■ **NET**  Internet Service Providers
- ■ **GOV**  Non-military government organizations
- ■ **MIL**  Military
- ■ **NUM**  Phone numbers
- ■ **ARPA**  Reverse DNS lookup
- ■ **XX**  Two-letter country codes

Beneath the top level are second-level domains that can contain both hosts and other domains known as *subdomains.* For example, a second-level domain may be GM (General Motors) and its domain may have subdomains such as Buick, Chevrolet, Oldsmobile, etc. Second-level domains and subdomains contain the hosts. The top-level domains are controlled on the Internet. Second-level domains are assigned by the InterNIC. Owners of the second-level domains control subdomains below that level. They may create whatever subdomains they want. Following the prior example, the domain GM.COM is registered with and assigned by the InterNIC to General Motors. GM creates a subdomain named Buick. They may do this without asking the InterNIC. They can also create a subdomain for Buick named Trucks, if so desired.

Host names are added to the beginning of a domain name followed by the subdomains, second-level domain, and then the top-level domain name. This convention is called the *fully qualified domain name (FQDN).* For example, WWW is the host name; MICROSOFT is the second-level domain; COM is the top-level domain; and the period after COM signifies the root. You do not have to use the period after the top-level domain since the top-level domains are known entities and do not change (or at least do not change that often). The software automatically appends the period for you.

## The Changing Structure of DNS

In order to be on the Internet, you must have a domain name. Domain names are kept in the domain name system, which is currently administered by Network Solutions, Inc. (NSI). NSI has a virtual monopoly on the registration of domain names. The federal government has moved to introduce competition in the area of domain name registration. Today, domain name registration is a fairly simple and straightforward task. You check to see if the name you want for your second-level domain is registered. If not, you complete a registration form, send in a relatively small amount of money, and NSI registers your domain name and puts it into their DNS server structure.

Since 1992, Internet traffic has jumped an incredible 3500 percent. There has been a corresponding jump in the number of domain registrations as well. In 1992, there were only 5000 registered domains on the entire Internet. Now some sources say that many new domains are added each day, straining the current DNS system to its limits.

There are few fail-safe measures in the BIND (Berkeley Internet Name Domain) protocol system. In addition, there are additional constraints in the current system. One such constraint is that there are only a few top-level domain names. Top-level domain names are probably recognizable to most of you. They are the names .COM, .NET, .ORG, .EDU, .MIL, etc.

In addition to the limitations imposed by having so few top-level domain names, there are many requests for what might be the same domain name. For example, if your company name is Comet, it may already have been registered by another individual or firm, leaving it unavailable to you.

To address this and some other concerns, the Department of Commerce released a document in early 1998 known as "The Green Paper." The Green Paper lays out the federal government's plan to move from a single-source system for the DNS to a name registration system that is competitive. The Green Paper, sponsored by the White House and put together by the Department of Commerce, is more of a proposal at this point than a mandated plan.

The main issue that stirs controversy in the DNS system is the registration fees being charged and the tight control of the process being maintained by NSI. NSI currently charges $50 per year to renew a domain name registration. NSI's share of the $50 is $35. NSI does two things for its $35 share of the registration fee:

- Registers domain names.
- Puts domain names in the zone file of the computer known as Root Zone Server A.

This zone server maintains the master copy of the Internet's top-level DNS zone file.

There are 11 other root zone servers. They copy the master file contained on Root Zone Server A. These 11 other root zone servers use this file to resolve names for top-level domain inquiries. The registration process ensures exclusive use of the domain name, and the root zone server guarantees that the domain name will work.

One of the proposals in The Green Paper is to split this into two separate directory service functions. A group of for-profit companies would act as registrars, each company maintaining the root zone file for the individual domains it controls. For example, one company would act as the registrar for the .COM top-level domain zone, and another for the .ORG top-level domain zones, etc.

While The Green Paper is not clear, it appears there could be a different set of for-profit companies, also known as registrars, who would be able to register domain names in any of the top-level domains and deal directly with companies or individuals that want to establish an Internet identity.

The Green Paper also proposes significant requirements for registrars in terms of the type of equipment they would need and the operations they would be required to run. A typical registrar would be required to have a 24-hour-a-day operation, physical security of the computer systems and premises, all equipment on uninterruptible power supplies, and be "globally positioned" to back up their root zone servers in the event of failure of equipment or of communication links. They would also be required to have multiple redundant communication links of at least T1 capacity to different Internet Service Providers. The registrars would also be required to design and implement a process whereby they would resolve trademark disputes.

The Green Paper outlines the government's plan to create new top-level domains. The names of these new top-level domains have not yet been specified, but leading candidates are .WEB, .NOM, .STORE, .FIRM, .RETAIL, .CATALOG, etc. Some of these new names were proposed last year by the Internet Society (ISOC) and were endorsed by the Council of Registries. The Council of Registries is a group of 88 companies from around the world. The Green Paper does not address the ISOC proposal to create and run new top-level domains itself.

The creation of new top-level domain names clears up some of the restrictions on having a name on the Internet that more closely resembles your company. For example, in the current top-level domain, .COM, there can be only one registered company called TheComputerStore. There may well be dozens, and perhaps even hundreds, of companies around the world called "The Computer Store," but only one of them can own the registered Internet name "TheComputerStore.COM." Having multiple top-level domains allows for more of TheComputerStore.*extension.*

On the other hand, there are certain names that have been trademarked, like IBM, AT&T, Coca-Cola, etc. While there can be only one IBM.COM, IBM is pretty safe from having people encroach on its trademark name. However, the organization known as the International Brotherhood of Magicians could now have an IBM.FIRM presence on the Internet, and it would be very difficult for users of the Internet to distinguish between IBM.COM, the computer makers, and IBM.FIRM, the group of magicians.

With more domains and more registrars now in the process, there is no mechanism for ensuring that trademark names are not abused in the domain name registration system. Further to that point, the Green Paper notes that U.S. trademark law "imposes no general duty on a registrar to investigate the propriety of any given registration." Nevertheless, The Green Paper states that the domain name registrars would be required to create trademark dispute resolution procedures. However, The Green Paper does not propose a comprehensive legal solution to resolve trademark issues.

The Green Paper proposes three aids for assisting in the resolution of trademark disputes. The first proposed aid is a better search tool than the one currently available. WHOIS is used to determine which domain names are registered. However, WHOIS was never intended to be more than a basic utility capable of doing a string search on a specific database.

Second, to aid in dispute resolution, The Green Paper proposes that should litigation occur, the litigation should be conducted in the company that maintains the top-level domain registry (which would probably be in the United States). This proposal would prevent someone from trying to register another company's trademark and then have it litigated in a country where the local courts might be more favorable to them, say in Somalia or Iraq.

Third, The Green Paper suggests an on-line trademark resolution process to assist in the effort, but then fails to specify how the process should work or who would maintain it.

**CERTIFICATION OBJECTIVE 7.02**

# DNS Zones

A DNS server is called a *name server.* Name servers store information about the domain name space, and they are generally responsible for one or more zones. When a name server is responsible for a zone, it is said to have *authority* for the zone. In other words, a zone of authority is that portion of a domain name space for which a particular server is responsible. The name server stores all the IP addresses and host names for the entire domain space within the zone. Name servers answer resolvers' queries for host name-to-IP address resolution.

A DNS server can be configured to manage one or multiple zone files. A *zone* is a physical file on the DNS comprised of the records in the database that define the domain. These database records are managed in the zone file. Each zone is anchored at a specific domain node called the zone's *root domain.* In other words, the DNS server's zone of authority encompasses at least one domain, and this domain is referred to as the zone's root domain. The DNS server's zone of authority may also include subdomains of the zone's root domain. However, a zone does not necessarily contain all of the subdomains under the zone's root domain.

All DNS servers must work in conjunction with other DNS servers. A DNS server in a subdomain must know that there is a DNS server in the domain above it, and so forth. When you configure a DNS server, you must specify the names of all the name servers in the same domain. There are three types of DNS servers:

- Primary name servers
- Secondary name servers
- Cache-only name servers

# Primary Name Servers

The *primary name server* obtains zone information from the local zone file. Changes to the file, which is at a domain server, are done at the primary name server.

# Secondary Name Servers

A *secondary name server* obtains the data for its zone from another name server in the network that has authority for that zone. Obtaining the zone information across the network is referred to as a *zone transfer*.

There are three reasons to use a secondary name server:

- **Redundancy**  When you have one computer performing a role, then you probably want a second computer performing the same role in order to provide redundant operations. Each zone should have at least one primary and one secondary name server.

- **Remote locations**  If you have clients in remote locations using WAN links, using secondary name servers at these locations means that resolvers do not have to cross the slow WAN links for host name-to-IP address resolution.

- **Reduction of workload**  Secondary name servers can reduce the workload of the primary server.

Interestingly enough, because information for each zone is stored in its own separate zone file, the designation of a primary or secondary server is defined at the zone level. In other words, it is entirely possible that the primary name server for one zone could be a secondary name server for another zone.

When you create a secondary name server, you have to indicate where that secondary name server is to obtain its zone information. The DNS server that provides the secondary name server with zone information is referred to as the *master name server*. The master name server may be either a primary or a secondary name server in that zone. When a secondary name server is initialized, it contacts the master name server for the zone and issues a zone transfer with the master.

## Cache-Only Name Servers

There is another type of DNS server that doesn't use zone files, known as *cache-only name servers*. Although all DNS servers cache queries that they have resolved, a cache-only name server performs queries and caches the answers. They do not keep zone data locally and therefore, are not authoritative for the domain. If you shut down a cache-only name server, the resolutions that were cached are lost, and the cache-only name server begins rebuilding its cache table after it is restarted.

Using a cache-only name server may be more efficient on a slow WAN link in the long run because the cache-only name server does not do a zone transfer of the zone database when it starts up. However, caching servers increases traffic in the near term because it must go out for name resolution across the WAN link each time.

### CERTIFICATION OBJECTIVE 7.03

# DNS Records

Part of the information in the name server's file is put there manually by the administrator of the domain server. This information stored in the zone file is stored in the form of database records. These database record types are described in RFC 1040 and 1035 and 1183. There are several types of resource records defined:

- SOA
- A
- NS
- TTR
- CNAME
- MX
- HINFO

Microsoft has added the WINS and WINS-R specific record types. These record types are specific only to Microsoft networks.

The first record type in the DNS database must be the Start of Authority record (SOA). The SOA defines the parameters of the DNS zone. The following rules apply to all SOA records:

- The "at symbol" ("@") in the database file indicates "this server."

- The IN indicates an Internet record.

- Any host name not ending with a period will be appended with the root domain.

- The @ symbol is replaced by a period in the e-mail address of the administrator.

- Parentheses must enclose line breaks that span more than one line.

Each name server zone file contains one or more name server records. The following is an example of a name server record:

@ IN NS server01.fun01.com

In order to resolve host names to IP addresses, the hosts must be listed in the DNS name server. A host record (A) statically associates the host name with its IP address. The following are examples of host records:

```
Host01        IN      A      201.200.189.33

Local Host    IN      A      127.0.0.1
```

You may refer to a server by a name different than its host name. To do so, you must have a *canonical name record (CNAME)* in the zone file. This is also known as an *alias*. The following is an example of a CNAME record:

```
www     CNAME      server02

ftp     CNAME      server02
```

A PTR record is a pointer record that provides an IP address-to-host name mapping to do a reverse lookup in the zone.

An MX record is a record pointing to a mail exchange server (not necessarily the Microsoft Exchange Server). The MX record is necessary so that the Internet can find your SMTP and POP3 servers effectively.

**CERTIFICATION OBJECTIVE 7.04**

# DNS Name Resolution

When users try to contact a host on the Internet, they typically use a fully qualified domain name (FQDN). The resolver presents this request to the DNS name server for resolution. This request is presented in the form of a query. There are three types of queries that a resolver might make to the name server:

- Recursive
- Iterative
- Inverse

A recursive query occurs when the name server is queried by the resolver and is required to respond with the requested IP data or send back an error stating that the data of the request type does not exist or that the domain name specified does not exist. In a recursive query, the name server cannot refer the request for resolution to a different name server.

With an iterative query, the query's name server either returns the resolution to the query or it generates a referral to another name server that might be able to resolve the original request. For example, a client within your organization sends a query to your DNS for the IP address of www.microsoft.com. Here is how that request is processed with an iterative query:

1. The resolver sends a recursive query to the name server asking for the IP address of www.microsoft.com. The name server responds and is unable to resolve the query. It cannot refer the resolver to another name server.

2. The local name server checks its zone file and the requested domain name that it cannot find. It sends an iterative query for www.microsoft.com to a root name server.

3. The root name server has authority for the root domain and replies with an IP address of a name server for the .COM top-level domain.

4. The local name server sends an iterative query for www.microsoft.com to the .COM name server.

5. The .COM name server replies with the IP address of the name server servicing the microsoft.com domain.

6. The name server sends an iterative query for www.microsoft.com to the microsoft.com name server.

7. The microsoft.com name server replies with the IP address corresponding to www.microsoft.com.

8. The local name server sends the IP address of www.microsoft.com back to the original resolver.

With an *inverse query*, the resolver sends a request to the name server to resolve a host name with an associated IP address. For example, you have an IP address 201.200.199.252 and you want to know what the host name is for this IP address. This is the inverse of a normal DNS query where you know the host name and are looking for the IP address. There is no correlation between host names and IP addresses in the DNS name space.

To assist with queries of this type, a special domain was created, known as *in-addr.arpa*. Nodes in the in-addr.arpa domain are known by their IP addresses whereas nodes in the DNS zone file are known by their host names. An interesting situation occurs because IP addresses get more specific from left to right. The fourth octet of the IP address is typically the host name in a class C network, for example. However, domain names get less specific from left to right. For example, in the FQDN www.microsoft.com, the www is the actual host name. Microsoft is a subdomain, and .com is the top-level domain. To accommodate this difference, the order of the IP address octets must be reversed when building the in-addr.arpa domain. For example, if the resolver is querying for a name associated with the IP address 201.200.199.252, this becomes a query for 252.199.200.201.in-addr.arpa.

Once the in-addr.arpa domain is built, special resource records called *pointer records (PTR)* are added to the database to associate the IP address with the host name. Part of the administration of the name server is ensuring that pointer records are created for the host names.

When a name server resolves a recursive query, the name server may be required to send out several other queries to find the answer. The name server caches all of the information it receives during this process. This information stays in the cache for only a certain period of time. The amount of time that the information stays in the cache is referred to as the *time to live (TTL)*. The TTL is determined by the TTL entry from the non-local name server. Smaller TTL values help ensure that data about the domain remain consistent across a large network. This is important if data changes often. However, the smaller the TTL value, the more that server will have to go out of the local network to resolve requests. This will increase the load on some name servers.

Once the data is cached by the local name server, it must start decreasing the TTL from its original value toward zero so that it knows when to remove this piece of data from its cache. If a query comes in that can be satisfied by the data in the cache, the TTL that is returned with the data is the current amount of time left, not the original TTL value. Resolvers also have data caches and they honor TTL values so that the resolver knows when to remove its data from the cache.

## Configuring the DNS Files

There are several files associated with a typical DNS server. These files are:

- Database file
- Reverse lookup file
- Cache file
- Boot file

The *database file* (ZONES.DNS) contains the records for the hosts for a domain. For example, if your zone is fun.com, then the database file is named FUN.COM.DNS. This file is stored in the Winroot/system32/dns folder.

This file is created automatically for you when you create a zone using the DNS server manager.

Microsoft also supplies a sample database file called PLACE.DNS with the Windows NT 4.0 distribution files. You can use this sample database file as a template. You edit this file with a text editor, and it should be renamed before you use it on your production name server. It is generally a good practice to give this file the same name as the zone it represents. This is the file that is replicated between master name servers and secondary name servers. Remember, you only need to edit this file if you are going to build your DNS by manually editing and creating the associated text files. If you are using the GUI interface DNS Manager, you do not have to do any of this manually. The DNS Manager creates all of the necessary files for you.

The *reverse lookup file* associates IP addresses with the respective host names. Remember, this is the inverse of what the DNS zone file does, which is to associate host names with their IP addresses. Recall that the IP addresses in the reverse lookup file are entered in reverse order. If you enter a normal IP address using the example x.w.y.z, then in the reverse lookup file, the IP address is entered as z.y.w.x.in-addr.arpa. The in-addr.arpa is a domain name given to reverse lookups.

The *cache file* is essentially the same on all name servers on the Internet, and it must be present. The name of the cache file is CACHE.DNS. This file contains the names and the IP addresses for all of the name servers that maintain the root domain. No matter what else happens, your DNS server must be able to contact the root domain servers.

The *boot file* is normally used by DNS servers for startup configuration. This file contains host information needed to resolve names outside of authoritative domain. The boot file is seldom used with Microsoft DNS name servers.

The boot file controls how the DNS server starts. There are several commands that may be used in the boot file. These commands are:

- Directory command
- Cache command
- Primary command
- Secondary command

The Directory command specifies a directory where other files referred to in the boot file can be found.

The Cache command specifies a file used by the name server to contact other name servers for the root domain. Remember, the cache file must be present.

The Primary command specifies a domain for which this name server is authoritative. It also specifies the database file that contains the resource records for the domain. This is your zone file. Multiple primary command records may exist in the boot file.

The Secondary command specifies a domain for which the name server is authoritative. It provides a list of master server IP addresses. This list provides information to the name server in order to download the zone information, called a zone transfer, rather than reading this information in a file. Multiple Secondary command records could exist in a boot file.

## Planning a DNS Implementation

Many organizations, especially those organizations with a small network, find it easier and more convenient to have a DNS name server maintained by another organization such as their Internet Service Provider (ISP). Most ISPs will maintain domain information for a small fee. Of course, you can lower that small fee if you want to endure the chore of maintaining your own DNS. When an organization wants to connect to the Internet, the InterNIC must be informed of the domain name for that organization and the IP addresses of at least two DNS servers that service the domain.

For reliability and redundancy, at least two DNS servers should be configured per domain: a primary name server and a secondary name server. The primary name server maintains the database information, and the secondary name server receives this information from the primary name server. The process of replicating the database information allows name queries to be serviced even if one of the name servers is down. The replication schedule can be configured, depending on how often names change in the domain. Replication should occur often enough so that both servers know the changes, but not so frequently that excessive traffic caused by the replication consumes network bandwidth.

**CERTIFICATION OBJECTIVE 7.05**

# Installing Microsoft DNS Server

Microsoft DNS Server is a fully RFC-compliant implementation. It offers a convenient GUI interface with which to configure DNS.

Before you install DNS, make sure your computer is correctly configured for your domain name. You do this from the Network applet using the Protocol tab. From there, you select the TCP/IP properties and then select the DNS tab.

There are three important items to configure, as illustrated in Figure 7-1. First is your host name. The host name that Windows NT suggests is your NetBIOS computer name. You may use this name or you may change it to

**FIGURE 7-1**

Configuring the host name and DNS search order

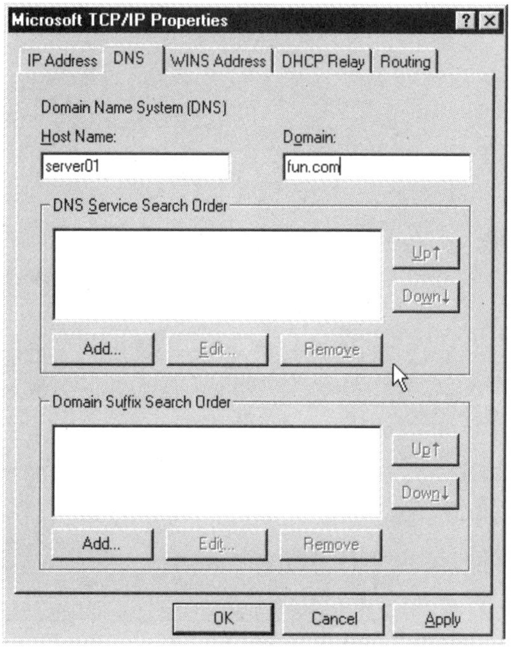

whatever you wish. There is no requirement that the Internet host name and the NetBIOS computer name be the same.

Second is the domain name. This is the name you registered with the InterNIC. This name must include the top-level domain name as part of the string.

The third item to configure is which DNS servers you will use to resolve your queries. You must have at least one DNS listed in the box. It is desirable to have two DNS servers listed, in case one server is down or unavailable; then your queries will be sent to the other DNS server listed for resolution.

To install the DNS, use the Network applet in the Control Panel. DNS installs just as most other Windows NT services. In the Network applet, select the Services tab illustrated in Figure 7-2.

**FIGURE 7-2**

Services tab

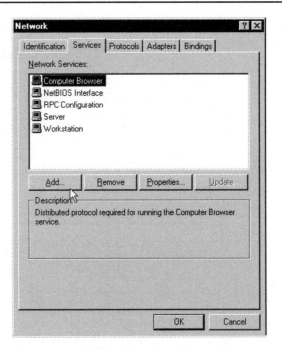

After clicking the Add button and selecting Microsoft DNS Server from the resulting list, specify the location of the distribution files and Windows NT takes care of the rest. Figure 7-3 illustrates how you select the DNS server.

Once the DNS server is installed, you are ready to configure the server to support your network. You do this by using the GUI interface DNS Manager. This tool is in the Administrative Tools group.

**FIGURE 7-3**

Selecting the DNS Server

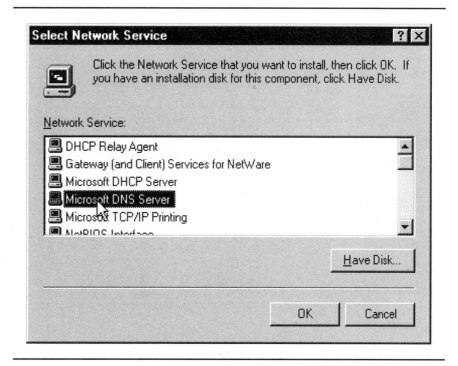

**EXERCISE 7-1**

### Installing DNS

Purpose: To install the Microsoft DNS.

*Do this exercise from both computers.*

1. Ensure you are logged on as Administrator.
2. Right-click Network Neighborhood.
3. Click Properties.
4. Select the Protocols tab.
5. Select TCP/IP.
6. Click Properties.
7. Select the DNS tab.
8. In the Domain box, enter **FUNXX.COM** (where *XX* is the number of your server).
9. Under the DNS Service Search Order, click Add.
10. In the DNS server box, enter the IP address for your computer.
11. Click Add.
12. Click OK.
13. Select the Service tab.
14. Click the Add button.
15. Enter your path to the Windows NT distribution files.
16. Click Continue.
17. Click Close.
18. Click No when asked to restart your computer.
19. Reinstall Service Pack 3 (SP3).
20. The system will restart after SP3 has been installed.

**CERTIFICATION OBJECTIVE 7.06**

# Configuring DNS Server

Configuring the DNS begins with opening DNS Manager, as illustrated in Figure 7-4.

The first step is to add a DNS server to the DNS Manager using the dialog box in Figure 7-5. You can manage any Microsoft DNS server from the DNS Manager.

**FIGURE 7-4**

Opening DNS Manager to begin configuration

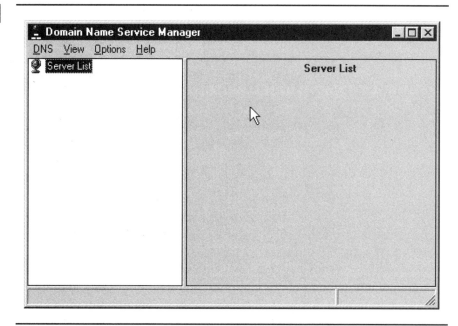

**FIGURE 7-5**

Adding your server to DNS Manager

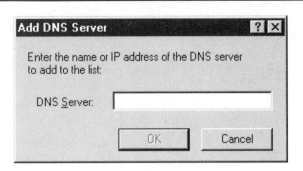

After adding the server to the DNS manager, create a zone using the dialog box in Figure 7-6. This creates the ZONENAME.DNS file to hold the host records for your domain.

**FIGURE 7-6**

Creating a new zone

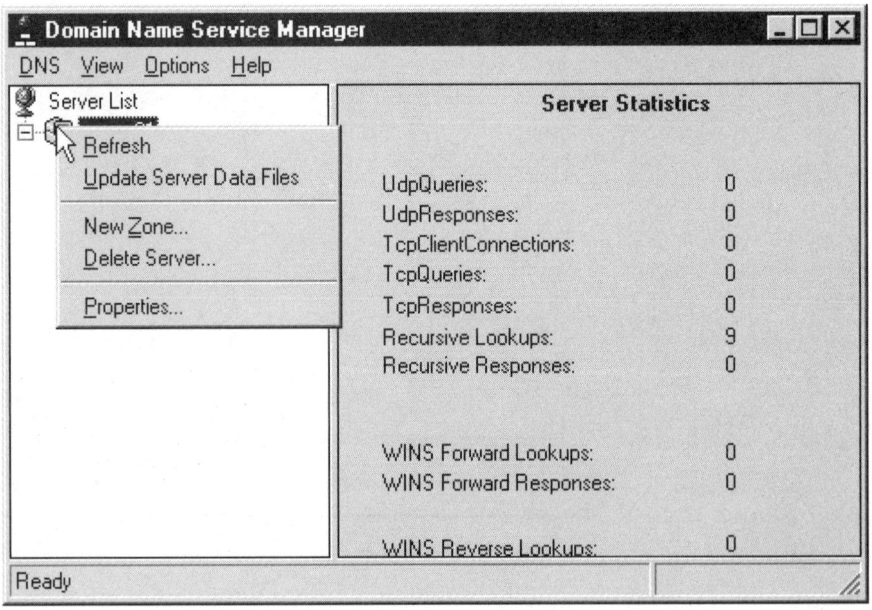

The first step in creating the new zone is to specify whether this will be a primary or secondary DNS server, as illustrated in Figure 7-7.

If you have elected to create a primary DNS server, the next step is to specify the zone name. After completing the dialog box in Figure 7-8, DNS manager automatically creates the zone file for you. The zone file is called *DOMAIN_NAME*.DNS and is located in the DNS folder in the system32 folder.

At this point you are essentially done with the zone creation. All that is left is to click Finish, as illustrated in Figure 7-9.

The zone creation creates the SOA record, the NS record, and an A record for the primary DNS server. After that, you manually create all of the other zone records as appropriate.

**FIGURE 7-7**

Selecting primary or
secondary server roles

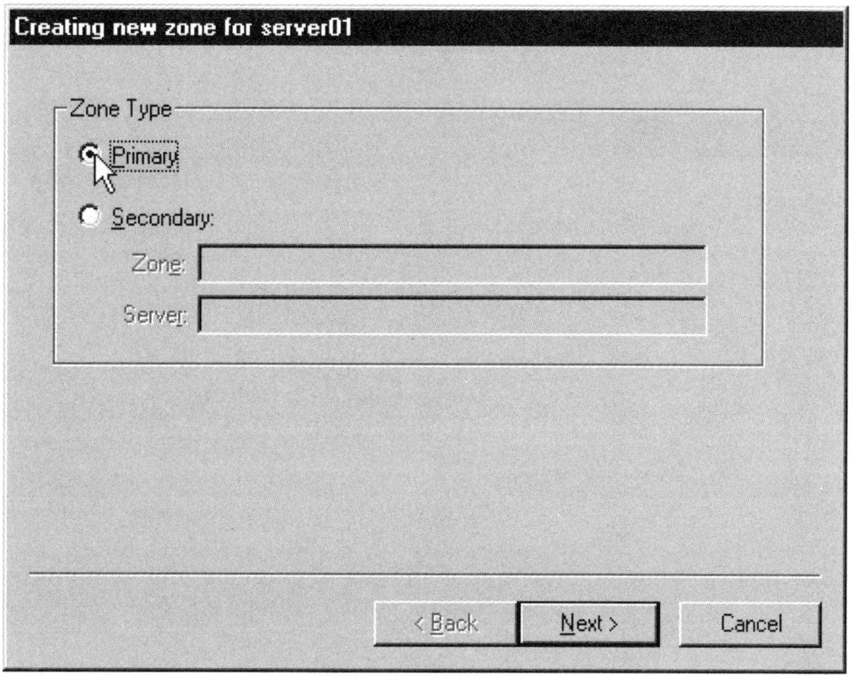

**FIGURE 7-8**

Specifying the zone name

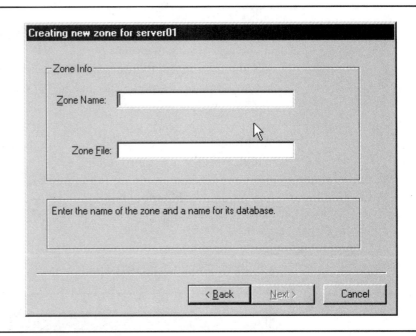

**FIGURE 7-9**

Finishing the zone creation

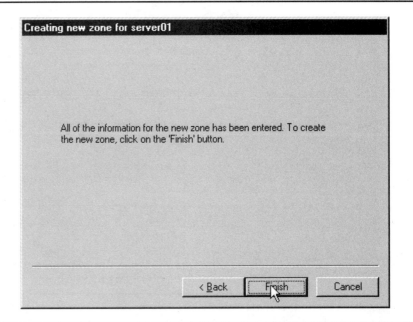

| EXERCISE 7-2 | **Configuring DNS** |
|---|---|

Purpose: To configure the DNS server to make it ready for use.

*Do this exercise from both computers.*

1. Ensure that you are logged on as Administrator.
2. Click Start.
3. Point to Programs.
4. Point to Administrative Tools.
5. Click DNS Manager.
6. Click the menu item DNS.
7. Click New Server.
8. Enter **Serverxx** in the dialog box.
9. Right-click your server name.
10. Click New Zone.
11. Click the Primary radio button.
12. Click Next.
13. In the Zone Name box, enter **FUNXX.COM** (where *XX* is your computer number).
14. Press the TAB key.
15. Notice that FUNXXCOM.DNS was entered into the Zone File box.
16. Click Next.
17. Click Finish.

## CERTIFICATION OBJECTIVE 7.07

# DNS and WINS Integration

You can also use Windows Internet Naming Service (WINS) for host name resolution but you don't have to choose between WINS and DNS. Integrating WINS and DNS utilizes the best of each system to create a dynamic DNS.

The integration of WINS and DNS is automatic when DNS is configured to resolve names that are not listed in the zone file. In this configuration, the DNS resolves the upper layers of the domain name and passes the resolution to WINS for the final resolution.

# FROM THE CLASSROOM

## Making DNS Easy

Many students come to class with previous experience configuring a DNS server in a non-Windows NT environment. Other students have no experience configuring any type of DNS server. Each student may have a different perception of installing and configuring Microsoft DNS based on their previous experience.

Students with previous experience are amazed how easy it is to install and configure Microsoft DNS while others may have a difficult time making the jump from working with a text editor and editing the files manually to using the GUI interface of DNS Manager. These students typically have UNIX experience and may have the same aversion to the GUI DNS Manager as they may have with other "I can't do this from the command line" frustrations. One of the keys to successfully using a new system of any type is to do things the way that system is structured and not the way you did it with the other system. If you fall

into this category, don't underestimate the "cognitive map" issue. We all try to put new experiences into a familiar frame so that we can understand and deal with them. Sometimes this is good and sometimes it gets in the way. For the good news, if you are comfortable and wish to continue manually editing the DNS files, you can do so. As one of our students was heard to remark upon completing the DNS exercise, "I like the way I do it and Microsoft can't make me change!"

If you don't have a wealth of experience, using the GUI interface of DNS Manager can make configuring DNS much easier. Everything is done from one place at one time. You get a view of all of the components that comprise your DNS system. Your hardest task may be in understanding how DNS does its job and what records are required for proper name resolution to occur. Armed with that understanding, the mechanical process of creating the configurations is easy.

## QUESTIONS AND ANSWERS

| | |
|---|---|
| Do I need a DNS server? | You do not have to host the DNS server; your ISP can do that for you. |
| If I don't have an ISP and I'm not on the Internet, do I need a DNS server? | Not necessarily. However, somewhere there must be some way to resolve domain names to IP addresses. You could use the hosts file, but the DNS server might be easier. |
| I already have a UNIX computer acting as a DNS. Do I need to set up the Microsoft DNS? | No, you can make the appropriate entries in any DNS server. |
| Can I get rid of the UNIX DNS and just use the Microsoft DNS and have it work for the UNIX computers as well? | Absolutely. The Microsoft DNS service, if fully RFC compliant, will support your entire organization if you wish. |
| Do I need both a DNS and a WINS server? | That depends on what you are trying to accomplish. Strictly speaking, if you just have a Web server or a FTP server and are only offering Internet services, then you don't need a WINS server. |

# CERTIFICATION SUMMARY

DNS does IP addresses to fully qualified domain name resolution. When an application addresses a host name, the resolver forwards a request, in the form of a query, to the DNS name server for resolution to an IP address. The DNS can use either a recursive or an iterative query in an attempt to resolve the request.

There are three types of DNS servers: primary, secondary, and cache-only name servers. Primary servers hold the zone database file. Secondary servers get the zone file from the primary server and cache servers have no zone file, but build a database dynamically by resolving requests and keeping the information in memory (cache) to reuse as required. Each domain must be listed in a DNS server somewhere on the Internet. If you want to be able to contact a host, it must also be listed in a DNS server.

# ✓ TWO-MINUTE DRILL

❑ Domain Name System (DNS) is used to list the names of hosts around the world.

❑ There is a root domain managed by the InterNIC.

❑ There are a few top-level domains managed by the InterNIC.

❑ DNS servers used for those domains are managed by NSI.

❑ There are DNS clients called resolvers.

❑ Microsoft DNS Server is fully RFC compliant.

❑ You manage Microsoft DNS through the DNS Manager.

❑ The resolver sends a query to the DNS server.

❑ The query contains a request to find the IP address of a host.

❑ The host is referred to by its friendly name.

❑ The complete host name is called the fully qualified domain name (FQDN).

❑ The DNS sends the IP address of the host back to the resolver.

❑ There are three types of DNS name servers: primary, secondary, cache-only.

❑ The primary DNS server contains a database of host names.

❑ This database is kept in a zone file.

❑ Every domain must be in a zone.

❑ DNS servers may have more than one zone.

❑ A domain may have more than one zone.

❑ There can only be one root authoritative server for the zone.

❑ Secondary zone servers get their zone file from the primary name server; this process is called a zone transfer.

❑ A CNAME record is an alias that refers back to a host name already created in the DNS.

❑ There are three types of queries: recursive, iterative, and inverse.

❑ An inverse query sends the DNS an IP address and asks to resolve it to a host name.

❑ Resolved queries are cached in memory.

❑ Cached queries remain in memory for their time to live (TTL) period.

❑ You can manually configure the DNS server by editing the DNS files directly, rather than using the GUI interface.

❑ There are four files in a typical DNS: database (or zone) file, reverse lookup file, cache file, and boot file.

❑ You install DNS server from the Network applet.

❑ You configure DNS server from the DNS Manager.

❑ DNS server can be integrated with WINS servers.

# SELF TEST

The following Self Test questions will help you measure your understanding of the material presented in this chapter. Read all the choices carefully, as there may be more than one correct answer. Choose all correct answers for each question.

1. Which of the following statements are true about DNS?

    A. Host name resolution is a client/server process.

    B. The resolver resolves the query for a host name to an IP address.

    C. The Microsoft computer name is the same thing as a host name.

    D. DNS is a hierarchical name system.

2. Which of the following statements are true?

    A. Domain Name Service (DNS) contains a root domain.

    B. There is a potentially unlimited number of top-level domains.

    C. You create second-level domain names as you need them.

    D. DNS queries only use the TCP protocol.

3. Which of the following is not a current top-level domain name?

    A. .COM

    B. .GOV

    C. .CA

    D. .ARMY

4. Which of the following statements are true of zones?

    A. A DNS server can manage more than one zone.

    B. A DNS server may only manage one zone.

    C. A zone and a domain are the same thing.

    D. Each subdomain must have its own zone.

5. Which of the following is not a DNS server type?

    A. Primary

    B. Backup

    C. Secondary

    D. Cache-only

6. Which of the following statements may be valid reasons for creating a secondary name server?

    A. You want to provide redundancy.

    B. You want to speed resolution for clients on remote WAN links.

    C. You have multiple IP segments in the building and need queries resolved on each segment.

    D. You want to balance the workload for resolving queries.

7. You have created a secondary server at one of your remote offices. What do you need

to do to ensure that the secondary server gets a copy of the zone database?

- A. Configure the directory replication service.
- B. Use the AT schedule service.
- C. Copy the database file manually.
- D. Nothing.

8. Which of the following statements is true of a cache name server?

- A. The cache server gets its database from the primary.
- B. The cache server sends its database to the secondary.
- C. A cache server loads the zone database file into memory for faster resolution.
- D. A cache server builds its database in memory from previously resolved queries.

9. Which of the following records must appear in the database, at a minimum?

- A. SOA record

- B. NS record
- C. MX record
- D. An A record for the primary DNS server

10. Which of the following is not a type of query that a resolver might make of the name server?

- A. Inverse
- B. Iterative
- C. Simple
- D. Complex

11. Which of the following statements are true of a reverse lookup?

- A. A reverse lookup sends an inverse query.
- B. A reverse lookup asks for a host name by presenting an IP address.
- C. A reverse lookup sends a recursive query.
- D. You can only do a reverse lookup if WINS is installed.

# 8

# Virtual Servers and Virtual Directories

I nformation is vital and the ability to access that information is critical. Where the information is stored is not important to the person accessing the information. Stated another way: Do you really care what the directory structure of the server is, or do you care that when you click on the hyperlink, the information you requested is displayed on your monitor?

# What Are Virtual Directories?

When you install Internet Information Server (IIS), publishing directories are created. The default directory structure begins with the \InetPub folder. Under this folder, you have the root or home directories for the WWW and FTP servers, as illustrated in Figure 8-1.

**FIGURE 8-1**

Root directory structure

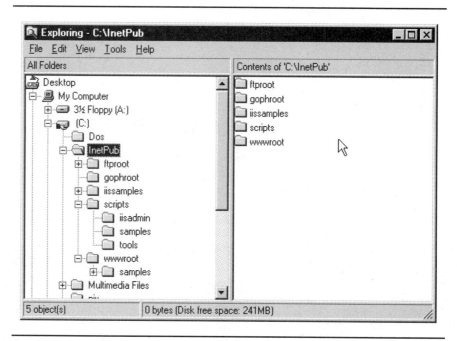

*Virtual directories* extend the capabilities of IIS to include additional directories that are not part of the IIS root structure. Virtual directories reside outside the root structure of the server. They can be located anywhere on any server and are referenced by an alias that points to the relative file locations. The alias gives you, the IIS administrator of the site, tremendous flexibility when determining where files will be stored. Without virtual directories, all the files would need to be stored on the IIS server, within the root structure. If the disk that contains the \wwwroot folder becomes full, for example, another disk needs to be added to that server. You need to shut down the server to install the new drive, making it unavailable for that period of time. A virtual directory does not allow you to add a new drive without shutting down the server if that drive is not already on your system and configured. Virtual directories allow you to store files on a different drive or even on a different computer and reference those files as though they were in the root structure. If you use file services on another server, you may be able to keep the server running and eliminate the need to add a hard disk.

Another case where virtual directories are helpful is when you have information (files) that are already stored on another server and you want to publish them on your Web server. You copy them from that server to your Web server. Now the files exist in two places on your network, on the original server and on your Web server. Whenever a file is updated on the original server, some mechanism is required to ensure that the updated file is also copied to the Web server.

You can create a virtual directory on the Web server that references the file location on the other server. Now the files are stored in only one location on the network and there is no need to make sure that updated files are copied to the Web server. Clients connecting to the Web server have access to the latest updates.

Virtual directories can be created for both FTP and WWW sites. The administrator specifies the physical location of the directory and an alias of the virtual directory.

exam
ⓦatch

***Virtual directories can be created for both FTP and WWW servers.***

Virtual directories do not appear in the directory listings. On an FTP server, the client needs to know the virtual directory alias in order to access the directory. Using the directory name does not work because you cannot go outside the root structure.

Virtual directories on the Web server do not show up in a directory listing either. Remember that if there is no default page or the client does not specify a filename in the URL, they will not get a directory listing. You need to create explicit hyperlinks in Hypertext Markup Language (HTML) files so that the client can access the virtual directories.

## Local and Remote Virtual Directories

A local virtual directory is on the local computer. A remote virtual directory is on another host. You can point to either using an alias. You assign the alias using Internet Service Manager (ISM). The directory may be a remotely shared folder or on any disk, including the disk that contains the wwwroot or ftproot folders.

*Virtual directories may be on the local or remote servers.*

You access the virtual directory by specifying it in the URL. Let's assume that you created a virtual directory on drive D: in a folder named Data. To access a file named default.htm, the access request is:

http://server01/data/default.htm

*Virtual directories must be referenced by their URL. On a Web server, the virtual directory contents may be accessed by a hyperlink as well.*

A remote virtual directory is located on another computer, not on the Web server. You point to the remote virtual directory using the Universal Naming Convention (UNC). The syntax for the UNC is:

\\server_name\share_name

If you create a virtual directory on a server named server01, and server01 had a share named co_info, then the UNC is:

\\server01\co_info

You specify the previous UNC in the alias that points to it. Let's assume that you created alias information to point to the previous UNC. Users connect to the remote virtual directory using the following access request:

http://server01/information/example.htm

The user connects to the IIS server. The IIS server accesses the remote server's share and provides a pathway for the user's request. There may be a small performance drop when accessing virtual directories located on remote servers.

## CERTIFICATION OBJECTIVE 8.02

# Configuring IIS for Virtual Directories

You configure a virtual directory with Internet Service Manager. Right-click the site to which you want to add the virtual directory and select New from the menu. Select Virtual Directory. This process is illustrated in Figure 8-2.

This starts the New Virtual Directory Wizard. At the first screen, you enter the alias by which you will refer to the virtual directory, as illustrated in Figure 8-3.

**FIGURE 8-2**

Configuring a virtual directory

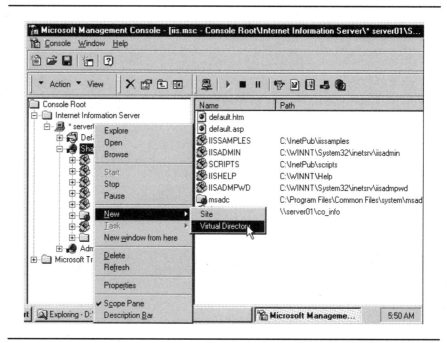

**FIGURE 8-3**

New Virtual Directory
Wizard

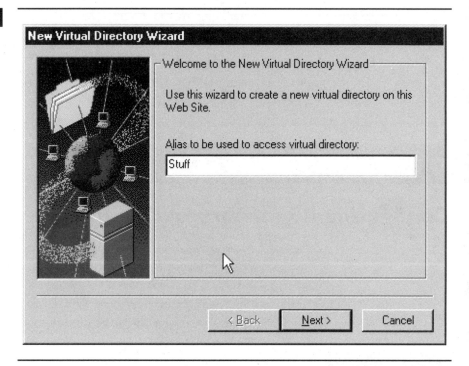

The next screen asks you for the path of the folder that will be the virtual directory. You can either type the path or click the Browse button and select the desired folder (see Figure 8-4).

The next dialog box of the New Virtual Directory Wizard allows you to set access permission for the virtual directory, as illustrated in Figure 8-5. You have the following choices:

- Allow Read Access
- Allow Script Access
- Allow Execute Access (includes Script Access)
- Allow Write Access
- Allow Directory Browsing

After this, click the Finish button and you are done. You have created a virtual directory on your Web server.

FIGURE 8-4

Specifying the path to a
new virtual directory

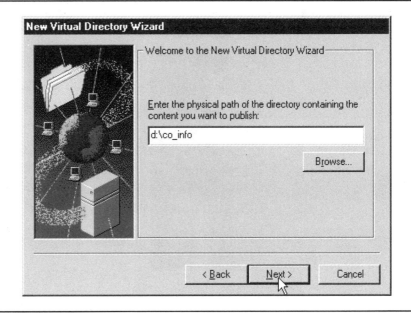

FIGURE 8-5

Setting access permissions

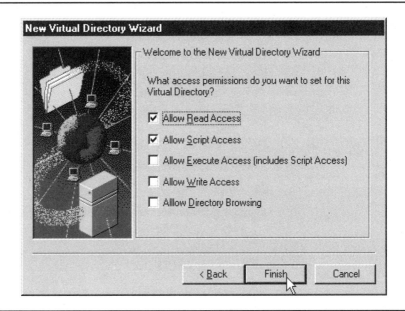

---

**EXERCISE 8-1**

### Configuring a Virtual Directory

Purpose: To configure both a local and a remote virtual directory.

*Do this exercise from both computers.*

1. Ensure that you are logged on as administrator.

2. Click Start, click Programs, and click Administrative Tools.

3. Open Disk Administrator.

4. Click OK or Yes if you receive messages about this being the first time Disk Administrator has been run, or it needs to write a signature to the disk. If you do not get these messages, it is of no concern.

5. Select the free space area of the disk.

6. Click Partition.

7. Click Create.

8. Create a partition of at least 250MB in size.

9. Click OK.

10. Click Partition.

11. Click Commit Changes Now.

12. Select the new partition area.

13. Click Tools.

14. Click Format.

15. In the File Systems drop-down list, select NTFS.

16. Click Quick Format from the Format Options area.

17. Click Start.

18. Click Close when the formatting is done.

19. Close Disk Administrator.

20. Open Windows NT Explorer.

21. Using Windows NT Explorer, create a folder named CO_INFO at the root of the D: drive (or whichever drive letter you assign this partition).

22. Create a folder named Certification in the \INETPUB\WWWROOT folder.
23. Close Windows NT Explorer.
24. Start Internet Service Manager.
25. Expand Internet Information Server.
26. Expand the server.
27. Right-click your Web site.
28. Select New.
29. Select Virtual Directory.
30. Enter the name **Stuff** in the first dialog box of the New Virtual Directory Wizard.
31. Enter the path **D:\co_info**.
32. Click Next.
33. Uncheck Allow Script Access.
34. Click Finish.
35. You should now see a folder named Stuff in the tree of your Web site.
36. Repeat steps 27–29 to create another virtual directory.
37. Enter the name **Information** in the first dialog box of the New Virtual Directory Wizard.
38. Enter the path **\\serverxx\rmtinfo**.
39. Click Next.
40. Enter **Webmgr** in the Username box. This account's password was blank, so you do not enter a password here.
41. Click Next.
42. Accept the defaults.
43. Click Finish.
44. You should now see a folder named Information in the tree of your Web site.

**CERTIFICATION OBJECTIVE 8.03**

# What Are Virtual Servers?

A *virtual server* is a server that appears on the Internet as a WWW (or FTP) server as though it is an actual physical computer. In reality, the virtual server is being hosted by another Internet Information Server. This IIS computer can host any number of virtual servers.

*Virtual servers are different than virtual directories and serve a different purpose. Be clear on the differences before the test.*

Multiple domain names can be hosted on a single IIS server using virtual servers. There are two common techniques that can be used to host virtual servers. Virtual servers may be used to extend Internet services by allowing a company to host multiple servers at a single IP address. You accomplish this by using *host headers*. If you select this technique for your virtual Web servers, your users will require a Web browser that is HTTP 1.1 compliant.

If the Web browser is not HTTP 1.1 compliant, it can still access URLs with host headers. Internet Information Server presents the Web browser with a list of servers that are tied to the IP address. The user makes the selection (which Web server) from the list. IIS places a *cookie* on the user's hard disk. When the user reconnects to the site, the cookie redirects the request to the appropriate virtual server.

A cookie is a text file (usually) that is created by the Web server on your machine to store information specific to your machine but relative to this server site, such as your preferred server choice, last connection time, length of connection, places visited on site, or anything else. Like any access to your machine from a remote host, a cookie may be malevolent. Many browsers can be set to warn you about systems setting cookies on your machine. In general, there is no harm done in accepting a cookie from well-known sites. Be wary of all others.

The second technique you can use to host virtual servers is to assign unique IP addresses for each domain name assigned to the server. To do this, you may need to get a unique IP number from the InterNIC. You may also need to register the other domain names for the virtual servers.

*Virtual servers may use a single IP address, or each virtual server may have its own unique IP address.*

Virtual servers also need an entry in the DNS so clients can connect using fully qualified domain names (FQDNs) instead of IP addresses.

## CERTIFICATION OBJECTIVE 8.04

# Configuring IIS for Virtual Servers

Before you configure a virtual server, you need a new folder to act as the virtual server's root directory. You can create this folder using Windows NT Explorer, as illustrated in Figure 8-6. You may create this folder on any local disk. You may also create the folder on another server.

To begin the process of creating the virtual server, select the site server icon in the display and right-click it. Then point to New and point to Site. The screen in Figure 8-7 appears.

This starts the New Web Site Wizard. Enter the name of the new virtual server (see Figure 8-8). This is the name that will show up in Internet Server Manager. This may or may not be the name that you register with DNS.

### FIGURE 8-6

Creating a root folder for a virtual server

**FIGURE 8-7**

Creating a new site as a
virtual server

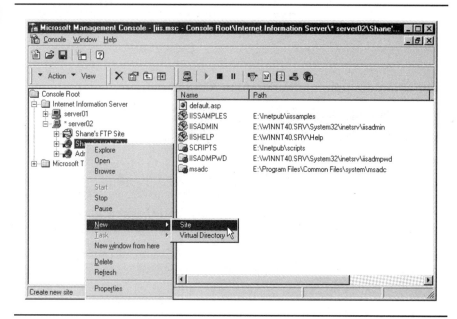

**FIGURE 8-8**

Naming the virtual server

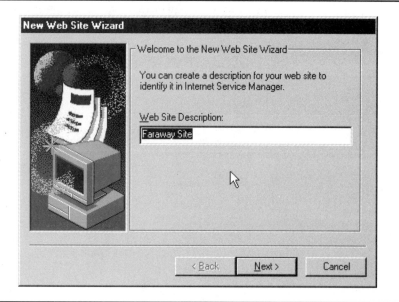

The next screen allows you to choose the IP address and the port number for the new virtual site, as illustrated in Figure 8-9.

On the next screen, you specify the root folder for the virtual server. This is the folder that was created in the prior example using Windows NT Explorer. Each Web server has its own root folder. This allows you to keep the content of one Web server separate and distinct from the contents of other virtual Web servers on the same Internet Information Server. Figure 8-10 contains the dialog box where you name the root folder.

In the previous screen, you set the access permissions. The default is to Allow Read Access and to Allow Script Access. See Figure 8-11 for the details.

**FIGURE 8-9**

Setting the IP address and
port number for the virtual
server

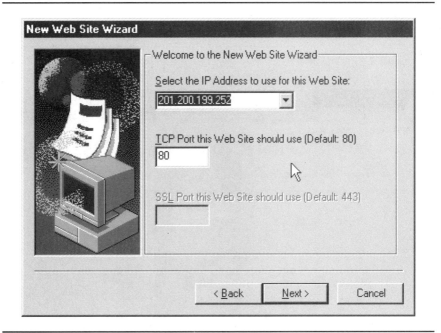

FIGURE 8-10

Specifying the root folder

FIGURE 8-11

Setting access permissions

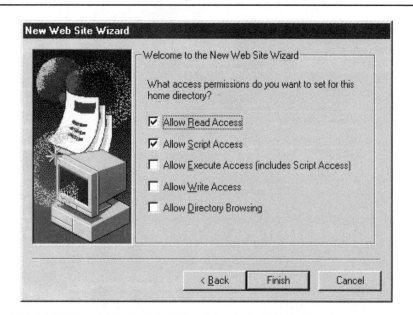

<table>
<tr><td>EXERCISE 8-2</td></tr>
</table>

## Configuring a Virtual Server

Purpose: To set up and configure a virtual server.

*Do this exercise from both computers.*

1. Ensure that you are logged on as Administrator.
2. Start Windows NT Explorer.
3. Create a folder named D:\VirRoot.
4. Copy the contents of C:\Intepub\wwwroot to D:\VirRoot.
5. Start Internet Service Manager.
6. Right-click your computer icon.
7. Click New.
8. Click Web Site. The New Web Site Wizard should start.
9. In the Web Site Description box, enter **Farawayxx Site**.
10. Click Next.
11. In the IP address box, click on your IP address.
12. Ensure that the TCP port value is set to 80.
13. Click Next.
14. In the Enter the path to your home directory box, enter **D:\VirRoot**.
15. Click Next.
16. Ensure that the Allow Read Access and Allow Script Access boxes are checked.
17. Click Finish. The new Web site Faraway*xx* Site should appear in the left pane.

<table>
<tr><td>EXERCISE 8-3</td></tr>
</table>

## Setting the Host Header Information

Purpose: To set the host header information so that the new Web site can be found.

*Do this at both computers.*

1. Right-click the Faraway*xx* Site.
2. Click Properties.
3. Click the Advanced button on the Web Site tab.
4. Select your IP address from the dialog box.

5. Click the Add button.

6. In the IP address drop-down list, select your IP address.

7. In the TCP Port box, enter **80**.

8. In the Host Header Name, enter **Farawayxx**.

9. Click OK.

10. Click OK.

11. Click OK to return to Internet Service Manager.

12. Right-click the Farawayxx Site.

13. Click Start. The stopped indication goes away.

**CERTIFICATION OBJECTIVE 8.05**

# Configuring the DNS for Virtual Servers

After you create a virtual server, you need an entry in a DNS server in order for clients to find the virtual server on the Internet. You do this by creating a *canonical name* (CNAME for short). A canonical name is an alias that refers back to the original server. You associate the name of the virtual server with the physical server name using the canonical name. You may have multiple canonical names associated with any server.

Start the DNS manager utility for your DNS service, then right-click the zone name, as illustrated in Figure 8-12.

By selecting New Record, you can enter the specifics for the CNAME, as illustrated in Figure 8-13.

**EXERCISE 8-4**

### Configuring the DNS for the Virtual Server

Purpose: To configure the DNS to resolve requests for Farawayxx.

*Do this exercise at both computers.*

1. Open a command prompt.

2. Ping Farawayxx.funxx.com.

**FIGURE 8-12**

Selecting the zone

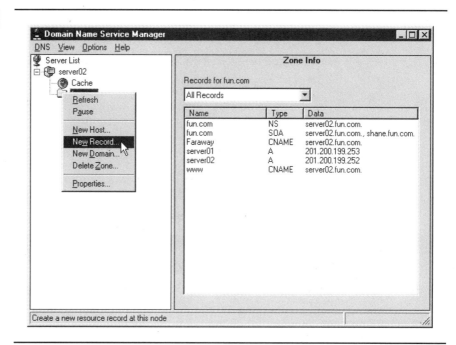

**FIGURE 8-13**

Creating the CNAME

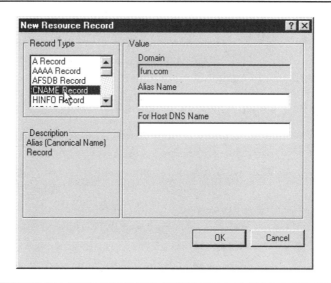

3. You should get a Bad IP address message.

4. Open the DNS Manager.

5. Expand your server by double-clicking on the icon.

6. Right-click Fun*xx*.com.

7. Select New Record.

8. Select CNAME Record from the list.

9. In the Alias Name box enter **Faraway*xx***.

10. In the For Host Name box, enter **Server*xx*.com**.

11. Click OK.

12. Return to the command prompt.

13. Ping Faraway*xx*.fun*xx*.com.

14. You should now get a response from the ping.

15. Close the command prompt.

---

**EXERCISE 8-5**

### Testing the New Virtual Site

Purpose: To verify the work that you have done.

*Do this exercise from both computers.*

1. Open Internet Explorer.

2. In the address box, enter **Faraway*xx*.fun*xx*.com**.

3. Close Internet Explorer.

## Configuring Windows NT for Multiple IP Addresses

You can configure your DNS to support multiple domains by configuring different zones for the DNS. This allows you to have multiple virtual servers with different domain names hosted on the same physical machine. Each virtual server has a different IP address.

You start by adding another IP address to your NIC. This address can be on your current network ID or on another network ID (see Figure 8-14). Pay close attention to the first three octets in the IP address: This number indicates the network ID in a class C network with a natural subnet mask. A natural subnet mask means the network is not divided into subnetworks.

**FIGURE 8-14**

Adding another IP address

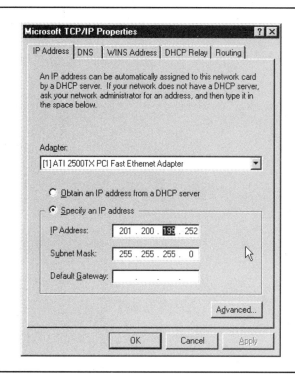

By left-clicking the Advanced button on the IP protocol properties, you can add other IP addresses to the NIC cards. One of the nice features of TCP/IP on Windows NT is that you can have multiple IP addresses assigned to one NIC. This means you do not need multiple network cards installed on the same machine to support multiple IP addresses. Figure 8-15 contains the Advanced IP Addressing dialog box.

Note that a different IP address, which has a different network ID, was assigned to the same network card. When supporting multiple virtual servers, it is not only possible to support multiple domain names, but it is possible to have them on different networks as well.

Microsoft documentation states that you are restricted to a maximum of five IP addresses per NIC, but this is not entirely true. Some Microsoft documentation states that only five IP addresses may be configured via the graphical user interface (GUI) interface; others must be configured via the

**FIGURE 8-15**

Assigning multiple IP
addresses

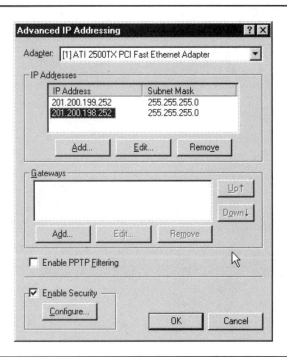

registry. Even this is not entirely accurate. Despite the Microsoft documentation, I have personally configured as many as seven IP addresses via the GUI interface.

You can find these entries in the HKEY_LOCAL_MACHINE under the Services key, [*your NIC*] \parameters\TCP/IP subkey. The addresses are listed in the IPAddress value and the appropriate net mask is located in the same key, SubnetMask value.

Note that these values are a data type known as *multi*. You must use the registry-editing tool Regedt32 to properly add or adjust these values. The registry-editing tool Regedit is the Windows 95 registry editor and is not fully compatible with the Windows NT registry. (This compatibility discussion is outside the scope of this book, so trust me on this one.) You cannot properly add or edit the multi data type using the Regedit tool because of this incompatibility. Windows 95 does not use the multi data type and therefore the editing tool does not support it. Use the Windows NT registry-editing tool Regedt32 for adding or modifying multi data types.

| **EXERCISE 8-6** |

### Configuring Windows NT for Multiple IP Addresses

Purpose: To add another IP address to the NIC.

*Do this exercise from both computers.*

1. Ensure that you are logged on as Administrator.
2. Open the Network applet.
3. Click the Protocols tab.
4. Select TCP/IP.
5. Click Properties.
6. Click the Advanced button.
7. Click the Add the button in the IP Addresses box.
8. In the IP Address box, enter 201.200.198.*xxx*, where *xxx* is the fourth octet of the current IP address for your server. This NIC now has an IP address on two different networks.
9. Click OK.
10. Select the DNS tab.
11. Add the other computer's IP address to your DNS Service Search Order list.
12. Click OK.
13. Click OK to close the Network applet.

## Configuring DNS to Support Virtual Servers Using Different IP Addresses

Once you have another IP address added, you are ready to configure your DNS to support a virtual server using that IP address. This is done using DNS Manager.

Of course, you can't just use any IP address you want. IP addresses need to be carefully coordinated and assigned, just as domain names are registered and assigned. You start the configuration by creating a new zone to support the new domain name. Once you have done this, you create records and CNAMEs just as you did previously. After this, you are ready to create the new virtual server.

### Creating a New Zone

Purpose: To create a new zone and associated records to support a new virtual server in a new Internet domain.

*Do this exercise from both computers.*

1. Open DNS Manager.

2. Right-click your server.

3. Select New Zone.

4. Click Primary.

5. Click Next.

6. Enter **Publishingxx.com** in the Zone Name box, where *xx* is your server number.

7. Press TAB. The zone file default appears and should be the zone name with a .DNS extension. In this case, the wizard enters publishing*xx*.com.dns.

8. Click Next.

9. Click Finish.

10. Right-click Publishing*xx*.com.

11. Select New Host.

12. Enter **Serverxx** in the Host Name box.

13. Press TAB.

14. Enter **201.200.198.xx** in the IP address.

15. Click Add Host.

16. Click Done. This creates a record for Server*xx*.

17. Right-click Publishing*xx*.com.

18. Select New Record.

19. Select CNAME.

20. In the Alias Name box, enter **www**.

21. Press TAB.

22. In the For Host DNS Name box, enter **Serverxx.publishingxx.com**.

23. Click OK. This creates a CNAME record for www.publishingxx.com.

24. Close DNS Manager.

## Creating a Virtual Server for the New Zone

Now that you have set things up from the DNS perspective, you can create the new virtual server. This is similar to the work you did in a previous exercise. In this case, you will use the 198-network IP address instead of the 199 network ID, as illustrated in Figure 8-16.

Configuring the IP address for the new virtual Web site

# FROM THE CLASSROOM

## The Difference Between a Virtual Directory and a Virtual Server

In many classes, the students are very interested in virtual directories and virtual servers and when to use them. In addition, students want to learn about IP addresses and what virtual "thing" gets an IP address and when.

You create a virtual directory when you want to extend the publishing capabilities of a Web server. When you install IIS, root-publishing directories are established. You will put your content in these directories. If the disk becomes full, then using a virtual directory to point to another local disk allows you to extend the reach of the root by using this other disk. Another scenario occurs when you have information that is already stored on another server, for example. Since only the information that is contained in the publishing root folder is available to your WWW or FTP clients, you need to copy the existing information from the other server to the Web server's root structure. This means that there are two copies of the same information in your organization. This could lead to version control problems with the information. When you change the information in one place, you need to change it in the other

place to ensure that the files are consistent in the organization. Or, you need a data replication scheme in process. These schemes can be tedious to manage in their own right. Using the virtual directory, you should point your Web server and clients to the server with the existing information so that you do not need to copy the information to the Web server. This eliminates the version control problems. Virtual directories are managed as part of the physical IIS server.

You do not need an IP address for a virtual directory, even when the virtual directory is on a remote server. Interestingly, the server that contains the remote virtual directory does not need to have the TCP/IP protocol installed. It could be using NetBEUI, for example.

Virtual servers, by contrast, appear as a "physical" server on the Internet or intranet, even though they are not separate physical servers. Virtual servers reside on one physical IIS server. There are several motivations for using virtual servers. One instance is when you do not want your clients to know what physical server they are connecting to or how many

# FROM THE CLASSROOM

physical servers you have in your organization. For example, www.your_co.com and ftp.your_co.com could be the same physical server, even though they have different FQDNs and perhaps even different IP addresses.

Another scenario allows one physical server to host virtual servers for different domains. In the previous scenario, both servers are in the same domain. Virtual servers allow you to host www.this_co.com and www.that_co.com on the

same physical server. Using this technique, you can host Web servers from multiple departments in your organization or from multiple companies on the same physical server.

You can assign multiple virtual servers to the same IP address. You can also assign a unique IP address to each virtual server. When you use unique IP addresses depends upon what you want to accomplish.

---

**EXERCISE 8-8**

## Configuring the New Virtual Server

Purpose: To configure a new virtual server that has its root directory on another server.

*Do this exercise from both computers.*

1. Open Windows NT Explorer.
2. Create a folder named C:\INETPUB\PUBROOT.
3. Share the folder as pubroot.
4. Create two folders in pubroot named Folder1 and Folder2.
5. Close Windows NT Explorer.
6. Open Internet Service Manager.
7. Expand your server by clicking on the plus (+) sign next to the server name.
8. Right-click the Faraway*xx* Site.
9. Click New.

10. Click Site.

11. In the Web Site Description box, enter **Publishing Site**.

12. Click Next.

13. In the IP address box, click on the 201.200.198.*xx* IP address.

14. Ensure that the TCP port is port 80.

15. Click Next.

16. In the Enter the path to your home directory box, enter **\\Serverxx\pubroot**, where **xx** is the *other* computer's number.

17. Click Next.

18. Ensure that the Allow Read Access and Allow Script Access boxes are checked.

19. Click Finish. The new Web site Publishing Site should appear in the left pane.

---

**EXERCISE 8-9**

## Configuring the Properties of the New Site

Purpose: To set the host header information so that the new Web site can be found.

*Do this at both computers.*

1. Right-click the Publishing Site.

2. Click Properties.

3. Click the Advanced button on the Web Site tab.

4. Select the 201.200.198.*xx* IP address from the dialog box.

5. Click the Add button.

6. In the IP address drop-down list, select the 201.200.198.*xx* IP address.

7. In the TCP Port box, enter **80**.

8. In the Host Header Name, enter **Publishing**.

9. Click OK.

10. Click OK.

11. Select the Home Directory tab.

12. Check the Directory Browsing Allowed box.

13. Click OK to return to Internet Service Manager.

14. Right-click the Publishing Site.

15. Click Start. The stopped indication goes away.

16. Close the MMC.

17. Open Internet Explorer.

18. In the Address box, enter **www.publishingxx.com**, where **xx** is the other computer number. You should connect to the other computer's Web site.

19. Close Internet Explorer.

# CERTIFICATION SUMMARY

This chapter covered a number of key concepts, starting with the fact that both the FTP service and WWW service support virtual directories and virtual servers.

Virtual directories allow you to have information outside the root structure and have it appear as though it were in the root structure. Virtual directories must be accessed by a hyperlink if they are virtual directories of a Web server, or by explicitly entering the directory from the FTP prompt.

Virtual directories may be contained on the local disk or on a remote server. Virtual servers may have their root structure on the local computer or on a remote server. Virtual servers may use the same IP address as the IIS server, or they may be assigned another IP address.

Virtual servers are a different concept than virtual directories. Virtual directories expand the capabilities of the local server while virtual servers allow the local server to "impersonate" other Internet servers. You need to configure the DNS for the appropriate entries to support virtual servers. You add the host name for each of the virtual servers to the DNS zone database so that Internet (and intranet) clients can connect to the server using the fully qualified domain name (FQDN). You may also wish to configure the server with a unique IP address for each of the virtual servers. Or, you can use one IP address for all of the virtual servers.

Virtual servers are created and configured through the Internet Service Manager. Properties for each virtual server may be unique to that server.

# ✓ TWO-MINUTE DRILL

❑ Virtual directories reside outside the IIS root.

❑ Virtual directories may be on a local disk.

❑ Virtual directories may be on a remote disk.

❑ You can have multiple virtual directories on a server.

❑ Virtual directories can be created for both the FTP and the WWW services.

❑ When managing the virtual directories, you refer to them by their alias.

❑ You must create a hyperlink to access virtual Web directories.

❑ To access FTP virtual directories, you must know the directory name and use it in the cd command.

❑ You can access the WWW virtual directory by including it in the URL request.

❑ You can assign multiple virtual directories to one IP address.

❑ You use HTTP headers to specify the virtual server name to the IIS server.

❑ Virtual servers need a root structure for their publishing information.

❑ The root structure can be on the local server.

❑ The root structure can be on a remote server.

❑ Virtual servers need an entry in a DNS table.

❑ Microsoft DNS supports multiple zones.

❑ Microsoft DNS supports multiple domains.

❑ You can assign multiple IP addresses to a single NIC.

❑ These IP addresses can be on different networks.

# SELF TEST

The following Self Test questions will help you measure your understanding of the material presented in this chapter. Read all the choices carefully, as there may be more than one correct answer. Choose all correct answers for each question.

1. Which of the following statements is true of virtual directories?

    A. Virtual directories allow you to use directories that are not part of the Internet Information Server root structure.

    B. Virtual directories cannot be on remote servers.

    C. Virtual directories can be on any disk.

    D. Virtual directories are referenced by an alias.

2. Which of the following statements is true of virtual directories on a Web server?

    A. Virtual directories can be on a remote server.

    B. Virtual directories can be accessed by a hyperlink.

    C. Virtual directories can be accessed by specifying the directory in the URL request.

    D. Virtual directories can only be accessed by Internet Explorer.

3. You are building a Web server. Some of the data you want to publish is on another server in your organization. How can you publish this data?

    A. Create a folder in the wwwroot folder and copy the data from the other server.

    B. Create another folder outside the wwwroot folder and copy the data to that folder.

    C. Create a virtual server.

    D. Create a share point on the other server and create a virtual directory that points to the share point using the UNC.

4. How do you create a virtual directory?

    A. Create a share point.

    B. Use Internet Service Manager.

    C. Create a folder for the virtual directory.

    D. Create a URL.

5. Which of the following is not an access permission to a virtual directory?

    A. Allow Read

    B. Allow Write

    C. Allow Take Ownership

    D. Allow Directory Browsing

6. Which of the following statements is true of a virtual server?

    A. A virtual server is another term for the IIS.

    B. A virtual server shows up in the computer browser.

    C. A virtual server needs a unique domain name.

    D. An IIS server can host multiple virtual servers.

7. You are the IIS administrator. Your organization has several divisions. Each organization wants its own presence on the Internet and has registered its own domain name. They want to use your IIS server to host their Web pages. How can you accomplish this?

   A. Create a virtual directory for each division.

   B. You cannot do this.

   C. Create one virtual server for all the divisions.

   D. Create a virtual server for each of the divisions.

8. You have a small ISP and want to host the Web pages for your clients. You do not want to dedicate servers to each client. How can you host each client on the same server when each client has its own domain name and its own IP address assigned to them? Select all correct answers.

   A. You cannot do this.

   B. Create virtual directories for each of your clients.

   C. Create virtual servers for each of the clients.

   D. Assign their IP addresses to the NIC.

9. You want to create virtual servers with their own IP addresses. What do you need to do?

   A. Assign multiple IP addresses to the NIC.

   B. Use multiple network interface cards.

   C. Make entries in the DNS for each virtual server.

   D. Configure a root directory for each virtual server.

10. You have created a virtual server. How do you create a host header for the server?

   A. Select the property sheet.

   B. Select the HTTP Headers tab.

   C. Select the Advanced button on the Web Site tab.

   D. Select the Advanced button on the HTTP Headers tab.

MICROSOFT CERTIFIED SYSTEMS ENGINEER

# 9

# Microsoft Active Server

Web authors have many choices when it comes to publishing content on the World Wide Web (WWW). Microsoft documentation lists publishing methods in degrees from *static* to *active*. Static content does not change, regardless of who the client is. Active content can change either as a result of input from the client or by recognizing who the client is and providing a preconfigured page to that client.

**CERTIFICATION OBJECTIVE 9.01**

# Categories of Web Publishing

The following are categories of content published on the Web:

- Basic linked content
- Dynamic HTML
- Data bound applications
- Interactive applications
- Personalization and transaction processing

## Basic Linked Content

Basic linked content is the most common type of Web content. It is static; all users see the same content. This type of Web page may also contain links to other pages. Using these links is called *navigation*. The links and the format of the page are usually created with Hypertext Markup Language (HTML) tags.

## Dynamic HTML

Microsoft's Internet Explorer (IE) 4.0 supports a feature called Dynamic HTML. Using Dynamic HTML, Web authors can change page elements, styles, and content at any time. This is true even after the client has loaded the page. Dynamic HTML executes on the client's computer rather than on the server.

exam

ⓦatch

*Remember that Dynamic HTML executes at the client's computer and not at the server.*

## Data Bound Applications

Data bound applications are Web applications that access data, usually large amounts of data. Active data objects (ADOs) and Open Database Connectivity (ODBC) are technologies that allow clients the ability to access data from databases. Using ADO and ODBC, the Web author can create interactive and customized Web content.

## Interactive Applications

With a standard Web page using HTML tags, each client receives the same content on the page. With interactive Web technologies like Active Server and Active Client, the Web author can create an environment where the contents of a page change depending on input from the client. Applications such as making an airline flight reservation or ordering products on-line are examples of interactive applications.

## Personalization and Transaction Processing

Microsoft's Personalization Server and Microsoft's Transaction Server (MTS) allow users to personalize and control Web-based applications. The Personalization Server uses the Active Server Pages (ASP) tool to generate a Web page dynamically, based on preferences the client had stored previously.

MTS allows an application to be developed as though it will run on a single computer instead of a network. This approach speeds the development process by simplifying what needs to be done. The program author does not need to account for such issues as security, different users, or network access. MTS takes care of these issues.

The next section describes Active Server Pages (ASP). This tool is not designed to make you a programmer. It is designed to make you familiar with ASP, how the pages are constructed, what their benefits are, and how to manage them using IIS.

**CERTIFICATION OBJECTIVE 9.02**

# Active Server Pages

ASP is a server-side scripting tool. Web authors can use ASP to create powerful Web-based applications. ASPs are dynamic pages that contain HTML tags, text, and script commands. ASPs can call ActiveX components, which are reusable objects that perform functions such as connecting to a database or performing a calculation.

*exam*
*Watch*

***ASPs are executed at the server and not at the client.***

ASP provides support for scripting languages like VBScript (Microsoft Visual Basic Scripting Edition), Microsoft JScript (Java Script) and Practical Extraction and Reporting Language (PERL). ASP files are text files with HTML code that is customized using the scripting language. ASP files are saved with an .asp extension.

VBScript is a subset of Visual Basic. JScript is not a subset of Java.

## What's New in ASP

There are several new features in this version of ASP. They are:

- Microsoft Script Debugger
- Transactional scripts
- Administration
- Isolating ASP applications
- File upload

- New components
- Application root changes
- Support for channels
- Support for HTTP 1.1 protocol

## Microsoft Script Debugger

A *script* is a type of mini-program. You write instructions (code) that are interpreted by the engine. "Things" happen as a result of the instructions that you have written. The more instructions in the script, the greater probability that errors may exist. These script errors are also known as *bugs*. The process of finding and correcting these errors is called *debugging*. Being able to quickly and effectively debug a script is crucial to the successful development of an ASP application.

The Microsoft Script Debugger is a tool designed to help you locate and correct errors in the server-side scripts. You use this tool through Internet Explorer (Version 3.*x* and later). The Script Debugger allows you to:

- Run the script one line at a time.
- Monitor the value of variables.
- Set a pause at a particular line of instructions.
- Trace procedures.
- You can view the script, but you cannot make edits with this tool.

## Transactional Scripts

A *transaction* is an operation that succeeds (or fails) as a whole, but doesn't affect the data or the integrity of the application. For example, you might have an HTML page in which you enter your name and address. When you click the Send button (a button provided by the programmer), the success or failure of that transaction does not affect the whole program or data contained elsewhere (such as in an ODBC database). Should your transaction fail, the program is unaffected. Your data on that page may be lost, but other clients who are connected and entering their data are not affected by your failure.

*If a transactional script fails, the application and the data are unaffected.*

You can also create an ASP script within the transaction so that if a portion of that script fails, the entire transaction is aborted. This type of ASP transaction processing is based on the Microsoft Transaction Server (MTS). IIS supports transactional scripts.

### Administration

Application settings are directly accessible from Internet Service Manager (ISM). Certain properties may be configured for each ASP application on the server. Application properties apply to all pages in the application, unless you override the settings with specific properties on a given page. You configure the application using the property sheet and the Home Directory, Virtual Directory, or Directory tab, as illustrated in Figure 9-1.

---

**FIGURE 9-1**

Setting ASP application properties

Application Configuration

App Mappings | App Options | App Debugging

Application Configuration

☑ Enable session state
    Session timeout: 20   minutes
☐ Enable buffering
☑ Enable parent paths
Default ASP language: VBScript
ASP Script timeout: 90   seconds

OK    Cancel    Apply    Help

---

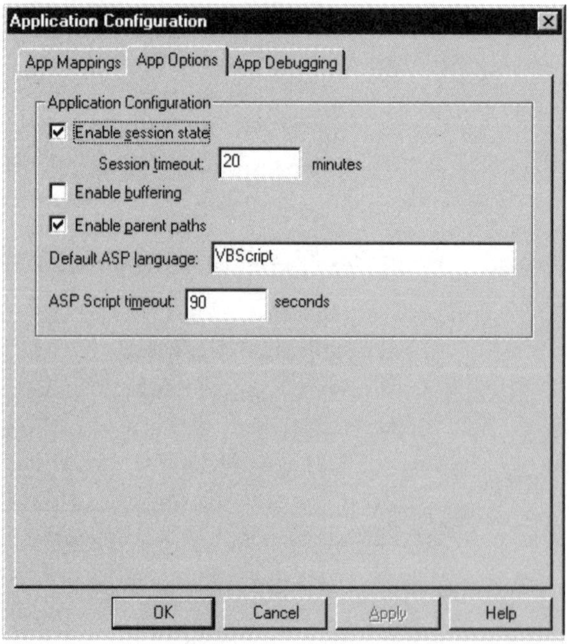

This dialog box contains the following options:

- **Enable session state**   When this box is checked, Active Server Pages creates a session for each user who accesses the application. You identify the user across pages in the application with this session information. Specify the session timeout value so that the session ends if the client has not requested (or refreshed) a page in the application by the timeout value expiration. You can also disable a session, even when the session state is enabled, using the <% @ ENABLESESSIONSTATE = False %> command in the script.

- **Enable buffering**   When you set this option, all of the output generated by the ASP page is buffered and sent to the client's browser at one time. By selecting this option, you can set HTTP headers from anywhere in the ASP script. If the option is unchecked, then the output is sent to the browser as it is generated.

- **Enable parent paths**   Selecting this option allows the ASP script to use relative paths to the parent directory. Use caution if you enable this option; if you give the parent directories Execute access, a script might be able to run an unauthorized program from the parent directory.

- **Default ASP language**   Specify the primary scripting language here. ASP has two active scripting engines: VBScript and JScript. The default value is VBScript.

- **ASP Script timeout**   Set the timeout value for the script to be running. If the script does not finish running by the time value specified here, then the script is stopped and an event is written to the application log in Windows NT. Microsoft documentation states this value may be set from 1 to 2147483647 seconds. Let me save you the time at your calculator: At the maximum value, your script must finish running just outside of 68 years or it will be aborted!

## Isolating ASP Applications

You can run each ASP application in its own memory space. This allows you to protect other applications from the errant behavior of any application. By running applications in their own protected memory space, if one application fails, it does not adversely affect other active ASP applications. Nor does it adversely affect the Web server.

*ASP applications run in their own separate memory space, which protects one application from another.*

## File Upload

Users can, through their browsers, upload files to the Web server. This is accomplished using the Posting Acceptor application. Use an ASP script to send e-mail through the Posting Acceptor with information such as the location and filename of the uploaded file. The file upload component is RFC 1867 compliant.

## New Components

ASP provides the base for ActiveX components. Some of the new components are:

- **Database Access**   This provides you with access to your database from inside the ASP application. You can view tables, run queries, and perform other database operations.

- **Ad Rotator**   You use this object to automatically rotate a new advertisement each time the user opens up the page. This is done based on the information that you specify in the Rotator Schedule File. You can also keep a record of how many users click an advertisement.

- **Content Rotator**   Similar in operation to the ad rotator, the content rotator displays changing content strings. These strings contain HTML tags so you can display any content that HTML can represent such as text, images, or hyperlinks. Use the content rotator to display a quote of the day or other information that you specify in your content schedule.

- **Browser Capabilities**   You can determine what the capabilities of the client's browser are. This is useful for determining what types of pages you want the browser to receive. When a browser connects to the Web server, it sends a header called the *User Agent HTTP header*. This is an ASCII string that identifies the browser and the browser version number. This information is passed to the object called BrowserType. This object compares the header information to the information contained in the browscap.ini file, located in the <winnt_root> \system32\inetsrv folder. Figure 9-2 shows a partial listing of the contents of this file.

- **File Access**   The file access component provides objects that you can use to retrieve and modify files on a computer's file system. Examples of these objects are drive objects, file objects, and folder objects.

- **Content Linking**   Using content linking, it is easy to navigate logically through the .asp files in an application. You specify the organization of the .asp files in a single text file. This is easier than trying to maintain URL references in all of the .asp files.

- **Page Counter**   Use the page counter to display the number of times a Web page is requested. This object writes the number of hits to a text file periodically so that you have a persistent record of the information.

- **Permission Check**   Use the permission check to test a user's right to access a page. You use this component to control if a user can use a hyperlink on a page.

---

**FIGURE 9-2**

Partial listing of the browscap.ini file

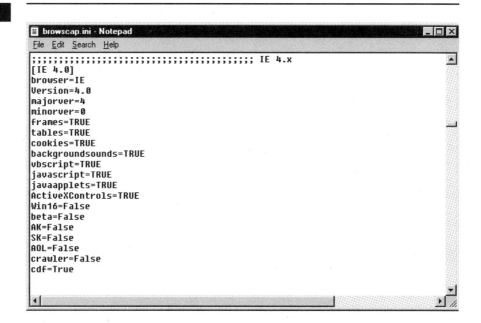

```
browscap.ini - Notepad
File  Edit  Search  Help
;;;;;;;;;;;;;;;;;;;;;;;;;;;;;;;;;;;;;;;; IE 4.x
[IE 4.0]
browser=IE
Version=4.0
majorver=4
minorver=0
frames=TRUE
tables=TRUE
cookies=TRUE
backgroundsounds=TRUE
vbscript=TRUE
javascript=TRUE
javaapplets=TRUE
ActiveXControls=TRUE
Win16=False
beta=False
AK=False
SK=False
AOL=False
crawler=False
cdf=True
```

### Application Root Changes

The root directory of an ASP application can be the physical directory at the Web server. Previously, the root directory had to be a virtual directory. You use Internet Service Manager to indicate the root of an ASP application.

### Support for Channels and Web Casting

The ASP application can generate *channel definition files*. A channel definition file has a .cdf extension. Channels are a feature of Internet Explorer 4.0. They are described in more detail in Chapter 22.

### Support for HTTP 1.1 Protocol

IIS supports HTTP 1.1 protocol. ASP takes advantages of the efficiencies of the new protocol when responding to browsers such as Internet Explorer 4.0.

## State Management

HTTP is a stateless protocol. This means that the Web server does not maintain information about the state of the client. Dynamic applications may have various states. When you create a dynamic Web application, ASP can provide state management for the application.

You can accomplish this by using the application and session objects. The state of these objects can be determined. A separate session object is created for each user of the application. The session object maintains information about each user session.

## ASP Built-in Objects

ASP provides six built-in objects:

- **Server Object**   This object provides access to methods and properties on the server itself.

- **Application Object**   An ASP application includes all the .asp files in a directory. Since the application may be used by more than one user at a time, there are methods for locking and unlocking objects to prevent users from altering an object concurrently.

■ **Session Object**    The session object stores user variables for use as the user jumps from page to page. Session state is only maintained for browsers that support cookies.

■ **Request Object**    A request object retrieves the values the client browser passed to the server during an HTTP request.

■ **Response Object**    The response object sends the output to the client's browser.

■ **ObjectContext Object**    The ObjectContext object is used to either commit or abort a transaction initiated by an ASP script.

## CERTIFICATION OBJECTIVE 9.03

# Creating an Active Server Page

An Active Server Page is a text file with the appropriate tags and saved with a file extension of .asp. ASPs contain HTML tags, text, and script commands. ASPs can call ActiveX components to perform tasks. These tasks can include connecting to a database or performing calculations. With ASP, you can add interactive content to your Web pages. You can also build entire ASP applications that use HTML pages as the interface to your customer.

An ASP application must have all related ASP files in one folder.

## Script Tags

An ASP page is a script page that uses script tags. Text is enclosed between the tags. The tags tell the script engine that the text is to be interpreted and not displayed. All HTML documents use tags as well.

Scripting may be done at the client and the server. Client scripting is different than server scripting and is not an Active Server Page. Client scripting depends on the browser for implementation.

Angle brackets (<>) are used to indicate a tag. Tags are used in pairs. One of the pair tags indicates the start of the function. The other tag in the pair indicates the stop of the function. The end tag uses a slash (/) placed just after the angle bracket.

For example, to declare that a document is an HTML document, use the HTML tag. You position the tag

```
<HTML>
```

at the beginning of the section to contain the HTML text. At the end of the HTML text, you add the end tag

```
</HTML>
```

Everything between these tags is displayed as text on the screen (assuming no other tags) except "HTML" because it is between the angle brackets. Figure 9-3 contains an example that uses HTML tags.

You also have to declare that the HTML document is an ASP document and what scripting language you want to use. You do that with a tag such as:

```
<%@ LANGUAGE = "VBScript"%>
```

**FIGURE 9-3**

Sample use of HTML tags

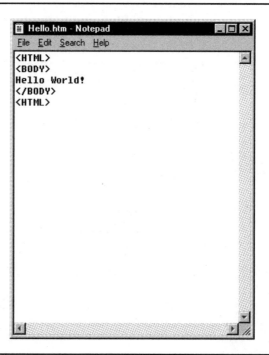

```
<HTML>
<BODY>
Hello World!
</BODY>
<HTML>
```

### Creating an HTML Page

Purpose: To create a simple HTML document in preparation to make it be an ASP document.

*Do this exercise at both computers.*

1. Ensure that you are logged on as administrator.
2. Open Notepad.
3. Enter the following lines of code (refer back to Figure 9-3):

```
<HTML>
<BODY>
Hello World!
</BODY>
<HTML>
```

4. Click File.
5. Click Save As.
6. Locate the Inetpub\wwwroot folder.
7. Name the file Hello.htm.
8. Open Internet Explorer.
9. In the Address box, type **localhost/hello.htm**.
10. You should see "Hello World!" in the browser.
11. Switch back to Notepad.
12. At the end of the line containing "Hello World!" enter the following tag:

```
<BR>
```

13. Press the ENTER key to create a new line.
14. Type the following line:

```
<H3>Hello World!</H3><BR>
```

15. Press the ENTER key to create a new line.
16. As illustrated in Figure 9-4, type the following line:

```
<H2>Hello World!</H2><BR>
```

17. Click File.
18. Click Save.
19. Switch back to the browser.

**FIGURE 9-4**

Hello.htm file with multiple
"Hello World!" lines

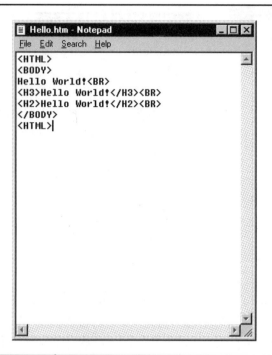

```
Hello.htm - Notepad
File  Edit  Search  Help
<HTML>
<BODY>
Hello World!<BR>
<H3>Hello World!</H3><BR>
<H2>Hello World!</H2><BR>
</BODY>
<HTML>
```

20. Click the Refresh button.

21. You should observe the text "Hello World!" three times displayed in increasing font size. The <H#> tag specifies a header font size. The <BR> tag creates a line break.

**EXERCISE 9-2**

## Creating an ASP Page

Purpose: To create an ASP page to perform an action similar to action performed by the .htm page you just created.

*Do this exercise at both computers.*

1. Open another instance of Notepad.

2. As illustrated in Figure 9-5, enter the following lines of code:

```
<%@ LANGUAGE = "VBScript"%>
<HTML>
<BODY>
<% For i = 3 To 7 %>
```

```
<FONT SIZE=<% = i %>>
Hello World!<BR>
</FONT>
<% NEXT %>
</BODY>
</HTML>
```

3. Click File.

4. Click Save As.

5. Locate the Inetpub\wwwroot folder.

6. Name the file Hello.asp.

7. Switch to the browser.

8. Click an insertion point at the end of the line in the Address box.

9. Change the .htm extension to .asp.

10. Press ENTER.

11. You should see the ASP script execute and see five lines of "Hello World!" in increasing font size.

---

**FIGURE 9-5**

Code listing for ASP file

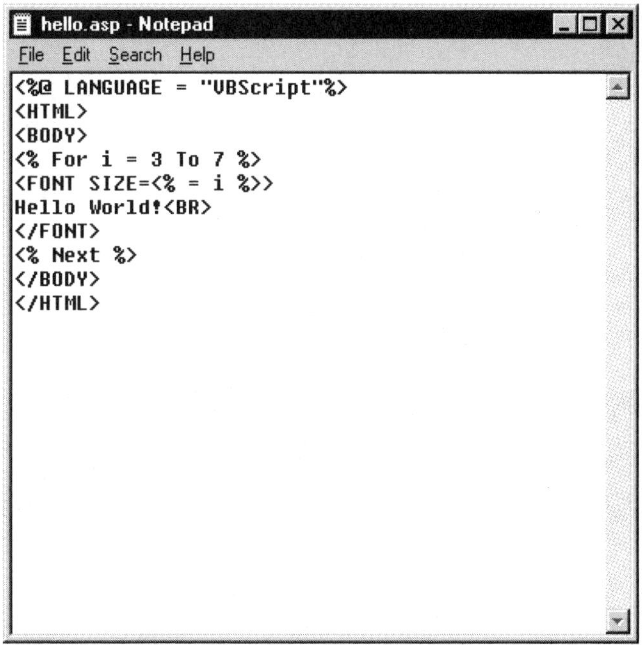

```
<%@ LANGUAGE = "VBScript"%>
<HTML>
<BODY>
<% For i = 3 To 7 %>
<FONT SIZE=<% = i %>>
Hello World!<BR>
</FONT>
<% Next %>
</BODY>
</HTML>
```

## FROM THE CLASSROOM

### Out of Their Element

Several students in one of the IIS classes had done quite well during the first part of the course. A few students had significant experience with Windows NT Server. Setting up IIS and configuring the Web server and the FTP server to take advantage of the integrated Windows NT Server security features was just a "walk in the park" for them. Life was good, the sun was shining, and these students had a certain bearing in class. One may call it cocky.

On the other side of the classroom were some students hunched over the Windows NT computers. What is this IUSR account? How do you get to User Manager? What is a SID again? And oh man, setting NTFS permission, what an ordeal! All before we had discussed integrated Windows NT domain security. These students did not have a background in Windows NT Server. They had never installed a server before, much less designed a domain

model and security policy for their organizations. They were programmers who had come to class to learn about administering IIS. Their skills were in Java, Visual Basic, and other programming languages.

Then we came to the chapter on Active Server Pages. The attitudes and body language changed. The students who had Windows NT administrative experience had no programming background. They were lost. Meanwhile on the other side of the room, you couldn't hold back the enthusiasm now found among the programmers. Finally, something they could relate to in their frame of reference. They were all smiles as they experimented with ASP pages and coding different elements.

The moral of this story is that Windows NT Server and IIS have something for everyone and something new that everyone can learn.

**CERTIFICATION OBJECTIVE 9.04**

# ODBC Connections

Microsoft Data Access Components (MDAC) provides easy-to-use, programming access to all types of data. Data-driven client/server applications deployed over the Web or a LAN use MDAC to easily integrate information from a variety of sources, both relational (SQL) and nonrelational.

MDAC includes Open Database Connectivity (ODBC) and the Microsoft OLE DB Provider for ODBC. These components provide access to SQL Server, Access, and Oracle when used in conjunction with an appropriate ODBC driver.

The Microsoft ODBC 3.5 Driver Manager is a library that manages communication between applications and ODBC drivers. The Driver Manager is a dynamic link library (DLL). The Driver Manager exists mainly as a convenience to application writers and solves a number of problems common to all applications.

## ODBC Driver for SQL Server

The SQL Server ODBC driver provides a native interface used by ODBC-based applications to access SQL Server databases. The driver provides optimal application performance by using native SQL Server network protocols and by taking advantage of all available SQL Server features.

## ODBC Driver for Access

The ODBC driver for Microsoft Access databases allows applications to create and modify data in an Access database. This driver may be used with OLE DB enabled applications, remote data objects (RDOs), and ADOs.

## Microsoft's Oracle ODBC Driver 2.0

The Oracle ODBC driver allows you to connect your ODBC-compliant application to an Oracle database. This version adds additional performance and control features, including access to PL/SQL packages, XA/DTC integration, and Oracle access from within Internet Information Server (IIS).

## Configuring ODBC Connection

You need to configure a data source name (DSN). A DSN is the name that the application uses to request a connection to an ODBC data source. It specifies the computer name and the database name to where the DSN maps.

A DSN for the Web server must be a system DSN. A system DSN is available to any process using the computer.

You start by configuring the DSN in the Control Panel using the ODBC applet (see Figure 9-6). Using the System DSN tab, click the Add button and select the appropriate ODBC driver, as illustrated in Figure 9-7.

Now specify the name and location of the database, as illustrated in Figure 9-8.

In the next step, you configure the login information in the dialog box shown in Figure 9-9.

Finishing this dialog box returns you to the system. You are now ready to go with a DSN.

---

**FIGURE 9-6**

ODBC applet

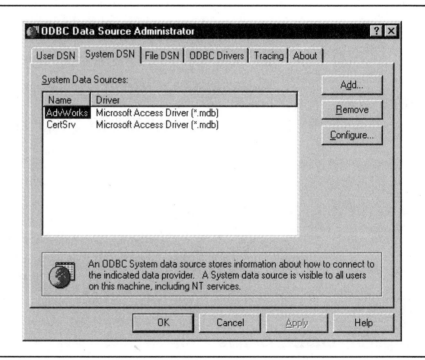

**FIGURE 9-7**

Selecting a driver

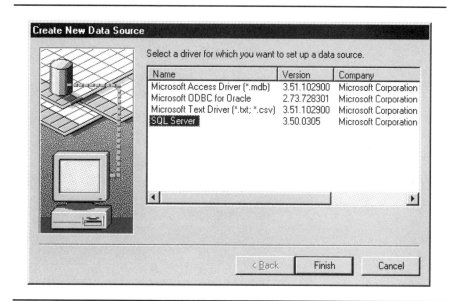

**FIGURE 9-8**

Specifying the parameters

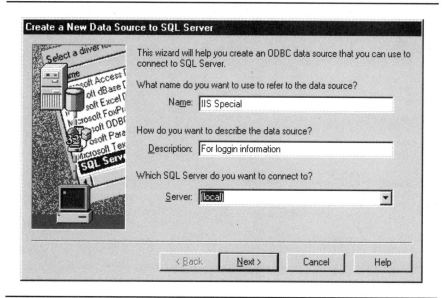

FIGURE 9-9

Setting login credentials

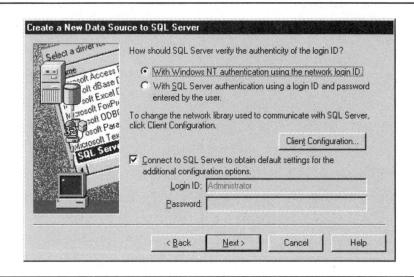

## QUESTIONS AND ANSWERS

| | |
|---|---|
| Do I need to know how to write ASP pages to use my IIS server? | No. ASP pages make it easier to do certain things with your Web pages. You can use ASP to make the pages interactive or to get information from a database, for example. |
| Is ASP a replacement for HTML? | No, ASP supplements HTML tags. You can still use HTML tags in your Web pages. |
| I have installed SQL Server. What else do I need to do so that I can use it with IIS? | You want to do several things: configure a data source name with the ODBC applet, build your database tables, and structure and build the front end to access the database, like ASP pages, query forms, etc. |

# CERTIFICATION SUMMARY

This chapter covered the types of Web publishing supported by IIS. There are new features in Active Server Pages that make it a more complete and powerful tool for sending content information to the browser clients. Included in the new tools is a script debugger, the ability to upload files to the Web server, and many new ActiveX controls.

The built-in ASP objects were discussed as well as script tags. The chapter also discussed the ODBC connections available to IIS. ODBC databases are relevant here because you can create ASP pages that contain information that is held in the databases.

ASP is an important technology within IIS. Understanding ASP is important in managing your IIS server and in passing the certification test.

 # TWO-MINUTE DRILL

❑ Static Web content stays the same regardless of who is accessing it.

❑ Active Web content can change when accessed by different clients.

❑ The evolution of Web content has migrated from basic linked content which is static to more dynamic and customizable content.

❑ Dynamic HTML is executed on the client's computer rather than on the server.

❑ ADO and ODBC allow access to information kept in databases.

❑ MTS allows applications to be developed quickly on the Web server.

❑ Active Server Pages is a server-side scripting tool.

❑ ASP allows for VBScript and JScript languages for scripting the ASP pages.

❑ ASP pages are text files with the appropriate tags.

❑ ASP files have an .asp extension.

❑ VBScript is a subset of Visual Basic.

❑   JScript is not a subset of Java.

❑   ASP supports file uploads to the Web server.

❑   Script Debugger is new.

❑   There are new ActiveX controls.

❑   ASP supports transaction-based scripts.

❑   Transaction scripts run within themselves. If the transaction fails, it does not affect the whole program.

❑   Each ASP application runs in its own memory space.

❑   If one ASP application fails, it does not affect other ASP applications.

❑   The ad rotator displays a different advertisement each time the client connects.

❑   The ad rotation is done based on the rotator schedule file.

❑   The content rotator is similar to the ad rotator except that it displays content strings.

❑   The page counter control tells you how many users have accessed a page.

❑   HTTP 1.1 protocol is supported by ASP.

❑   HTTP is a stateless protocol.

❑   ASP can provide state management.

❑   ASP has six built-in objects.

❑   ASP uses tags.

❑   Tags tell the script engine not to display the text within the tags.

# SELF TEST

The following Self Test questions will help you measure your understanding of the material presented in this chapter. Read all the choices carefully, as there may be more than one correct answer. Choose all correct answers for each question.

1. Which of the following are not publishing methods?

   A. Basic linked content

   B. Dynamic HTML

   C. ODBC

   D. Interactive applications

2. Which of the following statements are true?

   A. Dynamic HTML is a server-side script.

   B. ASPs are executed at the server.

   C. ASPs can contain no HTML tags.

   D. ASPs are static pages.

3. Which of the following scripting languages does ASP support?

   A. Visual C

   B. VBScript

   C. JScript

   D. PERL

4. Which of the following statements are true about the Script Debugger?

   A. You run the Script Debugger at the server.

   B. You must start the Script Debugger tool using the Services applet in the Control Panel.

   C. You use the Script Debugger through the browser.

   D. You can edit the script with the Script Debugger.

5. Which of the following statements are true about transaction scripts?

   A. A transaction script and an ASP program are the same thing.

   B. The failure of a transaction should not affect the whole program.

   C. You can create an ASP script within the transaction.

   D. A transaction may be viewed as an operation that succeeds or fails as a whole.

6. Which of the following statements are true of ASP applications?

   A. An ASP application includes all of the .asp files in a directory.

   B. An ASP application runs in its own memory space.

   C. ASP applications run in the same memory space.

   D. You can script an ASP application.

7. Which of the following statements are not true?

   A. The ad rotator is an ActiveX component.

   B. The ad rotator displays various content strings each time a user accesses a page.

C. You can determine what the browser capabilities are.

D. The content rotator uses the rotator schedule file.

8. Which of the following statements are true?

A. Tags are enclosed in angle brackets.

B. Text to be displayed must be enclosed in quotation marks.

C. You may declare what scripting language you want to use.

D. ActiveX components are reusable objects.

MICROSOFT CERTIFIED SYSTEMS ENGINEER

# 10

# Index Server

## CERTIFICATION OBJECTIVES

T his chapter describes Microsoft Index Server 2.0. Index Server is part of the Windows NT 4.0 Option Pack. The function of Microsoft Index Server creates a list of documents on your Web server and indexes the contents of those documents. This allows users of your server to search for the information they need quickly and efficiently.

**CERTIFICATION OBJECTIVE 10.01**

# Overview

Microsoft Index Server indexes the contents of an Internet Information Server Web site. The contents may be on an intranet or the Internet. The contents may be on the local IIS server or on a remote server.

After the server is indexed you create a query form. This query form is an HTML document and contains fields. Clients connect to the Web server, fill out the fields in the query form, and send the form to the Web server. The Web server forwards the information contained in the fields (the information filled in by the clients) to the query engine.

The query engine takes the information, looks through the indexed documents, and finds the matching information. It then formats the result in an HTML-formatted Web page and returns the page to the client.

Index Server can be used to index the contents of multiple Web servers or file servers, including Novell and UNIX servers. The file system of the server is unimportant; it can be FAT or NTFS. You support multiple servers by creating share points on the servers where the documents reside. You then create a virtual directory to the remote server.

## Supported File Formats

Index Server indexes the contents of HTML (.htm) files directly. In addition, Index Server indexes the contents and properties of documents formatted in formats other than HTML. This saves the administrator the time of converting other documents to HTML format.

Index Server can index the following file formats directly:

- Text files
- Word 95
- Word 97
- Excel 95
- Excel 97
- PowerPoint 95
- PowerPoint 97
- The properties of binary files

You can install content filters provided by other independent software vendors (ISVs). The ISV writes a content filter that reads the proprietary format of that vendor's software. When Index Server creates its index, the content filter supplies the words in a text format and then Index Server creates the appropriate indexes for the documents.

## Network News Transfer Protocol

Index Server can index the contents of Network News Transfer Protocol (NNTP) messages. NNTP is defined by RFC 975. NNTP allows users to post articles and have others read those articles. Readers can respond to posted articles or post articles of their own for others to read. NNTP is described in more detail in Chapter 1.

exam
Ⓦatch     *Index Server can index the contents of NNTP.*

## Language Support

One of the most useful features of Index Server is that it can index multilingual documents. Index Server switches back and forth between the languages as required without user intervention. One document may contain English, German, and Spanish in the same document and Index Server can index the document without a problem. Index Server stores its index information as Unicode characters. When a client executes a query, the query is converted to Unicode before Index Server executes the query.

Index Server supports the following languages:

- Chinese, Traditional and Simplified
- Dutch
- French
- German
- Italian
- Japanese
- Spanish
- Swedish
- U.K. English
- U.S. English

## Index Maintenance

Another useful feature of Index Server is *automatic indexing*. Once Index Server is installed and started, it takes care of itself. Once you create the index, the system is ready to go. When you make changes to the content, Index Server "sees" those changes and automatically indexes the changes and incorporates them into the searchable index. This happens whether the changes are modifications to existing documents, new documents, or existing documents being deleted. The benefit of this feature is that very little time is required on the part of the administrator to keep the searchable index up to date.

exam
ⓦatch

*Index maintenance is fully automatic. When content is changed, added, or deleted, the index is updated automatically.*

**CERTIFICATION OBJECTIVE 10.02**

# Installing Index Server

You can install Index Server during the installation of Internet Information Server. You can also install Internet Information Server without installing

Index Server; there is no requirement to install Index Server with Internet Information Server.

You can install Index Server after you have installed IIS using the Windows NT 4.0 Option Pack setup program, as illustrated in Figure 10-1.

## Index Server Requirements

The minimum hardware and software requirements to support Index Server are:

- Windows NT Server 4.0

- Internet Information Server 4.0

- 3 to 12MB of disk space, depending on which language options you install. This disk space is higher than that required for Windows NT Server and IIS but it does not include disk space for the catalog.

**FIGURE 10-1**

Installing Index Server

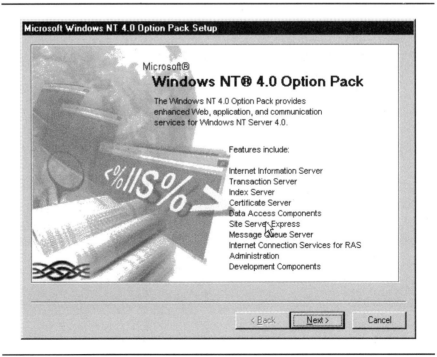

- Sufficient disk space for the catalog file. This space could be as much as 40 percent of the space used by the corpus. (The *corpus* is defined as all of the documents stored that are indexed. See the next section for more details.)

Consider using the NFTS file system for the Index Server data. This will improve the security and protection of the data.

The amount of RAM that you want depends on the following factors:

- The size of the corpus
- Number of documents to be indexed
- Number of simultaneous queries

Table 10-1 summarizes the memory requirements for Index Server.

Another factor that affects the speed of the query is the nature of the query. A more complex query runs faster on a server with a faster CPU.

Microsoft documentation suggests that a 486/DX4-100 with 32MB of RAM may do well as an Index Server platform if there are not too many concurrent queries. Practical experience suggests that any 486 computer does not make a very robust Windows NT platform.

The setup program does several things during installation. First, it copies:

- Program files
- Administration files
- Documentation files
- Sample HTML files

**TABLE 10-1**     Memory Requirements for Indexing Documents

| Number of Documents | Minimum Memory (MB) | Recommended Memory (MB) |
|---|---|---|
| Less than 10,000 | 32 | 32 |
| Less than 100,000 | 32 | 32 |
| Up to 250,000 | 32 | 64–128 |
| Up to 500,000 | 64 | 128–256 |
| Greater than 500,000 | 128 | 256 and up |

The Setup program also creates a default catalog file in the folder specified during the Setup Wizard (see Figure 10-5 later in this section). This file is named catalog.wci. This file is used to store the index and property cache. You need to plan for enough disk space for this file. If you have 1GB of documents to be included in the index, the catalog file could be as large as 400MB. That is a substantial amount of disk space. It is possible for this file to be as large as 40 percent of the size of the corpus.

exam
ⓦatch

*Know that the space required for the catalog can be as much as 40 percent of the size of the corpus.*

If you are installing Index Server after installing Internet Information Server, from the second screen of the Installation Wizard, select the Add/Remove program button, as illustrated in Figure 10-2.

**FIGURE 10-2**

Selecting the Add/Remove button

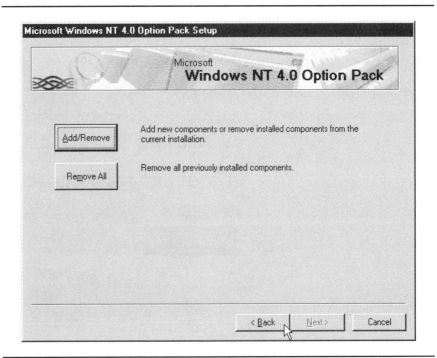

Microsoft Windows NT 4.0 Option Pack Setup

Microsoft
**Windows NT 4.0 Option Pack**

Add/Remove — Add new components or remove installed components from the current installation.

Remove All — Remove all previously installed components.

< Back    Next >    Cancel

You can see which subcomponents can be installed with Index Server by selecting Index Server and clicking on the Show Subcomponents button (see Figure 10-3).

There are four individual components that may be installed, as listed in Figure 10-4. They are:

- Index Server System Files

- Language Resources

- Online Documentation

- Sample Files

The next step is to specify the location of the folder to contain the default catalog file (see Figure 10-5). Remember, you want to have enough space available for this file. It can be as large as 40 percent of the corpus.

**FIGURE 10-3**

Selecting Index Server for installation

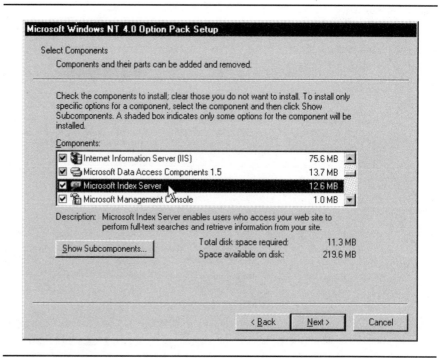

**FIGURE 10-4**

Selecting individual components of Index Server for installation

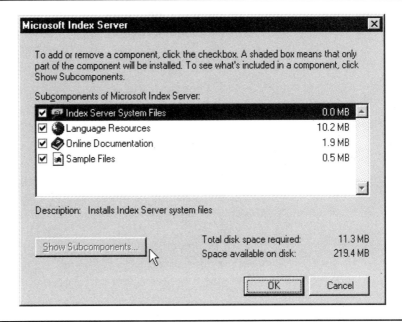

**FIGURE 10-5**

Specifying where to create the catalog

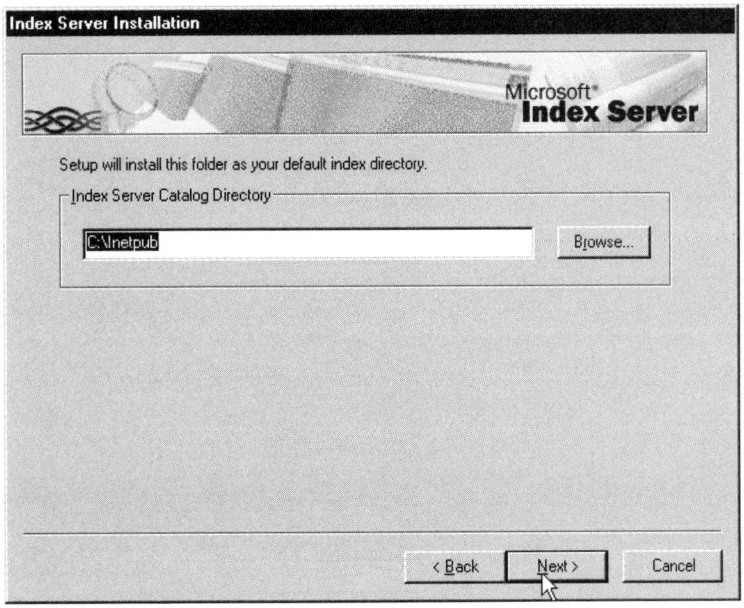

At this point, the Installation Wizard installs the files. All that is left is to click the Finish button (see Figure 10-6).

The installation process for Index Server installs the Content Index service. You can view the status of this service through the Control Panel, Service applet, as Figure 10-7 illustrates.

The Content Index service is started after installation. Its startup mode is set to Automatic. At this point, the Content Index service begins to index all of the documents on the Internet Information Server, including virtual directories on local drives and virtual directories on remote servers.

The Content Index service continues to index new documents placed into the publishing folders on the Web server, including new documents placed into virtual directories.

exam
ⓦatch

**The Content Index service is responsible for indexing.**

---

Finishing the Installation
Wizard

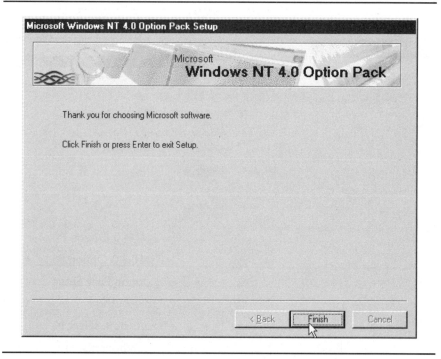

FIGURE 10-7

Content Index service

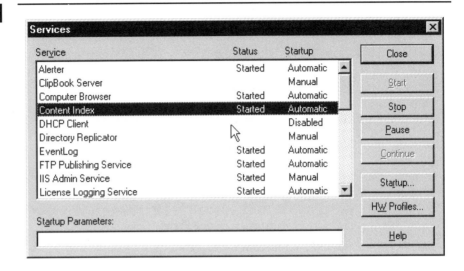

If you create new virtual directories, both locally or on a remote server, and place new documents into these new virtual directories, these new documents will also be indexed automatically. In addition, the Content Index service indexes documents even if the World Wide Web (WWW) service is stopped.

EXERCISE 10-1

## Installing Index Server

Purpose: To install Index Server after IIS has been installed.

*Do this exercise at both computers.*

1. Ensure that you are logged on as Administrator.
2. Click Start.
3. Point to Programs.
4. Point to Windows NT 4.0 Option Pack.
5. Click on Windows NT 4.0 Option Pack Setup.
6. Click Next on the Option Pack Setup screen.
7. Click the Add/Remove button.
8. From the Components box, select Microsoft Index Server.
9. Click the Show Subcomponents button.

10. Ensure that all of the components are selected.

11. Click OK to return to the Select Components dialog box.

12. Click Next.

13. Click Next to accept the default location for the catalog files.

14. Click Finish after the files are installed.

15. Open the Control Panel.

16. Start the Services applet.

17. Make sure that the Content Index service is started and that the startup mode is automatic.

18. Close the Service applet.

19. Close Control Panel.

---

**EXERCISE 10-2**

## Exploring Index Server Manager

Purpose: To introduce you to the Index Server Manager.

*Do this exercise at both computers.*

1. Ensure you are logged on as Administrator.

2. Point to Start.

3. Point to Programs.

4. Point to Windows NT 4.0 Option Pack.

5. Point to Index Server.

6. Click on Index Server Manager.

7. What is the name of the .msc file that was opened? (Hint: Look in the title bar.)

8. Left-click the plus sign ("+") to expand Index Server on Local Machine.

9. Left-click the plus sign ("+") to expand Web site.

10. What is the location of the catalog?

11. How many documents are in the catalog?

12. Close the MMC.

*Answers to steps in this exercise.*

7. ciadmin.msc.

10. c:\Inetpub.

11. 4134. Your count may vary depending on how many components are installed and how many help files are installed. Do not be concerned if your number does not match this number.

## CERTIFICATION OBJECTIVE 10.03

# Indexing

Indexing is the process of taking documents and keeping track of the words in those documents in such a way that users can ask what is contained in those documents. The user asks this question by completing a query form and submitting it to the Index Server. The Index Server processes the query by looking at the "key" words the user is interested in and finding which documents contain those words. Index Server knows which documents contain those words because the server indexed the documents. It is the indexing of the documents that makes the query fast.

There are some definitions that are important:

- Corpus
- Scope
- Content Filters
- Word Breakers
- Normalizer
- Indexes
- Catalog
- CiDaemon

## Corpus

A *corpus* is the collection of all documents that are stored on an IIS site. The corpus is the *body* of all documents. The corpus may be located on local disks or on remote servers defined as either virtual directories or virtual servers. Remember that one Index Server can index documents for more than one IIS server.

## Scope

A *scope* is defined by those documents from the corpus that are indexed. The administrator defines the scope by stating which directories should be indexed. You do not need to index all documents in the corpus. The documents in the scope create the catalog.

## Content Filters

A *content filter* is a small program that recognizes the proprietary format of a document. For example, Microsoft Word and Microsoft Excel have different file formats. WordPerfect has a different file format than either Word or Excel. The content filter understands how to read the information stored in the format of the file. Each separate file format has its own content filter. Index Server uses these content filters to index the files. Content filters perform the following functions:

- Extract text
- Recognize multiple languages within the same document
- Handle embedded objects

When an embedded object is encountered, the correct content filter for that object is called to index that object. For example, if a Word document that contains an Excel spreadsheet is being indexed, the content filter for the Excel data is called; Index Server indexes the text contained in the Word document and the text contained in the embedded Excel document.

Independent software vendors supply content filters for their proprietary file formats for Index Server to use. This means that Index Server is extendable and able to accommodate new file formats. The ISV simply needs to include a content filter for the file format.

exam
**W**atch

*Content filters are file format specific.*

## Word Breakers

Documents are "fed" to their respective content filters. The content filters, in turn, send out a stream of characters. Index Server indexes words, not characters, so there must be a mechanism to tell Index Server what group of characters constitutes a word. In addition, different languages view words and breaks between words differently.

Index Server includes *word breakers.* These are language-specific devices that understand how a particular language views words. Word breakers know a language's syntax and structure.

The function of the word breaker is to take in the character stream from the content filter and break the characters into words and output these words to the normalizer.

## Normalizer

The function of a *normalizer* is to take the words produced by the word breaker and clean them up. The normalizer corrects the words for such things as:

- Capitalization
- Punctuation
- Extraneous word removal

Some languages contain extraneous words that add no meaning to the word or the sentence, for example, words like "the," "of," "a," and "it." Microsoft refers to these words as *noise words.* Indexing these types of words adds no value to the index and Index Server does not store information about such words in the content index.

One of the benefits to removing noise words is they may constitute a substantial part of the written text and removing them can substantially reduce the size of the index. This makes the storage space requirement less.

You can customize the noise word list to accommodate specific language usage such as slang words.

Once words are normalized, they are put into their content index.

**exam**
**ⓦatch**

*Know what noise words are and how they are removed.*

## Indexes

There are two types of indexes. They are:

- Word lists
- Persistent indexes

There are two types of persistent indexes:

- Shadow indexes
- Master indexes

**exam**
**ⓦatch**

*Know what the index types are.*

When words are first indexed from a document, they are put into a *word list*. A word list is a small index contained in memory. Creating a word list is fast and does not require that any data be written to disk. A word list is a temporary holding place during the indexing process.

You can control the behavior of word lists by editing the registry. The word list parameters are contained under:

```
HKEY_LOCAL_MACHINE
    \SYSTEM
        \CurrentControlSet
            \Control
                \ContentIndex
```

The parameters are:

- MaxWordLists
- MaxWordlistSize

- MinSizeMergeWordlists
- MinWordlistMemory

## Shadow Indexes

The default value for MaxWordLists is 20. This is the maximum number of word lists that can exist at any one time. Once the number of word lists exceeds this value, then the word lists are merged. This process is called a *shadow merge*. The outcome of a shadow merge is the creation of a *shadow index*.

A shadow index is one of the persistent indexes. There may be multiple shadow indexes in a catalog. A shadow index is written to disk.

## Master Indexes

The *master index* is a persistent index, which means that it is written to disk. The master index data is in a highly compressed format. Under ideal conditions, the master index is the only persistent index that exists in the catalog; there would be no shadow indexes and no word lists.

A master index is created by a process called the *master merge*. During a master merge, the source indexes for any existing shadow indexes are combined with the master index. After the master merge is completed, only the master index remains.

Depending upon the size of the source indexes, running a master merge may take a long time and is a resource-intensive operation. A master merge uses CPU, memory, and disk space resources while it is running. After the master merge is complete, these resources are freed. The server and queries run faster if there is only a master index (no shadow indexes or word lists).

A master merge is fully restartable. If it is interrupted, it automatically restarts where it left off.

A master merge can be done several ways:

- A nightly master merge can be set up by changing the value in the registry parameter MasterMergeTime. This value indicates the number of minutes after midnight for the master merge to occur.

- When the value contained in the MaxFreshCount is exceeded, a master merge occurred. This count is the number of documents that have changed since the last master merge.

- When disk space is low. When the disk space on the catalog drive is less than the value specified in MinDiskFreeForceMerge and the cumulative space used by shadow indexes is greater than the value contained in MaxShadowFreeForceMerge parameter, a master merge is started. By combining the shadow indexes, space is freed on the disk.

- When the total disk space used by all shadow indexes exceeds the value contained in the parameter MaxShadowIndexSize, a master merge starts. This condition has a higher precedence than the previous condition.

- The administrator can force a master merge.

### Forcing a Merge

You can force a merge from Index Server Manager. You start by selecting the catalog that you wish to merge, and then select Merge from the Action menu, as illustrated in Figure 10-8.

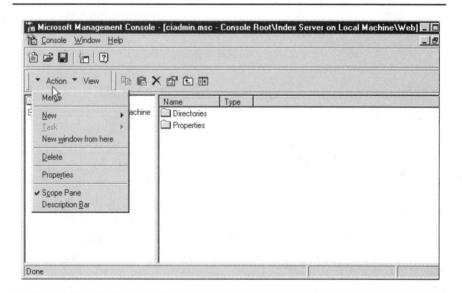

After that, click Yes to begin the merge, as shown in the following illustration:

## To Merge or Not to Merge, That Is the Question

We receive the most questions during the class about the indexes and the index processing and what happens during the merge. It is important to understand how the indexes are created and what is happening and when.

When you index documents, the content index engine accesses the document and takes it apart. It uses the content filter to do this. This simply outputs a stream of characters. All of the document formatting is stripped away. The content filter sends this to the word breaker. The job of the word breaker is to take this stream of characters and assemble them into words. This, of course, leads some students to wonder why the index engine would take a Word document which is full of words and make them non-words just to feed them to another process which makes words out of them again. Some students find this scenario pretty funny.

The next issue that confuses students is what the actual indexes are and when they are created. When you make modifications to the scope, by adding a new document for example, the words derived from this document are put into a word list. Word lists reside in memory. At some point, the word list is written to the disk in what is called the shadow index. A shadow index is called a persistent index because it is written to the disk.

The next step is to combine the shadow indexes into the master index. At least once a day, at midnight by default, the master merge occurs automatically and the shadow indexes are merged into the master index. There are some other things that can trigger the master merge, including the administrator forcing the merge to happen.

It takes students a while to become accustomed to the way this works, but they generally find it worth their while to work through the process, especially if they are going to use the product extensively and take the certification test.

## Catalog

A catalog is a completely self-contained entity. It has an index and cached properties for the scope. It is at the top of the hierarchical structure. An Index Server may contain more than one catalog. However, a query may not span multiple catalogs.

exam

ⓦatch

*Remember that queries may not span multiple catalogs.*

## The CiDaemon Process

The Index Server gives a list of documents to the *CiDaemon process*. The Index Server engine spawns the CiDaemon process. This process is responsible for identifying the document format and selecting the proper content filters and word breakers.

Filtering is done in the background. If another process needs a document opened by CiDaemon, CiDaemon closes the document as soon as possible so the other process can access the document. It automatically retrieves the document for filtering at a later time. This feature is only available on local disks. It is not available for remote content.

---

**EXERCISE 10-3**

### Combining an Index

Purpose: To combine indexes by forcing a merge to happen.

*Do this exercise at both computers.*

1. Ensure you are logged on as Administrator.

2. Point to Start.

3. Point to Programs.

4. Point to Windows NT 4.0 Option Pack.

5. Point to Index Server.

6. Click on Index Server Manager.

7. In the left-hand pane, select the folder named Web.

8. Click the Action menu.

9. Click Merge.

10. Click Yes.

11. Close the MMC.

# Index Server Manager

Index Server provides seven functions for the management of Index Server. These tools are:

- Checking Status
- Setting Global Properties
- Creating and Configuring Catalogs
- Adjusting the Property Cache
- Adding and Removing Directories
- Forcing a Scan
- Forcing a Merge

## Checking Status

The Index Server snap-in allows you to check the status and view the properties of directories that are indexed. To do this, select the Index Server folder and view the information in the right-hand pane, as illustrated in Figure 10-9.

## Setting Global Properties

You can set the properties for all catalog settings. You can do this at the Index Server level or at the catalog level. Values set for the catalog override the values set at the server. You can also turn off characterization. With characterization turned off, you will not get summaries or abstracts when the result pages are generated.

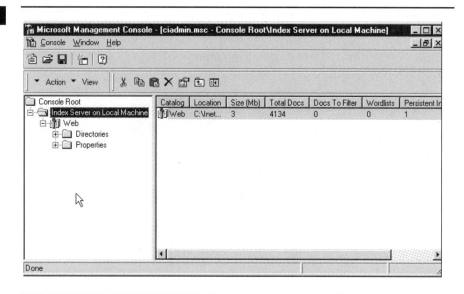

You can also set the characterization size under the Generation tab. The default size is 320 characters.

## Creating and Configuring Catalogs

When you install Index Server, it creates one catalog for you. You can create other catalogs and you can separate which content is indexed to which catalog.

You create a catalog from the Index Server Manager. Select Index Server and right-click to display the menu system. Then point to New, as illustrated in Figure 10-10.

After you select Catalog, supply the name for the new catalog and location of the catalog files. The following illustration shows the dialog box where you supply the catalog name and location.

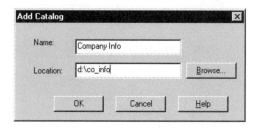

FIGURE 10-10

Creating a new catalog

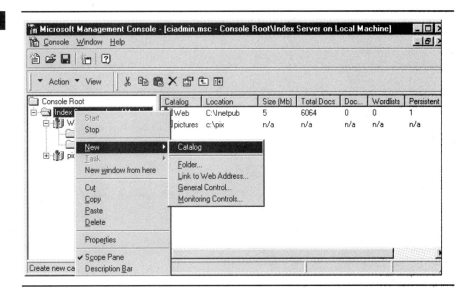

The final step is the notification that the catalog will not be active until Index Server is stopped and started again as shown next.

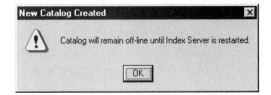

**EXERCISE 10-4**

## Creating a Catalog

Purpose: To gain experience in creating a catalog.

*Do this exercise from either machine.*

1. Ensure that you are logged on as Administrator.

2. Click the Start button.

3. Point to Programs.

4. Point to Windows NT 4.0 Option Pack.

5. Point to Microsoft Index Server.

6. Click on Index Server Manager.

7. Select Index Server on Local Machine.

8. Right-click Index Server on Local Machine.

9. Click New.

10. Click Catalog.

11. In the resulting dialog box, type **Company Info** and press TAB.

12. Type **d:\co_info**. This is the directory we created earlier.

13. Click OK.

14. Click OK on the Offline message.

15. Ensure that Index Server is still selected.

16. Click the Action menu.

17. Click Stop.

18. Repeat steps 15 and 16 and start the service.

19. The catalog will build automatically. This process will take several minutes. When the process is done, close the MMC.

## Adjusting the Property Cache

You can configure the property cache to add values that may be frequently searched. This may speed up query times. Property cache is an on-disk cache. If the property is not cached, then Index Server accesses the documents directly and retrieves the properties at the time of the query. Properties that are not indexed by default can be added later and used in queries.

## Adding and Removing Directories

You can use the Index Server Manager to add directories to or exclude directories from the indexing process. This instruction tells Index Server to include or exclude a given directory, or files in that directory, in the index. Doing this does not physically delete (or add) directories at the server.

## Forcing a Scan

If you want to re-inventory a virtual directory, you cause Index Server to do this by forcing a scan. You should do a scan after making global changes such as:

- Adding or removing a filter
- Adding a new word breaker

■ Changing the characterization size

■ Changing the filter of unrecognized extensions

## Forcing a Merge

You force a merge to speed up queries and to combine smaller indexes to free up disk space or memory space. Refer to the section on master indexes earlier in this chapter.

**CERTIFICATION OBJECTIVE 10.05**

# Querying with Index Server

Clients use a form to query the Index Server index for documents that meet the criteria they select. You start with a *query scope*. A query scope is a set of documents that the search engine uses to match the criteria.

You can further narrow the search by using *content query restrictions* and *property query restrictions*. With a content query restriction, you narrow the search by specifying the content to find. With a property query restriction, you narrow the search by specifying file attributes such as:

■ File size

■ File creation date

■ Last modification date

■ File author

## Hit Highlighting

Index Server highlights the exact text that meets the query criteria. This simplifies the task of seeing what it was that qualified. You can view an HTML page with a list of hits. The words that make up the hit are displayed in a different color and will be italicized. Figure 10-11 contains an example of a query return after successfully finding matches. Figure 10-12 contains an example of how the document looks with the key words highlighted.

**FIGURE 10-11**

A successful query

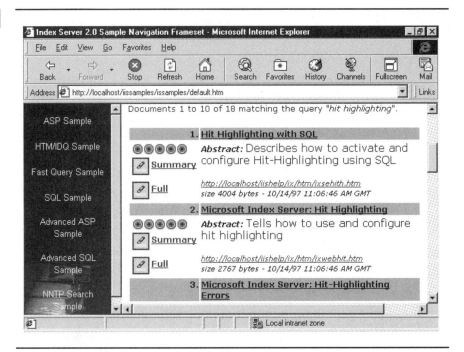

**FIGURE 10-12**

Documents with key words highlighted

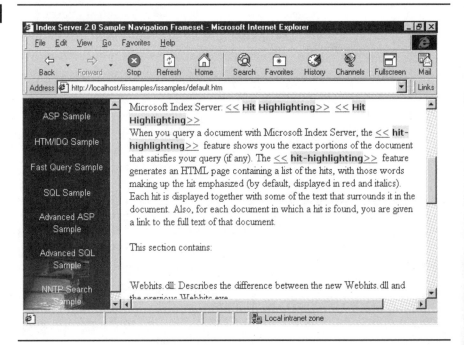

# Query Language

You search for information that has been indexed by the server by filling out a query form and sending it to the server. The server executes the query based on instructions you sent along with the form. Index Server supports the following:

- **Boolean operators**   such as "and," "or," and "not."

- **Proximity operators**   The proximity operator is "near." The near operator returns a match if both words are in the same page. The near operator differs from the "and" operator in that it assigns a ranking to how close the words are together on a page. The "and" operator only looks to see if the two words are on the same page. The closer the words are together, the higher the ranking. If the two words are separated by 50 words or more, then the page is assigned a rank of zero and is excluded from the data set. The "near" operator can only be applied to words (or phrases).

- **Wildcards**   The wildcard character ("*") matches words that contain the specified prefix.

- **Free-text queries**   A free-text query looks for meanings rather than exact words. A free-text query ignores Boolean, proximity, and wildcard operators. Free-text queries must begin with "$contents," for example, "$contents how do I query with Index Server?"

- **Vector space queries**   A vector query matches words and phrases. You separate the words with a comma. You can also specify the relative weight of the word in the query by using the [weight] syntax. For example, the queries "index[10]," "server[25]," "index server[100]" rank results with the phrases with "index server" above pages with the words "index" and "server" on the same page.

- **Property value queries**   You construct a property value query using the operators and the following rules:

  - Consecutive words are treated as a phrase; they must appear in the same order in the document.

  - Queries are not case sensitive.

- You can search for words in the exception list, such as "a," "an," "and," etc.

- Punctuation marks are ignored.

- To use special characters, you must enclose the query with double quotes ("").

- To search for a word in double quotes, enclose the entire word (including the double quotes) with another set of double quotes.

**CERTIFICATION OBJECTIVE 10.06**

# Query Forms

A *query form* is an HTML document that a client submits to the Index Server. The query form contains criteria supplied by the user. The server matches the criteria and returns the results to the user in the form of a *results page*, which is an HTML document. The client initiates this process from their browser.

When you install Index Server, the Installation Wizard installs several sample query forms. There are:

- ASP sample form
- HTM/IDQ sample form
- Fast Query sample form
- SQL sample form
- Advanced ASP sample form
- Advanced SQL sample form

You may provide these forms to your users, or use them as samples for developing your own forms. You can access the forms from the Windows NT 4.0 Option Pack and then from the Microsoft Index Server (see Figure 10-13).

FIGURE 10-13

Accessing the sample
query forms

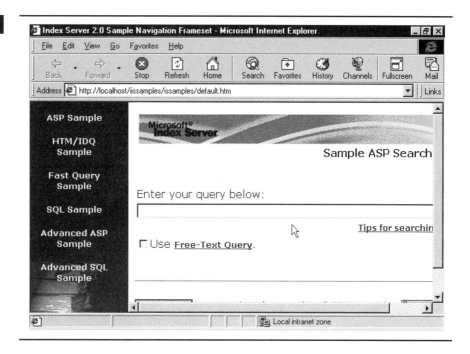

## CERTIFICATION OBJECTIVE 10.07

# .idq and .htx Files

The query form has several elements. These are:

- HTML file
- Internet Data Query file (.idq)
- HTML Extension file (.htx)

These files must all be located in one virtual directory. The directory must have Read and Execute (or scripts) permissions. Index Server installs three sample files that you can use to create your own query forms. These files are stored in the /iissamples/issamples folder. They are:

- ixtourqy.htm
- ixtourqy.idq
- ixtourqy.htx

## HTML File

This file displays the Web page where the user enters the query parameters. The results are also returned to the user via an HTML page.

## Internet Data Query File

The Internet data query (IDQ) file is a file with an .idq extension. It is an intermediate form that the server uses to execute the search request.

*Know what the .idq and .htx files do.*

The IDQ file is comprised of two sections:

- Name section
- Query section

The name section is optional and does not need to be included in the file for standard queries to operate. The name section defines nonstandard column names. These column names may be referred to in the query.

The query section contains the parameters that may be used in the query. It may contain form variables. It may also contain conditional expressions that change the value of a variable, depending upon the condition.

## HTML Extension File

The HTML extension (HTX) file is a file with an .htx extension. It is an HTML file that contains the query result data set. The data is added to an HTML page and sent to the browser.

## Other Query Forms

You can use Active Sever Pages (ASP) and SQL with Microsoft's ActiveX Data Objects (ADO) to create query forms.

### ASP Queries

You can build forms with Active Server Pages. This technique allows you to use the power and flexibility of ActiveX scripting. The queries have the file extension .asp and add flexibility in displaying query results.

While creating query forms with ASP is more powerful than using basic forms, there is a price to pay for this power and flexibility. These queries are slower on a very active site that receives many queries at the same time. For that type of site, queries are faster as .idq and .htx files rather than .asp files.

### SQL Queries

As an alternative method of running queries, you can write SQL queries that use ActiveX Data Objects (ADO). You can use this method instead of the standard forms. You use SQL extensions to form the query. ADO retrieves the data and you use a scripting language, such as VBScript, to display the data.

Like ASP forms, SQL queries consume more machine resources at the server and tend to be slower than the queries that use basic forms. This will be evident on a heavily queried server.

**CERTIFICATION OBJECTIVE 10.08**

# Resolving Index Server Problems

For the most part, Index Server is self-sustaining and maintenance-free. There are several error conditions that Index Server finds and corrects by itself. Other than hardware failures, Index Server does not need manual intervention for most other problems.

Common errors include:

- **Lost file notification**   When you make changes to documents or to the scope, Index Server automatically incorporates those changes. If the rate of those changes becomes very high, it is possible that Index Server will not see the changes. Index Server automatically sets up an incremental scan for that scope.

- **Dropped network connection**   If you are using a virtual directory and lose the network connection, Index Server periodically scans to determine if the network connection is available again.

- **Corrupted files and faulty DLLs**   If the CiDaemon process detects that a file is corrupt, that file is left unfiltered. You can get a list of unfiltered files. If there is a faulty DLL, you will be able to determine this because the file type with that filter will not be processed.

- **Disk full condition**   If the disk that contains the catalog becomes nearly full, the indexing process is suspended. When the disk approaches 3MB of free space, then filtering is temporarily suspended until you relieve the space shortage issue.

- **Corrupted property cache**   If index server is interrupted abnormally, or for any reason the property cache becomes corrupted, it is marked as corrupted. This condition can be fixed by stopping and starting Index Server. During recovery, queries can still be executed but filtering is suspended until the recovery is complete.

- **Data corruption and internal inconsistencies**   If you suffer a catastrophic failure, the index data may become corrupted to the point where it cannot be repaired. When this happens, the index data is deleted and the documents are refiltered. If this corruption occurs during normal operations, then you need to manually stop and start the Content Index service to initiate recovery.

- **Query doesn't return documents known to exist**   If you issue a query and it doesn't return documents you know exist, one cause can be that the documents were indexed in one language and queried in another. Another cause might be that the document has not been filtered yet. A third cause might be that an error occurred during filtering.

## QUESTIONS AND ANSWERS

| | |
|---|---|
| Does Index Server have to be installed on the file server where the documents are located? | No, you can install Index Server on your IIS server machine and have it index documents anywhere in your organization. |
| How many documents can be indexed on a server? | There is no hard limit to the number of documents you can have in a scope. The limiting factor is one of performance. |
| Are there always word lists in memory? | Not necessarily. As the number of words increases, the words are written to the disk in the shadow index. |
| What network protocol do I use for index server? | TCP/IP. The query process uses the HTTP protocol. |

# CERTIFICATION SUMMARY

This chapter described the features of Microsoft Index Server 2.0. Index Server installation and using Index Server Manager were covered. How the server performs and how much memory might be required was also discussed.

This chapter described the indexing process in detail. We covered the major components in indexing and what their roles in the indexing process were. The main purpose of indexing is to be able to find information quickly that contains data important to you. You find this data by constructing a query. You send the query to the server, which executes the query and returns to you the resulting data.

This chapter discussed how queries are performed and what sample query forms are available to you. We described additional query forms and their advantages and disadvantages, query elements, and query operators that can be used to construct a query statement.

 # TWO-MINUTE DRILL

❏  Index Server is part of Windows NT 4.0 Option Pack.

❏  Index Server allows you to create a catalog of documents on the server.

- ❏ You can search these documents using a query form.
- ❏ Index Server can index the contents of multiple servers, including UNIX and Novell.
- ❏ Index Server supports various file formats.
- ❏ You can add file formats to cover additional files.
- ❏ You can index the contents of a newsgroup.
- ❏ Index Server supports multiple languages and even indexes documents when they contain multiple languages.
- ❏ When you add documents, they are automatically indexed.
- ❏ The space required for the catalog can be as much as 40 percent of the size of the corpus.
- ❏ The name of the catalog file is catalog.wci.
- ❏ By default, the catalog is created at installation.
- ❏ The corpus refers to all of the documents stored on the server.
- ❏ A scope is the set of documents to be indexed.
- ❏ Content filters are programs that "look" inside a document at the words in the documents.
- ❏ A word breaker is a program that takes the output from the content filter, which is just one character after another, and breaks them up into words.
- ❏ The normalizer is a program that takes the words from the word breaker and cleans them up.
- ❏ A word list is contained in RAM.
- ❏ A shadow index is created when too many word lists exist.
- ❏ A shadow index is written to disk.
- ❏ A master index is updated by incorporating the shadow indexes.
- ❏ A master index is updated by a master merge.
- ❏ A master merge happens automatically.
- ❏ You can force a master merge.
- ❏ Queries can contain wildcards. Queries are not case sensitive.
- ❏ A query form is an HTML document.

# SELF TEST

The Self Test questions will help you measure your understanding of the material presented in this chapter. Read all the choices carefully, as there may be more than one correct answer. Choose all correct answers for each question.

1. Which of the following statements about Index Server is true?

   A. Index Server can index the content of multiple Web servers.

   B. The file system of the partitions that contain the data is unimportant.

   C. Index Server only indexes content on NTFS partitions.

   D. You cannot index information on a remote server.

2. Which of the following file formats is indexed without installing additional content filters?

   A. HTML

   B. Microsoft Word

   C. Oracle database files

   D. WordPerfect

3. Which of the following statements about Index Server is true?

   A. Index Server can be used with any Web server.

   B. Index Server automatically indexes documents that contain multiple languages.

   C. Index Server automatically indexes documents that contain multiple languages only if the document was created in Microsoft Word.

   D. A Unicode character is a character that is unique to a particular language.

4. What are the minimum requirements to install Index Server?

   A. Windows NT 4.0 with SP3 installed

   B. 3 to 12MB of free disk space

   C. CD-ROM drive

   D. IIS 4.0

5. Which of the following characteristics is not important concerning the amount of RAM desirable for Index Server?

   A. The size of the corpus

   B. The number of documents to be indexed

   C. The number of simultaneous queries

   D. The amount of free space on the disk that will contain the catalog file

6. Which of the following is true about catalogs?

   A. There can only be one catalog per Index Server.

   B. A catalog may be as large as 40 percent of the size of the corpus.

   C. A catalog must be on an NTFS partition.

D.   A catalog must be manually
constructed.

7.   You receive a call from a user who states
that they appear to be unable to run any
queries. What can you do to help determine
if Index Server is functioning properly?

A.   Check to see if the WWW service is
running.

B.   Ping the Web server.

C.   Check the Content Index service in the
Services applet.

D.   Ping the user's station to see if they are
on the network.

8.   Which of the following statements are true
about the way documents are indexed?

A.   An index contains all of the
recognizable words from a document.

B.   If a document contains multiple
languages, an index is created for each
language.

C.   Word breakers are employed to decide
which words to index if a document
contains words with similar meanings.

D.   Content filters are specific to file format
types.

9.   Which of the following is not a type of
index?

A.   Word lists

B.   Primary index

C.   Shadow index

D.   Master index

10.   Which of the following statements is true of
a shadow index?

A.   There is no such thing as a shadow
index.

B.   A shadow index is created when the
MaxWordLists parameter is exceeded.

C.   A shadow index is held in memory until
a master merge is run.

D.   There can be multiple shadow indexes.

11.   Which of the following statements is true
about a master index?

A.   There is only one master index per
catalog.

B.   Merging word lists creates a master
index.

C.   An administrator cannot update the
master index.

D.   A master index is updated with shadow
indexes.

12.   You are the system administrator. You
notice that queries seem to be running slow
at your Index Server. You start a master
merge when you have to shut down the
server to address another issue. What do
you have to do about the master merge that
was running?

A.   Nothing, it will restart when the service
restarts.

B.   You must start the master merge again.

C.   You must rollback to the previous index
and then restart the master merge.

D.   Recreate the shadow indexes and then
stop and start the content service. Then
force the master merge again.

13.   How can a master merge occur?

A. Automatically at midnight

B. When the MaxFreshCount parameter is exceeded

C. When forced by an administrator

D. When there are too many word lists in the directory

14. Which of the following statements is not true about catalogs?

   A. There can only be one catalog per Index Server.

   B. There can be multiple catalogs per Index Server.

C. Queries can span multiple catalogs.

D. Queries cannot span multiple catalogs.

15. Which of the following statements is true about .idq and .htx files?

   A. The .idq file receives the query from the client.

   B. The .htx file receives the query from the client.

   C. The .idq file formats the results.

   D. The .htx file formats the results.

# 11

# Microsoft
# Certificate
# Server

Certificate Server is a standards-based, server application for managing the issuance, revocation, and renewal of digital certificates. Certificate Server is part of the Windows NT 4.0 Option Pack. Digital certificates are used in a security scheme. The purpose of this security scheme is to be able to tell, with a high degree of certainty, who is on the other end of the communication process.

Certificate Server generates certificates in standard X.509 format. These certificates can be used for public-key applications including, but not limited to, the following:

- Server and client authentication under the Secure Sockets Layer (SSL) protocol
- Secure e-mail using Secure/Multipurpose Internet Mail Extensions (S/MIME)
- Secure payment using Secure Electronic Transaction (SET)

The Certificate Server product consists of:

- The server engine
- The server database
- Administrative tools
- An HTTP client for performing certificate enrollment
- Software development files and sample code
- Product documentation

The product documentation is designed to assist administrators and Web masters who install, configure, operate, administer, and customize Certificate Server. The documentation also assists corporate developers and independent software vendors (ISVs) who need to write custom modules and applications that interact with Certificate Server.

# Certificates and Authentication

It is highly desirable, especially in an environment where security is a concern, that you be able to determine with whom you are communicating. You cannot see or hear the person on the other end when you communicate electronically. With electronic communication, it is difficult to ensure secure communication because it happens so fast and at such great volume.

*Digital certificates* are a form of authentication. They provide the mechanism necessary to conduct private communications in an open environment. They also provide a method to "prove" the origin of the communications. These requirements work both ways. As a user, you want to be sure that the host and processes you are accessing are, in fact, what you think they are. The same logic holds true for the host. The host processes also need to validate who is on the other end of the communication process.

In addition to knowing who is on the other end, the data that is sent back and forth needs to be secure. Data encryption and decryption provides this security. This type of security is highly desirable in a nonsecure environment such as the Internet.

There are three types of security mechanisms:

- Data encryption
- Digital signatures
- Digital certificates

## Data Encryption

*Cryptography* is the science of devising communication methods that take ordinary information and scramble it. The objective is to make the information accessible only to those who know how to unscramble it. Cryptography is centuries old in its practice and is not new to computers and digital information. The old art of making it information hard to access is being applied to the relatively new technology of computers.

Cryptography provides a set of techniques for scrambling messages so that they are stored and transmitted securely. This technique is also known as *encryption*. Encryption can achieve secure communication even when the transmission medium is not trustworthy. This is the case with the Internet. Encryption can also scramble sensitive files so an intruder cannot understand them.

Cryptography also provides techniques for unscrambling the encrypted data to reveal its original state. This technique is known as *decryption*.

Without knowledge of the secret encryption key necessary to decrypt a message, reconstruction of the original message is extremely difficult, even for experienced hackers.

Data encryption techniques employ a set of *keys*. These keys are created in pairs. One of the keys is called the *public key*. The other key is called the *private key*.

When using encryption, the only parts that must remain secret are the encryption keys, with the exception of the public keys. Other items such as algorithms, key sizes, and file formats can be made public without compromising security.

In using data encryption, a plain text message is scrambled to appear like random data. Such a message is difficult to unscramble without a secret key. (The term *message* refers to any piece of data designated for encryption.) This message can be ASCII text, a database file, or any data designated for secure transmission. The term *plain text* refers to data that has not been encrypted, while the term *cipher text* refers to data that is encrypted.

After a message has been encrypted, it can be stored on nonsecure media or transmitted on a nonsecure network, and still remain secret. Later, the message can be decrypted into its original form.

When a message is encrypted, an encryption key is used. This is analogous to a key used to lock a safety deposit box in a bank. To decrypt the message, the corresponding decryption key must be used. It is important to properly restrict access to the decryption key, because anyone who possesses it can decrypt all messages that were encrypted with the matching encryption key.

There are several different techniques used to encrypt and decrypt data. *Symmetric algorithms* are a common type of encryption algorithm. Symmetric algorithms use the same key for both encryption and decryption. In order to communicate using symmetric algorithms, both parties must share a secret key.

*Public-key (asymmetric) algorithms* use two different keys:

- A public key
- A private key

The private key is kept private to the owner of the key pair. The public key can be distributed to anyone who requests it, often through a certificate. If one key is used to encrypt a message, then the other key is required to decrypt the message. The private and public keys are matched in a pair. To decrypt the message that was encrypted with a private key, you would need the corresponding public key. You can use any public key.

Consider the following example: John wants to send a message that is secure. The software program uses John's private key as a seed for the algorithm to scramble the data. The data gets scrambled and is then sent.

The recipient of the message needs to decrypt it in order to read it. To decrypt the message, the recipient asks the holder of the public keys for John's public key. The key is sent and the message is decrypted.

To encrypt a reply, the process is reversed. The recipient uses John's public key to encrypt the message and sends the message to John. Remember, the message is encrypted with John's public key. If another public key is used, John cannot have access to the corresponding private key and cannot decrypt the message.

When John receives the message, he uses his private key to decrypt the message. Only his private key can decrypt the message.

Symmetric algorithms are much faster than public-key algorithms. They are often used for encrypting large amounts of data. However, because the keys must remain secret, distribution of the keys to large numbers of people is not practical. Public-key algorithms solve this problem and can be used in conjunction with symmetric algorithms to achieve optimal performance when large amounts of data are involved.

## Digital Signatures

*Digital signatures* are used to verify who sent the message. A digital signature does not encrypt the data. It is entirely possible to send a message with a digital signature (so the recipient can verify who sent the traffic) and not encrypt the data.

Digital signatures can be used when a message is distributed in plain text form, and the recipients need to verify that no unauthorized individual has tampered with the message. Signing a message does not alter the message; it simply generates a digital signature string that is bundled with the message. This digital signature may also be transmitted separately.

Digital signatures can be generated using public-key signature algorithms. This is when the transmitting (sender) private key is used to generate the signature. The message is sent in an e-mail message. Upon receipt of the message, the recipient uses the sender's public key to validate the signature. Because only the sender's public key (received by the recipient earlier) can be used to validate the signature, the digital signature is proof that the message sender's identity is authentic.

If the traffic that has been digitally signed is open en route, the digital signature is automatically recalculated. When the intended recipient gets the message, the digital signature won't match. The recipient knows that the message is not authentic or that the message was diverted en route. Either way, the recipient knows that something is not right.

## Digital Envelopes

*Digital envelopes* are used to send private messages that can only be understood by a specific recipient. This method is similar to data encryption. The message is encrypted using the recipient's public key. You can only decrypt the message using the recipient's private key, so only the recipient can read the message.

# Digital Certificates

The previous sections assume that the identity of the owner of the public key used to encrypt or decrypt a message is established beyond doubt. But in practice, how can the recipients of a message sent by John (accompanied by a digital signature that can be validated with a public key that belongs to John) be sure that they are really using John's public key? John's public key is accompanied by a *digital certificate* from a "trusted authority."

In the physical world of documents, you have a certain interaction that assures you (at least at some level) of the authenticity of the documents and the process. For example, consider the use of a passport. The customs official who looks at your passport and then accepts it as proof of your identity, trusts that your government did an adequate job of identifying you before issuing you a passport. There has to be a level of trust in the certifying authority.

In order to guarantee authenticity of public keys, Microsoft uses a Certificate Server to provide digital certificates (commonly known as *certificates*) as a secure method of exchanging public keys over a nonsecure network. In other words, just like the customs official that trusted the government's process of issuing a passport, you are going to trust the process of receiving keys by using the certificate.

## What Is a Digital Certificate?

A certificate is data that completely identifies an entity (a user, for example). The digital certificate is issued by a *certificate authority (CA)*. The certificate is only issued after that authority has verified the requestor's identity. The data includes the public encryption key tendered to the requestor. When the sender of a message signs the message with its private key, the recipient of the message can use the sender's public key (retrieved from the certificate sent with the message) to verify that the sender is legitimate.

Digital certificates are virtual documents that authenticate individuals and entities on a network. The use of certificates on a network is more complex than the use of a physical document because the communicating parties most likely will not physically meet. Therefore, it is not necessarily a one-to-one exchange, as with the case of the passport.

As a result, you need a method to attain a high level of trust despite the lack of physical verification. Also, on a nonsecure network it is much easier to intercept messages and present fictitious identities. To prevent these problems, security protocols employing the cryptographic techniques described earlier make it very difficult, if not impossible, for someone to falsify a certificate and present a false identity.

In other words, the primary goal of a digital certificate is to confirm that the public key contained in a certificate is the public key belonging to the person who sent the message, the one that was encrypted using the private key.

For example, a CA may sign a special message digitally containing the name of a user; in this case John. The CA is your *certificate server* and this message is known as *certificate information*.

This message contains a public key that may be used in such a way that anyone can verify that the certificate information message was signed by no one other than the CA. Thereby, trust in the public key designated for John is confirmed.

The typical implementation of digital certification involves a *signature algorithm* for signing the certificate. The process follows these steps:

- John sends a certificate request containing his name and public key to a CA.

- The CA creates a special message from this request, which constitutes most of the certificate data. The CA signs the message with its private key and obtains a separate signature. The CA then returns the message and the signature to John. Together, the two parts form a certificate.

- John sends the certificate to the recipient, which conveys his public key.

- The recipient verifies the signature using the CA public key. If the signature is verified, the public key designated for John is accepted.

As with any digital signature, anyone can verify that the CA signed the certificate, without accessing the privileged information.

## Certificate Revocation

Certificates have a time duration. It is possible for the certificate to expire and no longer be valid. A certificate is valid only for the period of time specified by the CA that issued the certificate. The certificate itself contains information about expiration date.

If a user attempts to access a secure server using an expired certificate, server authentication software automatically rejects the access request. Users can renew certificates before the expiration date to avoid this situation.

It is also possible for certificates to be revoked by the CA for other reasons. To handle this situation, the CA maintains a list of revoked certificates. This list is called a *certificate revocation list (CRL)*, and is available to network users to determine the validity of any given certificate.

In summary, certificates may be revoked for two reasons: One, the certificate's time period is no longer valid, and two, the administrator revoked the certificate, making it no longer available for use.

exam
ⓦatch

*Know that certificates can be revoked or can expire, making them invalid.*

## Certificate Authority Hierarchies

Within large organizations composed of multiple business units, each unit needs to manage their own resources on the corporate intranet. Each unit must enforce the policies under which approval is granted to requesters to gain access to their intranet resources.

You can give these corporate units the ability to set policies and issue certificates themselves by allowing them to become certifying authorities, each with their own CA server.

Misuse of authority is addressed through use of a *CA hierarchy*. The CA hierarchy begins with an ultimate certifying authority called the *root*. The root authority certifies CA servers within the parent organization to enforce security and control throughout the entire system. There may be multiple levels of CA servers. For example, a level 1 CA is certified by the root CA, and in turn, the level 1 CA certifies level 2 CAs.

The use of a CA hierarchy provides organizations with the flexibility needed to manage policies and grant certificates throughout a certification system composed of multiple certificate authorities. A CA hierarchy enables a certification system to be managed from a single control point.

When a certificate issued by a level 1 or level 2 CA is transmitted on a network, the recipient must verify that the issuing CA has been certified by each level above it, until a chain of authority exists between the lower level CA and the root CA.

If, for some reason, a lower level CA mismanages the issuance of certificates, the root authority can revoke the relevant server certificate. This effectively invalidates the certificates issued by the lower level CA, but it ignores any other certificates issued within the greater organization.

## FROM THE CLASSROOM

### How the Security Keys Work

One of the main topics of interest for students with regard to security is the concept of the keys. The security system being used here has two facets: One facet is encrypting and decrypting data. The other facet is identification and authentication.

For encrypting and decrypting data, two keys are used. One key is called the public key. The public key is given to anyone who asks for the key; it is publicly available. The students want to know how a public key can be secure. If anyone can get the public key then where is the security? But not anyone can get the public key. You have to have a reason to have access to the public key. For example, if I send you an e-mail message and encrypt it, I use my private key to encrypt the message. To read the message, you have to decrypt it. To do that, you need my public key, not just any public key. To get my key you go to the key server (electronically) and ask for it. The server knows which public key to give you by looking at the private key you are

holding. So, if you do not have a private key to start, then you won't be issued a public key. And, the public key that is generated for you is based on the private key code you present. Therefore it is unique and won't be any good for anything else.

You can enhance and supplement the key system by using certificates. Some students wonder what the differences are between the keys and the certificates. Don't they do the same thing?

Certificates do not modify the data. Certificates do not encrypt the data. Certificates are used to ensure that the computer on the other end is what you think it is. When you connect to the host at Microsoft, how do you really know that it is the host at Microsoft and not somebody spoofing you by impersonating the Microsoft host? This is where the certificate comes in; it provides a way to ensure that you are communicating with the genuine article and not an imposter.

**CERTIFICATION OBJECTIVE 11.02**

# Certificate Server Features

Certificate Server has a number of important characteristics:

- Policy independence
- Transport independence
- Standards based
- Key management
- High reliability

## Policy Independence

Certificate Server gives out certificates based on defined policies. The requestors must also meet the criteria defined in the policy to receive a certificate. The policies are implemented in *policy modules* written in Visual Basic, C, C++, or Java. Writing or modifying policy modules does not affect the certificate server functions. These functions are independent of the policies.

## Transport Independence

Certificates are requested and certificates are given out to requestors. This may be done through any transport mechanism. These transport mechanisms may include:

- HTTP (Hypertext Transfer Protocol)
- RPC (Remote Procedure Call)
- Disk file
- Custom transport (a transport mechanism that you write or create)

## Standards Based

Certificate Server accepts Public Key Cryptography Standards (PKCS) #10 requests. Certificate Server issues X.509 compliant (Version 1.0 and Version

3.0) certificates. Because Certificate Server is based on standards, it works with non-Microsoft clients that are also standards based. You can get additional information about these standards from http://www.rsa.com.

*Certificate Server issues X.509 certificates.*

## Key Management

Private keys are an important part of the security system. The security of the certificate system depends upon how well the private keys are protected. Certificate Server can help you protect your private keys by relying on the Microsoft CryptoAPI to perform key management. With the CryptoAPI, you can use software-based and hardware-based key engines for the generation and protection of keys.

## High Reliability

Certificate Server runs on Windows NT Server and has the same high reliability that Windows NT Server has. Certificate Server is a cornerstone for implementing public-key-based security on enterprise networks. Using Certificate Server, it is easier to support large numbers of users since there is no need to distribute password databases. Certificate Server can be deployed on multiple servers in an organization, giving the flexibility of more than one CA.

## CERTIFICATION OBJECTIVE 11.03

# Certificate Server Architecture

Certificate Server has several architectural components. The server engine is the core of the system. Each of the other modules performs a distinct function. The modules are:

- Server engine
- Intermediary
- Server databases

- Administration tools
- Policy module
- Extension handlers
- Exit modules

## Server Engine

The *server engine* is the core component of Certificate Server. The engine acts as the data pump for the requests it receives from the other modules. It pushes the information between the components during request processing and certificate generation. The engine monitors each request through the various processes to ensure that appropriate actions are being taken.

## Intermediary

The *intermediary* is the component that receives the request for a new certificate from the requestor. The intermediary submits the request to the server engine on behalf of the requestor.

The intermediary has two components:

- The intermediary application that handles the request from the requestor (the client)
- The Certificate Server Client Interface, which handles the interaction between the request and the server engine

Internet Information Server is an intermediary that handles requests from HTTP clients and forwards the requests to the server engine. Intermediaries can be written to be client specific, transport specific, or policy criteria specific.

## Server Database

Certificate Server has a *server database*. The server database maintains status information and a log of all issued certificates. It also maintains the CRLs.

The database has two components:

- Server log
- Server queue

### Server Log

The server log stores all certificates and CRL certificates issued by the server so administrators can track, audit, and archive server activity. In addition, the server log is used by the server engine to store pending revocations prior to publishing them in the CRL.

The server log stores recent certificate requests for a period of time in case a problem is encountered when issuing a certificate. An example of such a situation would be a delivery failure of the certificate. This time period is configurable by the administrator. The Certificate Log Utility provides administrative access to this part of the Certificate Server database.

### Server Queue

The server queue maintains status information as the server is processing a certificate request. The status information includes:

- Receipt
- Parsing
- Authorization
- Signing
- Dispatch

The Certificate Queue Utility provides administrative access to this part of the Certificate Server database.

exam
ⓦatch

*The Certificate Server Database is composed of the server log and server queue.*

## Administration

Administration of Certificate Server is done through Web-based administration tools. These tools provide access to the data contained in the server database. The two tools are:

- Certificate Log Utility
- Certificate Queue Utility

*There are two utilities for viewing the log files kept by Certificate Server:*
*the Log utility and the Queue utility.*

The server database has two parts to it. A record of all certificates requested is kept in the server queue. Copies of all issued certificates are kept in the server log. You access these logs from the Certificate Server Administration Tools Web page.

### Certificate Log Utility

You access the Certificate Log Utility from the Web browser. Point the browser to the http://localhost/certsrv page. The Log utility accesses the database and provides a listing of all of the certificates that have been issued or revoked.

### Certificate Queue Utility

You access the Certificate Log Utility from the Web browser. Point the browser to the http://localhost/certsrv page. At the page, click the link Certificate Administration Queue Utility. This provides a list of the request for certificates that are currently being processed, as illustrated in Figure 11-1.

## Policy Module

The policy module contains the set of rules governing the issuance of certificates. The policy module also contains the requirements for the renewal and the revocation of certificates. All requests received by the server engine are passed to the policy module. The policy modules are also used to parse any supplemental information provided within a request and set properties on the certificate accordingly.

The policy module is fully replaceable and customizable through an automation interface to the server engine.

## Extension Handlers

Extension handlers work with the policy module. They allow the process to set custom extensions on a certificate. An extension handler is a template with the custom extension that appears in the certificate. The policy module loads the proper extension handler when it is needed.

Viewing the Web page for server administration

# Exit Modules

Exit modules publish completed certificates through any number of transports or protocols. By default, the server notifies each exit module installed on the server whenever a certificate is published. It also notifies the exit module when a certificate is revoked.

A Component Object Model (COM) interface is used for writing custom exit modules. These exit modules may be written for different transports (protocols) or custom delivery options.

For example, an LDAP (Lightweight Directory Access Protocol) exit module might be used to publish only client certificates in a directory service and not server certificates. In this case, the exit module uses the COM interface to determine the type of certificate that the server is issuing and filter out any certificates that are not appropriate client certificates. You can find out more about COM and LDAP from the Microsoft Web site and related sites.

## CERTIFICATION OBJECTIVE 11.04

# Installing Certificate Server

Installing Certificate Server is done through the Windows NT 4.0 Option Pack, assuming that you did not install Certificate Server when you installed IIS. There is no requirement to install Certificate Server in order to use IIS or the other options that come with the Option Pack. There are no special requirements for the installation of Certificate Server beyond the requirements for Windows NT Server. Figure 11-2 illustrates how you use the Windows NT 4.0 Option Pack to install Certificate Server.

The next step is to select the Add/Remove button, as illustrated in Figure 11-3.

The Add/Remove button takes you to the screen that lists the various components available within the Option Pack. Select the Certificate Server and then select Show Subcomponents to view what subcomponents will be installed when you install Certificate Server (see Figure 11-4).

---

**FIGURE 11-2**

Using Windows NT 4.0 Option Pack setup to install Certificate Server

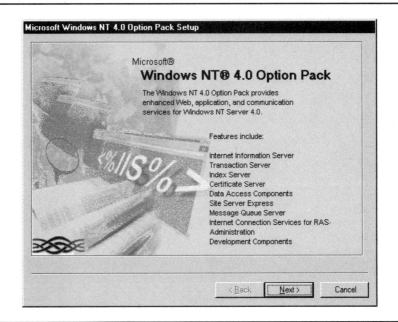

**FIGURE 11-3**

Selecting the Add/
Remove button

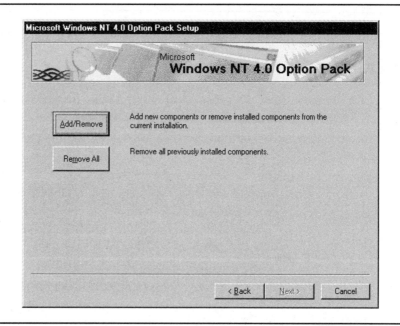

**FIGURE 11-4**

Viewing the Certificate
Server subcomponents

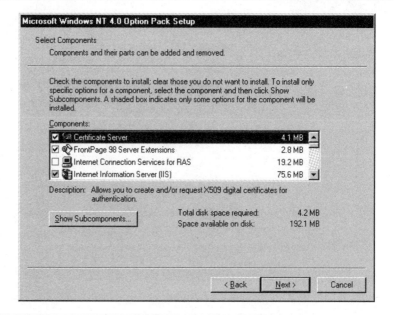

After you select the desired components, you need to complete the certificate information, as illustrated in Figure 11-5.

Click on Next and the files will be installed. Click on Finish and you are done. Certificate Server is now installed.

### Installing Certificate Server

Purpose: To install Certificate Server on the computer running IIS.

*Do this exercise at both computers.*

1. Ensure that you are logged on as Administrator.
2. Click Start.
3. Point to Programs.
4. Point to Windows NT 4.0 Option Pack.
5. Click on Windows NT 4.0 Option Pack Setup.

FIGURE 11-5

Completing the information for Certificate Server

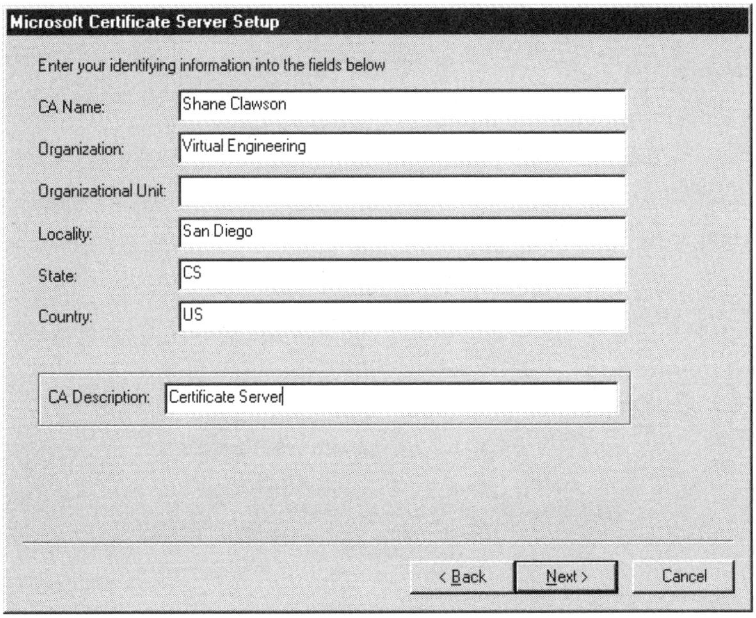

6. Click Next on the Option Pack Setup screen.

7. Click the Add/Remove button.

8. From the Components box, select Certificate Server.

9. Click the Show Subcomponents button.

10. Ensure that all of the components are selected.

11. Click OK to return to the Select Components dialog box.

12. Click Next.

13. In the Configuration Data Storage Location box, enter **c:\inetpub\certdata**.

14. Click Next and accept the default location for the log files.

15. Click OK if you get a dialog box asking to create the directories.

16. Fill out the Certificate Server Setup information box as follows:

   ■ CA Name: Your Name

   ■ Organization: Your company name

   ■ Organizational Unit: Your department name, or any piece of information if you do not have a department.

   ■ Locality: Your City

   ■ State: Your State

   ■ Country: US

   ■ CA Description: CA Server*xx*

17. Click Finish after the files are installed.

18. Open the Control Panel.

19. Start the Services applet.

20. Make sure that the service Certificate Authority is present and the startup mode is automatic. The service will not be started. Start the service.

21. Close the Services applet.

22. Close Control Panel.

23. Restart Windows NT Server.

**CERTIFICATION OBJECTIVE 11.05**

# Generating a Certificate Request File

After installing Certificate Server, you still need to do a couple of things to render it usable. In order to use Certificate Server to deliver certificates to your clients, you need to get a certificate. There are several firms that specialize in providing certificates and you should contact one of them for your certificate. These certificates are critical; you cannot just make this part up as you go along.

You start the process from Internet Service Manager (ISM). Right-click the Web site and select Properties (see Figure 11-6).

In the Secure Communications box, click Edit and it will bring you into the Secure Communications dialog box, which is illustrated in Figure 11-7.

Selecting the Key Manager begins the process. Right-click the WWW icon and select Create New Key, as illustrated in Figure 11-8.

| FIGURE 11-6 |
| --- |

Directory Security screen

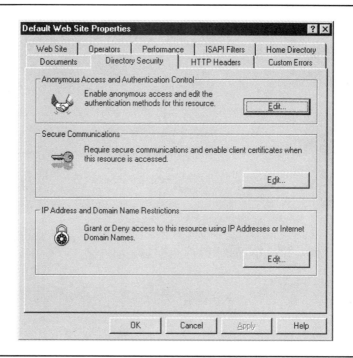

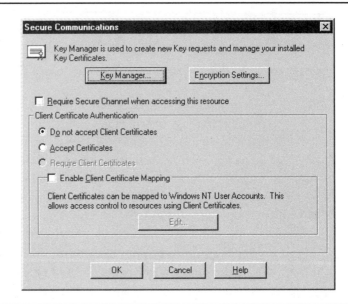

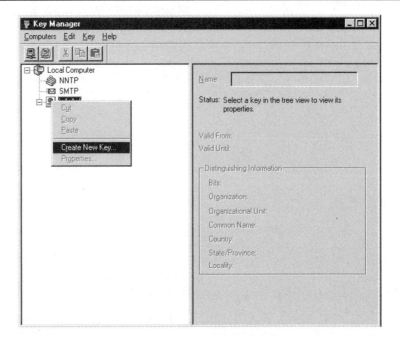

The next step is to specify how you want to register. You can elect to automatically send the request for a certificate, or you can generate a file and send it in manually to obtain the certificate. Figure 11-9 contains the Create New Key dialog box.

The next step is to name the new key and supply a password in the dialog box illustrated in Figure 11-10.

Next, you need to fill out some contact information. The system generates the new key for you (see Figure 11-11).

## Installing Certificates on the Server

If a server has clients connect to it and the server needs to authenticate those clients, the server must install a CA certificate from the same CA that issues the certificate to the clients. This certificate allows the server to validate the client certificates.

**FIGURE 11-9**

Specifying certificate request file

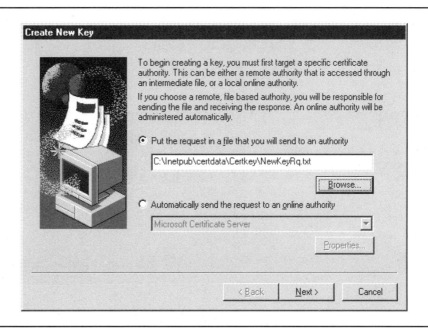

**FIGURE 11-10**

Giving a name and a
password to the new key

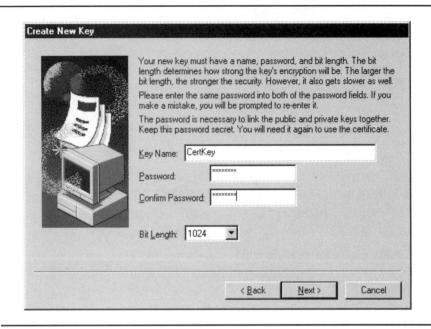

To install the certificate on the server, install Microsoft Internet Explorer (IE). You use IE to connect to the CA server and install the certificate the same way you would for the client.

**FIGURE 11-11**

Generating the new key

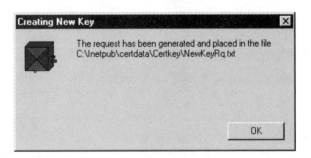

# Installing Certificates on the Clients

In order for the browser to connect to a server that uses certificates, the browser must obtain and install a certificate from the CA that issued the server its certificate. The browser uses the certificate to validate the server.

To install the certificate using IE, load the Certificate Authority Certificate List Web page in the shared folder location.

| EXERCISE 11-2 |

## Generate a Certificate Request File

Purpose: To generate the file to be sent to obtain your authority. You will generate a new key.

*Do this exercise at both computers.*

1. Start Internet Service Manager.
2. Expand your computer icon.
3. Select your Web site (the default Web site).
4. Right-click the Web site.
5. Click Properties.
6. Select the Directory Security tab.
7. Click the Key Manager button.
8. Right-click the WWW folder.
9. Click Create New Key.
10. Click the radio button that begins with "Put the request in a file...".
11. Click the Browse button.
12. Select the c:\inetpub folder.
13. Click the second icon to the right of the Save in: dialog box. This is the "Create new directory" icon. You can also do this by a right-click in the browser window, clicking New, and clicking on the folder name.
14. Enter the name CertKey in the new folder box.
15. Click Save.
16. Click Next.

17. Enter the following values:
    - Key Name: CertKey
    - Password: password
    - Confirm Password: password
    - Bit Length: 512

18. Click Next.

19. Enter the following values:
    - Organization: Your company
    - Organizational Unit: Your department
    - Common Name: Serverxx.funxx.com

20. Click Next.

21. Enter your information for the Country, State, and City.

22. Click Next.

23. For the next screen, enter the following values:
    - Name: Administrator
    - Someone@somewhere
    - Telephone number: 888.555.1212

24. Click Next.

25. Click Finish after you read the message in the dialog box.

26. Click OK when it says the key has been created.

27. Close Key Manager.

28. Click Yes if asked "Commit all changes now?" You may need to attempt to close Key Manager again.

29. Click OK on the Secure Communications dialog box.

30. Click OK to close the Web Site Properties dialog box.

**EXERCISE 11-3**

## Submitting the Certificate Request

Purpose: To simulate sending and receiving the certificate. This will enable you to generate certificates for requestors.

*Do this exercise at both computers.*

1. Open Internet Explorer.

2. In the address box, type *localhost/certsrv*.

3. Press the ENTER key. This connects you to the Microsoft Certificate Server page.

4. Click the link Certificate Enrollment Tools.

5. Click the link Process a Certificate Request. This brings up the Web Server Enrollment Page (krenroll.asp).

6. Open Notepad.

7. Click File.

8. Click Open.

9. Go to the \inetpub\certkey folder.

10. Open the file named certkey.txt.

11. Click an insertion point to the left of the line that begins "----BEGIN NEW...".

12. Select all of the text from that point to (and including) the line that begins "----END NEW...". Be sure to highlight both the "BEGIN" and the "END" lines as well as all of the unintelligible text in between.

13. Click on Edit.

14. Click on Copy.

15. Return to the browser.

16. Click on the insertion point in the white box below "Paste certificate request file here:".

17. Click Edit.

18. Click Paste. This copies all of the text that was selected from Notepad into the area.

19. Scroll down and click on Submit Request.

20. If you receive a Security Alert dialog box, click Yes.

21. You should get a page that has Certificate Download. Scroll down and click on Download.

22. Ensure that the radio button next to "Save this file to disk" is selected.

23. Click OK.

24. Select the \inetpub\certkey folder.

25. Click Save.

26. Click OK on the Download Complete dialog box.

27. Close Internet Explorer.

28. Close Notepad.

### Installing a New Certification Key

Purpose: To install and activate the new key.

*Do this exercise from both computers.*

1. Internet Service Manager should still be open from a previous exercise. If not, open it.

2. Right-click your Web site.

3. Click Properties.

4. Select the Directories Security tab.

5. Click Edit from the Secure Communication box.

6. Click Key Manager.

7. Right-click CertKey, underneath WWW.

8. Click Install Key Certificate.

9. Go to the \inetpub\certkey folder.

10. Select the file newcert.cer.

11. Click Open.

12. Enter the password you used to create the request file.

13. Click OK.

14. Click OK on the Server Bindings dialog box.

15. Close Key Manager.

16. Click Yes if asked "Commit all changes now?" You may need to close Key Manager again.

17. Click OK on the Secure Communications dialog box.

18. Click OK to close the Web Site Properties dialog box.

19. Close the MMC.

## QUESTIONS AND ANSWERS

| | |
|---|---|
| Do I need to install Certificate Server to operate a Web site? | No, you never need to install Certificate Server. Certificates add to security but their absence does not affect functionality. |
| If I only have an intranet, should I install Certificate Server? | Maybe. The functionality that certificates offer can be useful on a large internal network. On smaller networks, the need to authenticate at this level may not be so critical. |
| How do certificates keep unauthorized users from gaining access? | Certificates ensure that known computers are talking to each other. Remember that you installed the certificate in the browser. Any user who can gain access to the computer will be able to use the browser. |
| If public keys are available to everyone, how can the system be secure? | It takes two keys to make the system work. If you don't have both keys, you can't decrypt. |

# CERTIFICATION SUMMARY

This chapter discusses how to implement security and encryption using Microsoft's Certificate Server. Certificates issued by Certificate Server can be used by applications such as secure e-mail, secure electronic transmissions, or applications using the SSL protocol.

Digital certificates are a form of authenticating the person or process on the other end. You can also encrypt (and decrypt) data as part of the security mechanism for your network. You can also use digital signatures and digital envelopes as a means of ensuring the sender's identity and that the message has not been tampered while en route to you.

Certificate Server uses the public key/private key algorithm. Keys are issued in matched pairs of one public key and one private key. To decrypt a message encrypted with a key (either public or private), you must have the other key to the matched set.

Certificate Server sends the public and private keys using a certificate. The certificate is issued by a Certificate Authority. These digital certificates can have an expiration date set. Certificates may also be revoked. Certificate Server keeps a list of the certificates that have been revoked in the certificate revocation list.

You can have more than one certificate server. When you have more than one certificate server, you arrange them in a hierarchy so that coordination is maintained between the certificate servers. The hierarchy begins with a root authority server and continues down for as many levels as you care to have.

# TWO-MINUTE DRILL

- ❏ Certificate Server is part of the Windows NT 4.0 Option Pack.
- ❏ Certificate Server generates standard X.509 certificates.
- ❏ Certificate Server product consists of a server engine, a server database, administration tools, HTTP clients, software development files, and product documentation.
- ❏ Digital certificates provide the mechanism necessary to conduct private communications in an open environment.
- ❏ Data encryption/decryption involves scrambling the data to make it hard for a hacker to read.
- ❏ Digital signatures provide a mechanism for verifying the sender of the message.
- ❏ Digital signatures provide a mechanism for verifying that a message has not been tampered with along the way.
- ❏ Encryption schemes employ a dual key technology.
- ❏ There is a public key and a private key for each key holder.
- ❏ These keys are unique and are paired with each other.
- ❏ The sender encrypts the data using his/her private key.
- ❏ The recipient requests the sender's public key, so that they may decrypt the message.
- ❏ Certificate Server verifies the recipient's request for the public key and sends the public key using a certificate.
- ❏ Once the recipient has the public key (the mate to the sender's private key) the recipient may decrypt the message.

❏ The private key only exists at the individual computer that was used to generate the key request.

❏ In a digital signature, the sender's private key is used to create a unique (encrypted) algorithm.

❏ The recipient of the message that has been digitally signed uses the sender's public key to generate the signature.

❏ After this, the recipient's version of the signature is compared to the sender's version of the signature. If the two match, the message is authentic.

❏ A digital envelope is created when the sender uses the recipient's public key to encrypt a message.

❏ The recipient uses his/her private key to decrypt the message.

❏ A trusted authority issues digital certificates.

❏ Certificate Server is this trusted authority.

❏ Certificate Server issues a digital certificate to guarantee the authenticity of the public key.

❏ The digital certificate completely identifies the sender.

❏ The certificate is only issued after the requestor's identity has been verified.

❏ The primary objective of the certificate is to assure the recipient of the authenticity of the public key they just received.

❏ Certificates can have an expiration date.

❏ Certificates can be revoked.

❏ Certificate Server keeps a list of certificates that have been revoked.

❏ This list is called a certificate revocation list (CRL).

❏ Revoked and expired certificates are not valid and are not honored when presented.

❏ You may have multiple certificate authorities in an organization.

❏ The top level CA is known as the root.

❏ You may create policy modules for a certificate server.

❏ The policy module tells the certificate server what to do when it receives a request for a certificate.

❑ Certificate Server has several components.

❑ The server engine is the coordinator of the processes.

❑ An intermediary is software that takes a request and gives it to the server engine.

❑ IIS is an example of an intermediary. Exchange Server is another example.

❑ The certificate server maintains a database.

❑ There are two components in the database: the server log and the server queue.

❑ Certificate server administration is done through the browser.

❑ You access the log files form the Certificate Server Administration Tools Web page.

# SELF TEST

The following Self Test questions will help you measure your understanding of the material presented in this chapter. Read all the choices carefully, as there may be more than one correct answer. Choose all correct answers for each question.

1. Which of the following are components of Certificate Server?

   A. Server engine

   B. Server database

   C. Internet Service Manager

   D. Windows NT 4.0 Option Pack

2. Which of the following is not a data security mechanism?

   A. Data encryption

   B. Logon authentication

   C. Digital signatures

   D. Digital certificates

3. Which of the following statements are true about data encryption?

   A. Encrypt and decryption are the same thing.

   B. Encryption can be used to protect data even if the medium for transmitting the data is not secure.

   C. It is easy to unscramble the encrypted data if a hacker captures the data packet.

   D. Data encryption can employ a set of keys.

4. How do you install Certificate Server?

   A. Log on as administrator.

   B. Open the Network applet, Services tab, and click Add Service and select Certificate Server.

   C. Open Control Panel, Add/Remove Software applet, and select Have disk.

   D. Use the Windows NT 4.0 Option Pack Setup program, Add/Remove button.

5. What is the primary administration tool for Certificate Server?

   A. Internet Service Manager

   B. Server Manager

   C. Web browser from the Certificate Server Administration Tools Web page

   D. Microsoft Management Console

6. Which best describes the function of the server queue?

   A. It is an indicator of how busy the server is.

   B. It allows an administrator to see what the server has done.

   C. It records what certificates have been issued.

   D. It maintains status information as a certificate request is being processed.

7. What information is contained in the server log?

   A. All of the logon activity

B. A list of the certificates sent and revoked

C. Only a list of the revoked certificates

D. How many users are currently accessing the server for certificates

8. Which of the following is true of an intermediary in the process of granting a certificate?

A. An intermediary is an application that handles the request for a certificate from a requestor.

B. IIS is an example of an intermediary.

C. The intermediary sends the certificate to the requestor.

D. An intermediary is created and stored as a policy module.

9. Which of the following are not features of Certificate Server?

A. It is transport independent.

B. It is standards based.

C. It uses Windows NT domain authentication.

D. It provides key management.

10. Which of the following statements are not true of CA hierarchies?

A. An organization can only have one certificate authority.

B. The top-level CA is known as the root.

C. Each level of CA is certified by the level above.

D. A higher level CA can revoke a lower level CA.

# 12

# Transaction Server

**M**icrosoft Transaction Server (MTS) is a transaction-based processing system used for developing, deploying, and managing high-performance applications. MTS defines a programming model and provides a run-time environment for these scalable and robust applications. Also included with MTS is a graphical administration tool for managing enterprise applications.

MTS contains the following components:

- MTS run-time environment.
- MTS Explorer. This is the user interface for deploying and managing the applications you create.
- Application programming interfaces (APIs) and resource dispensers. A resource dispenser manages a pool of database connections for MTS components that make standard ODBC calls.

exam
Ⓦatch

*Know the three parts of MTS: run-time environment, MTS Explorer, and APIs.*

<hr>

**CERTIFICATION OBJECTIVE 12.01**

# MTS Model

The client makes a request for an object on MTS. MTS creates an object context and associates it with the object. When the task is completed, the object uses a SetComplete call to indicate that the transaction was successful.

If the transaction was not successful, the object calls SetAbort, instead of SetComplete, which indicates a failure and MTS rolls back the transaction.

This basic pattern is always in effect.

A *transaction* is defined as a unit of work. This unit of work is treated as a whole entity. The transaction either succeeds or fails. But it succeeds or fails as a whole entity or transaction.

For example, you are filling out a form that has your name, company, and city location. You enter all the information but forget to enter the zip code. When you submit the transaction, the transaction fails. None of the information that you sent is accepted because the transaction must either succeed or fail as a whole.

*Transactions succeed or fail as a whole if any information is incorrect or omitted.*

A transaction is a way to coordinate changes being made to a resource. These changes are done through a central point known as a *resource manager*.

## Transaction Properties

Transactions have the following properties:

- Atomicity
- Consistency
- Isolation
- Durability

These properties can be referred to by the memory aid ACID.

### Atomicity

Atomicity means that all of the actions of a transaction must happen, or none of the actions will be allowed.

### Consistency

The consistency property ensures that actions taken do not violate any integrity constraints on any of the objects. MTS checks the permissions of each object involved in a transaction to make sure that no violations occur to any object as a result of the transaction. If a transaction has permission to some but not all of the objects, the transaction will fail the consistency check.

### Isolation

Isolation prevents actions from happening concurrently. This way, conflicting changes cannot occur to the same object. Actions are executed sequentially, one after the other.

### Durability

The durability property means the changes to a resource will survive a network or operating system failure.

## Components of a Transaction

Microsoft defines a transaction as a "discrete unit of code built on Microsoft ActiveX technologies that delivers a well-specified set of services through well-specified interfaces." Components of a transaction include:

- Client logic
- Configuration manager
- Connection manager
- Context manager
- Data
- Database connection manager
- Network protocol
- Network receiver
- Queue manager
- Security manager
- Service logic
- Synchronization manager
- Thread pool

Having listed these components, it is enough that the administrator knows they exist. It is beyond the scope of this work to explain what they do and how you might use them. Consult a book on how to write programs for MTS.

**CERTIFICATION OBJECTIVE 12.02**

# MTS Features

MTS has a number of features that make it easy to develop and deploy transaction-based applications across your network. This section discusses some of the features of MTS, including:

- New features of MTS
- Application development
- A reliable application environment

## New Features of MTS

MTS Version 2.0 is tightly integrated with IIS 4.0. New features from this integration include:

- **Transactional Active Server Pages**   ASP scripts can run in the context of an MTS-managed transaction.

- **Crash protection**   Applications execute within their own MTS environment. This provides process isolation and crash protection from other processes.

- **Transactional events**   You can embed commands in ASP scripts, allowing the application to respond based on the transaction outcome.

- **Object context**   Object context frees the application developer from the complexity of managing user state information.

- **Common installation and management**   IIS and MTS share a common installation procedure and both use Microsoft Management Console.

- **XA protocol support (including native Oracle support)**   MTS supports the XA transaction protocol which means that it will interoperate with IBM DB2, Informix, Oracle, and other XA-compliant databases.

- **Microsoft cluster server support** MTS 2.0 supports cluster server technology (MSCS). That provides for automatic fail-over for MTS application.

- **Support for CICS and IMS transactions** MTS offers support for both CICS and IMS transactions on MVS systems (LU 6.2 Sync level 2).

- **Administration** MTS explorer is an MMC snap-in component.

# Application Development

Server application development is less complex because of the three-tier model employed. The three tiers are:

- Presentation
- Business/data components
- Data source

## Presentation

The client consists of a GUI interface (browser) used to display the Web pages. Other services, such as a database connection, are done at the middle level (business/data components), making less work for the client.

## Business/Data Components

You use this middle level to implement data rules or business rules. These rules provide the logic necessary between the client and the data source.

*Data rules* are the rules that keep data structures intact within the same database as well as between databases. *Business rules* are rules such as government regulations or other business algorithms.

## Data Source

This is the DBMS access layer. It is the computer where the database is kept. You access this layer only by coming through the middle layer.

## Scalable Applications

MTS supports scalable applications. Scalable applications must deal with three issues:

- Multiple clients can generate multiple messages across the network. These messages must be queued and processed and then sent back to the proper client. This must happen in a timely manner. A *message* in this context is a piece of information being passed by the client/server process. This is not a message in the context of e-mail that you might send or receive.

- Scalable applications must accommodate user context. When multiple users access a program, it is possible that the users will have different properties that relate to which objects they have permission for and what that permission is. The application must provide for a user context so those individual users have their unique properties and are not accorded the properties of another user (or users in general).

- Understanding the service logic layer. The service logic layer accommodates mechanisms for database record locking and other synchronization. This is also called a *line-of-business logic* and it sets the rules for accessing shared data.

## Other Development Tools

MTS supports other development tools:

- **ActiveX support**    Software developers write an MTS application using tools that build on ActiveX components. These are tools such as Visual Basic.

- **Automatic thread and process management**    MTS manages the low-level processes and threads for the software developer. This frees the software developer from having to write those complexities into the program.

- **Object management** MTS manages the objects to simplify client interactions. When a client expects an enhanced object and encounters an older object without the enhancements, the process does not fail.

- **Component packaging** MTS has a packaging service that manages the integration and deployment of many components of an application.

- **Database connection pool** MTS manages a pool of IDBC connections to a database, thus freeing the software developer from having to write code in the application to handle these connections.

- **Shared property manager** MTS allows data to be shared among multiple executing objects. This relieves the programmer of writing the code necessary to do state sharing and synchronization.

MTS also provides a command-line environment. You can use these utilities to automate certain tasks from batch files. Table 12-1 lists these utilities and their purposes.

**TABLE 12-1**

MTS Command-line Utilities

| Utility | Purpose |
|---------|---------|
| MTXSTOP | Stops all MTS processes. |
| MTXTEST | Tests component marshalling outside the run-time environment. Marshalling is the process of packaging interface parameters across threads. |
| MTXTSTOP | You need to look closely at this command to distinguish it from the first command. This is the MTX'T'STOP command and is installed only with the Development option. |
| SAMPDTCCC | Tests the DTC installation with a sample client. DTC is the Distributed Transaction Coordinator, which manages transactions that span multiple resource managers. |
| SAMPDTCCS | Tests the DTC installation with a sample server. |
| MTXREREG | Refreshes components registered at the server. |
| MTXREPL | Replicates an MTS server to a designated computer. |
| TestOracleXAConfig | Tests an Oracle configuration to validate transactions involving MTS components. |

## Reliable Application Environment

MTS provides a reliable environment for running applications. It also provides error protection for applications that are running on IIS 4.0.

MTS provides automatic failure isolation and recovery for transactional applications. This support is provided transparently, without the need to explicitly write such controls into your program.

Critical to this support is the program isolation where each program runs in its own environment as a separate process.

## Multiple Deployment Choices

MTS is designed for flexibility. It provides businesses with deployment options for their changing business requirements.

MTS uses the *Distributed Component Object Model (DCOM)*. DCOM is a fast object transport native to Windows NT. This allows components to be located anywhere on the network. The locations of the components are transparent to the client, since the client does not need to know where the components are physically located on the network in order to work. DCOM also supports a technique called *application partitioning*, where applications are spread across multiple servers.

MTS works with any resource manager that is capable of supporting a transactional, two-phase commit process, including:

- Relational databases
- File systems
- Image stores

**CERTIFICATION OBJECTIVE 12.03**

# Installation and Setup

MTS provides a programming model and a run-time environment for transaction-based applications. MTS is an integral part of the Window NT 4.0

Option Pack. MTS installs its components by default when you install IIS 4.0. While it is possible to install IIS 4.0 without also installing MTS, you do not have Microsoft Management Console (MMC) or its functionality to administer IIS.

exam
ⓦatch

*Know that you can install MTS by itself and that if you install IIS, it installs MTS as well.*

You can install MTS as part of the IIS 4.0 installation (or other components). You can also use the Option Pack to install just MTS. You do not need to have IIS installed to install and use MTS.

MTS runs on any Windows NT or Windows 95 computer that has DCOM support.

## System Requirements

The requirements for MTS are essentially the same requirements for IIS, with the exception that DCOM support is required for MTS but it is not required for IIS. Below is a list of the software and hardware requirements:

■ Windows NT 4.0 with Service Pack 3

■ DCOM support installed

■ 30MB of free disk space

■ 32MB RAM

There are other requirements depending on the environment in which you are operating. For example, if you use SQL Server, you must have Version 6.5 or higher. You must also install SQL Server first and then install MTS. If, at a later time, you reinstall SQL Server, you must also reinstall MTS. Microsoft has stated that this requirement will be fixed in a later revision.

## Performing the Installation

You begin the installation of MTS from the Windows NT 4.0 Option Pack. Click on the Add/Remove button if you already have components installed from the Option Pack. If you are just installing MTS and are using the Option

Pack for the first time, select the Custom option. Either way you begin the installation, you have the opportunity to select Transaction Server and the MTS subcomponents, as illustrated in Figure 12-1.

From this dialog box, you can elect to display the subcomponents available with MTS (see Figure 12-2).

The third item in the subcomponents list is Transaction Server Development. There are three subcomponents of this component, as displayed in Figure 12-3:

■ **Transaction Server Development**   Installs the MTS server development tools.

■ **Transaction Server Development**   ocumentation. Installs the development documentation.

■ **Visual Basic Transaction Server Add-In**   Installs the Visual Basic add-in for Transaction Server.

---

**FIGURE 12-1**

Selecting Transaction
Server for installation

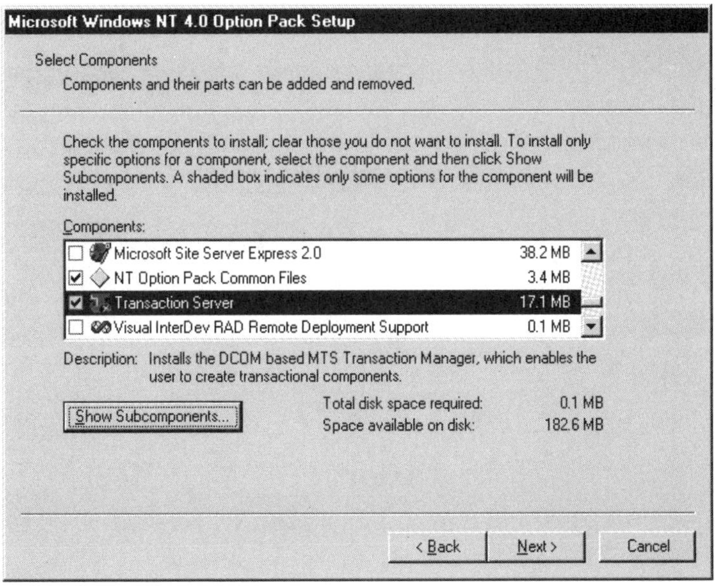

Microsoft Windows NT 4.0 Option Pack Setup

Select Components
Components and their parts can be added and removed.

Check the components to install; clear those you do not want to install. To install only
specific options for a component, select the component and then click Show
Subcomponents. A shaded box indicates only some options for the component will be
installed.

Components:

| | | |
|---|---|---|
| ☐ Microsoft Site Server Express 2.0 | 38.2 MB | |
| ☑ NT Option Pack Common Files | 3.4 MB | |
| ☑ Transaction Server | 17.1 MB | |
| ☐ Visual InterDev RAD Remote Deployment Support | 0.1 MB | |

Description:  Installs the DCOM based MTS Transaction Manager, which enables the
user to create transactional components.

Show Subcomponents...

Total disk space required:        0.1 MB
Space available on disk:        182.6 MB

< Back    Next >    Cancel

**FIGURE 12-2**

Subcomponents available to
Transaction Server

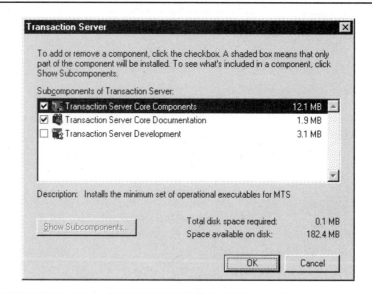

**FIGURE 12-3**

Subcomponents for
Transaction Server
Development

EXERCISE 12-1 **Verifying the MTS Components**

Purpose: To ensure that the MTS components have been installed.

*Do this at both computers.*

1. Ensure that you are logged on as Administrator.

2. Start the Windows NT 4.0 Option Pack Setup.

3. Click Next.

4. Click on the Add/Remove button.

5. Scroll down until you find Transaction Server.

6. Left-click the name Transaction Server. This should highlight the name. There should be a check mark in the box and the box should be gray indicating that there are subcomponents that have not been chosen for installation. Make sure the check mark remains in the box.

7. Click Show Subcomponents.

8. Make sure that the first two boxes are checked and that Transaction Server Development is unchecked.

9. Click OK.

10. Click Next.

11. If any of those components were not installed, they will be installed now. If they were already installed, you may still see the Completing Installation dialog, which looks as though an installation is happening. This is not a concern.

12. Click Finish when present. The Option setup program will close.

## CERTIFICATION OBJECTIVE 12.04

# Microsoft Messaging Queue (MSMQ)

Some applications may need to send communications. Client/server applications are an example of such an application. In addition, applications may need to communicate with other processes as well as with the client portion of the program. This communication takes the form of *messages*. For obvious reasons, these messages must be passed back and forth reliably; otherwise the application won't work properly.

The most common type of client/server communication is *synchronous communication*. In synchronous communication, a message is generated and then the message is forwarded to the recipient right now, in real time. This type of communication is fast but may not be necessary for transactional processing. And, it can be inefficient on a slow communication link.

There is another type of communication method known as *asynchronous communication*. This method is also called the *store-and-forward method*. In asynchronous communication, the message is delivered to a queue for later delivery. The "later" part of this delivery depends on several factors: scheduled time intervals, number of messages accumulated, demand for other resources, etc. Internet e-mail is an example of an asynchronous communication. Asynchronous communication provides near real-time behavior.

## What Is MSMQ?

MSMQ (Microsoft Message Queue) provides the mechanism for applications to communicate with other application programs over a network. The message is received by MSMQ and placed in a queue. The intended receiver looks in the message queue for any messages destined for it. It reads the message, responds accordingly, and the response may go to the message queue where it will be picked up later.

MSMQ keeps messages while they are in transit between the sender and receiver. These queues protect messages from being lost in transit and provide a convenient place for receivers to look for new messages when they are ready. The benefit of this is that the applications may continue processing even if the receiver is unable to reach the network at that time.

Receivers may be unavailable for many reasons. Some of these conditions may be intentional, such as a remote user disconnecting. Some may be unintentional, such as a network segment becoming isolated due to router failure. When the receiver comes back on the network and is ready to process requests, MSMQ delivers the messages in the queue. This process improves reliability in the system.

**e x a m**
**ᗯ a t c h**

*Know what the MSMQ is and what it does.*

## MTS and MSMQ

MSMQ is tightly integrated with MTS and can act as a resource manager within MTS. You can include transactional work in MSMQ operations. These operations will commit or abort in the transaction to preserve data integrity. Remember, transactions either succeed or fail as a whole. If you are sending an update to the database, any abort condition causes the database to roll back the updates. MSMQ also rolls back by canceling the send operation. In this case, since the update was never sent to the database, the database does not actually roll back because it never received the message. The update was handled by MSMQ. MSMQ never completes the send until the transaction commits.

The same type of activity occurs during a receive operation. If the transaction aborts, MSMQ puts the message back in the queue, thereby effectively doing a rollback. The message is still available for subsequent transactions. This is a big deal in database operations. If the receive operation does not roll back when the associated database operations are rolled back, the message will be lost because no database processing occurred.

## CERTIFICATION OBJECTIVE 12.05

# Configuring MTS

You configure MTS using MTS Explorer. MTS Explorer is a snap-in available in Microsoft Management Console (see Figure 12-4).

There are several ways you can access MTS Explorer. You can access just the MTS Explorer by selecting Microsoft Transaction Server and then selecting Transaction Server Explorer from the menu, as illustrated in Figure 12-5. This starts the MMC. When you start MTS in this fashion, you only have MTS in the MMC window.

**FIGURE 12-4**

Accessing MTS Explorer
with MMC

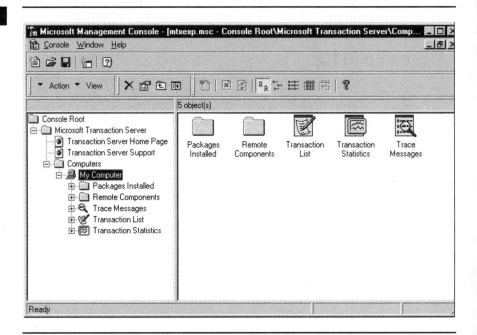

You can also access MTS Explorer by starting Internet Service Manager, as illustrated in Figure 12-6. This opens the MMC; you will have both the ISM and the MTS Explorer in the MMC window. You can manage both functions from this window. Remember, you can create custom consoles that have the snap-in programs that are useful to you.

**FIGURE 12-5**

Selecting Transaction
Server

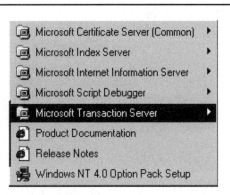

FIGURE 12-6

Using ISM to access the
MTS Explorer

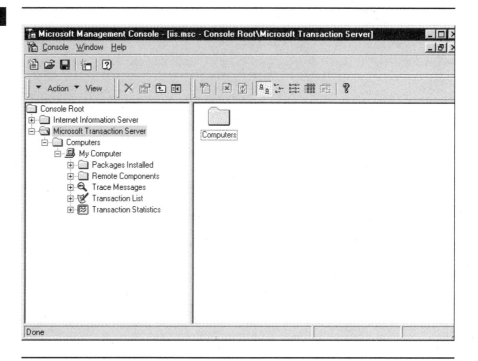

MTS Explorer contains several wizards to help you in assembling and configuring a solution from pre-built packages and components. A *package* is a defined set of components that perform related functions as an application. When you install IIS and MTS, several packages are pre-built for you. Those packages are shown in Figure 12-7.

There are several wizards to help you build packages. These wizards are:

- **Package Wizard**   Use this to create a package.

- **Component Wizard**   Use this to add components to a package. This wizard also lists all of the components registered with a system.

- **Add Server Wizard**   Use this wizard to export packages to a remote server. It also adds the server to a distributed solution.

- **Add Clients Wizard**   Use this wizard to add new clients to a distributed solution.

**FIGURE 12-7**

Viewing MTS components and packages

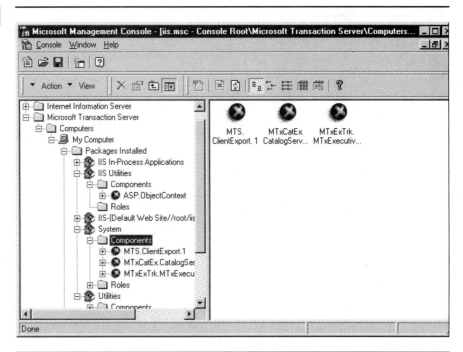

- **Configure Wizard**  Use this wizard to set the transactional properties of components contained in a package.

- **Security Wizard**  Use this wizard to configure the security attributes of components and packages.

MTS Explorer also includes three utilities. They are:

- **Trace Messages**  Use this utility to view the current status of MTS activities such as startup and shutdown. You may also be able to trace potential problems by viewing additional debugging information. You can use the trace slider from the computer's Property sheet, Advanced tab to indicate the level of tracing that is displayed in this window, as illustrated in Figure 12-8.

- **Transaction List**  Use this to list the properties of transactions that are running. This list also includes transactions whose status is in doubt. There are a number of different statuses that a transaction can have:

- Aborted
- Aborting
- Active
- Cannot Notify Aborted
- Cannot Notify Committed
- Committed
- Committing
- Forced Abort
- Forced Commit
- In Doubt
- Prepared
- Preparing

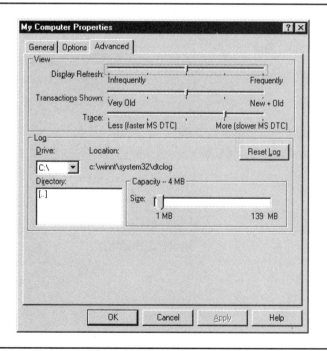

■ **Transaction Statistics**   Use this utility to display statistics for transactions on that computer. Some of the indices are cumulative and some indicate current performance. Figure 12-9 contains examples of transaction statistics.

## Configuring MTS

Purpose: To use MTS Explorer to access various components and packages.

*Do this exercise from either computer.*

1. Start Internet Service Manager.

2. Expand Microsoft Transaction Server.

3. Expand My Computer.

4. Right-click My Computer.

5. Select Properties.

FIGURE 12-9

Viewing transaction statistics

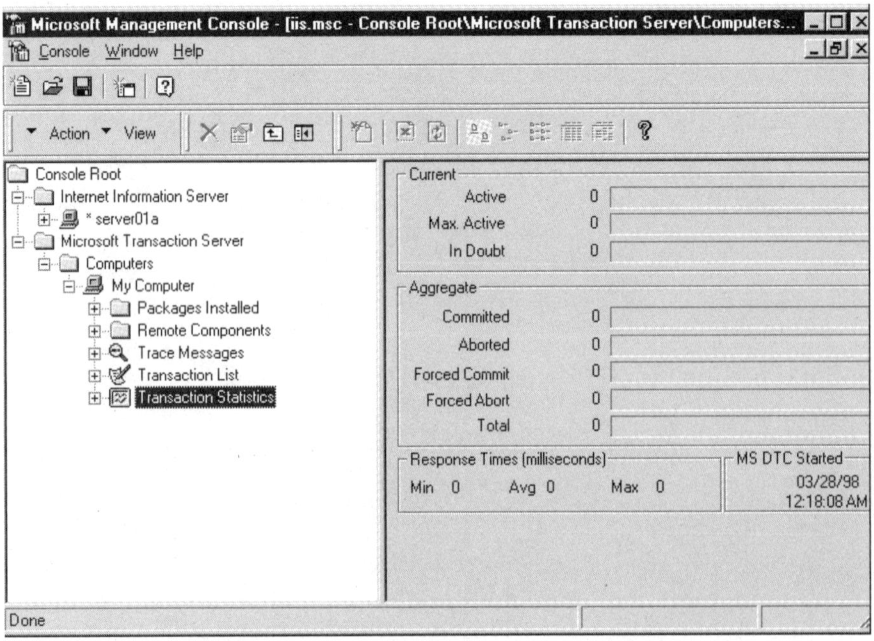

6. Select the Advanced tab.

7. Move the trace slider bar to the middle tick mark.

8. Select the General tab.

9. In the Description box, enter Serverxx.

10. Click OK.

11. Close the MMC.

12. Click No when asked to save the console settings.

# FROM THE CLASSROOM

## An Unfocus on Microsoft Transaction Server

While there are many types of students that attend our classes, most students have some things in common. Most students are IT professionals working to enhance their skills and add to their credentials. In the Web Tools and Internet Information Server 4.0 class, the majority of students are Windows NT administrators who need to learn how to install and support Internet Information Server within their organization.

These students typically come from a network background. Many of these students have Windows NT knowledge and TCP/IP. They are approaching the course from the network and Windows NT administration point-of-view. Many do not have an in-depth programming background. What they know is Windows NT. All these students need to know about Microsoft Transaction Server is that it gets installed when they install IIS.

There is another type of student that comes to the Web Tools and Internet Information Server class. These students are the Web masters and programmers. It is not unusual at all to find these students at a disadvantage during the other parts of the class. Many of these students are not Windows NT administrators and feel lost when we talk about Windows NT security, NTFS partitions, and setting up user accounts. On the other hand, they really shine when it comes to Active Server Pages and the programming environment of MTS.

The moral behind this story is there is something for almost everyone in the Windows NT 4.0 Option Pack. The breadth of the services available is amazing. It is difficult for one person to be an expert in all of the options. Everyone has his or her specialty.

## QUESTIONS AND ANSWERS

| | |
|---|---|
| When do I need MTS? | You don't necessarily need MTS anytime. When you install IIS, MTS is installed, so that you can use the MMC. |
| I am the administrator for our Windows NT Server and the IIS server. Will I be using MTS? | MTS is for programmers who wish to write programs to take advantage of the features that programming for MTS can provide. |
| What do I need to have installed at home to learn more about MTS? | Either Windows NT (Server or Workstation) or Windows 95 with DCOM support installed. |
| How does MTS work in my network? | MTS is used by software developers to build scalable applications on top of ActiveX components. This client/server application runs on the network. |

# CERTIFICATION SUMMARY

This chapter explored Microsoft Transaction Server (MTS). MTS provides an environment for developers to write applications quickly and effectively. You can use these applications to do more complex tasks than you might want to do with HTML Web pages. Microsoft includes two such applications as samples with the Option Pack. One application is a banking application and the other is the well-known game Tic-Tac-Toe.

Transactions either succeed or fail as a whole transaction. If a transaction fails, MTS rolls back the entire transaction.

MTS has several new features. MTS shares a common installation with IIS and like IIS, MTS uses the Microsoft Management Console (MMC). MTS also supports the XA protocol, including native Oracle support.

MTS server applications use the three-tier models: presentation, business/data components, and data source. Having the application in three tiers, instead of the traditional two tiers of the client/server model allows application developers to produce highly scalable applications. MTS takes care of the scalability issue for the programmer. These issues are generally categorized as keeping track of multiple messages, managing user context, and providing for service logic.

Microsoft Messaging Queue (MSMQ) provides a reliable storage location for messages. Senders and receivers use the message queue. With the message queue, processing can continue, even if contact with the other end of the communication is lost. When communication is re-established, messages are sent and received without a problem.

# ✓ TWO-MINUTE DRILL

- ❑ MTS is a transaction-based processing system.
- ❑ A transaction is a unit of work.
- ❑ A transaction is a way to coordinate changes to a resource.
- ❑ Atomicity means that all of the actions of a transaction must happen, or none of them will.
- ❑ Consistency means that actions do not violate the constraints of an object.
- ❑ Isolation prevents actions from happening concurrently.
- ❑ Durability means changes will survive a failure.
- ❑ MTS is tightly integrated with IIS 4.0.
- ❑ An ASP script can run in the context of an MTS transaction.
- ❑ MTS supports the XA transaction protocol.
- ❑ MTS is a client/server process.
- ❑ MTS supports scalable applications.
- ❑ Clients of an MTS application must have context.
- ❑ MTS rules provide user context when accessing objects.
- ❑ MTS has several command-line utilities.
- ❑ MTS provides a reliable environment for applications running on IIS 4.0.
- ❑ When you install IIS 4.0, you install MTS as well.
- ❑ You can install MTS without installing IIS.
- ❑ MTS runs on any computer that has DCOM support.
- ❑ MTS requirements for installation are essentially the same as for IIS.

❑ MTS requires DCOM support, where IIS does not.

❑ You can install MTS when you install IIS.

❑ You can install MTS at any time, with or without IIS.

❑ Applications use messages as a method of communicating with each other.

❑ These messages are not the same as e-mail.

❑ MSMQ is the mechanism for applications to communicate over the network.

❑ MSMQ keeps the messages while they are in transit between sender and receiver.

❑ Receivers can go to the message queue at any time and pick up their messages.

❑ Messages do not need to be picked up in real time.

❑ MSMQ is tightly integrated with MTS.

# SELF TEST

The Self Test questions will help you measure your understanding of the material presented in this chapter. Read all the choices carefully, as there may be more than one correct answer. Choose all correct answers for each question.

1. Which of the following is true about Microsoft Transaction Server (MTS)?

   A. MTS is a transaction-based processing system.

   B. MTS has a run-time environment.

   C. MTS is part of Windows NT Server.

   D. MTS is part of Windows NT 4.0 Option Pack.

2. Which of the following statements is not true of a transaction?

   A. A transaction is a unit of work.

   B. A transaction that has failed cannot be rolled back.

   C. A transaction succeeds or fails as a whole.

   D. Transaction changes are done through a resource manager.

3. What are the requirements to successfully install MTS?

   A. Windows NT 4.0

   B. DCOM support

   C. 16MB of RAM

   D. NTFS partition

4. How do you install MTS?

   A. From the Windows NT CD-ROM

   B. Control Panel, Add/Remove Programs

   C. Network applet, Services tab

   D. Windows NT 4.0 Option Pack Setup

5. Which of the following statements is true of MSMQ?

   A. You can install MSMQ without installing MTS.

   B. MSMQ uses synchronous messaging.

   C. MSMQ uses asynchronous messaging.

   D. MSMQ is a storage area for messages.

6. You are the system administrator of a Windows NT Server running MTS. You suspect that some of the transaction-based applications are no longer running on the server. How do you determine which transactions are running?

   A. Control Panel, Services applet and check to see which transactions are running.

   B. Open Transaction Explorer, choose My Computer properties, and select the Advanced tab.

   C. From within Transaction Explorer, choose Transaction List.

   D. From within Transaction Explorer, choose Trace message.

7. Which of the following statements is true about installing MTS?

   A. You must install MSMQ separately.

   B. You must install SQL Server 6.5 before you install MTS.

   C. You must install MTS before you install SQL 6.5.

   D. After installing MTS, you must manually create the message queue.

MICROSOFT CERTIFIED SYSTEMS ENGINEER

# 13

# Microsoft SMTP and NNTP Services

## CERTIFICATION OBJECTIVES

Internet mail is common among sites that are interconnected, especially to the Internet. Internet mail is typically sent using Simple Mail Transfer Protocol (SMTP). Internet Information Server 4.0 has an SMTP component. This component is dedicated to sending and receiving mail messages over the Internet.

The SMTP service provides facilities for you to customize its configuration to accommodate your security and delivery requirements. The SMTP service has been optimized to provide maximum-messages-per-second processing.

Network News Transfer Protocol (NNTP) allows clients to read articles posted to a common area called a *newsgroup*. If allowed, users may also post articles on the newsgroup for others to read. They may join in a conversation about a topic of interest to them called a *thread*.

NNTP service supports both client-to-server and server-to-server communication over the Internet.

## CERTIFICATION OBJECTIVE 13.01

# SMTP Service

The SMTP service uses the SMTP protocol to deliver messages. Remote mail servers transfer messages from themselves to the SMTP server designated as the domain.

The SMTP service uses TCP port 25 to listen for a connection. The SMTP service receives e-mail from other SMTP servers or directly from applications themselves. As a point of reference, POP3 (Post Office Protocol 3), a service that provides e-mail, uses port 110.

Some people refer to the OSI (Open Systems Interconnect) model when talking about services provided by Microsoft products. Microsoft and Novell products use a different model. The OSI model is irrelevant and for this purpose, out of date. The OSI model was defined in the mid-1970s to support the HDLC (High Level Data Link Control) protocol and derivatives such as X.25.

The Microsoft network model uses four layers. The top layer of the Microsoft network model is the *Application Layer*. This is where the SMTP service functions. For more information on the Microsoft networking model, visit the Microsoft Web site.

There are two types of SMTP message recipients:

■ Local domain

■ Nonlocal or remote domain

## Domains

SMTP domains are different than Windows NT domains and DNS (Internet) domains. On SMTP servers, domains are used to organize messages for delivery. Each SMTP site has at least one domain known as the *default domain*. Strictly speaking, having the one domain is sufficient to operate, but it may not always be desirable.

You can add domains by creating them and configure them as remote domains or local domains. You can also delete domains but you can never delete the default domain.

exam
ⓦatch

*Understand the difference between a Windows NT domain and an SMTP domain.*

If you do not have an in-depth understanding of Windows NT domains, consult other reference material such as *MCSE Windows NT Server 4.0 Study Guide* and *MCSE Windows NT Server 4.0 in the Enterprise Study Guide* (Osborne/McGraw-Hill). Windows NT Domain is a security scheme for organizing user accounts and controlling access to resources of the servers in the Windows NT Domain. It is critical that you be fluent in the planning, setup, and administration of Windows NT Domain to be successful with Windows NT Server. You should also be familiar with IIS and the Option Pack components.

### Local Domain

A *local domain* is a domain that is served by the local SMTP server. The local domain has an entry in the DNS table. When a message arrives at the SMTP server and it is addressed to the local domain, the SMTP server puts the message in a local Drop folder. The local SMTP server cannot send the message to a remote SMTP server. If it cannot put the message in a local Drop folder, it must return a non-delivery report (NDR) to the sender.

NDRs go through the same delivery process as regular messages and are subject to the same restrictions. If an NDR cannot be delivered to the sender, then the SMTP server places a copy of the message in the Badmail folder. You can also send NDR notification to another location as well. You should check the Badmail folder periodically. Deleting messages and NDRs from the Badmail folder helps system performance, especially if there are numerous messages.

## Remote Domains

A *remote domain* is a domain that is not local. This means there is no Drop folder for that domain on the local SMTP server. Mail addressed to remote domains are forwarded to the SMTP server specified for that domain. The SMTP uses DNS entries to locate the remote domain SMTP server.

SMTP server uses the following process to deliver remote mail:

1. **Sort messages**   SMTP sorts the messages by domains. This allows the service to send the messages to a group, optimizing the connection and the transfer.

2. **Queue the messages**   SMTP puts them in a queue ready to send.

3. **Connects to the remote server**   SMTP attempts to connect to the remote server. If the connection cannot be made or the server is not ready, the messages remain in the queue. The delivery is attempted again at a designated time, up to the maximum number of attempts specified.

4. **Verify recipients**   The message recipients are verified. If the recipient is not at the remote server (not verified), then an NDR is generated for that message.

5. **Send**   Once the verification is complete and the recipient is verified, the message is sent and acknowledged.

# SMTP Features

The Microsoft SMTP server that is part of the Windows NT 4.0 Option Pack is standards based and provides full support for the Simple Mail Transfer Protocol. It is also compatible with standard SMTP mail clients such as Outlook Express (bundled with Internet Explorer 4.0) and Eudora.

SMTP service has the following features:

- Standards based
- Scalable
- Ease of administration
- Security
- Mail drop and pickup

## Standards Based

The SMTP service is compliant with RFC 821 and RFC 822. It interoperates with all other compliant SMTP servers and clients on the Internet.

## Scalable

The SMTP service is fully integrated into the Windows NT Server environment and is highly reliable. It offers excellent performance and scales well. It can support thousands of users on a single server.

## Ease of Administration

Because the SMTP service is integrated with Windows NT Server, the administrator uses familiar tools from Windows NT Server such as Performance Monitor and Event Viewer. SMTP service also responds to standard Simple Network Management Protocol (SNMP) commands. To administer the SMTP server, use Internet Service Manager (ISM) or the HTML-based ISM that is included as part of IIS.

Using these tools, you can collect information about the usage and performance of the SMTP server. These tools may also be used to identify problems or potential problems.

## Security

SMTP service can make use of Windows NT security, including authentication and the NTFS file system. The Secure Sockets Layer (SSL) may also be used to give added security to the service.

## Mail Drop and Pickup

You configure the SMTP service for one or more domains. For each domain, SMTP places mail into the Drop folder. SMTP can also be used as a mail receiver for applications to drop their mail. Applications may also pick up messages. SMTP places messages for pickup in the Pickup folder.

### CERTIFICATION OBJECTIVE 13.03

# Installing SMTP Service

Installation of the SMTP service is done from the Windows NT 4.0 Option Pack. Internet Information Server must be installed before you can install the SMTP service. However, you can install IIS without also installing the SMTP service. You can also install the SMTP service at a later time (after you have installed IIS 4.0). The requirements for installing the SMTP service are the same as those for IIS.

If you are installing SMTP service after you have installed IIS, select the Add/Remove button from the Options Setup screen. Then select Internet

Information Server and click Show Subcomponents. The resulting screen (Figure 13-1) shows what is, and is not, installed with IIS.

The SMTP service has two components: the SMTP service and its accompanying documentation. You may install either one or both of these at any time, as illustrated in Figure 13-2.

The installation process creates at least five subdirectories. The Mailroot directory must be installed on the same drive as the SMTP service. Figure 13-3 shows the location of the Mailroot directory.

During the installation process, you can specify the directory structure. If at a later date you wish to move some of the directories, you may, except for the Mailroot directory, which must remain on the same drive as you installed it.

**FIGURE 13-1**

Selecting the SMTP service for installation

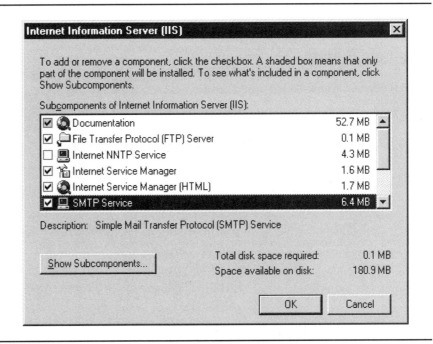

**FIGURE 13-2**

Selecting the SMTP
components

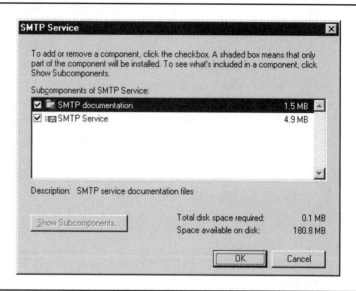

**FIGURE 13-3**

SMTP directory structure

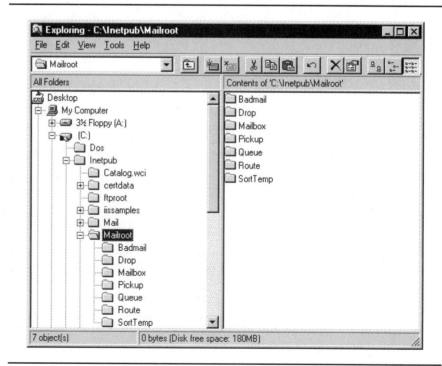

If the partition that contains the Mailroot directory is an NTFS partition, then the Badmail and Drop folders may be moved to a different partition. Otherwise, they must remain with the Mailroot folder. The other folders must remain with the Mailroot folder.

There is no clear reason why you can move some folders if the file system is NTFS. Microsoft documentation never states what happens if the file system is FAT instead of NTFS. You may want to move the Badmail and Drop folders to a drive that has more space. Most of the activity will be in the Badmail and Drop folders.

The following list describes the main folders of Mailroot:

- **Badmail**  Stores undeliverable messages and NDRs that are not returned to the sender.

- **Drop**  Receives all incoming messages. You can have a different Drop folder for each domain you host.

- **Pick up**  Pick up messages from the folder. These messages are created as text files and they are copied into the folder.

- **Queue**  Holds messages waiting for delivery. If a message cannot be delivered, it remains in the queue until it is delivered or until the maximum number of retries has been reached.

exam
Ⓦatch

*Know what the Drop, Badmail, and Queue folders are used for. The Drop folder is for mail pick up, which can be used by applications. If the mail is not picked up before the maximum number of retries is reached, then the mail is moved to the Badmail folder.*

**EXERCISE 13-1**

## Installing SMTP Service
Purpose: To install the SMTP service.

*Do this exercise at both machines.*

1. Ensure that you are logged on as Administrator.

2. Click Start.

3. Point to Programs.

4. Point to Windows NT 4.0 Option Pack.

5. Click Windows NT 4.0 Option Pack Setup.

6. Click Next on the Option Pack Setup screen.

7. Click the Add/Remove button.

8. From the Components box, select Internet Information Server (IIS).

9. Click the Show Subcomponents button.

10. Select the SMTP Service. Make sure that a check mark is in the box at the left.

11. Click the Show Subcomponents button.

12. Make sure all of the components are selected.

13. Click OK.

14. Click OK to return to the Select Components dialog box.

15. Click Next.

16. Click OK if you get a dialog box asking to create the directories.

17. Click Finish.

**EXERCISE 13-2**

## Starting the SMTP Service

Purpose: To start and explore the SMTP service.

*Do this exercise from both computers.*

1. Open the Internet Service Manager.

2. Expand ISM.

3. Expand your computer.

4. Select the Default SMTP Site.

5. Click the Action menu.

6. Click Start.

7. Observe that the SMTP site is now running.

8. Close the MMC.

**CERTIFICATION OBJECTIVE 13.04**

# Configuring SMTP Service

SMTP operates under the context of IIS. Like the WWW service, the SMTP service is administered using the Internet Service Manager (ISM-HTMLA).

## Starting and Stopping the SMTP Service

You can start, stop, and pause the SMTP Service by opening the Internet Service Manager and selecting the SMTP site. This installation creates one SMTP site called *Default SMTP Site.*

After you select the SMTP site, you can take these actions (start, stop, pause) through one of three techniques:

- Click the Action bar and select the action.
- Right-click the SMTP site and select the action, as illustrated in Figure 13-4.
- Click the action (Start, Stop, or Pause) from the rebar.

You may also start, stop, or pause the SMTP service from the Services applet found in the Control Panel, just as you would for other services running in Windows NT Server. Figure 13-5 illustrates this procedure. The drawback to this approach is that you need to be at the console of the server to use the Services applet from the Control Panel.

## SMTP Property Sheet

You use the SMTP Properties sheet to set the properties for the site. There are five configuration sheets for the SMTP site (see Figure 13-6):

- SMTP Site
- Operators
- Messages
- Delivery
- Directory Security

**FIGURE 13-4**

Starting, stopping, or
pausing the SMTP service
form ISM

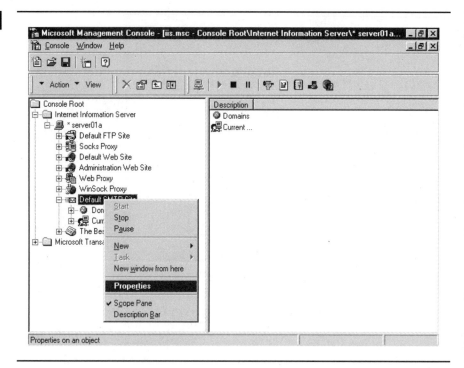

**FIGURE 13-5**

Using the Services applet

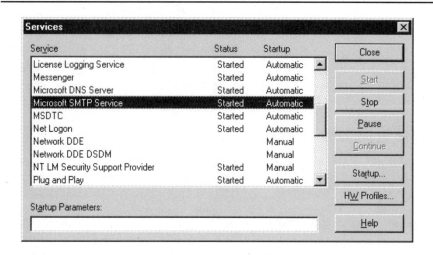

FIGURE 13-6

Default SMTP Site
Properties

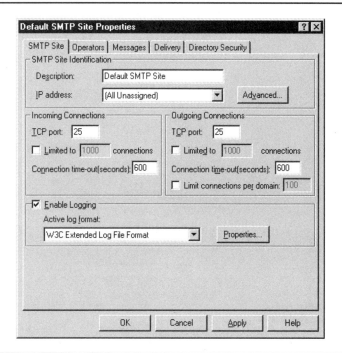

## SMTP Site

There are three sections to the SMTP Site property sheet:

■ **SMTP Site Identification**   Use this section to name your SMTP site. You can also assign which IP addresses monitors which TCP port. By clicking the Advanced button, you can change the selections to suit your requirements.

■ **Incoming and Outgoing Connections**   Use these boxes to specify which TCP port to monitor. You may also specify how many concurrent connections you will allow and what the connection timeout values will be.

■ **Enable Logging**   Use this to enable and select the log format you want. You have four options:

■ Microsoft IIS Log File Format

■ NCSA Common Log File Format

■ ODBC Logging

■ W3C Extended Log File Format (default)

If you use the W3C Extended Log File Format option, then you select which properties to log to the file. Figure 13-7 lists the extended logging options.

## Operators

On the Operators property sheet, you specify which user accounts have operator permissions. Figure 13-8 contains the Operators property sheet. These options can only be set from the Internet Service Manager, not using the HTML version.

Extended logging options available for W3C Extended Log

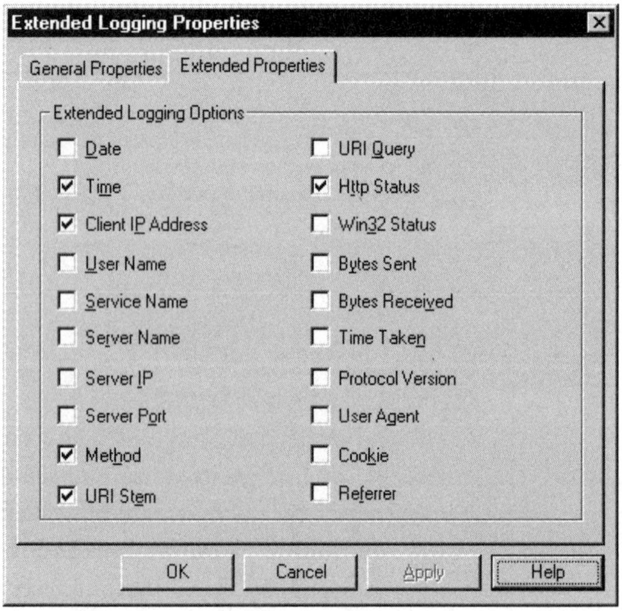

**FIGURE 13-8**

Granting operator
permissions

Operators are users or groups of users who are authorized to access the
service for the purpose of administration. By default, users in the Local
Administrators group are operators.

## Messages

Use the Messages property sheet to set the limits for messages. You can set
limits on the size of the message, the number of recipients, and the session size,
as illustrated in Figure 13-9. You can limit messages as follows:

- **Maximum message size** This indicates the maximum size of a
  message in kilobytes. An individual message may exceed this limit,
  provided that it does not exceed the maximum session size value. If a
  message exceeds the maximum session size, the session will be closed.
  This value should be less than the maximum session size.

■ **Maximum session size**   This is an absolute limit. When this limit is reached, the connection is automatically closed. This value must be equal to or greater than the maximum message size. Its default value is 10240KB. There may be multiple messages sent during a session.

You can also specify the maximum number of outbound messages per connection. This parameter and the maximum message size and maximum session size control the behavior for sending messages. The maximum message size is a soft limit as long as the session size limit has not been exceeded. You can further modify this by stipulating how many messages can be sent per connection.

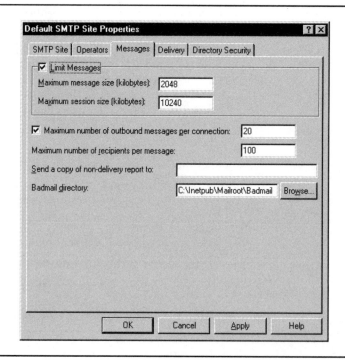

For example, you set the following parameters:

- **Maximum message size**   2048
- **Maximum session size**   10240
- **Maximum number of outbound messages per connection**   20

Now assume there are 43 messages in the queue, and that each message is 1024KB. The first 10 messages are sent, the session size limit is reached, and the connection is closed. The remaining messages wait in the queue for the configured interval.

Now vary the previous example and make the message size 420KB. After the first 20 messages, the total number of bytes transmitted is 8400KB, which is below the session limit. But the connection is closed because the maximum number of outbound messages per connections has been reached.

exam
ⓦatch

*Know how the maximum message size, maximum session limit, and maximum number of outbound messages per connection relate to each other.*

You want to set these parameters based on how many messages you have, what their average size is, how often the messages arrive, what the link speed is for outgoing connections, and how much bandwidth you want to use.

You may also specify the following parameters:

- **Maximum number of recipients per message**   This parameter can be any value greater than or equal to 1.

- **Send a copy of non-delivery report to**   Enter the e-mail address of a mailbox to which you want copies of NDRs sent.

- **Badmail directory**   Specify which folder to use as the Badmail folder. The Badmail folder must be a subdirectory of the Mailroot folder unless it was installed on an NTFS partition and you moved the folder to another partition.

## Delivery

Use the Delivery property sheet to specify the routing and delivery options, as illustrated in Figure 13-10. These settings may be grouped into three broad categories:

- Routing
  - Maximum hop count
  - Fully qualified domain name
  - Smart host
- Transmission
  - Maximum retries
  - Retry interval
- Security
  - Masquerade domain
  - Perform reverse DNS lookup on incoming messages
  - Outbound security

---

**FIGURE 13-10**

Delivery property sheet

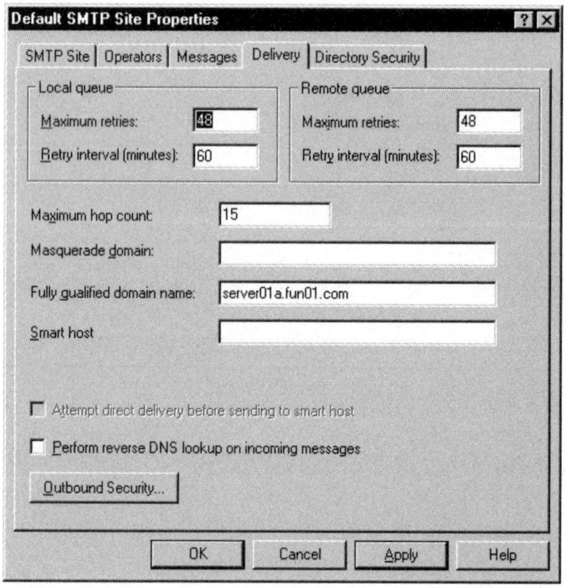

One of the routing options of interest is the smart host option. This option allows you to route outgoing messages to a single smart host. You do this instead of sending the messages directly to the remote domains. Once the smart host is set, the outgoing messages are routed to that server to take advantage of a more stable or less costly route.

## Directory Security

Use the Directory Security property sheet for specifying the access methods and authentication control (see Figure 13-11). There are four categories on this sheet:

- **Anonymous Access and Authentication Control**   This allows you to set:
  - Allow anonymous access
  - Basic authentication
  - Windows NT challenge/response

**FIGURE 13-11**

Directory Security property sheet

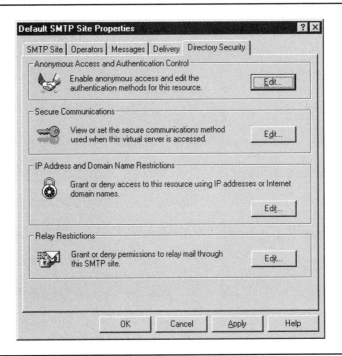

■ **Secure Communications**   This allows you to specify a secure channel using a valid key certificate.

■ **IP Address and Domain Name Restrictions**   This allows you to grant or deny access based on IP addresses or domain names. It also allows you to specify the address of a DNS name to use for lookup.

■ **Relay Restrictions**   Set this parameter if you are going to allow mail to be relayed through this SMTP site. By default, no relay is allowed to limit the proliferation of unsolicited commercial e-mail (UCE).

## CERTIFICATION OBJECTIVE 13.05

# NNTP Features

The Network News Transfer Protocol (NNTP) service is a robust and scalable newsgroup server. NNTP allows you to host and participate in newsgroup-style discussion. NNTP allows users to read articles and to post articles for others to read.

To support this functionality, NNTP has the following features:

■ Standards support

■ Windows NT Server integration

■ Administration

■ Site integration

■ Security

## Standards Support

NNTP service supports both client-to-server and server-to-server communication over the Internet. NNTP supports popular extensions and is fully compatible with other NNTP clients and servers.

NNTP supports the following content formats:

- Multipurpose Internet Mail Extension (MIME)
- Hypertext Markup Language (HTML)
- Graphics Interchange Format (GIF)
- Joint Photographic Experts Group (JPEG)

For additional information on NNTP standards, see RFC 975.

# Windows NT Server Integration

The NNTP service takes advantage of the standard tools that are available in Windows NT Server, such as Performance Monitor and Event Viewer. Installing NNTP also installs the performance counters. NNTP writes service states and error messages to the system log file. NNTP service also responds to SNMP commands.

# Administration

You can manage the NNTP service from either the ISM or the HTMLA version of ISM. The advantage of using the HTMLA version of ISM is that the only tool you need installed is a Web browser. You can manage the NNTP service from a browser anywhere in the world.

# Site Integration

NNTP supports full text and property indexing when using Microsoft Index Server. There is also an optional content replication system that automatically updates the Windows NT Access Control List (ACL) across multiple servers. This makes security administration easier.

# Security

The NNTP service manages access to newsgroups using the Windows NT Server ACL. You set permissions for the folder that contains the newsgroup and control access by assigning permissions to the folder. The NNTP service supports three security options:

- Anonymous access
- Standard NNTP security extension (AUTHINFO)
- Windows NT challenge/response

# NNTP Process

NNTP operates as a service running under Windows NT Server. You find the service by using the Services applet in the Control Panel.

The NNTP service is a client/server process. Microsoft provides their Internet Mail and News client to connect to an NNTP server. You may also use Outlook and Outlook Express to make a connection to a news server. Outlook Express is part of IE 4.0; Outlook Express can also be used as your news client.

The news client uses the TCP/IP protocol and makes the connection to the NNTP server through port 119. When the inbound connection is made, the server authenticates the client. After authentication takes place, the user then gets a list of available newsgroups from the server. The user selects which newsgroups to view, but no articles from the newsgroup have been sent yet. The server verifies that the client is authorized to access this newsgroup and sends the client a list of articles available in the newsgroup.

The client selects and requests certain news articles. The NNTP server sends the client the contents of the selected articles.

## NNTP Data Structures

Each newsgroup has its own folder. Each article is stored as a file in that folder. There may be as many newsgroup folders as you wish.

The top of the hierarchy is the root folder. The default location is inetpub\nntpfile\root but you can change this at any time. NNTP also supports the use of virtual directories. Figure 13-12 shows the NNTP root folder structure.

When you create a newsgroup, the service also creates a folder for that newsgroup. The folder has the same name as the newsgroup.

Newsgroup articles have an extension of .nws. The NNTP service also creates a list of subjects of the articles. It keeps this list in a file with an extension of .xix. It creates a list file for every 128 articles in the folder.

There are other files that NNTP uses that should not be removed. They typically have file extensions such as:

- .hsh
- .hdr
- .lst
- .txt

**FIGURE 13-12**

NNTP root folder structure

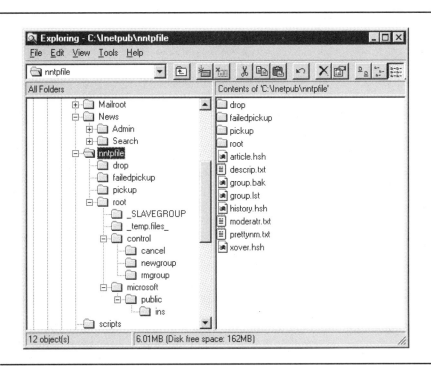

**CERTIFICATION OBJECTIVE 13.07**

# Installing NNTP

You install NNTP using the Windows NT 4.0 Option Pack setup. NNTP
may be installed when you install IIS or it may be installed at a later time.
NNTP is one of the subcomponents of IIS. IIS must be installed before you
can install NNTP. After you start the Option Pack Setup program, select IIS
and click on Show Subcomponents. Select Internet NNTP Service, as
illustrated in Figure 13-13.

There are two subcomponents of the NNTP service: the service itself and
the documentation. You may install one or both of these components at any
time. Figure 13-14 lists these subcomponents.

---

**FIGURE 13-13**

Selecting NNTP for
installation

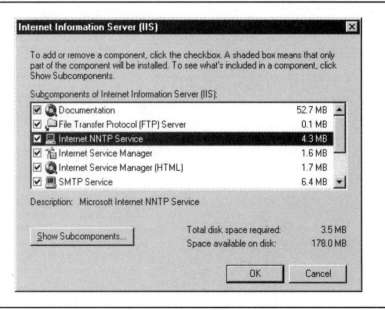

---

FIGURE 13-14

NNTP subcomponents

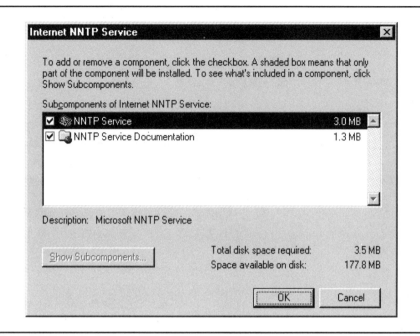

The requirements for installing NNTP are the same requirements as for Internet Information Server. You must have enough disk space to support the planned newsgroups.

## CERTIFICATION OBJECTIVE 13.08

# Configuring NNTP

You can start, stop, or pause the NNTP service from the Services applet in the Control Panel or by using the Internet Service Manager or the HTMLA version. When you pause a service, new connections may not be made. Existing connections will continue to be serviced.

## Creating a Newsgroup

You create newsgroups through the ISM. You start by selecting the property sheet for the NNTP server. You select the Group tab and then select Create new newsgroup. Figure 13-15 contains the dialog box where you enter the newsgroup properties.

You can configure the following newsgroup characteristics:

- **Newsgroup**  This is the name of your newsgroup. You specify the name by starting at the top-level folder. Separate names with a period (.). For example, if you want a newsgroup named Support, enter **Support**. If later you want to create a subgroup to that newsgroup (for example, a newsgroup about supporting Microsoft products), the newsgroup name might be Support.Microsoft. If later you want to add newsgroups for specific Microsoft products, such as IIS, you might specify the name Support.Microsoft.IIS. To create a newsgroup for Word 97, its name might be Support.Microsoft.Word97.

- **Description**  This entry is optional.

---

**FIGURE 13-15**

Creating a new newsgroup

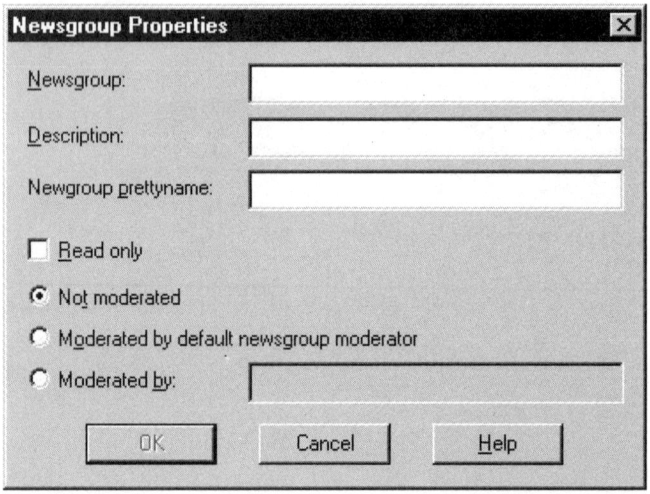

| Newsgroup Properties |
| --- |
| Newsgroup: |
| Description: |
| Newgroup prettyname: |
| ☐ Read only |
| ⦿ Not moderated |
| ○ Moderated by default newsgroup moderator |
| ○ Moderated by: |
| OK    Cancel    Help |

■ **Newsgroup prettyname**   Enter a display name for the newsgroup. This is the name that will be returned with the NNTP command list prettynames.

■ **Read only**   Sets the newsgroup for read-only mode.

■ **Moderated parameters**   When a newsgroup is moderated, the articles are sent to the moderator first. The choices are:

■ Not moderated

■ Moderated by default newsgroup moderator

# NNTP Property Sheets

There are six property sheets used to configure the NNTP service. They are:

■ News Site

■ Security Accounts

■ NNTP Settings

■ Home Directory

■ Directory Security

■ Groups

## News Site

Figure 13-16 contains the News Site property sheet. Use this property sheet to set:

■ **Description for the site**   The name displayed in the ISM.

■ **Path header**   The string used for the path line in each news posting.

■ **IP address**   The IP address for the service.

■ **TCP and SSL ports**   The TCP and SSL port numbers. The default TCP port is 119 and the default SSL port is 563.

■ **Connections**   The number of connections and the connection timeout period.

■ **Enable logging**   Enabling or disabling logging.

FIGURE 13-16

News Site property sheet

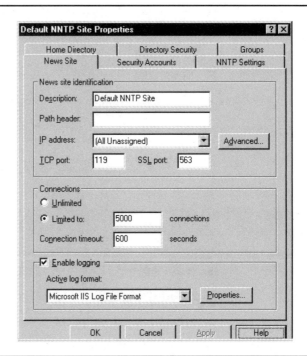

## Security Accounts

Use the Security Accounts property sheet to specify which Windows NT account will be used for anonymous connections. The default account is the IUSR_*servername* account. You also use this sheet to specify the site operators. Figure 13-17 shows the Security Accounts property sheet.

## NNTP Settings

Use the NNTP Settings property sheet to set posting limits for the clients. You can limit the size of articles that may be posted. You can also limit the size of all postings during a connection. You can specify if other servers will be allowed to pull articles from this server and what to do with control messages. You can post control messages or just log them in the log.

FIGURE 13-17

Security Accounts
property sheet

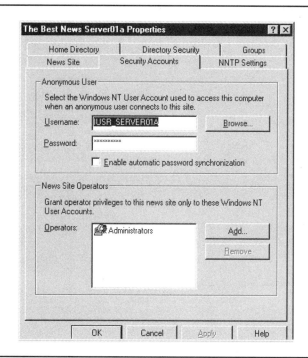

You can specify the SMTP server where postings for moderated groups are forwarded. This can be a host name or a path name. If you use the host name, the NNTP service needs to be able to find the host name in a DNS table. If you use the directory path, the path must either be on the local machine or a virtual directory.

## Home Directory

Use the Home Directory property sheet to specify where the home directory is located. It can be on the local machine or a remote computer. Use the UNC for the remote computer. You also use this property sheet to set access restrictions and content control.

Use the Edit button in the Secure Communications box to set Require Secure Channel for the home directory. Figure 13-18 contains the Home Directory property sheet.

FIGURE 13-18

Home Directory
property sheet

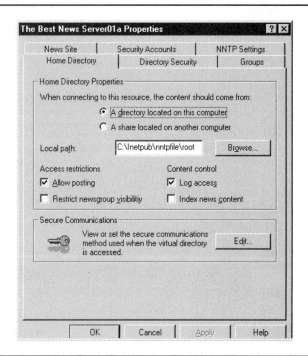

## Directory Security

Use the Directory Security property sheet to set the Password Authentication Method, as illustrated in Figure 13-19. This property sheet contains four check boxes:

- Allow Anonymous
- Basic Authentication
- Windows NT Challenge/Response
- Enable SSL Client Authentication

You also use this property sheet to set the IP address restrictions. The default is to Grant Access to all IP addresses.

FIGURE 13-19

Directory Security
property sheet

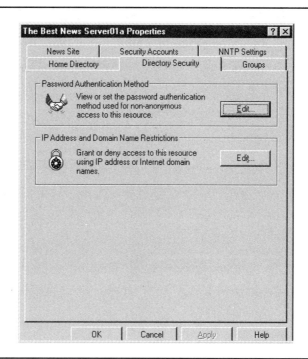

### Groups

Use the Groups property sheet to create, edit, and delete newsgroups from the server. Figure 13-20 shows this property sheet.

**CERTIFICATION OBJECTIVE 13.09**

# Moderated Newsgroups

When you want to have articles read by someone who will be responsible for approving or rejecting the article, consider creating a moderated newsgroup.

**FIGURE 13-20**

Groups property sheet

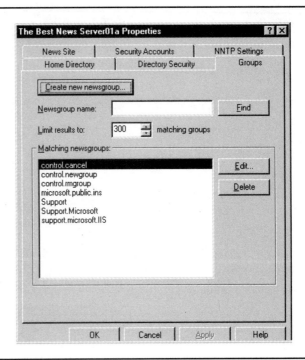

An article posted to a moderated newsgroup is not actually posted until the moderator posts it.

In a moderated newsgroup, when the user posts a message, the NNTP server sends that message to the moderator. The NNTP service uses the SMTP server to send messages to the moderator.

The moderator receives a message. The moderator reviews the article and either rejects it or posts it. When the moderator posts the article, it becomes available to all readers of the newsgroup.

If the moderator rejects the article, the moderator can elect to return the article to the sender with an explanation about why the article is being rejected. Otherwise, the moderator simply discards the message.

CERTIFICATION OBJECTIVE 13.10

# Newsgroup Limits and Expirations

You can establish a limit for the length of time an article may be kept through the New Expiration Policy Wizard. You can set this limit for expiration for one or more newsgroups. These policies can vary from newsgroup to newsgroup. Figure 13-21 illustrates how you set the limits and expiration.

You can specify to delete articles older than the specified number of days. You can also specify that articles be deleted when the newsgroup reaches a certain size. The oldest articles are deleted first. Figure 13-22 contains the New Expiration Policy Wizard dialog box.

**FIGURE 13-21**

Setting the limits and expiration

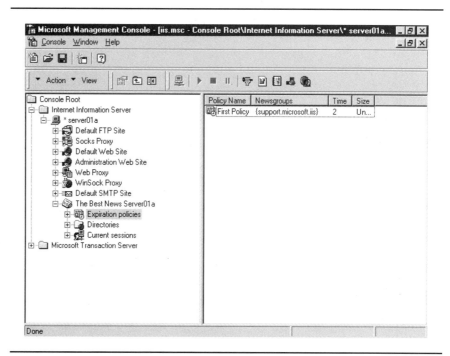

**FIGURE 13-22**

Specifying the number of days or newsgroup content size

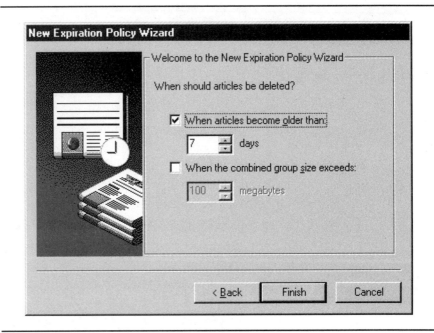

## Installing NNTP Service

Purpose: To install the NNTP service.

*Do this from both computers.*

1. Ensure that you are logged on as Administrator.
2. Click Start.
3. Point to Programs.
4. Point to Windows NT 4.0 Option Pack.
5. Click Windows NT 4.0 Option Pack Setup.
6. Click Next on the Option Pack Setup screen.

7. Click the Add/Remove button.

8. From the Components box, select Internet Information Server (IIS).

9. Click the Show Subcomponents button.

10. Select the Internet NNTP Service. Make sure a check mark is in the box at the left.

11. Click the Show Subcomponents button.

12. Make sure that all of the components are selected.

13. Click OK.

14. Click OK to return to the Select Components dialog box.

15. Click Next.

16. Click OK if you get a dialog box asking to create the directories.

17. Click Finish.

**EXERCISE 13-4**

## Configuring NNTP

Purpose: To configure the NNTP service.

*Do this at both computers.*

1. Open the Internet Service Manager.

2. Expand Internet Information Server.

3. Expand your server.

4. Start the NNTP service, if it is not started. You can start it just as you started the SMTP service.

5. Expand the NNTP site.

6. Right-click Default NNTP Site.

7. Click Properties.

8. In the Description box, type **The Best News Serverxx**, where *xx* is the number of the server.

9. Click the Groups tab.

10. Click Create new newsgroup.

11. In the Newsgroup Properties, enter the following information:
    - Newsgroup: Support
    - Description: blank
    - Newsgroup prettyname: blank

12. Click OK.

13. Create a newsgroup called Support.Microsoft and accept all other defaults.

14. Create a newsgroup called Support.Microsoft.IIS and check the radio button Moderated by default newsgroup moderator.

15. Click the NNTP Settings tab.

16. In the Administrators Email account, type **Webmgr@funxx.com**.

17. Click Apply.

18. Click OK.

19. Right-click Expiration policies.

20. Point to New.

21. Click Expiration Policy.

22. Type **First Policy** in the wizard's Expiration policy description box.

23. Click Next.

24. Check the radio button Only Select newsgroups on this site.

25. Click Next.

26. Enter **Support.Microsoft.IIS**.

27. Click the Add button.

28. Click Next.

29. Set two days for the expiration.

30. Click Finish.

31. Close the MMC.

# FROM THE CLASSROOM

## What SMTP and NNTP Bring to Your Table

One of the things you must assess is what a particular feature or option of a program can do for you, your users, and your operation. The Windows NT 4.0 Option Pack is packed with features and programs. Some of these may be of value to you and some may not. Sometimes it's hard to know how useful a particular feature is until you install it and use it for a while.

Many students who are familiar with the Internet know that Internet e-mail is sent to SMTP servers. The SMTP server for your organization might reside at your ISP, for example. Some students are delighted to see that IIS 4.0 also has an SMTP service. They visualize using this SMTP service on their server and moving from the ISP. Typically an ISP may charge a few dollars each month to host your user's personal mailboxes. This charge is quite small many times, but for a larger organization, the cost could be substantial. For example, the charge of $1 per month for every 10 mailboxes for an organization of 30 people is hardly worth the effort to convert from the ISP to managing on your own. On the other hand, if you have 20,000 users, the financials work a bit differently.

There is one 'gotcha' in the SMTP service that comes with IIS 4.0: It is not a POP3 service, not what you need to host personal mailboxes.

We had one student tell us that putting up the NNTP service was one of the worst things his organization had experienced. He came from a medium-sized company where the IT staff had relatively good control of the Internet access and services. The company management wanted to give the users a bonus by hosting newsgroups locally. The newsgroups were used for internal traffic, as well as taking some NNTP feeds from the Internet. At that point, the student said the workload on his part increased substantially in terms of supporting users about how to use newsgroups and the ever-present requests from users to have access to more and more newsgroups. He was frustrated.

Apparently so was his management. The boss came in one day and told him to stop the newsgroups, at least the newsgroup feeds from the Internet. It seemed that the group managers had complained about a loss of worker productivity. They had discovered that, in some cases, their workers preferred participating in newsgroups to doing the things their bosses had in mind for them!

**CERTIFICATION OBJECTIVE 13.11**

# Optimizing NNTP Performance

You use the Performance Monitor tool in Microsoft Windows NT Server to monitor Microsoft NNTP Service. The performance counters, which are installed with the Microsoft NNTP Service, enable you to build charts and reports that show critical performance data such as:

- Overall performance
- Service activity
- Security

## Performance Monitor Objects

The NNTP Service installs two objects in Performance Monitor: the NNTP Commands object and the NNTP Server object. This section describes the performance counters that are used most frequently. For more information on other available performance counters, consult Microsoft documentation or one of the two books mentioned earlier in this chapter.

The NNTP Commands object contains counters for client commands. The NNTP Server object contains counters for service performance.

In addition to charts and reports, you can define alerts to notify you when monitored values exceed thresholds that you specify. Consult the help information in Performance Monitor for more information.

## Monitoring Service Activity

You want to monitor service activity to make sure that the NNTP Service is accepting new connections and servicing existing connections. The following performance counters provide a good indication of service activity:

- **Bytes Total/Sec in the NNTP Server object**   This value should be greater than 0 when active users are connected.

- **Current Connections in the NNTP Server object**   This value should be greater than 0 when users are connected.

- **Logon Attempts and Logon Failures in the NNTP Commands object** The value of Logon Failures should be a small fraction of the value of Logon Attempts.

- **Logon Failures/Sec in the NNTP Commands object**   This value should be 0 when users are successfully connecting.

- **Maximum Connections in the NNTP Server object**   This value should be significantly less than the Limited to Value in the News Site property sheet.

## Monitoring Security

You can monitor the Logon Failures/Sec counter in the NNTP Commands object as a method of gauging the relative security of your NNTP site. A high number of logon failures might mean that unauthorized users are trying to gain access to your news site.

## Monitoring Overall Performance

In monitoring the overall performance of your news site, you may want to select processor and disk performance counters in addition to Microsoft NNTP Service performance counters. The following performance counters provide advance warning of performance problems:

- **% Processor Time in the Processor object**   The sustained value should be less than 75 percent.

- **Available Bytes in the Memory object**   You want this value to be more than 4,200,000 (4.2MB).

- **% Free Space in the LogicalDisk object**   This value should always be greater than 0. Set an alert at 10 for advance warning that you are running low on disk space.

- **Avg. Disk Queue Length in the LogicalDisk object**   This value should be less than the number of disks in the computer's disk array.

Before you can use the counters in the LogicalDisk object, you must enable disk counters by typing **diskperf –y** at the command prompt and then restarting the computer. Using the performance counters is a heavy resource drain, so disable them when you are done by typing **diskperf –n.**

## Monitoring Performance Trends

A chart view of the Performance Monitor object and counters is best used for monitoring current performance data. To monitor performance trends, use the log function of Performance Monitor. The log function uses the same performance counters as the chart display, but it collects the data at specified intervals. The information is written to a file on the disk that may be viewed at any time. For more information on how to set up a Performance Monitor log file, see either of the two books on Windows NT Server previously mentioned or consult the Windows NT documentation.

## QUESTIONS AND ANSWERS

| | |
|---|---|
| If I use the SMTP service, will my users have Internet mail addresses at my organization? | No. There are two components to Internet mail: SMTP server and a POP3 server. There is no POP3 server in the Option Pack. |
| What do I use the SMTP service for, if it is not for the users' e-mail? | SMTP service allows you to send and receive mail from other SMTP servers and to receive mail from an SMTP client or from other programs. |
| Do I have to use Microsoft Outlook Express as the NNTP news client? | No. You may use any news client. |
| Can I use NNTP service with Microsoft's Proxy Server? | Yes. You need to configure the Proxy Server to support the NNTP protocol and you are ready to go. |

# CERTIFICATION SUMMARY

This chapter explained how to install and configure both the SMTP service and the NNTP service. Both of these services run as services in Windows NT Server and require that Internet Information Server be installed and running prior to installation. You manage the services using the ISM, just as you would for the FTP or the WWW services.

The Microsoft SMTP server is a fully RFC 821-compliant and RFC 822-compliant mail server. The SMTP server supports one or multiple domains. It is a robust service that allows you to configure a variety of security options. Messages are delivered to the server. If they are local addresses, the server puts them in the Drop folder. If they are destined for a remote server, the server puts them in a queue until they are delivered. If a message cannot be delivered, the message is put in the Badmail folder.

Microsoft's NNTP service is a fully functional Network News Transfer Protocol (NNTP) server. It is compliant with RFC 975. You administer the NNTP service using the ISM, just as you would for the SMTP service. The NNTP allows you to configure a variety of security options, including using the NTFS Access Control List (ACL) to set permissions on articles and newsgroups. You can create newsgroups using the ISM. Newsgroups may be unmoderated or moderated at your discretion.

You can also set expiration policies and size limits for individual newsgroups or for all newsgroups as a whole.

 # TWO-MINUTE DRILL

- ❑ Internet mail is typically sent by using Simple Mail Transfer Protocol (SMTP).
- ❑ IIS has an SMTP component.
- ❑ There are two types of SMTP recipients: recipients in the local domain and recipients in a remote domain.
- ❑ SMTP domains are different than Windows NT domains.
- ❑ The SMTP service creates the default domain at installation.

❑ You can create other domains.

❑ You can delete domains that you created.

❑ You cannot delete the default domain.

❑ A local domain is served by the local SMTP server.

❑ Messages bound for a local recipient are put into the Drop folder.

❑ Messages that cannot be delivered are put into the Badmail folder.

❑ NDRs that cannot be delivered are put into the Badmail folder.

❑ You should delete the messages and NDRs from the Badmail folder periodically.

❑ Messages not destined for local addresses are sent to other SMTP servers.

❑ Messages are sorted by domains before they are sent.

❑ The sending SMTP server verifies that the recipient is at the destination before sending the message.

❑ If the recipient is not verified, an NDR is generated.

❑ An NDR is a non-delivery report.

❑ You can use SSL and secure channels with messages sent using the SMTP service.

❑ You install the SMTP service from the Option Pack.

❑ You must have IIS installed and running to install the SMTP service.

❑ You can install the SMTP service during the installation of IIS by selecting Custom from the menu.

❑ You can install the SMTP service after IIS has been installed by using the Add/Remove button.

❑ Both the SMTP and the NNTP services can be started, stopped, and paused using the Services applet found in the Control Panel.

❑ There are five property sheets for the SMTP service.

❑ The NNTP service is fully RFC 975 compliant.

❑ NNTP interoperates with other news servers on the Internet.

❑ NNTP supports full text and property indexing.

❑ You can index the newsgroups using Index Server.

❑ You can restrict access to newsgroups on NTFS partitions.

❑ NNTP is a client/server process.

❑ Each newsgroup has its own folder.

❑ The folder is created when you create the newsgroup.

❑ You create the newsgroup and do other administrative tasks using the ISM.

❑ You install NNTP from the Option Pack.

❑ IIS must also be installed.

❑ There are six property sheets used to configure the NNTP service.

❑ Newsgroups may be moderated.

❑ Articles for moderated newsgroups are sent to the moderator first.

❑ The moderator posts the articles.

❑ You can set time limits on articles and size limits on newsgroup content.

# SELF TEST

The Self Test questions will help you measure your understanding of the material presented in this chapter. Read all the choices carefully, as there may be more than one correct answer. Choose all correct answers for each question.

1. Which of the following statements are true of SMTP domains?

   A. An SMTP domain is the same as a Windows NT domain.

   B. Every site has at least one domain.

   C. A site may have multiple domains.

   D. Domains are created automatically when SMTP does a reverse lookup at the DNS.

2. Which of the following statements are true?

   A. A local domain is always on the same LAN segment as the SMTP server.

   B. A local domain has a Drop folder for messages.

   C. You configure the IP address of a remote domain through the SMTP property sheet.

   D. Messages bound for a local address are put in the queue folder while they await pickup.

3. You are the system administrator. You installed Internet Information Server last week and now you want to install the SMTP service. What is the best way to accomplish this?

   A. Uninstall IIS. Reinstall IIS and select the option to install the SMTP service.

   B. Use the Option Pack setup and select the Custom installation.

   C. Open the Network applet. Select the Services tab and select Add. Choose the SMTP service from the list.

   D. Use the Options Pack and select the Add/Remove button.

4. Which of the following folders are not part of the SMTP directory structure?

   A. Localmail

   B. Drop

   C. Badmail

   D. Pickup

5. How do you set the logging options for the SMTP service?

   A. Open the Network applet, select the Services tab, select the SMTP service, click Properties, and select the Log tab.

   B. Right-click the SMTP site in ISM and select the Log tab.

   C. Open Event Viewer, click on Log, click on settings, and select the SMTP log settings.

   D. Right-click the SMTP site in ISM, select the SMTP Site Identification tab, and set the log settings.

6. You want to keep a remote SMTP server from flooding your server with messages. How can you best do this?

   A. Set the maximum message size lower.

   B. You cannot do this.

C. Pause the SMTP server when the other server attempts to deliver messages.

D. Set the maximum session size smaller.

7. You have recently installed the SMTP service on your IIS site and are concerned that your server not be used to send spam (junk e-mail). What can you do to prevent this?

A. Set the relay restrictions in the Directory Security property sheet.

B. You cannot do this with Microsoft's SMTP service.

C. Set the relay restrictions in the Delivery property sheet.

D. Don't configure your server to send mail to remote SMTP servers.

8. Which of the following statements are true of the NNTP service?

A. The root folder is created during installation.

B. You must create the root folder after installation.

C. You must manually create folders for your newsgroups.

D. Newsgroups can be on either the local server or on remote servers.

9. What is a moderated newsgroup?

A. A newsgroup that does not allow extreme discussions.

B. A moderated newsgroup only allows so many articles to be posted each day.

C. Articles are posted to the newsgroup and a moderator may delete them if they are inappropriate for the newsgroup.

D. Articles are sent to a moderator. The moderator sends the articles to the newsgroup.

10. You are the newsgroup operator. Your server contains several newsgroups. Some of the newsgroups have articles that have a short time value and you want to remove them after a few days. Several newsgroups have content that should remain available for a long period of time, but you don't want the messages in these groups to consume too much disk space. How can you devise a policy to support both objectives?

A. You have to manually delete those articles that are no longer of value.

B. Use Windows NT Explorer to set quota limits on the folders for the newsgroups.

C. Set expiration limits for the newsgroups where the messages have a short life and set size limits for newsgroups where the messages need to remain for a long time.

D. You cannot set a policy that both restricts the number of days and the size limits differently for different newsgroups. What you set for one newsgroup will be effective for them all.

MICROSOFT CERTIFIED SYSTEMS ENGINEER

# 14

# Tuning and Troubleshooting IIS

T his chapter describes the following tools, and how to use them to tune, monitor, and troubleshoot common problems with Internet Information Server (IIS):

- Site Server Express
- Performance Monitor
- Log files

## CERTIFICATION OBJECTIVE 14.01

# Site Server Express

Microsoft's Site Server Express is a subset of the features found in the Microsoft product called Site Server. Some of the features of Site Server Express are:

- **Personalization System**  Site Server Express works with Active Server Pages to dynamically generate Web pages based on stored user preferences. It enables you to deliver targeted content to each site visitor.

- **Content Replication System**  This feature enables you to implement site staging and to mirror server Web sites into a corporate backbone. It provides a reliable, secure, and efficient way to move content within Web servers.

- **Web Publishing Wizard**  This feature provides you with the ability to post Web pages to almost any type of Web server.

- **Posting Acceptor**  Allows IIS to accept Web content from the Web Publishing Wizard. It also integrates with Content Replication System.

- **Usage Analyst**  With this feature, you can import Web server logs and provide a comprehensive suite of usage analysis reports.

- **Site Analyst**  This feature provides comprehensive site visualization, content analysis, link management, and reporting capabilities for managing Web sites.

Site Server Express allows you to:

- **Publish content**   Using the Posting Acceptor, you can provide a hosting service for users wanting to post Web content to your server.

- **Manage content**   Using the Quick Search feature, you can detect broken links, find objects with load sizes greater than 32KB, and perform other tasks.

- **Analyze usage**   Using Content Analyzer, you can find broken links, analyze site structure and object properties, manage local and remote sites, and perform a variety of other Web site management tasks.

Site Server Express has four components:

- **Content Analyzer**   Content Analyzer provides comprehensive site visualization, content analysis, link management, and reporting capabilities for managing Web sites.

- **Usage Import**   Usage Import reads the Internet server log files and reconstructs the actual requests, visits, users, and organizations that have been to your Web site.

- **Report Writer**   The Report Writer enables you to analyze and cross-reference properties of the requests, visits, and users who have visited your site.

- **Posting Acceptor**   As indicated previously, the Posting Acceptor allows your users to publish information on the Web site. The Posting Acceptor allows you to accept Web content from Microsoft Web Publishing Wizard/API and Netscape Navigator 2.02 (or higher) through any standard HTTP connection.

## Installing Site Server Express

You install Site Server Express from the Windows NT 4.0 Option Pack Setup. Select the Add/Remove button and then select Microsoft Site Server Express 2.0 from the choices presented, as illustrated in Figure 14-1.

**FIGURE 14-1**

Installing Site Server
Express

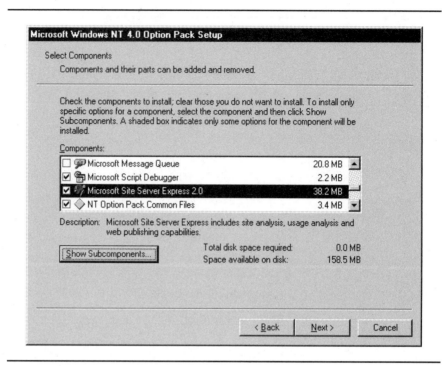

There are four subcomponents of Site Server Express that you may choose (see Figure 14-2):

- Analysis - Content
- Analysis - Usage
- Publishing - Posting Acceptor 1.01
- Publishing - Web Publishing Wizard 1.52

**EXERCISE 14-1**

## Installing Site Server Express

Purpose: To install Site Server Express.

*Do this from both computers.*

1. Ensure that you are logged on as Administrator.
2. Click Start.

3. Point to Programs.

4. Point to Windows NT 4.0 Option Pack.

5. Click on Windows NT 4.0 Option Pack Setup.

6. Click on Next on the Option Pack Setup screen.

7. Click the Add/Remove button.

8. From the Components box, select Site Server Express 2.0.

9. Click the Show Subcomponents button.

10. Make sure that all of the components are selected.

11. Click OK to return to the Select Components dialog box.

12. Click Next.

13. Click OK if you get a dialog box asking to create the directories.

14. Click Finish.

**FIGURE 14-2**

Site Server Express
components

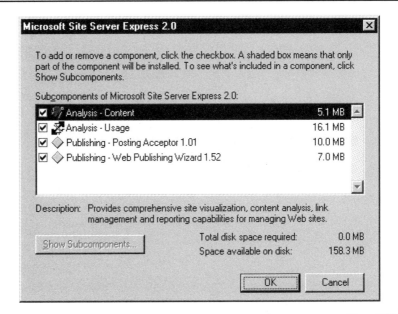

## Content Analyzer

The Content Analyzer allows you to visualize the Web site. Using the Content Analyzer, Web administrators can find broken links. The Content Analyzer also allows you to analyze site structure and object properties, manage local and remote Web sites, and perform other Web site management tasks. The goal of Content Analyzer is to allow you to manage your Web site more effectively. You can use the features of Content Analyzer to help you optimize your Web site.

A *WebMap* is a graphical representation of the resources in your site. These include resources such as HTML pages and graphic images, program files, Java, and Word files, etc. The map has easily identifiable icons and label colors, making it a powerful tool that helps you quickly identify your site's structure. The map provides you with information at a glance, information you might spend hours looking for.

There are two options for viewing the Web site from within Content Analyzer:

- The tree view, a hierarchical view of the site map.

- The Cyberbolic view that depicts the Web site, showing its interconnected structure.

You start the Content Analyzer from the Microsoft Site Server Express 2.0 group found inside the Option Pack group. When you launch Content Analyzer, it prompts you with the three choices illustrated in Figure 14-3. You can choose to view the User's Guide, create a new WebMap or open an existing WebMap.

As stated previously, a WebMap is a graphical view of your site. You use a WebMap to find and repair broken links, hypertext links, headings, and titles. A WebMap shows you the resources and objects in your Web site and the relationship between them.

The first step in creating a new WebMap is to specify whether to create the map from a URL or a file. Once you have created a WebMap, you can save it

FIGURE 14-3

Opening Site Server
Express

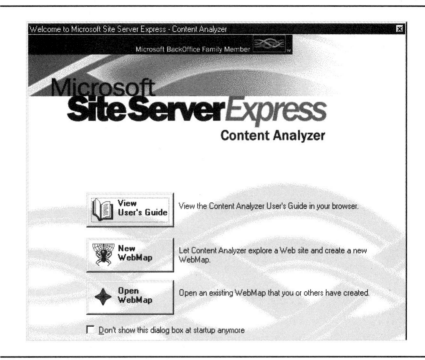

as a file and recall it for later use. This is faster than creating a new WebMap each time. This illustration shows how you create a WebMap.

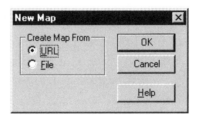

After the WebMap has been created, you may view the WebMap with the Content Analyzer. The default file location for storing a WebMap is

\Program Files\Content Analyzer Express\Webmaps. WebMap files have an extension
of .wmp. The Content Analyzer offers two views of the site, tree view and Cyberbolic view.

You can customize Content Analyzer after you have installed it using the Program Options menu under the View menu from inside Content Analyzer. There are five tabs in Program Options. They are:

- General
- Helpers
- Proxy
- Cyberbolic
- Passwords

## Tree View

The tree view displays the WebMap objects in a hierarchy listing, as illustrated in Figure 14-4. Each icon and its text label represent an object in the site. At the top of the tree is the home page. All objects directly under the home page are on the home page. All objects linked to the home page are considered second-level objects and appear indented. Third-level objects are indented from the second-level objects, and so on.

Some objects have a small gray box to the left. These are *control objects*. This box has three states:

- **Plus**   This indicates that there are objects contained within. This view may be expanded.
- **Minus**   This view is already expanded so you can view the objects.
- **Question Mark**   This means the page has not yet been examined to determine what objects are contained on the page.

A page with no icons indicates that the page has been examined and there are no links to other pages contained on that page.

FIGURE 14-4

Tree view of the WebMap

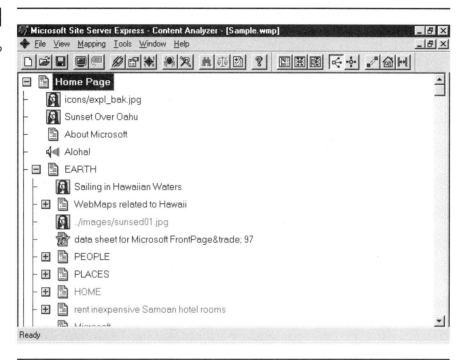

## Cyberbolic View

The Cyberbolic view is a dynamic view of the WebMap. Unlike the tree view, the Cyberbolic view is not linear. It is meant to be graphical in its presentation and to represent more closely how you might visualize the Web site in your mind. Figure 14-5 contains an example of the Cyberbolic view.

An interesting feature of the Cyberbolic view is you can left-click any object and move it around the view. This changes the perspective and gives a different feel for the site and object relationships.

You can set the object view to be at the center of the page or at the left of the page. When you select an object, that object becomes the focus point of the view. For example, if the view is set to the left and you select an object, the

**FIGURE 14-5**

Cyberbolic view of the
WebMap

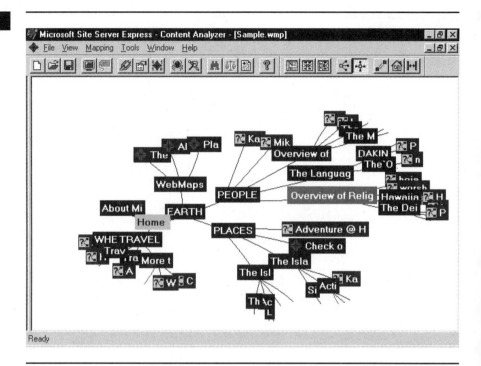

perspective changes so that you have a better view of the objects that relate to the object that you just selected.

The Cyberbolic view takes a little more real estate on your screen to display. Therefore, it uses short labels by default. Pointing to an object with your mouse causes the tool tips to come into view for 1.5 seconds. If you look away, you may miss the tool tip. If you move the cursor away and point to the object again, you will have another chance to view the tool tip.

The Cyberbolic view, by default, only displays Web pages and not all resources. This is done to reduce the clutter that might result from too many objects. Also, as all objects are displayed, there is no expanding or collapsing as there is in the tree view.

**EXERCISE 14-2**

## Using Content Analyzer

Purpose: To become familiar with Content Analyzer.

*Do this exercise at either computer.*

1. Click Start.

2. Point to Programs.

3. Point to Windows NT 4.0 Option Pack.

4. Point to Site Server Express 2.0.

5. Click on Content Analyzer.

6. Click on the New WebMap button.

7. Make sure that the URL radio button is selected and click OK.

8. Type your server name in the Home Page Address (URL): box. For example, **Serverxx.funxx.com.**

9. Observe the creation of the WebMap. This takes a couple of minutes. The larger and more complex the site, the longer it takes to create a WebMap.

10. Click OK on the Generate Site Reports dialog box to accept the default file location and name.

11. Internet Explorer (IE) should launch with a Site Summary Report. Review the information contained in the report.

12. Minimize IE.

13. Return to Content Analyzer.

14. Maximize Content Analyzer and the window.

15. You should have two panes in the window. The left pane is the hierarchical view and the right pane is the Cyberbolic view. On the toolbar, locate the button for Maximize Tree view and select it. The Cyberbolic view should disappear.

16. Left-click the plus key next to "Welcome to IIS 4.0!" This should expand the object.

17. Right-click Internet Information Server under the welcome, and select Properties. Take some time to explore the Properties dialog box.

18. Click Cancel.

19. Locate the Maximize Cyberbolic View button and click it. The Tree view should disappear.

20. From the toolbar, left-click the Center Orientation button.

21. Locate the tag "Welcome to Exploration Air On-line." If you hold the mouse pointer over the object, the full text label displays.

22. Left-click that object and observe the changes.

23. Left-click and slowly drag that object toward the lower right-hand corner of the screen. Observe the changes.

24. Close Content Analyzer. Click No if asked to save changes.

25. Close IE.

## Site Summary Report

You can generate a Site Summary Report (Figure 14-6) to assist in your understanding about the content of the site. The report includes:

■ **Object Statistics**   Counts and sizes for various objects such as pages, images, applications, etc.

**FIGURE 14-6**

Site Summary Report

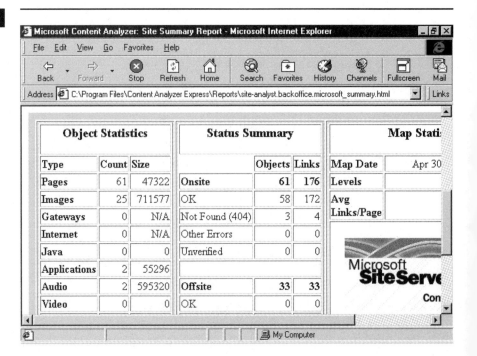

| Object Statistics | | | Status Summary | | | Map Stati: | |
|---|---|---|---|---|---|---|---|
| Type | Count | Size | | Objects | Links | Map Date | Apr 30 |
| Pages | 61 | 47322 | Onsite | 61 | 176 | Levels | |
| Images | 25 | 711577 | OK | 58 | 172 | Avg Links/Page | |
| Gateways | 0 | N/A | Not Found (404) | 3 | 4 | | |
| Internet | 0 | N/A | Other Errors | 0 | 0 | | |
| Java | 0 | 0 | Unverified | 0 | 0 | | |
| Applications | 2 | 55296 | | | | | |
| Audio | 2 | 595320 | Offsite | 33 | 33 | | |
| Video | 0 | 0 | OK | 0 | 0 | | |

- **Status Summary**   Counts of objects and links that are OK or missing or have some other error condition for both on-site and off-site links.

- **Map Statistics**   The map date, number of levels, and average number of links per page.

- **Server Summary**   The domain, server version, and HTTP version.

# Quick Search

You can search your site for weaknesses and errors. Content Analyzer has eight quick searches available for use. You access the Quick Search from the Tools menu within the program.

- **Broken Links**   You can search the site for links that do not successfully connect to their destination object.

- **Home Site Objects**   This search shows objects that share the same domain as your home page. It can determine if an object needing repair can be accessed locally.

- **Images without ALT**   This search finds images that do not have the optional ALT text string. This allows you to find graphic objects that do not display a placeholder label to text-only browsers because the ALT string is missing.

- **Load Size over 32KB**   This search shows which pages require more than 32KB of data to pass to your browser during the load. This helps identify which resources can be trimmed to reduce the download time.

- **Non-Home Site Objects**   This search shows you which objects do not exist in the same domain as your home page. You can use this to see which links are not under your control. You may want to check the links often for reliability.

- **Not Found Objects (404)**   This search finds objects that cannot be located. These objects give that ever-annoying HTTP 404 error message. These objects have links that have been removed or need to be repaired.

- **Unavailable Objects**   This search lists objects that cannot be located, or cannot be accessed when located. Reasons for this could be that the server may be down or the communication link may be down. It can also be because the object is password protected.

- **Unverified Objects**  This search shows objects that have not been checked to see if they are accessible or not.

# Report Writer

You can create reports on usage activity for your site. Before you can do this, enable logging for the site. Next, take the log file and import it into the database. Do the import from the Usage Import program. Initially, you need to configure the program for which Web site to monitor and where to get the log files. After this is configured, click the Start Import button and the data from the log files will be imported.

Now that you have imported the log files into the database, you can produce reports that help you analyze the activity for the site. You do this from Report Writer. With Report Writer, you create and save your own reports. You can also select from 20 already created report formats. These report formats include detailed reports and summary reports. You can also edit these reports to better reflect your needs.

There are nine separate detail reports for you to use:

- **Bandwidth**  This report shows the number of bytes transferred on an hourly, daily, or weekly basis.

- **Browser and Operating System**  This report shows trends about Netscape and Microsoft browsers and operating systems. This report requires the user agent.

- **Geography**  This report shows the top geographic areas of visitors to your site. This requires that the IP resolution and Who-is queries be done before analysis.

- **Hit**  This report shows the number of hits to a site by hour, day, or week. It also includes averages for hour-of-the-day or day-of-the-week analysis.

- **Organization**  This report is similar to the Geography report. It shows who may be visiting your site.

- **Referrer** This report shows the top external links that users went to from your site. This report requires referrer data and IP resolutions.

- **Request** This report highlights the least-requested documents and the most-requested documents on your site.

- **User** This report gives you user type information such as the number of users who visit your site, who the first-time visitors are, the requests, and the length of stay.

- **Visits** This report gives you the number of requests made by the busiest of your visitors.

# Performance Monitor

Performance Monitor is a major tool for tuning and troubleshooting your Windows NT Server and applications that are running on Windows NT Server. Anything that you might want to know about what is happening on your Windows NT system can be discovered using Performance Monitor.

Performance Monitor is a standard tool with Windows NT. You start Performance Monitor from the Administrative Tools Group. Everything in the Windows NT operating system is an object. An object may have various *instances*. An instance is a unique occurrence of an object. For example, if you have two CPUs in your system there are two instances of the processor object. You can monitor the performance of either or both instances of the processor.

Performance Monitor has a set of core objects that are installed when the operating system is installed. Which additional objects are installed depends on what else you install on Windows NT. For example, if the FTP service is installed, you have an object, the FTP service, installed in Performance Monitor. Likewise, if the Web service is installed, then you have the object Web service.

If you want to track disk performance by using the Logical and Physical Disk objects, you must enable the counters first by issuing the command diskperf –y at the command prompt and restarting the computer. Using the disk counters is a substantial performance drain. Therefore, you only want to use these counters while you are testing and then turn them off. The command to turn off the disk counters is **diskperf –n**.

Each object/instance has a unique set of counters associated with it. These counters are the actual statistics that are being collected or monitored. For example, Table 14-1 contains the counters for the HTTP Content Index object.

Which object and which counters you select depends entirely on the information you want, or what you are trying to discover. For example, if you are trying to determine how busy your Web server is and how many resources it is consuming, you might want to monitor objects such as:

- Active Server Pages
- Internet Information Services Global
- Web service

You may also want to monitor other objects such as memory, cache, server work queues, and processes such as CiDaemon. You will probably not be very interested in the objects server, redirector, or system.

It may take you some time to discover which objects are important to you and how they relate to each other. This trial-and-error process of determining

**TABLE 14-1**

Examples of Counters and Their Explanations

| Counter | Explanation |
| --- | --- |
| % Cache Hits | % of queries found in the query cache |
| % Cache Misses | % of queries not found in the query cache |
| Active Queries | Number of current queries running |
| Cache Items | Number of completed queries in cache |
| Current Requests Queued | Current number of query requests queued |
| Queries Per Minute | Number of queries per minute |
| Total Queries | Total number of queries run since service start |

which objects to use may take you some time to master. This is quite normal for Windows NT administrators. In addition, you have different sets of objects for different scenarios.

# Analyzing Performance

One of the keys to effectively using Performance Monitor is to establish core sets of objects to be monitored and use them periodically. The first time you should use them is before you put the server into production. This gives you a no-load performance measurement referred to as a *baseline*. You will refer to this baseline when you run subsequent tests on the server. By comparing the later tests to the baseline, you can monitor the performance of the server over time.

You can start Performance Monitor on any Windows NT computer (including Windows NT Workstation) and monitor another Windows NT computer. You can use this technique to reduce the overhead associated with Performance Monitor by running on a computer whose performance you are not monitoring. Of course, if you are attempting to analyze network performance, then this technique is not as good because you generate network traffic as the statistics.

## Identifying Bottlenecks

You can use Performance Monitor to help determine where *bottlenecks* exist. A bottleneck is any place there is a system shortage or a resource shortage. All computer systems will have resource shortages. Alleviating one resource shortage may cause another area to be identified as the bottleneck. You may then try to add more resources to shore up that area.

Generally speaking, you should monitor four categories of objects when you are monitoring the system and attempting to identify bottlenecks:

- CPU
- Memory
- Disk
- Network

## Identifying CPU-Related Performance Issues

*Know that a sustained CPU activity of greater than 75-80 percent indicates a bottleneck and the need for more CPU resources.*

Proxy Server is not CPU intensive, so improving the CPU performance is usually not required. However, tracking CPU activity can help you determine how busy your server is and how much work it is doing. In Windows NT, there are two factors to consider relative to CPU activity and the need to upgrade CPU performance:

- The speed of the CPU (clock speed generally stated in Mhz)
- The number of CPUs in the system

If you are running multithreaded processes, you might benefit more from adding additional CPUs to your system than from increasing the clock speed and only using one CPU. Of course, you must have the appropriate hardware platform to support multiple CPUs and the CPUs must match. You can use the following objects to help determine CPU performance:

- Processor
- Process
- Thread
- System

*Know that the System object gives you totals for the system.*

## Identifying Memory-Related Performance Issues

All of the processes inside Windows NT use memory to run. There is a general rule that states that Windows NT will use all the RAM that you can put in the computer. You can also tune the system to determine exactly how much memory is required to support your configuration.

Windows NT uses a virtual memory manager. *Virtual memory* is comprised of RAM and space allocated on the disk for the pagefile.sys file. Windows NT's virtual memory manager can address up to 4GB of virtual memory.

You can use the following objects to help determine which memory is being used and what processes are using the memory:

- Cache (system cache, not the Web Proxy cache, which is written to the hard disk)
- Memory
- Process
- Server
- Server Work Queues

### Identifying Disk-Related Performance Issues

The disk counters in Windows NT are disabled by default. You must enable them in order to get any information about disk activities. You enable disk counters by issuing the command **diskperf –y** from the command line. If you are using a RAID array, issue the command **diskperf –ye**. Disk counters are a significant performance drain on the system. You should only enable the counters when you want to collect information about disk performance and then turn the counters off. To disable the counters, issue the command **diskperf –n**. You need to restart the computer after you enable or disable the disk counters in order for the state to become effective.

exam
ⓦatch

*Know that the disk counters are disabled by default and how to enable them.*

The two primary objects for tracking disk performance are:

- Physical Disk
- Logical Disk

Each object has its own associated counters. Some of the counters can be found in either Physical Disk or Logical Disk. Some of the counters are unique. For example, the counters % Free Space and Free Megabytes can only be found in the Logical Disk object.

### Identifying Network-Related Performance Issues

There are several objects that you can use to help you identify network-related performance issues:

- IP
- NBT Connection
- Network Interface
- Network Segment
- Redirector
- Server
- Server Work Queues
- System. In particular, the counter Total Interrupts/Second. This is the rate at which the computer is receiving and servicing interrupts. Your network interface card (NIC) generates an interrupt when it has traffic it needs to process.
- TCP
- UDP
- HTTP
- FTP

For more details on how to use Performance Monitor, refer to *MCSE Windows NT Workstation 4.0 Study Guide* (Osborne/McGraw-Hill*), MCSE Windows NT Server 4.0 Study Guide* (Osborne/McGraw-Hill), and *MCSE Windows NT Server 4.0 in the Enterprise Study Guide* (Osborne/McGraw-Hill).

### Optimizing IIS Performance

There are several different types of counters available for monitoring HTTP sites usage and connections in Performance Monitor. There are counters related to:

- Bandwidth usage
- Throughput specific requests

■ Errors and counters related to users and connections.

Table 14-2 lists some of the counters related to connections. You can use some of these counters to monitor current sessions. You can also monitor current session status from the properties sheet of any of the Proxy services by selecting the Current Sessions tab.

**TABLE 14-2**

HTTP Counters

| Counter | Meaning |
| --- | --- |
| Anonymous Users/Second | The rate users are making anonymous connections using the Web server |
| Connection Attempts/Second | The rate that connection attempts to the Web server are being made |
| Current Anonymous Users | The number of users who currently have an anonymous connection at the Web server |
| Current Connections | The number of connections established with the Web server |
| Current NonAnonymous Users | The number of users who have a nonanonymous connection at the Web server |
| Logon Attempts/Second | The rate at which logon attempts are being made |
| Maximum Anonymous Users | The highest number of users who have established an anonymous connection at the Web server |
| Maximum Connections | The highest number of connections made at the Web server |
| Maximum NonAnonymous Users | The highest number of users who made nonanonymous connections using the Web server |
| Non Anonymous Users/Second | The rate at which nonanonymous users are connecting to the Web server |
| Total Anonymous Users | The total number of users who established an anonymous connection |
| Total Connection Attempts | The total number of attempted connections to the server |

| | |
|---|---|
| **TABLE 14-2**<br><br>HTTP Counters<br>(*continued*) | |

| Counter | Meaning |
|---|---|
| Total Logon Attempts | The total number of successful logons at the server |
| Total NonAnonymous Users | The total number of users who established a nonanonymous connection |

### Optimizing Index Server Performance

There are two objects that you can use to monitor the performance of Index Server: the Contents Index and the Content Index Filter. Table 14-3 lists the counters for the Content Index.

Table 14-4 lists the counters that may be used to monitor activities of the content filters.

### Optimizing SMTP Performance

The SMTP service for IIS 4.0 provides Windows NT Performance Monitor counters to measure responsiveness. Use these to assist in troubleshooting your SMTP service.

In addition to the SMTP service object counters, you might also want to monitor counters for objects that measure system capacity. These include:

- Logical Disk object (% Disk Time counter)
- Memory object (Available Bytes counter)
- System object (% Total Processor Time counter).

For more information on increasing performance using Performance Monitor, see the Windows NT Server documentation.

| | |
|---|---|
| **TABLE 14-3**<br><br>Content Index Counters | |

| Counter | Meaning |
|---|---|
| # Documents Filtered | The number of documents filtered since the indexing was started in the instant of the current process |
| Files to be Filtered | The remaining files waiting to be filtered |
| Total # of Documents | Total number of documents in the index |

**TABLE 14-4**

Content Index Filter
Counters

| Counter | Meaning |
|---|---|
| Binding Time | Average time (in milliseconds) to bind to a filter DLL |
| Filter Speed | Speed (in MB/hour) at which documents are filtered |
| Total Filter Speed | Speed (in MB/hour) at which documents are indexed |

## Optimizing NNTP Performance

You can use the Performance Monitor in Control Panel to monitor the NNTP service. The performance counters show critical performance data for:

- Service activity
- Security
- Overall performance

NNTP service includes two objects in Performance Monitor: the NNTP Commands object and the NNTP Server object. The Commands object contains counters for client commands. The NNTP Server object has counters for service performance. The NNTP Server object includes counters listed in Table 14-5.

**TABLE 14-5**

NNTP Server Counters

| Counter | Meaning |
|---|---|
| Bytes Sent/Second | The rate at which data bytes are sent by Microsoft NNTP service |
| Bytes Received/Second | The rate at which data bytes are received by Microsoft NNTP service |
| Bytes Total/Second | The sum of Bytes Sent/Second and Bytes Received/Second |
| Total Connections | The number of connections that have been made to NNTP service |
| Total SSL Connections | The number of Secure Sockets Layer (SSL) connections that have been made |
| Current Connections | The current number of connections to the NNTP service |

**TABLE 14-5**

NNTP Server Counters
(*continued*)

| Counter | Meaning |
|---|---|
| Maximum Connections | The maximum number of simultaneous connections |
| Current Anonymous Users | The number of anonymous users currently connected |
| Current NonAnonymous Users | The number of nonanonymous users currently connected |
| Total Anonymous Users | The total number of anonymous users who have ever connected |

Table 14-6 lists the NNTP Commands counters.

**TABLE 14-6**

NNTP Commands Counters

| Counter | Meaning |
|---|---|
| Article Commands | The number of Article commands received |
| Article Commands/Second | The number of Article commands per second received |
| Group Commands | The number of Group commands received |
| Group Commands/Second | The number of Group commands received per second |
| Help Commands | The number of Help commands received |
| Help Commands/Second | The number of Help commands received per second |
| Ihave Commands | The number of IHAVE commands received |
| Ihave Commands/Second | The number of IHAVE commands received per second |
| Last Commands | The number of LAST commands received |
| Last Commands/Second | The number of LAST commands received per second |
| List Commands | The number of LIST commands received |

**TABLE 14-6**

NNTP Commands
Counters (*continued*)

| Counter | Meaning |
|---|---|
| List Commands/Second | The number of LIST commands received per second |
| Newgroups Commands | The number of NEWGROUPS commands received |
| Newgroups Commands/Second | The number of NEWGROUPS commands received per second |
| Newnews Commands | The number of NEWNEWS commands received |
| Newnews Commands/Second | The number of NEWNEWS commands received per second |
| Next Commands | The number of NEXT commands received |
| Next Commands/Second | The number of NEXT commands received per second |
| Post Commands | The number of POST commands received |
| Post Commands/Second | The number of POST commands received per second |
| Quit Commands | The number of QUIT commands received |
| Quit Commands/Second | The number of QUIT commands received per second |
| Stat Commands | The number of STAT commands received |

## Optimizing IIS Performance

You can use Performance Monitor to monitor your IIS server's performance. Counters monitor activity that varies over time such as file transfer rates, bandwidth usage, or connection rates.

IIS installs special counters, including Web service counters, FTP service counters, Active Server Page application counters, and global counters for Internet Information Services. You can use these counters to monitor the behavior of your memory caching settings and bandwidth throttling settings.

Table 14-7 lists the counters used to monitor the bandwidth used by IIS.

**TABLE 14-7**

Bandwidth Counters for IIS

| Counter | Meaning |
|---------|---------|
| Current Blocked Async I/O Requests | Current number of requests that are temporarily blocked by the bandwidth throttle setting |
| Measured Async I/O Bandwidth usage | The number of bytes received and sent by your Web server, averaged over one minute |
| Total Allowed Async I/O Requests | The number of user requests allowed by the Web and FTP services |
| Total Blocked Async I/O Requests | The total number of requests that have been temporarily blocked by the bandwidth throttle setting |
| Total Rejected Async I/O Requests | The total number of user requests rejected (because of bandwidth settings) |

**EXERCISE 14-3**

## Using Performance Monitor

Purpose: To familiarize yourself with the techniques for using Performance Monitor.

*Do this exercise at either computer.*

1. Ensure that you are logged on as Administrator.
2. Click Start.
3. Point to Programs.
4. Point to Administrative Tools.
5. Click on Performance Monitor.
6. Click on View.
7. Click on Log. This should bring the log form into view.
8. Click the Add Counter button (the plus button).
9. Select the following objects:

   - Active Server Pages
   - Cache
   - Internet Information Services Global
   - Memory

- Processor
- Web Service

10. Click Add.

11. Click Done.

12. Click Options.

13. Click Log.

14. Select the C:\temp folder.

15. Set the periodic update interval to 1 second.

16. Type **Web usage1.log** as the log filename.

17. Click Start Log.

18. Observe that Status reads "Collecting" and the log file size is growing.

19. Minimize Performance Monitor.

20. Start IE.

21. Connect to your Web site.

22. Browse through several pages.

23. Connect to the other server's Web site and browse through several pages.

24. Close IE.

25. Return to Performance Monitor.

26. Click Options.

27. Click Log.

28. Click Stop Log.

29. Click the View a Chart button.

30. Click Options.

31. Click Data From.

32. Click Log File.

33. Click on the ellipsis (…) and select the log file you just created.

34. Click Open and then click OK.

35. Click the Add Counter button.

36. Add counters of your choice, at least one counter from each object, to the chart. Click Done.

37. View the log file to your satisfaction.

38. Close Performance Monitor.

# Log Files

There are a number of log files that can be used to help with management and troubleshooting tasks. Many of the applications in the Windows NT 4.0 Option Pack write to the Windows NT Server log files. These logs are:

- System Log
- Security Log
- Application Log

The Internet publishing service also makes use of log files. These files can be saved in several different formats. Saving the log files in the extended format allows you to enable extended logging options to have a more complete set of information recorded. The default folder for these log files is the <winnt_root>\system32\logfiles folder. The default is to create a new file each day.

# Common Problems

Another helpful utility is the netstat utility. netstat is run from the command prompt and shows you the status of active connections at the server and statistics about TCP, IP, and UDP connections, as illustrated in Figure 14-7. You can also use nbtstat, which displays NetBIOS protocol statistics and current connection information.

## FROM THE CLASSROOM

### Resolving Windows NT's Enhanced Security and Access Problems

There are two facets to Windows NT's security architecture that can pose problems for students and administrators when working with IIS and the HTTP and FTP services. These are in addition to setting access permissions with the Internet Service Manager, restricting who can access what files and folders.

One facet is the logon security. Users attempting to access resources on a Windows NT computer must have a valid account to do so. This is true whether the IIS server is on a stand-alone Windows NT Server or the IIS server machine is part of a domain. During the installation, IIS builds an account (IUSR_*servername*) to be used for FTP and HTTP logon access. By default, this account is granted the Log on Locally right so that users may be authenticated and have access to the resources. Users may also use any other valid Windows NT account to be authenticated. Of course, if you use an account other than the anonymous account, the authentication should

be encrypted to protect the logon credentials. This is easy to do for your HTTP sessions by using Microsoft's challenge/response and IE. FTP sessions are more difficult to set up encryption for the logon, especially if you connect from the command prompt.

The other facet of security aspect is using NTFS permissions to control which files and folders users will have access to. You set these permissions by using Windows NT Explorer. Select the object (folder or file) by right-clicking the object. Then select Properties from the menu and click the Security button. From that dialog box, you can fine-tune the NTFS permissions to be whatever you require. You can set different permissions for the folder than you set for the files. You can set the permissions on each of the files to be different than the permissions of other files in the folders. This allows you to set read access to a folder from ISM and then further restrict access at the NTFS level.

exam
**ⓦatch**    *Know how to use and understand the information from the nbtstat utility,*
*especially NetBIOS names.*

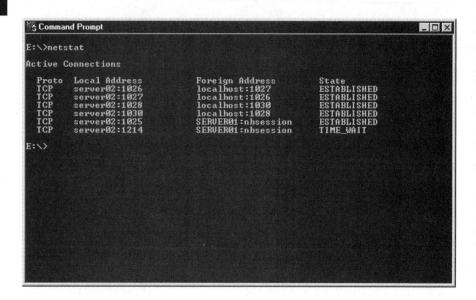

**FIGURE 14-7**

Using netstat

If you suspect trouble with your Active Server Pages, the following counters are useful:

- Debugging Requests
- Memory Allocated
- Request Execution Time
- Request Wait Time
- Request Total

If you are tuning memory and cache, the following Internet Information Server Global counters may be useful:

- Cache hits %
- Cache misses
- Directory Listing

- Objects

In terms of judging your hardware's performance capacity, the following Web server counters are helpful:

- Bytes Total/Second
- Connection Attempts
- Connections/Second
- Maximum CGI Requests
- Maximum ISAPI Extension Request

# CERTIFICATION SUMMARY

This chapter discussed programs and techniques that can help you tune and troubleshoot Windows NT Server and the Internet services that you use to publish your Web site content. The line between tuning a system for performance and troubleshooting can be thinly drawn at times. Not all "problems" with a system are outright hardware failures or software bugs. Many system problems manifest themselves in system slowdowns.

CPU slowness is often referred to as a bottleneck. All systems have bottlenecks. A bottleneck is defined as the limiting resource. This may also be thought of as the resource that is in short supply at the time that processes need that resource. Tuning is the process of identifying which resources are critically short and configuring the system to maximize its performance relative to these limited resources.

Often, discovering a bottleneck and eliminating that particular bottleneck simply means that another resource is now identified as the new system bottleneck. For example, discovering the memory is in short supply and adding more memory may relieve the memory bottleneck. Having done that, a new bottleneck is now identified at the network interface card. Relieving that bottleneck may lead to the discovery of yet another limiting resource, and so on.

In some cases, it may not be possible to eliminate the bottleneck due to physical constraints. For example, you identify that your system would perform faster if more physical RAM was installed but there is no room on the system motherboard for any more RAM. You have identified the bottleneck but cannot add more RAM. You may be able to tune other processes to be more efficient in using the available RAM. For example, ISAPI applications run in shared memory space and are therefore more efficient in their use of memory than CGI scripts. So minimizing the number of CGI scripts and using more ISAPI applications may yield better system performance with the available RAM.

In some cases, you may need to employ more of a given resource. In the previous example, you may need to use another server if the one server is at its performance capacity. Tuning to eliminate problems and increase performance can take on many different forms.

 # TWO-MINUTE DRILL

- ❑ Site Server Express is a subset of the Microsoft Commercial Internet Server (CIS).
- ❑ Site Server Express allows you to analyze and manage Web content.
- ❑ Site Server Express has four components.
- ❑ Content Analyzer allows you to see the content relationship within a site.
- ❑ Usage Import and Report Writer allow you to import log files and gets reports of the activities on the Web server.
- ❑ You install Site Server Express from the Windows NT 4.0 Option Pack.
- ❑ Content Analyzer allows you to visualize the Web site.
- ❑ There are two options for viewing the Web site from Content Analyzer.
- ❑ The tree view is a hierarchical view of the site.
- ❑ The Cyberbolic view shows you the interconnect structure of the Web site.
- ❑ The top of the tree view is the home page.
- ❑ Objects linked to the home page are second-level objects.
- ❑ The Cyberbolic view is a dynamic view of the site.
- ❑ Selecting an object in the Cyberbolic view makes this object the focus of the view and all other information is now relative to that object.

❑  The Cyberbolic view displays Web pages.

❑  The Site Summary Report can show you site objects, status summary, map statistics, and server summary data.

❑  You can search for certain types of information using one of the eight Quick Search queries.

❑  You can create reports using Report Writer.

❑  You first import the log files into the database.

❑  There are 20 existing report formats that you can use or modify.

❑  You can use Performance Monitor to track performance of the server and identify weaknesses and bottlenecks.

❑  Performance Monitor uses objects.

❑  There is a core set of objects.

❑  Additional objects are installed depending on which services and applications you have installed.

❑  netstat is a command-line utility that tells you the status of TCP connections and ports.

# SELF TEST

The following Self Test questions will help you measure your understanding of the material presented in this chapter. Read all the choices carefully, as there may be more than one correct answer. Choose all correct answers for each question.

1. Fred is the system administrator. He wants to see quickly who is connected, and at what port, on his server. How can he do this?

   A. Use the Event Viewer.

   B. Use netstat.

   C. He cannot do this.

   D. Use getstat.

2. You want to check to see if any significant events have occurred. Which log files should you check?

   A. System Log

   B. Security Log

   C. Application Log

   D. Internet Services Log

3. Which of the following is not related to Performance Monitor?

   A. CPU speed

   B. Objects

   C. Instances

   D. Counters

4. Which of the following statements are true of Report Writer?

   A. There are nine detail reports.

   B. There are 20 existing report formats you can use or modify.

   C. Reports are created from information contained in the System Log.

   D. You cannot edit the report formats.

5. Bill wants to show his supervisor statistics about activity on the Web server. What does he have to do?

   A. Use a report from Report Writer.

   B. Make sure that logging is enabled.

   C. Log on at the server and run the reports.

   D. Import the log files from Usage Import program.

6. Mary wants to check her Web server to see how many pages pass more than 32KB of data to the browser. How can she best do that?

   A. Use Windows NT Explorer.

   B. Use the Quick Search feature of Content Analyzer.

   C. Check the Application Log.

   D. Use Performance Monitor.

7. Which of the following statements are not true?

   A. Content Analyzer utilizes WebMaps.

   B. Content Analyzer has two views of the site.

   C. The tree view is dynamic.

   D. The Cyberbolic view is dynamic.

8. How do you install Site Server Express?

   A. Use the Network applet.

   B. From the Windows NT Server CD-ROM.

   C. From the Commercial Internet Server CD-ROM.

   D. Use the Windows NT 4.0 Option Pack Setup.

9. Which of the following is not a component of Site Server Express?

   A. Content Analyzer

   B. Usage Import

   C. Commercial Internet Server

   D. Report Writer

# 15

# Microsoft Proxy
# Server 2.0

This section of the book introduces you to Microsoft's Proxy Server Version 2.0, how to install, configure, and tune it. Proxy Server provides LAN clients with secure access to the Internet. Proxy Server can also be configured to allow Internet users to access servers on the internal LAN.

This section of the book provides you with the necessary skills to use Proxy Server and prepares you to take the Certified Exam, exam number 70-088. This certification exam measures your ability to administer, implement, and troubleshoot servers that are running Microsoft Proxy Server Version 2.0. Before taking the exam, you should be proficient in the following job skills:

- Planning
- Installation
- Configuration
- Managing resource access
- Integration
- Interoperability
- Optimization
- Monitoring
- Troubleshooting

To successfully complete this section of the book, you should have an in-depth understanding of:

- Implementing and administering Windows NT Server 4.0
- Implementing and networking with TCP/IP on Windows NT Server 4.0
- Implementing and administering Internet Information Server 4.0

**CERTIFICATION OBJECTIVE 15.01**

# What Is Proxy Server?

One of the primary functions of Microsoft Proxy Server is to act as a gateway to and from the Internet. Proxy Server 2.0 is called an *extensible firewall.* Being extensible means the functionality of the server can be extended or made to perform other functions, not necessarily included by Microsoft. Third-party programmers or others may add functionality.

Proxy Server also serves as a *content cache server.* A content cache server stores the Web pages most frequently accessed by the network users. This speeds up the return of Web pages to clients' browsers because they come from a local server rather than the Internet. In most cases, the access speed of the local network is faster than the Internet.

The Proxy Server acts as a *gateway.* A gateway is a system, hardware and software, that acts as an interface allowing two different systems to communicate. Using Proxy Server as a gateway, you can secure your network against unauthorized access. By using Proxy Server, your network users may be able to access other networks on the Internet but Proxy Server does not allow access to your network by unauthorized users.

One of the new features of Proxy Server 2.0 is its ability to allow users on the Internet to access the Web servers on your internal network through the Proxy Server. This is a feature known as *reverse proxy.*

exam
ⓦatch

*Proxy server now supports reverse proxy in Version 2.0.*

In addition to reverse proxy, Proxy Server has the ability to do *packet filtering.* Packet filtering can make your network more secure while providing you with greater control over how information is accessed.

Microsoft Proxy Server provides the following services, which are described in detail later in this chapter:

■ Web Proxy

■ WinSock Proxy

■ SOCKS Proxy

**CERTIFICATION OBJECTIVE 15.02**

# Proxy Server Architecture

In general terms, a proxy is the authority to act for another. In the context of a network, a proxy provides a path in and out of the network. Proxy Server has the authority to act on behalf of the local clients.

Clients connect to Proxy Server when they make a request for resources located on the Internet. Proxy Server gets the resource and returns it to the client. Proxy Server can also allow selective computers or protocols access the internal network. You only present one IP address to the Internet; Proxy Server hides your network. Figure 15-1 illustrates how clients can hide from the Internet behind Proxy Server.

## Proxy Server and the Internet

The Internet and its protocols comprise an *open system*. An open system in this case means that the protocols are published and equipment is interoperable. These open systems are all interconnected into what we call the Internet. There are numerous private LANs all tied into the public Internet.

Even though these organizations are interconnected, private networks still need to be isolated from the larger public network for reasons of security and safety. Proxy Server allows you to isolate your private network while still having some degree of manageable access to the Internet.

Proxy Server has one network card for the private network. It also has another adapter with which to connect to the Internet. This adapter may be

Hiding from the Internet
behind Proxy Server

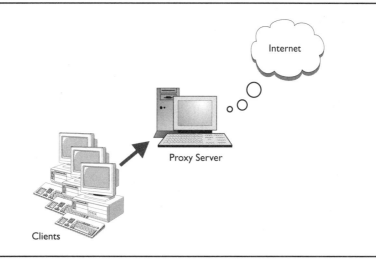

another network card or it may be an ISDN adapter. This (and other Proxy
Servers) are the only computer(s) attached to both networks.

In this configuration, the Proxy Server acts as the gateway between the
private network and the Internet. In larger networks, more than one Proxy
Server can be configured.

**CERTIFICATION OBJECTIVE 15.03**

# Proxy Server Services

Proxy Server has three services. They are:

- Web Proxy
- WinSock Proxy
- SOCKS Proxy service

exam
ⓦatch

*Know what the three Proxy Server services are and what they do.*

# Web Proxy Service

The Web Proxy service runs as a service on Windows NT Server. It runs as an extension to IIS 3.0 or higher. The Web Proxy service provides services to both the clients and the server. Clients contact the Web Proxy service and it contacts other Web servers on behalf of the client and then relays the information to the original client.

The Web Proxy service supports Hypertext Transfer Protocol (HTTP) and File Transfer Protocol (FTP) for computers on the local LAN using TCP/IP.

The Web Proxy service is implemented as a dynamic link library (DLL) and uses the Internet Server Application Programming Interface (ISAPI). The Web Proxy service runs as a process under the WWW Publishing service. Therefore, the WWW Publishing service must be installed before the Web Proxy service. The WWW Publishing service receives the requests from the client and passes them to the Web Proxy service through the ISAPI interface.

There are two components to the Web Proxy service. They are:

■ Proxy Server ISAPI filter

■ Proxy Server ISAPI application

### CERN Compliance

CERN stands for the Conseil Europeen pour la Recherche Nucleaire or the European Laboratory for Particle Physics. The CERN organization is based in Switzerland. Much of the support for HTTP and the Web libraries has their origins at CERN. As the products evolved, the CERN proxy protocol became the standard that was accepted by the Internet. The Web Proxy service is fully compatible with the CERN proxy protocol. Web browsers such as Internet Explorer and Netscape Navigator are examples of CERN-compliant applications.

Communications between CERN-compliant proxy servers and clients is done using the HTTP protocol. HTTP has commands that clients send to the server. Among these commands are Get and Post.

The Get command is used to forward the URL to the server requesting the resource named in the URL. The Post command is used to send the request containing the URL and the data. The user provides this data, generally by using an HTML form.

### Proxy Server ISAPI Filter

An ISAPI filter is called every time a request is made of the server. ISAPI filters can monitor, modify, and redirect (among other things) requests.

An ISAPI filter is called on every request. These DLLs register their entry points, which the Web Proxy service calls when it receives a request. Proxy Server's ISAPI filter DLL is the W3proxy.dll file. This file and other files are located in the Inetpub\scripts\proxy folder.

This filter looks at every request in order to determine the request type and then selects the appropriate action. If the request is a CERN proxy request, the filter adds instructions to route the response to Proxy Server. If the request is a standard HTTP request (not a CERN request) then the filter makes no changes to the request and passes the request through for normal processing.

exam
ⓦatch

*Know what the ISAPI filter does and how it works.*

### Proxy Server ISAPI Application

The other component of the Web Proxy service is the ISAPI application. The ISAPI application takes the following actions when it receives a request:

- Authenticates the client
- Checks the domain filter
- Checks the local cache
- Obtains objects from the Internet
- Makes entries in the log

The ISAPI application may be processing many simultaneous requests. Relatively speaking, Proxy Server may require a longer period of time to process a request. To aid this situation, IIS can use a feature called a *keep-alive*. Normally, a TCP connection is torn down after each request is completed and then re-established for the next request. The keep-alive feature allows the TCP request to remain after the request has been fulfilled. By not having to make a new connection each time, performance is improved.

## Caching

The Web Proxy service maintains a local copy of HTTP and FTP objects on the local hard disk. This is called *caching*. Not all objects are cached. Some objects change frequently, even each time they are accessed, so caching them is a waste of processing time. Some objects have a security context and are cached for the security reasons.

Proxy Server performs two types of caching:

- Passive caching
- Active caching

**exam**
**ⓦatch**

*Know what the cache types are and how they work.*

*Passive caching* is the predominant cache method used. It is also known as *on-demand caching* because it is available on demand when the client makes the request. As mentioned before, a request is the URL of the desired resource.

In a normal (no Proxy Server) situation, the client contacts the Web server on the Internet. The Web server responds to the request and sends the requested objects directly back to the client. Proxy Server sits in the middle of this process. The Proxy client contacts Proxy Server with the request. Proxy Server goes to the Internet with the request and retrieves the requested object. It caches that object. If you, or any other client, requests the object again, Proxy Server gets the object from the local cache rather than from the Web server on the Internet.

In order to ensure that the cached information is still current, several techniques are used. One technique is to set an expiration time on the object. This expiration time is known as the time to live (TTL). When a client requests an object that is cached, Proxy Server checks the TTL to determine if the requested object is still valid. If the TTL has not expired, then the object is returned to the client. If the TTL has expired, then Proxy Server goes out to the Internet and retrieves the object and the TTL process begins again.

In order to manage disk space, Proxy Server deletes older cached objects to make room for new objects to be cached if the disk becomes too full.

*Active caching* supplements passive caching. The intent of active caching is to maximize the probability that an object will be in the local cache when the client requests the object from Proxy Server. To accomplish this, Proxy Server may automatically retrieve objects from the Internet. It chooses objects by considering such factors as:

- **Frequency of request**   Objects that are more frequently requested are kept in the cache. If the TTL on one of these objects expires, a new object is requested.

- **Time to live**   Objects having a greater TTL are better to cache than objects with shorter TTLs. In other words, if an object has a short TTL and is seldom requested, it is not advantageous to cache it because the TTL will have expired by the time the next request arrives.

- **Server activity**   Proxy Server seeks to cache more objects during times of low activity than it does during periods of high activity.

# WinSock Proxy Service

Windows Sockets (WinSock) is a set of application programming interfaces (APIs) that applications can use to communicate with other applications in the network. Many applications may be running on the same computer even though the processes are being conducted across the network. The APIs support the following functions:

- Initiating an outbound session as a client
- Accepting an inbound session as a server
- Transferring data on the established connection
- Terminating the session

WinSock is a port of the Berkeley Sockets API for UNIX. It has extensions for the Win16 and Win32 message-based application environments. It supports the Windows TCP/IP protocol stacks and supports other protocols such as IPX/SPX.

WinSock supports a point-to-point connection-oriented session. It also supports a point-to-point or multi-point connectionless session.

The WinSock Proxy service supports the following features:

- Support for WinSock 1.1-based applications (for example, Telnet)
- Secure IP
- Control of inbound and outbound access
- Filtering of Internet sites by domain or IP address
- Data encryption through SSL

The WinSock Proxy service works with Windows-based client computers. The WinSock Proxy service allows WinSock applications to run remotely. However, the WinSock Proxy service does not support Windows Sockets 2.0 API.

The Winsock Proxy service is a client/server process that runs only on Windows NT 4.0 Server running Proxy Server. It allows client applications to run as if they are directly connected to the Internet.

On the client computer, WinSock DLLs are replaced with the WinSock Proxy client DLLs. During installation, the original DLLs are renamed and the proxy DLLs are given the same name. This allows the WinSock applications to link to the proxy DLLs when the application is run.

The WinSock Proxy service sets up a control session between the client and the server to allow for messages. The session uses the UDP protocol with a simple acknowledgement protocol added for reliability. The control session uses UDP port number 1745 on both the WinSock Proxy Server and client. This control session serves the following functions:

- **Routing information**  When the session is first established, the server sends the client the LAT (local address table). This table contains the list of internal IP addresses and subnets.

- **Establishing the TCP connection**   When the client makes the connection to the remote application, the server uses the control session to establish this virtual connection. After the connection is established, the control session is not used for data.

- **Message traffic**   The control session is used for non-data requests such as a request for a host name resolution (DNS).

### TCP/IP and IPX/SPX

There are several important points you need to know about using TCP/IP or IPX/SPX protocols and the WinSock Proxy service. When you are using TCP/IP on your LAN and an application wants to communicate with a server, that server may be local or remote to the application. When the WinSock client initializes, it receives the LAT from the WinSock Proxy service.

Based on the addresses contained in the LAT, the application can tell if the requested server is local or remote. If the address is local, the client WinSock DLL forwards the request to the original WinSock DLL, the one that was renamed. In this situation, there is no special processing.

If the address is not local, then the WinSock DLL does the processing and the WinSock Proxy service is involved. If the WinSock Proxy DLL cannot determine if an address is local or remote, it processes the request as if it is a local address. This is the more secure assumption to make.

If your LAN is running the IPS/SPX protocol, the scenario changes. In this case, the WinSock Proxy service is also acting as a protocol gateway. It converts the IPX/SPX protocol to the TCP/IP protocol and back again.

Since you are not running TCP/IP, there is no LAT table to be downloaded to the WinSock Proxy client at initialization time. Since there are no TCP/IP hosts on the local network, all attempts to connect to a TCP/IP host are considered requests for a remote host and are processed according to those rules.

## SOCKS Proxy Service

The SOCKS Proxy service is a cross-platform mechanism used to establish secure communications between the server and the client. This service allows for transparent access to the Internet using Proxy Server. This service does not support applications that use UDP, nor does it support the IPX/SPX protocol.

The SOCKS protocol acts as a proxy. It allows a host on one side of a SOCKS server to be able to access a host on the other side of a SOCKS server. You do not need a direct IP connection to do this. Microsoft Proxy Server supports SOCKS Version 4.3a, which means that most SOCKS applications will be able to run remotely through the SOCKS Proxy service.

SOCKS has two operations:

- Connect
- Bind

The Connect operation is used when the SOCKS client needs to connect to an application server. This connection request includes information such as the SOCKS protocol version number, command code, destination IP address and port number, and a user ID.

The SOCKS Proxy service receives the request. The server replies to the client with a status such as granted, rejected, or failed. If the client request was rejected or failed, the server may return an error code indicating why and closes the connection without further action.

If the request to connect is successful, the server executes the Bind operation. The Bind operation provides access control.

### CERTIFICATION OBJECTIVE 15.04

# Security Features and Benefits

Proxy Server 2.0 is a firewall that provides security. It does this by preventing users outside your network from gaining access to your network.

# The Guardian Between You and the Internet

The computer that runs Proxy Server has two network interface cards (NICs). One card is connected to your network and one card is connected to the Internet. This physically isolates your LAN from the Internet. The processes within Proxy Server monitor all interactions and requests for access between your LAN and the Internet.

# IP Address Masking

You can configure Proxy Server to disable IP forwarding. In this manner, the only IP address that is visible externally to the Internet is the IP address of the Proxy Server itself. Since the only address visible to the Internet is that of the Proxy Server, hackers have no target IP addresses, except the address of the most secure computer on your network. In other words, the client computers "hide" behind the address of the Proxy Server and the Proxy Server masks the IP addresses of the clients. Don't confuse this concept with a subnet mask, which is entirely different.

exam
ⓌＷatch

*If you have IP forwarding enabled, Proxy Server will disable it.*

# Packet Filtering

*Packet filtering* is a scheme whereby only certain packets are passed through to the network and other packets are discarded. You can block or enable reception of certain types of packets through certain ports. Proxy Server 2.0 has a dynamic packet-filtering feature. This feature is implemented as a kernel mode service.

Ports are only opened as needed. Packets are allowed in for only the minimum duration required and only on specified ports.

# Benefits of Proxy Server

Proxy Server is fully integrated with the administrative and security interfaces of Windows NT Server operating system and with IIS. This integration allows you to take advantage of the ease of administration through the already familiar tools of Windows NT Server and IIS when administering Proxy Server.

## Bandwidth Utilization

Proxy Server allows your network clients to access the Internet through the single connection provided by Proxy Server. Proxy Server also supports dial-up access. It is possible for a small office using multiple dial-up lines to consolidate those lines into a single ISDN line and share that access through Proxy Server.

In a larger company of thousands of employees, you can trade the dial-up circuits for fast, dedicated circuits such as a T-1 or a T-3 connection. Depending upon the number of dial circuits installed, this can be less expensive and can provide faster access, because each employee no longer needs a modem and a dial-up circuit.

## Web Support

There are two main benefits derived from Proxy Server and the Web. The first benefit is that through the caching of frequently accessed Web pages at the Proxy Server, users who access these pages do so faster because the page comes from the local server, reducing the overall traffic on the Internet.

The second benefit comes with the ability to publish information on a server and have it available to users on the Internet through Proxy Server. There are two techniques used:

- Reverse proxy
- Reverse hosting

These techniques are described in detail in Chapter 20.

# FROM THE CLASSROOM

## What's Going On?

Many students come to the Proxy Server class without a good idea of the capabilities of Proxy Server. This is not unusual in itself, since students come to class to find out about the capabilities of the product and how to administer it. But it is not unusual for students in a Windows NT class or an IIS class to come to class with a good understanding of the capabilities of the IIS or Windows NT Server.

What makes the Proxy Server scenario unusual is the degree to which some of the students are unaware of the capabilities of Proxy Server. One of the first surprises for some of the students is that Proxy Server is a firewall. When the students hear the word "firewall," light bulbs go off. Suddenly Proxy Server begins to come into focus for many students who may already have firewalls or are exploring the use of firewalls in their organizations.

A new feature of Proxy Server 2.0 is its ability to support reverse proxy and reverse hosting.

Reverse proxy is the process by which the Proxy Server takes a request for a resource located on the internal LAN and forwards that request to the server internal LAN. Computers outside the Internet do not have direct access to the servers on the internal LAN. All communication is through the Proxy Server.

Reverse hosting takes this to the next level. In the process, Proxy Server maintains a list of internal computers that have permission to publish on the Internet. In this case, Proxy Server listens and responds on behalf of the computers on the internal network. Again, there is no direct contact with internal computers and computers from the Internet.

There is one other interesting surprise for you and Microsoft Proxy Server. Have you checked the price of other firewalls lately?

# QUESTIONS AND ANSWERS

| | |
|---|---|
| When do I need Proxy Server? | When you want to isolate your private network from other networks, such as the Internet. Using Proxy Server allows you to stay connected to the Internet while keeping your network isolated. |
| I already have a Web server on UNIX and want to use Proxy Server. Do I still need IIS? | Yes, Proxy Server requires that IIS be installed and running. This won't interfere with your UNIX-based Web server however. Everything should operate as before. |
| Do I have to use the content cache with Proxy Server? | No, you are not required to use the cache feature, although you might find it a benefit for frequently accessed sites. |
| How can I control the TTL times to make them longer for the objects that are cached? | You cannot. The TTL parameter is controlled at the other end. Your systems are simply going to react to it. When the TTL expires, the object is no longer considered valid. |
| Well, if I can't increase the TTL of cached objects, how can I ensure that I have objects in cache? | The active cache feature does this for you under certain conditions. While content cache can be very useful, if some objects have short TTLs, there may be a good reason for this (i.e., they change often) and you won't want them in cache. |
| Why shouldn't I use TCP/IP if I am going to connect to the Internet? | Proxy Server can act as an IPX/SPX gateway for your internal IPS/SPX LAN. This can save you time in configuring your systems for both protocols, relieve memory constraints, and make it a little more difficult for unauthorized users to come crashing through to your internal network. |
| I am not using NetWare. Can I still use the IPX/SPX protocol and Proxy Server? | Yes, you do not need NetWare to run Microsoft's NWLink protocol, which is the compatible IPX protocol from Microsoft. |

# CERTIFICATION SUMMARY

This chapter covered the basic concepts and architecture of Microsoft's Proxy Server. A proxy is a go-between. Proxy Server acts as a go-between from your private LAN to the Internet. By doing this, you can keep your internal network hidden and secure from users on the Internet.

Proxy Server runs as a service under Windows NT Server and IIS. Proxy Server supports three different types of proxy services: the Web Proxy service, the WinSock Proxy service, and the SOCKS Proxy service. Each service is used to accomplish specific tasks.

The Web Proxy and the WinSock Proxy services can be configured so that they compliment each other. You configure the client's Internet browser to use the Web Proxy service. You configure the client computer to use the WinSock Proxy service.

By doing this, when the browser attempts to connect, the request is handled by the WinSock Proxy service, which routes the request through IIS to the Proxy ISAPI process. The Proxy Server ISAPI application issues the Internet request for resources and returns them to the client.

 **TWO-MINUTE DRILL**

- ❏ Microsoft Proxy Server acts as a gateway to the Internet.
- ❏ Proxy Server 2.0 is an extensible firewall.
- ❏ Proxy Server also acts as a content server.
- ❏ Proxy Server supports reverse proxy.
- ❏ Reverse proxy is when users on the Internet access your Web server through Proxy Server.
- ❏ There are three services with Proxy Server: Web Proxy, WinSock Proxy, and SOCKS Proxy.

- ❑ The Web Proxy service allows CERN-compliant applications to access WWW and FTP servers.
- ❑ Internet Explorer is a CERN-compliant application.
- ❑ CERN-compliant applications must be configured to use the Proxy Server.
- ❑ The WinSock Proxy service allows clients to run WinSock applications without directly accessing Internet resources.
- ❑ The Winsock Proxy service is accessed through the WinSock Proxy client installed on the client computer.
- ❑ The original WinSock DLLs are renamed when you install the WinSock Proxy client.
- ❑ The WinSock Proxy client DLLs are installed and named as the original DLLs.
- ❑ Application programs communicate normally and the WinSock Proxy DLL determines what to do with the request.
- ❑ Some requests are handled by the WinSock Proxy DLL and are sent to the Proxy server, if the request is for a remote resource.
- ❑ Requests for local resources are sent to the original DLLs by the WinSock Proxy DLL.
- ❑ You can use IPX/SPX on your internal LAN and use Proxy Server as a gateway to the Internet.
- ❑ SOCKS Proxy service allows host-to-host communication to occur in a secure fashion.
- ❑ Proxy Server supports SOCKS Version 4.3a.
- ❑ The Web Proxy service caches requests on the local disk.
- ❑ Content remains cached until the content expires.
- ❑ Expiration is controlled by the TTL.
- ❑ There are two types of caching techniques: passive caching and active caching.
- ❑ Passive cache is storing Internet objects on the local disk.
- ❑ Active caching attempts to predict which objects will be requested frequently and stores those objects on the local disk before they are requested by a client.

# SELF TEST

The following Self Test questions will help you measure your understanding of the material presented in this chapter. Read all the choices carefully, as there may be more than one correct answer. Choose all correct answers for each question.

1. Which of the following statements are not true of Proxy Server?

   A. Proxy Server is a gateway.

   B. Proxy Server is a Web server.

   C. Proxy Server is a firewall.

   D. Proxy Server is a content cache server.

2. Which of the following is not a service of Proxy Server?

   A. Web Proxy

   B. WinSock Proxy

   C. SOCKS Proxy

   D. Reverse proxy

3. What are the two components of the Web Proxy service?

   A. Proxy Server ISAPI filter

   B. SOCKS Proxy

   C. Proxy Server ISAPI application

   D. WinSock DLL

4. Which of the following statements are not true of the Web Proxy service?

   A. Web Proxy service runs as a service under Windows NT Server.

   B. Web Proxy service is an extension of IIS.

   C. Web Proxy service uses ISAPI.

   D. Web Proxy service can be hosted on either Windows NT or UNIX.

5. Which of the following are caching techniques used by Web Proxy service?

   A. Active caching

   B. File caching

   C. Access token caching

   D. Passive caching

6. Which statements best describe how passive caching works?

   A. You must configure the cache size manually.

   B. You must manually refresh the cache.

   C. Proxy Server periodically sends cache updates to the clients.

   D. When a client requests an object, Proxy Server checks the cache to see if the object is available from cache.

7. Which of the following is not a consideration for active caching of objects?

   A. How often an object is requested

   B. The size of the object

   C. TTL

   D. Server activity

8. Which of the following is not a function of WinSock Proxy service?

A. Transferring data between the client and the server

B. Accepting an inbound session as a server

C. Caching requested objects

D. Terminating a session

9. Which of the following statements best describes IP masking?

A. IP masking uses the IPX protocol for communication.

B. IP masking hides the IP addresses on the local LAN from the Internet.

C. IP masking is a technique used by WINS server.

D. IP masking hides the Internet from the internal LAN.

10. Which of the following statements describes a benefit of Proxy Server?

A. Dial-up access

B. Reverse proxy

C. Reverse hosting

D. Data encryption

# 16

# Planning Considerations for Proxy Servers

T his chapter discusses planning issues and examines factors that can affect the performance of your network and your Proxy Servers. You will discover techniques to do a site analysis to determine what type and how many Proxy Servers you may need. You will also see how to estimate volume and server usage.

# Gathering Information

Planning for anything can involve the practice of modeling. A model in this context is a simulation of how an environment acts. Once the model is defined, you can introduce variables into the model and see the effects that the changes have on the other factors in the model. We all do this in our daily lives to some level or another, consciously or subconsciously.

First, you establish a goal that you want to reach. Then you determine what factors might affect reaching that goal. You can also use historical data to help you in the analysis. If you do not have any historical data, then you make projections about the impact of these factors. When you roll these all up, you have a model.

Some models are relatively simple and may be done in your head. Other models can be quite complex and require sophisticated software programs to design.

An example of a simple model is when you want to take a trip to another city and do not want to stop for gas. In this scenario, you establish the objects (go to another city and not stop for gas). You look at your gas gauge to determine how much gas you have; you know how far the distance is to the city. From historical evidence (you have been driving the car and know the mileage it gets), you calculate whether your objectives can be met.

While this example is simple (something you have probably done before), the process is the same for more complex scenarios. Set your goals, identify the variables, and modify the variables until the goal is achieved.

In gathering information to develop your plan, you should interview the users in your organization. You may find conflicting goals and schedules among them. One of your tasks may be to prioritize who gets which services and who gets them first during your implementation.

## Goals

Setting goals helps you plan your Proxy Server. You should answer the question: What am I trying to accomplish? Use the following checklist to help.

What type of applications will be used?

- HTTP, FTP
- Streaming audio and video
- E-mail
- Internet Relay Chat (IRC)
- Other applications

What services will these applications need?

- Web Proxy
- WinSock Proxy
- SOCKS Proxy

What protocols do you need to support?

- TCP/IP
- IPX/SPX

## Volume

After you analyze what type of activities that you need to support to accomplish your goals, try to estimate the volume of activity on the Proxy Server and the network.

Once you have estimated the volume, either by extrapolating historical data or by estimating the volume, evaluate how much bandwidth is available to you. If you have more than one site, determine the bandwidth between the sites. Some of your sites may be connected by a WAN. Even though you may have a fast link between the sites, you probably need to share that bandwidth with other activities such as file transfers.

When determining what factors can affect the demand on the Proxy Server, you should analyze:

- How many users you have
- How often they will attempt to connect
- What type of access they require
- Where they are located in relation to the Proxy Server

## CERTIFICATION OBJECTIVE 16.02

# Rollout Issues

After you have determined what your goals are and what the volume of traffic will be, you can begin to size a server to the task. Earlier in this book, you learned the minimum hardware requirements for supporting Proxy Server. While the minimum is enough to get Proxy Server up and running, it may not be enough to adequately serve your organization. Microsoft breaks organizations up into four broad categories. They are:

- Small business
- Medium business
- Large business
- Internet Service Provider (ISP)

Table 16-1 summarizes disk space and memory recommendations based on organization size.

exam
watch

*Understand that there are different cache and memory recommendations for different size operations.*

| TABLE 16-1 | Hardware Requirements Based on the Number of Desktops Connected to the Network |

| Business Type | Processor | Disk Space | RAM |
|---|---|---|---|
| Small business, up to 300 desktops | P-133 | For caching, up to 2GB | At least 32MB |
| Medium business, up to 2,000 desktops | P-166 | For caching, up to 4GB | At least 64MB |
| Large business, up to 3,500 desktops | P-200 or a P-Pro 166 | For caching, up to 16GB | At least 128MB |
| ISP with 1,000 or more simultaneous connections | P-Pro 200 or Alpha AXP 300 | For caching, 16GB or more | At least 128MB |

## Connecting to the Internet

There are two factors with regard to connecting to the Internet. One factor is the hardware that interfaces to the circuit that connects you to the Internet. There are different types of hardware, depending upon the connection requirements. The other is the type of circuit itself. In some cases, the type of hardware you use depends on the type of circuit employed.

The following discussion describes some but not all of the hardware devices and data circuits possible or supported by Proxy Server. Equipment and circuit choices you make can vary from what is listed here, based on your location and what is available in your area or on your budget.

### Hardware Devices

There are many different hardware devices that you can use to connect to the Internet. As mentioned previously, the hardware device that you would select depends on the type of circuit being used. Another factor is the desired speed or bandwidth. Different types of hardware (and circuits) support different network speeds. Obviously, you have to match the appropriate hardware device to the circuit and circuit speed. As a point of reference, data transmission speeds are always measured in bits per second (bps). Data file sizes are referenced in bytes.

This section describes common hardware devices:

**MODEMS**    Modem is an acronym for modulator/demodulator. Its job is to modulate a digital signal from the computer into an analog signal that travels along a voice grade circuit. Modems are slow communication devices with connection speeds ranging in the neighborhood of 20,000 bps. Some modem manufacturers claim higher speeds. There are standard modem speeds, such as 2400, 9600, 14400, 28800, and most recently 56000.

Modem speeds are difficult to measure because many manufacturers speak in different terms. In recent studies, modems tested seldom connected at their top speed. In other words, a 28.8 modem can theoretically connect at that speed, but oftentimes will not. You likely see connection speeds like 26,000 or 24,600.

Some modem manufacturers describe techniques like data compression, for example, when they talk about how "fast" their modem is. Of course, the use of data compression affects not the link speed but the effective throughput. But if the data being transmitted does not compress (or compress much), you will not experience improved throughput.

There is a difference between bits and baud. They are not the same. Technically speaking, your 28.8 modem is a 9600 baud modem transmitting 28,800 bits per second. This is achieved by a technique called "adding more points in the constellation."

You don't need to worry about all of this. Just focus on the fact that modems are slower than other alternatives and that speeds that modem manufacturers claim may or may not have anything to do with how much data you can actually transmit in a given timeframe.

**ISDN DEVICES**    An *Integrated Switched Digital Network (ISDN)* offers higher speeds for connecting than you might typically get with a modem. This is a digital service and the device used to connect to the service is referred to as an *ISDN modem*. This is technically not a "modem" because the circuit is a digital circuit so there is nothing to modulate and no way to carry the analog signal even if you did modulate. The typical ISDN circuit has two channels for transmitting and receiving data. Each channel is capable of speeds at 56/64 Kbps. If you use both channels, you will have an aggregate speed of 128 Kbps.

**DSU/CSU**    A *data service unit/channel service unit (DSU/CSU)* is used to connect to a leased data circuit. This type of circuit is usually a full-time connection. The typical DSU/CSU does not care about the transmission speed of the circuit because it is an electro-mechanical interface to the telephone company circuit. However, some manufacturers offer DSU/CSU equipment for the fractional T-1 and the full T-1 circuits. The cost is the differentiating factor.

**ROUTER**    A *router* is a hardware device that connects two or more networks (or network segments) together. These networks may be local or remote, or a combination of both. A *bridge* also serves the same purpose. The router differs from a bridge in that a router is a protocol-specific device. A bridge is a protocol-indifferent device. There are other differences. Unlike the other devices listed in this section, a router does not attach directly to a telephone company circuit. A router attaches to the LAN on one side and to the DSU/CSU on the other side. Some routers have built in a DSU/CSU or ISDN interface.

## Circuits and Connections

In selecting the type of service or circuit you want to connect to the Internet, estimate the amount of traffic you will be sending over that link. Generally speaking, network traffic is nonlinear and random over time. The amount of traffic is characterized by periodic high usage spikes, times of minimal traffic, and the majority of the time, a "normal" amount of traffic. One thing to consider is how many of the heavy usage periods you want to accommodate.

A network's capacity to move data, measured in bits per second, is called *bandwidth*. When you contract for a data circuit, the cost of that circuit is directly proportional to the circuit's bandwidth. In other words, the faster the circuit, the higher the cost of that circuit. There are several types of circuits, the most common of which are described in the following sections.

**DIAL-UP ANALOG MODEM LINES**   *Dial-up analog modem lines* are the most common types of circuits. They are also known as *voice lines* and *POTS (Plain Old Telephone System)*. This is classified as a slow link. Modems can accommodate speeds up to 56 Kbps, although most phone company circuits, due to design limitations, cannot accommodate speeds quite that high. Analog lines are relatively inexpensive. In the Washington, DC metro area, you can lease a CENTREX line (from the telephone company) for about $11/month; a standard business line is about $45/month.

**DIGITAL DATA SERVICE (DDS)**   A DDS circuit is a leased line, point-to-point circuit. The circuit is exclusively yours and is not shared with anyone else. It was common several years back but has lost popularity due to availability of frame relay circuits and ISDN lines. DDS speed is 56 Kbps. This is considered a slow speed circuit. Prices vary depending upon the distance to the other point. They usually start at several hundred dollars per month and go up from there.

**ISDN**   ISDN is a digital circuit and is typically used in a dial-up, switched circuit environment. Each ISDN circuit has three channels. Two of the channels are known as B channels and the third is known as a D channel. Each B channel is 56/64 Kbps and is used for data. The D channel is used for signaling and control. There is a monthly charge for ISDN circuits. Some carriers also charge based on the amount of time you are connected. The charge is calculated per channel. This is a slow speed circuit.

**T-1**   A T-1 circuit is a leased line, point-to-point circuit. It is comprised of 24 individual channels (these channels are referred to as *DS0*) bonded together to form one data path whose speed is 1.544 Mbps. In the past, this was considered a high-speed circuit. Based on the enormous amount of information that is moved in today's environment, especially considering HTTP and typical Web pages, the T-1 circuit is on the verge of being considered a slow link.

**FRACTIONAL T-1**   As the name suggests, the circuit speed of fractional T-1 is a fraction of the speed of the T-1 circuit. It is technically possible to construct a fractional T-1 circuit with any number of DS0 channels, giving you speed ranges from 64 Kbps up to the maximum speed. Each DS0 is 64 Kbps of bandwidth. The cost of the circuit increases as the speed of the circuit increases. In practice, most providers offer speeds of:

- 64 Kbps
- 128 Kbps
- 256 Kbps
- 512 Kbps
- 768 Kbps
- 1024 Kbps

**T-3**   This circuit has a rated speed in excess of 45 Mbps. This type of circuit is used mainly by carriers and high-end service providers. The cost of the T-3 circuit is very high compared to other choices available.

## Cost Analysis

Two factors that can influence the cost of circuits are bandwidth (or speed) and persistence of the connection. This section describes these factors in more detail.

**BANDWIDTH (SPEED)**   You must decide how much user demand you want to accommodate. Do you purchase enough bandwidth to accommodate peak demand and then have excess bandwidth during normal operations? Do you buy bandwidth to satisfy normal operations and then tolerate slow operations during peak demand? Once you have selected the desired speed, you can expect to pay more for higher speed circuits. Some circuits are also distance sensitive; the greater the distance, the greater the cost. Some circuits, such as dial analog and ISDN, may also carry long distance charges. Some providers may also charge you for the amount of traffic you send in addition to the monthly lease on the circuit.

**PERSISTENCE OF THE CONNECTION**   You have two choices for the connection: dial-up circuits and leased lines. With a dial-up circuit, you pay a small monthly fee and additional charges for the time you are connected. Some services allow you a fixed amount of connection time as part of your monthly fee. Others may charge you for all connected time. For example, you may pay a small monthly fee for an ISDN circuit. You may also pay a connection charge (for example, seven cents per minute) for each channel. If you use both channels, then your connect charge will be twice as much. At some point, if you are connected for long periods of time, you can pay more for the dial-up circuit than you would for a dedicated leased circuit. You need to calculate the crossover point (the point at which you pay more) based on your situation. You also need to anticipate how your use of the lines might change over time.

## Licensing Proxy Server

You must have a license for each copy of Proxy Server that you install. You do not need to license the computers that connect to the Internet through Proxy Server.

Consider a scenario where your organization has two remote sites, each with a Proxy Server, and a central site with four Proxy Servers in an array. You have six Proxy Servers installed and therefore, you need six licenses.

**CERTIFICATION OBJECTIVE 16.03**

# Implementation Scenarios

Microsoft lists three environments to consider when implementing Proxy Server. The environments are:

- Small networks
- Medium-sized networks
- Large networks

Networks can vary in size, configuration, and complexity. In the Microsoft environment, your network may be comprised of one or more Windows NT Domains. You may have more than one physical location. These locations may employ multiple connectivity options to connect to each other and to the Internet.

As a point of reference, Proxy Server can control access to your intranet even though you may not need or want to access the Internet. Proxy Server can also control what your users can access from internal resources just as it can control what external resources your users can access. The caching features of Proxy Server can improve performance for remote users wanting access to your Web servers.

## Small Networks

In a small network, there is a single LAN segment. It services up to 200 clients and uses dial-out facilities such as an ISDN circuit. You might have a single Windows NT Server that serves as your file and print server as well as the Proxy Server. Or the network may have multiple servers. You configure one Proxy Server to support the network.

You should enable the caching feature and configure it to minimize the number of times it needs to dial to the Internet. Properly configuring the cache is the key to maximizing the effectiveness of the Proxy Server.

## Medium-Sized Networks

A medium-sized network, in this context, might have a centrally located site. It might have one or more branch offices. You have 200–2000 users to support on the network. At the central location, there is a dedicated high-speed link (such as a T-1) to the Internet. The central locations and the branch offices may have Internet servers.

To support this scenario, you configure a Proxy Server array at the central location. This array provides distributed caching. It also provides the central security policy for all clients.

At the branch offices, depending on their size and activity, you can install a single Proxy Server. You configure the Proxy Server to use the AutoDial feature, which provides dial-on-demand access to the central location. Once connected to the central locations, the branch clients go through the Proxy Server array and on to the Internet. The Proxy Server AutoDial uses the RAS phone book. The Proxy Server needs to be configured as a RAS client to support this. You need to be a RAS server at the central location to receive the inbound call.

## Large Networks

In a large organization, the network environment may be comprised of many network segments at one or more central locations and several large regional locations. Many branch offices can be involved. The central office has a dedicated high-speed link to the Internet, such as a T-1 link. There may be dedicated links between the regional offices and the central location. For redundancy and fault tolerance, the central location may have multiple links to the Internet and there may be links between the regional offices themselves. Branch offices might have dial-on-demand access to the central location, or depending upon circumstances, to one of the regional locations. There may be extranets involved in the organizational network.

Implementing Proxy Server in a large network is similar to implementing it on a medium-sized network environment in some respects. However, there are some differences. In the large network there may be more than one transport protocol. The network may be using both TCP/IP and IPX/SPX protocols. Your network structure, such as routers, needs to accommodate both protocols.

At the central location (and perhaps at the regional offices as well) there may be a backbone network to which departmental LANs are connected. Each departmental LAN may have its own Proxy Server, each with two network adapters. The Proxy Server array and the connection to the Internet are on the backbone network.

**exam**
**ⓦatch**

*Have an understanding of the general characteristics of each network type. Branch offices dial into the central location.*

## Extranets

An *extranet* is a private network that connects two or more LANs or intranets from different organizations. You have the LAN in your own organization and you can be connected to the network of another organization. This connection is regular and frequent and can even be on a dedicated circuit between the two organizations. An example of an extranet is that of a buyer-supplier relationship. A manufacturer of personal computers may have an extranet with the supplier of the components used in assembling the personal computers.

Another example of an extranet is a network between a retailer and the manufacturer or wholesaler. An automobile dealership may be online full time with the manufacturer of the automobiles they sell. The dealer configures a Proxy Server and connects directly to the manufacturer without going through the Internet. This type of relationship has existed at automobile dealers for decades; they just used different technology. They used terminal-to-host technology support by dial-on-demand technology or relatively low-speed dedicated circuits. Today, they might use LAN-to-LAN connectivity support through Proxy Server.

**CERTIFICATION OBJECTIVE 16.04**

# Using Multiple Proxy Servers in an Organization

You configure multiple Proxy Servers in your organization to support two objectives:

- Redundancy
- Load sharing

Having more than one Proxy Server allows you to have multiple gateways to the Internet. Designing a plan to share the load among the gateway computers is an important issue. You can configure this load sharing in several ways. They are:

- Load sharing using DNS
- Load sharing using WINS
- Load sharing using multiple WinSock Proxy Servers

For clients using the Web Proxy service, you can configure the clients to use a specific Proxy Server or you can configure them to use all Proxy Servers. For clients using the WinSock Proxy service, you configure them to use a specific Proxy Server.

For additional information on how to configure multiple Windows NT Server gateways to the Internet, refer to the Windows NT Server 4.0 Resource Kit and the Windows NT Server 4.0 Resource Kit Supplement 1.

exam
ⓦatch

*Understand the ways to implement load sharing with multiple Proxy Servers.*

## Load Sharing Using DNS

Domain Name System (DNS) servers are responsible for providing host name-to-IP address resolution. For example, a client wants to contact a host named "training" in the domain microsoft.com. To accomplish this, the client software needs the IP address. There are several ways to get the IP address. One way is to query the DNS server for the IP address. This request can be in the form of a URL.

Before the Web browser can establish the session with the Web server, it must have its IP address. If you are using multiple servers, you can configure the DNS in such a way that it distributes the workload of the servers by supplying a different IP address for each successive request.

Let's say, for example, that you have particular information that is accessed heavily by users. That information is on three different Web servers. Clients access that information using the URL, but since the URL contains the host name and each of the three servers has a different host name, each client needs to specify a different URL. This is undesirable because you want all clients to specify a single URL. The clients have no idea to which of the three hosts they are connected and they do not care. This process needs to be transparent to the user.

The Microsoft DNS server supports a process known as *round robin*. This process balances the workload of the servers, in this case, the three Web servers. To do this, you must create an alias that points to multiple IP addresses. This alias record is a CNAME record entry in your DNS server file, as illustrated in Figure 16-1.

In this case, you have three servers, Server10 through Server12, with resource (A) records configured in the DNS. Then you create three CNAME records of "www," each pointing to a host resource record.

When a client issues a request for a URL containing www.*something*, DNS gives the client the IP address of the first host in the list. The DNS then moves that host to the bottom of the list. When the next request for www.*something* arrives, DNS gives the IP addresses of the second server, now at the top of the list, and moves that server name to the bottom of the list, and so on.

Load sharing using DNS

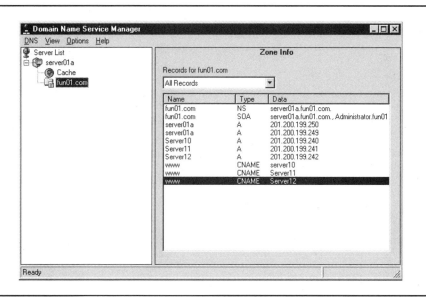

In this manner, each host receives its share of client requests and the process is transparent to the client.

The process is the same for Proxy Server. For the Web Proxy service, you configure the browser with a host name. You can do this in the browser, or have it done by the Proxy Server when the browser connects, as illustrated in Figure 16-2. You configure the server name, "Proxy," for example. You then create the CNAME records in the DNS table for "Proxy" to point to each of the Proxy Servers.

## Load Sharing Using WINS

If you are using Windows and the TCP/IP protocol, then you should have at least one Windows Internet Name Service (WINS) server deployed. WINS is Microsoft's implementation of an RFC NetBIOS Name server. WINS serves a similar, but different function than DNS. DNS resolves FQDNs (Fully Qualified Domain Names) to IP addresses. WINS resolves NetBIOS names to

**FIGURE 16-2**

Settings in the IE browser
for Proxy Server

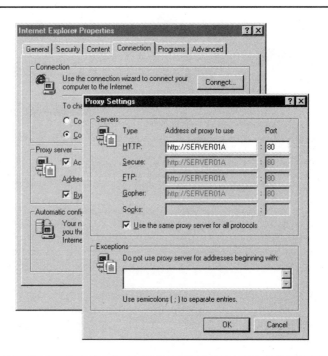

IP addresses. All Microsoft operating systems rely on NetBIOS for their networking.

For more information on how to configure Windows NT Server to be a WINS server, consult the Windows NT Resource Kit or the *MCSE Microsoft TCP/IP on Windows NT 4.0 Study Guide* (Osborne/McGraw-Hill).

You can use WINS in the same manner as you use DNS to share the load of your Proxy Servers. You create a static entry in your WINS server table for the Proxy Server alias and map it to multiple IP addresses. Figures 16-3 and 16-4 show how to view and create static mappings in WINS.

*Know how to configure WINS to support load sharing.*

## Load Sharing Using WinSock Proxy

You install the WinSock Proxy client from a Proxy Server. Thereafter, that client attaches to and uses the WinSock Proxy service of the Proxy Server from which the client was installed. Figure 16-5 contains the dialog box for client installation and configuration.

---

**FIGURE 16-3**

Viewing static mappings in WINS

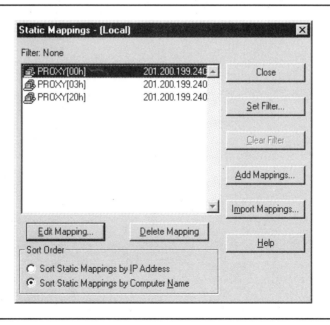

---

**FIGURE 16-4**

Creating static mappings
in WINS

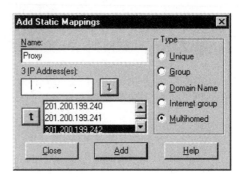

To balance the workload of the WinSock Proxy services, configure the clients from different Proxy Servers. This distributes the load among the Proxy Servers in the organization. You can also boost the processing capacity of a particular Proxy Server to help speed the processing. However, this is only effective to a certain point. Eventually, you will want to add more Proxy Servers and balance the load sharing by configuring clients from multiple servers.

**FIGURE 16-5**

Specifying the Proxy Server

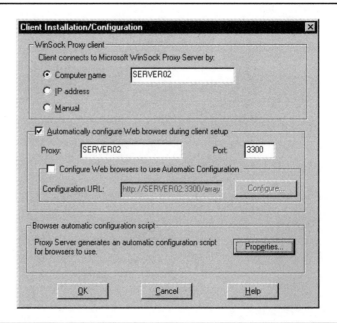

# FROM THE CLASSROOM

## Load Sharing

Does load sharing mean I don't have to work as hard?

You may have to still work as hard, but life may be a little easier for your Proxy Servers.

It is interesting to watch the students' reactions to the discussion about load sharing. The concept seems clear enough for them. Then we start talking about how load sharing is implemented and the students' eyes glaze over as some of them go far away.

But the implementation can be clear to implement as well as to understand, if you organize your thought process into a one-two-three approach.

First, how are you doing name resolution on your network? How do the client computers get the IP addresses for the Proxy Servers? There are typically two choices: DNS or WINS (or a combination of both). (I am going to deliberately ignore the issue of HOSTS and LMHOSTS files, otherwise your eyes will glaze over and you will go far away. What you want to do is simplify first, before you make it complex. Considering HOSTS and LMHOSTS files makes it complex before you understand how it works in simple form.)

Two, if you are using a DNS server, then you should configure the DNS server so that

it provides an IP address for a different Proxy Server for each successive client request.

Let's simplify this with an example. You have two Proxy Servers called MPS1 and MPS2. You want to configure your client's browser to contact a Proxy Server named "Proxy." But we don't have a server named "Proxy" you exclaim! I know; don't go away just yet because the really cool stuff is about to come. So your clients are going to ask for a server named "Proxy" and you are going to create an alias (CNAME) record that points the request for "Proxy" to MPS1. Now when the client queries for "Proxy," they get the address for MPS1 and are connected to that server. OK? No problem!

Third, you are going to add a second alias pointing the name "Proxy" to MPS2. Now you have two records for "Proxy" pointing to two different servers. This might look strange, but from here, DNS takes over and keeps track of which Proxy Server (MPS1 or MPS2) is next in line. In other words, the first client gets sent to MPS1, the next client gets sent to MPS2, the third client gets sent to MPS1, and so forth. Do you have 10 Proxy Servers? The process is the same.

# Using Distributed Caching

You can configure caching to be distributed among multiple Proxy Servers in the organization. This improves both the active and passive caching. You distribute the cached objects and provide for fault tolerance if one Proxy Server fails or becomes unavailable. Distributed caching is implemented by one of two methods, or by combining and using both methods:

■ Chaining

■ Arrays

## Proxy Server Routes

Using Proxy Server to route to another proxy server is a technique that involves a process called *upstream routing*.

By configuring upstream routing, a Web Proxy client request can be routed to an upstream Proxy Server, to a Proxy Server array, or directly to the Internet. The term "upstream," from a data flow point-of-view, refers to being closer to the Internet, closer to the Internet resource that is your ultimate destination.

You can route the access request to any CERN-compliant Proxy Server, including another Microsoft Proxy Server.

This technique is also known as *chaining*. The Microsoft documentation incorrectly states that you can route SOCKS Proxy. This is incorrect. You can get more information about this from a TechNet article or from the Microsoft Web site.

You can also specify a backup route to use in the event that the upstream Proxy Server is unavailable. The backup route is fully functional and provides for automatic transfer transparently. From time to time, the primary route Proxy Server is queried to see if it is available. When the primary Proxy Server is available, the primary route is re-established automatically.

To configure routing, take the following steps:

1. Open the Internet Service Manager (ISM).

2. Expand the server.

3. Right-click the Web Proxy icon.

4. Click Properties.

5. Select the Routing tab, as illustrated in Figure 16-6. In this dialog box you can enable a backup route and specify if you are going to use an array.

6. To specify the upstream Proxy Server parameters, click Modify. The dialog box in Figure 16-7 appears.

**FIGURE 16-6**

Setting up routing in the Web Proxy service

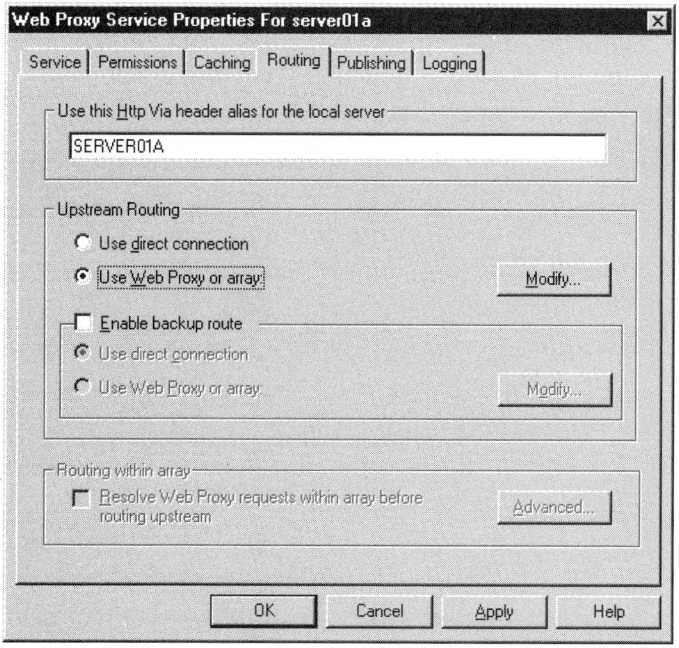

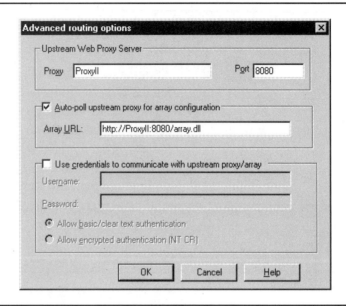

**FIGURE 16-7**

Specifying the route to the
upstream Proxy Server

## Configuring a Proxy Server Array

An array is a group of Proxy Servers bound together by an array name. Proxy
Servers in an array are administered as a single element. Configuring an array
provides for load sharing, fault tolerance, and easier administration. Arrays can
be useful in the following environments:

- Branch offices
- Networks that are too large to be serviced by a single Proxy Server
- Consolidating multiple Internet connections

You must create an array. You do this from the ISM. An array is common
to all Proxy services. Each Proxy Server maintains a list of which members of
the array are available and which members are not available.

Each individual member in the array uses the *hash* to make routing
decisions. The hash is a mathematical algorithm that uses three factors:

1. Available servers

2. The URL of the client request

3. A load factor

The end result of this hash is predictable; given the same input factors, a URL request is routed to the same array member cache each time.

You should only administer one member of the array at any time. If more than one person attempts to administer an array at the same time, an array configuration conflict message appears. Only system administrators are allowed to configure the array membership. The configuration for a single array member may be propagated and synchronized to all members of the array. The following parameters are propagated when auto-synchronization is enabled:

- Advanced caching options
- Client configuration files
- Domain filters
- LAT
- Logging information
- Publishing information
- Upstream routing options
- Web Proxy user permissions
- WinSock protocol definitions

Use the following steps to create or join an array:

1. Open the Internet Service Manager (ISM).

2. Expand the server.

3. Right-click the Web Proxy icon. Select any service.

4. Click Properties.

5. Click the Array button (see Figure 16-8).

Preparing to create or join
an array

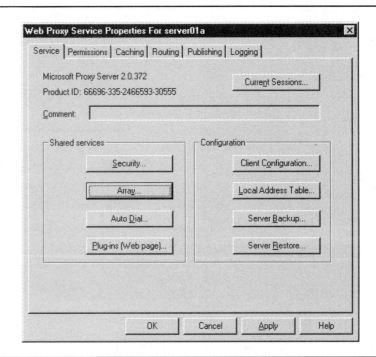

6. Click the Join button. A list of arrays available appears, as illustrated in
   Figure 16-9. If there are no arrays, you have to create one by specifying
   the name of another server to use to start the array, as in Figure 16-10.

To leave an array, the server must be part of the array and you must
perform the leave operation at the server being removed from the array. You
can also remove a server from an array. You can remove any member from the
array using the same dialog box you use to leave an array. The leave and
remove functions effectively perform the same function; the specified
computer is no longer part of the array.

Use the following procedure to remove a server from an array:

1. Open the Internet Service Manager (ISM).

2. Expand the server.

**FIGURE 16-9**

Joining an array

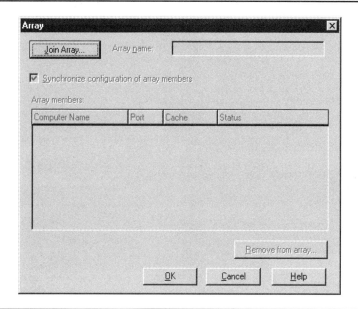

3. Right-click the Web Proxy icon. Select any service.

4. Click Properties.

5. Click the Array button.

6. Click Leave Array, as illustrated in Figure 16-11.

**FIGURE 16-10**

Creating an array

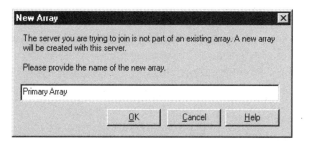

**FIGURE 16-11**

Leaving an array

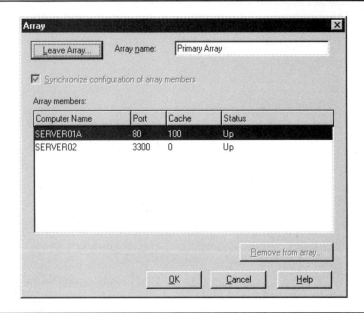

# Cache Array Routing Protocol (CARP)

Proxy Server 2.0 supports Cache Array Routing Protocol (CARP). This is an enhancement of the Internet Cache Protocol (ICP) developed in 1995. The purpose of this protocol is to allow a Proxy Server to query other Proxy Servers to see if those servers have cached copies of requested objects before the Proxy Server goes to the Internet for the object.

One of the issues with the ICP protocol is that the Proxy Servers in the array query the other Proxy Servers to determine where an object is. This results in additional network traffic. It also can produce a "self-feeding" condition; the more Proxy Servers in the array, the more queries are sent to determine if an object is cached within the array. This increases network traffic. Another issue is that arrays built on the ICP tend to become redundant in caching objects over a period of time.

CARP expands on the ICP protocol in several ways:

- CARP uses a "queryless" hash-based algorithm. The hash-based routing results in the URL being resolved to the same Proxy Server. This means there is a single hop resolution for the requested object.

- CARP becomes faster the more Proxy Servers are added. This is because the location of each cached object is known within the array, unlike ICP, which must query for each requested object.

- CARP prevents multiple servers from caching the same object. This makes the CARP array much more efficient than an ICP array.

exam
**W**atch

***Know how CARP works and what its benefits are.***

Proxy Servers are tracked through an array membership list. This list is automatically updated whenever servers are added to or removed from the array. A hash is computed for the name of each Proxy Server.

A hash is computed from the name of each requested URL. The hash value of the Proxy Server name and the URL are added together. Whatever server + URL results produces the greatest hash value becomes the owner of the object. This process eliminates the need to maintain and update massive tables detailing where cached objects can be found. The browser calculates the same hash value to determine where an object is.

## QUESTIONS AND ANSWERS

| | |
|---|---|
| Does Proxy Server care what type of Internet connection I have or what its speed is? | No. The speed of the link or the link type only affects the performance of Proxy Server. |
| I have a small network at home and I am connected to the Internet using the TV cable company and a cable modem. Can I use Proxy Server? | Absolutely. One of the drawbacks of this type of connection scheme is that cable companies only provide you with one IP address. If you have multiple computers on the network, you should install Proxy Server so that all your computers can access the Internet through the cable modem. |
| What does it mean if my network is not defined as one of the three types of networks that Microsoft categorizes? | It is not important if your network doesn't "look" exactly like the examples. They are only meant to be generic models. |
| Do I have to use multiple Proxy Servers? | No. Multiple Proxy Servers offers many advantages to the way your network can support users and Internet access efficiency, but there is no requirement to implement multiple Proxy Servers. |

# CERTIFICATION SUMMARY

This chapter outlined the factors to consider when setting your goals for what you want from your technology. It discussed some of the typical options available to you for hardware devices for connecting to the Internet. There are many different circuit choices for connecting to an ISP, not all of which are available from every ISP. Speed and distance are the primary cost factors when contracting for a data circuit.

This chapter also discussed the three network size classifications that Microsoft uses. Remember not the "hard" characteristics of each network type, but the types of functions that you might have to support and what type of Proxy Servers you might implement to accommodate a given network configuration.

You can install multiple Proxy Servers to add speed and efficiency to your network. Using multiple servers allows you to implement load sharing among the servers while providing fault tolerance to cover instances of one (or more) Proxy Servers being unavailable.

The chapter also described the Cache Array Routing Protocol (CARP) and some of the benefits of CARP over the ICP protocol.

 # TWO-MINUTE DRILL

❑ Gathering information helps you set goals.

❑ Setting goals gives you a clear idea of what you need to do.

❑ Goals may be simple and easy to establish.

❑ Goals may be complex and take a long time and a great deal of thought to establish.

❑ Analyzing the anticipated network traffic volume allows you to select proper equipment and services.

❑ Microsoft breaks networks into three categories, plus a fourth category: ISPs.

❑ The network categories are small, medium, and large.

❑ The more users you support, the more RAM and cache space you need.

❑ You use a hardware device and a telephone company circuit to connect to the Internet.

❑ Data speed is measured in bits per second.

❑ Modems are slow, even "high-speed" modems.

❑ The faster the link, the greater the cost.

❑ You can configure multiple Proxy Servers.

❑ You should do this for load sharing.

❑ You should also do this for redundancy.

❑ You can implement load sharing using DNS, WINS, or WinSock clients.

❑ You can implement distributed caching.

❑ You can configure Proxy Servers in an array.

❑ You can chain Proxy Servers.

❑ Microsoft uses Cache Array Routing Protocol (CARP).

# SELF TEST

The following Self Test questions will help you measure your understanding of the material presented in this chapter. Read all the choices carefully, as there may be more than one correct answer. Choose all correct answers for each question.

1. Which device do you use to connect to an existing voice line to support dial-on-demand Proxy Server?

   A. ISDN modem

   B. Router

   C. Modem

   D. Parallel cable

2. What type of hardware do you need to fully support interconnecting two IP LANs using a T-1 circuit and a leased line?

   A. Modem

   B. DSU/CSU

   C. Router

   D. ISDN modem

3. Which of the following circuits offers the greatest bandwidth?

   A. High-speed modem

   B. ISDN

   C. Fractional T-1 using four DS0 channels

   D. DDS circuit

4. Which of the following characteristics is not a factor in the cost of a leased data circuit?

   A. Speed of the circuit

   B. Number of concurrent sessions

   C. Distance between the locations

   D. Time of day

5. Which of the following is not a method of load sharing Proxy Servers?

   A. Configuring DNS

   B. Configuring WINS

   C. Configuring clients to use a specific WinSock Proxy server

   D. Configuring DHCP

6. You have a network with only Windows 95 and Windows NT as clients. You are connected to the Internet through an ISP. Both your DNS servers are maintained by the ISP and are located at the ISP. How do you configure your network to provide optimally for load sharing across your multiple Proxy Servers?

   A. Have the ISP add the Proxy Server's IP addresses to their DNS table.

   B. Configure the Proxy Servers in an array. They will automatically load share.

   C. Configure static mappings in the WINS server for the multiple Proxy Servers.

   D. Configure the Proxy Servers to use DHCP.

7. Which of the following are methods that you can use to implement a distributed cache?

   A. Configuring the DNS with a CNAME that points to multiple IP addresses

   B. Adding static entries into the WINS server

C. Chaining

D. Arrays

8. Which of the following statements are not true of an array?

A. An array is comprised of two or more Proxy Servers acting together.

B. You can have multiple people administer the array concurrently.

C. The configuration for a member of the array may be propagated to other members in the array.

D. An array is common to all proxy services.

9. You have 10 Proxy Servers configured in an array in the central locations. You support 5 branch offices, each with its own Proxy Server. There are 3000 users in your organization. How many Proxy Server licenses do you need?

A. 1

B. 6

C. 15

D. 3015

10. Which of the following are advantages of CARP?

A. It uses a queryless protocol for a single-hop resolution for the requested object.

B. It tends to become faster the more Proxy Servers are added.

C. It prevents multiple servers from caching the same objects.

D. It allows multiple servers to cache the same objects for faster response.

# 17

# Installing Proxy Server

This chapter describes the installation of Proxy Server. It also describes the client installation. You must have at least one Proxy Server installed at your site. You may have more than one Proxy Server configured in an array. (Chapter 16 describes multiple Proxy Servers and arrays in detail.)

This chapter describes the server installation and the construction of the local address table (LAT) during the installation. The differences between internal and external IP addresses are critical to the success of using Proxy Server. This chapter describes the LATs on the server and the LATs on the client systems.

**CERTIFICATION OBJECTIVE 17.01**

# Server System Requirements

Most of the requirements to support Microsoft Proxy Server are similar to the requirements for Windows NT Server 4.0, which is required to run Proxy Server. Internet Information Server 2.0 (or higher) must also be installed on the same computer where you are going to install Proxy Server.

## Hardware

Table 17-1 lists the minimum hardware requirements for installing Proxy Server.

exam
ⓦatch    *Know how to calculate the cache drive space requirements.*

| Component | Minimum Requirements |
| --- | --- |
| CPU | 486/33 or higher. |
| RAM | 24MB for an Intel system; 32MB for RISC. |
| Disk space | 10MB for the Proxy Server system files, for content caching, NTFS volume, and enough free space. Recommend 100MB plus .5MB for each Proxy Server client. |
| Network adapter | For connection to the internal LAN. |
| Second network interface | A network adapter, ISDN adapter, modem, or other device for connecting to the Internet (or other network). |

## Software

Table 17-2 summarizes the minimum software requirements to install Proxy Server. Proxy Server must be installed on a computer that has both Windows NT Server 4.0 and Internet Information Server 2.0. Service Pack 3 is required, since when you install Service Pack 3, it automatically upgrades IIS 2.0 to IIS 3.0. You can also use IIS 4.0, which you install from the Windows NT Option Pack.

| Software Component | Version |
| --- | --- |
| Windows NT Server | 4.0 |
| Windows NT Service Pack | 3 |
| Internet Information Server | 2.0 |
| TCP/IP | n/a |
| Proxy Server | 2.0 |

**CERTIFICATION OBJECTIVE 17.02**

# Installing Proxy Server

Before you begin, make sure that everything is in order so that your installation can proceed without any stumbling blocks. The following is a quick checklist:

- Make sure you have an NTFS partition available for your content cache. At least 100MB of free disk space is required. You may want to have more disk space available if you anticipate heavy use.

- Network connectivity and adapters are installed and configured.

- You have installed and configured the necessary protocols.

You begin the installation by running Setup from the Proxy Server CD-ROM. If you have Microsoft Back Office or the Solution Developers Kit, Proxy Server is located in the msp folder. This brings you to the Welcome screen, illustrated in Figure 17-1.

**FIGURE 17-1**

Starting the Proxy Server installation

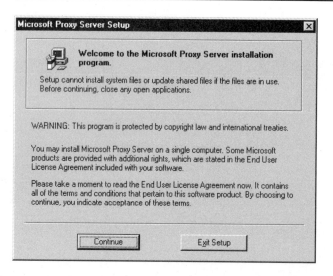

Clicking Continue takes you to the screen asking you for your CD-ROM key. This is the 10-digit code located on the CD-ROM case. After you enter the key, the product identification window appears (see Figure 17-2).

Next, specify where you want to install the Proxy Server system files. The default is in the C:\msp folder. You can change this folder by selecting the Change Folder button (see Figure 17-3). You do not have to install the server files on an NTFS partition. There is only one button for the installation of Proxy Server. Click it and the installation continues.

The next dialog box (Figure 17-4) allows you to select the installation options. Specify which components you want to install. You can install Proxy Server, the Web Administration Tool, and the documentation.

Click on the Install Microsoft Proxy Server option and then click Change Option. The dialog box in Figure 17-5 appears. Here you select which client subcomponents to install.

Once you have set the installation options, the Setup program proceeds. It shuts down the Web service while you are doing the installation and restarts it at the end of the installation. After shutting down the service, you specify the cache drive (see Figure 17-6). Caching is enabled by default. You can have more than one cache drive. The minimum cache size is 5MB but you will want more. The default is 100MB. Microsoft recommends that you add .5MB

---

**FIGURE 17-2**

Product identification
number

Microsoft Proxy Server Setup

Product ID:      66696-335-2466593-30555

This is your Microsoft product identification number. If you want to call Microsoft for technical support, you will be asked for this number.

For your records, please write down this number in the designated portion of your registration card. After the software has been installed, you can access the number by clicking the About... command on the Help menu.

OK

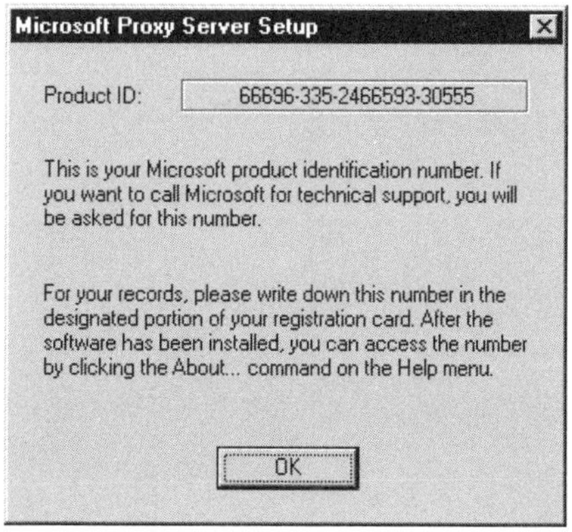

Specifying the Proxy Server
folder for installation

per user. If there are 100 proxy clients accessing this server, then the cache size
should be 150MB. You can only use an NTFS partition for caching.

*Know that you can only have cache on an NTFS partition.*

Selecting the Proxy
Server components

**FIGURE 17-5**

Selecting which client
subcomponents to install

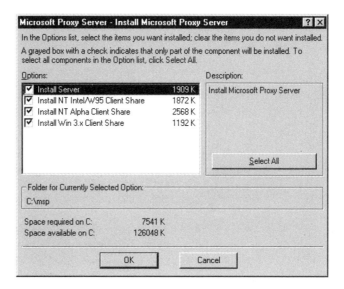

**FIGURE 17-6**

Setting up a cache drive

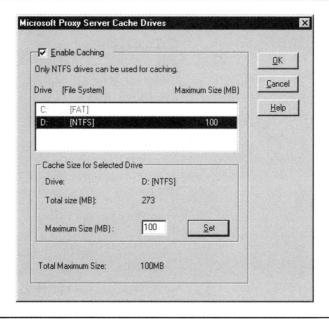

After assigning the cache drive, your next task is to set up and configure the LAT. Define all the local IP addresses in your network in the dialog box in Figure 17-7. You do not want IP addressees that are external to the network defined here. This chapter will discuss LATs in more detail later.

You can add the IP addresses manually or have Proxy Server construct them for you. After clicking the Construct Table button, the dialog box in Figure 17-8 appears, where you specify the characteristics of the LAT.

If you know which adapter is connected to the internal network, select Load from NT internal Routing Table; IP addresses are added from that source. If you don't know which adapter is for the internal network and which adapter is for the external network, select the button next to Load known address ranges from all IP interface cards. This constructs the LAT from all IP addresses. It is a good idea to know this beforehand. If you are installing and it is convenient at this point, you should obtain this information now. You can modify the LAT table later to exclude the external network IP addresses that were loaded here, but that is more work.

There is also a check box for loading private ranges of IP addresses. Three ranges of IP addresses have been reserved by the InterNIC for use on private

---

**FIGURE 17-8**

Constructing the LAT

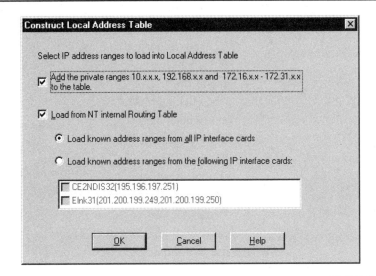

networks. These addresses are never assigned to users of the Internet. You use one of these addresses if you are building an internal IP network and are not connecting to the Internet. Using Proxy Server allows you to keep your private network addresses (not change them now that you are going to access the Internet) while accessing the network. There is one private address range for each class of networks.

If you know which network cards are for internal networks and which are external, then check the box next to Load known address ranges from the following IP interface cards. You can select multiple network cards. If you have a multi-homed computer (a computer with more than one network card is known as a *multi-homed computer*), then use this technique.

After the IP range has been constructed, you may get a message that states the IP address ranges have been loaded into the LAT and if they contain external network addresses, you will need to remove these addresses later. Figure 17-9 shows this message.

Your next choice is about Proxy client installation and configuration for the WinSock Proxy clients (see Figure 17-10). Enter the name of the computer, or the IP address, of the Proxy Server to which the client will connect to access the Internet.

**FIGURE 17-9**

Reminder to remove
external network IP
address range

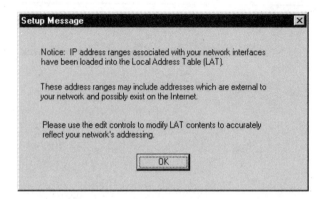

You can select to have the client's browser automatically configured to use
the named Proxy Server and you can specify the port number. You can also
select to have the client connect to an array of Proxy Servers. (Chapter 16
describes Proxy Server arrays in detail.)

**FIGURE 17-10**

Information used by the
client setup program

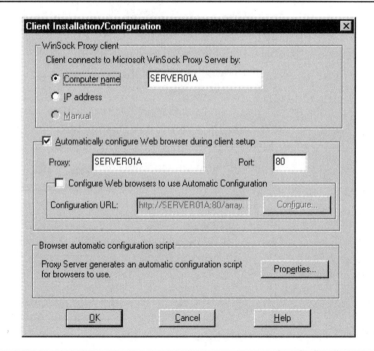

By clicking on the Properties button in the Browser automatic configuration script box (Figure 17-11), you can specify:

- Whether Proxy Server will be used for local servers

- Which IP addresses to exclude

- Which domains to exclude

- Whether to use a backup route. You can route a client request upstream to a Proxy Server or directly to the Internet. This provides an automatic transfer, thereby eliminating a single point of failure.

At this point, the Access Control Dialog box appears. Use this box to enable access control for the WinSock Proxy service and the Web Proxy service, as illustrated in Figure 17-12. By default, access control is enabled for both services. This means that the Proxy Server services validate connections from clients.

**FIGURE 17-11**

Advanced client configuration options

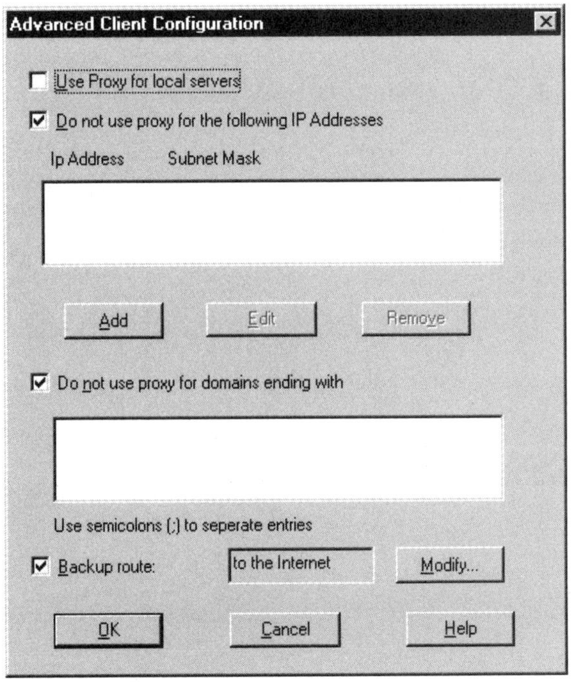

FIGURE 17-12

Enabling access control

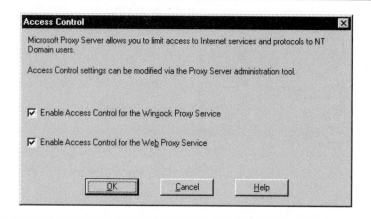

Using the Web Proxy or WinSock Proxy service without access control enabled is considered nonsecure. In this condition you cannot set any password authentication settings.

exam
ⓦatch

*Know that without enabling access control, your Proxy Server cannot attempt to authenticate clients.*

After configuring, the access control files are copied and a Setup Information dialog box appears (Figure 17-13). A new feature of Proxy Server 2.0 is *packet filtering*. Packet filtering is disabled by default. You can enable it using the Internet Service Manager (ISM) to configure the Proxy Service.

At this point, the IIS services are restarted. The installation is now complete and you should get the dialog box in Figure 17-14, stating that the installation was successful.

FIGURE 17-13

Information about
packet filtering

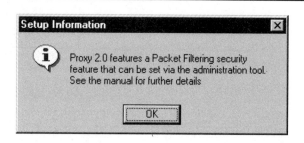

**FIGURE 17-14**

Successful installation

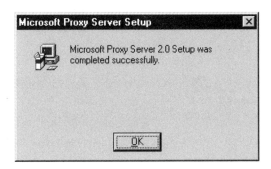

**EXERCISE 17-1**

## Configuring TCP/IP for Two Network Adapters

Purpose: To configure the Proxy Server computer so that the two network cards have the proper IP addresses. The IP addresses for the network card connected to the internal network must be on a different network than the network card connected to the Internet, or the simulated Internet. Use the following IP addresses:

- 201.200.199.*xx* for the internal network (intranet)
- 195.196.197.*xx* for the external network (Internet)

*Do this exercise from the primary domain controller only.*

1. Ensure that you are logged on as Administrator.
2. Click Start.
3. Point to Settings.
4. Click Control Panel.
5. Double-click the Network icon to launch the Network applet.
6. Click the Adapters tab and make sure you have two network adapters installed.
7. Click the Protocols tab.
8. Select TCP/IP protocol in the window.
9. Click the Properties button.
10. In the Adapter drop-down list, select the adapter that is connected to the internal network.
11. The Specify an IP address radio button should be checked.

12. The IP address should be 201.200.199.*xx*.

13. The subnet mask should be 255.255.255.0.

14. The default gateway must be empty on the adapter for the internal network.

15. From the Adapter drop-down list, select the adapter that is connected to the external network.

16. Select the Specify an IP address radio button.

17. Enter the IP address **195.196.197.*xx***.

18. The subnet mask should be 255.255.255.0.

19. The default gateway should be empty, or if you are using a live network, then the gateway for the ISP should be present.

20. Click OK.

21. Click Close.

22. Click Yes when asked to restart your computer.

**EXERCISE 17-2**

### Installing Proxy Server

Purpose: To install Proxy Server 2.0.

*Do this at the domain controller only.*

1. Ensure that you are logged on as Administrator.

2. Open Windows NT Explorer.

3. Change to the root directory of the Proxy Server CD-ROM.

4. Double-click Setup.

5. Click Continue on the Welcome dialog box.

6. Enter your CD-ROM key and click OK.

7. Click OK when the product identification number dialog box is displayed.

8. Accept the default location for the Proxy Server files and click the Installation Options button.

9. Select Install Microsoft Proxy Server option.

10. Click the Change Options button.

11. Deselect the Alpha client and the Windows 3.1 client.

12. Click OK.

13. Click Continue. The Setup Wizard stops the Web service.

14. Click OK to accept the defaults for the cache drive.

15. When the Local Address Table Configuration dialog box appears, click the Construct Table button.

16. Check the Add the private ranges box.

17. Check the Load from NT internal Routing Table check box.

18. Select the network adapter that has the 201.200.199.0 network assigned to it.

19. Deselect any adapters with external IP addresses.

20. Click OK.

21. Click OK on the Setup Massage dialog box that tells you the IP addresses have been loaded into the LAT.

22. Click OK on the LAT Configuration dialog box.

23. Click OK on the Client Installation/Configuration dialog box to accept the defaults.

24. Click OK on the Access Control dialog box to accept the defaults.

25. Click OK on the information box for packet filtering.

26. Click OK on the Setup box stating that setup was successfully completed.

## Installing Documentation

You can just install the product documentation for Proxy Server 2.0 if you wish. You do not need to install the documentation on a computer running Windows NT Server to use the documentation. This option allows you to study the documentation so that you can plan your Proxy Server environment prior to installation.

To install the documentation, run the Proxy Server Setup program. Clear all of the installation options except the Install Documentation option. After the Setup program is complete, you have a group named Microsoft Proxy Server. The documentation uses your Internet browser, as illustrated in Figure 17-15.

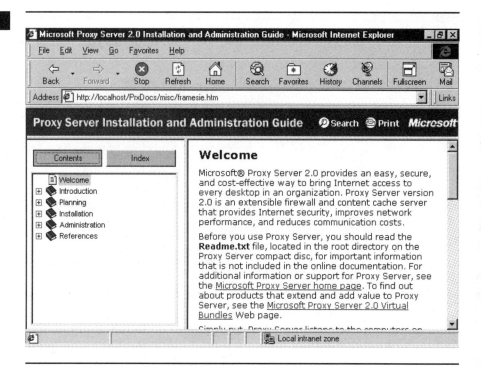

## Reinstalling or Removing Proxy Server

There are three tasks that you can accomplish after Proxy Server is installed by
running Setup again (see Figure 17-16):

- **Add or Remove Select Components**   Use this option to either add or
  remove components. For example, if you no longer want the
  documentation installed on the server, you can remove it.

- **Restore Missing Files or Settings**   Use this option if there are files
  that were not installed during the original installation.

- **Remove Proxy Server**   Use this option to remove Proxy Server and all
  its components and program groups.

FIGURE 17-16

Removing Proxy Server

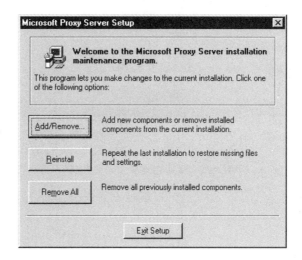

## Changes Made by the Installation Process

As a point of reference, the installation of Proxy Server makes some changes to your Windows NT Server:

- The Web Proxy, WinSock Proxy, and SOCKS Proxy services are added to ISM.
- The HTML Proxy documentation file is added to the <winnt_root>\help\proxy folder.
- A cache is created.
- A LAT is constructed.
- Counters for Proxy Server are added to Performance Monitor.
- The client software is copied to the \msp\clients folder.
- The WSP applet is added to Control Panel.
- The Proxy Server Administration, WinSock Proxy, Protected Storage, and the Proxy Alert Notification services are added.

## CERTIFICATION OBJECTIVE 17.03

# Local Address Table (LAT)

The function of the LAT is to define the addresses on the internal network. Network addresses not contained in the LAT are considered external addresses.

exam

ⓦatch

***There will be questions on the exam about the LAT, what are proper network addresses, and how to create a local LAT file for the clients.***

The LAT entries are pairs of IP addresses. Each pair defines an address range. This address range can be an entire network ID or a single IP address. The LAT is built when you install Proxy Server. The LAT is generated from the Windows NT Server routing table. This method may not record all the addresses of the internal networks. You can review the LAT table at any time. You may have subnets that need to be added. There may also be external network addresses that need to be removed. It is important to remove external network addresses from the LAT.

When you install the Proxy client, the Setup program installs a file named msplat.txt. This file is installed in the \mspclnt folder. This file contains the LAT file. The contents of this file are identical to the LAT on the server. To keep this file consistent, the server regularly updates the msplat.txt file on the client.

Consider the following: You have a LAN in the big city and three other LANs connected to your LAN by a 56K router. Your local LAN IP is 192.168.5.*x*, each of the other sites are .6.*x*, .7.*x*, and .8.*x*. Draw a topographical overview of the locations to outline your point. The .6, .7, and .8 ranges must be added because they aren't likely to appear from the routing table.

When a WinSock application needs to establish a connection using an IP address, the msplat.txt file is consulted to determine if the requested IP address is internal or external. If the address is listed in the msplat.txt file, then it is considered to be on the internal network and the connection with the resource is made directly. If the address is not listed in the msplat.txt file, then it is considered to be on an external network and the connection is made through the Proxy Server.

If the LAT at the server does not contain all of the internal network addresses, you can modify the msplat.txt at the client to include the other internal network addresses. However, these address modifications are lost when the server periodically sends the LAT to the client.

To overcome this, you can create a custom LAT for the client using a text editor. You add the additional address pairs that are on the internal network so that the client recognizes them as part of the internal network. You then save the file in the \mspclnt folder. The file must be named Locallat.txt. The WinSock client checks both files, if they are present in the \mspclnt folder, for local IP addresses. Here is an example of the contents of the msplat.txt file:

| 10.0.0.0 | 10.255.255.255 |
|---|---|
| 172.16.0.0 | 172.31.255.255 |
| 192.168.0.0 | 192.168.255.255 |
| 201.200.199.0 | 201.200.199.255 |
| 224.0.0.0 | 255.255.255.254 |
| 127.0.0.0 | 127.255.255.255 |

exam
ⓦatch

*Know how to create the Locallat.txt file and what folder to put it in.*

**CERTIFICATION OBJECTIVE 17.04**

# Client Installation

When you install Proxy Server, the Setup Wizard creates the \msp\clients folder. Client software utilities are installed in their respective folders. For example, the Alpha folder contains Alpha-specific files and the I386 folder contains the Intel-specific files. The Setup Wizard also shares the \msp\clients as a mspclnt share name.

You install the WinSock client software on the client computer. The client setup program configures the computer to be a client of the WinSock Proxy

---

# FROM THE CLASSROOM

## Understanding the LAT

One of the most significant issues about properly configuring the Proxy Server is properly configuring the LAT. The LAT contains the IP addresses and address ranges of all of the IP addresses that are to be considered as internal IP addresses. Any address not specifically identified as an internal address is considered an external address. This is significant because only internal addresses have access to Proxy Server; all external addresses are blocked from access. If you get this wrong, you can cripple the security functionality of the Proxy Server or valid internal addresses will not be served by the Proxy Server.

To illustrate the point, consider the following scenario. You have two branch offices connected to the corporate office with leased lines. You have three IP subnets as listed here:

- Corp HQ     192.168.5.0
- Branch1     192.168.6.0
- Branch2     192.168.7.0

When you configure Proxy Server, it may not detect the .6 and the .7 subnets. You need to add them to the LAT manually in order for Proxy Server to accurately identify which addresses are internal and which are external. Otherwise, Proxy Server will perceive that 192.168.6 and .7 are external addresses.

---

service from where the setup was initiated. Also, as part of the installation, the Web browser is also configured as a client of the Web Proxy service.

You can start the client setup program using one of two techniques. You can connect to the UNC \\server_name\mspclnt and run the client setup program. Alternatively, you can use a browser, such as Internet Explorer, point it to http://computer_name/msproxy, and click the Install WinSock Proxy 2.0 client link, as illustrated in Figure 17-17. If you are installing the client on a Web server, the setup program stops the Web service while the installation is in progress.

FIGURE 17-17

Installing the WinSock
Proxy client from
the browser

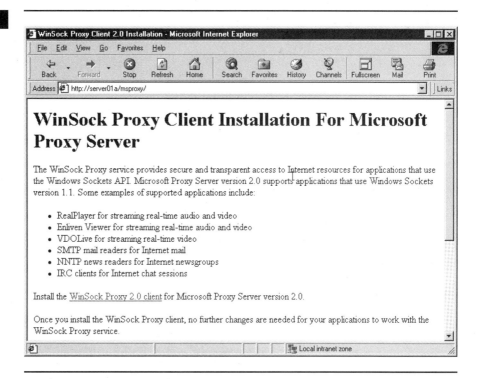

# Installing the WinSock Client Software

If you start the installation using the browser, the next dialog box (Figure 17-18) asks if you want to save the file or run the file from the current location. If you save the file to disk, then you have to run Setup from the local drive.

If you select Run this program from its current location, a command window appears and the Setup Wizard begins. This first dialog box is the Welcome to the Microsoft Proxy Client installation program (see Figure 17-19).

The next dialog box (Figure 17-20) allows you to change the folder where the client files will be installed and select the installation button.

After clicking Install, the files are copied to the client folder and you see the message illustrated in Figure 17-21 indicating the installation was successful.

**FIGURE 17-18**

Starting the installation
from the browser

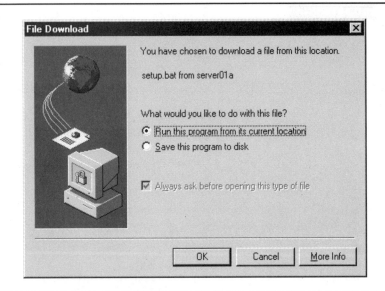

**FIGURE 17-19**

The client setup
welcome dialog box

**FIGURE 17-20**

Selecting the
installation folder

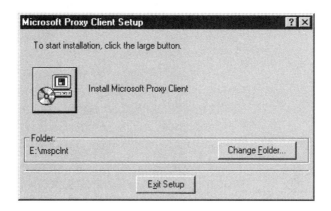

## Configuring Netscape Navigator

Take the case where you are going to use the Netscape Navigator as your Web
browser for your computer. You run the client setup program and Netscape
Navigator is configured as a Web Proxy client to the Proxy Server.

You can also set this up inside Netscape Navigator with its own
configuration interface. In Navigator for Windows NT and for Windows 95,

**FIGURE 17-21**

Successful installation

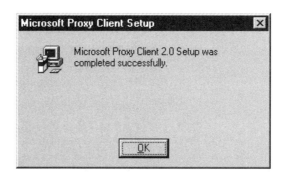

you define the name of the computer being used as the Proxy Server and the port number using the following options:

- Options menu
- Proxies tab
- Network tab
- Manual Proxy Configuration
- View

### Configuring Browsers for Other Clients

If you are using Web browsers for other non-Windows operating systems, such as Macintosh and UNIX, consult the specific product documentation for detailed information on how to configure the browser application to use a Proxy Server.

There is usually some point in the program or in the associated support files where you need to enter the Proxy Server computer name and a port number to use to contact the Proxy Server.

Name resolution is also important. If you are using a non-Windows operating system and the Web browser is a SOCKS client, you need to provide a DNS Proxy Server to your clients for name resolution. The DNS proxy server resolves the names by passing the request to a server on the Internet.

## Force IPX/SPX Option

There may be times that you are running both the TCP/IP and the IPX/SPX protocol. IPX/SPX may be the primary protocol and TCP/IP is there to support RAS, for example. The problem exists because the WinSock Proxy client attempts to use the TCP/IP protocol to make its connection. Disabling the TCP/IP protocol is not effective, because the WinSock Proxy client still detects the protocol stack. Deleting the protocol means that it is unavailable for RAS and you need to reinstall it.

You can also use this option if you are running only the IPX/SPX protocol to configure a client computer on an IPX-only network. Proxy Server does not support IPX on Windows 3.1 (or Windows for Workgroups 3.11) running IPX. The computers need to access Proxy Server using TCP/IP. There are also some settings that need to be correct in the mspclnt.ini file. Check the Proxy Server documentation for these settings. Chapter 16 also discusses how to modify the mspclnt.ini file.

You can use the Force IPX/SPX protocol option instead. Open Control Panel and open the WSP applet. Check the Force IPX/SPX protocol box, illustrated in Figure 17-22.

### Configuring for an IPX/SPX Network

Certain parameters need to be set correctly on all computers running Proxy Server in order for them to operate correctly. Different parameters may need to be configured depending on whether you have NetWare servers or not, and whether your topology is Ethernet or Token Ring. You must also configure your Windows NT and Windows 95 clients properly as well.

If you are using NetWare servers, then both the Proxy Server and clients' IPX frame type can be set to Auto. If you do not have NetWare servers on the network, the IPX clients do not automatically configure their IPX settings correctly. Proxy Server does not respond to client broadcast for IPX external network number. How you deal with that depends on whether you are using Ethernet or Token Ring. There are procedures listed in your Proxy Server online documentation for configuring for these situations.

**FIGURE 17-22**

Selecting the Force
IPX/SPX protocol option

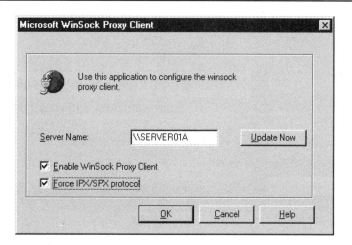

## Using JavaScript to Configure a Client

When a Web browser client is started, you can specify that a client configuration script be downloaded to the client computer. This configuration script is written in JavaScript and is located on the Proxy Server computer to that client computer. Remember, every client contacts a specific Proxy Server.

The script is downloaded to the browser on the client computer and is executed against every URL that the browser requests. The output of the script is an ordered list of Proxy Servers that is used by the browser to retrieve the object specified by the URL. This can reduce some of the routing work performed by the Proxy Server array.

## Removing or Disabling the WinSock Proxy Client

You can remove the Winsock Proxy Client software by running Setup from the Microsoft Proxy Server group. You can also Add/Remove components from the same Setup program.

You can also disable the client instead of uninstalling it. You do this from the WSP applet in the Control Panel.

**EXERCISE 17-3**

### Installing the WinSock Client

1. Ensure that you are logged on as Administrator.
2. Click Start.
3. Click Run.
4. Type **http://server01/msproxy** and press ENTER. This starts Internet Explorer and connects to the server.
5. Click the Install WinSock Proxy 2.0 client link.
6. Select Run this program from current location.
7. Click Continue.
8. Click the Install Microsoft Proxy Client button.
9. Click Yes if asked to create the folder.
10. Click OK in the Completed successfully dialog box.
11. Click the Restart Windows Now button.

## QUESTIONS AND ANSWERS

| | |
|---|---|
| Do I need to install a Web Proxy client separately? | No. When you install the WinSock client, Internet Explorer is configured as well and you can contact Internet resources using the Proxy Server. The Web Proxy service will cache objects you call for you. |
| Can I install Proxy Server on an NTFS partition? | Of course. You can also install it on a FAT partition. However, you must have an NTFS partition if you want to have a cache drive. |
| Do I need TCP/IP installed on my network? | Yes and no. The Proxy Server itself must have TCP/IP installed so that it may communicate with the Internet. Client computers may use either IP or IPX protocol. |
| During installation, I check "Load...from all...cards." Is this OK? | Yes, but you need to make a change. When you load IP addresses from all the cards, you probably load external network addresses as well. You need to edit those out of the LAT, either during installation or afterwards. |
| Do I need to create the Locallat.txt file? | Not necessarily. You only need it if there are internal IP addresses not contained in the LAT. |

# CERTIFICATION SUMMARY

This chapter described how to install both the Proxy Server and the WinSock Proxy client. Proxy Server is not part of Windows NT Server so it is not included with the Windows NT Server distribution files. Proxy Server is a separate program that you purchase separately from Microsoft. Proxy Server runs on top of Windows NT Server and must have IIS installed as well.

Microsoft Proxy Server is very popular as a cost-effective firewall solution, compared to the price of other firewalls.

Proxy Server installs three services: Web Proxy, WinSock Proxy, and SOCKS Proxy. You manage these services using the Microsoft Management Console (MMC) and the Internet Service Manager (ISM).

During the installation, you build the local address table (LAT). This table contains all the IP addresses that are on your internal network. These addresses are entered in pairs of IP addresses; a beginning address and an end address define an address range. An address range may be a single IP address. It is important that only internal addresses be in the LAT. There should be no external addresses.

You can install the WinSock client software by connecting to the Proxy Server using the UNC or by using a browser and connecting to the URL http://computer_name/msproxy. The processing of installing the client software also installs a copy of the LAT on the client. You can supplement this LAT with a text file that can include other local IP addresses not contained in the LAT. If you want to connect to the Internet directly, you can disable the client.

 **TWO-MINUTE DRILL**

❑ The system requirements for Proxy Server are pretty much the same as for IIS.

❑ You need 10MB of disk space.

❑ You need disk space for cache.

❑ For cache, use 100MB plus .5MB for each Proxy client.

❑ Proxy Server is installed from the msp folder on the CD-ROM.

❑ You can only have cache on a NTFS partition.

❑ You must set up the LAT during installation.

❑ The LAT is very important to you.

❑ You will see several questions on the LAT on your Proxy Server exam.

❑ You should not have any external IP addresses in the LAT.

❑ You can modify the LAT at any time.

❑ You can have Proxy Server attempt to discover the network addresses.

❑ Do you get the idea that having the proper addresses in the LAT is important?

❑ Access control is enabled by default during installation.

❑ Packet filtering is disabled by default during installation.

❑ During client installation, the file msplat.txt is copied to the client computer.

❑ This is a local copy of the LAT table and it is refreshed periodically.

❑ You can create a custom LAT for the client by creating a text file named Locallat.txt.

❑ You can install the WinSock client from the browser.

❑ You can install the WinSock client from the UNC \\server\mspclnt, running the Setup Wizard.

❑ You can configure Netscape Navigator the same way.

❑ You can configure Netscape Navigator manually.

❑ You can force the IPX/SPX protocol to be used instead of TCP/IP.

❑ You cannot use IPX only on Windows 3.1 clients.

# SELF TEST

The following Self Test questions will help you measure your understanding of the material presented in this chapter. Read all the choices carefully, as there may be more than one correct answer. Choose all correct answers for each question.

1. Which of the following is not a minimum requirement for installing Proxy Server 2.0?

   A. Windows NT Server with SP3

   B. 32MB RAM

   C. NTFS partition for caching

   D. Internet Information Server

2. You are the system administrator. You are planning to install Proxy Server 2.0 to support 220 users. You want to make sure you have enough drive space for cached objects. What is the recommended cache space to support your users?

   A. 100MB

   B. 10MB

   C. 110MB

   D. 210MB

3. Which of the following are not options that you select during the installation of Proxy Server?

   A. Transaction Server

   B. Proxy Server

   C. Web Administration Tool

   D. Documentation

4. Which of the following is necessary for caching, at a minimum?

   A. NTFS partition

   B. 100MB of free space

   C. 5MB of free space

   D. Either a FAT or NTFS partition

5. Which of the following statements are true about the LAT IP addresses?

   A. The LAT should contain internal IP addresses.

   B. The LAT should contain external IP addresses.

   C. You can have the Installation Wizard construct the LAT for you.

   D. You can manually build the LAT.

6. Which of the following is not installed or enabled by default?

   A. Web Proxy service

   B. WinSock Proxy client software for distribution

   C. Packet filtering

   D. Access control

7. Which of the following changes are not made by the Proxy Server installation process?

   A. Proxy services

   B. IUSR_Proxy account

   C. Counters for Performance Monitor

   D. WSP applet

8. You are a local administrator but you do not administer the Proxy Server. You have added another subnet to your network and want to access the IIS servers on that network. Since you cannot modify the LAT at the Proxy Server, what can you do to allow client browsers to access the new subnet?

   A. Nothing. You have to wait until the Proxy Server administrator modifies the LAT.

   B. Modify the mspclnt.txt file on the client.

   C. Modify the Locallat.txt file on the client.

   D. Modify the msplat.txt file on the client.

9. What installation techniques can you use to install the WinSock client?

   A. Download the client software from the Microsoft Web site.

   B. Run Setup from the inetsrv\clients folder.

   C. Connect to the UNC mspclnt at the Proxy Server.

   D. Connect to the URL http://computer_name/msproxy.

MICROSOFT CERTIFIED SYSTEMS ENGINEER

# 18

# Controlling Access

T his chapter describes the concepts and configurations for controlling outbound access and inbound access. The chapter also discusses encryption using the Secure Sockets Layer (SSL). This chapter prepares you to describe the security functions of Proxy Server. You can also configure and implement security for Proxy Server.

# Outbound Access

You can allow your clients complete access to the Internet. Microsoft Proxy Server provides several methods for controlling outbound access to the Internet as well. These methods allow you to configure as granular a control as you require in order to determine what your clients can and cannot access on the Internet. Granularity in this context means a fine setting; the ability to control finitely, like fine grains of sand.

There are three primary methods for configuring outbound access:

- Controlling access by Internet service
- Controlling access by IP parameters
- Controlling access by TCP port

**exam**
**Ⓦatch**

*Know the three primary methods of controlling outbound access.*

## Controlling Access by Internet Service

One of the key tenets of security is to allow access to resources and services only by those who need them.

In the context of Proxy Server, you limit specific services to only those users who need to use the service. You can set the access control permissions individually for the Web Proxy, WinSock Proxy, and the SOCKS Proxy services. You set the permissions from inside the ISM using the property sheet of the specific service.

By right-clicking on the Web Proxy icon and selecting Properties (see Figure 18-1), you can set the access permissions for the following services:

- **WWW (HTTP)**    This is for access to HTTP protocol.

- **FTP Read**    This is for access to FTP services.

- **Gopher**    Gopher is a menu-based system used to supplement FTP. Remember that IIS 4.0 dropped support for Gopher, although it is still in use on the Internet.

- **Secure**    This is the SSL service. If you have access granted, then you can use SSL security.

**FIGURE 18-1**

Controlling access to the Web Proxy service

Click the Edit button, and you can add users and groups to the access box, as illustrated in Figure 18-2.

You use the same procedure to set the permissions for using the WinSock service, as illustrated in Figure 18-3. Note that the WinSock Proxy service has a special selection in the protocol list titled "Unlimited Access." This allows access to all protocols and all ports of this server without restriction. This option allows a user full control to use any protocols or ports with WinSock Proxy service, including those ports that are not defined. For this reason, be careful in assigning this option to users. Remember that users granted **this access** are not affected by WinSock Proxy domain filtering. The users and groups are built using User Manager for Domains, a Windows NT administrative tool. You use this tool to set the security policies for your users such as passwords, password expiration, etc.

You use the same procedure to set the permissions for using the SOCKS service. Figure 18-4 shows the dialog box you use to configure this service. The source specifies the origin of the request. You do this either by IP address and subnet mask, for a particular domain (Internet domain and not a Windows NT Domain) or for all computers. The destination side is where you allow (or deny) the destination of the permitted entry.

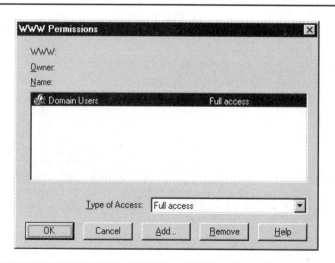

Setting access permissions
for the SOCKS Proxy
service

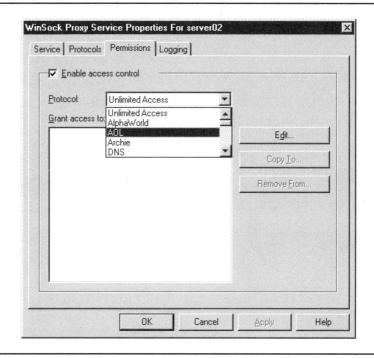

Configuring access to the
SOCKS service

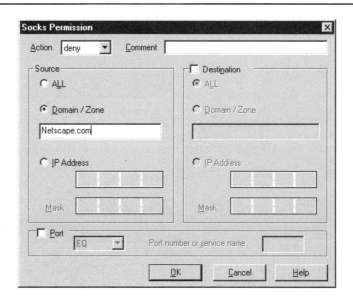

## Controlling by IP Parameters

Proxy Server allows you to control access by specific IP parameters such as:

- IP address
- IP subnet
- Internet domain

This is done by enabling filtering and then specifying the appropriate IP address, subnet, or domain.

When configuring this security, there are two methods you can use. You can grant access to everyone and then restrict access by denying certain IP addresses, subnets, or domains. Or, you can deny access to everyone and then grant access by exception by specifying the IP address, subnet, or domain. Figure 18-5 contains the dialog box you use to set this access.

**FIGURE 18-5**

Setting access by IP address, subnet, or domain

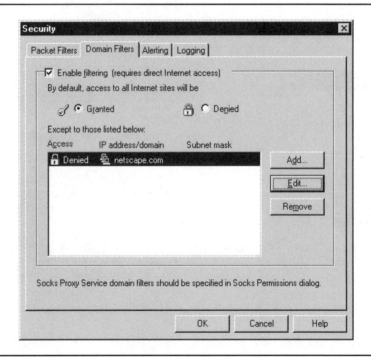

*Know that you can either grant or deny access by exception.*

Just as with configuring access by Internet service, you can set these parameters for each individual Proxy Server.

## Controlling by Port

You can configure which port is used by the TCP and UDP protocols and thus control the access of the WinSock Proxy service. Proxy Server comes with a default set of protocol definitions. You can add your own protocol definitions or modify the definitions of the default protocols to suit your requirements.

Proxy Server uses application service ports for the WinSock Proxy and SOCKS Proxy services. WinSock-based applications work through a network connection. Ports are used in combination with IP addressing to form socket connections. A socket is an endpoint in the communication process. The WinSock Proxy service can also redirect a **listen**() call. The implication of this is that Proxy Server can listen to Internet requests on behalf of your application. It then redirects the request from the Internet to your application.

Earlier, this chapter discussed the special setting called Unlimited Access. You can also enable access to inbound and outbound service ports selectively for users on your network. You do this through the ISM by selecting the WinSock property sheet and then selecting the Protocols tab, as illustrated in Figure 18-6.

You can create definitions and modify existing protocol definitions. You can save these definitions and load them at a later date. You can save this file from one Proxy Server and load it at another Proxy Server. You may use any legal filename, including an extension. Proxy Server does not append the filename with an extension. It is saved as a text file.

By selecting the Edit button, you can change the parameters of the inbound and outbound connections for that protocol (see Figure 18-7).

You can also create new protocol definitions in WinSock Proxy service properties for the purpose of controlling access. Consider the following scenario: You want to allow both outbound and inbound port access for FTP

**FIGURE 18-6**

Selecting protocols under the WinSock service

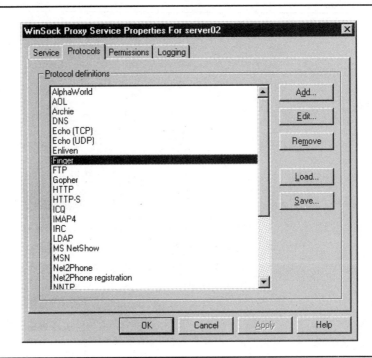

service to all internal users on your network. However, you want to allow only inbound FTP logon for the single Internet (non-internal) client user called FTPSpec1.

In this scenario, you use the predefined protocol definitions for FTP. This grants all the internal users permission to this protocol because inbound and outbound port access is enabled.

To allow only inbound port access for the FTPSpec1 user account *only*, you create a new protocol definition called "FTP Special" and define only the inbound TCP port 0 for it. The FTPSpec1 account can then be assigned permissions to the "FTP Special" protocol permission list.

Table 18-1 summarizes the parameters for the default protocols. You can modify the initial connection, specify TCP or UDP, and specify whether it is

**FIGURE** 18-7

Editing the parameters

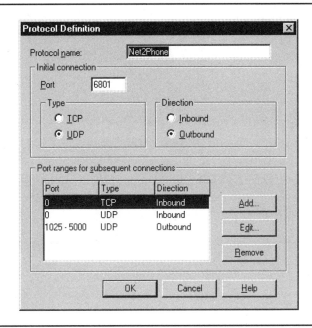

inbound or outbound. You can also set the parameters for subsequent connections, which do not have to be the same as the initial connection.

Refer to the RFCs at www.internic.net, the Microsoft Web site, and TechNet for further information on these protocols and their use.

**TABLE** 18-1     Matrix of the Default Protocol Initial Parameters

| Protocol Name | Initial Connection | Type | Direction |
|---|---|---|---|
| Alpha World | 5670 | TCP | Outbound |
| AOL | 5190 | TCP | Outbound |
| Archie | 1525 | UDP | Outbound |

**TABLE 18-1**    Matrix of the Default Protocol Initial Parameters (*continued*)

| Protocol Name | Initial Connection | Type | Direction |
|---|---|---|---|
| DNS | 53 | UDP | Outbound |
| Echo (TCP) | 7 | TCP | Outbound |
| Echo (UDP) | 7 | UDP | Outbound |
| Enliven | 537 | TCP | Outbound |
| Finger | 79 | TCP | Outbound |
| FTP | 21 | TCP | Outbound |
| Gopher | 70 | TCP | Outbound |
| HTTP | 80 | TCP | Outbound |
| HTTP-S | 443 | TCP | Outbound |
| ICQ | 4000 | UDP | Outbound |
| IMAP4 | 143 | TCP | Outbound |
| IRC | 6667 | TCP | Outbound |
| LDAP | 389 | TCP | Outbound |
| MS NetShow | 1755 | TCP | Outbound |
| MSN | 569 | TCP | Outbound |
| Net2Phone | 6801 | UDP | Outbound |
| Net2Phone registration | 6500 | TCP | Outbound |
| NNTP | 119 | TCP | Outbound |
| POP3 | 110 | TCP | Outbound |
| Real Audio (7070) | 7070 | TCP | Outbound |
| Real Audio (7075) | 7075 | TCP | Outbound |
| SMTP (client) | 25 | TCP | Outbound |
| Telnet | 23 | TCP | Outbound |
| Time (TCP) | 37 | TCP | Outbound |
| VDOLive | 7000 | TCP | Outbound |
| Vxtreme | 12468 | TCP | Outbound |
| WhoIs | 43 | TCP | Outbound |

# FROM THE CLASSROOM

## I Can't Get Access to the Web!

There is a scenario that we see both in the classroom and at client sites that is interesting to observe. It seems to be a common oversight that can be made by almost anyone. I watch experienced people and rookies make the same mistake.

If you are used to setting up Windows NT systems, you know that default access is wide open. This is especially true with Windows NT Workstation. By default, the group "Everyone" can log on locally and access the computer from the network. The guest account is even enabled in Windows NT Workstation by default! You can install the operating system and walk away from the machine with people having access.

It is up to the administrator to lock down the computer by implementing the proper security controls. This is not a problem, but you have to do something.

So, armed with this experience, you installed Proxy Server. The installation went smoothly.

You rushed to your computer, opened the browser, selected the Proxy Server URL, and installed the WinSock client. You checked the browser and found it was set to use the Proxy Server.

You now point your browser to your favorite Web site and ... you get back a blank screen. That's all, just a blank browser screen. No error messages; no 404 "URL not found;" no access denied message; just a blank screen. In fact, for the next three hours you get back blank screens from every Web site. What is the problem, you ask?

When Proxy Server is installed, everything is locked down. The default is Enable Access Control. There are no users or groups listed in the Grant access to box. No one is going outside your network until you configure the Proxy Server. It is a little bit different than the usual Windows NT setup.

**CERTIFICATION OBJECTIVE 18.02**

# Inbound Access

There are good site design and implementation guidelines that you can adhere to that lessen the security risks when using Microsoft Proxy Server. Use the following checklist for items to consider:

- **Disable IP forwarding**   Setting this parameter disables the forwarding of IP packets.

- **Enable Access Control**   This is the default during installation. Without access control enabled, you will not be able to set password authentication. This is considered unsecured.

- **Local Address Table**   The LAT details what addresses Proxy Server considers internal network addresses. This point is critical. Internal addresses have access to the internal network. Never put external addresses in the LAT.

- **Disable Server Service**   Consider disabling the Windows NT Server service on the Proxy Server system. This service provides file and print services to network clients. These services are not necessary for the Proxy Server or its clients to function adequately. If you choose not to disable the service, then make sure that any shares that you created have the proper permissions assigned to them. You should also use the NTFS file system because it greatly enhances security for this situation.

- **Drive Mappings**   Do not use drive mappings to connect to remote resources if you are running Proxy Server and IIS on the same server and you are publishing content. The issue with mapped drives is that if, for any reason, the drive letter designator should change, the resource will not be available. If you use the UNC syntax, this cannot happen. In addition, you are limited to the number of drive mappings you can have, based on the characters in the alphabet. This technique holds true for administration of Windows NT as well.

- **Configuring the Client**   Remove gateway references and DNS references from the IP parameters from the client computers. This prevents clients from bypassing Proxy Server to access the Internet. Don't forget to remove these parameters from your DHCP scope properties as well.

- **Disable RPC ports**   Ports 1024 through 1029 are used by TCP/IP services for Remote Procedure Call (RPC) listening. You can disable all ports used for RPC listening on the external network interface. Then these ports are no longer visible to the Internet. You make these changes through the registry. The Proxy Server documentation provides more information about these settings.

There is additional information in a white paper located at the Microsoft Web site. Point your browser to http://www.microsoft.com/proxy to find Proxy Server white papers.

## Controlling Access to the LAN

The default installation configuration of Microsoft Proxy Server has the network fully secure from outside access by Internet users. Interestingly enough, if, during installation, you accept the defaults that enable access control, internal access to the Internet is also prevented. In other words, users inside cannot access the Internet and users outside cannot access the internal network.

Access control is enabled by installation, but no users or groups are specified yet. The administrator must explicitly do this. This is true for both the Web Proxy and WinSock Proxy services.

There are two factors to consider:

1. Your Proxy Server has two network cards. Proxy Server disables IP forwarding on the server. External users connect to one network card.

The internal network is connected to the other network card. All connections between the two networks are done by referencing the routing information contained in the LAT. With IP forwarding disabled, external users cannot access the internal network.

2. Listening on inbound service ports is disabled. If ports are not available, then connections cannot be made. You must specifically enable which application service port you wish to use. This means that you cannot publish from the Web server to the Internet using the default configuration.

If you install Remote Access Service (RAS) after you install Proxy Server, IP forwarding is enabled. You must manually disable it to re-establish tight security on your network.

## Controlling Access by Packet Type

You can use Proxy Server to control access to the internal network using a technique known as *packet filtering*. With packet filtering enabled, Proxy Server accepts or denies packets based on packet type. You can also block packets originating from specific Internet hosts.

Proxy Server supports both dynamic and static packet filtering. With dynamic packet filtering, designated ports are automatically opened for outgoing and inbound traffic. The ports are automatically closed after the session has been terminated. This minimizes the number of ports that are open at any time and minimizes the length of time a particular port is open. Dynamic packet filtering is automatic and requires no work on your part.

Static packet filtering involves manually configuring the filter. You do this using ISM and the property sheet for the service. Click the Security button to display the dialog box in Figure 18-8. Packet filtering is covered in more detail in Chapter 20.

## Encryption

Proxy Server takes advantage of authentication and the security architecture of IIS. The Web Proxy service uses the same password authentication methods

**FIGURE 18-8**

Enabling packet filtering

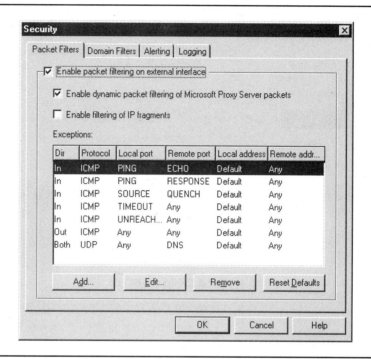

for client requests as those configured in the WWW service of IIS. These authentication methods include:

- Anonymous logon
- Basic authentication
- Windows NT challenge/response authentication

Using challenge/response authentication with any Web browser other than Internet Explorer (IE) 4.0 might result in rejection of client configuration scripts (JScripts) or incorrect display of HTTP pages that use the Secure Sockets Layer (SSL). You should use basic authentication if you are using a Web browser other than IE 4.0. Basic authentication is sent clear text. If you use basic authentication along with SSL, then the user's name and password are encrypted.

SSL supports data encryption and authentication. Data sent to and from a client using SSL is encrypted both ways.

There are some performance penalties associated with SSL encryption both on the server and on the link.

### Isolating the Internal and External Networks

Purpose: To verify the settings of IP forwarding.

*Do this exercise at the Proxy Server.*

1. Ensure that you are logged on as administrator.
2. Open the Network applet.
3. Click the Protocols tab.
4. Select TCP/IP.
5. Click Properties.
6. From the resulting dialog box, select the Routing tab.
7. Make sure that the Enable IP forwarding check box is cleared.
8. Click OK until all dialog boxes have been closed.

### Configuring Access in Web Proxy Service

Purpose: To learn to configure the Web and Web Proxy services. You are going to change the access authority scheme. In the exercise, you will revoke anonymous access and grant access to the global group Domain Admins.

*Do this exercise from the domain controller.*

1. Start the Internet Service Manager.
2. Expand your server.
3. Right-click your Web site.
4. Select Properties.
5. Click the Directory Security tab.
6. Click the Edit button.
7. Clear the Allow Anonymous Access check box.

8. Click OK to close the Web Site Properties dialog box.

9. If you receive the Inheritance Overrides dialog box, click Cancel.

10. Right-click the Web Proxy icon.

11. Select Properties.

12. Select the Permissions tab.

13. Make sure that the Enable Access Control check box has a check mark.

14. In the Protocol box, select WWW.

15. Click the Edit button.

16. Click the Add button.

17. Double-click Domain Admins.

18. Click OK.

19. Click OK.

20. Click OK.

| EXERCISE 18-3 | ### Configuring a Domain Filter |

Purpose: To gain experience configuring a domain filter.

*Do this exercise from the domain controller.*

1. Right-click the Web Proxy icon.

2. Select Properties.

3. Click the Security button.

4. Click the Domain Filters tab.

5. Check the Enable filtering (requires direct Internet access) box.

6. Click the Add button.

7. Click the Domain radio button.

8. In the Domain text box, type **Junkmail.com** and click OK. This restricts internal users from accessing the domain "Junkmail.com."

9. Click the Add button.

10. Click A Group of Computers.

11. Type the IP address **131.107.2.0.** This entry, in combination with the subnet mask, establishes the range of IP addresses that are unavailable to internal users.

12. Type the subnet mask **255.255.255.0.**

13. Click OK.

14. Click OK.

15. Click OK to close the Web Proxy Service Properties dialog box.

EXERCISE 18-4 ### Backing Up Proxy Server Configuration

Purpose: To become familiar with backing up and restoring the server configuration. You will back up the Proxy Server configuration files. They will be stored in the msp\config folder with the file names "msp*[date/time from your system]*.mpc. You should do these backups periodically, like any other type of backup. You can then use the restore feature. This file is a text file and can be used to set the configuration parameters for any Proxy Server.

*Do this exercise from the domain controller.*

1. Ensure that you still have the d:\co_info folder. If not, create it.

2. Right-click the Web Proxy icon.

3. Click the Server Backup button.

4. Use the Browse button to select the d:\co_info folder.

5. Click OK.

6. Open Windows NT Explorer.

7. Select the d:\co_info folder. You should see a file there ending in the .mpc extension. The filename will be in the format *yyyymmdd.* If you created a second file on the same day, it would be *yyyymmdd*a, and then "b," and so on with the .mpc extension.

8. Close Windows NT Explorer.

9. Return to the MMC (ISM).

10. Click the Server Restore button.

11. Use the Help button to learn more about the restore options.

12. Click Cancel.

13. Click OK.

14. Close the MMC.

---

**CERTIFICATION OBJECTIVE 18.03**

# Using Proxy Server to Dial Up

Proxy Server has a feature called AutoDial. This feature allows you to configure Proxy Server to automatically dial to your ISP, or dial back to your central location. Proxy Server uses RAS to establish the dial-up connection. AutoDial is event driven and makes the connection only when needed. Proxy Server autodials:

- When Web Proxy cannot find a requested object in cache
- For all client requests of WinSock
- For all client requests of SOCKS

To support Proxy Server AutoDial, you must do the following:

- Install and configure RAS and DUN (Dial-Up Networking).
  - Install RAS.
  - Make a phonebook entry.
  - Configure the RAS service.

- Configure Proxy Server AutoDial.
  - Configure the AutoDial credentials.
  - Set the AutoDial dialing hours.
  - Stop and start the Proxy Server services.

There are advantages and disadvantages to using the AutoDial feature. One of the benefits is that you don't need a dedicated circuit that may cost more.

The disadvantage is that dial-up access tends to be slow, but only as measured by the link speed. When users access an outside resource, there is a time delay as the Proxy Server makes the connection.

You can get faster dial services such as ISDN lines. But you must use caution here as well. While ISDN access may be faster, it may also carry charges based on the connect time. The more you connect, the greater the cost. At some point, the cost of an ISDN circuit that is frequently accessed will be greater than the cost of a leased line.

## Installing Remote Access Service (RAS)

In order to use Proxy Server AutoDial, you must install RAS and configure the services. You must also set up at least one phonebook entry. If you are unfamiliar with RAS and how to configure the services, refer to the Windows NT Server Resource Kit or Windows NT Online help. Other resources that are helpful are two study guides, *MCSE Windows NT Workstation 4.0 Study Guide* and *MCSE Windows NT Server 4.0 Study Guide* (Osborne/McGraw-Hill).

e x a m
ⓦatch

***You need to know how to configure the RAS services and phonebook entries for the test.***

RAS can be installed during the Windows NT Server installation. RAS can also be installed at any time after the installation. When you install RAS, be prepared with certain information to make the installation go smoothly:

- If you are going to use a modem, know what the modem type is. If that model is not listed in the modem.inf file, you may need to create a custom entry for that model.

- Know which communication port you are connecting the modem to. I prefer to use external modems because of their status lights. I can diagnose many modem communications problems quickly by observing the status lights. Don't underestimate the difficulty of troubleshooting this type of problem.

- If you are using ISDN as your dial equipment, be prepared with the same type of information. You can get more insight from the Windows NT Server Resource Kit Supplement One.

RAS should be configured for dial-out only. This makes it a RAS client. If you configure RAS to receive calls or for both dial-out and to receive calls, you are making the computer a RAS server capable of receiving incoming calls. This is something that you do not want to happen.

After you have RAS installed, you need to do the following:

■ Stop the Remote Access AutoDial Manager service.

■ Disable the AutoDial Manager service.

■ Stop and Start the Remote Access Connection Manager service.

■ Make sure that the Connection Manager is set to automatic startup mode.

exam
Ⓦatch

*Remember that you must disable the RAS AutoDial Manager so it does not conflict with the Proxy Server AutoDial.*

## Building a Phonebook Entry

You use Dial-Up Networking (DUN) to connect as a client through RAS. A phonebook entry is used to store the parameters necessary to connect to a remote network. Again, you can refer to the same resources described in the previous section to get more information on how to configure a phonebook entry.

You configure the phonebook entry from DUN, found in My Computer. When you double-click DUN for the first time, you receive a notice that the phonebook is empty and it will ask if you want to create an entry, as shown in the following illustration.

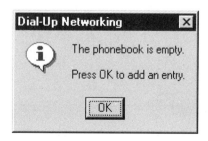

After you click OK, the New Phonebook Entry Wizard is launched (see Figure 18-9). The wizard walks you through the basic phonebook configuration, or you can check the box and configure the phonebook parameters yourself without the wizard.

## Configuring AutoDial Credentials

After installing RAS and setting up the phonebook entries, you need to configure the AutoDial credentials in Proxy Server. You supply the credentials necessary to be authenticated at your ISP. If these logon credentials change, you need to change them in Proxy Server also.

You begin by configuring the Proxy services from the ISM. By selecting the Web Proxy properties sheet, you can select the AutoDial button, as illustrated in Figure 18-10.

**FIGURE 18-9**

Running the New
Phonebook Entry Wizard

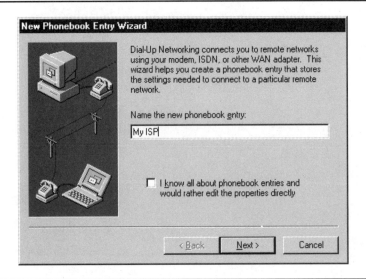

**FIGURE 18-10**

Selecting the AutoDial
button from the Web
Proxy properties sheet

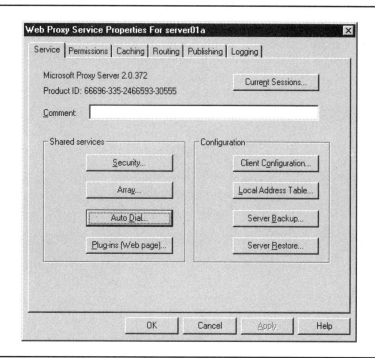

There are two tabs in the AutoDial sheet. They are:

- **Configuration tab**   Here you set what times are allowed for dialing.
  This section works similarly to the Logon Hours box in Windows NT
  User Manager. You also enable the specific services that AutoDial will
  support. Figure 18-11 contains this dialog box.

- **Credentials tab**   You use this tab to specify the logon credentials for
  the connection to the ISP. Figure 18-12 contains this dialog box.

**FIGURE** 18-11

Setting the AutoDial times
on configuration

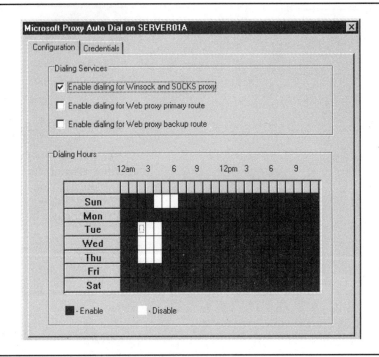

**FIGURE** 18-12

Specifying logon credentials
for the ISP

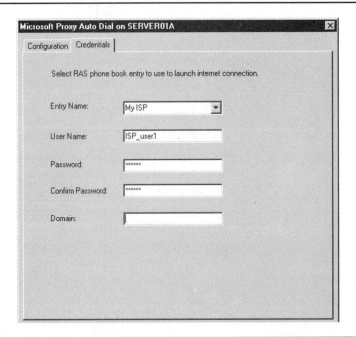

## QUESTIONS AND ANSWERS

| | |
|---|---|
| If I am going to use RAS to support Proxy Server AutoDial, does my ISP need a RAS server? | No. Your ISP needs a PPP server to receive the RAS client connection. |
| Why would I want to control outbound connections? | Not everyone in your organization may need access to the Internet. One of the security tenets is not to allow what is not needed. |
| Can I restrict users from accessing multiple Internet domains? | Yes. In the MMC, specify which Internet domains they are not allowed to access. You cannot restrict access to Windows NT Domains with this process. Access to a Windows NT Domain is controlled by the Windows NT Domain security policies. |
| I have hundreds of domains that I don't want my users to access. Is there an easy way to set this? | Perhaps. You can deny access to all domains, then grant access to domains by exceptions, if you don't have too many domains to access. |

# CERTIFICATION SUMMARY

This chapter described how to control outbound and inbound access using Proxy Server. There are three ways to control outbound access. One way is by controlling by Internet service type. You can set access permissions for each of the three Proxy services, Web Proxy, WinSock Proxy, and SOCKS Proxy. You can also control access using IP parameters. You can restrict the sites your users may visit by restricting certain Internet domain names, network addresses, or individual IP addresses. And finally, you can restrict access by port number.

The chapter discussed how to control inbound access. You do this using one of two techniques. One technique is packet filtering. The other technique is properly configuring the network adapters and which ports Proxy Server listens to for connections.

You can use Proxy Server's AutoDial feature to connect to an ISP or to your central location. Using the AutoDial feature requires that RAS be installed and a phonebook entry be configured.

✓ **TWO-MINUTE DRILL**

❑ You can control what Internet resources your users may access.

❑ You can control user access by limiting the type of Proxy service they may use.

❑ You can set access permissions by groups or by individual users.

❑ WinSock Proxy service has a special access permission called Unlimited Access.

❑ Access control is enabled by default during installation.

❑ By default, no users have outbound access until you configure it for them.

❑ You can restrict users from accessing a particular domain

❑ You can restrict users from accessing a given network ID or subnet.

❑ You can restrict users from accessing an IP address.

❑ WinSock applications communicate using TCP ports.

❑ You can configure which ports the WinSock application has access to.

❑ You can create new protocol definitions for your WinSock applications.

❑ You can edit and modify existing WinSock protocol definitions.

❑ To control inbound access, disable IP forwarding.

❑ Disabling IP forwarding is done using the Network applet.

❑ You control inbound access by ensuring that no external addresses are listed in the LAT.

❑ Disabling the Server service on your Proxy Server is a good idea to protect it from unauthorized inbound access.

❑ You can control access using packet filtering.

❑ Proxy Server supports dynamic packet filtering.

❑ Proxy Server supports static packet filtering.

❑ Dynamic packet filtering closes the port when not in use.

❑ Proxy Server supports SSL encryption of authentication.

❑ Proxy Server has a feature called AutoDial.

❑ AutoDial calls the ISP when an HTTP object is not in cache.

❑ AutoDial calls the ISP when a WinSock application needs access.

❑ AutoDial calls the ISP when a SOCKS application needs access.

❑ You must install RAS to use the AutoDial feature.

❑ You must configure a phonebook entry.

❑ You must disable the Remote Access AutoDial Manager service.

❑ You must configure the Proxy Server AutoDial logon credentials for the ISP.

# SELF TEST

The Self Test questions will help you measure your understanding of the material presented in this chapter. Read all the choices carefully, as there may be more than one correct answer. Choose all correct answers for each question.

1. Which of the following is not a primary method of controlling outbound access?

   A. Internet service

   B. IP address

   C. TCP port

   D. Time-of-day access

2. You have users on your network who want to access the Microsoft Web site. How do you configure Proxy Server to allow this?

   A. You don't need to do anything; the users can access Internet Web sites. Internet users cannot access your internal Web sites.

   B. Use the Web Proxy properties sheet and add those users who need access through the Permissions tab.

   C. Use the Web site properties sheet and add those users who need access to the Grant To dialog box.

   D. Use the WinSock Proxy properties sheet and add those users who need access through the Permissions tab.

3. Which of the following is not true about access control for WinSock Proxy service?

   A. Unlimited Access allows users access to all protocols.

   B. You can create your own protocol definitions.

   C. You can edit the default protocol definitions.

   D. You can edit the definitions that were installed, but you cannot create new definitions.

4. Which of the following IP parameters cannot be used to control outbound access?

   A. DHCP client status

   B. IP addresses

   C. IP subnets

   D. IP domains

5. Which of the following is not a variable that you can change for a WinSock protocol?

   A. Initial connection port

   B. Inbound/outbound direction

   C. Time-to-live

   D. Subsequent connection ports

6. Which statement best describes the function of IP forwarding?

   A. It sends packets to the Internet.

   B. It forwards SMTP e-mail to the Internet.

   C. It takes packets from the Internet and gives them to the internal network.

   D. It forwards packets from one network card to another.

7. Which of the following packet filtering techniques does Proxy Server support?

   A. Dynamic

   B. Static

   C. Active

   D. Passive

8. You want to use Proxy Server AutoDial. Which of the following RAS parameters do you not need to configure?

   A. Type of modem

   B. What communication port to use

   C. Which users can dial out

   D. Disable the RAS AutoDial Manager service

9. Which of the following do you configure for the Proxy Server AutoDial function?

   A. Allowed times for dialing out

   B. Which users can dial out

   C. Logon credentials for the ISP

   D. Which transport protocol to use

# 19

# Administering and Configuring Proxy Server

## CERTIFICATION OBJECTIVES

A fter Microsoft Proxy Server is installed, you administer and configure the various features using Microsoft Management Console (MMC). You configure the Web Proxy, WinSock Proxy, and Socks Proxy services using the Internet Service Manager (ISM).

Proxy Server also works closely with Internet Information Server (IIS) and Windows NT Server settings. By using these settings together, you can develop an appropriate administrative configuration for Proxy Server.

This chapter describes the configuration parameters of the three proxy services:

- Web Proxy
- WinSock Proxy
- SOCKS Proxy

**CERTIFICATION OBJECTIVE 19.01**

# Proxy Server Administrative Tasks

Many administrative tasks can be performed from any of the three Proxy Server services. Proxy Server administrative tasks include:

- **Setting server parameters** This is configuring items such as:
  - Auto dial-out
  - Local address table (LAT)
  - Caching
  - Backup and restore properties.
- **Setting security policies** This is configuring such items as:
  - Password authentication
  - User permissions
  - Protocol and port permissions

- Domain filters
- Packet filters
- Alerts
- **Configuring multiple servers**   This includes configuring items such as:
    - Proxy Server arrays
    - Chained Proxy Servers
- **Configuring logs**   This includes configuring properties for the three services logs and the packet log.
- **Administering clients**   This includes configuring client application and client LAT properties.

You can use the following tools to administer the Proxy Server services:

- **Internet Service Manager**   ISM is provided with the MMC. Proxy Server installs additional software components in ISM that you can use to administer the Proxy Server services.
- **Command line**   You can also administer Proxy Server from a command line with two utilities: RemotMsp and WspProto. These utilities allow you to use scripts to configure multiple Proxy Server computers.
- **Web Administration Tool (WAT)**   This tool allows you to administer Proxy Server using a Web browser.

## Using Internet Service Manager

You can administer Proxy Server from the MMC. The Proxy services are listed under the ISM, as illustrated in Figure 19-1. (Chapter 3 describes the details of using MMC and ISM.)

exam
ⓦatch

*The MMC is an integral part of managing IIS and Proxy Server and the future of where Microsoft is taking its administrative tools. Have plenty of hands-on experience with the MMC before you take the exam.*

**FIGURE 19-1**

Using ISM to configure
Proxy services

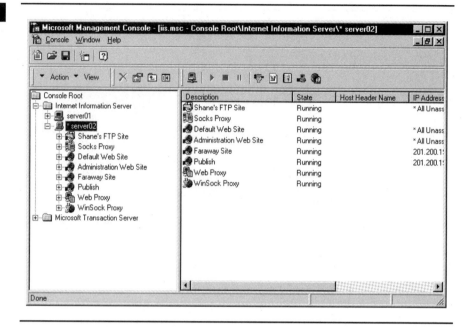

When you install Proxy Server, a program group called Microsoft Proxy Server is created. Inside that group is a selection for MMC. Starting that program calls the file iis.mmc. This is the same console used for IIS, which has its own separate group. You can start the ISM from either IIS or MMC. Figure 19-2 shows how MMC is available from the Proxy Server group.

Note the following information about stopping the Web Proxy service and the WWW service: If you stop the Web Proxy service, you also stop the WWW service but you do not receive a message stating that the WWW service has been stopped. In addition, the Web site in the ISM does not state that the WWW service has been stopped. But if you look in the Services applet, the WWW service is stopped.

FIGURE 19-2

The Proxy Server group
and MMC

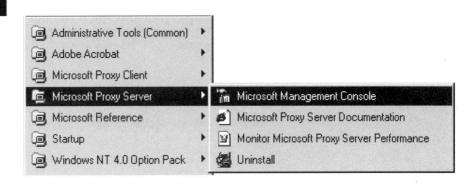

Examine Figure 19-3. The Web site is selected and the Stop Item button on
the rebar is available. You might conclude from this figure that the WWW
service is running; otherwise it would say (Stopped) as the Web Proxy service
does and the Stop Item button would not be available.

FIGURE 19-3

The Web Proxy service is
stopped, but not the
WWW service

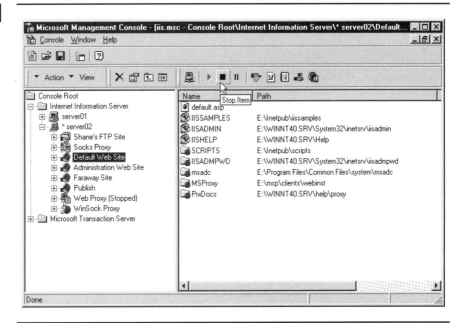

### Trying to Figure It Out

There are some interesting quirks about using the ISM and how it updates the screen display for the Web site and Web Proxy status. Stopping the Web Proxy service stops the WWW service, but the display never says that the WWW service was stopped. The really interesting part is if you press the F5 key, the screen refreshes and the Web Site status changes to Stopped and the Stop button becomes unavailable to you. But you have to select the Web site icon first, then press F5.

You have the same problem in reverse. If you refresh the status of the Web site and start the Web Proxy service, this also restarts the WWW service but the screen won't update. You need to refresh the screen for this also.

Note that if you restart the WWW service, the Web Proxy service is not restarted. You need to manually restart the Web Proxy service.

If you carefully inspect the menu bar, there is no "Refresh" menu item available. You must use the F5 key to perform this function. In many Windows programs, the F5 key does a refresh, but not in all programs. Is this tip worth the price of the book, or what?

## Using the Command Line Utilities

You can also administer Proxy Server using the command line. This is useful if you need to configure many Proxy Server computers identically using scripts.

Two command-line utilities are installed during Proxy Server setup:

- RemotMsp
- WspProto

The RemotMsp utility helps you configure and administer a remote Proxy Server computer. The WspProto utility adds, edits, and deletes the WinSock Proxy service protocol definitions. Refer to the online documentation for more information about configuration options.

The command-line options for RemotMsp include a [common options] section, which has the following syntax:

```
[-c:server name [ -v -h ]]
```

The options are:

- **-c**   specifies a remote Proxy Server computer
- **-v**   specifies verbose output
- **-h**   returns help for usage

## Using the Web Administration Tool

The Web Administration Tool (WAT) allows you to administer Proxy Server from your Web browser. WAT provides the same functions as ISM.

To use WAT, you need a Web browser that supports JavaScript. You should be running at least Microsoft Internet Explorer (IE) 3.02, Netscape Navigator 3.0, or Netscape Communicator 4.04. In addition, your browser should be configured to enable cookies. (Cookies are a means by which a server stores information about clients that connect to the server's Web site.)

You can get the WAT from the Microsoft Web site. Point your browser to www.microsoft.com/proxy and follow the links presented. You must install the WAT on the computer running Proxy Server.

**CERTIFICATION OBJECTIVE 19.02**

# Configuring the Web Proxy Service

The Web Proxy service supports proxy requests from any browser that is compatible with the standard CERN protocol. These browsers include Microsoft Internet Explorer and Netscape Navigator.

The Web Proxy service supports the Hypertext Transfer Protocol (HTTP), Gopher, and File Transfer Protocol (FTP) protocols. The Web

Proxy service also supports the HTTP-S protocol for secure sessions using Secure Sockets Layer (SSL) connections.

Configuring the Web Proxy service is done through the ISM. The property sheet (illustrated in Figure 19-4) contains the following tabs:

- Service
- Permissions
- Caching
- Routing
- Publishing
- Logging

Web Proxy service properties sheet

## Service Properties

The Service property sheet (Figure 19-4) contains information about the system, such as the Proxy Server version number and the product ID. It also contains information about the shared services and configuration for any of the Proxy Server services.

The items contained in the Shared services box and the Configuration box are common to all three Proxy services. Setting the parameters on any service's property sheet sets the parameters for them all.

You can view the current session of users at any of the three Proxy services, as illustrated in Figure 19-5. This feature is handy when you are performing administrative tasks for a service. You do not have to close the Web Proxy property sheet to see who has sessions with the WinSock Proxy service or the SOCKS Proxy service. This function is available from the other services as well.

**FIGURE 19-5**

Viewing current sessions
for any of the services

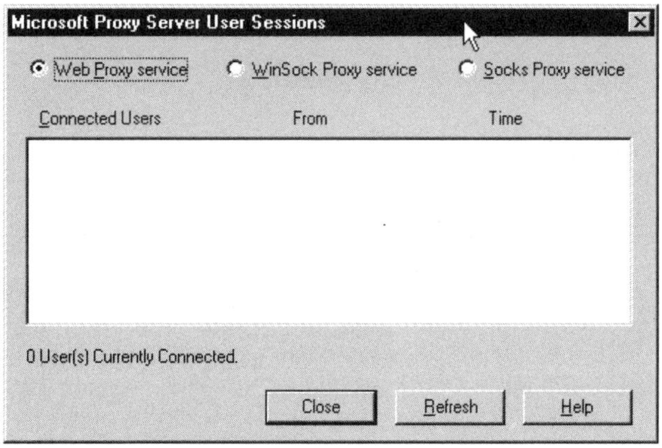

## Permissions Properties

You use the Permissions property sheet to grant or deny access to use the Internet protocols. These protocols are:

- FTP Read
- Gopher
- Secure
- WWW

You set the permissions for each protocol independently. You can allow one user access to the WWW protocol while not allowing that same user access to the FTP Read protocol (see Figure 19-6). In order to set these permissions, the Enable access control box must be checked. This is the default from the installation.

Setting Web Proxy access to Internet protocols

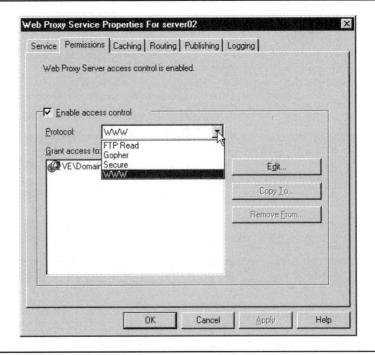

*By default, no user has any access through Web Proxy after you install Proxy Server. You need to manually configure this; otherwise the users do not have access to the Internet.*

## Caching Properties

Use the Caching property sheet to enable or disable the cache. Figure 19-7 contains this property sheet. You can only cache on an NTFS partition.

You can also change the configuration of the cache and set advanced options for the TTL of objects in the cache. Use the Advanced button to access the Cache Filter button. From there, you specify which URL you want cached and invoke Proxy Server to do it. Figures 19-8 and 19-9 illustrate this process. (Chapter 18 discusses caching in detail.)

*Know how to configure the cache size and location.*

---

**FIGURE 19-7**

Enabling the cache

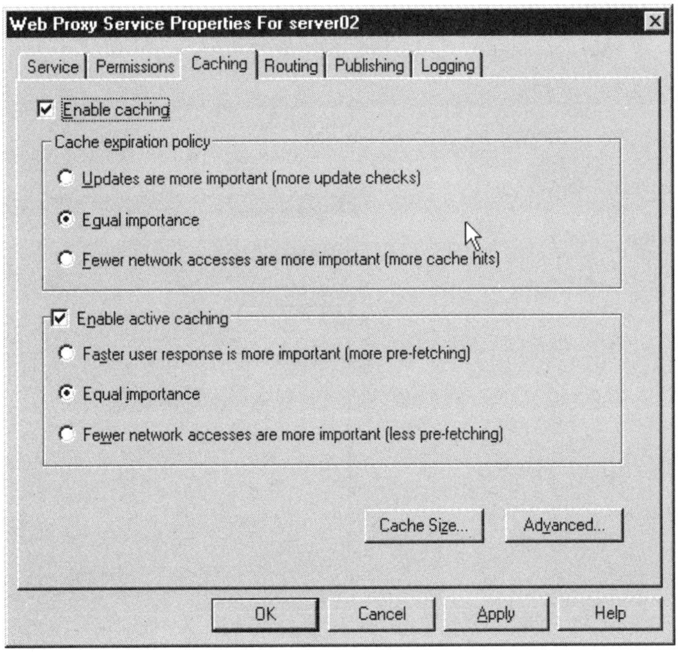

Web Proxy Service Properties For server02

Service | Permissions | Caching | Routing | Publishing | Logging

☑ Enable caching

Cache expiration policy

○ Updates are more important (more update checks)

◉ Equal importance

○ Fewer network accesses are more important (more cache hits)

☑ Enable active caching

○ Faster user response is more important (more pre-fetching)

◉ Equal importance

○ Fewer network accesses are more important (less pre-fetching)

Cache Size... | Advanced...

OK | Cancel | Apply | Help

---

**FIGURE 19-8**

Configuring the cache size
and location

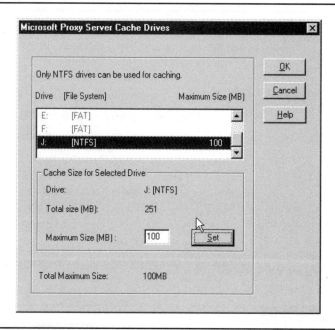

**FIGURE 19-9**

Setting advanced options

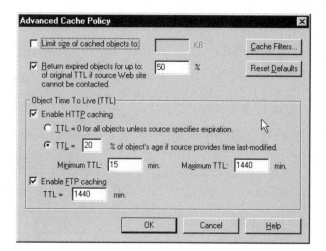

## Routing Properties

Use the Routing property sheet to specify how Web Proxy routes the requests for objects. Figure 19-10 contains this property sheet. You can set upstream routing to another Proxy Server or to an array, as illustrated in Figure 19-11.

You can also set the service to resolve URL requests within the array before requesting the object from the Internet. This box is checked by default if you have an array configured.

## Publishing Properties

Use the Publishing property sheet (Figure 19-12) to configure Proxy Server to support reverse proxy and reverse hosting. (Chapter 20 discusses Proxy Server in detail.)

**FIGURE 19-10**

The Web Proxy
Routing tab

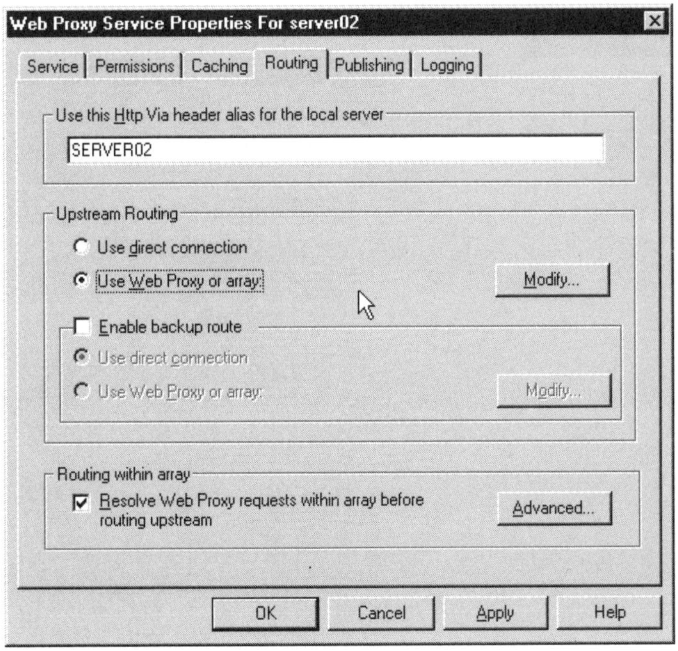

**FIGURE 19-11**

Specifying the upstream
Web Proxy Server

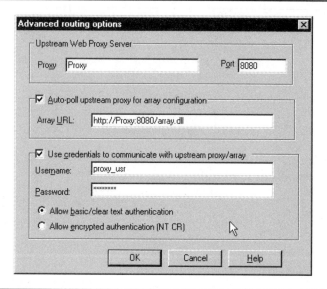

**FIGURE 19-12**

Configuring for reverse
proxy and reverse hosting

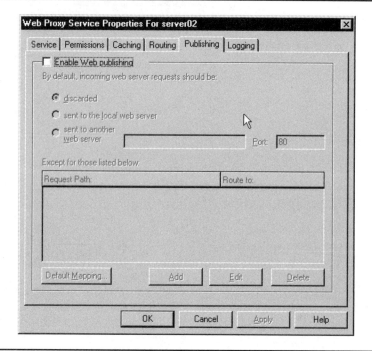

## Logging Properties

Use the Logging property sheet to set the log options to track errors when they occur (see Figure 19-13). The default log file settings are:

- Enabled
- Format is regular instead of verbose.
- New log file daily
- Log files are recorded in the system32\msp folder.
- Log file starts with the name W3 and then the date.
- Stop the service if the disk is full.

*Know how to configure the log settings.*

**FIGURE 19-13**

Setting the logging options

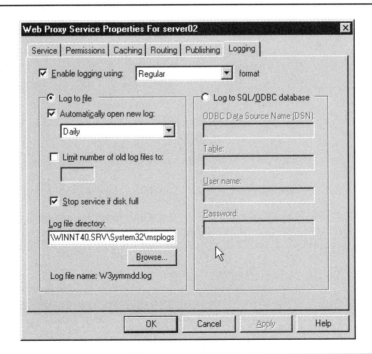

# Configuring the WinSock Proxy Service

The WinSock Proxy service allows a Windows Sockets (WinSock) application to access the server as if it is directly connected to the Internet. Examples of such applications are:

- E-mail
- IRC
- NetShow
- NNTP news
- RealAudio
- Telnet

The client application makes a WinSock API call to communicate with an application running on an Internet host. The WinSock Proxy components redirect the necessary APIs to the Proxy Server. This establishes a communication path from the internal application to the Internet host through the Proxy Server computer.

The WinSock property sheet has the following tabs:

- Service
- Protocols
- Permissions
- Logging

## WinSock Service Properties

The Service property sheet is identical to the property sheet found in the Web Proxy (and the one for the SOCKS Proxy service); it has all the same configuration options. Remember that you can use this sheet from any service to make the configuration changes. These changes affect all the services.

**exam** ⓦ**atch** *You can use the Service tab from any Proxy service to implement a change.*

## WinSock Protocols Properties

Use the Protocols property sheet (Figure 19-14) to set the parameters for the Internet protocols. By default, Proxy Server installs 30 protocols during the installation. (Chapter 18 contains a table describing these services and how to configure them.)

You control access by port number, protocol, and user (or groups of users). Each port is enabled or disabled for communications by a specific list of users. The list of users that can initiate outbound connections on a port can be a different list than the list of users that can listen for inbound connections on the same port.

**FIGURE 19-14**

WinSock Protocols

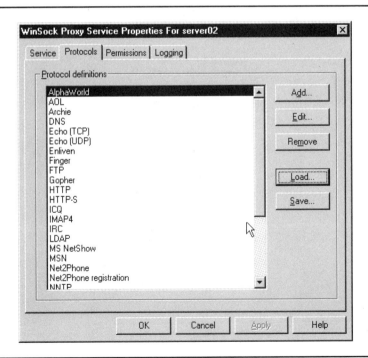

You can create new protocol definitions and modify existing protocol definitions. You can save these definitions in a text file using any legal filename and extension and load the definitions from that file at a later date. You can save the definitions file from one Proxy Server and load it at another Proxy Server. Figure 19-15 contains an example of a protocol definition file.

You can configure the logging options to audit who is accessing the server and using which protocol.

## WinSock Permissions Properties

Use the Permissions property sheet (Figure 19-16) to set permissions for the various Internet protocols. By default, Enable access control is set by the

**FIGURE 19-15**

Viewing a protocol
definition file

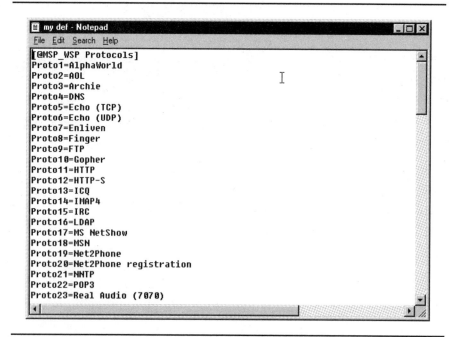

**FIGURE 19-16**

Viewing and setting
WinSock permissions

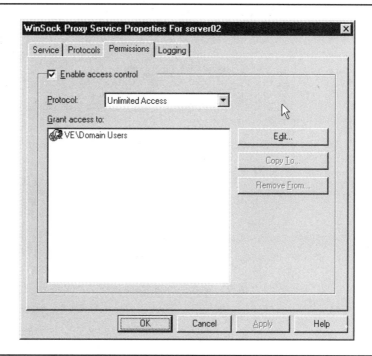

installation. No one has outbound permissions for any of the protocols. You
must explicitly grant users permissions.

If you create a new protocol definition, no one has permission to access the
new protocol to get to the Internet. You need to explicitly set the user
permissions.

# WinSock Logging Properties

The logging options for the WinSock service are identical to those of the Web
Proxy service. The only difference is that the filename for the WinSock log file
begins with "WS" and the rest of the filename is identical to that of the
Web Proxy.

**CERTIFICATION OBJECTIVE 19.04**

# Configuring the SOCKS Proxy Service

The SOCKS protocol is a cross-platform mechanism that establishes secure communication between client and server computers. The SOCKS Proxy service supports SOCKS Version 4.3a. (See Chapter 15 for more details on the SOCKS Proxy service.)

Windows applications use the WinSock Proxy service. The SOCKS Proxy service extends the redirection provided by the WinSock Proxy service to non-Windows platforms.

SOCKS Proxy service uses the TCP/IP protocol and can be used for such non-windows applications as:

■ Telnet

■ FTP

■ Gopher

■ HTTP

The Socks Proxy service does not support applications that rely on the UDP protocol.

Security is based on IP addresses, port numbers, and destination hosts. The SOCKS Proxy service does not perform client password authentication and it does not support the IPX/SPX protocol.

The SOCKS Proxy property sheet has three tabs. They are:

■ Service

■ Permissions

■ Logging

The Service and Logging property sheets are identical to those of the other two services in every respect except one. The SOCKS log filename begins with "SP" and the rest of the file syntax is the same.

*Know how to identify the various log files by their filenames. For example, SOCKS log files start with "SP" and WinSock log files with "WS."*

## SOCKS Permissions

The WinSock Proxy and the SOCKS Proxy services support similar functions. They redirect API calls and send them to a remote site. Figure 19-17 contains the dialog box used to set these permissions.

WinSock Proxy service has a client-side component to redirect API calls. This means that Windows NT challenge/response authentication can be used for client identification.

On the other side, the SOCKS Proxy service supports the SOCKS Version 4.3a standard. The SOCKS Proxy service uses IP addresses and the

**FIGURE 19-17**

SOCKS permissions dialog box

Identification (Identd) protocol to identify and authenticate SOCKS Proxy clients.

It is interesting to note that the SOCKS Proxy service depends on the Web Proxy service running. If you stop the Web Proxy service, the SOCKS Proxy service also stops running.

The SOCKS Proxy service can open only a primary port for an application; it does not support secondary port connections. By default, the Proxy Server installation sets all SOCKS client requests to "denied."

SOCKS permission is a rule entry in an ordered list. Each rule specifies a source and a destination address. The rules also specify whether a request satisfying the rule entry should be permitted or denied.

The first rule entry in the list that matches the incoming client request is used, and from that, it is determined if the request is permitted. However, if a client request does not match any rule entry in the list, the request is denied.

The source address of a request is specified to be an address-and-mask combination. The destination address is specified by an address-and-mask combination and a port range. The destination is optional. Figure 19-18 shows how you specify these addresses.

# QUESTIONS AND ANSWERS

| | |
|---|---|
| I installed Proxy Server, but I did not get the Web Administration Tool. What happened? | You only get the Web Administration Tool if you install it separately. It is not part of Proxy Server installation. |
| How do I install the Web Administration Tool? | You must first download it from the Microsoft Web site. Run the self-extracting executable file. |
| I have installed the first of five planned Proxy Servers. I want to create an array so that when I install the others, they can join the array, but I can't create the array. Why not? | Don't you just hate it when machines won't let you do what you want? You must first have at least two Proxy Servers installed and running to create the array. Install your second Proxy Server and try again. |
| I installed Proxy Server and configured the client's browsers but no one can access the Web. What's wrong? | You have to enable access control and you have not granted any users permission for the Web Proxy service. Fix that and your users will be able to access the Web. |

FIGURE 19-18

Setting SOCKS permission

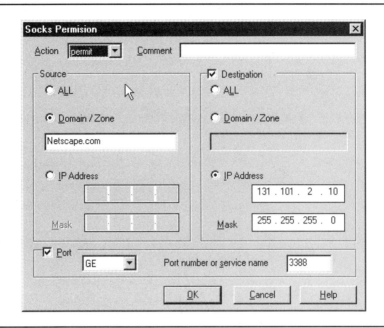

# CERTIFICATION SUMMARY

This chapter discusses configuring and administering Proxy Server. Each of the three Proxy services are discussed, along with their properties sheets. Each of the three Proxy services has a Service property sheet and a Logging property in common. Parameters set in the Service property sheets are effective for all three Proxy services. Configuring the logging options is done in the same manner for each service. If you know how to configure the logging options for one of the services, you know how to do it for any service.

There are three ways to administer Proxy Server. You can use the ISM, a command-line utility, or the Web Administration Tool. You can use the ISM from the MMC, which may be installed on any Windows NT computer. You can administer any Proxy Server to which you have permission from the ISM.

You can use the command-line utility to perform administrative functions. The command-line utility makes it easy to script tasks and run them remotely or unattended. You could use this technique to efficiently and quickly configure multiple Proxy Servers that need to have identical configurations.

You can use the Web Administration Tool to access Proxy Servers and perform administrative tasks from your Web browser.

 **TWO-MINUTE DRILL**

❑ There are three services that may be configured: Web Proxy, WinSock Proxy, and SOCKS Proxy.

❑ There are three administrative tools that may be used to administer Proxy Server: ISM, command-line utilities, and the Web Administration Tool.

❑ There are two command-line administrative utilities: RemotMsp and WspProto.

❑ The Web Administration Tool allows you to administer Proxy Server from your Web browser.

❑ The Web Administration Tool does not come with Windows NT 4.0 Option Pack. You must download it from the Microsoft Web site.

❑ Proxy services are accessed under IIS in the ISM.

❑ The Proxy Server installation also installs a Microsoft Proxy Server group under Programs.

❑ If you stop the Web Proxy service, you also stop the Web Publishing service.

❑ The Web Proxy service is CERN compatible.

❑ There are five property tabs for the Web Proxy service.

❑ The Services tab is the same for all Proxy services.

❑ The technique for configuring logging options is the same for all Proxy services.

❑ The option Enable access control is checked by default during installation.

❑ No users can access the Internet by default.

❑ You must explicitly grant users permissions to access the Internet.

- ❏ Users may have different permissions for different Internet protocols.
- ❏ You configure caching in the Web Proxy service.
- ❏ Routing allows you to chain to an upstream Proxy Server.
- ❏ You can chain to any CERN-compliant Proxy Server.
- ❏ Routing allows you to configure a Proxy Server array.
- ❏ You can configure Proxy Server to support reverse proxy and reverse hosting.
- ❏ There are four property sheets for the WinSock Proxy service.
- ❏ You can modify existing protocol definitions.
- ❏ You can create custom protocol definitions.
- ❏ You can save protocol definitions as a file.
- ❏ You can load a protocol definition file into any Proxy Server.
- ❏ There are three property sheets for the SOCKS Proxy service.
- ❏ The SOCKS Proxy service does not support UDP.
- ❏ The SOCKS Proxy service does not support IPX/SPX.
- ❏ SOCKS permissions are rule-based permissions.

# SELF TEST

The following Self Test questions will help you measure your understanding of the material presented in this chapter. Read all the choices carefully, as there may be more than one correct answer. Choose all correct answers for each question.

1. Which of the following is not a Proxy service?

   A. Web Publishing

   B. WinSock

   C. Web Proxy

   D. SOCKS

2. Which of the following cannot be used to configure Proxy Server?

   A. ISM

   B. WinMSD

   C. RemotMsp

   D. Web Administration Tool from Microsoft

3. Which Internet protocols are not supported by Web Proxy?

   A. NetBIOS

   B. FTP

   C. HTTP

   D. HTTP-S

4. You are setting up a private network at your home. You have four PCs on a 10Base2 network. You have contracted with your cable company to provide Internet access and they have installed the cable modem. You need to configure your Proxy Server to send requests to the cable company Proxy Server. How do you configure this?

   A. Open Control Panel, Network applet and select Services. Click Microsoft Proxy Server and select Properties. Enter the IP address of the other Proxy Server.

   B. You cannot do this if the cable company is using a Microsoft Proxy Server.

   C. From the Web Proxy service property sheet, select the Routing tab and click the Auto Detect button. Proxy Server will search for the upstream server.

   D. From the Web Proxy service property sheet, select the Routing tab and enter the name and port number of the upstream Proxy Server.

5. You want to configure the cache on your Proxy Server. When you select the Caching tab, all of the options are grayed out. What is causing this?

   A. You are not logged on as administrator.

   B. You did not install the cache option during installation.

   C. You can only cache if the server is part of an array.

   D. There is no NTFS partition available.

6. You have the ISM open and are in the WinSock property sheet. You want to know

who is connected and currently using the Web Proxy service. What is the easiest way to find that out?

A. Close ISM and restart it. Then right-click Web Proxy icon and click Properties.

B. Close the WinSock property sheet. Open the Web Proxy property sheet and click the Current Sessions button.

C. From within WinSock, select the Services tab, click the Current Sessions button, and click the Web Proxy Service radio button.

D. Open Server Manager, double-click the server, and click the Users button.

7. You have gone to the \msp folder to access the Web Proxy log file and there are many files in the folder. Several files are dated today. How do you know which file is the latest log file?

A. You cannot tell because you did not empty the folder each day.

B. Find the files with today's date/time and open them one at a time and look at the first line in the file.

C. Web Proxy log filename starts with "W3." Find the latest file that begins that way.

D. Web Proxy log filename starts with "WS." Find the latest file that begins that way.

8. Which of the following is not a WinSock property sheet?

A. Caching

B. Service

C. Logging

D. Permissions

9. Which of the following statements are true about WinSock protocols?

A. You can create new protocol definitions.

B. You cannot create new protocol definitions.

C. You can save protocol definitions to a file.

D. You can load protocol definitions from a file.

10. Which of the following statements are not true about the SOCKS Proxy service?

A. SOCKS does not support UDP.

B. SOCKS supports TCP/IP.

C. SOCKS Proxy supports SOCKS Version 4.3a.

D. SOCKS supports IPX/SPX.

MICROSOFT CERTIFIED SYSTEMS ENGINEER

# 20

# Secure Publishing and Packet Filtering

**P**ublishing, as the word is used in this chapter, refers to placing objects (documents, images, etc.) on a Web server so they can be reached by anyone with access to the Web server. Of course, the concept of publishing applies to intranet users as well as Internet users.

Even if you are only publishing to employees on your internal network, there may be reasons why you do not want everyone to be able to connect to any server. One such reason could be that the server is located in an unsecured area of the building where potentially anyone could have access to it. So the techniques for securing your Web content against external forces can apply to internal forces as well.

Proxy Server 2.0 implements both reverse proxy and reverse hosting as a means of helping you publish to the Internet while not compromising network security or the flexibility you want for your published information.

The reverse proxy and reverse hosting features allow virtually any server on your internal network that is running an HTTP server application such as Internet Information Server (IIS) to publish to the Internet. Security is not compromised because all incoming requests and outgoing responses pass through Proxy Server first so there remains only a single path to the Internet.

## CERTIFICATION OBJECTIVE 20.01

# Being Secure with Web Publishing

Publishing to the Internet using a Web server increases the exposure of your internal network to external forces. Proxy Server makes your outbound proxy connections and as a result, your network is not visible to Internet users. As your Web server maintains a continuous presence on the Internet, this allows outside users to try various techniques to break into your server.

On Web servers where interactive scripts or programming extensions are used to make dynamic changes in Web published content, unauthorized users can use programs to search out and exploit server security leaks caused by poorly designed Web server applications.

There are publishing features in Microsoft Proxy Server that allow you to publish to the Internet without compromising the security of your internal network. One of the features that Proxy Server uses is *reverse proxy.* Reverse proxy is used to service requests from IIS on the Proxy Server to send requests to Web servers located downstream from the Proxy Server computer. The Proxy Server impersonates a Web server to the outside world, while your Web server maintains access to internal network services. In this context, "publishing" refers to placing material on a Web server so it can be reached by anyone with Web access. This applies to intranet users as well as Internet users.

When Proxy Server is used to service only outbound proxy connections, your network is not visible to Internet users. When you use external Web publishing, your Web server maintains a continuous presence on the Internet, which can result in outside users trying to break into your network. There are Web servers where interactive scripts or programming extensions, such as Common Gateway Interface (CGI) or Internet Server Application Programming Interface (ISAPI) DLLs, are used to make dynamic changes in Web published content. On those servers, external users can use programs to exploit server security leaks caused by poorly designed Web server applications.

## Reverse Proxy

Reverse proxy is Proxy Server's ability to process incoming requests to an internal Hypertext Transfer Protocol (HTTP) server and to respond on its behalf. This is the reverse of the normal process where the proxy takes a request from the internal network and passes the request to the Internet. With reverse proxy, Proxy Server takes the request from the Internet and responds to it as the internal Web server. This is the reverse of the usual forwarding of internal requests out to the Internet.

exam
**Ⓦatch**

### Know how reverse proxy functions.

To configure reverse proxy and reverse hosting, open the ISM and select the Web Proxy service. Right-click and select properties to bring up the Web Proxy service properties sheet, as illustrated in Figure 20-1.

The next step is to select the Publishing tab (see Figure 20-2). The default condition is that Web publishing is disabled. Check the box Enable Web

**FIGURE 20-1**

ISM with Web Proxy
service selected

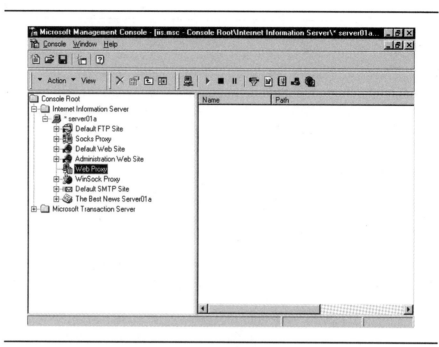

**FIGURE 20-2**

Web Proxy service
properties with the
Publishing tab selected

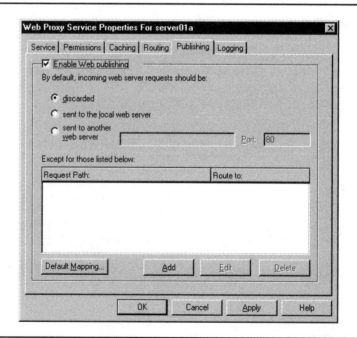

publishing and the rest of the box lights up. In the top part of the dialog box, you have the following choices:

- **discarded**    Click this to ignore all incoming Web server requests.

- **sent to the local web server**    By selecting this, all incoming Web server requests will be forwarded to the IIS located on the Proxy Server computer.

- **sent to another web server**    Select this option to forward incoming Web server requests to a specific downstream server (including an IIS server) that will be used for Web publishing. You need to enter a valid server name and TCP port number; the default is port 80.

e x a m
ⓦ a t c h

*Know how to configure Proxy Server to send packets to the local Web server and to downstream servers.*

Next, select one of the roles and specify the default local server. The default local server is usually the IIS server located on the Proxy Server. Figure 20-3 and the illustration that follows show how you do this. Setting Default Local Host Name will reroute older Web clients and legacy Internet applications to the Web server where

**FIGURE 20-3**

Specifying that requests be sent to the local server

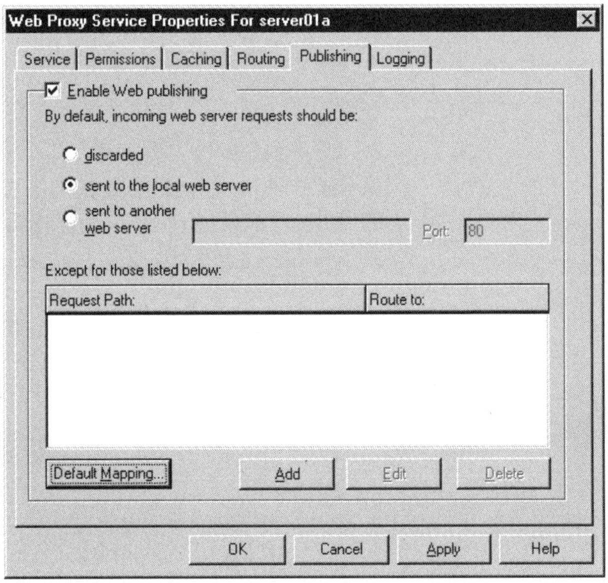

> **Web Proxy Service Properties For server01a**                         ✕
>
> Service | Permissions | Caching | Routing | Publishing | Logging |
>
> ☑ Enable Web publishing
>
> By default, incoming web server requests should be:
>
> ○ discarded
>
> ● sent to the local web server
>
> ○ sent to another
>   web server _____   Port: 80
>
> Except for those listed below:
>
> | Request Path: | Route to: |
> | --- | --- |
> |  |  |
>
> [Default Mapping...]     [Add]     [Edit]     [Delete]
>
> [OK]     [Cancel]     [Apply]     [Help]

the requested content resides. These older clients and applications may not support the extensions being currently used by that Web server.

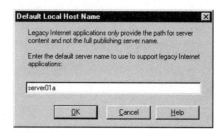

## Configuring Reverse Proxy

Purpose: To enable Web publishing and to specify the default local host.

*Do this exercise from the domain controller.*

1. Ensure that you are logged on as Administrator.
2. Open the Internet Service Manager.
3. In ISM, expand the computer name.
4. Right-click the Web Proxy icon.
5. Select the Web Proxy Service Properties.
6. Click the Publishing tab.
7. Select the Enable Web publishing check box.
8. Click the radio button next to "sent to the local web server."
9. To set the default Web server host, click Default Mapping.
10. In the Default Local Host Name dialog box, enter the default server. This host name is usually the name of the Proxy Server computer.
11. Click OK.
12. When finished, click Apply.
13. Click OK.

# Reverse Hosting

Reverse hosting takes publishing to the next logical step. In reverse hosting, Proxy Server maintains a list of servers on the internal network that have permission to publish to the Internet. This enables Proxy Server to listen and respond on behalf of multiple servers that are located behind it. To the Internet client, this process is transparent. There is no evidence that the request passes through Proxy Server before being forwarded to the applicable Web server. Proxy Server merely redirects the incoming Uniform Resource Locator (URL) to the appropriate server.

To configure reverse hosting, from the Publishing tab of the properties sheet, click the Add button, as illustrated here.

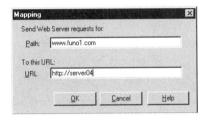

You specify the URL of the incoming request and set the path for the outgoing request. The outgoing URL is the Web server that has the requested resource. This can be any Web server; you are not limited to IIS servers. You can view the routes that you have configured in the Publishing tab (see Figure 20-4). This is called the *reverse hosts map*.

**FIGURE 20-4**

Viewing the reverse hosts map

| EXERCISE 20-2 | **Configuring Reverse Hosting** |
|---|---|

Purpose: To configure the Proxy Server to support reverse hosting. You can create a reverse host route by mapping a URL to a specific Web server on your internal network. For example, you can set up host route mapping so that a URL, such as http://www.fun01.com, can be mapped to the internal server, http://server04.

*Do this exercise from the domain controller.*

1. Right-click the Web Proxy icon.

2. In the Web Proxy Service Properties dialog box, click the Publishing tab.

3. To add a reverse host route, under Except for those listed below, click Add.

4. In the Path box on the Mapping dialog box, enter **http://www.fun01.com.**

5. In the URL box, enter **http://server04.**

6. Click OK.

7. When the Publishing tab returns, click Apply.

8. Click OK.

## CERTIFICATION OBJECTIVE 20.02

# Packet Filtering

*Packet filtering* occurs when Proxy Server intercepts incoming packets. Proxy Server evaluates packets before they are passed to higher levels in the protocol layers or to an application. Proxy Server gives you the ability to automatically apply predefined dynamic filters. Sometimes this is referred to as *stateful filtering. Dynamic filtering* occurs when Proxy Server evaluates which TCP/IP packet types are accessible to specific internal network services. With dynamic filtering enabled, Proxy Server is acting as a firewall.

A *firewall* is a hardware/software product that acts as a barrier. Its purpose is to prevent entry into a network by unauthorized users, processes, or data.

The security features of Proxy Server allow you to control the flow of traffic to and from the network. In addition to authenticating client requests with packet filtering, you can:

- Intercept packets destined to specific services on your Proxy Server computer. You can then either allow those packets through or block them.

- Send an alert when dropped packets or suspicious events occur. You can either forward a record of alerts to a log file or send alerts through e-mail.

You can configure packet filters to reject any type of packet and thereby prevent them from being processed through the Proxy Server. This provides a high level of security for your network. Packet filtering can block packets originating from specific Internet hosts. You can specify that Proxy Server reject packets associated with many common attacks, such as address spoof, SYN, and FRAG attacks.

Packet filtering only applies to the external network adapter. The internal network adapter is not affected.

exam
Ⓦatch     *Remember that packet filtering only applies to the external adapter.*

## Creating and Modifying Packet Filtering

Proxy Server can provide both dynamic and static packet filtering modes. These modes control which protocol ports are opened for communication. With dynamic packet filtering, you do not need to specifically unbind individual services from the external network adapter. Ports are opened for either transmit, receive, or both operations. Ports are then immediately closed after any of the Proxy Server services terminates a connection.

For a finer level of control and maximum security, you can manually configure *static packet filters* (also known as *persistent packet filters*) through the user interface. For a finer level of control and maximum security, you can configure static packet filters through the ISM.

You configure packet filters through the ISM interface, using any of the three Proxy services' properties page, using the Security button (see Figure 20-5).

FIGURE 20-5

Viewing the Service tab

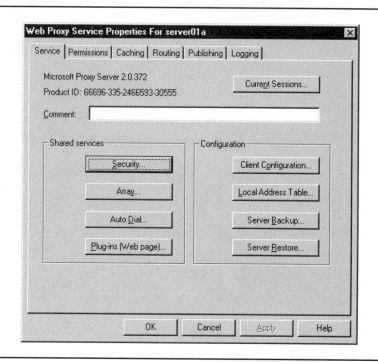

The list of packet types applies to all requests issued to the server, regardless of whether the request originated from the Internet or from an intranet client. You cannot specify packet filtering on a user basis, although different Proxy Servers on your network can offer access to different protocols and ports for different users. You can use ISAPI to implement additional custom filters that might provide for a user filter.

When you select the Security button from the Service tab, you can enable packet filtering. Figure 20-6 contains this dialog box. Select the Enable packet filtering on external interface box. The box next to Enable dynamic packet filtering of Microsoft Proxy Server packets is checked by default when you enable packet filtering. Unchecking this box gives you greater control of the

**FIGURE 20-6**

Enabling packet filtering

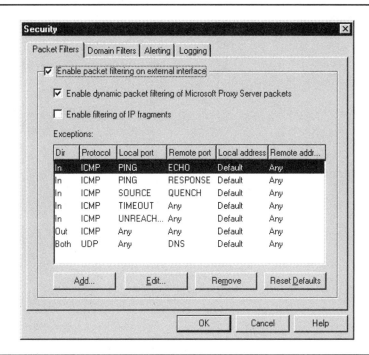

ports being used in external communication. But it also increases the potential for configuration errors. Microsoft recommends that if packet filtering is enabled, dynamic filtering should also be enabled.

Selecting the box next to Enable filtering of IP fragments allows you to filter datagrams or IP fragments. The book *MCSE Microsoft TCP/IP on Windows NT 4.0 Study Guide* (Osborne/McGraw-Hill), describes datagrams and fragments.

The Exceptions box in the dialog box in Figure 20-6 lists the packet types that will be allowed. All others will be rejected. To add additional packet types to be allowed, click the Add button. Select from a list of predefined filters or you can create custom filters, as illustrated in Figure 20-7.

**FIGURE** 20-7

Defining additional
packet filters

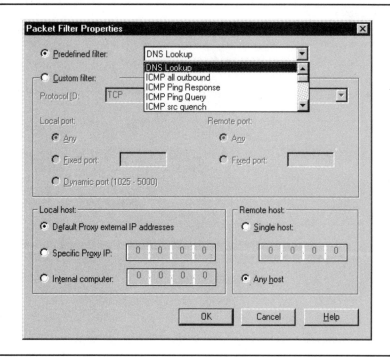

There are predefined filters for:

- DNS lookup
- ICMP all outbound
- ICMP ping response
- ICMP ping query
- ICMP src quench
- ICMP timeout
- ICMP unreachable
- PPTP call
- PPTP receive
- SMTP
- POP3

- Identd
- HTTP server (port80)
- HTTPS server (port 443)
- NetBIOS (WINS client only)
- NetBIOS (all)

## Creating New Packet Filters

Purpose: To allow you to create packet filters. You must create new packet filters for cascaded configurations. A cascade is where you employ an upstream, chained Proxy Server. This allows you to packet to the downstream Proxy Server computer. You must also create filters if you have other services running on the Proxy Server. Your Proxy Server supports multiple IP addresses assigned to the same external network adapter card.

*Do this at the domain controller.*

1. In ISM, right-click any of the Proxy Server services.
2. Click Properties.
3. On the Service tab, under Shared services, click Security.
4. Click the Packet Filters tab.
5. Check the Enable packet filtering on external interface check box. This blocks all packets except the ones listed in the Exceptions box.
6. Verify that the check box next to Enable dynamic packet filtering of Microsoft Proxy Server packets is selected.
7. On the Packet Filters tab, click Add.
8. In the Packet Filter Properties dialog box, click Predefined protocol and select POP3 from the drop-down list.
9. Click OK.
10. On the Packet Filters tab, click Add.
11. In the Packet Filter Properties dialog box, make sure that Custom filter is selected.
12. In Protocol ID, select TCP.
13. In Direction, select In.
14. Under Local port, click Dynamic port (1025-5000).

15. Under Remote port, click Fixed port and enter **119.**

16. Under Remote host, click Single host and enter **201.200.199.200.**

17. Click OK.

18. To remove a protocol, select ICMP Source Quench from the list.

19. Click Remove.

20. To restore the default configuration, click Reset Defaults.

21. Click OK.

22. Click OK to return to the ISM.

23. Click OK on the message about restarting Proxy Server.

## CERTIFICATION OBJECTIVE 20.03

# Alerts

Events that can compromise your system should be monitored. If such an event occurs, the server can be configured so that an alert is generated. Events for which you can generate alerts include:

- **Rejected packets**   Watches the external network interface for dropped IP packets.

- **Protocol violations**   Watches for packets that do not follow the allowed protocol structure.

- **Disk full**   Watches for failures caused by a full disk.

If any of these events occurs, Proxy Server writes the event in the system log. Use the Windows NT Event Viewer to view the log file.

exam
ⓦatch

*Know which three events are written to the log file.*

An alert can also be sent as an e-mail message to a designated recipient. In addition, Proxy Server can generate reports on packets where no system service was listening. You must enable packet filtering first for alerting to be operational. Figure 20-8 contains the dialog box for configuring alerts.

**FIGURE 20-8**

Configuring aerts

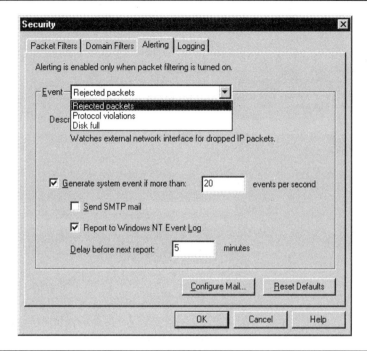

**EXERCISE 20-4**

## Configuring Alerts

Purpose: To practice setting an alert condition.

*Do this from the domain controller.*

1. In ISM, right-click any of the Proxy Server services.
2. Click Properties.
3. On the Service tab, under Shared services, click Security.
4. In the Security dialog box, click the Alerting tab.
5. In Event window, select Protocol Violations from the drop-down list.
6. Make sure that the check box next to Generate system event if more than is checked.
7. Enter **2** in the events per second window.
8. Make sure that the check box next to Report to Windows NT Event Log is checked.

9. Set a value of 1 minute in the window.

10. Click OK to return to the Service tab.

**CERTIFICATION OBJECTIVE 20.04**

# Logging

Packet filter alert events may be stored in the dedicated log file used by Proxy Server. They may also be stored in an Open Database Connectivity (ODBC) database such as SQL Server. For performance reasons, SQL server is preferable to using Microsoft Access.

By default, only dropped packet events are logged. In addition to the dropped packets, a count of accepted SYN frames is also kept. Proxy Server can record information on packets after they are received and examine packets that are sent to a non-listening port.

The log configuration procedure is like that for the Web Proxy, WinSock Proxy, and SOCKS Proxy service logs. The log file is stored in %winnt_root%/system32/msplogs/pf*yymmdd*.log. The various Proxy Server log files all include the now-familiar *"yymmdd"* format and they all begin with a unique identifier, in this case, "pf" for packet filter.

***Know what the log file naming convention is and where the log file is kept.***

The packet log records information related to the following areas:

- Service information
- Remote information
- Local information
- Filter information
- Packet information

## Service Information Fields

The following log fields pertain to service information:

- **Date**   The date the packet was received
- **Time**   The time the packet was received

## Remote Information Fields

The following log fields pertain to the remote computer:

- **Src IP**   The IP address of the source (remote) computer. The source computer is the computer from which the data packets originate.
- **Src port**   The service port number that the source computer is using to maintain the connection with the destination computer. This field is only valid if the TCP, UDP, or ICMP protocol is used.
- **Protocol**   The particular transport-level protocol (such as TCP, UDP, or ICMP) used during the connection.

## Local Information Fields

The following log fields pertain to the local computer:

- **Dest IP**   The IP address of the destination (local) computer. The destination computer is usually the Proxy Sever computer.
- **Dest port**   The service port number that the destination (local) computer uses to maintain the connection with the source computer. This field is only valid if the TCP, UDP, or ICMP protocol is used.

## Filter Information Fields

The following log fields pertain to packet filters:

- **Action**   Possible values are drop and accept. By default, only dropped packets are logged.
- **Interface**   The interface, usually only one, on which the packet was received. This field is reserved for future use.

## Packet Information Fields

The following log fields pertain to packet information:

- **Raw IP header (hex)** The entire IP header of the data packet that generated the alert event. The IP header is logged in hexadecimal format.

- **Raw IP packet (hex)** A listing of a portion of the data packet that generated the alert event. A registry key sets how many bytes of the IP packet to capture. The IP packet is logged in hexadecimal format.

## FROM THE CLASSROOM

### Denial of Service (DoS)

A denial of service (DoS) attack is one where your system is not penetrated or breached but is made unavailable for use because it is too busy responding to bogus requests. In late 1996, several underground magazines published code to conduct denial of service attacks by creating TCP half-open connections. Although discovering the origin of such an attack is difficult, it is possible.

In a normal process, the client makes a connection request and the server responds. The client accepts the response and the transaction begins. The attack arises at the point where the server has sent an acknowledgment (SYN-ACK) back to the client but has not yet received the ACK message. This is called the *half-open connection.* The server has allocated memory for all pending connections. The memory for this is of limited size, and it can be made to overflow by intentionally creating too many half-open connections.

A SYN attack creates each SYN packet in the flood with a bad source IP address, which, during routine use, identifies the original packet. All responses are sent to the source IP address. But the bad source IP address either does not actually exist or is down. Therefore, the ACK that should follow a SYN-ACK response never comes back. This creates a backlog queue that's always full, making it nearly impossible for legitimate TCP SYN requests to get into the system.

Generally, there is a timeout associated with a pending connection, so the half-open connections eventually expire. However, the attacking system can simply continue sending bogus packets, requesting new connections faster than the server can expire the pending connections.

The result is that your server is too busy servicing these bogus requests to respond to legatee requests from users.

## QUESTIONS AND ANSWERS

| | |
|---|---|
| Am I required to implement reverse proxy in order to use Proxy Server? | No. When you install Proxy Server, reverse proxy and reverse hosting are disabled by default. You must enable them. Proxy Server protects your network with or without reverse proxy enabled. |
| I heard that I still need a firewall even if I use Proxy Server. Is that true? | What are you trying to accomplish that Proxy Server cannot do for you? The answer to that question will help determine the answer to the first question. Proxy Server is a functional firewall. |
| Do I still need a Proxy Server and firewall for my UNIX servers, even if I install Proxy Server? | No. Microsoft's Proxy Server is fully functional. It will serve as a Proxy Server for your UNIX operating systems as well. |

# CERTIFICATION SUMMARY

This chapter described secure Web publishing and packet filtering. Using reverse proxy and reverse hosting, you can configure Proxy Server to allow inbound access to your Web servers. Reverse proxy and reverse hosting serve the same function but with a different scope. Reverse proxy allows the Proxy Server to respond and reverse hosting allows Proxy Server to forward requests to servers on the internal network.

Using packet filtering, you can allow or reject packets based on the packet type. You can also restrict packets destined for specific computers on your network, or servers that provide specific services.

Proxy Server allows you to configure alerts. These alerts may be sent to a Proxy Server log file or to an ODBC-compliant database. You can also configure alerts to be sent via an e-mail address.

 # TWO-MINUTE DRILL

- ❑ Proxy Server supports reverse proxy.
- ❑ Proxy Server supports reverse hosting.

- ❑ Using reverse proxy, Proxy Server impersonates an internal Web server to the outside world.
- ❑ Reverse proxy is a technique where Proxy Server takes incoming HTTP requests to an internal server and responds on its behalf.
- ❑ You configure reverse proxy through the ISM.
- ❑ You use the Web Proxy properties sheet to enable reverse proxy.
- ❑ By default, Web publishing is disabled.
- ❑ You can set Web publishing to ignore all Web server requests.
- ❑ You can forward incoming Web server requests to the IIS on the Proxy Server.
- ❑ You can forward incoming requests to a downstream server.
- ❑ Proxy Server responds on behalf of multiple servers located behind it.
- ❑ For reverse hosting, specify the URL of the incoming request.
- ❑ For reverse hosting, specify the URL to the outgoing server.
- ❑ You build a list of the servers known as a map.
- ❑ Packet filtering intercepts inbound packets.
- ❑ Packet filtering evaluates the packets to determine whether or not to pass them on.
- ❑ Packet filtering only applies to the external network adapter.
- ❑ You can configure a dynamic packet filter.
- ❑ You can configure a static packet filter.
- ❑ You configure packet filters through the ISM.
- ❑ You can configure packet filtering by using the properties sheet of any of the proxy services.
- ❑ You cannot configure packet filters on a per-user basis.
- ❑ You can use predefined filters.
- ❑ You can define custom filters.
- ❑ You can send an alert when dropped packets occur.

❑ Dropped packets are packets that have been rejected by the Proxy Server.

❑ You can set an alert to watch for protocol violations.

❑ You can set an alert to notify you when your hard drive becomes full.

❑ Proxy Server writes the events to the system log.

❑ Packet filter alert events may be stored in an ODBC-compliant database.

❑ By default, only dropped packet events are logged.

# SELF TEST

The following Self Test questions will help you measure your understanding of the material presented in this chapter. Read all the choices carefully, as there may be more than one correct answer. Choose all correct answers for each question.

1. You have enabled Web publishing on your Proxy Server. What else must you do to forward packets to a specific Web server?

   A. Nothing. Packets are forwarded to the first Web server on your network.

   B. Select send to another server.

   C. Select send to local computer.

   D. Nothing. The packets can only go to the Web server located on the Proxy Server.

2. You want to know when Proxy Server is dropping packets. What do you need to do to configure this?

   A. Turn on auditing in User Manager.

   B. Nothing. Alerting is turned on when you enable packet filtering.

   C. Configure the Alert tab in any one of the Proxy Server properties page.

   D. Configure the Alert tab in the Web Proxy service properties page.

3. You want to be sure that Internet users do not have access to any of your Web servers. How can you configure Proxy Server to accomplish this?

   A. Enable Web publishing in the Web Proxy service.

   B. Set a domain filter to deny access.

   C. Enable Web publishing in the WinSock Proxy service.

   D. Make sure that Web publishing is not enabled.

4. You want to forward all incoming requests for HTTP objects to the IIS located on your Proxy Server. How do you configure this?

   A. Check the box Enable Web publishing.

   B. Select send to the local web server.

   C. Configure a packet filter to allow HTTP access on port 443.

   D. Disable access control.

5. You have installed and configured your Proxy Server. Now you want to prevent Internet users from viewing your NetBIOS name table. How should you configure Proxy Server?

   A. Enable Web publishing to preclude user access to NetBIOS functions while using the HTTP protocol.

   B. Nothing, since you are using TCP/IP protocol and not the NetBEUI protocol.

   C. Enable packet filtering.

   D. Make sure there are no NetBIOS filters listed in the Exceptions list.

6. Which of the following is not true of Web publishing?

   A. It is enabled by default when you install Proxy Server.

   B. You can forward incoming HTTP requests to the IIS server located on the Proxy Server.

   C. You can only forward packets to IIS servers.

   D. You can forward packets to multiple downstream Web servers.

7. Which of the following statements are not true about packet filtering?

   A. A dynamic filter closes the TCP port for use by users on the Internet.

   B. You can configure custom filters.

   C. You can use predefined filters.

   D. Filtering a protocol and port means that those packets will be rejected by Proxy Server.

8. For what events does Proxy Server not write an event in the system log?

   A. Disk full

   B. Logon failure

   C. Protocol violations

   D. Rejected packets

9. Which of the following statements are true about logging information?

   A. Proxy Server can log to an ODBC-compliant database.

   B. Proxy Server logs the number of connection attempts.

   C. You can have items logged to a log file.

   D. The log file is named pf*yymmdd*.log.

# 21

# Tuning and Troubleshooting Proxy Server

T his chapter describes how to tune and troubleshoot Microsoft Proxy Server.

Proxy Server provides counters that you can use to monitor its performance and monitor how users are connecting. You can use Performance Monitor to view Proxy Server activity.

Windows NT Server uses Performance Monitor for tracking computer performance and processes. When you use Performance Monitor, you actually monitor the behavior of its components. These components are known as *objects*. Examples of objects are the processor, memory, cache, hard disk, services, and other components. Each object has a set of counters that are unique to it.

When Proxy Server is installed, the following counter objects are installed into Performance Monitor. These objects contain all the performance counters that are used to monitor Proxy Server.

- **Web Proxy Server Service**   This object includes counters specific to the Web Proxy service and the SOCKS Proxy service

- **Web Proxy Server Cache**   This object includes counters specific to caching performed by the Web Proxy service.

- **WinSock Proxy Server**   This object includes counters specific to the WinSock Proxy service.

- **Packet Filtering**   This object includes counters specific to packet filtering.

**CERTIFICATION OBJECTIVE 21.01**

# Tuning Cache

If you are configuring to use a single Proxy Server, the main performance issues are the expected usage of the server and the configuration of the cache.

For optimal performance, you should tune the cache based on the expected usage of the server. You should adjust active caching so that it is sufficiently aggressive.

Other things you should check include the following:

- Make sure that you have enough disk space.

- Ensure proper usage of your cache by configuring it for maximum performance.

- Review the time to live (TTL) for HTTP and FTP objects to ensure that the appropriate expiration occurs.

- Limit the size of cached objects to allow for the maximum number of objects in the cache.

- Distribute your cache to different physical disks to optimize performance.

## Cache Issues

Although you can simply increase the size of the cache, you should monitor it on a regular basis to determine the best size.

If, after comparing the cache performance at a later date to the baseline, you see that the hit rate is low, then you can conclude the cache is not being used optimally. Consider tuning the cache to improve the hit rate. When tuning the cache, look at the following issues:

- Hard disk space allocated to caching
- Expiration settings
- Optimizers
- Active cache

**CERTIFICATION OBJECTIVE 21.02**

# Performance Monitor

Performance Monitor is a major tool for tuning and troubleshooting your Windows NT Server and applications that are running on Windows NT Server. Just about anything that you might want to know about what is happening on your Windows NT system can be discovered using Performance Monitor.

Performance Monitor is a standard tool provided with Windows NT. You start Performance Monitor from the Administrative Tools Group. Everything in the Windows NT operating system is an object. An object may have various *instances.* An instance is a unique occurrence of an object. For example, if you have two CPUs in your system, there are two instances of the processor object. You can monitor the performance of either or both instances of the processor.

To successfully monitor your Proxy Server computer, first create a baseline. A baseline provides an anchor point that allows you to measure future performance. You then compare the future performance to the baseline in order to identify changes.

Performance Monitor has a set of core objects that are installed when the operating system is installed. Which additional objects are installed depends on what else you install on Windows NT. Refer to the online documentation for more information about the objects and counters available.

The Performance Monitor log files help you determine if you have the appropriate configurations for your Proxy Server. This chapter will describe some relevant objects and counters that you can use to track Proxy Server performance.

exam
ⓦatch

*You may get a question or two about using Performance Monitor and its important counters.*

## Identifying Bottlenecks

Performance Monitor can help determine where *bottlenecks* exist. A bottleneck is any place there is a system shortage or a resource shortage. All computer systems will have resource shortages. Alleviating one resource shortage may cause another area to show up as the bottleneck. You may then try to add more resources to shore up that area.

You should monitor four categories of objects when monitoring the system and attempting to identify bottlenecks:

- CPU
- Memory
- Disk
- Network

e x a m
ⓦatch

*Know what a bottleneck is. Understand that you want to include the previous categories, as well as Proxy Server-specific categories, when you run Performance Monitor.*

## Identifying Network-Related Performance Issues

There are several objects that can help you identify network-related performance problems:

- IP
- NBT Connection
- Network Interface
- Network Segment (see Table 21-1 for a list of counters for this object).
- Redirector
- Server

| Counter | Meaning |
|---------|---------|
| % Broadcast Frames | Percentage of network bandwidth being used by broadcast frames |
| % Multicast Frames | Percentage of network bandwidth being used by multicast frames |
| % Network Utilization | Percentage of network bandwidth being used on network segment |
| Broadcast Frames Received/Second | Number of broadcast frames received per second |
| Multicast Frames Received/Second | Number of multicast frames received per second |
| Total Bytes Received/Second | The number of bytes received per second |
| Total Frames Received/Second | The number of frames received per second |

- Server Work Queues

- System. In particular, Total Interrupts/Second. This is the rate at which the computer is receiving and servicing interrupts. Your network interface card (NIC) generates an interrupt when it has traffic it needs to process.

- TCP

- UDP

- HTTP

- FTP

You can get information about who is connected to the Proxy Server. You can also monitor current session status from the properties sheet of any of the Proxy services by selecting the Current Sessions tab. This is in addition to information that you collect using Performance Monitor.

To get more information on any particular counter, select the counter and click the Explain button in Performance Monitor. There are additional objects that are specific to Proxy Server that are covered later in this chapter.

### Monitoring FTP Sessions

There are several different types of counters available for monitoring FTP sites and connections in Performance Monitor. There are counters related to

- Bandwidth usage
- Throughput
- Users and connections

Table 21-2 lists some of the counters related to connections. You can use some of these counters to monitor current sessions.

| TABLE 21-2 | Counter | Meaning |
| --- | --- | --- |
| FTP Counters Related to Connections | Current Anonymous Users | The number of users who currently have an anonymous connection using the FTP service |
| | Current Connections | The current number of connections established with the FTP service including anonymous and nonanonymous users |
| | Current NonAnonymous Users | The number of users who currently have a nonanonymous connection using the FTP service |
| | Maximum Anonymous Users | The highest number of users who have established an anonymous connection since FTP service started last |
| | Maximum Connections | The largest number of simultaneous connections established with the FTP service since service startup |
| | Maximum NonAnonymous Users | The highest number of users who have established a nonanonymous connection since FTP service last started |
| | Total Anonymous Users | The total number of users who established an anonymous connection with the FTP service |

| Counter | Meaning |
| --- | --- |
| Total Connection Attempts | The total number of connections to the FTP service that have been attempted since the service last started |
| Total Logon Attempts | The total number of successful logons to the FTP service since the service started |
| Total NonAnonymous Users | The total number of users who established a nonanonymous connection with the FTP service |

## Monitoring HTTP Sessions

There are several different types of counters available for monitoring HTTP sites usage and connections in Performance Monitor. There are counters related to

- Bandwidth usage
- Throughput
- Specific requests and errors
- Users and connections

Table 21-3 lists some of the counters related to connections. You can use these counters to monitor current sessions. You can also monitor current session status from the properties sheet of any of the proxy services by selecting the Current Sessions tab.

| Counter | Meaning |
| --- | --- |
| Anonymous Users/Second | The rate users are making anonymous connections using the Web server |
| Connection Attempts/Second | The rate that connection attempts to the Web server are being made |
| Current Anonymous Users | The number of users who currently have an anonymous connection at the Web server |
| Current Connections | The number of connections established with the Web server |

**TABLE 21-3**

HTTP Counters Related
to Connections (*continued*)

| Counter | Meaning |
| --- | --- |
| Current NonAnonymous Users | The number of users who have a nonanonymous connection at the Web server |
| Logon Attempts/Second | The rate at which logon attempts are being made |
| Maximum Anonymous Users | The highest number of users who have established an anonymous connection at the Web server |
| Maximum Connections | The highest number of connections made at the Web server |
| Maximum NonAnonymous Users | The highest number of users who made nonanonymous connections using the Web server |
| NonAnonymous Users/Second | The rate at which nonanonymous users are connecting to the Web server |
| Total Anonymous Users | The total number of users who established an anonymous connection |
| Total Connection Attempts | The total number of connections to the server that have been attempted |
| Total Logon Attempts | The total number of successful logons at the server |
| Total NonAnonymous Users | The total number of users who established a nonanonymous connection |

## Network Monitor

Using Performance Monitor may not be sufficient to get more detailed information on network performance and what is actually happening at the protocol level or the packet level. To do that, Windows NT Server comes with a tool called Network Monitor. This is a functional network diagnostic tool and protocol analyzer. Network Monitor is only available on Windows NT Server and must be installed using the Network applet (located in the Control Panel) and the Services tab. You can use the Network Monitor to

■ Perform Internet and intranet traffic analysis

- Look at packets on both sides of the network

- Collect statistical information about the type and characteristics of the network traffic. The Network Monitor that ships with Windows NT is limited to viewing traffic between the server and one other station on the network.

For more details on how to use Performance Monitor and Network Monitor, refer to *MCSE Windows NT Workstation 4.0 Study Guide* (Osborne/McGraw-Hill), *MCSE Windows NT Server 4.0 Study Guide* (Osborne/McGraw-Hill)*, and MCSE Windows NT Server 4.0 in the Enterprise Study Guide* (Osborne/McGraw-Hill).

## Identifying Disk-Related Performance Issues

The disk counters in Windows NT are disabled by default. You must enable them in order to get any information about disk activities. You enable the counters by issuing the command **diskperf –y** from the command line. If you are using a RAID array, issue the command **diskperf –ye.** Disk counters are a significant performance drain on the system. You should only enable the counters when you want to collect information about disk performance and then turn the counters off. To disable the counters, issue the command **diskperf –n.** You need to restart the computer after you enable or disable the disk counters in order for the state to become effective.

exam
ⓦatch

*Know that the disk counters are disabled by default and know how to enable them.*

The two primary objects for tracking disk performance are:

- Physical Disk
- Logical Disk

Each object has its own associated counters. Some of the counters can be found in either Physical Disk or Logical Disk. Some of the counters are unique. For example, the counters % Free Space and Free Megabytes can only be found in the Logical Disk object.

## Identifying CPU-Related Performance Issues

Proxy Server is not CPU intensive, so improving the CPU performance is usually not required. However, tracking CPU activity can help you determine how busy your server is and how much work it is doing. In Windows NT, there are two factors to consider relative to CPU activity and the need to upgrade CPU performance:

- The speed of the CPU (clock speed generally stated in MHz)
- The number of CPUs in the system.

*exam*
*ᗯatch*

*Know that a sustained CPU activity of greater than 75–80 percent indicates a bottleneck and the need for more CPU resources.*

If you are running multithreaded processes, you might benefit from adding more CPUs to your system than increasing the clock speed and only using one CPU. Of course, you must have the appropriate hardware platform to support multiple CPUs and the CPUs must match. You can use the following objects to help determine CPU performance:

- Processor
- Process
- Thread
- System

*exam*
*ᗯatch*

*Know that the System object gives you totals for the system.*

## Identifying Memory-Related Performance Issues

All of the processes inside Windows NT use memory to run. There is a general rule that states that Windows NT will effectively use all the RAM that you can put in the computer. You can also tune the system to determine exactly how much memory is required to support your configuration.

Windows NT uses a virtual memory manager. *Virtual memory* is comprised of RAM and space allocated on the disk for the pagefile.sys file. Windows NT's virtual memory manager can address up to 4GB of virtual memory. You can use the following objects to help determine what memory is being used and what is using the memory:

- Cache (this is system cache and not the Web Proxy cache, which is written to the hard disk)
- Memory
- Process
- Server
- Server Work Queues

## Increasing Throughput

If network traffic exceeds local area network (LAN) or wide area network (WAN) bandwidth, then network performance will suffer. To detect this situation, it is important to watch network traffic levels, particularly on devices such as bridges and routers. You may need to upgrade the hardware on the network or the routers. You may also want to upgrade an existing WAN connection to one with a higher bandwidth or switch from a 10MB network and components to 100MB.

You can configure the routing between Proxy Servers to optimize both response times to users and network traffic. One technique is to configure a local Proxy Server with cache and then chain that server to a Proxy Server array at the central location. See Chapter 16 for more information on multiple Proxy Servers.

## Proxy Server Default Counters

When you install Proxy Server, an icon for Monitor Microsoft Proxy Server Performance is added. Clicking on this icon starts Performance Monitor with msp.pmc. A .pmc file is a preconfigured Performance Monitor workspace. It already has the objects and counters installed so you do not need to configure Performance Monitor each time you want to monitor the same set of conditions. Table 21-4 lists the Proxy Server default counters.

**TABLE 21-4**

Proxy Server Default Counters

| Counter | Meaning |
| --- | --- |
| % Processor Time - Inetinfo and WSPSRV | These counters monitor the time used by these two processes. They help you identify problem areas and indicate processor usage by the service. If they are increasing, install a faster processor. When these get to 100 percent, the system is at maximum capacity. |
| Active Sessions | This counter tells you how many people are using the server at one time. |
| Cache Hit Ratio (%) | This counter indicates what percent of requests the cache is serving by telling you how effective the caching is. The goal should be to increase this number. |
| Requests/Second | This counter displays the rate of incoming requests that have been made to the Web Proxy Server. |
| Current Average Milliseconds/Request | This counter displays the number of milliseconds required to service a request. |

| TABLE 21-5 | Counter | Meaning |
|---|---|---|
| Web Proxy Service Counters | Sites Denied | This counter indicates if access limits are working and whether limits are necessary. |
| | Sites Granted | Compare this counter to Sites Denied. |
| | Total Users | This is a cumulative counter of the total number of users that have ever used the server. |
| | Current Users | This counter indicates the number of users currently using the server. This helps to determine when it is convenient to stop the server. |
| | Maximum Users | This is a cumulative counter that indicates the maximum number of users simultaneously connected to the server. |
| | Inet Bytes Total/Second | This counter indicates the amount of data that is processed between the server and the ISP. |

## Web Proxy Server Service Object

Table 21-5 lists some of the counters for monitoring Web Proxy service performance.

## Web Proxy Server Cache Object

Table 21-6 lists some of the counters for monitoring Web Proxy service's cache performance.

Using the counters in Table 21-4, 21-5, and 21-6, you can judge if you have the proper configuration for your server in a given situation. Remember, you are comparing current Performance Monitor information to the information contained in Performance Monitor log files to identify trends.

| TABLE 21-6 | Counter | Meaning |
|---|---|---|
| Web Proxy Service Cache Counters | Bytes in Cache | This indicates the current amount of data in the cache. If this is near the maximum, increase the size of the cache. |
| | Max Bytes Cached | This indicates the maximum number of bytes that have ever been stored in the cache. |
| | Active Refresh Bytes Rate | This counter determines whether you should increase or decrease the active caching. |

### Chasing Problems

When troubleshooting, the most important thing to remember is to change just one variable at a time. This is especially true if you are chasing intermittent hardware problems. You want to change one thing at a time and observe the effect of the change on the symptoms. If the change seems to make no difference to the symptom, then set the condition back to its original state and make another change. Each time reset the variable and try another until you isolate the problem hardware component.

One of the more difficult problems to find is intermittent bad memory. Some memory failures do not manifest themselves as a direct failure of the bank of memory. Sometimes the memory failure results in corrupted data. This data corruption can be in memory cache and is propagated to the file itself when saved to the disk.

Some disk controllers have memory that they use for their own cache operations. This makes running down memory corruption problems even harder. In addition, many times these symptoms are mistaken for disk or disk controller problems. I have watched clients format drives in an attempt to alleviate the problem. In one case, I observed the client change out the drive controller and take the cache memory from the old controller and put it on the new controller. Now, I agree with that procedure because he only changed one variable at a time. When that did not fix the problem, he began replacing memory on the system board. He had forgotten about the memory on the controller. Replacing the memory on the motherboard did not help and he was on his way to replacing the motherboard when I reminded him about the controller cache. Changing the controller cache fixed the problem.

## CERTIFICATION OBJECTIVE 21.03

# Transaction Log Files

Your log files let you know how your equipment is doing and how the organization uses the Internet. Log files are located in the subfolder specified in the Logging tab. The log files are ASCII text files.

If you log on to an Open Database Connectivity/Structured Query Language (ODBC/SQL) data source, you must use an ODBC-compliant client front end to view and print the data. Microsoft Access is an example of such a front end.

You can set the logging service to write transactions in an abbreviated format to reduce the size of the log files. You can also write the full transactions to the log files and filter the logs for display and reporting by using a batch file, an application, or a Microsoft SQL Server table filter.

You can use daily, weekly, and monthly analysis of logs to see patterns. You can produce the reports on a regular schedule. You can distribute these reports to members of your organization who need to monitor the logs. By distributing this information, your management and users become more aware of their use of the resources.

## Logging to a Text File

When you install Proxy Server, logging to a file is the default logging method. Logging to a file records all Internet accesses to a text file. This text file can be viewed with a text editor or with an application such as Microsoft Word. Log files can also be exported into a spreadsheet or to a database for analysis.

The following options are available:

- **Automatically open new log**   This creates a new log file periodically using the interval specified by the Daily, Weekly, or Monthly options. When a new log file is started, the old log file is closed. When the Automatically open new log check box is cleared, the same log file is used. When it is selected, and a new log file is opened. The filename format is wsb*nnnn*.log.

- **Daily, Weekly, or Monthly**   Selecting one of these indicates that a new log file should be started at the designated intervals.

- **Limit number of old logs to**   This option enables you to set the number of log files that are stored on the hard disk.

- **Stop service if disk full**    Under the Logging tab for the service. If the hard disk is full, Proxy Server stops the service. You need to delete files from the disk before you can restart the service.

- **Stop all services if disk full**    Logging tab for packet filtering in the Security dialog box. Selecting this check box for packet filter logging stops all Proxy Server services if the hard disk runs out of space.

- **Log file directory**    Use this to set the directory where the log files should be written; Proxy Server generates the log file name for you. The filename has the format ws*yymmdd*.log. The name varies depending if you have daily, weekly, or monthly options selected.

There are two log file formats available:

- **Regular**    This is the default. It records only a subset of all available information for each Internet access. Using this option reduces the disk space needed.

- **Verbose**    This format records all available information for each Internet access.

## Logging to a Database

Logging to a text file is the default. However, if you prefer to save logs in a database, you can configure the Web Proxy and WinSock Proxy services to log information to a database instead.

Proxy Server supports ODBC for logging service information to databases. Logging to any ODBC Version 2.5-compliant database is possible. It does not need to be a Microsoft database.

Database logging increases the amount of time and resources needed by Proxy Server. You may want to consider logging to a text file and then importing the text file into the database as a means of enhancing performance. Writing log data to a database allows for data querying and reporting is enhanced.

Log files are stored in one table. Each transaction generates one record in the table. The database can exist on a Proxy Server computer or on any other computer on your network.

You must supply the following information to log on to a database:

- **ODBC Data Source Name (DSN)** This is the ODBC Data Source Name (DSN) for the database to which Proxy Server logs data. You configure this through the ODBC applet in Control Panel.

- **Table** This is the name of a table in the database to which Proxy Server logs information.

- **User Name** A valid user name for the database table.

- **Frequency** Use daily, weekly, and monthly analysis of logs to identify patterns of how your users typically browse the Internet.

- **Password** Use this if the table is to be password protected.

**CERTIFICATION OBJECTIVE 21.04**

# Troubleshooting

When troubleshooting, gather information specific to your computer. There are several helpful commands that may be executed from the command prompt. These commands may be referred to by the service they affect. They are the following:

- **TCP/IP commands** You can use nbtstat, which displays NetBIOS protocol statistics and current connection information. Another command is netstat, which displays TCP, UDP, and IP statistics. The ipconfig and ipconfig /all commands display server IP configuration information.

- **IPX command** The ipxroute config command displays the information on all of the bindings for IPX, such as network number, IPX frame type, network card address, and IPX address. The ipxroute servers command displays the SAP table, which includes IPX address, Server type, and Server name.

■ **WinSock Proxy commands**

# WinSock Proxy Commands

The utilities described in this section provide configuration information that is useful when you troubleshoot WinSock Proxy conditions. You can run these utilities at the client computer to determine which parameters are set.

### CHKWSP32

This command is executed on either Windows NT or Windows 95 computers. It is installed to the \mspclnt\i386 folder during Setup. It identifies the WinSock Proxy client configuration and includes the following information:

■ Protocols installed

■ WinSock path and filename

■ WinSock version

■ Name of the Proxy Server

■ Status of connection to server

### CHKWSP16

This command is executed on Windows 3.x client computers. It is installed to the \mspclnt\i386 folder during Setup. It identifies information similar to that displayed using CHKWSP32.

### Proxy Server Connectivity

The CHKWSP16 and CHKWSP32 utilities check connectivity with the Proxy Server computer. If the connection succeeds, the following message displays:

"Client control protocol matches the server control protocol"

You can use the verbose mode switch, /f, with CHKWSP32 or CHKWSP16 to see full diagnostics information.

## Registry Entries

In troubleshooting, you may need to find and verify registry entries. There are two registry-editing tools packaged with Window NT. They are:

- **Regedt32**   This is the preferred registry-editing tool. It has some features not found in its counterpart, regedit. The features included are the option to set read-only mode and a Security menu item that allows you to set permissions. You access this tool from the Run command, or you can create an icon to point to regedt32.exe.

- **Regedit**   This is the Windows 95 registry-editing tool. It lacks the features of the regedt32 tool in all respects except one: it has a superior search facility. With regedit, you can search for a string in the key, value, or data fields in the registry. This feature is invaluable.

There are several locations for the various registry entries for Proxy Server. To view the keys, start at HKEY_LOCAL_MACHINE, System, CurrentControlSet, Services. Table 21-7 lists the keys and their locations.

There are several registry keys that are shared by the Web Proxy service, the WinSock Proxy service, and the SOCKS Proxy service. You can find these keys under HKEY_LOCAL_MACHINE, System, CurrentControlSet, Services. Table 21-8 lists these keys and their locations.

For more information about registry entries, refer to the Proxy Server documentation, *Installation and Administration Guide,* Appendix A, Registry Entries.

**TABLE 21-7**

Registry Entries for Proxy Server

| Key | Location |
|-----|----------|
| Web Proxy service | W3Proxy, Parameters |
| Web Proxy service cache | W3Pcache, Parameters |
| Reverse proxy | W3Proxy, Parameters, ReverseProxy |
| WinSock Proxy service | WSPSrv, Parameters |
| SOCKS Proxy service | W#Proxy, Parameters, SOCKS |

| | Key | Location |
|---|---|---|
| **TABLE 21-8** | Domain filtering | W3Proxy, Parameters, DoFilter |
| Shared Registry Entry Keys | Packet filtering | MSPAdmin, Filters |
| | Array membership | W3Proxy, Parameters, MemberArray |
| | Chained array | W3Proxy, Parameters, ChainedArray |
| | Logging | MSPAdmin, Parameters |

A word of caution about the registry and making modifications, either intentional or unintentional. If you mess up the registry, your server and services may not work or even run at all.

## Resolving Proxy Server and Client Installation Problems

The Proxy Server client setup program creates a log file. This log file is named C:\mpcsetup.log on the client computer. It contains information about the setup process. If you run into a problem during setup, you can view this file using any text editor. It contains information beyond any error messages that the users may get. You can use this file to help identify client installation problems.

There is a utility located on the Proxy Server CD-ROM in the msproxy directory that can be of some help in determining common configuration problems. The utility is called mspdiag; copy the executable file to the C:\msp folder and run the utility. If the setup completed successfully, then the utility was already installed for you.

Proxy Server also creates a setup log file named mspsetup.log. This file is saved in the root folder of the C: drive.

## Resolving Proxy Server and Client Access Problems

You can use the commands CHKWSP32 and CHKWSP16, described in an earlier section, to check the status and connection of the client to the Proxy Server.

Other client access issues can come about from several sources. If you try to connect to a Web site and immediately receive an access denied message, the most probable cause is that there is a domain filter in place denying access to that site.

This scenario is different than access authentication problems in that the domain filter returns an immediate access denied message. Authentication issues take a little time to work through the process of authenticating before it returns the access denied issue.

exam
ⓦatch

*Know how to troubleshoot connection problems that arise from the various authentication settings and know what the messages will be at the client side.*

## Resolving Proxy Server Client Computer Problems

The mspclnt.ini file contains configuration information about the client. This is a text file and can be edited with any text editor. By default, the client configuration file is downloaded to the client each time a client computer is restarted and is updated every six hours after an initial refresh. When a refresh occurs, the order of server share paths, listed in the [Master Config] section of mspclnt.ini, is used to determine the location of updated configuration files.

At least one entry must be present. Entries are tried in the order listed. Additional path listings are tried only in the event that preceding paths are not available.

For mspclnt.ini changes made on the server to be reflected on a client, you either have to manually update the WinSock Proxy client or wait for the client to be automatically updated.

Keep in mind that if you change the client's mspclnt.ini file and want the changes to remain, you should also modify the file on the server as well.

If you are experiencing a "Failure to Refresh Configuration Files" or "Failure to Connect to the Server," there are several things to check. These conditions indicate a problem connecting to the \mspclnt share on the Proxy Server computer. This share must be available at all times for Proxy Server clients to refresh their configuration files. Make sure that the client has permissions to the share.

The following is an example of an mspclnt.ini file:

```
[Internal]
scp=9,10
Build=2.0.372.12
[wspsrv]
Disable=1
[inetinfo]
Disable=1
[services]
Disable=1
[outlook]
Disable=0
[raplayer]
RemoteBindUdpPorts=6970-7170
LocalBindTcpPorts=7070
[rvplayer]
RemoteBindUdpPorts=6970-7170
LocalBindTcpPorts=7070
[net2fone]
ServerBindTcpPorts=0
[icq]
RemoteBindUdpPorts=0
ServerBindTcpPorts=0,1025-5000
NameResolutionForLocalHost=P
[Common]
WWW-Proxy=SERVER02
Set Browsers to use Proxy=1
Set Browsers to use Auto Config=0
WebProxyPort=3300
Configuration
Url=http://SERVER02:3300/array.dll?Get.Routing.Script
Port=1745
Configuration Refresh Time (Hours)=6
Re-check Inaccessible Server Time (Minutes)=10
Refresh Give Up Time (Minutes)=15
Inaccessible Servers Give Up Time (Minutes)=2
Setup=Setup.exe
[Servers Ip Addresses]
Name=SERVER02
[Servers Ipx Addresses]
[Master Config]
Path1=\\SERVER01A\Mspclnt\
```

## Resolving Security Problems

If the user is not a member of the same Windows NT domain as the Proxy Server (or if the Proxy Server is a stand-alone server) you must enable the Guest account on the Proxy Server computer so the user may access it. You also need to give the account permission to the share for downloading the WinSock client.

You can create an account on the Proxy Server computer that matches the username and password of the user on the client computer as an alternative. This latter approach is less desirable than using the Windows NT Domain security strategy. However, if you do not have Windows NT Domains and are using Proxy Server, this is another way.

You can also configure Windows NT Server so that certain events are audited and records placed in the security log. You view the security log with the Event Viewer tool. You configure auditing through User Manager (for Domains) by selecting the Policies menu and then selecting Audit.

## Resolving Caching Problems

There are several issues with regard to caching. There are cache configuration issues and there is the issue of not having an NTFS partition to install cache on. If you install Proxy Server on a system that only has FAT partitions, you will not be able to enable caching until you convert at least one of the partitions to an NTFS file system. After that, you should stop the Web Proxy service, enable caching, and set the cache size. After you apply the changes, you need to restart the service for caching to take effect for the first time.

When you configure the cache, you have a number of available configuration options:

- Setting passive caching parameters and general expiration policy for object freshness
- Setting active caching parameters
- Changing the cache disks or the total cache size

- Setting advanced caching parameters, including the ability to set object size, object TTL, and the ability to create cache filters

You can implement passive caching in several ways:

- You can choose the option Updates are more important, which will increase the amount of traffic.
- You can choose the option Fewer network accesses are more important, which will balance the traffic and may provide better user response.

Active caching properties determine how often Proxy Server automatically retrieves data from the Internet and stores it in the cache. You can configure active caching in several ways:

- For best cache response and therefore best user response, choose the option Faster user response is more important (more prefetching).
- For equal importance between freshest cache data and best cache performance, choose the option Equal importance.
- For the least amount of traffic on your server and therefore the stalest cache date, choose the option Fewer network accesses are more important (less prefetching).

# Troubleshooting WINS to Provide Client Access

If the client can browse internal HTTP servers but is unable to browse an external HTTP server, try to ping the Proxy Server. If the response is "Bad IP Address" then the problem is in name resolution.

Check to see if the client is configured to use WINS and that the IP address for the WINS listed in the client configuration is actually the valid IP address for the WINS server.

If the IP address is correct for the WINS server, then check the WINS server database to make sure that the Proxy Server registered its NetBIOS names. If the NetBIOS names for the Proxy Server are not registered, then check the WINS configuration parameters at the Proxy Server to make sure that the server is a WINS client.

## Troubleshooting Hardware Problems

Troubleshooting hardware problems can be interesting and difficult. Hardware problems fall into two categories: hard failures and intermittent problems.

The hard failures are sometimes the easier category to troubleshoot. For example, you know when you have a CPU failure, especially in a single CPU system. If you lose a bank of memory, be prepared to see the Stop screen (sometimes called the Blue Screen of Death). Hard failures are easy to spot.

Intermittent hardware problems are more difficult to see. Often it is difficult to fix a problem that you cannot conclusively identify. Windows NT Server provides some tools that can make this job easier. One of the first things is to check the System Log using the Event Viewer. Many times clues show up there. If you have the Event Viewer in its default configuration, then the most recent event is at the top of the list. The most recent event is probably not the one that you are interested in, but an older event (or failure) whose failure has also caused the most recent event (or failure).

For example, you receive calls from users stating they can no longer access the computers using the host name, but they can access them using the IP addresses. You suspect that the DNS server is not working. You check the system log and, sure enough, the first entry in the list is the DNS service failed to start. Your impulse might be to open DNS manager and see what's happening.

However, if you check further down the log, you will see that the Messenger service did not start, the Alerter service did not start, the TCP/IP protocol did not bind, the network adapter driver did not bind, and all the way at the bottom of the list, the message that states "could not find adapter at location such and such." Bingo. The problem may not be the DNS server but a bad NIC. Fix the NIC problem and the rest of the problems will probably clear up as well.

Performance Monitor can help isolate intermittent hardware errors. Hardware devices, like the NIC card, generate an interrupt to process the data. If you notice that the number of interrupts per second is high, suspect a malfunctioning piece of hardware. How do you know what is a high number of

## QUESTIONS AND ANSWERS

| | |
|---|---|
| I want to be able to query my log records. How can I do that and not have to log to the SQL database? | You can log to the text file and import the text file into the database. This way, you have the speed of logging to the text file and the flexibility of keeping the history in the database. |
| Why do I want to keep Performance Monitor logs? | You might want to keep the logs that you created with Performance Monitor so that you can clearly see any potential performance trends. This might help you anticipate configuration changes in the future. |
| Why don't I just monitor all of the objects and counters instead of only selecting a few? | There are a couple of reasons. There can be an overwhelming number of counters to deal with. When sorting through all types of data, it can be harder to find the relevant parts. Additionally, the more objects you monitor, the larger your log file will be. |
| How do I know which counters to select? | Determine what information you are trying to collect. Study the available counters and make your choices. You might run some controlled tests to validate that the counters that you have selected actually measure what you hope they measure. Once you are sure, collect live data. |

interrupts for your system? Because you compare the number that you just got to the baseline number that you created. You did create a baseline, didn't you?

There are techniques that you can use to lessen the impact of malfunctioning hardware. For example, you can use a RAID 5 array to lessen the impact of a single disk failure. You can have multiple NICs installed so that if one is bad, the other is still working.

## Troubleshooting Internet/Intranet Routing Hardware and Software

There are two error messages that you can find in the system log concerning Remote Access Service (RAS):

- **Error 136, Proxy dial out connection failed**   For this condition, check that RAS and Auto Dial out are configured correctly.

- **Error 142, a dial out to the Internet failed**   This typically means that a chained Proxy Server is unavailable or the connection to your ISP is not working.

When you want to use RAS to connect your Proxy Server to an ISP, don't forget to create a phonebook entry for the dial connection to the ISP. You must also provide your logon credentials in the phonebook entry in order to successfully connect.

In order to use Routing and Remote Access Service (RRAS) with Proxy Server, you must download the RRAS hot fix from the Microsoft Web site. After you download it, you must apply the fix.

# CERTIFICATION SUMMARY

This chapter described how to tune cache in order to optimize the performance of Proxy Server and the Proxy Server clients.

The chapter also described how to use Performance Monitor to identify bottlenecks, network-related performance issues, disk-related performance issues, and memory-related performance issues. You can use Performance Monitor to establish a baseline of performance by saving the performance information in a log file. By repeating this procedure periodically, you can determine trend information about usage patterns, software configurations, and hardware requirements. You can do this across the broad categories such as CPU, disk, network, and memory as well as fine-tuning it for FTP, HTTP, and the Proxy Server services.

Several categories of troubleshooting were discussed, including how to identify and resolve problems with Proxy Server installation, client installation, and related client computer problems.

# TWO-MINUTE DRILL

- ❑ Tune cache based on expected usage.
- ❑ Adjust active caching so it is sufficiently aggressive.
- ❑ Allocate sufficient disk space for cached objects.
- ❑ Review the TTL settings to confirm that they are appropriate.
- ❑ Use Performance Monitor log files to determine trends.
- ❑ Reviewing the log files helps determine if Proxy Server is configured correctly.

❑ A bottleneck is a resource shortage.

❑ Use various objects and counters when you run Performance Monitor.

❑ Always include counters from CPU, memory, disk, and network objects.

❑ Use other objects and counters to get specific information about FTP, HTTP, and Proxy Server services.

❑ You can monitor FTP connections and statistics.

❑ You can monitor HTTP connections and statistics.

❑ Use Network Monitor to further analyze network traffic.

❑ Network Monitor is a tool available with Windows NT Server.

❑ You install Network Monitor using the Network applet.

❑ The Network Monitor that ships with Windows NT is limited to viewing traffic between the server and one other station on the network.

❑ You can use Performance Monitor to track disk-related activity.

❑ Disk counters are disabled by default.

❑ You enable them by entering **diskperf –y** at the command line.

❑ Disk counters are a substantial performance drain.

❑ Disable the disk counters when you are finished.

❑ Proxy Server is not normally CPU intensive.

❑ There are several things you might do to increase performance on the network.

❑ Using 100MB components may increase network throughput.

❑ Effectively configuring cache can increase network performance.

❑ Effectively using Proxy Server arrays can increase network performance.

❑ When you installed Proxy Server, a Proxy Server group was created.

❑ In the Proxy Server program group is an icon for starting Performance Monitor with Proxy Server-specific counters already configured for you.

❑ This icon launches Performance Monitor using the msp.pmc workspace.

❏ The Active Sessions counter tells you how many users are on the system at one time.

❏ The Cache Hit Ratio counter tells you how effective your caching configuration is.

❏ The higher the cache hit ratio, the better it is.

❏ You can log activities to a Proxy Server log file.

❏ You can log activities to an ODBC-compliant database.

❏ You must configure the system with a DSN to use the ODBC database.

❏ You must configure the database with the proper fields.

❏ You can use TCP/IP commands such as ping, ipconfig, nbtstat, and netstat to help isolate problems.

❏ You can use CHKWSP32 to help confirm configuration.

❏ You can check the mpcsetup.log and mspsetup.log files to help debug setup problems.

# SELF TEST

The following Self Test questions will help you measure your understanding of the material presented in this chapter. Read all the choices carefully, as there may be more than one correct answer. Choose all correct answers for each question.

1. You have configured Proxy Server to auto-dial to your ISP. You installed RAS and configured RAS. When you access the Web Proxy Server, you do not get connected to the Internet and the modem never dials. What can be causing this problem?

   A. You cannot use RAS to dial out.

   B. You do not need to use RAS to dial out. You can dial out using the Auto Dial feature of Proxy Server.

   C. You did not configure a phonebook entry.

   D. You have access control enabled.

2. You installed Windows NT Server, IIS Server, and Proxy Server. You have no other Windows NT Servers on your LAN, nor do you have a Windows NT Domain. What must you do to ensure that clients can connect to the Proxy Server?

   A. Install another Windows NT Server as a domain controller.

   B. Add the Proxy Server to a Windows NT Domain.

   C. Nothing.

   D. Enable the Guest account on Proxy Server.

3. You made several modifications to the mspclnt.ini file on one of the local computers. When you came back the next day, the modifications were not there. You are using the NTFS file system. What is the most probable cause of this problem?

   A. You cannot modify the file on an NTFS partition.

   B. The mspclnt.ini file is being overwritten during the refresh cycle.

   C. You must have the mspclnt.ini file on a FAT partition.

   D. The user is changing the file after you change it.

4. You have configured Proxy Server to use Windows NT challenge/response protocol. When you try to connect to a site on the Internet, you immediately receive back an error message saying "Access Denied." What is the cause of this problem?

   A. You have a domain filter configured at the Proxy Server.

   B. Your browser does not support challenge/response.

   C. You do not have an account at the Proxy Server.

   D. You supplied the wrong password.

5. You are attempting set up the WinSock client on a Windows 95 computer. You are

having trouble getting the installation to complete successfully. What can you check to help determine the source of the problem?

A. Check the system log on the client.

B. Check the mspsetup.log on the Proxy Server.

C. Run mspdiag.

D. View the mspsetup.log file on the client.

6. You want to view the registry settings for Proxy Server. What tool can you use to do this?

A. Windows NT Diagnostics

B. Regedt32

C. System Policy Editor, Registry Mode

D. Performance Monitor

7. You want to check the parameters for the WinSock software on a client. What utility can you use to do this?

A. CHKWSP16/CHKWSP32

B. Mspdiags

C. Performance Monitor

D. Windows NT Diagnostics

8. You are sitting at a Windows NT Workstation computer attempting to determine why you cannot connect to the Proxy Server. You try to ping the Proxy Server by name and receive the message "Bad IP Address." You cannot ping the Proxy Server by using the IP address. What can you do to help isolate this problem?

A. Add the server name to the DNS.

B. Use ipconfig.

C. Use ipxroute.

D. Make the computer be a WINS client.

9. You want to know how efficient your cache is. What object/counter do you use?

A. Cache/% Data Hits

B. Memory/Proxy Cache

C. Memory/Web Proxy Cache

D. Web Proxy/Cache Hit Ratio (%)

10. You ran Performance Monitor and recorded the information to a log file. You selected the objects Physical Disk and Logical Disk. When you open the log file, all of the counters for those objects display zero activities. Why?

A. There was no disk activity to record.

B. You did not enable the disk counters.

C. This is normal.

D. You do not have permission to access the disk objects.

MICROSOFT CERTIFIED SYSTEMS ENGINEER

# 22

# Internet Explorer Administration Kit 4.0 (IEAK)

W hat is the IEAK? The Internet Explorer Administration Kit (IEAK) is Microsoft's tool for packaging and deploying custom implementations of Internet Explorer 4.*x* (IE). Whether you are a corporate administrator, an Internet Service Provider (ISP), or an Internet Content Provider, you will find that IEAK is an invaluable tool.

If you have previously used IEAK 3.02, you will find several new features added to Internet Explorer 4.0, including the ability to customize the bitmaps for Active Setup (branding) and the ability to set system policy information and restrictions.

This chapter describes the process of deploying and maintaining IE 4.0 for end-user browser and desktop configurations. It covers each of the necessary skills for exam preparation. This chapter can also serve as a primer for your own production environment.

This chapter covers only IEAK. You should already be familiar with installing and configuring Internet Explorer 4.0, Outlook Express, NetMeeting, and IE 4.0's other components. If you are not fluent with these programs, study them before launching into this chapter.

**exam**
**ⓦatch**

*You will need to know how to install and work with Internet Explorer 4.0, Outlook Express, and NetMeeting before attempting to take the IEAK exam.*

IEAK is not just a great tool. It is a required core exam to pass for certification if you are currently seeking Microsoft's MCSE+I. Microsoft expects you to be proficient in six areas:

- Planning
- Installation and Configuration
- Configuring and Managing Resource Access
- Integration and Interoperability
- Monitoring and Optimization
- Troubleshooting Internet Explorer 4.*x* solutions that utilize IEAK

For a complete list of all required skills, visit http://www.microsoft.com/mcp/exam/prep/PG70-079.htm.

# How to Get IEAK

You can download IEAK from Microsoft at the URL http://www.microsoft.com/ie/ieak/. However, you must first register to download. After registering, you will be given instructions on how to get the customization key and download IEAK. There are four steps to getting the IEAK:

1. **Register to use the secure pages of this Web site**   You need to register your e-mail address and fully qualified domain name (FQDN). Your verification, with a password, will be sent to you via e-mail.

2. **Choose License**   You have three choices:
   - To customers outside your organization (ISP, ICP)
   - To company employees within your organization (corporate administrator)
   - To meet special requirements (128-bit browser, dial-up networking)

3. **Download or order the software you want to distribute**   You can download IEAK, or you can order it on CD-ROM.

4. **Make sure you report your distributions**   Microsoft expects you to report the first distribution of IE 4.0 that you make immediately and then quarterly thereafter.

# Modes of Operation

Which agreement you accept for licensing determines what you will be able to use IEAK to do. If you intend to use IEAK for both corporate administration and ISP services, you need to register two separate times. Microsoft calls these differences *modes of operation*.

When you run the IEAK Wizard, you enter your customization key and then select one of the following modes of operation:

- Content Provider/Developer
- Internet Service Provider
- Corporate Administrator

Note that the ability to select Corporate Administrator is not be available if you chose "To customers outside your organization" for the licensing agreement.

**CERTIFICATION OBJECTIVE 22.03**

# System Requirements

First and foremost, you must have Internet Explorer 4.0 loaded on the machine you are running IEAK on. IEAK does not work otherwise.

## Internet Explorer 4.0

The minimum system requirements needed to install Internet Explorer for Windows 95 and Windows NT 4.0 are:

- **Processor**   486/66 or better
- **Operating system**   Windows 95 (all Service Packs), or Windows NT 4.0 with Service Pack 3 (SP3)
- **Memory (Windows 95)**   8MB minimum, 16MB with Active Desktop
- **Memory (Windows NT)**   16MB minimum, 24MB with Active Desktop
- **Disk space**
  - 39MB for a minimal installation
  - 51MB for a standard installation
  - 70MB for a full installation
  - Peripherals: mouse, modem, or network interface
  
    Adding 5MB to the previous numbers will aid in troubleshooting.

## IEAK Configuration Wizard

The minimum system requirements needed to install IEAK and run the Wizard on Windows 95 and Windows NT 4.0 are:

- **Processor**   486/66 or better

- **Operating System**   Windows 95 or Windows NT 4.0

- **Memory (Windows 95)**   8MB

- **Memory (Windows NT)**   16MB

- **Disk Space**   40MB to 60MB at installation; 40MB to 100MB per custom package. Warning! The amount of hard disk space required also depends on the different distribution media you select.

- **Connection**   Must have Internet access active to run first instance of the Wizard.

Note that for a full installation of IE 4.0 with all of its components, you need 100MB free disk space per package.

Microsoft has plans to release versions of IEAK for the Macintosh and Windows 3.*x* machines.

## CERTIFICATION OBJECTIVE 22.04

# Planning

Before installing IEAK, become very familiar with Internet Explorer and components. There are many sources that can help you obtain a good working knowledge of IE 4.0:

- IEAK help

- Microsoft's Internet Explorer Web site (http://www.microsoft.com/ie/)

- Internet Explorer Customer Support Web site (http://www. microsoft. com/iesupport/)

- Internet Explorer Help

Once you are familiar with Internet Explorer, the functionality of IEAK becomes self-evident. However, there are many issues to consider before proceeding with building a distribution package.

The following areas of consideration should be given a great deal of thought when planning your custom package.

## Operating System

IEAK 4.01 supports distribution packages for Windows 95, Windows NT 4.0, Windows 3.1, Windows for Workgroups 3.11, Windows NT 3.51, UNIX (Solaris 2.5 or higher), and Macintosh 68K and PPC. The options for each operating system vary as well as the options for ISPs and Corporate Administrators in each operating system. To see a complete list of options, visit http://ieak.microsoft.com/xplatform.asp.

## Network Configuration

Document all client and server hardware/software configurations. Try to determine the initial needs of the end users. Define which groups of users need custom configurations of their browsers. You can allow the users to choose from up to 10 custom installations for each custom package that you distribute.

Determine which components are necessary to meet the users' work requirements. In addition, determine security levels on a per-group basis as needed. Think about how company policies can be incorporated into the settings for each package.

## Migration

IE 4.0 installs on top of IE 3.x. However, they cannot exist on the same machine unless it is a dual-boot system. IE 4.0 imports proxy settings, bookmarks, and cookies from Netscape Navigator 3.x, but it cannot import plug-ins.

Coexistence with Netscape Navigator is possible. If Netscape Navigator is already loaded, IE 4.0 does not use the Active Setup component to install. Instead, it loads its own Active Setup component and runs Setup from there.

If Outlook Express is being installed as part of the migration deployment, the following options are imported from Netscape Navigator:

- SMTP server information
- POP3 server settings
- Name, e-mail address, reply address, organization, signature information
- Personal address book (PAB)
- Web phonebook
- Send and post settings if different from the Navigator default
- Messages refresh setting if different from the Navigator default

If the Web Publishing Wizard is installed as part of the migration deployment, the following options are imported from Netscape Navigator:

- Author name
- Document template location
- Publisher username
- Publisher password

If you are migrating from any browser other than IE or Netscape, you have to reconstruct your favorites list.

Beware of compatibility issues. Software that was present before the installation of IE 4.0 may not be compatible. For example, Web pages and scripts for proprietary browsers and HTML may not operate properly.

## Method of Distribution and Type of Media

Decide on a distribution strategy that fits the needs of your end users. You can create a download site on an intranet/Internet, create a distribution CD-ROM, create a distribution on multiple floppy disks, or if you are an ISP, you can distribute on a single floppy disk.

### Distribution Servers

Regardless of which distribution media you select, IEAK always creates a downloadable copy of your distribution package to be placed either on the local machine or directed to a network connection. If you decide to use a download site, sometimes referred to as a *kiosk*, you need to have the path to the server available and you need the appropriate URLs.

To prepare a server, create a folder such as "CIE" in every server to which you plan to publish. CIE (for Custom Internet Explorer) is just a recommendation; you can choose another name for this folder.

For example, let's say you created the paths C:\Inetpub\Wwwroot\Cie and C:\Inetpub\Ftproot\Cie on the hard disks. The URLs would be http://*computername*/cie and ftp://*computername*/cie, respectively.

### Network Capacity

You can use the different distribution methods to reduce the network bandwidth. IEAK allows you to set up to 10 different download sites for your end users to choose from.

*You will start to notice that the number 10 is used a lot with IEAK. The number of download sites is 10. The number of custom installations is 10. The number of custom applications that can be included with a package is 10. Yes, 10 seems to be Microsoft's magic number for IEAK.*

### Internet Access

Make sure that you have sufficient access rights to the Internet as an administrator to be able to download the most current components of Internet Explorer 4.0 for the IEAK. Also, consider your end users' access rights when deciding on a distribution method.

## Languages

For each language you intend to support, you must create separate distribution packages for each one. In addition, create a subdirectory for each language in your distribution directory. IEAK does this automatically. If you have a similar configuration for each package, you can shorten the length of time it takes to create a new package by using an existing .ins package and modifying the target language.

If your bilingual users will be accessing Web sites that are hosted in a different language, you do not have to create another package. Users can add languages to their browsers.

Here are the steps for adding languages to your browser:

1. Click on View from the menu bar in IE 4.0.

2. Select Internet Options.

3. On the General tab, click on the Languages button.

4. Click on Add.

5. Select all the languages for your browser to read, in order of preference.

## Automatic Version Synchronization (AVS)

When you run IEAK for the first time, you cannot deselect AVS (Automatic Version Synchronization). AVS automatically checks for the latest versions of Internet Explorer and other components as you run the IEAK Wizard. To keep all of your components current, use AVS for each package you create.

After the initial synchronization of all IE 4.0 components, you can disable AVS and create additional packages based on the first synchronization.

Make sure you have a connection to the Internet the first time you run the Wizard. This ensures that AVS can use the Synchronize All Components option.

Table 22-1 is a checklist of all of the components that are synchronized using AVS. You can also use this list to help prepare your custom package.

| **TABLE 22-1** | Component | Function |
| --- | --- | --- |
| Internet Explorer 4.0 Component Suite Selection Guide | Microsoft Internet Explorer 4.0 Web Browser | Allows users to browse the World Wide Web |
| | Microsoft Internet Explorer Core Fonts | Core fonts: Comic Sans, MS, etc. |
| | Microsoft NetMeeting | Enables real-time communication and collaboration |
| | Microsoft Outlook Express | Enhanced e-mail and news client |

**TABLE 22-1**

Internet Explorer 4.0
Component Suite
Selection Guide
(*continued*)

| Component | Function |
|---|---|
| Microsoft Chat 2.0 | Updated Comic Chat |
| Microsoft NetShow | Allows broadcasting to the desktop |
| Intel Indeo 5 | Intel's Digital video captures, compression, and decompression driver |
| VDOLive Player | Allows audio and video streaming over limited bandwidth |
| Microsoft Interactive Music Control | An ActiveX control that plays music in response to a user's actions |
| Microsoft Internet Explorer Sound Pack | Sound scheme for IE 4.0 to play sounds for different events |
| Macromedia Shockwave Director | Allows you to create multimedia productions (kiosk productions, CD-ROM titles, Web content, advertising, and business presentations) |
| Macromedia Shockwave Flash | Allows you to create efficient, vector-based Flash movies to enhance Web pages |
| RealPlayer by Progressive Networks | Multimedia player (animation, audio, video, 3-D images, MIDI, presentations, and text) |
| Microsoft FrontPage Express | A graphical user interface (GUI) for creating HTML pages |
| Microsoft Web Publishing Wizard | Walks you through the steps of publishing your Web pages to nearly any Web server |
| Microsoft Visual Basic Run Time | Allows you to distribute ActiveX controls with your custom package |
| Microsoft Wallet | Allows you to conduct secure financial transactions over the Web with supporting sites. It also stores items such as credit card numbers securely |
| Task Scheduler | Scheduling for IE 4.0 |
| Microsoft Internet Explorer Supplemental Fonts | TrueType fonts that can be used with IE 4.0 (Arial, Comic Courier, Impact, and Times New Roman) |

To verify whether the components are current, Microsoft provides you three symbols:

| Symbol | Meaning |
|---|---|
| Green check mark | The latest version of this component has already been downloaded. |
| Yellow exclamation point | An outdated version of this component has been downloaded or you have not selected AVS. |
| Red X | This component is not currently downloaded. |

**exam**
**ᗯatch**

*The meaning of the AVS symbols will pop up a few times on the exam. Know, for example, what it means if a component has a yellow exclamation point after AVS completes.*

## Branding

One of the most celebrated new features in IEAK is the ability for an organization to *brand* their custom setup (which is created and distributed using IEAK) and the browser (which the end user installs).

Branding options are:

- Customize the CD-ROM Autorun splash screen.
- Brand the Setup Wizard to include the organization's logo and name.
- Brand the browser with the organization's logo.

Customize backgrounds for title bar text and toolbar icons. More instructions on how to use the bitmaps are in the IEAK Help files. Table 22-2 lists some of the graphical enhancements you can customize to brand the browser build to your corporate and/or business specifications.

## Silent Installation (CA only) vs. Multi-Option Installations (Up to 10)

As a corporate administrator (CA), you have to decide whether to perform a silent installation. A silent installation does not allow the end user to select

**TABLE 22-2**

Branding Options

| Type of .bmp File | Size | Use |
|---|---|---|
| Static Logo | 38x38 and 22x22 | Brand IE 4.0 browser with your logo |
| Animated Logo | 38x38 | Brand IE 4.0 browser with your animated logo |
| Active Setup | 120x239 (256 colors) | Brand Active Setup |
| Toolbar | No specific size | Custom toolbar for Control Panel, IE 4.0, Windows 95/Windows NT Explorer, and My Computer |
| Autorun Splash Screen | 540x357 (256 colors) | Provides branded introduction to IE 4.0 for CD-ROM installations |
| Channels | 32x32 (Channel) 80x32 (Channel Bar) 194x32 (Channel Pane) | Custom channels |
| LDAP Service | 134x38 (16 color) | Internet White Pages look-up service |

his/her options or interact with Setup. However, the drawback is that you can have only one custom configuration and one download site. This requires a high degree of maintenance on an administrator's part if there are multiple packages, and it can easily become confusing.

On the other hand, if you have only one set configuration for your entire organization, you know what the default configuration should be, and this becomes handy for help-desk troubleshooting.

The other option is to use the built-in capability to have up to 10 unique configurations that your end user can choose from during Setup. You define the custom configurations while running the Configuration Wizard.

exam
ⓦatch

*Remember that during a silent installation (corporate administrator only) there can only be one download site configured in the custom build.*

# Applications

Iexpress is a tool that comes with IEAK and is used to package a custom application or a third-party application into a .cab file that is self-installing and self-extracting.

If you want to add custom applications to your distribution package, use Iexpress to create the .cab file and add it using the Wizard. IEAK Wizard allows up to 10 custom applications to be added.

# Custom Browser Settings

The following list shows the general options you need to plan for when customizing browser settings.

- Title bar and toolbar bitmaps
- IE4 animated logo (upper right-hand corner)
- Start page
- Support page*
- Search page
- Default favorites
- Welcome page
- Active channels (CDF files)
- My Computer (HTML for Web View)
- Control Panel (HTML for Web View)
- Proxy Server settings
- User agent string

*It is recommended that you create a support Web site to support your end users and add that URL to your custom browser settings.*

Details for corporate administrators and ISPs are provided later in the chapter.

## Centralized Management of Browser Settings

Corporate administrators have the option to automatically configure their users' browsers from a single point. When you enable Automatic Browser Configuration, you can specify a URL for users to connect to so they can download the latest updates to their package. The options you must plan for are:

- Enable automatic browser configuration for end users
- Specify the URL containing user Internet setting (.ins files)
- Specify the URL containing auto-proxy (.js or .pac files)
- Specify a schedule for when automatic configuration occurs, in addition to when the browser is started

INS files are centralized Internet setup files that are checked each time the browser is started to see if anything needs to be updated or reconfigured for the users' browser such as favorites and software updates.

JS, JVS, and PAC script files (JScript and JavaScript) allow you to configure and maintain advanced proxy settings from a central location for client proxy management. Script files can be used independently of, or in conjunction with, IEAK.

By specifying the URLs for both automatic configuration and automatic proxy using the Wizard, you incorporate the settings into the .ins package. Because the script files are incorporated into the .ins file, the correct form for the auto-proxy URL path uses a .ins filename for the script to run properly.

## Security Zones and Site Certificates

IE 4.0 is enhanced by its built-in security. IE 4.0 has security zones. This structure allows an administrator to restrict access to Internet sites by placing them in a zone. Zones range from trusted to restricted. They come with default settings based on common sense utilization of the Internet/intranet. Additionally, an IEAK administrator can customize settings as well. The zones and their default security levels are:

- Local Intranet Zone    Medium
- Trusted Sites Zone    Low
- Internet Zone    Medium
- Restricted Sites Zone    High

*Be prepared to know what the default setting is for each option in every zone. Many of the scenario questions on the exam will test your ability to configure security zones to meet the required and optional results.*

When planning the appropriate security settings for the zones, consider the types of sites in that zone. Sites can vary from Publish Kiosks to Business to End User sites. Security settings vary greatly based on your users' needs. You can create multiple custom security packages for various groups of users with similar needs.

For corporate administrators that must manage both an intranet and Internet, the layers of complexity increase to the $n^{th}$ degree. Make sure you know what solution you need to provide. The settings will follow suit. For example, if you have a team of developers that beta test unsigned ActiveX controls that they get off the Internet on a day-to-day basis, it doesn't make any sense to restrict them from downloading unsigned ActiveX controls.

Another overlooked aspect to planning security strategies is the fact that IE 4.0 fully supports NTLM or Windows NT challenge/response authentication. This is a wonderful way to make sure that passwords are not jeopardized. There are, of course, some drawbacks to using NTLM. For instance, since the actual password is never used in a challenge/response, the IIS server cannot use it to connect to another resource on the network (file server or application). User authentication can be set to high, medium, low, or custom. If you wish to disable authentication and use the Guest account only, use the custom settings and select anonymous logon. The low setting uses NTLM by default.

Table 22-3 lists the security options for IE 4.0.

For security reasons, many users running IE 4.0 have customized security zones. In many cases, they cannot install unsigned ActiveX controls. For this reason and others, use digital signatures to identify where your custom package and any custom programs you may have are from. This allows users to

**TABLE 22-3** Security Options for IE 4.0

| Security Option | High | Medium | Low |
|---|---|---|---|
| **ActiveX Controls and plug-ins** | | | |
| Download unsigned ActiveX controls. | Disable | Disable | Prompt |
| Script ActiveX controls marked safe for scripting. (Active Desktop will not function without this option enabled.) | Enable | Enable | Enable |
| Initialize and script ActiveX controls not marked as safe. | Disable | Prompt | Prompt |
| Download signed ActiveX controls. | Disable | Prompt | Enable |
| Run ActiveX controls and plug-ins. | Disable | Enable | Enable |
| **User Authentication** | | | |
| Logon | Prompt for username and password | Automatic logon only in intranet zone | Automatic logon with current username and password |
| **Downloads** | | | |
| Font download | Prompt | Enable | Enable |
| File download | Disable | Enable | Enable |
| **Java** | | | |
| Java permissions | High safety | High safety | Low safety |
| **Miscellaneous** | | | |
| Software channel permissions | High safety | Medium safety | Low safety |
| Launching applications and files in an IFRAME | Disable | Prompt | Enable |
| Installation of desktop items | Disable | Prompt | Enable |

| TABLE 22-3 | Security Options for IE 4.0 (*continued*) | | |
|---|---|---|---|
| **Security Option** | **High** | **Medium** | **Low** |
| Submit nonencrypted form data | Prompt | Prompt | Enable |
| Drag and drop or copy and paste files | Prompt | Enable | Enable |
| **Scripting** | | | |
| Scripting of Java applets | Disable | Enable | Enable |
| Active scripting | Enable | Enable | Enable |

download your package without warnings. To sign your programs or custom package, first obtain a site certificate. For more information on certificates, visit http://www.microsoft.com/security/ or read Chapter 11.

## Internet Mail and News

Internet mail and news options are:

- Set your Internet POP3 (incoming mail) server, SMTP (outgoing mail) server, domain server, and news servers. If you have a different server for your incoming mail (POP3) and outgoing mail (SMTP), know the names and network paths to these servers.

- Set Outlook Express as the default mail and news client. If you would like to have a standardized e-mail and news client, set Outlook Express as the default.

- Secure Password Authentication (SPA) can be set to authenticate users' logons.

- Set Lightweight Directory Access Protocol (LDAP) settings. If you want your clients to be able to access the information contained in the directory structure of an Exchange Server on your network, include LDAP in your custom package.

- Set the InfoPane and welcome message for Outlook Express. The InfoPane allows ISPs and corporate administrators to have important information placed where the user has immediate access, for example: a URL for a support page, company name and phone number, logos, and more. This information is located at the bottom of the Outlook Express window.

  If you plan to customize the InfoPane and provide content and support information to your users, the Wizard is the only place you can do this. If you are trying to cut down on bandwidth used on your network, choose a local file instead of a URL. This way, the Wizard imports the file into your package, and the file is placed on the users' hard disks during installation. By default, the user can turn this option on or off.

- Set default signature files for e-mail and news messages.

## System Policies and Restrictions (IEAK Configuration Wizard)

You can restrict and customize these areas:

- NetMeeting
- Active Desktop
- Internet Properties
- Outlook Express
- Shell
- Channels and subscriptions
- Microsoft Chat
- Internet Explorer advanced settings
- Internet code download

If you are not familiar with any one of these components, spend some time with them. This chapter discusses the major components in more detail later.

exam
ⓦatch

*Microsoft expects you to be proficient at configuring and planning in all of these areas for the exam.*

The majority of work in the planning stage is information gathering. Even in a small organization, this can be a time-consuming task. When going through the Configuration Wizard, being familiar with the previous issues can save you much time and energy.

# Additional Planning Considerations for ISPs

As an ISP, you do not have as much control over restrictions and policies that a corporate administrator has, but that does not mean that you do not have as much to plan for. In both cases, test your distributions in a lab until they work across all necessary platforms. For an ISP, consider what type of sign-up process your customer should perform.

There are two types of sign-up methods:

- Server-Based
- Non-Server-Based

Non-server-based sign-up is via CD-ROM or multiple floppy disks. The user only has to change the username, password, and connection configuration to set up an account and use your browser.

The server-based method uses a single floppy disk to configure the connection to a server by using a generic .isp file. Once connected, the server gathers information from a user and then sends a unique configuration file (.ins file) to the user. The Internet Explorer Setup then uses the file to configure the desktop computer.

For more information on this, see the IEAK Help on preparation for running the Wizard.

## Using the IEAK Configuration Wizard

Additionally, an ISP administrator must be able to use the Internet Connection Manager in ISP mode. Plan for:

- Modem detection
- Stack installation
- Dial-up connections

In order to create the single floppy disk option, these settings must be configured using the IEAK Configuration Wizard in ISP mode.

**CERTIFICATION OBJECTIVE 22.05**

# Using the Wizard

Microsoft divides the Wizard into five stages:

- Gathering Information
- Specifying Active Setup Parameters
- Customizing Active Setup
- Customizing the Browser
- Component Customization

This section takes you through the five stages screen by screen. In each stage contains at least four dialog boxes. Depending on whether you are an ISP, ICP, or corporate administrator, and what options you select, you are presented with additional screens. For this example, we will show how a corporate administrator builds a custom package.

For exam study purposes, I will comment on the differences between what options you have as an ISP compared to a Corporate Administrator.

The first time you run the Wizard, expect it to take approximately one hour. If you are a corporate administrator and you have already obtained your 10-digit customization code, please use this as an exercise. If you have not yet obtained your customization code or your license agreement is ISP, continue reading. All screen shots are provided for you to see the complete process.

If you plan to use this as an exercise, you should have:

- One server and one client machine that are networked

- Obtained a customization code for the corporate administrator role

The server should have:

- Windows NT Server 4.0 with SP3
- Access to the Internet (dial-up or network)
- Installed IE 4.0 (full installation with Active Desktop)
- Installed IEAK
- Have Internet Information Server (IIS) 3.0 or higher installed on the same machine as IEAK and IE 4.0 with all the default paths and directory names
- At least 200MB of free hard disk space for your custom packages

The client should have:

- Windows 95 or Windows NT Workstation
- IE 3.*x* (installs by default with Windows NT)

You can start IEAK Configuration Wizard using the Run command:

1. On the Start menu, click Run.
2. Type **C:\Program Files\IEAK\ieakwiz.exe** inside the Run dialog box.
3. Click OK.

If you have not loaded IE 4.0, the Wizard warns you that this is the time to stop and do it, as illustrated in Figure 22-1.

Use the standard navigation keys to get around in the Wizard. Use the Next button to accept the values and display the next page. Use the Back button to return to a previous screen to view or edit entries. Use the Cancel button to exit the Wizard.

Heed the licensing warning, and continue by clicking on Next, as shown in Figure 22-2.

**FIGURE 22-1**

IEAK Configuration Wizard
welcome page

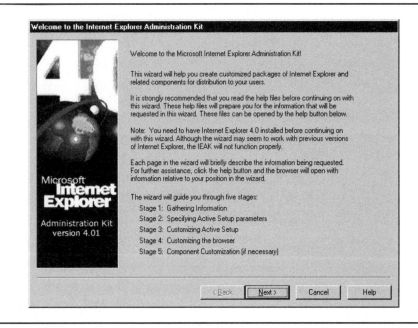

**FIGURE 22-2**

Stage 1: Gathering
information

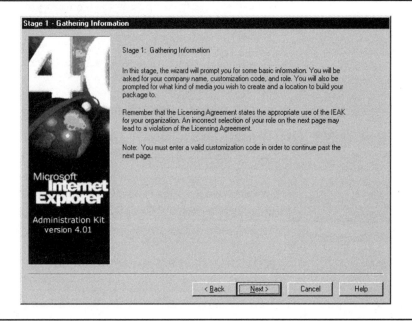

For the following steps, refer to Figure 22-3.

1. Enter your company name. This name is placed in the registry and will be used by future custom packages.

2. Enter your customization code (the 10-digit code provided by Microsoft).

3. Select the role of corporate administrator.

4. Leave AVS selected. If you are not connected to the Internet, do not select AVS.

5. Click Next.

You will not be able to continue without the customization code.

Select English (the default target language), as shown in Figure 22-4. Remember that if you want to support multiple languages, you must create a custom package for each one. It is not possible to select more than one language at a time. Click the Next button to continue.

**FIGURE 22-3**

Stage 1: Enter company name and customization code

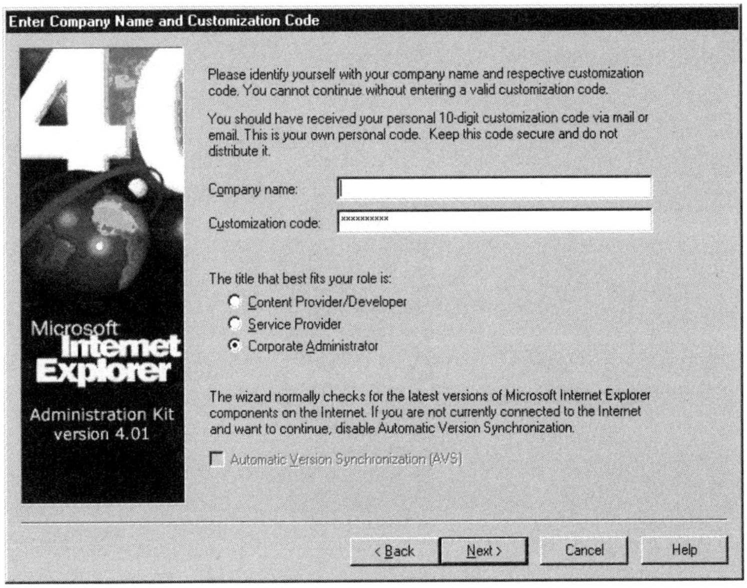

Stage 1: Select a language

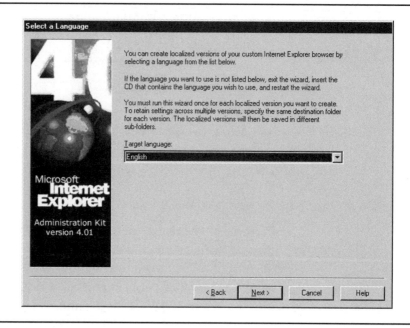

Now you decide how to distribute your custom package (see Figure 22-5). Enter a local path or a path for a network drive. For now, use a local path and let the Wizard create the directory.

If your goal is to create multiple browser packages for each group of users in your organization, where the differences between the packages are slight, you can use your .ins file as a template in the following manner: For each modified package, create a new folder, copy the .ins file from the original destination folder, and then specify the new folder as the destination folder for the new package.

1. Type **c:\inetpub\wwwroot\cie** in the Destination Folder field.

2. Select CD-ROM.

3. Click on Next to continue.

Active Setup has several components. Each component can be added or removed from your custom setup. Active Setup is dynamic. If Active Setup terminates due to a connectivity issue, it can resume where it stopped because

Stage 1: Select media to distribute your browser

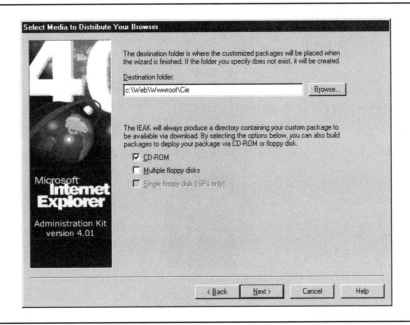

it installs each component separately by utilizing self-extracting, self-installing .cab and .exe files. Active Setup tracks the progress by utilizing log files and registry keys.

*For the exam, understand how Active Setup works and how you use IEAK to customize it.*

Follow Figure 22-6 and the other screen shots carefully as each stage is described. Pay close attention to the process of building a package. Knowing at which stage each item is customized will help you when taking the exam. After reading the page, click Next to continue.

IEAK provides a drop-down list of sites to choose from (see Figure 22-7). Select the download site closest to your geographic location from the drop-down list. Click on Next to continue.

Now that you've selected a download site, the Wizard automatically begins to download the most current versions of all the available components. If AVS had not been selected, all icons would appear with yellow exclamation points.

**FIGURE 22-6**

Stage 2: Specifying Active
Setup parameters

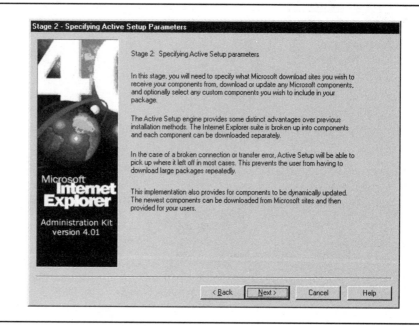

**FIGURE 22-7**

Stage 2: Select a Microsoft
download site

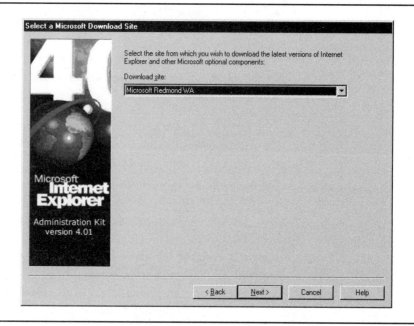

This process can take a great deal of time, especially for the larger components if they are out of date.

After the first time you run the Wizard, you can deselect AVS and synchronize only the components you want to add to your custom package. Each subsequent time you create a package takes less time because you need to modify only the original package.

Once synchronization has completed, green check marks appear next to all Microsoft components, as illustrated in Figure 22-8.

exam
ⓦatch

*Microsoft uses green check marks to represent that a component is current; yellow exclamation points represent components that are outdated; and red Xs represent components that are unavailable.*

The dialog box in Figure 22-9 is where you can specify up to 10 custom components to install with your package. The name you type for the component appears on the user's screen during Active Setup. These custom

---

**FIGURE 22-8**

Stage 2: Automatic Version
Synchronization (AVS)

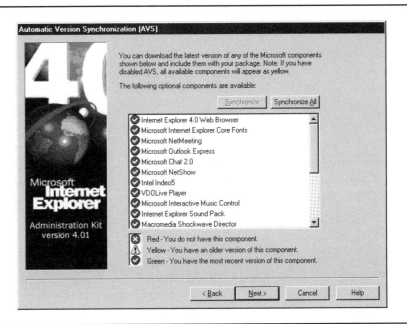

FIGURE 22-9

Stage 2: Specify custom
Active Setup components

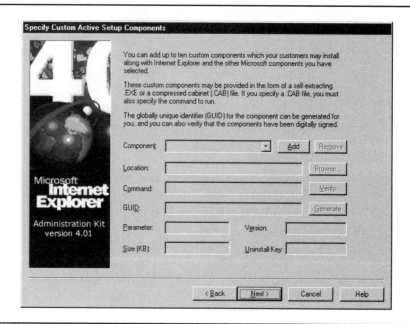

components need to be in either the .cab or .exe formats. The tool for creating .cab files is Iexpress.

Your custom .cab files will not work unless you enter a command for each one. If you have custom .exe files, enter parameters or switches to be run with your executable. You also have the option to test the executables and commands at this point.

Microsoft recommends signing your custom code. This assures the end user that they are receiving trustworthy code. If you plan to distribute your custom package, you must sign custom components. When you sign your custom package, obtain a digital certificate from a Certificate Authority (CA). You must sign custom .cab files for distribution. However, if you do not, the package still works. A warning just informs the user that the package is untrustworthy. Here are the files that must be signed:

- Branding.cab
- Desktop.cab

- IE4cif.cab
- IE4Setup.exe
- All Folder(*x*).cab files
- All chl(*xxxx*).cab files
- All custom applications (.cab and .exe)

If you have not generated a globally unique identifier (GUID), you can click on the Generate button to have IEAK create one for you. A GUID is an identifier that is used to distinguish a program or object from others. Because of the method used to derive the GUID, it can never be re-created and therefore is always unique.

If you are adding custom components, select a publisher to sign your files and then select that publisher or CA from the list of trusted publishers on the machine on which you are running IEAK, as illustrated in Figure 22-10. Click on Next to continue.

---

**FIGURE 22-10**

Stage 2: Specify
trusted publishers

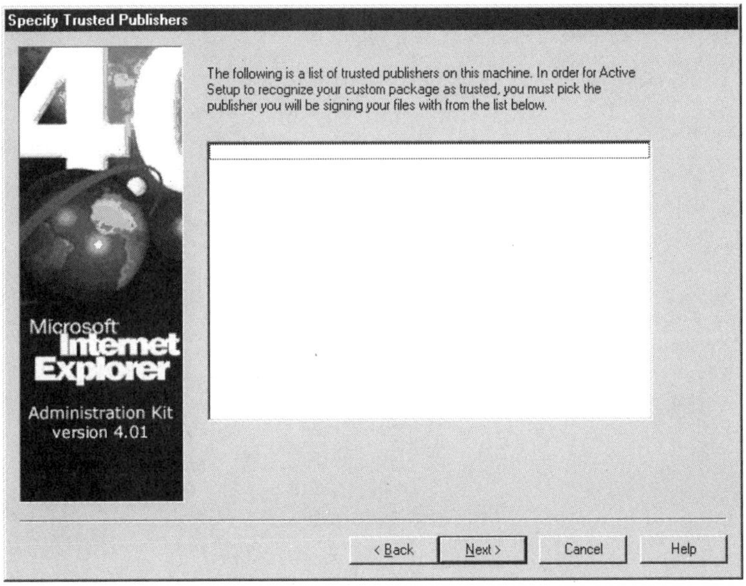

In Stage 3, you need to configure Active Setup. From branding to distribution media to distribution servers' URLs, you specify the look, feel, and functionality of your package (see Figure 22-11).

Since we selected CD-ROM as a distribution medium, there is an additional screen in this stage as well (see Figure 22-12). This dialog box lets you customize the Autorun screen to assist the user with installation of your CD package. Take the following steps:

1. Type **My Custom CD Package** in the title bar text field.

2. Leave all other settings at their defaults.

3. Click on Next to continue.

In the dialog box in Figure 22-13, enter what the user will see in the title bar of Active Setup:

1. Type **My Custom Setup** in the Active Setup wizard title bar text field.

2. Leave the bitmap path blank.

3. Click on Next to continue.

---

**FIGURE 22-11**

Stage 3: Customizing
Active Setup

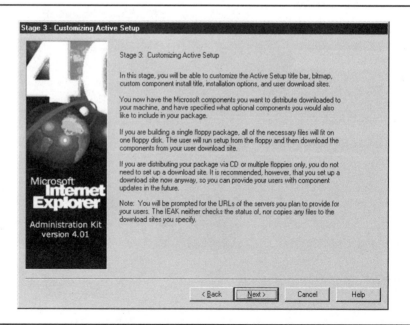

**FIGURE** 22-12

Stage 3: Customize the
Autorun screen for
CD-ROM installations

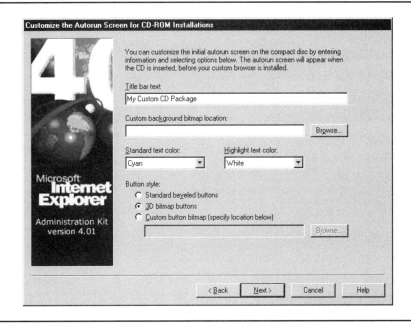

**FIGURE** 22-13

Stage 3: Customize the
Active Setup Wizard

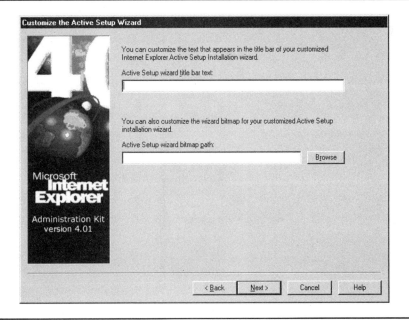

For more information on creating custom bitmaps, see IEAK Help.

In the dialog box in Figure 22-14, you can "install package silently" (the default). You are also reminded of what the limitations are to your users and yourself. This option is not available to ISPs or ICPs. There are only two options that require creating a separate package: One is language and the other is a silent installation.

■  Deselect the option, Install package silently.

■  Click on Next to continue.

In conjunction with the three preset options (Minimal, Standard, and Full), you may specify a total of 10 installation options. Corporate administrators can use this feature to create custom setups for different user groups. ISPs can use this feature to deliver IE 4.0 to different types of customers.

**FIGURE 22-14**

Stage 3: Select silent installation

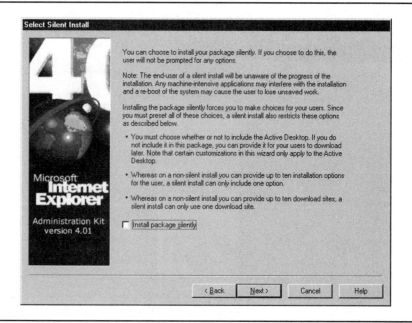

The components you can add are all those you have downloaded for IE 4.0 and any custom components you added during Stage 2 (see Figure 22-15).

1. Select Full Installation from the Option list box.

2. Review the components you are installing in the Components to install list box.

3. Highlight Internet Explorer 4.0 Web Browser.

4. Click on the < button. Note that you cannot remove the browser.

5. Click on the << button. Note that everything except the browser is removed.

6. Click on the >> button. All components are now back.

---

Stage 3: Select
installation options

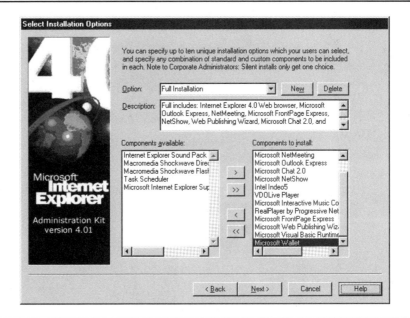

7. Remove the following by selecting the component from the right pane and clicking on the < button (they will appear in the left-hand pane):

   ■ Internet Explorer Sound Pack

   ■ Macromedia Shockwave Director

   ■ Macromedia Shockwave Flash

   ■ Task Scheduler

   ■ Microsoft Internet Explorer Supplemental Fonts

8. You now have restored "Full Installation" to its original configuration.

9. Click on Next to continue

In the Specify Download URLs dialog box (Figure 22-16), you must specify at least one URL. If you are performing a silent installation, you may only choose one. If you are an ISP or you want multiple download sites to balance your network load, you can add up to 10 sites.

1. Click the Add button.

2. Type **Corporate HQ WWW** in the Site Name field.

3. Type **http://**_computername_/**cie** where "_computername_" is your distribution server name in the Site URL field.

4. Click on the Add button again.

5. Type **Corporate HQ FTP** in the Site Name field.

6. Type **ftp://**_computername_/**cie** where "_computername_" is your distribution server name in the Site URL field. Note that the Wizard will append the subdirectory /IE4site to this URL. You should not add this yourself as it will still include it and you will find yourself with two IE4site directories specified.

7. Verify that both entries appear in the Custom Download Sites box.

8. Click on Next to continue.

Failure to properly enter the URL at this stage will cause your users' installation process to fail. There are two files that store the URL information:

FIGURE 22-16

Stage 3: Specify
download URLs

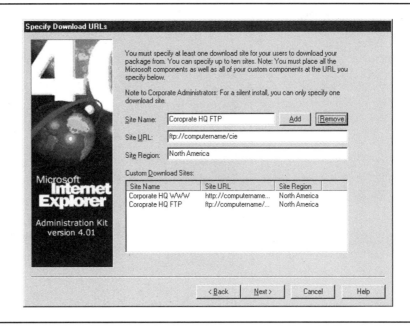

ie4setup.inf and ie4setup.dat. If at some point the IE4site folder is moved, you need to update the URL in the ie4setup.dat file.

The built-in version numbering mechanism provides you with the means to guarantee that the proper build of your customized package is installed, as illustrated in Figure 22-17. You must have a version number to keep users from loading an older build on top of a newer one. For example, version 2*0*0*0 is newer than 1*0*0*1.

You use the configuration identifier to prevent older custom versions of the browser from overwriting a newer one. However, for this to work properly, the company name (entered in Stage 1) must be the same for the two custom packages.

Use the Add-On Component URL to allow users to update IE 4.0 via Help or Control Panel, Add/Remove Programs. If you leave this blank, the default URL is determined by using the first download site you specified and Addon95.htm or Addonnt.htm. This will result, in our case, to be http://*computername*/cie/addon95.htm or http://*computername*/cie/addonnt.htm.

**FIGURE 22-17**

Stage 3: Select version
information and Add-On
Component URL

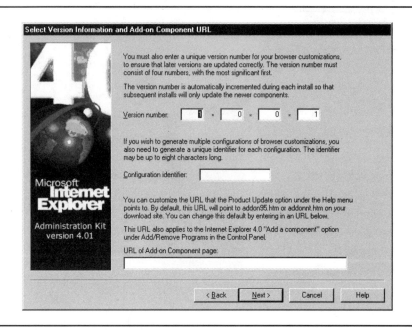

For more information on customizing the Add-On Components, see the IEAK
4.0 Help "Add-On Components."

When you modify an existing version of a package, IEAK will automatically
increment the version number of the modified package:

1. Verify that the version number is 1*0*0*1.

2. Click on Next to continue.

Only a corporate administrator can specify a custom path for IE 4.0 on the
user's machine (Figure 22-18). If the user doesn't have the custom path already
on his/her PC, it is created during Setup. If you are upgrading from IE 3.*x*, IE
4.0 installs over the existing directory. This means that for upgrading
purposes, your specified custom path is not used.

1. Verify that the default, Install in the specified folder within the
   Program Files folder, is selected.

2. Click on Next to continue.

**FIGURE 22-18**

Stage 3: Specify where
you want to install
your browser

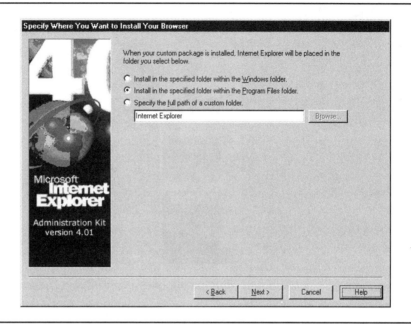

The Windows Desktop Update merges your Internet browser with your
standard desktop and integrates the functionality of both. It enhances the
taskbar and Explorer windows as well. When the update is installed with your
package, users can browse their local machines like they browse the Internet.
Active content can be placed on the desktop, and you can specify later in the
Wizard which custom channels to make available. Figure 22-19 contains an
example of this.

If you are a corporate administrator and you have not opted to perform a
silent installation, your users can install the Desktop Update, as illustrated in
Figure 22-19.

1. Verify that User choice is selected.

2. Click on Next to continue.

Figure 22-20 is an example of how the look and feel of a Web browser has
been merged with a standard window folder. There are Back and Forward
navigation buttons and the folder itself has a customized background.

**FIGURE  22-19**

Stage 3: Integrating the
Windows Desktop Update

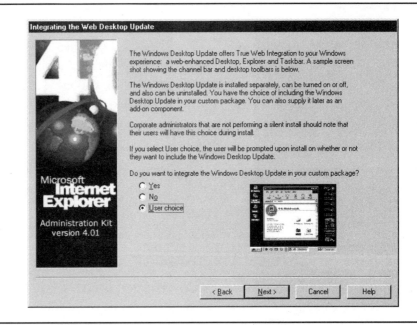

**FIGURE  22-20**

Web-enhanced folder

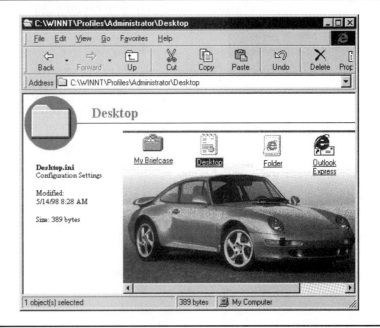

Note that the selected file (desktop.ini) properties are shown in the left pane. A desktop.ini file is generated for each folder using Web view. The underlined filenames represent a single-click Web-like action for opening them.

Table 22-4 contains a list of all available options in Stage 4. You will be expected to be an expert on which options are uniquely available to each role and which ones are standard. Go through this portion on the Configuration Wizard (Figure 22-21) several times and use this table as a guide to acquaint yourself with all the different options.

The ICP is not in the table. The ICP can:

■ Set Start, Search, and Support pages.

■ Customize Favorites list.

■ Change the title bar and logos of the browser.

■ Add a channel and delete a channel.

**TABLE 22-4**  Custom Browser Settings

| General Settings | Corporate Administrators | Internet Service Providers |
|---|---|---|
| Browser title bar and toolbar background bitmap | Custom active channel bar | Add one custom channel and delete direct competitors. |
| Internet Explorer logo in the upper right-hand corner of the browser | Desktop toolbar settings | Add one custom desktop component. |
| Star, Search, and Online support pages | Software distribution channels | Sign-up method: Server or Server-less |
| Favorites, Favorites folders, and links for the Links bar | Proxy settings | Custom sign-up files |
| Welcome messages and desktop wallpaper | Settings for site certificates and Authenticode Security | Customize dial-up networking connection settings. |
| Active Desktop items | Settings for security zones and ratings | Provide path for logon scripting script file. |
| My Computer and Control Panel | | |
| User agent string | | |
| Automatic Browser Configuration | | |

**FIGURE** 22-21

Stage 4: Customizing
the browser

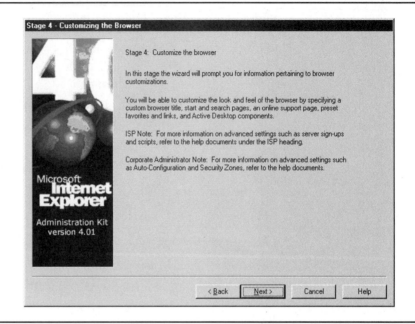

- Customize the appearance of the Setup program and configure types of installation (such as Standard, Minimal, and Full).

- Point users to Internet or intranet servers to access the latest product versions with Active Setup.

- To specify the language version of Internet Explorer; you must create a custom package for each language version you want to create.

- Enable automatic software distribution over the Internet.

In the dialog box in Figure 22-22, you can brand your custom browser and Outlook Express. By default, this option is not selected.

1. Select Customize Title Bars.

2. By default, the name of your company appears as you entered it in Stage 1. If it is not there, enter it now.

3. Leave the Toolbar background bitmap blank. If you wish to create a background bitmap, follow the guidelines in the IEAK Help documents.

4. Click on Next to continue.

**FIGURE** 22-22

Stage 4: Customize the
window title and toolbar
background

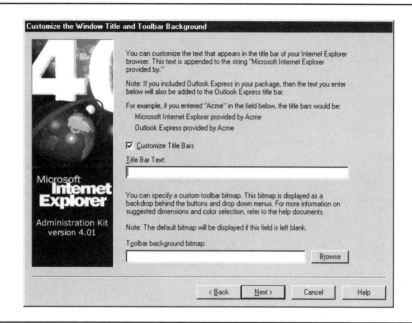

You can now select what URLs your users will use to search the Web and
what home page they will get when they start IE 4.0 (see Figure 22-23). If you
are using your own home page and search engine, take time at this point to
test the URLs you have supplied. This will save you from post-installation
troubleshooting. If you typed the URL incorrectly or there is a connectivity
problem, you can troubleshoot before the package is completed.

If you are upgrading from IE 3.*x*, the Search pane is a new feature of IE 4.0
and replaces the Search page. The Search pane gives the user the ability to
search in the left-hand pane of the screen and read the content of a Web page
in the right pane.

Following the dialog box in Figure 22-23:

1. Make sure you are connected to the Internet.

2. Click on the Test URL button for home page URL.

3. Close IE.

4. Click on the Test URL button for Search pane URL.

**FIGURE 22-23**

Stage 4: Customize the
start and search pages

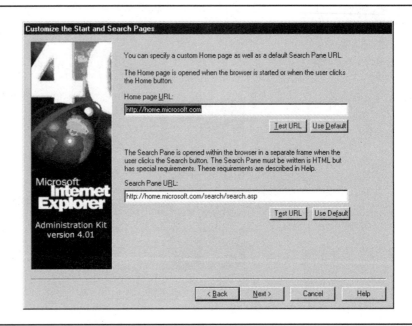

5. Close IE.

6. Click on Next to continue.

If you plan to provide full support to your end users, you cannot leave this part out during distribution of your custom browser (see Figure 22-24). Your support page should take as much time to develop as it did to prepare your custom package. If you do not have a complete help site set up now, leave this blank. By leaving it blank, your users are directed to Microsoft's online Help.

1. Leave the Online support page URL blank.

2. Click on Next to continue.

Use this page to build a hierarchy of folders for your users to store their favorite URLs. You can also add links to sites that are critical to your own organization in addition to your online Help. All URLs can be tested by highlighting a URL and clicking on the Test URL button, as illustrated in

FIGURE 22-24

Stage 4: Specifying an
online support page for
your browser

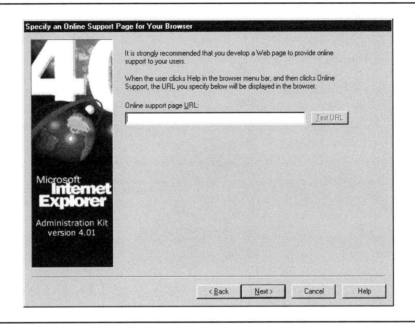

Figure 22-25. You can specify up to 200 favorites to be included with your
custom package. You also can import a folder of favorites.

1. Expand each folder.

2. Test each URL.

3. Click on Next to continue.

When a user starts IE 4.0 for the first time, a welcome message appears.
This is quite different from the home page. You can use Microsoft's default
welcome message or create your own and set the URL here (see Figure 22-26).
If your users choose to install the Windows Desktop Update, they are
welcomed to IE 4.0 with a welcome message. Using the Wizard, you can turn
this message on or off.

The other thing you can do in this dialog box is to brand your custom
package to set the desktop wallpaper to be used by all of the users who install
your custom package. However, this option does not work if you use the same
filename for wallpaper that is currently on the users' desktops.

**FIGURE 22-25**

Stage 4: Favorites folder
and links customization

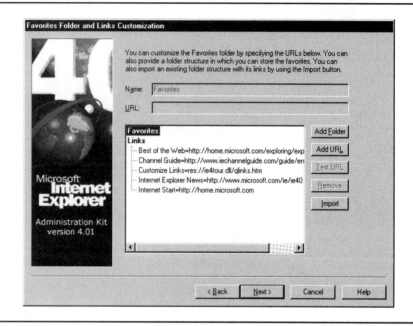

**FIGURE 22-26**

Stage 4: Customize the
welcome message and
desktop wallpaper

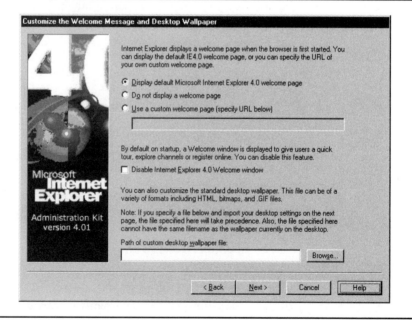

We recommend that you allow the welcome message to appear to the user. It links them to the tour of IE 4.0 and to the Help documents.

1. Verify that the option, Display default Microsoft Internet Explorer 4.0 welcome page, is selected.

2. Click on Next to continue.

Customizing the Active Channel bar (Figure 22-27) is a three-step procedure. First, delete unwanted channels (corporate administrator role) or channels that are a competitor's channel (ISP/ICP role). For more information, refer to your licensing agreement and to Table 22-1.

Second, add the channels from the Channel Guide provided by the Wizard. For the third step to work, you must configure your current desktop to represent what you want your users to have.

Third, specify that the Wizard import that configuration. In Stage 5, you have the ability to set a policy that keeps users from changing the Active Channel configuration. You can limit even what they can add or remove from

**FIGURE 22-27**

Stage 4: Customize the Active Channel bar

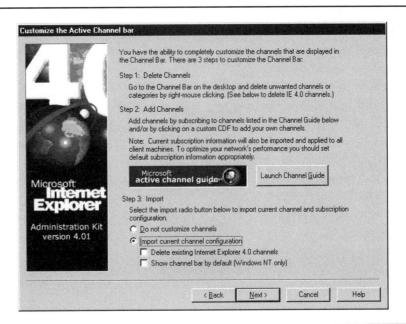

it. If your installation is on Windows NT, you can also show the channel bar by default.

1. Verify that the option, Import current channel configuration, is selected.

2. Click on Next to continue.

3. Verify that the option, Do not customize channels, is selected.

4. Click on Next to continue.

Configuring the Open Software Distribution (OSD) section of a .cdf file creates a Software Distribution Channel (see Figure 22-28). There must be a SOFTPKG reference for each application to be distributed. The Setting AUTOINSTALL=YES and STYLE=Active Setup within the SOFTPKG reference causes the applications to be updated automatically. In addition, a USAGE VALUE=Software Update must appear in the .cdf file.

---

**FIGURE 22-28**

Customize Software
Distribution Channels

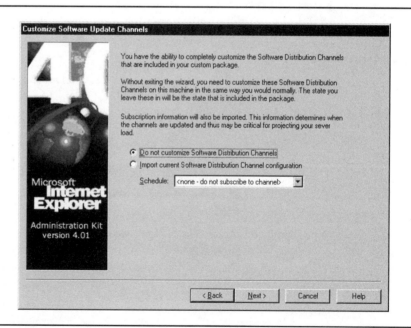

The corporate administrator's custom Software Distribution Channels should be configured on the computer and imported into the Wizard. If you choose to import from your desktop, you must choose one of the following schedules for the channels: <None -- do not subscribe to channel>, Auto, Daily, Monthly, Weekly. Auto uses the preconfigured times set by the Channel Definition Format (CDF) file, so you need to find out if the .cdf file has scheduling information in it. Be very careful that you do not select the default Schedule Option by accident. This forces the user to subscribe before he/she receives updates. The Schedule options are:

- <None -- do not subscribe to channel> (default)
- Auto
- Daily
- Monthly
- Weekly

The next three dialog boxes from the Wizard appear only if you have Windows Desktop Update (Active Desktop) installed and running on the same machine. If you plan to create custom desktop configurations for your users, you need to make the changes directly on your desktop and then import them while running the Wizard.

Before you import the current Active Desktop components, you have two ways to verify/change the settings. Use the Modify Settings button or make the changes directly to the desktop. You do not need to exit IEAK to do this. Figures 22-29 and 22-30 illustrate these two options.

1. Select Import the current Active Desktop components.

2. Click on the Modify Settings button.

3. View the options in each of the tabs (Background, Web, and Plus).

4. Click on Cancel.

5. Click on Next to continue.

Active Desktop allows you to add toolbars to your Windows taskbar. If you have created any custom toolbars or you want to create a standard toolbar for

FIGURE 22-29

Stage 4: Specify Active
Desktop components

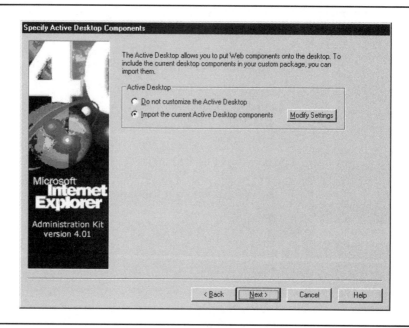

FIGURE 22-30

Display properties accessed
by the Modify Settings
button (Web tab)

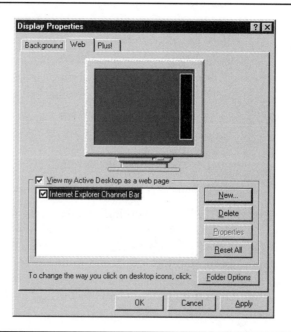

all your users, configure the toolbars the way you want them on your desktop and import them into your package, as illustrated in Figure 22-31.

1. Select the option, Do not customize Desktop Toolbars.

2. Click on Next to continue.

If you plan to use Explorer Web View, you can customize how My Computer and Control Panel look and function (see Figure 22-32). Web View is when My Computer and Control Panel appear as Web pages. You can customize the Web View to include your company logo, instructions on use, links to support sites, and more.

There are two template files that you must customize:

- Mycomp.htt
- Controlp.htt

**FIGURE 22-31**

Stage 4: Customize
desktop toolbars

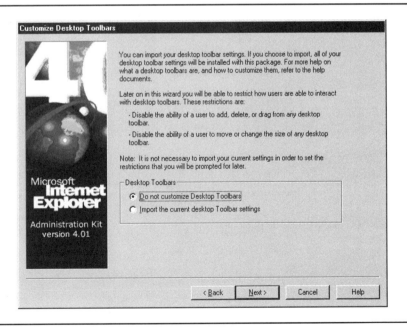

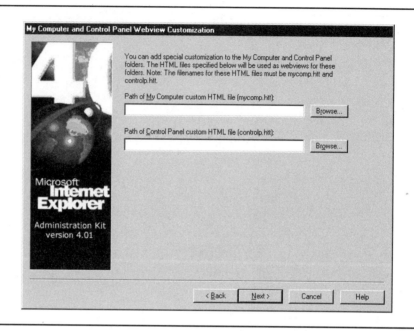

For more information on customizing these two files, see IEAK Help, My Computer and Control Panel Web View customization. After you have customized these files, specify the paths to the files so that they are included in your custom package.

1. Leave both path statements blank.

2. Click on Next to continue.

User agent strings allow administrators of Web servers that your browser visits to track information about the users that are visiting. Adding a custom appendage to this allows you to track different groups of users and gather statistics from other Internet sites.

By default, the user agent string (Mozilla/4.0-compatible, MSIE 4.0, Windows NT) provides:

- **Browser type**    Mozilla/4.0-compatible

- **Browser version**    MSIE 4.0

- **Operating system**    Windows NT

If you want to track the username (%USERNAME%) or package version number, add those to the string on the User Agent String Customization dialog box (Figure 22-33). By adding a custom string, you are making information about your users available to the world.

1. Leave the default string.

2. Click on Next to continue.

If you want your users' configurations to be updated automatically, dynamically, or on a regular schedule, and/or you have advanced proxy settings (using script files) that must be maintained, enable Automatic Browser Configuration (ABC), as illustrated in Figure 22-34. The script formats can be .js, .jvs, or .pac files. ABC is also useful if you need to block a range or group of Web addresses from your users.

The custom package (.ins file) incorporates the proxy script files if both auto-configure and auto-proxy URLs are entered. To create an auto-configuration file, you can use an existing .ins file as a template. Once the

---

**FIGURE** 22-33

Stage 4: User agent string customization

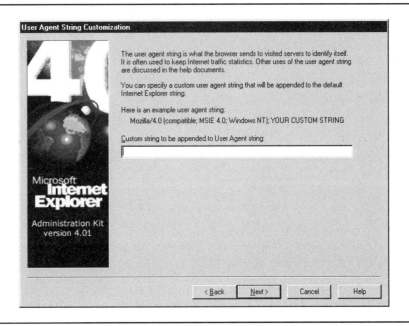

FIGURE 22-34

Stage 4: Automatic
browser configuration

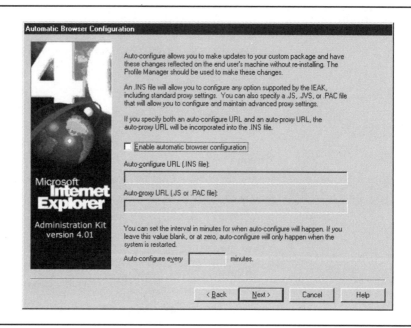

auto-configuration file is created, it can be placed on a server, and a reference
can be made to it using the Auto-Configure URL (.ins file) field in the
Automatic Browser Configuration page. When the user opens IE, their
browser is updated. You can also specify the interval at which auto-
configuration occurs. Leaving the Auto-configure every field blank sets
auto-configuration to happen when the system is restarted. The client will be
configured with these settings in the Internet Properties dialog box in the
Connection tab for the Automatic Configuration option. See Figures 22-35A
and 22-35B for more detail.

There are two reasons not to use the proxy settings on the dialog box in
Figure 22-36: you do not have a proxy server or you are using auto-proxy
scripts. If you have a proxy server and you do not use scripts, then you can

**FIGURE 22-35A**

Internet Properties

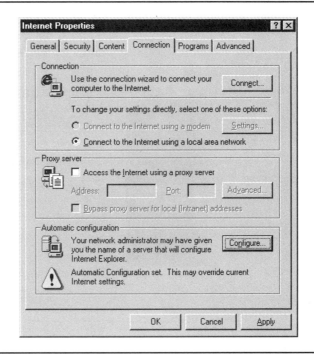

**FIGURE 22-35B**

Automatic Configuration

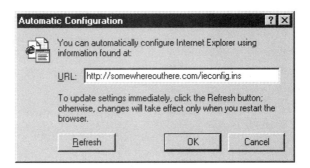

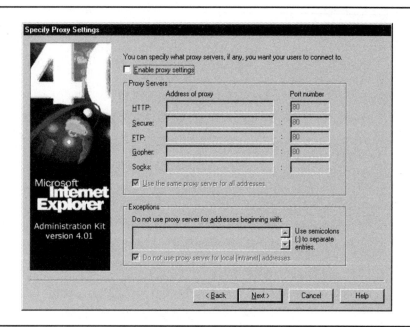

**FIGURE 22-36**

Stage 4: Specify proxy settings

select Enable proxy settings and enter the settings on this page for these protocol services:

- HTTP
- Secure
- FTP
- Gopher
- SOCKS

Note that you use the Secure option when you need to specify a server and port for HTTPS (HTTPSecure).

If all of these services are on the same server, enter the address once in the HTTP Address field and select the option, Use the same proxy server for all addresses. Otherwise, enter the URL for the server and the port number. In the Exceptions box, you can specify URLs that do not use the proxy. Valid entries in the Exceptions box are:

- FQDNs with wildcards (*.company.com); Internet address must have FQDNs
- IP addresses
- Computer names

For local access, select the option, Do not use proxy server for local (intranet) addresses, as illustrated in Figure 22-36.

1. Remove the check mark from Enable proxy settings.

2. Click on Next to continue.

On this dialog box, you can import site certificates and Authenticode settings that you have preconfigured on your computer to become part of your custom package (see Figure 22-37). This is the first step toward securing IE 4.0.

Digital certificates and Microsoft Authenticode have become a standard for ensuring that individuals and organizations can be identified and trusted with

Stage 4: Site certificate and Authenticode settings

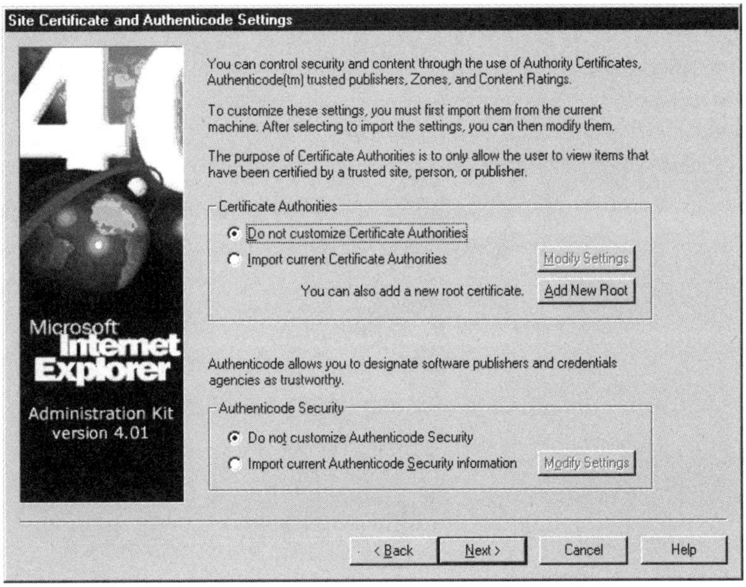

the code they are providing on the Web. They are the electronic equivalent to shrink-wrapping a product. This is to show the customer that the code has not been tampered with since it came from the manufacturer.

There are two possible reasons a user might have trouble downloading trusted code from a Web site: One is if the user is still using Authenticode 1.0. The second is if the author of the code has an expired certificate.

1. Leave all the defaults.

2. Click on Next to continue.

The second part of securing IE 4.0 is to import your preconfigured security zones and content ratings. If you have not preconfigured these settings, use the Modify Setting buttons for zones and ratings provided on this page of the Wizard (see Figure 22-38). Table 22-3, earlier in this chapter, provides all of the default settings for High, Medium, and Low security levels to help you decide which is best for your different zones. You may need to develop custom

---

Stage 4: Security zones
and content ratings
customization

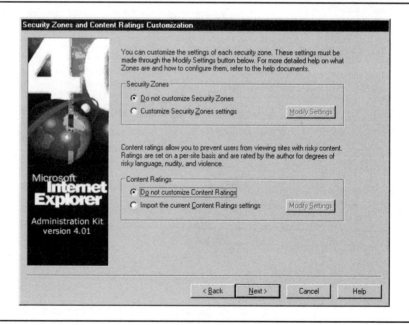

---

settings for one or more of the four zones. The zones and their default security levels are:

- **Local Intranet Zone**   Medium
- **Trusted Sites Zone**   Low
- **Internet Zone**   Medium
- **Restricted Sites Zone**   High

exam
ⓦatch

*Be prepared to know what the default setting is for each option in every zone. Many of the scenario questions on the exam will test your ability to configure security zones to meet the required and optional results.*

The security zones settings are made in the Internet Properties dialog box under the Security tab (see Figure 22-39). You can configure a zone by

---

**FIGURE 22-39**

Internet Properties
Security tab

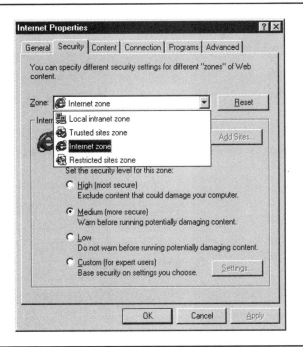

selecting it from the "zone" list box and then selecting High, Medium, Low, or Custom.

Another advantage IE 4.0 has over its predecessor is the ability to customize the security level for each item individually. With IE 3.0 your only choices were High, Medium, or Low. Custom is a new setting. Only advanced users with a clear understanding of Internet security should use the Custom setting. Figure 22-40 contains the dialog box for specifying these settings.

To finish securing IE 4.0, set a Content Rating policy using the dialog box in Figure 22-41. By default, ratings are not enabled. To successfully implement content ratings, you need to understand how the rating system works.

Table 22-5 lists the categories and their corresponding rating levels. Use this table to develop your security policy in combination with security zones, site certificates, and Microsoft Authenticode.

Of the five levels, Level 4 is the highest rating and gives users the most access. By default, when content ratings are enabled, they are set to 0 (least amount of access) for each category.

---

**FIGURE 22-40**

Security tab Custom
Settings dialog box

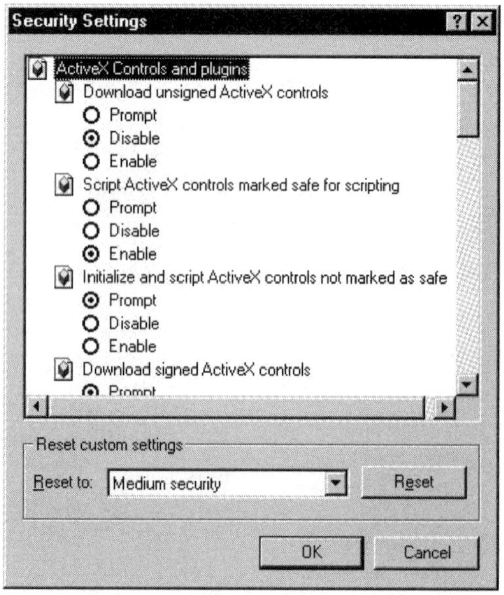

**FIGURE 22-41**

Content Advisor

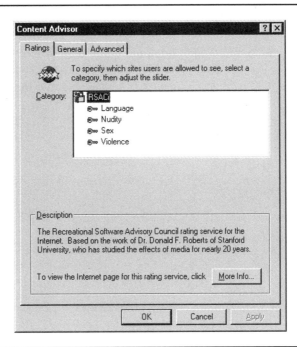

**TABLE 22-5**     Content Ratings

| Category | Level 0 | Level 1 | Level 2 | Level 3 | Level 4 |
|----------|---------|---------|---------|---------|---------|
| Language | Inoffensive slang | Mild expletives | Moderate expletives | Obscene gestures | Explicit or crude language |
| Nudity | None | Revealing attire | Partial nudity | Frontal nudity | Provocative frontal nudity |
| Sex | None | Passionate kissing | Clothed sexual touching | Nonexplicit sexual touching | Explicit sexual activity |
| Violence | No violence | Fighting | Killing | Killing with blood and gore | Wanton and gratuitous violence |

Under the General tab, there is the option, Users can see sites that have no rating. The rating system was developed by the Recreational Software Advisory Council (RSAC). Only a site that has been rated is validated. Be very careful with this selection. Many corporate intranet sites are not rated. Therefore, you may be restricting critical sites. On the other hand, if you select this option, you can open a hole in your security policy.

For the next two steps, refer to Figure 22-38.

1. Verify that you are not importing zones or ratings.

2. Click on Next to continue.

Stage 5 is the final stage of building a custom package (see Figure 22-42). If you chose Outlook Express as an option for your package, you need to complete the next four dialog boxes in the Wizard:

- Specify Internet Mail Server, Domain, and News Server
- Specify LDAP Server Settings
- Outlook Express Customizations
- Include a Signature

The second-to-last dialog box is the System Policies and Restrictions dialog box. On this dialog box, specify information that would be cumbersome to an end user. Outlook Express is a dynamic Internet client; it gives you great versatility. However, with that versatility comes a great deal to configure. Fortunately, the IEAK Wizard simplifies your life a great deal. You can preset in your custom package:

- POP3 server name for inbound mail
- IMAP server name for inbound mail
- SMTP server name for outbound mail (can be the same as incoming POP3 or IMAP)
- Internet news server name

FIGURE 22-42

Stage 5: Customizing
components

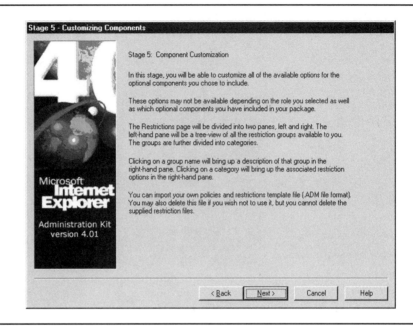

Know the names of your POP3 (incoming mail) server and SMTP (outgoing mail) server and enter them correctly. If your servers are in your intranet, you use the machine name, i.e., Server1.

If your clients need to connect to other mail servers, instruct them to map to the other servers from Outlook Express. You cannot specify more than one set of inbound/outbound servers using the IEAK Wizard or Profile Manager.

You can also make Outlook Express the default mail and news client, which means that your users do not have to switch to a different application to do both.

Secure Password Authentication (SPA) can be set to authenticate users' logons (see Figure 22-43).

1. Leave all fields blank.

2. Click on Next to continue.

**FIGURE 22-43**

Stage 5: Specify Internet
Mail Servers, Domain, and
News Server dialog box

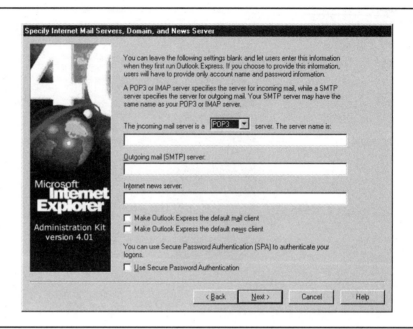

The dialog box in Figure 22-44 allows you to configure a specific server for your users to connect to for Internet Directory Services. Lightweight Directory Access Protocol (LDAP) is a powerful tool for finding people on the Web. It is used by several key components, including Outlook Express. There are many servers to choose from. Two common choices are Switchboard and Four11 (411, i.e., Information, of the Internet). It can also be configured to obtain information from an Exchange Server's directory.

You also can select the option, Check names against this server when sending mail, for an added level of name resolution. You need to specify how your users will be authenticated as well. The default is Anonymous.

If you plan to customize the InfoPane and provide content and support information to your users, the Wizard is the only place you can do this, using the dialog box in Figure 22-45. If you are trying to cut down on bandwidth used on your network, choose a local file instead of a URL. This way, the Wizard imports the file into your package, and the file is placed on the users' hard disks during installation.

**FIGURE 22-44**

Stage 5: Specify LDAP
Server Settings dialog box

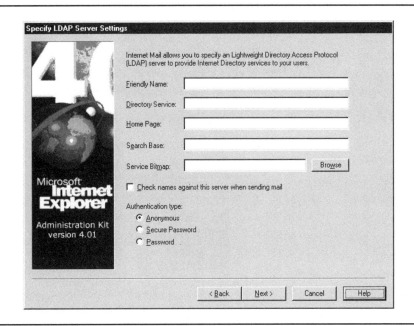

**FIGURE 22-45**

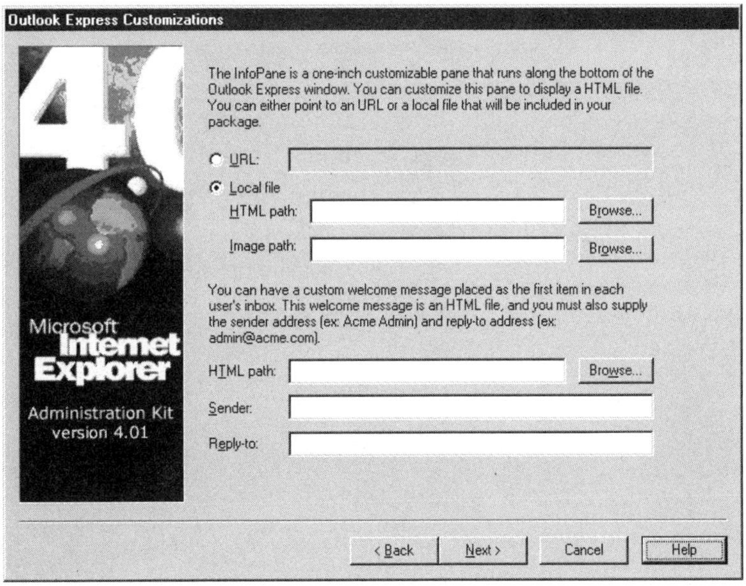

InfoPane and welcome
message settings

A nice customer service touch is to create a welcome e-mail that the users receive when they first run Outlook Express. You can make the HTML e-mail as informative as you like, giving the users a place to start. Provide some handy information like your name (person or organization sending the e-mail) and a return e-mail address for the user to reply to.

1. Leave all fields and check mark boxes blank.

2. Click on Next to continue.

If your company's reputation is at stake by having your technical people interact with newsgroups, you may want to reconsider using the dialog box in Figure 22-46. You can append a message to a user's signature stating that this person's remarks, suggestions, or beliefs do not represent the company's in any way, shape, or form. You can specify this for e-mail, newsgroups, or both.

1. Leave the check mark boxes blank.

2. Click on Next to continue.

**FIGURE 22-46**

Stage 5: Include a signature

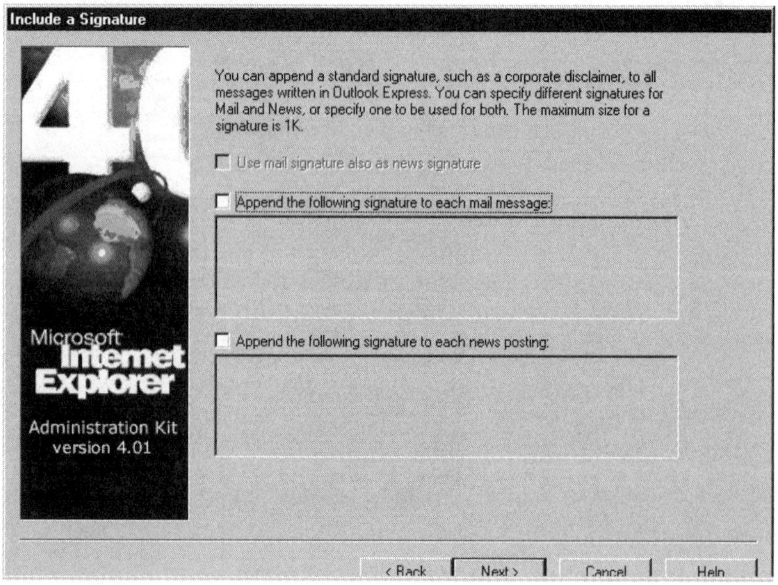

The dialog box in Figure 22-47 allows you to specify what functionality users have when using IE 4.0 and the components included in your distribution package. These settings can be assigned for individuals, computers, groups, and organizations. When you select Options from the right-hand pane, you are customizing an .adm file. This .adm file overwrites settings in the user's registry. Carefully consider the implications of each setting before implementing them.

To modify a component, select it from the hierarchical tree in the left-hand pane. The related options appear in the right-hand pane as check marks. Select the options you want, and continue until you have completed them.

1. Browse through the tree structure and the options for each component. *Do not change any settings.*

2. Click on Next to continue.

You are now finished. *Do not click on the Finish button unless you are certain that all information is correct.* If you are positive that all is configured correctly, click on the Finish button (see Figure 22-48) to generate your package.

Stage 5: System policies and restrictions

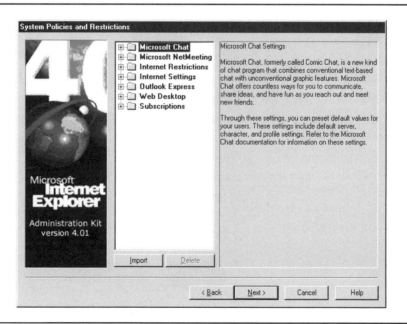

**FIGURE 22-48**

Stage 5-Generate your
custom Internet Explorer
package

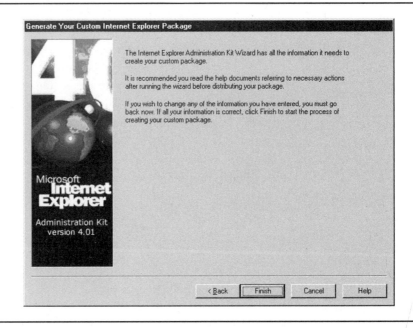

IEAK now builds your package. First, it prepares the files for the package. This includes all custom components you have added and/or modified. Then it creates the package by creating .cab files, placing them in the destination path you typed in Stage 1. Figures 22-49, 22-50, and 22-51 illustrate this process.

**FIGURE 22-49**

IEAK building a package:
Task 1 of 3

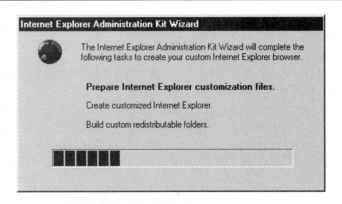

FIGURE 22-50

IEAK building a package: makecab.exe

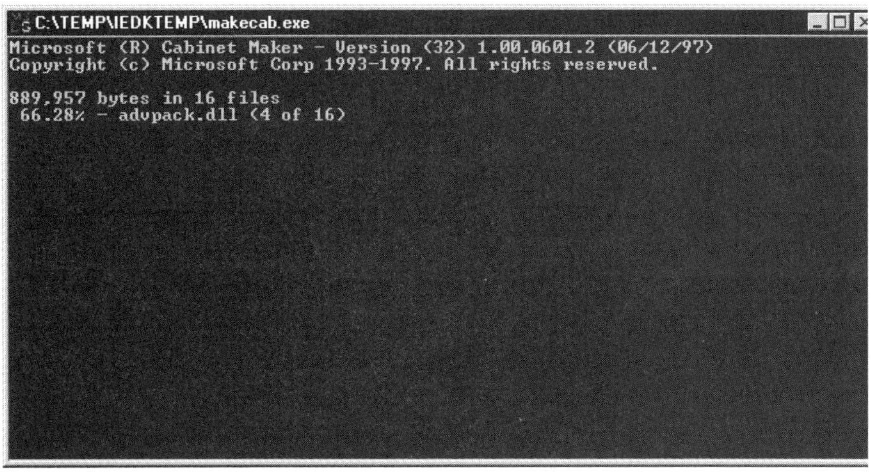

```
C:\TEMP\IEDKTEMP\makecab.exe                                    _ □ ×
Microsoft (R) Cabinet Maker - Version (32) 1.00.0601.2 (06/12/97)
Copyright (c) Microsoft Corp 1993-1997. All rights reserved.

889,957 bytes in 16 files
 66.28% - advpack.dll (4 of 16)
```

---

**CERTIFICATION OBJECTIVE 22.06**

# Delivering Your Package

When the Wizard has completed building your package, it notifies you that it has placed it in your destination folder (see Figure 22-51). If you specified a path to the actual distribution server, then you do not have much left to do. However, if you specified a local or network path that is not the same as the URL for your distribution server, then you must move your package.

FIGURE 22-51

IEAK building a package: IEAK finished

**Internet Explorer Administration Kit Wizard**                    ×

The Internet Explorer Administration Kit has finished building your custom package.

Your customized files have been placed in:  c:\inetpub\wwwroot\cie

[ OK ]

In the package you just built, you specified the folder c:\intepub\ wwwroot\cie. This local path happens to be the distribution server. What exists there now are all of the necessary files and folders for an Internet/Intranet downloadable package and a CD-ROM package.

If you specified that the package be placed in another directory, you need to know what to move to your distribution server. IEAK creates an \IE4site folder and a language subfolder for each package you build for different languages. For example, you will find \IE4site\En for English. Move the localized language folder and all of its contents to the \IE4site folder on your Internet or intranet server.

For example, c:\IE4site\En\*.* on your local machine or network server needs to be moved to \\webserver\c:\inetpub\wwwroot\cie\IE4site\En\*.*. In addition, make sure you move the c:\IE4site\ie4setup.dat file to \\webserver\c:\inetpub\wwwroot\cie\IE4site\ie4setup.dat.

## Compact Disks

All folders and files you need for the CD-ROM distribution are located in the CD directory created by IEAK. Follow the instructions with your CD-ROM image software on how to create the CD-ROM itself.

When you place your CD-ROM in a client machine, the Autorun program searches for an existing browser. If it finds IE 4.0 already installed, it brings up a splash screen in what is called *kiosk mode* (start.htm). For Autorun to work properly, it needs to be in the root folder of your CD-ROM.

## Floppy Disks

Floppy disks and CD-ROMs both come with IE4setup.exe located on Disk 1 of the floppy disks. This executable file starts Active Setup. You can also provide a hard copy of instructions on how to install with your floppy disk. Active Setup uses the distribution to get all necessary files.

Compact disks and multiple floppy disks do not require that you have any files on a server. Internet/intranet and single floppy disk distribution require files on a distribution server.

# Post-Installation and Using the Profile Manager

For corporate administrators, Profile Manager is an advanced tool for building and maintaining multiple custom versions of IE 4.0.

You have already built a package using the Wizard. By default, the filename is install.ins and is found in the \INS\En folder where IEAK placed your distribution files. You can open this and any other .ins file to make updates to any of the settings you made using the Wizard.

You can also increase the functionality of Profile Manager by utilizing custom .adm files. These .adm files are used as templates for building policies and restrictions. If you have pre-existing .adm policies, import them to add options to the hierarchy. Once you make the desired changes, the settings are incorporated into the .ins file and packaged into the auto-configuration cabinet (.cab) files. The user's machine in turn is reconfigured by the .cab file when it is expanded.

The Profile Manager screen has two panes, the same as the Systems Policy and Restrictions dialog box of the Wizard. To modify a component, select it from the hierarchical tree in the left-hand pane. The related options appear in the right-hand pane as check mark boxes. Select the options you want, and continue until you have completed them.

To start Policy Manager from the command line:

1. Click on the Start button.

2. Click on Run.

3. Type **c:\Program Files\IEAK\profmgr.exe.**

4. Click OK.

One of the most popular uses of policies and restrictions is to lock down the settings you have made for your custom setup. For example, you have imported custom security zone settings and you do not wish them to be compromised, so you use Profile Manager to prevent users from changing those settings (see Figure 22-52).

In Figure 22-52 you see only one portion of the Systems Policy and Restrictions page. You can effectively lock down every option you customized while building your .ins file. But remember, every restriction you make has several consequences. Weigh carefully your liberties and restrictions. Remember to consider the use of different packages for different groups of users. With the flexibility IEAK provides, you can find the right balance. I encourage you to explore all of the settings for all of the options in Profile Manager because, "Knowledge is Power."

Profile Manager is also used if you plan to implement Automatic Browser configuration. Open a copy of the INS file from the central location and make your modifications. Test the modified version and then replace the old INS with the new one. Then the users' browsers will automatically update.

**FIGURE 22-52**

Profile Manager:
Maintaining a .ins file

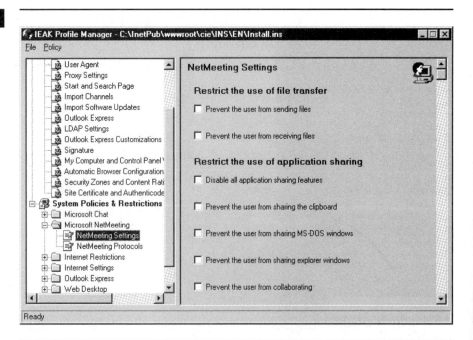

**CERTIFICATION OBJECTIVE 22.08**

# Troubleshooting

TCP/IP is the "Internet Protocol" so it makes sense that Microsoft expects you to be skilled in TCP/IP when dealing with IE 4.0. If you are concerned that the IEAK exam will test you on subnetting and configuring routing tables, you can lay your fears to rest.

However, you will need to know how to use the utilities that come with the TCP/IP protocol suite, when to use them, and what information they give you. Also, be prepared to know about DHCP (Dynamic Host Control Protocol), WINS (Windows Internet Name Service), and DNS for the server and the client. You can get more information on these topics in *MCSE Microsoft TCP/IP on Windows NT 4.0 Study Guide* (Osborne/McGraw-Hill).

exam
 ⓦatch

*The troubleshooting portion of the exam will not just be on TCP/IP. You will need to be able to diagnose and resolve problems with IE 4.0, IEAK, etc.*

## Internet Explorer 4.0

Here are some common problem areas related to installing/uninstalling IE 4.0:

- Successful IE 4.0 deployments depend on both the operating system and the target language settings of the custom package. If you attempt to install on a machine where the settings for the package do not match the user machine's settings, you will be unsuccessful.

- The Desktop Update is also sensitive to the target language of a custom package. If the Desktop Update fails to start when you bring up IE 4.0 for the first time, you have loaded the wrong language version. To correct the problem, you must uninstall IE 4.0 and reinstall with the correct language.

*You can't run IE 4.0 on a Windows NT machine that does not have SP3 installed.*

For many device drivers and Windows NT services to run properly, you must reapply SP3 after installing them. If you find you have to reapply SP3 after you have installed IE 4.0, follow these steps:

1. Run Update.exe (executable file for SP3).

2. Select No, I do not want to create an Uninstall directory.

3. Select No when prompted to replace newer files.

The rationale for this procedure is that the code that comes with IE 4.0 supercedes SP3. If you choose to replace the newer files with older ones, IE 4.0 is rendered inoperable. By not creating an Uninstall directory for SP3, you eliminate the ability to remove SP3 out from underneath IE 4.0. Removing SP3 after you have installed IE 4.0 renders IE 4.0 inoperable.

If you attempt to remove IE 4.0 on Windows 95 or Windows NT using the Add/Remove program from Control Panel and it fails, you are missing one or more of these files:

■ IE4bak.dat

■ IE4bak.ini

■ Integrated Browser.dat

■ Integrated Browser.ini

In this case, you have two separate procedures for removing IE 4.0. Use the IERemove.exe command as a last-case scenario. On Windows NT, this involves IERemove.exe and the Emergency Repair Disk (ERD) utility. For Windows 95, this involves IERemove.exe and a registry entry (System 1$^{st}$).

For each installation of IE 4.0 on a machine, an Active Setup log.txt file is created. If IE 4.0 has previously been installed, the existing Active Setup log.txt is renamed to Active Setup log.bak. This file can be used to pinpoint setup problems.

## IEAK Wizard

When you troubleshoot problems relating to the Wizard, understand the limitations of the Wizard that exist after you have created a custom package. Also, know when it is easiest to use the Wizard to change settings post-installation.

For example, if you want to add a component like Active Desktop to a user's computer after he/she has installed the custom package, would you use the IEAK Wizard or the Add/Remove program? In one scenario, you use the Add/Remove program and add the Desktop Update component. However, if the package has not been delivered and installed, you can modify the package using IEAK.

Opening your Custom Install.ins file in Profile Manager is a good way to explore the Wizard's functionality for .ins maintenance.

## Outlook Express

Outlook Express is two clients in one: mail and news. Troubleshooting a connection problem tests your knowledge of the software and network configuration. You must know your IP address, DNS address, and incoming/outgoing mail server information. You can find the IP and DNS information using the Ipconfig command for Windows NT and Winipcfg for Windows 95. For the mail server configuration, you need to ask an administrator.

exam
ⓦatch

*You will need to know that you use Winipcfg for Windows 95 troubleshooting and Ipconfig for Windows NT.*

## NetMeeting

NetMeeting problems may also test your troubleshooting techniques. You can use Ipconfig and Winipcfg as previously mentioned. Additionally, use nslookup to check the DNS name resolution for connection problems to the Internet Locator Service (ILS) servers and ping to determine TCP/IP connectivity.

Since NetMeeting is a multimedia collaboration application, there are many hardware components to coordinate. Check out Microsoft's online support for the latest issues on NetMeeting and IE 4.0 at www.microsoft.com/support and click on the link to Online Support.

In particular, if you are using a proxy server, you have some additional considerations. Some proxy solutions do not support the opening of ports dynamically as needed for voice communications. If you decide to use NetMeeting over the Internet, you also will be faced with some security issues.

# Webcasting

Before you can effectively troubleshoot Webcasting, you need to know the basics of Webcasting, in particular, how site subscriptions work. For example, how does a user subscribe to a site? How can a Web author use Webcasting to reduce the amount of time a user spends browsing and opening up connections to his or her server?

Practice using the Custom Schedule configuration for subscriptions. It can be found on the Favorites menu by selecting a site to subscribe to, right-clicking on the site, and selecting Properties. In the Properties box for the site, select the Schedule tab.

Once you are comfortable with the basics, you can understand and troubleshoot the configuration of .cdf files for Active Channels. In particular, the HTML tags for:

- Automatic download scheduling of channels
    - <SCHEDULE>   The SCHEDULE tag is used to specify when the best time is to check for any changes to the defined channel.
    - <EARLIESTTIME>
    - <LASTTIME>
    - <INTERVALTIME>
- Channel content
    - <ITEM>

The PRECACHE=Yes/No attribute can be used to specify that channel content be downloaded to a user's hard disk. If it is set to No, the content is not downloaded to cache. If you are using the .cdf file for a Software Distribution Channel, you can use the attribute AUTOINSTALL=Yes/No to have the software automatically installed on a user's machine or to have the user choose. AUTOINSTALL overrides the PRECACHE attribute.

## Active Desktop Items

Many problems with desktop items are self-inflicted ones. When you run the IEAK Wizard and you reach Stage 6, you have the ability to lock down the Active Desktop items using the System Policies and Restriction page in the Web Desktop item. When troubleshooting Active Desktop items, check that the following options are not causing your problem:

- Disable all desktop items
- Disable adding any new desktop items
- Disable deleting any desktop items
- Disable editing any desktop items
- Disable closing any desktop items

Know the two types of desktop items: the Icon Layer items and the HTML Layer items. The Icon Layer is the standard Windows shell. The Active Desktop is the HTML Layer.

The HTML Layer contains:

- Desktop components (HTML frames)
- ActiveX controls (for move/resize)
- HTML wallpaper (can be a custom HTML file)

If a package for one target language, i.e., French, is installed on a computer with a different language, i.e., English, as the default Local, the Active Desktop cannot install properly. One workaround is to change the Local setting in the

Keyboard option in Control Panel, then add the Desktop Update using the Add/Remove program in Control Panel.

# Caching

When you troubleshoot caching on a user's PC, you look in one specific place. The General tab for Internet Options has three sections: Home Page, Temporary Internet Files, and History. The two things you need to know for caching are:

- Temporary Internet files
- History

Every time you visit a Web site, it is copied to your hard disk in the Temporary Internet Files folder. The user, by default, can change his/her settings to specify how the cached pages are updated by:

1. Clicking on the Settings button.

2. Selecting one of the following from the Check for newer versions of stored page options:

   - Every visit to the page
   - Every time you start Internet Explorer (default)
   - Never

If the option, Never, is selected, this could explain why a user sees only outdated information from every Web site they revisit.

In the Settings dialog box, there is also a slider bar available to set the amount of hard disk space to be used for temporary Internet files. If your users are experiencing long delays accessing regularly visited sites, consider raising this setting.

The History folder does not house any files. It stores the URLs to the pages you visit for a set amount of days (0-999). A new feature of IE 4.0 that depends on this folder is the AutoComplete feature. This is what you will see when you enter a URL to a page you have already visited, and it completes the link automatically. If a user wants to remove a site that they no longer visit or that has changed names, they need to know where the History folder is. You can find it on any Windows NT or Windows 95 machine by taking the following steps:

1. Click on the Start menu.
2. Point to Find.
3. Click on Files or Folders.
4. Type History in the Named field.
5. Select C: from the Look In list box.
6. Select Include subfolders.
7. Click on Find now.

On Windows NT machines, you have a History folder for each Profile.

# Connectivity

Some examples of when to use Ipconfig, Winipcfg, PING, and nslookup were discussed earlier in this chapter. Additionally, know how to use Trace Route and Network Monitor. The next few paragraphs summarize each utility.

### Ipconfig

Ipconfig is used to display a host machine's IP configuration for each network adapter present. Ipconfig displays:

- IP address
- Subnet mask
- Default gateway

### Ipconfig/all

Ipconfig/all displays the following additional information:

- Description (of NIC)
- Physical address (MAC address of NIC)

- DHCP enabled (yes or no)
- DHCP server address (IP address)
- Primary WINS server (IP address)
- Secondary WINS server (IP address)

If you are using DHCP to assign IP addresses to your clients, know two additional switches for this command: /release and /renew. See the *MCSE Microsoft TCP/IP on Windows NT 4.0 Study Guide* (Osborne/McGraw-Hill) for more information about these commands.

### Winipcfg

Winipcfg is the Windows 95 GUI version of Ipconfig. Ipconfig will not run on a Windows 95 machine.

### PING (Packet Internet Groper)

PING uses ICMP echo packets to verify TCP/IP connections between two IP addresses. The proper methodology for troubleshooting with PING is:

1. Ping the loopback address. This is the address with the network ID of 127.0.0.1.

2. Ping the address of the host where you are. You also can ping the host name if you do not know the host's IP address. You also can run Ipconfig to find the host IP address.

3. Ping other hosts on the same network.

4. Ping the default gateway.

5. Ping a remote network address (an address on the other side of your default gateway).

Steps 1-3 determine if you have a proper TCP/IP configuration of your local network. Steps 4 and 5 determine your connectivity to the outside world.

### Tracert (Trace Route)

Tracert reports the route that an ICMP request takes to get to an address. It does this by counting the hops or routers that the request goes through. Tracert is useful in diagnosing where a link to a Web site fails, for example, if you can get to your ISP but you cannot connect to www.microsoft.com.

### Network Monitor

Network Monitor is not a TCP/IP utility in the sense that it is part of the protocol suite. It is a network diagnostic tool that allows you to monitor network packets on local and remote networks with a GUI interface. It can monitor the data flow of a network to look for servers that are unavailable and look for bottlenecks.

You can customize Network Monitor in many ways. The two main ways are to set a capture filter and/or a display filter. Know how to configure both. For more information on Network Monitor, refer to *MCSE Windows NT Server 4.0 Study Guide* and *MCSE Windows NT Server 4.0 in the Enterprise Study Guide* (Osborne/McGraw-Hill). For example, know that when you configure a capture filter between two computers, you must specify what traffic to capture:

- The **<--->** symbol tells Network Monitor to capture all traffic that is passed in either direction between the two selected addresses.

- The **-->** symbol tells Network Monitor to capture only the traffic that is passed from the address in the left-hand pane to the address in the right-hand pane of the Network Monitor window.

For more information on configuring Network Monitor, see the Microsoft Knowledge Base Article Q148942 *How to Capture Network Traffic with Network Monitor.*

### Nslookup

Nslookup can requisition host information in a domain or change the configuration of host records on a DNS server. Use nslookup if you can ping an IP address, but you can't access it by its FQDN (www.*companyname*.com, for example). For more information on nslookup, see "TCP/IP Procedures Help" in Control Panel Help.

None of these utilities, excluding Network Monitor, is available on a machine that is not running TCP/IP.

# What Else Do You Need to Know?

This section contains information that is not easily classified elsewhere, but is probably important for you to know to help you pass your test.

## Internet Explorer 4.0

IE 4.0 requires that a member of the Local Administrators group be logged on during installation of IE 4.0 on a Windows NT machine. If you are in a domain, members of the Domain Administrators group are placed in the Local Administrators group by default when a machine joins a domain.

When the system reboots after Active Setup, it requires that the same Administrator account be used to log on and finish the installation and desktop configuration.

This is not true of Windows 95. Any user who can log onto a Windows 95 computer can install IE 4.0.

When a newer package is loaded over an older package, only items that are shared with other applications are replaced, like the Favorites folder, for example.

For users to subscribe to sites, they use the Favorites menu, and select Add to Favorites. Then they must choose from three options:

- No, just add the page to my favorites.

- Yes, but only tell me when the page is updated (partial subscription).

- Yes, notify me of changes and download the page for offline viewing (full subscription).

If you want to reduce the amount of time a user spends on your Web server, instruct them to make a full subscription to your Web server. A full subscription lets the user's browser download the content for offline use, and it only has to access the server when a change is made to the site. The browser will connect at predefined intervals.

If you want users to subscribe to a channel, they need to link to a .cdf file. You can create a single HTML page with multiple .cdf hyperlinks. The title of each channel must be unique. The user subscribes to the channels by clicking on the hyperlinks. When a user subscribes to a channel, the channel's icon is placed in the channel bar on the Active Desktop.

Profile Assistant is a feature of IE 4.0 that stores common information like your screen name and password. It then makes it available to a Web site that requests it without you having to enter it each time you visit. Cookies do the same thing, but require you to enter the information for each cookie. The Profile Assistant cannot be configured in the IEAK Wizard.

## Outlook Express

When migrating from Eudora Pro, use the Outlook Express Wizard to import the address book. In order for Outlook Express to access the addresses, you need to exit Outlook Express and restart the system.

To secure your e-mail messages, use a digital ID. A digital ID is composed of a public key, a private key, and a digital signature. The public key is given to other users so they can encrypt messages sent to you. The private key is used to decrypt those messages. The digital signature provides proof that the message is actually from you.

## NetMeeting

Microsoft NetMeeting enables real-time audio, video, and data communication over the Internet/Intranet. It also supports peer-to-peer communications on LANs.

To use NetMeeting, you need one of the configurations listed in Table 22-6.

For the multimedia features of NetMeeting to function, you need a sound card and a video-capture card. (Consult hardware vendors for optimal configuration.)

| TABLE 22-6 | Microsoft Windows 95 or Windows 98 (BETA 3 or Later) | Microsoft Windows NT Version 4.0 |
|---|---|---|
| NetMeeting Configuration Requirements | At least a 486/66 processor with 8MB of RAM (Pentium with 12MB of RAM recommended) | At least a 486/66 processor with 16MB of RAM |
| | | Microsoft Windows NT 4.0 Service Pack 3 (you will not be able to share applications without SP3) |

Windows NT clients cannot share applications unless SP3 is loaded before NetMeeting is installed. Errors will occur if SP3 is installed after NetMeeting.

NetMeeting utilizes directory servers to locate other NetMeeting clients for you to conference with on the Internet. LDAP is used to access servers like ils.microsoft.com or ils.four11.com. You can use these servers and others to locate people on the Internet. However, if you connect to a list server via a proxy server, it does not function properly unless your proxy supports Remote WinSock.

Up to 32 users can use NetMeeting 2.1 to share a single application. Only two users can connect at a time for audio and video meetings.

System policies are fully supported by NetMeeting in both Windows 95 and Windows NT. Using the IEAK Wizard, you can restrict NetMeeting functionality and client settings for your distribution package.

When calculating the strategy for locking down (restricting) the user settings for NetMeeting, have a clear understanding of the effect of each setting you make. Cruising through the NetMeeting section of Profile Manager gives you an idea of how complex a strategy can be. Here are a couple of common configurations:

- Disabling video features:

  1. Restrict the use of video.

  2. Prevent the user from sending video.

  3. Prevent the user from receiving video.

  4. Disable the video option page.

- Disallow directory services:

    1. Prevent the user from using directory services.

    2. Disable the calling options page.

NetMeeting is a very dynamic application in its own right. Its use on the Web is growing. One of the best resources for implementing NetMeeting is the NetMeeting Resource Kit, which is free on the web at: www.microsoft.com/netmeeting/reskit/.

## Proxy Server

It is important to emphasize again that you will encounter questions concerning Proxy Server on the exam.

*Due to the role a proxy can play on the functionality of IE 4.0 and its components, expect to know how to configure proxy settings on the server, client, and IEAK Wizard. As mentioned previously in this chapter, you need to know how to configure advanced proxy settings and you need to know the different compatible scripting formats.*

## NetShow

NetShow is a component that can be included in a package to take advantage of streaming technology. Multimedia presentations such as corporate meetings and technical seminars can be multicast or unicast across the Internet/intranet to a client using NetShow, who in turn can either watch a live data stream or control the playback using VCR-like buttons. The file types that can be streamed are:

- ASF Active Streaming Format
- RPT Live audio files
- RPT WAVE audio files

## QUESTIONS AND ANSWERS

| | |
|---|---|
| Why do I need to know how to use IE to use the administration kit? | With the administration kit, you are building packages that deliver Internet Explorer configured to users. Know how to configure IE so that the packages are configured correctly. |
| How do I get the IEAK? | You must go to the Microsoft Web site and register for the kit. |
| What if I am not going to distribute any IE packages and I just need IEAK to study for my test? Do I still need to register and do all the forms? | Yes. Currently the only way to get the IEAK is to sign the licensing agreement and fill out the forms, even if you never intend to distribute a single copy of IE. |

# CERTIFICATION SUMMARY

This chapter discussed the requirements for IEAK and encouraged you to become intimately familiar with Internet Explorer 4.0. Planning issues for your deployment of the IEAK were outlined. Migration points were discussed. Automatic Version Synchronization (AVS) was explored.

The five stages of using the Wizard were discussed at length. There are many variables that can lead to different deployments. You were exposed to the different options to deliver your package.

The troubleshooting section discussed troubleshooting IE and the IEAK kit, Outlook Express, NetMeeting, caching, etc.

Finally, a bonus section at the end discussed tips and other information that may come in handy when you are taking the exam.

 # TWO-MINUTE DRILL

- ❑ Know how to install and configure IE 4.0 before taking the test.
- ❑ You get the IEAK by downloading it from Microsoft.
- ❑ There are four steps in the downloading and registering process.
- ❑ There are three choices of IEAK kits you can download.

❑ There is an ISP kit.

❑ There is a Corporate Administrator kit.

❑ There is a Content Developer kit.

❑ The previous three are called modes of operation.

❑ Know how to use IE 4.0.

❑ You can order IEAK on a CD-ROM.

❑ You must report how many IE programs you distribute to Microsoft.

❑ You make this report quarterly.

❑ You must have IE 4.0 installed to use IEAK.

❑ You need 16MB RAM with Windows 95.

❑ You need 24MB of RAM with Windows NT.

❑ A full package can be as big as 100MB.

❑ Know how to configure IE 4.0.

❑ IEAK always creates a downloadable copy of your distribution package.

❑ IEAK packages are language sensitive.

❑ The first time you run IEAK, you cannot deselect AVS.

❑ The IEAK package is built from your knowledge of how to configure IE 4.0.

❑ You can brand your IEAK distribution package.

❑ A silent installation does not allow the user to interact with the installation.

❑ You can have up to 10 unique configurations that the user may choose during installation.

❑ You can add up to 10 custom applications to be installed with IE.

❑ You can configure system policies and restrictions.

❑ For an ISP, you must consider what type of sign-up process your customers will use.

❑ An ISP must be able to use the Internet Connection Manager in ISP mode.

❑ Running the IEAK is divided into five stages:

    ❑ Stage 1: Gathering Information.

- ❑ Stage 2: Specifying Active Setup Parameters.

- ❑ Stage 3: Customizing Active Setup.

- ❑ Stage 4: Customizing the Browser.

- ❑ Stage 5: Component Customization.

❑ The Profile Manager screen has two panes and is the same as the Systems Policy and Restrictions page of the Wizard.

❑ Uh, did I mention that you are probably going to need to know how to use and configure IE 4.0 to pass the test?

# SELF TEST

The Self Test questions will help you measure your understanding of the material presented in this chapter. Read all the choices carefully, since there may be more than one correct answer. Choose all correct answers for each question.

1. You are creating a package for distribution that will include the Windows Desktop Update. How much RAM do you need on your client's stations? Select all that are correct.

   A. 8MB for Windows 95

   B. 16MB for Windows NT

   C. 16MB for Windows 95

   D. 24MB for Windows NT

2. You are planning a deployment of IE 4.0 in a global organization where English is the corporate standard for desktop. There are nine different departments that need custom configurations. What is the minimum number of distribution packages you must create?

   A. 1

   B. 2

   C. 9

   D. 10

3. AVS has just completed. How can you verify that all components are current?

   A. They all have yellow exclamation points next to them.

   B. There are no red, yellow, or green icons.

   C. There are only green check marks.

   D. There is no way to tell; just click on the Next button to continue.

4. You are running the IEAK Wizard with an ISP customization code. Which of the following will you be able to accomplish?

   A. Create a CD-ROM for distribution

   B. Create a multiple floppy disk distribution.

   C. Create a single floppy disk distribution.

   D. Create a server-based distribution.

5. In which stage of the IEAK Wizard do you specify the download URLs?

   A. Stage 1

   B. Stage 2

   C. Stage 3

   D. Stage 4

6. The default setting for the Internet Security Zone is

   A. Level 0

   B. Medium

   C. High

   D. Level 4

7. In the Exceptions box for the Proxy Settings page, you can specify the URLs

that do not use the Proxy Server. Valid entries in the Exceptions box are:

A. FQDNs

B. IP addresses

C. Computer names

D. Usernames

8. Profile Manager is used to maintain or customize which type of file?

A. .js

B. .bmp

C. .ins

D. .cab

E. .adm

9. Which of the following pieces of configuration information do you receive by typing Ipconfig at the DOS prompt on a Windows NT machine?

A. IP address

B. Default gateway

C. DHCP server address

D. Primary WINS server

10. Your company wants to take advantage of streaming technology to broadcast live product seminars to all members of the sales department. You have been asked to create a custom package for them. What component must you include to allow the sales department to receive these broadcasts?

A. NetMeeting

B. Desktop Update

C. Outlook Express

D. NetShow

# A

## Self Test
## Answers

# Answers to Chapter 2 Self Test

1. Which operating systems support IIS 4.0? Select all answers that apply.
   **C.** Just knowing the answer is Windows NT Server 4.0 is not sufficient. IIS 4.0 will not run on Windows NT Server 3.5x, Windows NT Workstation, or UNIX. Even though you need SP3 installed first, the question asks you about the operating system version, not the service pack.

2. What are the minimum hardware requirements for IIS 4.0? Select all answers that apply.
   **A, D.** B and C are recommended but are not the minimum.

3. Which service would you use if you wanted to send and receive files using IIS?
   **B.** WWW and HTTP are the same thing and while they allow you to receive files, you cannot send files with either service. RAS (Remote Access Service) allows you to send and receive files, but it has nothing to do with IIS. TFTP is a command-line utility that uses FTP service.

4. Which service that was supported under previous versions of IIS is no longer supported under IIS 4.0?
   **D.** TFTP is a command-line utility that uses FTP service.

5. Which transport protocol should be installed for IIS?

   **A.** While having NetBEUI installed doesn't hurt, it is not necessary.

6. Which items need to be installed prior to IIS 4.0? Select all correct answers.
   **A, B, D.** You need to know this; it is fundamental.

7. You have IIS 2.0 installed on your server and want to upgrade to IIS 4.0. What steps are required?
   **C.** None of these actions is required. Of course, you must run setup.exe, but that is not listed.

8. During an installation of IIS 4.0 on a server with a previous version of IIS installed, which installation options are available to you? Select all answers that apply.
   **B, C.** Typical and Custom are from a new installation, not an upgrade.

9. Which command do you run to upgrade IIS 3.0 to IIS 4.0?
   **C.** Most Microsoft products use the setup command for installation.

10. Where do you find the IIS 4.0 distribution files for installation?
    **A.** IIS 4.0 is an inseparable part of the Option Pack. SP3 is how you might upgrade IIS 2.0 to IIS 3.0.

11. During a Typical installation, what publishing services are installed by IIS 4.0?
    **A, D.** Gopher is no longer supported. TFTP is a command-line utility that uses FTP service.

12. Which three installation options are available when you install IIS 4.0 on a server that does not have a previous version of IIS installed? Select three answers.
**A, C, D.** You only get an upgrade option when you have a previous version of IIS installed.

13. Which browsers can connect to an IIS 4.0 server? Select all correct answers
**B, D.** Any browser can connect to IIS 4.0. Frames and browser compatibility may affect what the client can see, but the client will still connect.

# Answers to Chapter 3 Self Test

1. What tools are available to manage IIS?
**C, D.** These are the only tools available to manage IIS.

2. Which tool provides the framework for snap-ins?
**B.** The MMC is the framework for snap-ins. IIS is a snap-in.

3. Which of the following statements are true of MMC?
**A, D.** The MMC does not make modifications to anything; that is the job of snap-ins.

4. Which of the following characteristics are benefits of MMC?

**A, B, C.** Only transportability is not a benefit as listed by Microsoft.

5. How do you start the MMC?
**B, C.** MMC is not in Administrative Tools and there is no ISM.EXE command.

6. What is contained in the scope pane of the MMC?
**A, B.** You cannot see registry entries. You see files in the results pane, not the scope pane.

7. Which of the following statements is true of the MMC menu bars?
**B, C.** MMC has three menu bars and you cannot add other menu bars.

8. Which of the following is true of the MMC?
**A, B, C.** D cannot be true. You can save console configurations.

9. What is the best way to make configuration changes to IIS?
**B.** The registry does contain configuration entries for this version of IIS. While you can edit the metabase directly, it is not wise.

10. How do you add another server to your console view?
**C.** Adding a computer through Server Manager is fine for creating computer accounts in a domain. Adding a computer to the console view is kept in the .msc file, not the metabase.

# Answers to Chapter 4 Self Test

1. Which of the following statements describes good password policies?
   **B, D.** Having the same password for all users is not a good idea if you are concerned about security, nor is having the username and password be the same.

2. Which of the following are good practices for Windows NT accounts?
   **A.** You do not want to delete the IUSR account because this is the account that IIS uses for user logon. For security, you want to remove the group Everyone from use and administrators should only log on using their admin accounts when they are going to do administration. Otherwise they should log on with their user-level account.

3. Under which DOD security classification can Windows NT be made to be compliant?
   **D.** Windows NT can only be certified under C-2.

4. Which of the following statements best describes IP spoofing?
   **B.** Firewalls can restrict outside IP addresses from accessing the local network because you tell it what the addresses are on the local network. In IP spoofing, an intruder sends a packet as though the packet originated on the local network, thereby circumventing the firewall.

5. Which of the following is true of a denial of service attack?
   **D.** A denial of service attack is aimed at making your server inaccessible to the network community.

6. Which accounts does IIS create during installation?
   **A, C.** The Administrator account is created when you install Windows NT. There is no Anonymous account in Windows NT.

7. Which of the following is true about the IUSR account?
   **A, B, D.** This is a tricky one. The IUSR account is granted Log On Locally rights during creation. By default, Windows NT installation allows the group Everyone access the computer from the network. All users are a member of the group Everyone, including the IUSR account, which means the IUSR account has access to the computer from the network. You must change this manually.

8. Which of the following are valid FTP authentication methods?
   **A, B, D.** You cannot use Windows NT Challenge/Response with an FTP logon. Challenge/Response is used with browsers and encrypts your logon. You can log on with your Windows NT account however, but it will not be encrypted.

9. Which of the following are valid HTTP authentication methods?
**A, C.** You can allow anonymous and use Windows NT Challenge/Response.

10. Which of the following security tools does IIS use?
**A, B, D.** There is no built-in FTP data encryption.

# Answers to Chapter 5 Self Test

1. To transfer files using FTP, what must be in place?
**B, D.** FTP is a client/server process. You don't need a default gateway if you are on the same network segment.

2. Which protocol does FTP use?
**C.** TFTP and NetBIOS are not transport protocols.

3. Which of the following are features of the TCP protocol?
**A, C.** TCP provides error correction and TFTP uses UDP, not TCP.

4. Which of the following statements about TFTP is true?
**A, C.** IIS cannot be a TFTP server.

5. How can you stop the FTP service?
**A, D.** You cannot use Server Manager, which is used to manage Windows NT Servers. Closing the MMC has no effect on FTP.

6. Which port does the FTP service monitor for a connection request?
**B.** The FTP service monitors port 21 for connections. It uses port 20 for data connections.

7. Which of the following statements is true about sockets?
**A, B, D.** The IP address and TCP port number identify the socket number, which is an endpoint.

8. Which of the following is not true of ports?
**B, D.** These are not true. Well-known ports are fixed and there are 65,535 ports.

9. Which ports does the FTP service use to transfer files?
**A.** The FTP service monitors port 21 for the connection and uses port 20 for data transfer connections.

10. Which of the following is not an FTP command?
**D.** Copy is a DOS command. It is also used by other operating systems.

11. You are preparing to set up several virtual servers on your IIS computer. You want these virtual servers to have properties in common. Which property sheet should you modify?
**B.** The Master property sheet provides inheritance for all FTP servers created. IIS is the server and MMC is the management console.

12. You want to set your FTP server to only allow anonymous connections. How can you accomplish this?
    **D.** If you disable the IUSR account, no one will be able to log on. Creating an anonymous user is not necessary; that is what the IUSR account is for. There is no Connections tab.

# Answers to Chapter 6 Self Test

1. What protocol does the WWW use?
   **B.** FTP is a service. IPX is a transport protocol and has nothing to do with Internet technologies.

2. Which of the following statements is true about a virtual server?
   **A, C.** Each virtual server must have its own IP address but you can use a single NIC to host many virtual servers.

3. Which of the following statements is true of virtual directories?
   **B, C, D.** You cannot create virtual directories using Windows NT Explorer. You create them from the Web property sheet.

4. Which port does the WWW service monitor for a client connection?
   **D.** FTP uses ports 21 and 20.

5. Which characteristics are necessary for you to specify access to a resource on a Web server?

**A, C, D.** While the communication will eventually need the MAC address, the ARP protocol takes care of this for you; you do not need to specify it.

6. You receive a call from a user stating that he is trying to connect to your Web server and receives the error message, "Internet Explorer cannot open the Internet site...". What may be causing this to happen?
   **C.** This is the best possible answer of the answers given. Either the client is specifying the wrong port number or your server is not monitoring port 80.

7. How do you modify which TCP port your Web server monitors?
   **A, D.** You modify this TCP port from the property sheet; there is no TCP port tab.

8. Jerry has been made responsible for managing the Web site recently. How can you make sure that Jerry will be able to administer the site?
   **A, D.** You could do either. However, making Jerry part of the administrators group has other implications.

9. You want to restrict the amount of bandwidth your Web server might use on the network. What is the best way to accomplish this?
   **B.** Using a slower network card is not a good idea. Limiting the number of concurrent users might have the desired effect and it might not.

10. Which of the following statements is correct about keep-alives?
    **D.** Keep-alives maintain the client connection so that the client's browser doesn't have to make a connection with each request.

# Answers to Chapter 7 Self Test

1. Which of the following statements are true about DNS?
   **A, D.** The resolver is the client asking for the IP address. The computer name is a NetBIOS name and is not the same as a host name.

2. Which of the following statements are true?
   **A.** There is a limited number of top-level domains. You register a second-level domain name, but you do not create it. It may create subdomains to your second-level domain as you see fit. DNS will use UDP first and TCP next.

3. Which of the following is not a current top-level domain name?
   **D.** CA is a valid top-level domain for Canada. .ARMY is a secondary domain to the top-level domain .MIL.

4. Which of the following statements are true of zones?
   **A, D.** A DNS server can manage more than one zone. A zone may include the entire domain but a zone and a domain are not the same thing.

5. Which of the following is not a DNS server type?
   **B.** Backup is not a DNS server type, although you might have a secondary server for the purpose of being a backup server in the case of a failure of a primary.

6. Which of the following statements may be valid reasons for creating a secondary name server?
   **A, B, D.** Even though you may have multiple IP segments, you do not need to have a DNS per segment.

7. You have created a secondary server at one of your remote offices. What do you need to do to ensure that the secondary server gets a copy of the zone database?
   **D.** When you set up the secondary server, it will get a copy of the database. It will also receive periodic updates.

8. Which of the following statements is true of a cache name server?
   **D.** Cache servers do not contain a zone file. They get their information by placing resolved queries into memory.

9. Which of the following records must appear in the database, at a minimum?
   **A, B, D.** You do not need an MX record. This is used for e-mail purposes, which might be required for you, but not for the DNS to function.

10. Which of the following is not a type of query that a resolver might make of the name server?
    **C, D.** There are three query types; simple and complex queries are not among them.

11. Which of the following statements are true of a reverse lookup?
    **A, B.** A reverse query looks for a host name while a standard query looks for an IP address.

# Answers to Chapter 8 Self Test

1. Which of the following statements is true of virtual directories?
   **A, C, D.** Virtual directories can be on remote servers.

2. Which of the following statements is true of virtual directories on a Web server?
   **A, B, C.** Any browser can access virtual directories. It is easier if the browser supports the HTTP 1.1 standard.

3. You are building a Web server. Some of the data you want to publish is on another server in your organization. How can you publish this data?
   **C, D.** The benefit to virtual directories in this case is that you can point directly to the other server. You don't need to copy files.

4. How do you create a virtual directory?
   **B, C.** You only need a share point if the directory is on a remote server. You use ISM to create the virtual directory. A URL is used in the request to open the virtual directory.

5. Which of the following is not an access permission to a virtual directory?
   **C.** This is not an access permission to a virtual directory. There is an NTFS permission called Take Ownership, however.

6. Which of the following statements is true of a virtual server?
   **D.** A virtual server does not show up in the computer browser list and it does not need a unique domain name.

7. You are the IIS administrator. Your organization has several divisions. Each organization wants its own presence on the Internet and has registered its own domain name. They want to use your IIS server to host their Web pages. How can you accomplish this?
   **D.** Virtual directories do not allow for unique identification. With only one virtual server, you cannot use all of the domain names registered by the divisions.

8. You have a small ISP and want to host the Web pages for your clients. You do not want to dedicate servers to each client. How can you host each client on the same server when each client has its own domain name and its own IP address assigned to them? Select all correct answers.

**C, D.** Virtual directories do not allow your clients to use their individual IP addresses and domain names.

9. You want to create virtual servers with their own IP addresses. What do you need to do?
**A, C, D.** You do not need to use multiple NICs.

10. You have created a virtual server. How do you create a host header for the server?
**A, C.** You do not use the HTTP Headers tab for this function and there is no Advanced button on the HTTP Headers tab.

# Answers to Chapter 9 Self Test

1. Which of the following are not publishing methods?
**C.** ODBC is not a publishing method. It is a standard that allows access to information contained in a database.

2. Which of the following statements are true?
**B.** Dynamic HTML is executed at the client. ASP pages do contain HTML tags and they are not static.

3. Which of the following scripting languages does ASP support?
**B, C, D.** Visual C is not a scripting language. All of the rest may be used for scripts and ASPs.

4. Which of the following statements are true about the Script Debugger?
**C.** You use the Script Debugger through the browser but you cannot edit the script using the Script Debugger.

5. Which of the following statements are true about transaction scripts?
**B, C, D.** A transaction script and ASP are not the same thing.

6. Which of the following statements are true of ASP applications?
**A, B, D.** ASP applications run their own memory space and not in shared memory space.

7. Which of the following statements are not true?
**B, D.** The content rotator sends content strings and the Ad rotator uses the rotator schedule file.

8. Which of the following statements are true?
**A, C, D.** Text does not need to be quotes to be displayed.

# Answers to Chapter 10 Self Test

1. Which of the following statements about Index Server is true?
**A, B.** You can index data on a FAT partition and on a remote server.

2. Which of the following file formats is indexed without installing additional content filters?
   **A, B.** You need additional content filters from other vendors for Oracle and WordPerfect.

3. Which of the following statements about Index Server is true?
   **B.** Index Server requires IIS. It can index data on any server run under IIS and Windows NT. Unicode is language independent.

4. What are the minimum requirements to install Index Server?
   **A, B, D.** You do not need a CD-ROM drive.

5. Which of the following characteristics is not important concerning the amount of RAM desirable for Index Server?
   **D.** The amount of free space on the disk that will contain the catalog file is not relevant to memory issues for Index Server.

6. Which of the following is true about catalogs?
   **B.** There can be multiple catalogs on any file system. A catalog is created by the Installation Wizard.

7. You receive a call from a user who states that they appear to be unable to run any queries. What can you do to help determine if Index Server is functioning properly?
   **C.** You cannot run queries if the WWW service is stopped. Pinging the Web server and the client may not help in determining why queries may not be executing.

8. Which of the following statements are true about the way documents are indexed?
   **D.** Not all words are indexed. The noise words are excluded. The function of a word breaker is to recognize words from the stream of characters generated by content filters.

9. Which of the following is not a type of index?
   **B.** There is no primary index. All of the rest are types of indexes.

10. Which of the following statements is true of a shadow index?
    **B, D.** There are shadow indexes, which are created when a word list becomes too large.

11. Which of the following statements is true about a master index?
    **A, D.** A master index is merged with shadow indexes, not word lists. The administrator can force a master merge, which updates the master index.

12. You are the system administrator. You notice that queries seem to be running slow at your Index Server. You start a master merge when you have to shut down the server to address another issue. What do you have to do about the master merge that was running?
    **A.** A master merge will restart automatically if it is interrupted.

13. How can a master merge occur?
**A, B, C.** All of these will cause a master merge to occur. Word lists are held in memory, not on the disk.

14. Which of the following statements is not true about catalogs?
**A, D.** Queries may not span multiple catalogs.

15. Which of the following statements is true about .idq and .htx files?
**A, D.** The .idq receives the query and the .htx formats the results.

# Answers to Chapter 11 Self Test

1. Which of the following are components of Certificate Server?
**A, B.** ISM has nothing to do with Certificate Server and Certificate Server is a part of the Option Pack.

2. Which of the following is not a data security mechanism?
**B.** Logon authentication is a security mechanism, but has nothing to do with data security.

3. Which of the following statements are true about data encryption?
**B, D.** Encryption and decryption are not the same thing. Without the key used to encrypt the data, it is very difficult to decrypt the data.

4. How do you install Certificate Server?
**A, D.** You need to install Certificate Server locally, so you need to be logged on at the console with sufficient authority to install software; being logged on as administrator will do. You do the installation from the Option Pack setup.

5. What is the primary administration tool for Certificate Server?
**C.** You do not administer Certificate server from the MMC or ISM. Server Manager is irrelevant for these programs.

6. Which best describes the function of the server queue?
**D.** It displays the status of certificates being requested. This may or may not be an indication of how busy the server is; absent any other information in the question, it is hard to tell.

7. What information is contained in the server log?
**B.** It contains both a list of sent certificates and revoked certificates.

8. Which of the following is true of an intermediary in the process of granting a certificate?
**A, B.** The intermediary takes the request and gives it to the server engine. IIS is an intermediary for HTTP clients requesting certificates.

9. Which of the following are not features of Certificate Server?
   **C.** Certificate Server functions outside the considerations of Windows NT domain security.

10. Which of the following statements are not true of CA hierarchies?
    **A.** An organization can have more than one certificate authority. That is the point to the hierarchy.

# Answers to Chapter 12 Self Test

1. Which of the following is true about Microsoft Transaction Server (MTS)?
   **A, B, D.** MTS is not part of Windows NT Server; it is part of the Option Pack.

2. Which of the following statements is not true of a transaction?
   **B.** MTS automatically rolls back a transaction that has failed.

3. What are the requirements to successfully install MTS?
   **A, B.** You need Windows NT 4.0 with SP3, DCOM support, and 30MB free disk space, plus 32MB RAM. You do not need an NTFS partition.

4. How do you install MTS?
   **D.** MTS is part of the Option Pack. It may be installed by itself or in combination with IIS 4.0.

5. Which of the following statements is true of MSMQ?
   **C, D.** MSMQ is part of MTS and cannot be installed without it. It uses asynchronous communication to support messaging.

6. You are the system administrator of a Windows NT Server running MTS. You suspect that some of the transaction-based applications are no longer running on the server. How do you determine which transactions are running?
   **C.** The Transaction List provides an indication of what transactions are running. The Services applet tells you what services are running. Transactions are not services.

7. Which of the following statements is true about installing MTS?
   **B.** If you are going to use SQL Server 6.5, you must install it before you install MTS.

# Answers to Chapter 13 Self Test

1. Which of the following statements are true of SMTP domains?
   **B, C.** You must create all domains except for the default domain, which is created automatically at installation.

2. Which of the following statements are true?
   **B.** A local domain is served by the SMTP server and has nothing to do with LAN segmentation. You specify the FQDN of

the remote domain and not the IP address. Nonlocal messages are put in the Pickup folder and local messages are put into the Drop folder.

3. You are the system administrator. You installed Internet Information Server last week and now you want to install the SMTP service. What is the best way to accomplish this?
   **D.** There is no reason to uninstall IIS first. You can only use the Custom installation if IIS has not been installed.

4. Which of the following folders are not part of the SMTP directory structure?
   **A.** Localmail is not a folder created at the installation. All of the other folders are created during installation.

5. How do you set the logging options for the SMTP service?
   **D.** Log settings are set in the SMTP Site Identification tab by checking Enable Log and setting the log format.

6. You want to keep a remote SMTP server from flooding your server with messages. How can you best do this?
   **D.** This is the best answer listed. Setting the message size smaller won't stop you from getting 10240KB of messages.

7. You have recently installed the SMTP service on your IIS site and are concerned that your server not be used to send spam (junk e-mail). What can you do to prevent this?

**A.** You set this parameter in the Directory Security property sheet and not the Delivery property sheet.

8. Which of the following statements are true of the NNTP service?
   **A, D.** You do not need to create any folders for your newsgroups. The NNTP service does that for you.

9. What is a moderated newsgroup?
   **D.** In a moderated newsgroup, users cannot post messages directly to the newsgroup.

10. You are the newsgroup operator. Your server contains several newsgroups. Some of the newsgroups have articles that have a short time value and you want to remove them after a few days. Several newsgroups have content that should remain available for a long period of time, but you don't want the messages in these groups to consume too much disk space. How can you devise a policy to support both objectives?
    **C.** You cannot set size limits or quotas using Windows NT Explorer. You can set a different policy for each newsgroup if you wish.

# Answers to Chapter 14 Self Test

1. Fred is the system administrator. He wants to see quickly who is connected, and at

what port, on his server. How can he do this?

**B.** The Event Viewer is used to view log files. There is no getstat utility.

2. You want to check to see if any significant events have occurred. Which log files should you check?

    **A, C.** Typically speaking, Internet services do not log to the Security Log, but they log to the System and Application Logs.

3. Which of the following is not related to Performance Monitor?

    **A.** CPU speed has nothing to do with Performance Monitor.

4. Which of the following statements are true of Report Writer?

    **A, B.** Reports are created from information contained in the W3 log files. You can edit the reports that come with Report Writer.

5. Bill wants to show his supervisor statistics about activity on the Web server. What does he have to do?

    **A, B, D.** You do not need to be logged on at the Web server to run the reports.

6. Mary wants to check her Web server to see how many pages pass more than 32KB of data to the browser. How can she best do that?

    **B.** There is a Quick Search available to check for pages that send more than 32KB of data.

7. Which of the following statements are not true?

**C.** The tree view is not dynamic but the Cyberbolic view is.

8. How do you install Site Server Express?

    **D.** You cannot install Site Server Express from CIS, only from the Option Pack.

9. Which of the following is not a component of Site Server Express?

    **C.** Site Server Express is a scaled-back component of Commercial Server.

# Answers to Chapter 15 Self Test

1. Which of the following statements are not true of Proxy Server?

    **B.** Proxy Server is not, of itself, a Web server. IIS is a Web server.

2. Which of the following is not a service of Proxy Server?

    **D.** Reverse proxy is a feature of Proxy Server but it is not a service.

3. What are the two components of the Web Proxy service?

    **A, C.** SOCKS is a peer service to Web Proxy service.

4. Which of the following statements are not true of the Web Proxy service?

    **D.** Proxy Server 2.0 can only run under Windows NT, not UNIX.

5. Which of the following are caching techniques used by Web Proxy service?

**A, D.** File caching is used by Windows NT Server but not directly by Proxy Server.

6. Which statements best describe how passive caching works?
   **D.** Proxy Server does not send updates to the client except when requested by the client.

7. Which of the following is not a consideration for active caching of objects?
   **B.** The size of the object is not a consideration for caching.

8. Which of the following is not a function of WinSock Proxy service?
   **C.** Caching requested objects is a function of the Web Proxy service.

9. Which of the following statements best describes IP masking?
   **B.** This has nothing to do with WINS and answer D is backwards.

10. Which of the following statements describes a benefit of Proxy Server?
    **A, B, C.** Microsoft lists all these as benefits of using Proxy Server.

# Answers to Chapter 16 Self Test

1. Which device do you use to connect to an existing voice line to support dial-on-demand Proxy Server?

   **C.** A modem is the device used to connect to an analog circuit, which is what a voice grade line is.

2. What type of hardware do you need to fully support interconnecting two IP LANs using a T-1 circuit and a leased line?
   **B, C.** The DSU/CSU is the device that interfaces to the telephone company circuit. The router routes traffic between your IP LANs over the telephone company circuit.

3. Which of the following circuits offers the greatest bandwidth?
   **C.** Modems are not "high speed" in relative terms. The maximum bandwidth on an ISDN circuit is 128 Kbps and a DDS circuit is 56/64 Kbps. Each DS0 is 64 Kbps, so using four DS0s is 256 Kbps.

4. Which of the following characteristics is not a factor in the cost of a leased data circuit?
   **B, D.** Speed and distance are the factors. When you lease a circuit, you own the entire circuit; you can have as many sessions any time of the day. Some shared circuits are traffic sensitive; the more data you send and receive, the greater your charges will be.

5. Which of the following is not a method of load sharing Proxy Servers?
   **D.** Using DHCP has nothing to do with load sharing Proxy Servers.

6. You have a network with only Windows 95 and Windows NT as clients. You are connected to the Internet through an ISP.

Both your DNS servers are maintained by the ISP and are located at the ISP. How do you configure your network to provide optimally for load sharing across your multiple Proxy Servers?
**C.** If you have only Windows clients on your network, then WINS implementation is preferred.

7. Which of the following are methods that you can use to implement a distributed cache?
**C, D.** The other two choices are how you might configure to support load sharing.

8. Which of the following statements are not true of an array?
**B.** You only want to have one person making changes to one member in the array at the same time.

9. You have 10 Proxy Servers configured in an array in the central locations. You support 5 branch offices, each with its own Proxy Server. There are 3000 users in your organization. How many Proxy Server licenses do you need?
**C.** You need one license per server. There are 10 servers in the array and one at each of the 5 locations.

10. Which of the following are advantages of CARP?
**A, B, C.** The advantage is that there is only one cached object, so requests for the object always know where to find the object.

# Answers to Chapter 17 Self Test

1. Which of the following is not a minimum requirement for installing Proxy Server 2.0?
**B.** 24MB of RAM is required for Proxy Server, according to the Microsoft documentation.

2. You are the system administrator. You are planning to install Proxy Server 2.0 to support 220 users. You want to make sure you have enough drive space for cached objects. What is the recommended cache space to support your users?
**D.** The recommended space for cache is 100MB plus .5MB for each client. You would need 210MB.

3. Which of the following are not options that you select during the installation of Proxy Server?
**A.** Transaction Server is an option in Windows NT 4.0 Option Pack.

4. Which of the following is necessary for caching, at a minimum?
**A, C.** 100MB is the default but 5MB is the minimum space required.

5. Which of the following statements are true about the LAT IP addresses?
**A, C, D.** The LAT should not contain external addresses.

6. Which of the following is not installed or enabled by default?

C. Packet filtering is a new feature in Proxy Server 2.0 and is disabled by default.

7. Which of the following changes are not made by the Proxy Server installation process?
B. There is no user account created to use Proxy Server. The IUSR_servername account is created when you install IIS.

8. You are a local administrator but you do not administer the Proxy Server. You have added another subnet to your network and want to access the IIS servers on that network. Since you cannot modify the LAT at the Proxy Server, what can you do to allow client browsers to access the new subnet?
C. This is the only appropriate choice. There is no mspclnt.txt file. If you modify the msplat.txt file, it is overwritten when the server makes its periodic updates.

9. What installation techniques can you use to install the WinSock client?
C, D. Either of these two techniques will work.

# Answers to Chapter 18 Self Test

1. Which of the following is not a primary method of controlling outbound access?
D. You do not control the time of the day a user can have Internet access. You can

control time-of-day access when using AutoDial, but this is not a primary method.

2. You have users on your network who want to access the Microsoft Web site. How do you configure Proxy Server to allow this?
B. You want to configure the Web Proxy permission. It is the Web Proxy service that brings you HTTP objects.

3. Which of the following is not true about access control for WinSock Proxy service?
D. This is not true. You can create your own protocol definitions.

4. Which of the following IP parameters cannot be used to control outbound access?
A. DHCP provides IP addresses and parameters to clients, but it cannot be used to directly control outbound access.

5. Which of the following is not a variable that you can change for a WinSock protocol?
C. You cannot change the TTL.

6. Which statement best describes the function of IP forwarding?
D. IP forwarding allows Windows NT to function as a router, routing traffic between NICs in the server.

7. Which of the following packet filtering techniques does Proxy Server support?
A, B. Dynamic and static filtering are supported. The terms active and passive apply to caching techniques.

8. You want to use Proxy Server AutoDial. Which of the following RAS parameters do you not need to configure?
C. You do not need to specify which users can use RAS because the users are not going to use RAS. Proxy Server takes care of that. If a user has outbound access for the Web Proxy service, for example, they can cause Proxy Server's AutoDial to activate and dial out.

9. Which of the following do you configure for the Proxy Server AutoDial function?
A, C. The default is to allow all hours for dial out. You may restrict that if you wish.

# Answers to Chapter 19 Self Test

1. Which of the following is not a Proxy service?
A. Web Publishing is an IIS service, not a Proxy service.

2. Which of the following cannot be used to configure Proxy Server?
B. WinMSD is a Windows NT diagnostic utility.

3. Which Internet protocols are not supported by Web Proxy?
A. NetBIOS is not an Internet protocol supported by Web Proxy service.

4. You are setting up a private network at your home. You have four PCs on a 10Base2 network. You have contracted with your cable company to provide Internet access and they have installed the cable modem. You need to configure your Proxy Server to send requests to the cable company Proxy Server. How do you configure this?
D. You configure routing from the Web Proxy service by specifying the upstream server name or IP address. There is no auto-detect.

5. You want to configure the cache on your Proxy Server. When you select the Caching tab, all of the options are grayed out. What is causing this?
D. The most likely cause of this scenario is there is no NTFS partition, which you need to support caching.

6. You have the ISM open and are in the WinSock property sheet. You want to know who is connected and currently using the Web Proxy service. What is the easiest way to find that out?
C. This is the easiest way. Remember that you can do these types of activities from any service. You can do B, but that would involve more work.

7. You have gone to the \msp folder to access the Web Proxy log file and there are many files in the folder. Several files are dated today. How do you know which file is the latest log file?
C. The Web Proxy log files begin with "W3" and then the date.

8. Which of the following is not a WinSock property sheet?
   **A.** Caching is a function of the Web Proxy service and is found in the Web Proxy property sheets, not in the WinSock property sheets.

9. Which of the following statements are true about WinSock protocols?
   **A, C, D.** You can create a new definition, which makes statement B false.

10. Which of the following statements are not true about the SOCKS Proxy service?
    **D.** SOCKS does not support IPX/SPX.

# Answers to Chapter 20 Self Test

1. You have enabled Web publishing on your Proxy Server. What else must you do to forward packets to a specific Web server?
   **B.** You can send packets to the local computer, but you can also forward them to other downstream servers.

2. You want to know when Proxy Server is dropping packets. What do you need to do to configure this?
   **B, C.** Alerting is enabled when you enable packet filtering. You should also configure the Alert tab to have the proper settings for your needs.

3. You want to be sure that Internet users do not have access to any of your Web servers.

How can you configure Proxy Server to accomplish this?
**D.** Enabling Web publishing, which is done through the properties sheet of the Web Proxy service, allows Internet users to have potential access. If you don't want this, you should make sure that this feature is disabled.

4. You want to forward all incoming requests for HTTP objects to the IIS located on your Proxy Server. How do you configure this?
   **A, B.** You must one, enable Web publishing and two, select where the packets are destined.

5. You have installed and configured your Proxy Server. Now you want to prevent Internet users from viewing your NetBIOS name table. How should you configure Proxy Server?
   **C, D.** By enabling packet filtering, you are blocking packets. By ensuring that there are no NetBIOS filters in the Exceptions list, you know these packets are going to be rejected. Without these filters, the nbtstat utility does not return the name table.

6. Which of the following is not true of Web publishing?
   **A, C.** By default, Web publishing is not enabled. You can forward packets to any Web server, not just IIS servers.

7. Which of the following statements are not true about packet filtering?
A. A dynamic filter opens and closes the port when needed. A persistent filter closes the port for use at all times.

8. For what events does Proxy Server not write an event in the system log?
B. Logon failures are recorded in the security log, if you have auditing enabled. Windows NT keeps track of this, not Proxy Server.

9. Which of the following statements are true about logging information?
A, C, D. Proxy Server does give the number of connection attempts. You might be able to derive such information by looking at some of the events, but don't expect to see an event that says *x* number of users attempt to connect.

# Answers to Chapter 21 Self Test

1. You have configured Proxy Server to auto-dial to your ISP. You installed RAS and configured RAS. When you access the Web Proxy Server, you do not get connected to the Internet and the modem never dials. What can be causing this problem?
C. You must configure a phonebook entry in addition to configuring RAS and Auto Dial. Don't forget to supply logon credentials as well.

2. You installed Windows NT Server, IIS Server, and Proxy Server. You have no other Windows NT Servers on your LAN, nor do you have a Windows NT Domain. What must you do to ensure that clients can connect to the Proxy Server?
D. Based on the information given, this is the best choice. You need a valid account to access the Proxy Server. You could install a domain and then add the Proxy Server to the domain, but this is more work and more equipment.

3. You made several modifications to the mspclnt.ini file on one of the local computers. When you came back the next day, the modifications were not there. You are using the NTFS file system. What is the most probable cause of this problem?
B. This file is refreshed from the server every six hours. The changes are being overwritten.

4. You have configured Proxy Server to use Windows NT challenge/response protocol. When you try to connect to a site on the Internet, you immediately receive back an error message saying "Access Denied." What is the cause of this problem?
A. If you get back an error message immediately, the most likely cause is that access to that site is denied.

5. You are attempting set up the WinSock client on a Windows 95 computer. You are having trouble getting the installation to

complete successfully. What can you check to help determine the source of the problem? **D.** The mspsetup.log is kept on the client and contains information about setup errors.

6. You want to view the registry settings for Proxy Server. What tool can you use to do this?
**B.** Regedt32 is the registry-editing tool of choice. None of the other tools allows you to view the registry parameters for Proxy Server.

7. You want to check the parameters for the WinSock software on a client. What utility can you use to do this?
**A.** You can use CHKWSP32 or CHKWSP16. Mspdiags is a utility that you can use to troubleshoot Proxy Service.

8. You are sitting at a Windows NT Workstation computer attempting to determine why you cannot connect to the Proxy Server. You try to ping the Proxy Server by name and receive the message "Bad IP Address." You cannot ping the Proxy Server by using the IP address. What can you do to help isolate this problem?
**B.** Using ipconfig will indicate that the IP address of this computer is 0.0.0.0, which means it has no IP address.

9. You want to know how efficient your cache is. What object/counter do you use?
**D.** The Cache object has nothing to do with the Proxy Server cache which is

written to disk. The Cache object refers to RAM cache used by Windows NT.

10. You ran Performance Monitor and recorded the information to a log file. You selected the objects Physical Disk and Logical Disk. When you open the log file, all of the counters for those objects display zero activities. Why?
**B.** The disk counters are disabled by default.

# Answers to Chapter 22 Self Test

1. You are creating a package for distribution that will include the Windows Desktop Update. How much RAM do you need on your client's stations? Select all that are correct.
**C, D.** The Windows Desktop Update requires additional RAM from the browser-only installation.

2. You are planning a deployment of IE 4.0 in a global organization where English is the corporate standard for desktop. There are nine different departments that need custom configurations. What is the minimum number of distribution packages you must create?
**A.** The key issue is that there is only one language. IEAK 4.0 supports up to 10 installation options for a single custom package.

3.  AVS has just completed. How can you verify that all components are current?
    **C.** Microsoft uses green check marks to represent that a component is current, yellow exclamation points for components that are outdated, and red Xs for components that are unavailable.

4.  You are running the IEAK Wizard with an ISP customization code. Which of the following will you be able to accomplish?
    **A, B, C, D.** As an ISP, you have the additional capability to use a single floppy disk to configure a client connection to a sign-up server.

5.  In which stage of the IEAK Wizard do you specify the download URLs?
    **C.** Stage 3, Configuring Active Setup, is where you specify the download URLs.

6.  The default setting for the Internet Security Zone is
    **B.** Level 0 and Level 4 refer to content ratings. High is the default setting for the Restricted Security Zone.

7.  In the Exceptions box for the Proxy Settings page, you can specify the URLs that do not use the Proxy Server. Valid entries in the Exceptions box are:
    **A, B, C.** Usernames are not supported for any of the advanced proxy settings.

8.  Profile Manager is used to maintain or customize which type of file?
    **C.** Although an .ins file incorporates .adm, .cab, .exe., and .js files, the Profile Manager is specifically used to maintain and customize .ins files.

9.  Which of the following pieces of configuration information do you receive by typing Ipconfig at the DOS prompt on a Windows NT machine?
    **A, B.** The DHCP server, WINS server, and description of the network interface card (NIC) appear only if you use the /all parameter with the Ipconfig command.

10. Your company wants to take advantage of streaming technology to broadcast live product seminars to all members of the sales department. You have been asked to create a custom package for them. What component must you include to allow the sales department to receive these broadcasts?
    **D.** NetMeeting allows live multimedia collaborations and application sharing. Outlook Express provides e-mail and news services. The Desktop Update provides Web integration with the desktop and allows active content to reside on the desktop. Only NetShow takes advantage of streaming or broadcasting technologies.

MICROSOFT CERTIFIED SYSTEMS ENGINEER

# B

# About the CD

# CD-ROM Instructions

This CD-ROM contains a full web site accessible to you via your web browser. Browse to or double-click **Index (Click.htm)** at the root of the CD-ROM and you will find instructions for navigating the web site and for installing the various software components.

## Electronic Book

An electronic version of the entire book in HTML format.

## Interactive Self-Study Module

An electronic self-study test bank is linked to the electronic book to help you instantly review key exam topics that may still be unclear. This module contains over 500 review questions, the same questions that appear at the end of each chapter. If you answer a multiple choice question correctly by clicking on the right answer, you will automatically link to the next question. If you answer incorrectly, you will be linked to the appropriate section in the electronic book for further study.

## Installing Sample Exams

Included on the CD-ROM are sample exams from some of the leading practice test vendors. Launch the web site by double-clicking on the **Index (Click.htm)** file in the root of the CD-ROM. This will launch your default browser and bring up the web's home page. From the Home Page, click on the "Sample Exams" button. You will be instructed that some of the exams can be launched directly from the web page by Internet Explorer by clicking on the hyperlinks and choosing the "open the file" option when prompted. Others exams will require additional installation steps. Carefully read the instructions for each exam.

If you have problems installing from Internet Explorer, or you are using another browser such as Navigator, you should install directly from Windows Explorer by opening the Demo Exams folder on the CD-ROM.

The demo exam, its subdirectory, and the file required to run the installation, are listed below:

| Product | Installation File |
|---|---|
| Microhard MCSE QUEST | ../Demo Exams/MCSEQuest/qustdemo.exe |
| Transcender CERT | ../Demo Exams/Transcender/setup.exe |
| VFX MCP Endeavor | ../Demo Exams/VFX Endeavor/setup.exe |
| Endeavor X* | ../Demo Exams/EndeavorX/setup.exe |
| Self-Test Software PEP | ../Demo Exams/Self-Test Software/pep.exe |

*Once you've installed EndeavorX, launch the program from your "Start" button. To see the IIS 4.0 demo, pull down the FILE\IMPORT menu to import the following IIS 4.0 data file: \Demo Exams\EndeavorX\EndeavorXIIS4\MS7087 Evaluation.mdbn

As of the printing of this book, the Microhard MCSE Quest, Transcender CERT, Self Test Software PEP, and BeachFrontQuizzer exams are current through Internet Information Server 3.0. Check the following sites for updated demos:

- www.microhard.com
- www.transcender.com
- www.stsware.com
- www.bfquiz.com

Once they are installed, you should run the programs via the "Start Programs" taskbar on your desktop.

# C

## About the
## Web Site

# Access Global Knowledge Network

As you know by now, Global Knowledge Network is the largest independent IT training company in the world. Just by purchasing this book, you have also secured a free subscription to the Access Global web site and its many resources. You can find it at:

http://access.globalknowledge.com

You can log in directly at the Access Global site. You will be e-mailed a new, secure password immediately upon registering.

## What You'll Find There. . .

You will find a lot of information at the Global Knowledge site, most of which can be broken down into three categories:

### Skills Gap Analysis

Global Knowledge offers several ways for you to analyze your networking skills and discover where they may be lacking. Using Global Knowledge Network's trademarked Competence Key Tool, you can do a skills gap analysis and get recommendations for where you may need to do some more studying (sorry, it just may not end with this book!).

### Networking

You'll also gain valuable access to another asset: people. At the Access Global site, you'll find threaded discussions as well as live discussions. Talk to other MCSE candidates, get advice from folks who have already taken exams, and get access to instructors and MCTs.

### Product Offerings

Of course, Global Knowledge also offers its products here—and you may find some valuable items for purchase: CBTs, books, courses. Browse freely and see if there's something that could help you.

# Glossary

**acknowledgment (ACK)**    An ACK is a packet of information sent from the recipient computer to the sending computer that verifies a successful transmission.

**Active Server Pages (ASPs)**    Active Server Pages are a server-side scripting feature. ASPs are HTML pages that contain scripts that are executed on the server before being downloaded to the client.

**ActiveX**    ActiveX is a set of object-oriented tools developed by Microsoft. A program developed in the ActiveX environment is called a component or an ActiveX control. A component is a stand-alone program that can be run anywhere in an ActiveX network. An ActiveX control is similar to a Java applet.

**administrator account**    This account is used to administer the settings on a Windows NT Server and network. This account is created during installation and has unlimited access to the server. Care must be taken when logged into a server as an administrator, because administrator access rights include the ability to shut down the server or erase critical data.

**alert**    An alert is generated if an event occurs that might compromise system integrity, application performance, or security. Alerts are recorded in the system log file and optionally, can be sent as e-mail. Proxy Server alerts are recorded.

**application gateway**    See proxy server.

**application partitioning**    Application partitioning occurs when an application runs on several servers to distribute the CPU time used.

**application programming interface (API)**    An API is a defined method that a programmer uses to write an application to interface with the operating system or another application.

**array**    An array is a group of Proxy Servers bound together to increase performance.

**asymmetric algorithm**   An asymmetric encrpytion algorithm uses a public key and a private key to encrypt and decrypt data.

**asynchronous communication**   In asynchronous communication, messages are delivered to a queue for delivery at a later time. The client performs other processing while waiting for the server to pick up and respond to the message. Also known as store-and-forward.

**authentication**   Authenticating users is a way to distinguish legitimate users from those trying to gain unauthorized access.

**AutoDial**   AutoDial is a feature that allows you to configure Proxy Server to automatically dial to your ISP, or dial back to your central location. Proxy Server uses RAS to establish the dial-up connection. AutoDial is event driven and makes the connection only when needed.

**back door**   A back door is a way into a computer system or network, sometimes through the legitimate system security and sometimes around the legitimate systems security.

**band**   A band is an area of the menu bar that contains additional tools.

**bandwidth**   Bandwidth is a network's capacity to move data, measured in bits per second (bps).

**baseline**   When monitoring system performance, a baseline is a series of tests that are run while the system is idle. The data collected during other times of system use can be compared to the baseline to determine if a problem exists.

**basic linked content**   Basic linked content is the most common type of Web content. It is static; all users see the same content. See also Dynamic HTML.

**bottleneck**   A bottleneck is any place there is a system shortage or a resource shortage.

**bps (bits per second)**   bps is a measurement of how fast data can be transferred across a network connection.

**branding**   In IEAK, branding is the ability to customize the bitmaps for Active Setup.

**bridge**   A bridge is a hardware device that connects two local area network (LAN) segments of either the same or different topologies. A bridge is protocol independent.

**bug**   A bug is an error in a script or program.

**business rule**   Business rules, in Microsoft Transaction Server, are rules that are applied, such as government regulations or other business algorithms.

**Cache Array Routing Protocol (CARP)**   CARP is an enhancement of Internet Cache Protocol (ICP). CARP allows a proxy server to query other proxy servers to see if those servers have cached copies of requested objects before the proxy server goes to the Internet for the object.

**caching**   Caching is the process of storing frequently-accessed data in temporary and easy-to-access storage.

**canonical name (CNAME)**   A canonical name is an alias that refers back to the original server. The name of the virtual server is associated with the physical server name using the canonical name. A server may have multiple canonical names.

**cascade**   A cascade is an upstream, chained Proxy Server. A cascade allows packets to be sent to the downstream Proxy Server computer.

**CD-ROM**   A CD-ROM is a device, similar to a musical compact disc, that stores data.

**CERN (Conseil Europeen pour la Recherche Nucleaire or the European Laboratory for Particle Physics)**   CERN is a Swiss organization that developed a proxy protocol that became the standard accepted by the Internet. Much of the support for HTTP and the Web libraries had their origins at CERN.

**certificate authority (CA)**   The certificate authority issues a certificate only after verifying the requestor's identity. The CA also keeps track of revoked certificates.

**certificate revocation list (CRL)**   The CRL is a list of revoked certificates maintained by the certificate authority. Certificates may be revoked if the certificate's time period is no longer valid or if the administrator revokes the certificate.

**certificate**   See digital certificate.

**Certificate Server**   Certificate Server is a standards-based, server application for managing the issuance, revocation, and renewal of digital certificates. Certificate Server is part of the Windows NT 4.0 Option Pack.

**CGI (Common Gateway Interface)**   A CGI is a predefined method that a Web server uses to pass control to an application program and receive data back when the application is done.

**chaining**   Chaining occurs when Proxy Server routes an access request to any CERN-compliant proxy server, including another Microsoft Proxy Server.

**channel service unit**   The CSU side of the device is connected to the telco circuit. See data service unit.

**checksum**   The checksum is a calculation attached to a packet by the sending computer. The recipient recalculates the checksum and compares that value to the checksum value contained in the packet.

**CiDaemon process**   The CiDaemon process is responsible for identifying the document format and selecting the proper content filters and word breakers.

**cipher text**   Cipher text refers to data that has been encrypted.

**command line**   The command line is a character mode interface for computer applications that relies on commands instead of a graphical interface to process information.

**component**   See ActiveX.

**connectionless protocol**   A connectionless protocol does not guarantee end delivery or set up a session. See connection-oriented protocol.

**connection-oriented protocol**   A connection-oriented protocol establishes a session between the client and the server before any information is exchanged. This session remains established until it is torn down, typically by the process that initiated the session. This is a bidirectional connection and the protocol provides for error recovery.

**container object**   In the context of MMC, container objects (in a tree) can contain other objects or tasks. See also leaf object.

**content cache server**   A content cache server stores the Web pages most frequently accessed by the network users. This speeds up the return of Web pages to clients' browsers because they come from a local server rather than the Internet.

**content filter**   A content filter is a small program that recognizes the proprietary format of a document. Each separate file format has its own content filter. Index Server uses content filters to index the files.

**control**   See Active X.

**cookie**   A cookie is a text file (usually) that is created by a Web server to store information specific to a computer but relative to the server site, such as preferred server choice, last connection time, length of connection, and places visited on site.

**corpus**   The corpus is defined as all of the documents stored that are indexed. The corpus may be located on local disks or on remote servers defined as either virtual directories or virtual servers.

**cracker**   A cracker is a person who gains access or attempts to gain access to a system or computer network with malicious intent. A cracker will illegally gain access to computer systems for fun, profit, or personal gain but does not always harm the system when gaining access.

**Data Access Components**   The Data Access Components from Microsoft make it easy to use databases with an expanded support for a variety of connections such as ActiveX data objects and OLEDB.

**data rule**   A data rule, Microsoft Transaction Server, is used to keep data structures intact within the same database as well as between databases.

**data service unit/channel service unit (DSU/CSU)**   A DSU/CSU is used to connect a communication device such as a router or a bridge to a leased data circuit. This type of circuit is usually a full-time, permanent connection.

**data source name (DSN)**   A DSN is the name that the application uses to request a connection to an ODBC data source.

**debugging**   Debugging is the process of finding and fixing bugs in scripts or software.

**decryption**   Decryption is the process of unscrambling data that has been encrypted. See also encryption.

**denial of service (DoS)**   A DoS attack is one where a computer is not penetrated or breached but is made unavailable for use because it is too busy responding to bogus requests.

**dial-up analog modem line**   Dial-up analog modem lines are the most common types of circuits. Modems can accommodate speeds up to 56 Kbps, although most phone company circuits, due to design limitations, cannot accommodate speeds quite that high.

**Dial-Up Networking (DUN)**   DUN is the remote access client of Windows NT operating systems that facilitates connections to remote hosts.

**digital certificate**   Digital certificates are a form of authentication. They provide the mechanism necessary to conduct private communications in an open environment.

**Digital Data Service (DDS)**   A DDS circuit is a leased line, point-to-point circuit. A DDS circuit is not shared with anyone else.

**digital envelope**   A digital envelope is created to send a private message that can be read only by the specific recipient intended. When creating the digital envelope, the sender encrypts the message using the recipient's public key. This message can only be decrypted by the recipient's private key.

**digital ID**   To secure e-mail messages, use a digital ID. A digital ID is composed of a public key, a private key, and a digital signature.

**digital signature**   A digital signature is used to confirm authorship and not to encrypt messages. Digital signatures are used to verify that the person who claims to be the author in fact sent the message.

**Distributed Component Object Model (DCOM)**   DCOM is a fast object transport native to Windows. DCOM allows components to be located anywhere on the network. The component locations are transparent to the client, since the client does not need to know their physical location on the network.

**domain**   A domain is a set of workstations and servers on a network that share a common security system.

**Domain Name Service (DNS)**   DNS is a hierarchical name service that translates Fully Qualified Domain Names to IP addresses. DNS is used with TCP/IP hosts.

**dynamic filtering**   Dynamic filtering occurs when Proxy Server evaluates which TCP/IP packet types are accessible to specific internal network services. A dynamic filter opens the TCP port only long enough to accept the connection and closes the port. See persistant filtering.

**Dynamic HTML**   Dynamic HTML is an emerging standard. Using Dynamic HTML, Web authors can change page elements, styles, and content at any time, even after the client has loaded the page. Dynamic HTML executes on the client's computer rather than on the server. See also basic linked content.

**Dynamic Link Library (DLL)**   A DLL is a module of executable code that is loaded on demand. Used in Microsoft Windows products.

**dynamic port**   A dynamic port is one whose value is selected at random by a computer. The port must be known to other computers.

**electronic mail (e-mail)**   Mail messages that are transmitted electronically from one network user to another, or across the Internet, are called e-mail.

**encryption**   Encryption is the process of scrambling data so that it can only be read by the intended recipient. See also decryption.

**Exchange Server**   Exchange Server is Microsoft's advanced e-mail and Groupware server. IIS integrates with Exchange Server and makes use of Exchange Server facilities such as SMTP server and POP3 server.

**extensible**   Programs that are extensible can have their functionality extended by external routines.

**extranet**   An extranet is a private internal network combined with another private network toward the purpose of facilitating inter-organization communication or business processes. An example of an extranet is linking a business's network with a customer's network so that the customer can process orders and access information without putting the traffic on the public Internet.

**firewall**   A firewall is a hardware or software product that protects a computer system from external intrusion. Firewalls have become more instrumental on computer systems as access to the Internet has grown more popular.

**flow control**   When two computers are transmitting packets back and forth, there must be some agreement about when to stop if one side gets too many packets. This process is called flow control.

**fractional T-1**   As the name suggests, the circuit speed of fractional T-1 is a fraction of the speed of the T-1 circuit. It is technically possible to construct a fractional T-1 circuit with any number of DS0 channels, giving you speed ranges from 64 Kbps up to the maximum speed.

**FTP (File Transfer Protocol)**   FTP is a TCP protocol that is used for sending files between the server and clients.

**gateway**   A gateway is a device that connects two or more dissimilar computer systems. Gateways can be electronic or software devices, and are becoming more common as the need for cross-platform communication increases.

**globally unique identifier (GUID)**   A GUID is an identifier that is used to distinguish a program or object from others.

**Gopher**   Gopher is the hierarchical structure of files on Internet FTP servers.

**Green Paper**   The Green Paper lays out the federal government's plan to move from a single-source system for the DNS to a name registration system that is competitive. The Green Paper, sponsored by the White House and put together by the Department of Commerce, is just a proposal at this point.

**guaranteed end delivery**   Guaranteed end delivery is a built-in mechanism to ensure that packets are delivered to their destination reliably.

**hacker**   A hacker is an independent-minded, generally law-abiding computer enthusiast who delights in gaining an intimate understanding of the internal workings of computer systems and computer networks in particular. Hackers are usually harmless.

**hash**   A hash is used by a Proxy Server array to make routing decisions. The hash is a mathematical algorithm that uses three factors: available servers, the URL of the client request, and a load factor.

**host**   On the Internet, a host is any computer that has full two-way access to other computers on the Internet. Each host has a unique host number that, together with the network number, forms its IP address.

**hyperlink**   A hyperlink is a location on a Web page that, when the user clicks on it, takes the user to another location on the Web.

**Hypertext Markup Language (HTML)**   HTML is a set of tags that are used to format information to be displayed on a Web site. A browser interprets the tags and presents the information accordingly.

**Hypertext Transfer Protocol (HTTP)**   HTTP is the protocol that is used when downloading (or uploading files with HTTP 1.1) on the World Wide Web. These files can contain text, graphics, sound, or video.

**Iexpress**   Iexpress is a tool that comes with IEAK and is used to package a custom application or third-party application into a .cab file that is self-installing and self-extracting.

**Index Server**   Microsoft Index Server creates a list of documents on your Web server and indexes the contents of those documents.

**instance**   In Performance Monitor, an instance is a unique occurrence of an object.

**Integrated Switched Digital Network (ISDN)**   ISDN is a set of CCITT/ITU standards for high-speed data transmission over telephone wires.

**intermediary**   The intermediary is the component of Certificate Server that receives the request for a new certificate from the requestor. The intermediary submits the request to the server engine on behalf of the requestor.

**Internet Connection Services for RAS**   Internet Connection Services for Remote Access Service (RAS) is a set of software components designed to help corporations and ISPs build comprehensive Internet access solutions, including dial-up virtual private networks (VPNs). With Internet Connection Services for RAS, subscribers and employees have a seamless connection experience, a global dial-up service, and secure connections over the Internet to a private network.

**Internet Explorer (IE)**   IE is Microsoft's Web browser.

**Internet Explorer Administration Kit (IEAK)**   IEAK is Microsoft's tool for packaging and deploying custom implementations of Internet Explorer 4.*x*.

**Internet Information Server (IIS)**   IIS is Microsoft's Web server software that services requests from Web browsers running on client computers. IIS runs on Windows NT Server and provides connectivity to an organization's Web site.

**Internet Server Application Programming Interface**   See ISAPI.

**Internet Service Manager (ISM)**   ISM is a tool used to configure IIS to improve performance, enforce security, monitor system use, and define directories for storing data.

**Internet Service Provider (ISP)**   An ISP is an organization that provides connectivity to the Internet for users and organizations. ISPs allow users to send and receive e-mail, upload and download files from the Internet, surf the World Wide Web (WWW), and host their own Web sites.

**internetwork**   An internetwork is two or more networks connected together.

**InterNIC**   (Internet Network Information Center) The InterNIC is the organization that is responsible for registering and maintaining the list of domain names for the World Wide Web.

**intranet**   An intranet is an internal network using Internet technology. By definition, an intranet is not connected to other networks or to the Internet. If an internal network is connected to the Internet, it is not an intranet.

**intruder**   Any person trying to break into a network.

**IP (Internet Protocol)**   IP is a commonly-used protocol that sets up the mechanism for transferring data across the network. Usually seen in TCP/IP.

**IP address**   The IP address identifies the computer on the network.

**IP masking**   IP masking hides the IP addresses on the local LAN from the Internet. This is not the same thing as a subnet mask.

**IPX**   IPX is the native transport protocol for Novell's NetWare. IPX is also available in the Windows NT environment.

**ISAPI (Internet Server Application Program Interface)**   ISAPI is a set of Windows application calls that allow programmers to write Web server applications that can run faster than a CGI application.

**ISAPI filter**   An ISAPI filter is called every time a request is made of a server. ISAPI filters can monitor, modify, and redirect requests.

**key**   A key is a mechanism used to encrypt data. The same key is required by the recipient to decrypt the data.

**keystroke grabber**   A keystroke grabber is software installed on a computer that records the user's keystrokes (keys on the keyboard that the user presses). It writes those keystrokes to a file. One purpose of a keystroke grabber is to record user login IDs and passwords.

**kiosk**   A download site is often called a kiosk.

**leaf object**   In the context of object oriented programming, an object that cannot contain other objects is known as a leaf object. See also container object.

**load sharing**   Load sharing is a technique where processing tasks are distributed among several computers so as not to overload any given computers while others remain idle.

**local address table (LAT)**   The function of the LAT is to define the addresses and address ranges on the internal network. Network addresses not contained in the LAT are considered external addresses.

**logging**  Logging is a mechanism that can be enabled to keep track of certain system events and store information about those events in a log file.

**marshalling**  Marshalling is the process of packaging interface parameters across threads.

**MB (megabyte)**  A megabyte is one million bytes. A byte is typically eight bits in PC systems.

**Mbps (megabits per second)**  Mbps is used to measure throughput or communication speed. Mbps is a communication rate of 1,048,576 bits per second.

**mean time between failures (MTBF)**  This represents the average time between component failures.

**metabase**  The IIS configuration parameters are stored in a database called the metabase.

**Microsoft Management Console (MMC)**  Management Console is a Microsoft product featured when IIS 4.0 is installed. It is intended to be the standard console in Windows NT 5.0. Applications written for managing services, called plug-ins, are written to run in MMC. MMC provides administrators with a common tool with which to manage all services running on Windows NT.

**Microsoft Message Queue (MSMQ)**  MSMQ gives applications the ability to communicate with each other by sending and receiving messages. MSMQ uses asynchronous communication and a store-and-forward methodology. MSMQ keeps messages in queues that protect messages from being lost while in transit. The queues are the place for recipients to look for new messages. MSMQ is integrated with Transaction Server (MTS).

**Microsoft Script Debugger**  See Script Debugger.

**Microsoft Site Server Express**   See Site Server Express.

**MIME (Multi-Purpose Internet Mail Extension)**   MIME is an Internet specification that lets computers exchange all types of data on the Internet: text files, audio files, video files, image files (.GIF, .JPEG), and executable files. The data type is specified in the MIME header, which is inserted at the start of every Internet transmission.

**MMC**   See Microsoft Management Console.

**mode of operation**   In IEAK, mode of operation refers to how IEAK will be used: for corporate administration or ISP services.

**modem (modulator/demodulator)**   A modem modulates a digital signal from the computer into an analog signal that travels along a voice grade circuit. Modems are slow communication devices with connection speeds ranging in the neighborhood of 20,000 bps.

**Mosaic**   Mosaic was the first graphical Web browser.

**MTS**   See Transaction Server.

**multi-homed computer**   A multi-homed computer is one with more than one network card.

**name server (NS)**   In the context of DNS, a name server is the record that designates the DNS server.

**namespace**   Namespace is the terminology used to describe the hierarchy of the objects.

**navigation**   The process of navigation is using links on one Web page to access another Web page.

**Navigator**    Navigator is Netscape's Web browser.

**negative acknowledgment (NACK)**    A NACK is a packet sent from the recipient computer to the sending computer to verify that a transmission was unsuccessful.

**network analyzer**    A network analyzer allows the network administrator to examine packets on a network and capture packets to determine the source address of the request that is attempting to busy out the server.

**network interface card (NIC)**    A NIC is the card that allows the computer to connect to and communicate across the network. The network cable attaches to the NIC.

**Network Monitor**    Network Monitor is only available on Windows NT Server. It is a functional network diagnostic tool and protocol analyzer.

**Network News Transfer Protocol (NNTP)**    NNTP is a standards-based server for hosting electronic discussion groups called newsgroups. NNTP supports secure authentication and can be encrypted.

**newsgroup**    A newsgroup is an online discussion group organized around a particular topic. Users can post messages to the newsgroup and other users can read and respond to those messages. Newsgroups can be private or public.

**node**    In the context of MMC, a node is an item or object in the tree view of the namespace.

**normalizer**    The function of a normalizer is to take words produced by the word breaker and clean them up. The normalizer corrects text for capitalization, punctuation, and removes extraneous words that do add to the meaning, such as "the" and "a".

**NT File System (NTFS)**    The file system used by Windows NT. NTFS supports large storage media and file system recovery, and, most importantly, local security for files and folders.

**object**    From the point of view of Performance Monitor, some examples of objects are the processor, memory, cache, hard disk, services, and other components.

**Open Database Connectivity (ODBC)**    ODBC is a standard for accessing database systems from different manufacturers.

**Orange Book**    The Orange Book provides technical criteria for evaluating hardware and software security, along with evaluation methodologies that support a data security model.

**package**    A package is a defined set of components that perform related functions as a single application.

**packet**    A packet is a unit of data that is transmitted across a network as a whole.

**packet filtering**    Packet filtering occurs when Proxy Server intercepts incoming packets. Proxy Server evaluates packets before they are passed to higher levels in the protocol layers or to an application.

**packet sniffer**    A packet sniffer for data monitors the network and captures each packet on the network. See Network Monitor.

**Performance Monitor**    Performance Monitor is a utility that provides performance information about a server to help locate bottlenecks, determine which resources are overtaxed, and plan upgrades to the system's capacity.

**phreak**    A phreak is a mischievous individual who delights in manipulating telephone equipment and other communications equipment. Phreaks have been around for several decades, and in their early existence, they broke into telephone systems in an effort to make long-distance calls without charges.

**Ping (Packet Internet Groper)**   Ping is a utility that verifies a computer's IP address and makes sure that the computer is properly connected to the Internet.

**plug-in**   A plug-in is an application that extends the capabilities of a browser.

**property sheet**   Property sheets are used by system administrators to set parameters for IIS services, such as the WWW service or the FTP service.

**protocol**   A protocol is a set of rules of formatting and interaction used to permit computers to communicate across a network. Networking software usually supports multiple levels of protocols.

**proxy**   A proxy provides a path in and out of the network. Microsoft Proxy Server has the authority to act as a proxy on behalf of local clients.

**proxy server**   A proxy server is a server that is entitled to act on behalf of other computers on the network. Proxy servers act as gateways between two systems attempting to communicate with each other across the Internet. Microsoft Proxy Server is an example of a proxy server.

**Proxy Server**   Microsoft Proxy Server provides LAN clients with secure access to the Internet. Proxy Server can also be configured as a firewall to allow Internet users to access servers on an internal LAN.

**public key encryption**   The Secure Sockets Layer (SSL) utilizes a technique known as *public key encryption* to shield the session key from interception during transmission. The public key algorithm is comprised of two keys: a public key and a private key.

**query**    A query is a request for information. In the context of DNS, a query might be a request for the IP address of a specified host.

**Remote Access Service (RAS)**    RAS is the dial-up service in Windows NT that allows users to access the network remotely by telephone lines.

**remote procedure call (RPC)**    RPC is a protocol that allows an application to request a service from a program located in another computer on a network without having to know the network details. The requesting application is a client and the application being asked to provide a service is the server.

**RemotMsp**    The RemotMsp utility is a command-line utility that helps you configure and administer a remote Proxy Server computer.

**Request for Comments (RFC)**    RFCs are public documents that define standards to be used by computers and networks connected to the Internet.

**resolver**    In the context of DNS, a client is called a resolver.

**resource manager**    A resource manager is software that coordinates changes to a resource (for example, a file) in order to prevent concurrent and conflicting access.

**retransmission**    Retransmission is the term used when the sender resends data packets that it sent previously.

**reverse hosting**    In reverse hosting, Proxy Server maintains a list of servers on the internal network that have permission to publish to the Internet. This enables Proxy Server to listen and respond on behalf of multiple servers that are located behind it.

**reverse proxy**   Reverse proxy is a feature of Proxy Server 2.0 that allows users on the Internet to access the Web servers on an internal network. Proxy Server processes incoming requests to an internal Hypertext Transfer Protocol (HTTP) server and responds on its behalf.

**rogue service**   A rogue service is an unwanted service that is running on a computer, consuming CPU time.

**router**   A router is a device that connects more than one physical network, or segments of a network, using IP (or other protocols) routing software. As packets reach the router, the router reads them and forwards them to their destination, or to another router.

**scope**   A scope is defined as those documents from the corpus that are indexed. The administrator defines the scope by stating which directories should be indexed. The documents in the scope create the catalog.

**script**   A script is a program written in an interpreted language, as opposed to a compiled language. A script contains commands, instructions to the interpreting application.

**Script Debugger**   Script Debugger from Microsoft is a built-in tool aimed at making it easier to follow script execution in order to find bugs in the script execution. Script Debugger can be used with client-based scripts or server-based scripts.

**second-level gateway**   Second-level gateways are similar to proxy servers except that second-level gateways verify the TCP or UDP session. Second-level gateways avoid any direct physical contact between the Internet and any host on the internal network (this describes Microsoft Proxy Server).

**secure socket**   Secure sockets provide a mechanism for transmitting and receiving encrypted traffic and for authenticating the client to the server.

**Secure Sockets Layer (SSL)**    SSL was developed by Netscape to ensure the secure transmission of messages in a network. The SSL resides between an application and the TCP/IP layers of the Internet.

**sequencing**    Sequencing is the process of dividing data into multiple packets and sending each packet separately. Each packet is given a sequence number in case they arrive out of order; the receiving station can reassemble them in the proper order.

**server**    A server is the computer running the network server software that allows it to offer the resources for use by other computers (users) on the network.

**server engine**    The server engine is the core component of Certificate Server. The engine pushes information between the components during request processing and certificate generation. The engine monitors each request through the various processes to ensure that appropriate actions are being taken.

**Simple Mail Transfer Protocol (SMTP)**    SMTP is a standards-based mail server and is used throughout the Internet. It is highly scalable and allows for the partitioning of mailboxes across multiple servers.

**Site Server Express**    Site Server Express is a tool from Microsoft that provides Web site administrators with the ability to analyze log files and Web site content on that server.

**SMTP service**    The SMTP service provides facilities for customizing a server's specific security and delivery requirements. The SMTP service has been optimized to provide maximum-messages-per-second processing.

**snap-in**    System management tools such as Internet Service Manager and Microsoft Transaction Server, when used with MMC, are called snap-ins.

The snap-in provides the actual functionality while the MMC provides the common environment for the snap-ins.

**socket**   A socket is a network endpoint.

**SOCKS**   SOCKS is a protocol used by non-Windows computers. A proxy server may accept requests from clients in a network and forward them across the Internet. The client side of SOCKS is built into Internet Explorer and Netscape Navigator. The server side of SOCKS can be added to a proxy server.

**spoofing**   Spoofing occurs when IP packets from one computer are made to look like packets from a trusted system. Spoofing lets an intruder on a TCP/IP network impersonate a computer as if it is on a local network.

**SQL Server**   SQL Server is part of Microsoft's Back Office suite of client/server applications. SQL Server is an ANSI-compliant SQL (pronounced "seeqwell") server. IIS provides a connector to SQL Server.

**store-and-forward**   See asynchronous communication.

**subnetwork (subnet)**   A subnetwork is a subset of an organization that is clearly identifiable. For example, a subnetwork might be a network for a particular group within the organization (Personnel) or a particular geographic location (New England area). This concept is not related to an IP subnet mask.

**symmetric algorithm**   Symmetric algorithms are a common type of encryption algorithm. Symmetric algorithms use the same key for both encryption and decryption. In order to communicate using symmetric algorithms, both parties must share a secret key.

**synchronous communication**   In synchronous communication, messages are generated and then forwarded to the recipient immediately. The recipient is interrupted and must respond to the messages in real time.

**T-1**   T-1 is a widely used digital transmission link that uses a point-to-point transmission technology with two 2-wire pair (or four wires where a modem uses only one pair or two wires). One pair is used to send data and one pair is used to receive data. T-1, also written as T1, can transmit digital, voice, data, and video signals at 1,544 Mbps.

**T-3**   T-3 is designed for transporting large amounts of data at high speeds. T-3, also written as T3, is a leased line that can transmit data at 45,154 Mbps.

**TCP port number**   The TCP port number identifies a process or application at the computer.

**TCP/IP (Transmission Control Protocol/Internet Protocol)**
TCP/IP is an industry standard set of protocols used to connect computers within a network, as well as to external networks, such as WANs and the Internet. TCP/IP is the most common networking protocol and can be used to connect many different types of computers for cross-platform communication.

**TFTP (Trivial File Transfer Protocol)**   TFTP is a file transfer protocol used when user authentication and directory visibility are not required. TFTP uses UDP instead of TCP.

**thread**   A topic of interest in a newsgroup to which one or more participants has posted. Also the smallest unit of execution of a program or a process.

**time-to-live (TTL)**   The amount of time that the information stays in the cache is referred to as the time to live (TTL). The TTL is determined by the TTL entry from the nonlocal name server.

**transaction**   In the concept of MTS, a transaction is a unit of information exchange that must be completed in its entirety. A transaction succeeds or fails as a whole. An example of a transaction is an update to a network database.

**Transaction Server (MTS)**   Transaction Server provides a stable run-time environment for high-performance applications. Transaction Server includes a graphical administration tool for managing these applications throughout an organization.

**tuning**   Tuning is the process of identifying which resources are critically short and configuring the system to maximize its performance relative to these limited resources.

**UDP (User Datagram Protocol)**   UDP is similar to TCP but it does not provide as much built-in data validation. The application program must be able to provide these services.

**Uniform Resource Locator (URL)**   A URL is the address of a page on the Web, for example, http://www.syngress.com.

**Universal Naming Convention (UNC)**   A UNC is an address used to identify a resource on a network computer.

**upstream routing**   Using Proxy Server to route to another proxy server is called upstream routing. The term "upstream," from a data flow point of view, refers to being closer to the Internet, closer to the Internet resource that is your ultimate destination.

**User Manager**   User Manager is the utility used by the system administrator to create users and groups, assign passwords, and set up security policies.

**virtual directory**   A virtual directory is a directory that appears to be in a server's root structure but can actually be located on any server in the same Windows NT domain.

**virtual server**   A virtual server can be used to host multiple domain names on the same physical Internet Information Server. Each virtual server must have a unique IP address.

**voice line**   See dial-up analog modem line.

**Web Administration Tool (WAT)**   The Web Administration Tool (WAT) allows system administrators to administer Proxy Server from their Web browser. WAT provides the same functions as ISM. To use WAT, the user needs a Web browser that supports JavaScript.

**well-known port**   A well-known port is a TCP port whose value and use are defined by industry standards.

**WINS (Windows Internet Name Service)**   WINS is the Windows NT service that provides a map between NetBIOS computer names and IP addresses. This permits Windows NT networks to use either computer names or IP addresses to request access to network resources.

**WinSock (Windows Sockets)**   WinSock is a set of application programming interfaces (APIs) that applications can use to communicate with other applications on a network.

**word breaker**   A word breaker is a language-specific device that understands how a particular language views words. Word breakers know a language's syntax and structure.

**WspProto**   The WspProto utility is a command-line utility that adds, edits, and deletes the WinSock Proxy service protocol definitions.

# INDEX

**Q**

**R**

## S

**Z**